W9-CCV-821

Professional Management *of* Housekeeping Operations

FIFTH EDITION

Professional Management *of* Housekeeping Operations

FIFTH EDITION

Thomas J. A. Jones, Ed. D., R. E. H.

William F. Harrah College of Hotel Administration
University of Nevada, Las Vegas

BICENTENNIAL
1807
WILEY
2007
BICENTENNIAL

JOHN WILEY & SONS, INC.

Library of Congress Cataloging-in-Publication Data:
Jones, Thomas J. A.
Professional management of housekeeping operations / by Thomas
J. A. Jones. – 5th ed.
p. cm.
Originally published: Profesional management of housekeeping
operations / Robert J. Martin. 1986.
Includes index.
ISBN 978-0-471-76244-7 (cloth)
1. Hotel housekeeping. I. Title.
TX928.M37 2007
647.94092–dc22

2007011319

To Humphrey S. Tyler,
a pioneer in the cleaning industry,
and to my family

Contents

Preface

If the **Fourth Edition** could be compared to a "major overhaul," then the **Fifth Edition** is definitely a "fine-tuning." Old wine is served up in new bottles in the form of ethical issues confronting the housekeeping department displayed as mini-case studies. It is hoped that these cases will inspire both students and the instructor to question the action (or inaction) of these fictional professionals and arrive at the conclusion that good business practices and ethical behavior are not mutually exclusive.

In the housekeeping department there are numerous traps waiting for the unwary executive housekeeper. So, another set of mini-case studies and cautionary tales has been introduced, called "Pitfalls in Housekeeping." These pitfall case studies are intended to stimulate the analytical problem-solving abilities of students. Students need to realize that snap decisions influenced by emotions and personal prejudice are not appropriate management practices.

Several sections have been updated to reflect prevailing trends and conditions affecting the housekeeping department. However, "green" remains our favorite color. The focus on environmental health has continued to grow in the industry since its introduction in these pages in the last edition.

In the last edition "Executive Profiles" from *Executive Housekeeping Today* were introduced, putting a human face on the executive housekeeper. In this edition discussion questions have been added so that students may more closely identify with these professionals and their management practices.

Acknowledgments

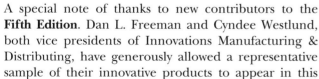

A special note of thanks to new contributors to the **Fifth Edition**. Dan L. Freeman and Cyndee Westlund, both vice presidents of Innovations Manufacturing & Distributing, have generously allowed a representative sample of their innovative products to appear in this edition. Another note of thanks to Roger McFadden, vice president of Technical Services at Coastwide Laboratories for his permission to reproduce a material data safety sheet (MSDS) from Coastwide's Sustainable Earth chemical product line.

I would also like to thank the following instructors, who provided helpful feedback through their reviews: Duncan Dickson of the University of Central Florida, Philip K. Ruthstrom of the Conrad N. Hilton College of Hotel and Restaurant Management at the University of Houston, and Susan Stafford of SUNY Tompkins Cortland Community College.

One more individual must be singled out for his lasting contribution, not only to this textbook, but to the entire cleaning industry. Humphrey S. Tyler, former owner of National Trade Publications, is without a doubt the industry's outspoken advocate of the need for education at all levels in the cleaning industry. Due to his efforts, and that of others such as Jim Harris, the Cleaning Industry Research Institute (CIRI) was formed two years ago. CIRI is intended to raise awareness of the importance of cleaning through scientific research and its mission is to create an enhanced positive public perception of the health benefits and productivity gains due to the cleaning industry. CIRI will act as a clearinghouse and central source for information, and will facilitate research and initiate scientific inquiry on the cleaning function and cleanliness. It is also hoped that CIRI will also advance techniques to improve indoor environmental quality for all types of buildings and uses, improve public understanding of the impact of the cleaning and building maintenance functions on public health, influence the development of public policy regarding cleaning and health at all levels of government, and provide credible research to help standards setting organizations develop and disseminate cleaning and maintenance best practices.

Even though Mr. Tyler has sold his publishing company and he has retired from business, he remains active as an officer and board member of CIRI. All of the industry and certainly this author owe Mr. Tyler a debt of gratitude for his unceasing commitment to the advancement of the cleaning industry. It is for this reason that this edition is dedicated to him.

PART ONE

THE HOUSEKEEPING PROFESSION AND THE PRINCIPLES OF MANAGEMENT

Since people have always traveled, there has always been a need for housekeepers and hospitality. The function of housekeepers has changed over the years, from doing specific tasks to managing the people, material, and other resources required for task accomplishment. In Part One we trace this change and see how the developing science of management relates to the profession of executive housekeeping. We continue Mackenzie's ordering of the principles of management, which include the sequential functions of planning, organizing, staffing, directing, and controlling. These sequential functions will be used as the organization structure for Parts Two and Three of the book. Part One of this edition also introduces Atchison's ''Preparing for Change,'' as he separates the management of systems and programs from the issues of leadership. (Part Four addresses special topics and offers a summary of the book.)

CHAPTER 1

The Executive Housekeeper and Scientific Management

LEARNING OBJECTIVES

After studying the chapter, students should be able to:

1. From memory, describe how the role of housekeepers has changed over the years.
2. Identify the management theorists mentioned in the chapter and describe each theorist's major contribution to the field.
3. From memory, list the three elements managers work with, according to Mackenzie.
4. From memory, list the continuous and sequential functions of management.
5. Given the basic activities associated with the sequential functions, define them and correctly associate each with its sequential function.
6. List and describe five normative characteristics associated with housekeeping employees.
7. Explain why delegation is the key to managerial success.
8. Describe the link between rewards and motivation.
9. Explain why there has been a shift away from cleaning for appearance to cleaning for health.
10. Differentiate between a manager and a leader.
11. Define the key terms and concepts at the end of the chapter.

Over the last 30 years the profession of executive housekeeping has passed from the realm of art to that of scientific management. Previously, professional housekeepers learned technical skills related to keeping a clean house. Now, the executive housekeeper and other housekeeping supervisory personnel are not only learning how to do such work but also how to plan, organize, staff, direct, and control housekeeping operations. They are learning how to inspire others to accomplish this with a high degree of quality, concern, and commitment to efficiency and cost control. In order to understand how the art melds with the science, we will trace the origins of professional housekeeping and of scientific management.

Origins of Hospitality and Housekeeping

Hospitality is the cordial and generous reception and entertainment of guests or strangers, either socially or commercially. From this definition we get the feeling of the open house and the host with open arms, of a place in which people can be cared for. Regardless of the reasons people go to a home away from home, they will need care. They will need a clean and comfortable place to rest or sleep, food service, an area for socializing and meeting other people, access to stores and shops, and secure surroundings.

Americans have often been described as a people on the move, a mobile society; and since their earliest history Americans have required bed and board. Travelers in the early 1700s found a hospitality similar to that in their countries of origin, even though these new accommodations may have been in roadhouses, missions, or private homes and the housekeeping may have included only a bed of straw that was changed weekly.

Facilities in all parts of young America were commensurate with the demand of the traveling public, and early records indicate that a choice was usually available at many trading centers and crossroads. The decision as to where to stay was as it is today, based on where you might find a location providing the best food, overnight protection, and clean facilities. Even though the inns were crude, they were gathering places where you could learn the news of the day, socialize, find out the business of the community, and rest.

With the growth of transportation—roadways, river travel, railroads, and air travel—Americans became even more mobile. Inns, hotels, motor hotels, resorts, and the like have kept pace, fallen by the wayside, been overbuilt, or been refurbished to meet quality demands.

Just as the traveler of earlier times had a choice, there is a wide choice for travelers today. We therefore have to consider seriously why one specific hotel or inn might be selected over another. In each of the areas we mentioned—food, clean room, sociable atmosphere, meeting space, and security—there has been a need to remain competitive. Priorities in regard to these need areas, however, have remained in the sphere of an individual property's management philosophy.

CREATING PROPER ATTITUDES

In addition to the areas of hospitality we discussed, professional housekeeping requires a staff with a sense of pride. Housekeeping staffs must show concern for guests, which will make the guests want to return—the basic ingredient for growth in occupancy and success in the hotel business. Such pride is best measured by the degree to which the individual maids (guestroom attendants or section housekeepers) say to guests through their attitude, concern, and demeanor, "Welcome. We are glad you chose to stay with us. We care about you and want your visit to be a memorable occasion. If anything is not quite right, please let us know in order that we might take care of the problem immediately."

A prime responsibility of the executive housekeeper is to develop this concern in the staff; it is just as important as the other functions of cleaning bathrooms, making beds, and making rooms ready for occupancy. Throughout this text, we present techniques for developing such attitudes in housekeeping staffs.

Origins of Management
✷

While the evolution of the housekeeping profession was taking place, professional management was also being developed. In fact, there is evidence that over 6000 years ago in Egypt and Greece, complex social groups required management and administration. It is even possible to derive evidence of the study and formulation of the management process as early as the time of Moses. Henry Sisk[1] reminds us that in the Bible (Exod. 18:13–26) Jethro, Moses's father-in-law, observed Moses spending too much time listening to the complaints of his people. Jethro therefore organized a plan to handle these problems that would in turn relieve Moses of the tedium of this type of administration. A system of delegation to lieutenants thus emerged. We can therefore assign some of the credit to Jethro for establishing several of the principles of management that we recognize today: the principles of **line organization**, **span of control**, and **delegation**.

SCHOOLS OF MANAGEMENT THEORY

Although it is beyond the scope of this book to provide an exhaustive examination and comparative analysis of all of the approaches to management theory that have appeared over the past 2000 years, the following discussion is an attempt to identify the major schools of management theory and to relate these theories to the modern housekeeping operation.

The Classical School

The **classical school** of management theory can be divided into two distinct concerns: **administrative theory** and **scientific management**. Administrative theory is principally concerned with management of the total organization, whereas scientific management is concerned with the individual worker and the improvement of production efficiency by means of an analysis of work using the scientific method. These two branches of the classical school should be viewed as being complementary rather than competitive.

Administrative Theory

Considered by many to be the father of administrative theory, Henri Fayol[2] (1841–1925) was a French engineer who became the managing director of a mining company. Fayol sought to apply scientific principles to the management of the entire organization. His most famous work, *Administratim Industrielle et General (General and Industrial Management)*, first published in 1916 and later in English in 1929, is considered by many to be a classic in management theory.

Fayol asserted that the process of management was characterized by the following five functions:

1. Planning—the specification of goals and the means to accomplish those goals by the company
2. Organizing—the way in which organizational structure is established and how authority and responsibility are given to managers, a task known as delegation
3. Commanding—how managers direct their employees

4. Coordinating—activities designed to create a relationship among all of the organization's efforts to accomplish a common goal
5. Controlling—how managers evaluate performance within the organization in relationship to the plans and goals of that organization[3]

Fayol is also famous for his Fourteen Principles of Management and his belief that administrative skills could be taught in a classroom setting.

Scientific Management

Fayol's counterpart in the management of work was Frederick W. Taylor[4] (1856–1915), the father of scientific management. Taylor was an intense (some would say obsessive) individual who was committed to applying the scientific method to the work setting. In 1912, Taylor gave his own definition of scientific management to a committee in the U.S. House of Representatives, by stating what scientific management *was not*:

> Scientific Management is not any efficiency device, nor a device of any kind for securing efficiency; nor is it any branch or group of efficiency devices. It is not a new system of figuring cost; it is not a new scheme of paying men; it is not a piecework system; it is not a bonus system, nor is it holding a stop watch on a man and writing down things about him. It is not time study, it is not motion study nor an analysis of the movements of men.

Although Taylor's definition of scientific management continued at length in a similar vein, he did not argue against using the aforementioned tools. His point was that scientific management was truly a *mental revolution*, whereby the **scientific method** was the sole basis for obtaining information from which to derive facts, form conclusions, make recommendations, and take action. Taylor's contribution was a basis for understanding how to administer a project and the people involved.

In his *Principles of Scientific Management*, published in 1911, he outlined four principles that constitute scientific management:

1. Develop a science for each element of a man's work, which replaces the old rule-of-thumb method.
2. Scientifically select and then train, teach, and develop the workman, whereas in the past he chose his own work and trained himself as best he could.
3. Heartily cooperate with the men so as to ensure all of the work being done is in accordance with the principles of the science which has been developed.
4. There is an almost equal division of the work and the responsibilities between the management and the workmen, while in the past almost all of the work and the greater part of the responsibility were thrown upon the men.[5]

Taylor also pointed out that the mental revolution had to take place in the workers' as well as the managers' minds.

The School of Management Science

An outgrowth of "Taylorism" is the school of **management science**, or, as it is alternatively known, **operations research**. Management science is defined as the application of the scientific method to the analysis and solution of managerial decision problems. The application of mathematical models to executive decision making grew out of the joint U.S. and British efforts during World War II to use such models in military decision making at both the strategic and the tactical levels.

The Behavioral School

A predecessor to the **human relations** school of management was the nineteenth-century Scottish textile mill operator Robert Owen.[6] He believed that workers needed to be "kept in a good state of repair." Owen urged other manufacturers to adopt his concern over improving the human resources they employed. He claimed that returns from investment in human resources would far exceed a similar investment in machinery and equipment.

Unfortunately, it was not until the second decade of the twentieth century that the results of Elton Mayo's Hawthorne Studies affirmed Owen's position and caught the imagination of American management.

Mayo[7] (1880–1949) was a faculty member of the Harvard University School of Business Administration when he began to study workers at the Hawthorne Works of the Western Electric Company in Chicago in 1927. From this study, Mayo and his colleagues concluded that there were factors other than the physical aspect of work that had an effect on productivity. These factors included the social and psychological aspects of workers and their relationships with managers and other workers.

Mayo's work effectively demonstrated to managers that in order for them to increase productivity in the work setting, they must develop human relations skills as well as the scientific management methods of Taylor and the other classical theorists.

MANAGERIAL TEMPERAMENT

The **behavioral school** does not end with Mayo. Douglas McGregor summarized certain assumptions about traditional, or work-centered, theory of management under the heading **Theory X**. McGregor's Theory X assumption is summarized in the following four statements[8]:

1. Work, if not downright distasteful, is an onerous task that must be performed in order to survive.
2. The average human being has an inherent dislike of work and will avoid it if he can.

3. Because of the human characteristic to dislike work, most people must be coerced, directed, controlled, or threatened with punishment to get them to put forth adequate effort toward the achievement of organizational objectives.
4. The average human being prefers to be directed, wishes to avoid responsibility, and has relatively little ambition, and wants security above all.*

Simply stated, Theory X indicates that there is no intrinsic satisfaction in work, that human beings avoid it as much as possible, that positive direction is needed to achieve organizational goals, and that workers possess little ambition or originality.

McGregor also presented **Theory Y**, which is the opposite of Theory X. His six assumptions for Theory Y are as follows[9]:

1. The expenditure of physical and mental effort in work is as normal as play or rest. The average human being does not inherently dislike work. Depending upon controllable conditions, work may be a source of satisfaction and will be voluntarily performed.
2. External control and the threat of punishment are not the only means for bringing about effort toward organizational objectives. Man will exercise self-direction and self-control in the service of objectives to which he is committed.
3. Commitment to objectives is a function of the awards associated with their achievements. The most significant aspects of such work (e.g., the satisfaction of ego and self-actualization needs) can be direct products of effort directed toward organizational objectives.
4. The average human learns under proper conditions not only to accept but even to seek responsibility. Avoidance of responsibility, lack of ambition, and emphasis on security are general consequences of experience, not inherent human characteristics.
5. The capacity to exercise a relatively high degree of imagination, ingenuity, and creativity in the solution of organizational problems is widely, not narrowly, distributed in the population.
6. Under the conditions of modern industrial life, the intellectual potentialities of the average human beings are only partially utilized.

An important point is that the opposite ways of thinking, as reflected in McGregor's Theory X and Theory Y, are what are actually conveyed by managers to their employees through everyday communication and attitudes.

---

*Assumptions 2, 3, and 4 are quoted directly from McGregor. Assumptions 1 has been added as an explicit statement of the nature of the work to which humans are reacting.

SATISFIERS AND DISSATISFIERS

Another leading theorist in the behavioral school was Frederick Herzberg. Herzberg and his associates at the Psychological Service of Pittsburgh[10] found that experiences that create positive attitudes toward work come from the job itself and function as **satisfiers** or motivators. In other words, satisfiers are created by the challenge and intrigue of the job itself.

A second set of factors related to productivity on the job are conditions outside of the job itself. Things such as pay, working conditions, company policy, and the quality of supervision are all a part of the working environment but are outside of the task of the job itself. When this second set of factors is inadequate, that is, when you believe that these conditions are not up to par, they function as **dissatisfiers**, or demotivators. When these factors are adequate, however, they do not necessarily motivate employees for a lasting period of time but may do so only for a short time.

Stated another way, Herzberg argued that the presence of satisfiers tends to motivate people toward greater effort and improved performance. The absence of dissatisfiers has no long-lasting effect on positive motivation; however, the presence of dissatisfiers has a tendency to demotivate employees.

PARTICIPATIVE MANAGEMENT

Rensis Likert,[11] another leading behaviorist, introduced the term **participative management**, which is characterized by worker participation in discussions regarding decisions that ultimately affect the worker.

Participation occurs when management allows hourly workers to discuss their own observances and ideas with department managers. (Such techniques have been seen as being one of the greatest motivators toward quality performance in a housekeeping operation.) More about this technique will be said when we discuss employee morale and motivation. **Theory Z**,[12] the highly vaunted Japanese management model, is heavily based on this participative management model.

THE MANAGERIAL GRID

Blake and colleagues[13] presented a revolutionary idea concerning the methods that underlie the thinking process involved in decision making. They found that a **managerial grid** could be established, whereby a maximum or minimum concern for production could be equated with a maximum or minimum concern for people. The managerial grid attempts to define the various ways in which people think through decisions. The way people think or feel can have a great influence on the quality of commitment from a group decision, especially when it comes to resolving conflicts. Blake and Mouton held that the best managers have both a high concern for production and a high concern for people in the organization.

One of the most recent attempts at group involvement in decision making has come out of a major concern for the loss of U.S. prestige in its own automobile market. Specifically, Japanese managers and workers have coined the term **quality circle**, which is a way of explaining total worker involvement in the processes as well as in the management decisions about production and quality that will ultimately affect worker welfare. Quality circles are now undergoing heavy scrutiny in the United States and are being used to help rekindle automobile production.

SITUATIONAL LEADERSHIP

Situational leadership,[14] or the **contingency approach**,[15] to management asserts that there is no one universally accepted approach to a management problem. It maintains that different problems require different solutions. This approach perhaps best reflects the complex nature of management in the organizational setting. Adherents to this approach agree that there is no ''one best'' way to manage; flexibility is the key to successful management. The works of Fred Fiedler,[16] Victor Vroom,[17] and Ken Blanchard and Paul Hersey[18] have contributed to this model.

SO WHAT DO MANAGERS DO?

Ask a manager that question and you will probably receive a hesitant reply, leading to responses such as ''What do I do?'' or ''That's hard to say,'' or ''I'm responsible for a lot of things,'' or ''I see that things run smoothly,'' none of which actually answer the question asked. After many years of researching the diaries of senior and middle managers in business, extended observation of street gang leaders, U.S. presidents, hospital administrators, forepersons, and chief executives, Mintzberg[19] was able to codify managerial behavior, as follows:

1. Managers' jobs are remarkably alike. The work of foremen, presidents, government administrators, and other managers can be described in terms of ten basic roles and six sets of working characteristics.

2. The differences that do exist in managers' work can be described largely in terms of the common roles and characteristics—such as muted or highlighted characteristics and special attention to certain roles.

3. As commonly thought, much of the manager's work is challenging and nonprogrammed. But every manager has his or her share of regular, ordinary duties to perform, particularly in moving information and maintaining a status system. Furthermore, the common practice of categorizing as nonmanagerial some of the specific

tasks many managers perform (like dealing with customers, negotiating contracts) appears to be arbitrary. Almost all of the activities managers engage in—even when ostensibly part of the regular operations of their organization—ultimately relate to back to their role as manager.

4. Managers are both generalists and specialists. In their own organizations they are generalists—the focal point in the general flow of information and in the handling of general disturbances. But as managers, they are specialists. The job of managing involves specific roles and skills. Unfortunately, we know little about these skills and, as a result, our management schools have so far done little to teach them systematically.

5. Much of the manager's power derives from his or her information. With access to many sources of information, some of them open to no one else in the organizational unit, the manager develops a database that enables him or her to make more effective decisions than the employees make. Unfortunately, the manager receives much information verbally and, lacking effective means to disseminate it to others, has difficulty delegating tasks for decision making. Hence, the manager must take full charge of the organization's strategy-making system.

6. The prime occupational hazard of the manager is superficiality. Because of the open-ended nature of this job, and because of the responsibility for information processing and strategy making, the manager is induced to take on a heavy workload and to do much of it superficially. Hence, the manager's work pace is unrelenting, and the work activities are characterized by brevity, variety, and fragmentation. The job of managing does not develop reflective planners; rather, it breeds adaptive information manipulators who prefer a stimulus-response milieu.

7. There is no science in managerial work. Managers work essentially as they always have—with verbal information and intuitive (nonexplicit) processes. The management scientist has had almost no influence on how the manager works.

8. The manager is in kind of a *loop*. The pressures of the job force the manager to adopt work characteristics (fragmentation of activity and emphasis on verbal communication, among others) that make it difficult to receive help from the management scientist and that lead to superficiality in his or her work. This in effect leads to more pronounced work characteristics and increased work pressures. As the problems facing large organizations become more complex, senior managers will face even greater work pressures.

9. The management scientist can help to break this loop by providing significant help for the manager in information processing and strategy making, provided he or she can better understand the manager's work and can gain access to the manager's verbal database.
10. Managerial work is enormously complex, far more so than a reading of the traditional literature would suggest. There is a need to study it systematically and to avoid the temptation to seek simple prescriptions for its difficulties.

Perhaps managers are not readily adept at answering the question about what they do because they are too mindful of what they are doing when they are actually performing their jobs. This writer also recalls once being asked, "What do you do?" I was stumped by the question, until many years later, when I discovered that a manager performs more than just the *sequential* functions. There are also those *continuous* functions—*analyzing problems, making decisions,* and *communicating*—as noted in the next section.

Principles of Management
❧

Executive housekeepers today recognize the need for a clear understanding and successful application of management principles. They may, however, feel overwhelmed by the many terms in the field of scientific management, both from the past and in the present. It is important for executive housekeepers to be familiar and comfortable with these terms and principles, since there is no department within the hospitality industry in general, and hotels in particular, that will provide a greater opportunity for applying management skills.

To help you understand the concept of management, we present an ordering of the management process as developed by R. Alec Mackenzie.[20] Building on the works of Fayol, he created a three-dimensional illustration relating the elements, continuous and sequential functions, and activities of managers. Refer to Figure 1.1, Mackenzie's diagram, when reading the following material.

ELEMENTS

According to Mackenzie, the **elements** with which today's managers work are ideas, things, and people. These are the main components of an organization and are in the center of the figure. The manager's task that is related to **ideas** is to think conceptually about matters that need to be resolved. The task related to **things** is to administer or manage the details of executive affairs. The task related to **people** is to exercise leadership and influence people so that they accomplish desired goals.

FUNCTIONS

The **functions** of a manager can be thought of as continuous functions and sequential functions. Many times a question may be asked: "But what does the manager do?" The manager should be seen to do several continuous functions, as well as several sequential functions.

The **continuous functions** relating to ideas and **conceptual thinking** are to *analyze problems.* Those related to things and **administration** are to *make decisions,* and those related to people and **leadership** are to *communicate* successfully. Problems are analyzed, facts gathered, causes learned, alternative solutions developed, decisions made, conclusions drawn, communications generated, and understanding ensured.

The **sequential functions** of management are more recognizable as a part of the classical definition of management. They involve the planning, organizing, staffing, directing, and controlling of ideas, things, and people. Mackenzie sets forth various activities in each of these sequential functions that should be studied and recalled whenever necessary.

ACTIVITIES OF SEQUENTIAL FUNCTIONS

According to Mackenzie, a manager's sequential functions are divided into five areas—planning, organizing, staffing, directing, and controlling.

Planning

The **management plan** involves seven basic activities:

1. *Forecasting:* Establishing where present courses will lead
2. *Setting objectives:* Determining desired results
3. *Developing strategies:* Deciding how and when to achieve goals
4. *Programming:* Establishing priorities, sequence, and timing of steps
5. *Budgeting:* Allocating resources
6. *Setting procedures:* Standardizing methods
7. *Developing policies:* Making standing decisions on important recurring matters

Organizing

Getting **organized** involves arranging and relating work for the effective accomplishment of an objective. Managers organize by making administrative or operational decisions. The four activities involved in getting organized are as follows:

1. *Establishing an organizational structure:* Drawing up an organizational chart
2. *Delineating relationships:* Defining liaison lines to facilitate coordination

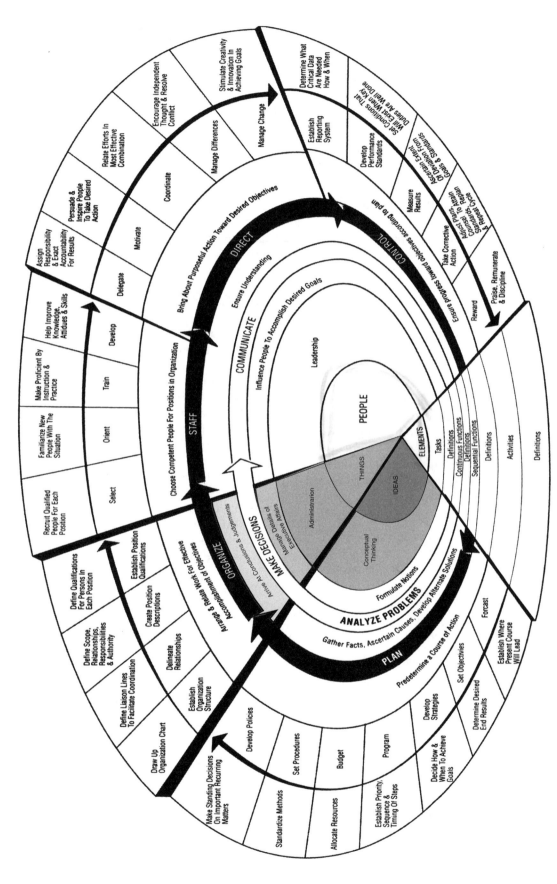

FIGURE 1.1 Mackenzie's management process, showing the elements, functions, and activities that are part of the executive job. (R. Alec Mackenzie, "The Management Process in 3-D," Harvard Business Review, November–December 1969.)

3. *Creating position descriptions:* Defining the scope, relationship, responsibilities, and authority of each member of the organization
4. *Establishing position qualifications:* Defining the qualifications for people in each position

Staffing

The third sequential function, **staffing**, involves people. Leadership now comes into play, and communication is established to ensure that understanding takes place. There are four activities:

1. *Selecting employees:* Recruiting qualified people for each position
2. *Orienting employees:* Familiarizing new people with their environment
3. *Training:* Making people proficient by instruction and practice
4. *Developing:* Improving knowledge, attitude, and skills

Directing

The first three sequential functions of management—planning, organizing, and staffing—might be performed before an operation gets under way. The last two sequential functions—directing and controlling—are carried out after the operation has begun or is in process. As with other managerial relationships involving people, leadership is accomplished through communication. In the **directing** of operations, there are five basic activities:

1. *Delegating:* Assigning responsibility and exacting accountability for results
2. *Motivating:* Persuading and inspiring people to take a desired action
3. *Coordinating:* Relating efforts in the most efficient combination
4. *Managing differences:* Encouraging independent thought and resolving conflict
5. *Managing change:* Stimulating creativity and innovation in achieving goals

Controlling

The final sequential function of management is to **control** organizations and activities to ensure the desired progress toward objectives. There are five basic activities in the controlling of operations:

1. *Establishing a reporting system:* Determining what critical data are needed
2. *Developing performance standards:* Setting conditions that will exist when key duties are well done
3. *Measuring results:* Ascertaining the extent of deviation from goals and standards

4. *Taking corrective action:* Adjusting plans, counseling to attain standards, replanning, and repeating the several sequential functions as necessary
5. *Rewarding:* Praising, remunerating, or administering discipline

Management Theory and the Executive Housekeeper

The question now is, "How can the executive housekeeper apply these diverse management theories to the job at hand, that being the management of a housekeeping department?"

Before we attempt to answer that rather encyclopedic question, perhaps we should first turn our attention to some of the inherent organizational and employee-related problems facing many housekeeping departments.

To begin, housekeeping is not a "glamorous" occupation. Cleaning up after others for a living is not, nor has it ever been, the American dream. No one wishes his or her child to become a guestroom attendant or a housekeeping aide. Housekeeping is viewed by a majority of the American public as being at the bottom of the occupational hierarchy in terms of status, pay, benefits, and intrinsic worth.

Even in the hotel industry, housekeeping employees are among the lowest paid of all workers in the hotel. Thus, the housekeeping department has traditionally attracted individuals who possess minimal levels of education, skills, and self-esteem.

Even the management positions in the housekeeping department have an image problem. In hospitality education, students normally tend to gravitate to the front office, marketing, food and beverage, and even human resource areas before they will consider housekeeping.

Normative Characteristics Exhibited by Housekeeping Employees

In order to manage housekeeping employees more effectively, we must understand their demographic and psychographic characteristics. As with most hotel departments, diversity among housekeeping employees is common. The following employee characteristics can be found in many housekeeping departments.

- Cultural diversity abounds in many housekeeping departments. It is not uncommon, especially in major U.S. urban centers, for people of different cultures to be found in the department.

- It is not uncommon for a variety of languages to be heard among the housekeeping staff and some employees may not be able to communicate in English.
- Housekeeping can often attract individuals with little or no formal education. Some housekeeping employees may be functionally illiterate. This can impact departmental efficiency and communications.
- Housekeeping employees may come from lower socioeconomic backgrounds and their attitudes and behavior may not be in parallel with the company's culture.
- A worker may have emotional or economic problems, or may even have a dependency problem. It is not suggested that the executive housekeeper is the only manager within the hotel who faces these problems, but many would argue that the frequency of these problems is higher in housekeeping than in other areas.

Although there are numerous lodging properties throughout the United States where these traits and characteristics are not found among the employees of the housekeeping department, as with any hotel department, it requires an astute housekeeping manager to prepare for such eventualities.

Motivation and Productivity

Motive is defined by Webster's[21] as "something (as a need or desire) that causes a person to act." The **motivation** of employees is accomplished by the manager creating an environment in which employees can motivate themselves. Managers cannot hope to directly motivate other human beings; however, they can provide a climate where self-motivation will take place.

What we as managers want our employees to do is to become more **productive**. We want them to accomplish their duties in a more effective and efficient manner. We want to substantially reduce **turnover**, **absenteeism**, and **insubordination** in the organization. We want our organization to be populated with happy, competent people who believe, as Douglas McGregor postulated, that "work is as natural as play or rest."[22]

To do that we must empower our employees with the abilities and inspiration to accomplish the mutually held objectives of the organization and the individual. There is no magic formula to achieve this goal. It takes dedication, perseverance, a plan, and plain hard work. What follows is not a fail-safe prescription for leadership success, but a series of approaches, methods, procedures, and programs that incorporate the best that the previously discussed schools of management theory have to offer the housekeeping department. Although not all of these applications may work in every setting,

they have been shown to positively affect the productivity of a number of housekeeping departments.

RESEARCHING THE MOTIVES

First, find out what motivates your best long-term employees to perform as well as they do. Find out why they stay with you. This can be done best by interviewing these people one on one (this is also a great opportunity to personally thank your best employees) in a distraction-free setting.

Second, find out why others leave. Conduct **exit interviews** with all persons being separated; but do not do it yourself and do not do it at the time of separation. Employees will be less than honest with you about the real reason for their resignation if you are part of the problem. Interviewing at the time of separation may also provoke the employee to be less than honest. They may give an "acceptable" reason for separation, such as more money, so they do not jeopardize a potential reference source.

The best approach is to have a third person call on the former employee a month after the separation. Make sure that the interviewer is able to convey an image of trust to the former employee.

Third, find out what current employees really want regarding wages, benefits, and working conditions. Administer a survey that ensures the anonymity of the respondent. If English is not the predominant language of the employees in your department, take the extra time to have a bilingual survey prepared. Also, form a committee of employees to assist you in designing the survey. This will help to lessen the effects of management bias and ensure that the survey reflects the attitudes of your department.

Have the employees mail the survey back to the company (be sure that the form has a stamp and return address), or have a ballot box for the forms. You may even want a third party, such as an outside consulting firm, to administer the survey.

Finally, administer this survey on a periodic basis—for example, twice a year—in order to remain current with the prevailing employee attitudes.

Use the information you have collected to assist you in strategic policy-making decisions and in the day-to-day operation of your department.

SELECTION

Far too often in housekeeping we take the first warm body that applies for the job. Recruiting is often viewed as a costly and time-consuming process for the management and the property. It is an endeavor fraught with failure; prospective employees don't show for interviews, newly hired workers quit during their first week on the job, and so on.

There is one method that can help to substantially reduce the cost and time involved in recruiting prospective employees. It can also help to reduce employee turnover and its associated costs.

This method is employee referral; that is, asking your employees (your best employees, in particular) to refer people whom they know (friends, family, and acquaintances) for entry-level position openings. In order for this procedure to work, the employer must be ready to pay a significant reward when a suitable candidate is presented. Typically, the reward is paid in installments over a time span of several months to a year or more to ensure the continued presence of both the employee who recommended the candidate and, of course, the candidate. One benefit to this system is that most conscientious employees will recommend only candidates whom they honestly feel will be good employees and will not reflect negatively on their recommendation.

However, safeguards must also be established to prevent unscrupulous employees from taking advantage of the system.

This author once observed an employee in a large hotel in Las Vegas asking an applicant, a stranger, who was in the waiting room of the personnel office in the hotel to put down his name on the referral line of the application blank. If the applicant was hired, the employee would then receive a bonus, which he offered to split with the applicant.

Other nontraditional sources of applicants for the housekeeping department include tapping into the disabled worker pool. Most communities have rehabilitation agencies where contacts can be established and cooperative programs initiated.

Senior citizens, young mothers, and legal immigrants are other potential sources of nontraditional labor.

TRAINING

As most housekeeping administrators know, a formal training program is an indispensable element in achieving productivity goals. There are, however, certain training approaches and concerns that are not being addressed by all housekeeping administrators.

These concerns include the educational background of the staff. As mentioned earlier, many housekeeping workers may be illiterate or may not be able to communicate in English. Written training materials, such as manuals, posters, and written tests, are quite useless when the staff cannot read, write, or speak the English language. Special audiovisual training materials are often required in housekeeping departments, and the written training materials must often be made available to the workers in Spanish or other languages.

The introduction of these materials does not rectify the problem, however. Consequently, many housekeeping departments have initiated remedial educational programs so that not only can employees learn to read and write in English, but they can also earn their

---

> **MOTIVATIONAL TIP**
>
> If you have an ESL (English as a second language) program for your housekeeping department, recognize those who successfully complete the program. Give them "diplomas" and have a graduation ceremony in their honor. Rent caps and gowns, invite their friends and relatives, and have a reception with cake and ice cream. According to Ronna Timpa of Workplace ESL Solutions, LLC, for many of your employees, it will be one of the proudest moments of their lives.

---

high school diplomas. The Educational Institute of the American Hotel and Lodging Association has recently developed a series of language-free videotapes for housekeeping. These World Trainer videos are superb training aids for any multilingual housekeeping department.

DELEGATION: THE KEY TO MANAGERIAL SUCCESS

According to Mackenzie, delegation is one of five activities of direction. Others view **delegation** as the most valuable activity. The other activities—motivation, coordination, managing differences, and managing change—can be seen as stemming from a manager's ability to delegate properly.

Too often we hear the phrase "delegation of responsibilities and authority." In fact, it is impossible to delegate a responsibility. To delegate actually means to pass authority to someone who will act on behalf of the delegator. The passing of such authority does not relieve the delegator of the responsibility for action or results, although there is an implied accountability of the person to whom power has been delegated to the person having that power. The responsibility of a manager for the acts or actions of his or her subordinates is therefore absolute and may not be passed to anyone else.

When an executive housekeeper is assigned overall responsibility for directing the activities of a housekeeping department, carrying out this responsibility may require the completion of thousands of tasks, very few of which may actually be performed by the executive housekeeper. It is therefore a responsibility of management to identify these tasks and create responsibilities for subordinates to carry them out. (The creation of these responsibilities is done during organization through the preparation of job and position descriptions; see Appendix A.) A good operational definition of delegation is the creation of a responsibility for, or the assignment of a task to, a subordinate, providing that person with the necessary authority (power) to carry out the task and exacting an accountability for the results of the subordinate's efforts. The lack of any one of the three

elements of this definition creates a situation whereby the manager abdicates the responsibility to manage.

Thorough and complete delegation, where possible, will free the manager from tasks that can be performed by subordinates, allowing the manager time to manage the operation. The manager is then left free to: 1) coordinate the activities of subordinates, 2) manage change (implies that the manager now has time to be creative and search for changes that will improve operations), and 3) manage differences (a form of problem solving).

How does one delegate? There are several methods, all of which will be useful to the executive housekeeper.

Methods of Delegation

1. *By results expected:* The manager can make a simple statement of the results that are to be obtained when the task has been completed properly.
2. *By setting performance standards:* The manager can create conditions that will exist when a task has been performed satisfactorily. An example of this type of delegation is found in inspection forms, which specify conditions that exist when the tasks are adequately performed. Figure 1.2 shows a room inspection form that sets forth standards that, if met, signify satisfactory performance.

    In hospitals and health-care institutions, standards may become stricter and even require that the institutions meet agency approval. Figure 1.3 is a list of standards, prepared by Charles B. Miller, that could be used as a guide in establishing standards and adding or deleting them as necessary in hospitals, health-care institutions, and hotels.
3. *By establishing procedures:* The major technique in dealing with routine matters is to prepare **standard operating procedures (SOPs)** in which the tasks to be performed are set forth in a routine procedure. The SOPs also indicate who will do what in the procedure, thus allowing for the delegation of appropriate tasks to people.

Another simple and equally important technique of delegation is to divide all tasks that must be done into three separate groups. Group 1 contains tasks that may be done by someone else immediately. Group 2 contains tasks that may be assigned to other people as soon as they have been properly trained. Group 3 contains tasks that must be done *only* by the manager. People are assigned group 1 tasks as soon as staff is available. Training is started for people to undertake group 2 tasks. As soon as training is complete and competence is shown, the tasks in group 2 are assigned. Group 3 tasks remain with the manager. The number of tasks remaining in group 3 is usually a measure of the manager's confidence to train people and let them become involved.

 A MINI CASE STUDY

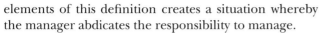
Ethical Dilemmas in ESL Training

"You want me to authorize what?" asks Tony Belcher, the hotel manager for the Seacoast Pines Resort & Convention Center. "Let me get this straight, you want me to contract with this English as a second language company, 'Espanola to English' to teach our housekeepers conversational English? Come on, Molly, is this really necessary?" Belcher responds to Molly Galloway, the executive housekeeper at the Seacoast Pines.

"Tony, over half of our housekeeping staff can't tell a guest how to get to the coffee shop. Aren't you concerned about customer service?" Galloway responds. "It would also help with communication within the department, too," Molly adds.

"All right, you know I want great service; we've built our reputation on friendliness and courtesy. But this is also going to benefit them personally. In fact, you will probably lose a few of them as their English improves," warns Belcher. "So, we improve their language skills and what we get out of it is higher turnover. Your department is already at an annual turnover rate of 200 percent."

"Does that turnover include the college students we hire in the summer when we're in our busiest season?" Galloway responds.

"O.K., your point is well taken," Tony admits. "But I am not going to pay your staff for training that benefits them as well as us. They will have to come in on their own time, after or before work."

1. If you were Galloway, how would you respond?
2. Is Belcher's proposal fair and equitable to your staff?
3. How do you think your staff will react to this offer?
4. Since you are not paying for their time, the training has to be optional. Do you think your staff will react favorably? If so, why would they react favorably, and if not, why not?

The executive housekeeper does not have to implement these remedial programs from scratch; he or she can turn to a number of sources of assistance found in most communities, such as the public school or the community college system. These sources can often provide qualified bilingual adult instruction at little or no cost to the company. Another tactic is to reimburse employee tuition if remedial classes are completed at the local community college.

The payoff to the housekeeping department is twofold. First, productivity improves because the level of communication has increased. Second, the employees' self-esteem should certainly increase when they begin to achieve their personal educational goals; and a self-assured workforce will ultimately become a more competent and productive workforce.

Why Managers Do Not Delegate

Often, managers do not delegate tasks properly. The reasons can be summed up as follows:

1. *Some managers do not understand their roles as managers:* This happens most often with newly appointed managers who have been promoted

GUESTROOM INSPECTION FORM

	Door	Clean, no dust on front, back, or top
	Door frame	Clean, no dust
	Connecting door	Clean, no dust, bolt locked
	Door chain	Fastened
	D.N.D. sign	Good condition
	Coat rack	Clean, no dust, no hangers missing, two laundry bags
	Carpet	Vacuumed, no debris (including behind drapes, between beds, and under spread, no dust around edges or under furniture, clean between connecting doors). Report *all spots and gum to supervisor*
	Furniture	No dust on tops or sides, including kneehole under desk, chair legs, and cushions, cushion turned regularly so the cover stays in place, drawers clean in c/o room, all furniture in proper position
	Pictures and mirror	No dust on frames, no streaks on mirror
	Wall lamps	No dust on bulbs, bulbs working, no dust on dish under bulb, seam on shade turned to the back, shade straight, correct wattage bulb
	Floor lamp	No dust (on arm, stand. or base), bulb working no dust on bulb, in proper position (12 inches from either wall with light extending over the chair), seam on shade turned to the back, shade straight, correct bulb
	TV	No dust on screen, front, back, stand, and restaurant ad on top
	Air conditioner	No dust on front, top, or control box; turned off

(a)

FIGURE 1.2 Guestroom Inspection Form. Checkmarks in boxes indicate satisfactory performance; N.I., needs improvement; U, unsatisfactory (condition must be corrected before renting the room).

	Tracks and patio door	Clean, no dust, locked
	Beds	Neat and smooth appearance, clean linen, sheet tucked under head of mattress, hospital corners, top sheet folded over blanket 6 inches from top edge of mattress, pillowcase seams turned to the wall, blanket clean, spread clean, mattress and box springs positioned properly on frame, no dust on headboard
	Nightstand	No dust (top, sides, and inside), phone book neat, name card
	Phone	No grease, makeup, or hair on receiver, clean dial and sides, clean cord, no dust at the back
	Waste basket	Clean and in good condition
	Desk drawer	Proper number of each in proper place (map, A.M. express, choose your credit, advance registration, stationery, two plastic bags, fly swatter)
	Dresser supplies	Proper number in proper places (Bible, we care, room service, menu, guest services directory, correct ashtray with matches, tray placed longway against back of right hand dresser with four glasses and pitcher cleaned and turned upside down)
Remarks:		Work orders:

(b)

FIGURE 1.2 (*Continued*)

from within as a reward for outstanding service. For example, the section housekeeper who has been doing an outstanding job as a room attendant is rewarded by being promoted to the position of supervisor, although he or she is given no supervisory training. Having been physically very busy in the act of cleaning guestrooms, the person is now in charge and, as such, feels out of place. The new supervisor (manager) has been moved from a realm in which he or she was very competent to a position in which he or she has little or no expertise. In Figure 1.1, we saw that a manager should be continually analyzing problems, making decisions, and communicating. Failing to understand this new role, the new supervisor does someone else's work. For this reason, supervisory training is an absolute must when promoting first-line workers into positions requiring managerial performance such as supervising.

2. *Managers who enjoy physically doing work are sometimes reluctant to let go of such tasks:* Again, this is a matter of training. The new manager needs to be reminded that doing the physical task is not what he or she is being paid to do. A new manager may need to be reminded that, by doing physical work that should be delegated, situations requiring management decisions may go unnoticed because the manager is too busy to observe, evaluate, and direct operations.

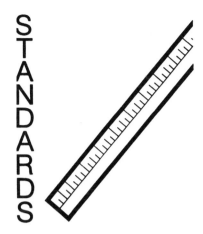

1. Ceilings - Clean, free of dust and spots, paint intact, vents clean and free of dust and lint, lights replaced.

2. Room Walls - Clean, no lint, paint intact, free of finger marks and stains.

3. Floors - Clean, free of dust, lint, and stains; no wax buildup or accumulation of soil in corners; free of heel and scuff marks; free of discolored wax.

4. Cove Bases - Clean and clear, no wax buildup, no mop marks, no accumulation of soil in corners, intact around room (firmly affixed to wall with no signs of being loose at juncture with floor).

5. Doors - Clean, free of marks, finish intact, kickplate clean and shiny, top free of dust and lint, edges clean, handle or knob clear and clean, hinge facing and door frame clean, door vent clean and free of dust and lint, window and frame clean and free of dust and lint (inside and outside).

6. Windows - Clear and clean, not in need of immediate washing, frame clean; glazing intact; sill clean; paint in good condition.

7. Window Drapes - Free of lint; properly hung on tracks; not faded; no stains, yellowing, or tears; pulleys and pull cords intact and working; pins installed correctly in drapes and on carriers.

8. Cubicle Curtains - Clean and free of stains, not faded, pull freely in tracks, properly mounted, no tears, adequate length and width.

9. Beds - Headboards and footboards clean, metal upright and horizontal frame members clean, control unit and cord clean and working, linen clean and free of stains and tears, bed properly made, undercarriage free of lint and soil, wheels clean and free of lint.

10. Mattresses - Clean, free of stains and lint, in good repair without rips or tears, thoroughly deodorized, mattress turned on each discharge.

11. Overbed Tables - Clean and free of dust; elevation controls working properly, drawer and drawer mirror clean and free of dust, lint, and streaks; base, frames, and wheels clean and free of dust and lint.

12. Bedside Console Units - Countertop, shelves, and facings clean and free of dust and spots; no accumulation of soil in corners; stainless steel sink and plumbing fixtures clean and free of spots and streaks; clothes closet clean and free of dust and lint.

13. Chairs - Clean, free of lint and dust.

14. Television Sets - Clean, free of dust and lint; shelf clean, free of dust and lint.

15 Toilets - Toilet bowl clean inside and outside; no stains, streaks, or residue, toilet seat clean, free of spots, stains, or streaks, and tightly fastened to toilet; plumbing fixtures clean, free of dust, spots, and streaks; plumbing connections to toilet free of alkali buildup and dirt; base of toilet free of soil buildup and stains.

16. Sinks - Clean, inside, outside, and underneath, free of spots and streaks; plumbing fixtures on top and underneath free of dirt, spots, and streaks; base of plumbing fixtures free of alkali buildup.

17. Mirrors - Clean, free of spots and streaks; frame top and edges free of dust and lint; shelf clean, free of spots and streaks.

18. Shower Stalls - Walls clean, free of soil buildup on caulking, caulking intact; fixtures free of spots and streaks; door frame and glass free of dust, lint, spots, and streaks, horizontal crossbars above door free of dust, lint, spots and streaks.

19. Dispensers - Soap, paper towel, and seat cover dispensers clean, free of dust and lint on top and underneath, free of spots and streaks, supplies replenished.

20. Refrigerators - Clean, free of dust spots and stains; shelves and facing clean and free of spots, spills, and stains, freezer clear and free of stains; motor vent clean and free of dust and lint.

21. Ovens - Stainless steel top, sides and metal or glass door clean and free of spots and streaks; interior shelf, sides and top free of stains; no accumulation of soiled food on surface of oven (interior).

22. Countertops - Clean free of dust, stains, and finger marks.

23. Telephones - Clean, free of dust and lint; receiver, mouthpiece, and dial free of dust and lint.

24. Drinking Fountains - Stainless steel free of spots and streaks.

FIGURE 1.3 A list of standards that can be used to develop an inspection form adapted to a specific institution. (*Charles B. Miller,* How to Organize and Maintain an Efficient Hospital Housekeeping Department, *reprinted with permission from American Hospital Publishing, 1981.*)

3. *Less competent people fear the consequences of being outperformed:* There are managers who refuse to delegate routine tasks for fear that their own incompetence will be magnified. Surprisingly enough, their incompetence will be in managing the activities of others, not in their ability to perform the task that they do not delegate. These people are uneasy because they fear that a stronger person will eventually be able to perform their jobs. What some managers forget is that they themselves cannot be promoted until someone is available and competent enough to replace them.

4. *Some managers feel that delegation is an all-or-nothing situation:* This may occur in spite of the fact that there are several **degrees of delegation**. Imagine the situation in which a manager needs to

investigate a situation, decide if action is needed, and, if so, take the appropriate action. This task, or portions of it, may be delegated to another person, depending upon the degree of training and demonstrated ability of the person. Here are several degrees of delegation, any one of which might be used, depending upon the skill level and reliability of the subordinate.

a. Investigate and report back
b. Investigate and recommend a course of action
c. Investigate and advise of intended action
d. Investigate, take action, and keep manager informed
e. Investigate and take action

5. *Some managers feel that if they do not do the task themselves, it will not be done properly:* This is synonymous with the often-heard phrase, "If you want something done right, do it yourself." Sometimes it is ego that prompts this type of thinking, but more often it is the mark of a Theory X thinker. This type of attitude encourages inaction on the part of the employees and a feeling that they are not trusted with important matters. More important, it is counterproductive to the creation of good morale-building environments. Many managers fear the possibility that some subordinate will rise to the occasion of being able to replace the manager. Said another way, some managers keep themselves in the position of being indispensable. Other managers recognize that until someone is capable of replacing them, they themselves are not promotable. What is important to remember is that until the manager trains people to act on his or her behalf, and delegates as much as possible to subordinates, the manager need not think of promotion, vacation, or even becoming ill, lest the operation crumble.

TANGIBLES VERSUS INTANGIBLES

Thomas Atchison[23] indentified a significant difference between the **tangibles** and the **intangibles** associated with management and leadership. He consulted with many organizations regarding the industrial downsizing that took place in the early 1980s, and he noted the tremendous pressures that befell many organizations beleaguered with the necessity of either downsizing or declaring bankruptcy. As a result of his investigations as a consultant, he was instrumental in helping several companies prepare for change as they moved toward new life in the twenty-first century. Atchison was able to identify the significant difference between the tangible and intangible **inputs** and **outputs** that occurred in the business world (Figure 1.4).

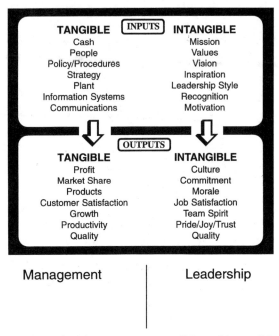

FIGURE 1.4 Atchison expresses tangible and intangible inputs and outputs in relation to their application to either management (producing predictable results) or leadership (producing inspired followers). *(Thomas A. Atchison, "Tangibles vs. Intangibles: Managing for Change," seminar notes; reprinted with permission.)*

Atchison recognized that tangible inputs and outputs are measurable and fairly predictable. Tangible outputs (e.g., profit, market share, growth, etc.) are the traditional goals of management, but it is the organization's intangible inputs and outputs that produce **inspired followers**. Intangible inputs, such as the company's mission and values, produce the intangible outputs, such as the organization's culture and the commitment of its employees. Leaders should focus on the intangibles rather than on the tangibles. To successfully deal with change, Atchison said, it is necessary for leaders to have followers who commit to achieving a vision by building teams to manage change.

Essential leadership activities must include:

1. Challenging the process by seeking out opportunities, without being afraid to take risks
2. Inspiring a shared vision by seeing the future and communicating it to others; making it their vision also
3. Enabling employees to act by fostering teams and empowering others
4. Modeling the way by setting an example, and remembering that success is gradual

Atchison concluded that when you lead well, others become willing followers in a new direction of *managed change*. He also concluded that management, in a sense, might be nothing more than a title. You are a manager until you get promoted, become retired, or are fired. Leadership, however, is earned, by having followers, and it is reearned every day. There is no accrual, no equity, no transfer in leadership. Every day, a leader must inspire followers.

The significance of these thoughts is that, as time goes on, you have only one choice. Are you going to *react* to change, or are you going to *manage* it, because change is going to happen at a continually accelerating rate. **Autocratic change** always produces **passive-aggressive behavior**, and this will destroy an organization. To the contrary, *managed change* is inspiring and what most employees actually hope for. Managed change has five ingredients:

1. Be specific in what change is desired.
2. Think small. Break the project into small increments.
3. Move quickly from one small increment to the next.
4. Evaluate whether progress is being made.
5. Celebrate the completion of each small segment.

It is important to put *fun* into work. Good work can be made enjoyable by remembering to grant *ownership* to the person who is responsible for the work being done. When the manager recognizes and passes credit to the person who performed well, and to that person's assistant, self-motivation emerges.

Consensus is the glue that seems to hold us back in America, but trust is the glue that binds leaders to followers. One has to work hard and steady to earn trust; and trust not cherished and protected can be easily destroyed.

Atchison provided six frameworks, each with four intangible items, as follows.

Leadership Style

Leaders are intelligent (which is nothing more than being flexible), are disciplined (have control of themselves, have compassion) care about people, and have energy (stay involved and participate).

Strength of Culture

Is there a mission?
Does everyone know the purpose of the unit? Employees must understand the *value* of what they do.
Vision—where will your unit be in ten years?
　Trust—work for it, earn it. Your unit must have it to move forward.

Personal Investment

Seek knowledge—people must know their roles and their jobs.
Skills—the leader must know how to do his or her job.
Attitude—the bad attitude is difficult to deal with; may warrant disconnecting.
Satisfaction—nothing more than happiness and being respected.

Team Spirit

Purpose—a good team knows why they come together.
Fit—everyone with a job must fit on the team and have value.
Communication—great teams know how to communicate.
Dynamic tension—great teams argue but keep their egos in check.

Managing Change

Focus—must change for something identifiable.
Barriers—focus and progress will always encounter barriers; remove them one by one.
Celebrate—every time a barrier is removed.
Courage—employees sometimes sense danger in progress; leaders set good examples.

Intangible Quality

Meaning—when put in employees' work lives, little guidance will be required.
Motivation—create the atmosphere in which employees can motivate themselves.
Harmony—like a great symphony, everyone fits together.
Commitment—requires three ingredients: pride, loyalty, ownership.

Rewards and Motivation

Recognizing and rewarding proper employee performance is essential. Virtually all employees want to know if their performance meets management expectations, and most want to see a linkage between that performance and rewards.

Managers often ask, "What form should these rewards take?" Some experts believe that although certain intangible rewards, such as recognition for achievement, may be nice, they are not as crucial to raising productivity as are the more tangible rewards (that is, money).[24]

MOTIVATIONAL TIP

One of the highlights of the Las Vegas International Hotel and Restaurant Show is the Hospitality Skills Competition. This event shows off the skills of the staff of 22 housekeeping departments. Games include the Bed-Making Competition, Vacuum Relay, Johnny Mop Toss, and Buffer Pad Toss. Each game has specific rules, and the contestants are judged on speed, accuracy, and the appearance of the contestant. Judges include top hotel management. Each team has a cheering section in the packed audience, holding up signs of support and cheering incessantly for its colleagues. In addition to the recognition received, the hotels donate dozens of great prizes to the winners (see Figure 1.5). The event is usually covered by the local news media, so contestants can see themselves on the evening news. Every state hospitality show should sponsor an event like this one.

FIGURE 1.5 A flyer asking for donations for the Hospitality Competition.

This theory seems to be borne out by some recent experiments linking pay to productivity levels. The Country Lodging by Carlson chain, a subsidiary of the Carlson Hospitality Group, pays its housekeepers by the rooms they clean rather than by the hour.[25] This approach has reduced the need for full-time housekeepers, and it has reduced the turnover and hiring costs in the housekeeping department. Housekeepers earn more, and they earn it, on average, in a shorter workday.

Three cautions regarding the implementation of a pay-per-room program should be addressed. First, management must not take advantage of the employee by raising the benchmark standards of how many rooms ought to be cleaned in an hour. As Country Lodging's Vice President Kirwin says, "The goal is to get your rooms cleaned, not to take advantage of people."[26] The productivity standard has been set at 2.25 rooms per hour at Country Lodging.

Second, an incentive program for room inspection should be implemented so that the hotel's room cleanliness standards do not erode because of the pay-per-room program.

Third, it is doubtful that this program could be adopted in most union environments at this time.

We stated in the beginning of this section that intangible rewards, such as recognition, may not be as crucial to the improvement of productivity as the more tangible effects of money. Although we believe this to be true, we certainly hold that recognition for employee achievement is an essential management technique.

Management Theory and Housekeeping Administration

✂

We have looked at the roles of employee participation, management delegation, training, and rewards in influencing productivity in housekeeping. Each of these practices evolved from management theories. The answer, then, to the question of which theory should be applied in the housekeeping department is, none of them, and at the same time, all of them. Each of them is appropriate at different times and under different circumstances (situational leadership).

Current research also seems to favor the situational leadership or contingency approach. Studies[27] have indicated that different circumstances demand different management approaches; an unchanging **leadership style** does not work as effectively as a flexible style. The key variable that influences a manager's style, according to the situational leadership theorists, is the ability and attitude of the follower.

Although a manager's behavior may change, or an approach to a problem may be dictated by the ability and attitude of the follower, we believe that a manager should always maintain a high level of concern for both the organization and the employee. This concern should be evident in everything that management says and does.

Reflecting that dual concern for productivity and people is the current shift from cleaning for appearance to cleaning for health. The emphasis on cleaning for health includes not only the health of the guest, but also the health of the employees—particularly the very employees who are cleaning the property. We are now discovering that many of the methods of cleaning, and the chemicals used in the cleaning process, negatively affect the environment, and the most immediate impact is on those who are implementing these processes and using these chemicals. If a worker's health is negatively impacted, that worker's productivity is either curtailed or eliminated and the business may incur unnecessary medical and legal expenses. Further in the text, there is considerable space devoted to this topic.

New Horizons in Management

Recent attempts to gain better guest acceptance of the service product being presented have yielded reports that the root problem noted by guests usually centered on the employee failing to perform adequately. Employee attitudes and motivations were also highly suspect; this was noticed when guests were asked to rank their most common complaints when visiting a hotel. Appearing at the top of most lists were the guests' concerns about employee attitudes. More detailed studies, however, have indicated that a clear 85 percent of all guest and service quality problems were the result of systems, policies, and procedures that were either outdated, inappropriate, or restrictive, and consequently did not take care of the guest. Only 15 percent of quality problems were associated directly with the employee's failure to perform properly in the employee's relationship with the guest. Basically, in our industry, employees have been overmanaged and underled.

Other studies addressed the issue of quality assurance in hotel operations. Such was the case of the American Hotel and Motel Association's sponsored study conducted at the Sheraton Scottsdale in Scottsdale, Arizona.[28] This study was primarily concerned with problem solving in areas where guest comments indicated a quality problem in rendering service to the guest.

Theory Z technique was applied at the Sheraton Scottsdale, and several focus groups (created from among several first-line employees who would be most conversant with the particular problem being discussed) were formed to address the problem areas identified by guest comments. (The terms *focus group* and *quality circle* are interchangeable.) The focus group concept, once and for all, took recognition of the fact that it was the front-line employee who was actually delivering the product or service being offered—not the company, the general manager, or the middle management of the property, or even the first-line supervisor. It is the front-line employee who, having the greatest contact with the guest, actually represents the entire organization to the guest. Too often in the past, when talking to the guest, the only response available to the employee was, "You will have to talk to the manager."

By placing the guest's problem in front of those employees (focus group) who had the greatest knowledge about how to solve a problem (because they did the work in the area of the problem), quality standards would be raised. Having been involved in creating the new and better-quality standard, the employees would be more inclined to personally commit themselves to meeting the new standards. These new standards then became the benchmarks for training or retraining of all employees: standards set by employees and agreed to by management.

The results of the changes developed through this sponsored study, as reported by Sheraton Scottsdale General Manager Ken MacKenzie, included "growth in revenue of twenty-eight percent in the first year of the program, twenty-five percent in the second year, and a group of supportive employees. You don't buy them or hire them, you develop them."[29]

EMPLOYEES RENAMED AND EMPOWERED

Further recognition of the results obtained with Theory Z and focus groups has resulted in many hotel companies now referring to their employees as **associates**.

In addition, associates are being **empowered** to do whatever is necessary to resolve problems for the guest, rather than to refer problems to management.

Empowerment is actually a form of ultimate delegation that allows the person who is delivering the product and is most closely in touch with the problem to do (within certain boundaries) whatever is necessary to "make it right" for the guest.

Empowerment as a program does not mean the employee simply takes power, but rather is granted power by the supervisor after being properly trained to meet written standards that have been prepared by the associates and have been accepted by management. Should an employee make a mistake through empowerment, he or she may be counseled or retrained.

These quality and empowerment concepts are now being developed by several hotel organizations into what is becoming known as Total Quality Management (TQM). According to Stephen Weisz, former Regional Vice President, Middle Atlantic Region, Marriott Hotels, "TQM encompasses having an understanding of customer requirements, and modifying product and service delivery to meet these requirements, customers being both external and internal to the company."

EXECUTIVE PROFILE
Bryan Cornelius *A Future CEO on the Go*

by Andi M. Vance, Editor, *Executive Housekeeping Today*

This article first appeared in the March 2003 issue of *Executive Housekeeping Today*, the official publication of the International Executive Housekeepers Association, Inc.

Depictions of young adults these days are filled with tales of apathy, hours on the PlayStation, laziness, misbehavior and overindulgence. For those young people who strive for something better for themselves, they follow the well-worn path from high school to college, which leads them to a career in something that oftentimes pertains little to what they studied in school.

It's a pretty safe bet to say that at age 22, Bryan Lee Cornelius is the youngest member of I.E.H.A.; however, he's really not your typical young adult. At the moment, he has no time for video games or college courses. Working ten hours a day, six days a week as the Executive Housekeeper at the Radisson Hotel in the Historic District of Savannah, Georgia, he is prevented from doing much even in terms of socializing with his friends. He spends his time managing the housekeeping department as well as cross-training in other departments. In fact, sleeping comprises much of his free time. By going against the grain, diligently working and learning everything within his reach, Bryan Cornelius continues to gain prominence in the hotel industry. He confesses that he's found his niche.

Many jobs in the service industry don't come without their fair share of challenges. Cornelius' persistence and dedication to his position has yielded many rewards throughout his short career. At the age of 18, he was completely green to hotels.

Looking to earn some spending money during high school, he worked as a shipping and receiving clerk at a local Marriott hotel. Fueled by an intense desire mixed and driven by foresight, Bryan anxiously pursued the countless opportunities available to him in the hotel business.

Unlike many of his younger peers, Bryan wholeheartedly dedicates himself to his job. His job is his life. Watching the construction of the 403-room Westin Savannah Harbor Resort across the river, Bryan anxiously submitted his application for employment along with half of the town of Savannah. An article in the local paper had revealed that over 20,000 people had applied at the hotel, so he was quite shocked to find he was one of only 300 who were selected.

With experience in shipping and receiving, he gained employment in this department, only to find they had overstaffed it. Cornelius volunteered himself to be transferred elsewhere, landing himself a supervisory position in Housekeeping at age 19. "After speaking with one of my friends and the Executive Housekeeper, I accepted the position," he anxiously recalls. "That was probably one of the best decisions I've made in my life. It was a daredevil opportunity. From then on, I knew Housekeeping was for me."

Equipped with little knowledge, but armed with a fierce work ethic, Cornelius set to face the many battles lying before him. Breaking down stereotypes

and misjudgments regarding his young age presented his biggest dilemma. "It's very tough when you are trying to work with room attendants and show them the proper way of doing something, and they just look at you and say, 'I have grandchildren as young as you. You're not going to show me anything about this job I don't already know.'"

GAINING RESPECT

Not only did Cornelius' work on the field gain recognition, but his diligence off the clock also brought attention. Little was Cornelius aware that his dedication on the hotel's softball team would help him later get a new job in Miami, Florida. At the time, the General Manager at the Westin was preparing to leave when he sat down with eight employees to make them aware of the opportunities available to them as he took over properties in Miami. Cornelius was a part of the group.

"He said one particular thing to me," Bryan remembers. "He said that even though we'd hardly worked together, he had watched me play softball. My dedication had shined through whenever I'd hit the ball. Even though I knew it was an easy catch, I ran right through first base."

Soon after, Cornelius accepted a supervisory position in Housekeeping at the Mandarin Oriental Hotel in Miami. "This hotel is just awesome," he relates with a sound of awe in his voice. "It's a 5-star hotel where rooms start at $600. If you want a suite, that runs you at $8,000 a night. It was a whole new ball game."

As if moving from Savannah to South Beach wasn't enough culture shock thrown at Cornelius, the carpets of the hotel were routinely studded with famous actors and movie stars who required particular attention. "I met Puff Daddy, and Michael Jackson stayed there for a month," he casually mentions. "It was fun; every day, you'd go up to the computer and print out the sheet of arrivals. When you saw Scooby Doo or Superman, you knew it was a celebrity. It was definitely exciting."

When a family situation beckoned his presence, Cornelius returned to Savannah eight months later. At the time, his identical twin brother, Ryan Lee Cornelius, continued to look for employment where he'd be happy. Seeing his brother's success in the hotel business, he sought employment in Bryan's former position at the Westin. Bryan's hard-working reputation at the hotel proceeded his brother, and Ryan was hired even without an interview. Ryan's hard work has also helped put him through the ranks as well.

Since his return home in February 2002, Bryan has enjoyed the amount of responsibility placed upon his shoulders in the

Housekeeping Department at the Radisson Hotel Historic in downtown Savannah. Hired initially as the Assistant Executive Housekeeper, he gained a promotion to Executive Housekeeper at the age of 21.

He remembers the day like it was yesterday. "Everyone was standing around and congratulating me when realization hit: I was now responsible for running the entire department. This was now my whole department.

The GM sat me down and acknowledged that while they could have hired anyone for the position, I was the first person who came to their minds. He wanted to enhance operations in the department and wouldn't have offered me the position if he didn't think I could do it."

STAFF

Turning the department around involved reducing turnover and keeping operations under budget. Cornelius admits that keeping people working can sometimes be difficult in Savannah, due to the poor economic conditions, but he found a way to establish loyalty. "If someone from up North were to try to come and handle some of these situations," he advises, "he might not be so effective. I grew up around this type of environment, so I know how to get them to work. You want to speak with them and stay on their level, never acting like you're better than them. They are Southern people and they do things a certain way, and they'll continue doing things that way. In Miami, I found the workers to be completely different. The work ethic between the two cities just varied greatly. In Savannah, they come to work because we make it a pleasant environment."

Bryan's interaction with his staff begins with their point of hire. During the interview, he details the Three Zero-Tolerance Rules, which are cause for termination: 1) If you pop sheets (don't change them), you're gone; 2) If you no call, no show, you're gone; 3) If you leave a room at the end of the day without cleaning it, you're gone. In his experience, over 95% of the housekeepers who are discharged leave for one of these three reasons.

After welcoming a new employee to his staff, Bryan makes an effort to spend time with an employee to better know him or her. "I get to know them on a personal level," he relates. "I want to know their favorite foods, interests, movies, and about their families. This shows them that you not only care about an employee as a worker, but a person as well. It pays off in the long run, because when you really need someone to come into work, they will respond to you a lot better."

BRYAN CORNELIUS ON SOUTHERN HOSPITALITY

Savannah, the oldest city in Georgia, is a Mecca for Southern Hospitality. When asked what comprises the essence of Southern Hospitality, Bryan summed it up with three things: cuisine, décor and attitude.

"[All the people at the hotel] have lived here for all their lives, so we exemplify Southern Hospitality to the core. Visitors come to Savannah and continually ask why everyone's so nice. That's just us," he admits. "We get tons of comment cards from people who are so impressed with the extra efforts our staff makes, but to us, we're not doing anything special. It's the way we were raised."

When guests are in need of certain items, Bryan rifles through his resources to see if he can find exactly what they need, or an item they can use to improvise. For example, the single most often left item in a room is a cell phone charger. He has a huge array of various chargers for every make and model of cell phone. When a guest calls Housekeeping on a whim, in dire need of a charger, Bryan asks which model is needed and sends one to the room immediately.

"Guests are always blown away by that," he says. "All I do is accumulate them, so if someone needs one, we can provide them. I've got tons; like 20 of the same type. Lost and found can be a really good thing."

He routinely advises his staff not to throw away the things for which they don't foresee a guest returning. Paperwork is a great example, says Cornelius. "I've probably had more paperwork sent out to guests than jewelry. This is a great area to show exemplary service. If I can find a number or a way to reach guests when they've left something, then I'll try to call them and let them know. Sometimes, it's even before they've realized that the article is missing. That's when they're really impressed!"

ST. PATRICK'S DAY

On St. Patrick's Day, pandemonium erupts on the streets of Savannah, and Bryan Cornelius' hotel is at the heart of it. Savannah is home to one of the largest St. Patrick's Day celebrations in the world, which presents countless issues for facilities housing the partygoers. "It's the one event none of us enjoy," Bryan admits. "I used to look forward to it because I used to be out in the

crowd. Now I'm in the hotel and it's mayhem. The two or three days they're here are the worst the hotel rooms look all year. It takes a lot of work to get cleaned up after that."

At the time of his interview, Bryan had been working for at least five months with other hotel personnel, party coordinators and vendors to assure the smoothest celebration possible. Security efforts are heightened during this time to assure the least amount of damage to property and injury to the participants possible.

"It's the most I work all year," says Bryan. "Last year, I worked a total of 23 hours in one day. I went from my normal duties to Manager on Duty to security. We all have to pitch in a hand to get through it."

AWARDS

Bryan Cornelius' early managerial success is the result of a perfect recipe of dedication, hard work, ambition and a willingness to learn everything he can from everyone around him. Much recognition has already been bestowed upon him as a result. In fact, the week prior to his interview, the Radisson awarded Bryan the Manager of the Year Award for 2002.

"I was so surprised," he admits. "Everyone had been saying that I would get it, but until my name came out of my GM, Whip Triplett's, mouth that night, I didn't believe it. It was amazing.

One of the first things I did was call my mother. She was so happy for me; I work so hard to make my mother proud."

Bryan has also received the Bill Tiefel Award of Excellence. Distributed by the Marriott, this award is given to employees

who show such exemplary service that a guest writes a letter to Bill Tiefel and expresses appreciation for the service. Bryan has no recollection of the guest who was impressed by his service, but was extremely honored by the award. He has also been honored as Employee of the Month.

Regardless of the facility or state where he works and the administration or staff with whom he works, Bryan Cornelius maintains five-star standards. He goes to every effort to ensure the best possible experience for everyone, while aiming to become a mogul in the hospitality industry. "I tell my friends who want me to go out and party that I'm a future CEO on the go. I spend a majority of my time working to advance my career."

Mentors have given him guidance along the way, steering him away from trouble and toward success. Mark Stratton, one of Bryan's current managers, sees Bryan's potential and assists in opening doors for him. Bryan really appreciates the recognition of his current G.M., Whip Triplett, as he's provided Bryan with great opportunities. "He's the one who disregarded my age as a consideration," he relates. "He had faith in me, and I have done an excellent job for him in return."

CONCLUSION

Bryan Cornelius' mom has always desired her son to go to college. While much of his drive and ambition is fueled by a desire to please his mother, Bryan has yet to step into a college classroom, although he advises that he will go at some point. Recognizing the plethora of opportunities available in hospitality, he's pursued his career with a zest that goes unparalleled. His commitment is to be admired and respected. Upon calling his mother regarding his award last week, she asked him if he realized what he had accomplished at such an early age. "I do realize," he says, "but I don't want to dwell on it too much. I'm constantly moving and I don't want to get a big head. I want to sharpen my skills and do a lot more in the future, so I don't have too much time to thinks about the present."

Bryan's advice to other young aspiring executive housekeepers and professionals

1. Set one goal at a time. If you set too many, you'll get discouraged. So set one and follow it through.
2. Always ask questions.
3. Listen. It's the most effective way to gain intelligence.
4. Keep your eyes open to opportunities.
5. Work hard.
6. Defy adversity and negativity.
7. Never set yourself above your coworkers.
8. Remember that age is only a number.
9. Always ask for additional responsibilities, when you can handle it.

DISCUSSION QUESTIONS

1. Bryan Cornelius has not pursued a college degree. He seems to have succeeded without it, but has he? What arguments could you make to Bryan for going to college?
2. Bryan is very focused for his age. Can a person be too ambitious? Do you see any possible pitfalls to this single mindedness?

CONCLUSION

In this chapter we briefly traced the origins of hospitality and housekeeping, as well as the development of management theory and its application to the housekeeping function.

Our exploration of housekeeping and management theory has by no means been exhaustive. It is impossible to discuss all of the contributors and their contributions to management here, but we will be referring to some of the major contributors throughout this text, particularly the sequential functions of management as revised and expanded by R. Alec Mackenzie. Keep these principles in mind and refer to them as you read this text. Also, compare these ideas with those of Tom Atchison.

KEY TERMS AND CONCEPTS

Hospitality
Line organization
Span of control
Delegation
Classical school
Administrative theory
Scientific management
Scientific method
Management science
Operations research
Human relations
Behavioral school
Theory X
Theory Y
Satisfiers
Dissatisfiers
Participative management
Theory Z
Managerial grid

Quality circle
Situational leadership
Contingency approach
Elements
Ideas
Things
People
Functions
Continuous functions
Conceptual thinking
Administration
Leadership
Sequential functions
Management plan
Organized
Staffing
Directing
Control
Motivation

Productive
Turnover
Absenteeism
Insubordination
Exit interviews
Delegation
Standard operating procedures (SOPs)
Degrees of delegation
Tangibles
Intangibles
Inputs
Outputs
Inspired followers
Autocratic change
Passive aggressive behavior
Leadership style
Associates
Empowered

DISCUSSION AND REVIEW QUESTIONS

1. How has the function of executive house-keepers changed over the years?
2. Explain Theory X and Theory Y. Why are these theories significant in the development of worker morale and job enrichment?
3. What are the three elements of delegation? Discuss the importance of each element. What are some of the reasons why managers do not delegate?

4. Alex Mackenzie provides us with a matrix that relates many management principles, terms, functions, and activities. Identify them as elements, continuous functions, sequential functions, or activities of these functions. In your opinion, which ones are the most important?
5. Is there a difference between managers and leaders? Please explain.

NOTES

1. Henry L. Sisk, *The Principles of Management: A Systems Approach* (Ohio: South-Western Publishing Co., 1969), p. 24.
2. Louis E. Boone and David L. Kurtz, *Principles of Management* (New York: Random House, 1981), pp. 82–83.
3. Patrick Montana and Bruce Charnov, *Management* (New York: Barren's Educational Series, 1987), p. 14.
4. H. F. Merrill (ed.), *Classics in Management* (New York: American Management Association, 1960), p. 77. The passage quoted is from Frederick W. Taylor's testimony at hearings before the special committee of the House of Representatives to investigate Taylor and other systems of shop management, January 25, 1912, p. 1387.
5. Boone and Kurtz, *Principles of Management*, p. 36.
6. Robert Owen, *A New View of Society* (New York: E. Bliss and F. White, 1825), pp. 57–62. Reprinted in H. F. Merrill, ed., *Classics in Management* (New York: American Management Association, 1960), pp. 21–25.
7. Montana and Charnov, *Management*, pp. 17–19.
8. Douglas McGregor, *The Human Side of Enterprise* (New York: McGraw-Hill Book Co., 1960), pp. viii, 33–34, 246.
9. Ibid., pp. 47–48, 246.
10. Frederick Herzberg, Bernard Mausner, and B. Snydeman, *The Motivation to Work*, 2nd ed. (New York: John Wiley & Sons, 1959).
11. Rensis Likert, *New Patterns of Management* (New York: McGraw-Hill Book Co., 1961), pp. 222–36.
12. Montana and Charnov, *Management*, pp. 26–28.
13. R. R. Blake, J. S. Mouton, L. B. Barnes, and L. E. Greiner, "Breakthrough in Organization Development," *Harvard Business Review* 42 (November–December 1964): 133–55. For a complete description of the managerial grid, see Robert R. Blake and Jane S. Mouton, *The Managerial Grid* (Houston: Gulf Publishing Co., 1964).

14. Kenneth H. Blanchard and Paul Hersey, *Management of Organizational Behavior: Utilizing Human Resources* (Englewood Cliffs, N.J.: Prentice-Hall, 1988).
15. J. M. Shepard and J. G. Hougland Jr., "Contingency Theory: 'Complex Man' or 'Complex Organization'?" *Academy of Management Review*, July 1978, pp. 413–27.
16. Fred E. Fielder, *A Theory of Leadership Effectiveness* (New York: McGraw-Hill Book Co., 1967).
17. Victor Vroom and Phillip W. Yetton, *Leadership and Decision-Making* (Pittsburgh: University of Pittsburgh Press, 1973).
18. Blanchard and Hersey, *Management of Organizational Behavior*.
19. Henry Mintzberg, *The Nature of Managerial Work* (Englewood Cliffs, N.J.: Prentice-Hall, 1973).
20. R. Alec Mackenzie, "The Management Process in 3-D," *Harvard Business Review*, November–December 1969.
21. *Merriam-Webster's 11th Collegiate Dictionary* (2003), s.v. "motive."
22. McGregor, *The Human Side of Enterprise*, p. 47.
23. Thomas A. Atchison. Atchison Consulting Group, Oak Park, Ill. (Seminar Notes, 1992).
24. Timothy Weaver, "Theory M: Motivating with Money," *Cornell Hotel and Restaurant Administration Quarterly* 29 (no. 3, November 1988).
25. Paul Kirwin, "A Cost-Saving Approach to Housekeeping," *Cornell Hotel and Restaurant Administration Quarterly* 31 (no. 3, November 1990).
26. Ibid., p. 27.
27. Blanchard and Hersey, *Management of Organizational Behavior*, pp. 197–99.
28. James Pearson, "A.H. and M.A. Observation Hotel in Quality Assurance: The Sheraton Scottsdale in Scottsdale, Arizona," *Lodging*, April–May 1985.
29. Ibid., April, p. 58.

PLANNING, ORGANIZING, AND STAFFING THE NEW ORGANIZATION

In Part One we introduced five sequential steps of management: planning, organizing, staffing, directing, and controlling. In Part Two you will see how the first three steps apply to the management functions of a newly assigned executive housekeeper in a soon-to-open hotel. Chapters 2–9 will take you through the management tasks of planning for a new hotel, establishing position and job descriptions both for environmental services departments in hospitals and for housekeeping departments in hotels, scheduling workers, planning for necessary materials, staffing for housekeeping operations, and operational planning.

CHAPTER 2

Conceptual Planning

LEARNING OBJECTIVES

After studying the chapter, students should be able to:

1. Describe, from the executive housekeeper's perspective, the planning that is required to open a new hotel.
2. Describe the intended use of the following documents: Division of Work Document, Area Responsibility Plan, House Breakout Plan, Department Staffing Guide, and the Table of Personnel Requirements.
3. List and describe the preopening priorities of a newly hired executive housekeeper at a new hotel.
4. List possible variables to consider when establishing workload criteria for a guestroom attendant.
5. Define the key terms and concepts at the end of the chapter.

As noted in Chapter 1, there are five sequential functions of management: planning, organizing, staffing, directing, and controlling. Planning to administer a housekeeping department affords one of the most classical experiences that might be found in the management profession. It is for this reason that Chapter 1 was devoted primarily to landmarks of professional management development. It would therefore be a good idea for you to refer to Mackenzie's chart of management terms, activities, and definitions while studying this chapter on conceptual development.

The New Executive Housekeeper

Being appointed **executive housekeeper** of an ongoing operation has its challenges. After a brief introduction and orientation, the new manager would normally be expected to improve upon and bring about changes in operations related to the management potential for which he or she might have been selected. Any executive housekeeper who has had this experience might comment about how trying the task of bringing about change can be and how much easier it would have been if the operation could be started over. There is considerable truth in such a statement.

Being involved in a soon-to-open operation in which department planning has yet to be undertaken gives a manager the opportunity to influence how a department will be set up. Involvement in such an experience is both rewarding and enlightening and, once experienced, can prepare managers to bring about changes in an ongoing operation systematically and efficiently. The important point to remember, as stated by John Bozarth, is "Good results without planning is good luck, NOT good management."[1] It is therefore essential that planning any operation, change, system, organization, or procedure be allotted a proper portion of the manager's energies.

Chapters 2 through 9 place you in the role of a newly assigned executive housekeeper in a soon-to-open hotel. You will learn about the management planning that must take place to initiate operations, as well as about organizing and staffing a new operation. Once systems are developed and understood, you will see how they may be applied systematically and efficiently to ongoing operations.

The Executive Housekeeper's Position within the Organization

In the model hotel that we present in this text, the executive housekeeper is in the position of a **department head**. This position and level of responsibility is not uncommon in most transient hotels or hospitals that range in size from 200 to 3000 rooms. However, some executive housekeepers are below the department head level, whereas others may rank even higher. Many become executive committee members (top management within the facility), and others reach corporate executive levels. Many seek careers that develop along housekeeping lines, and others choose to be executive housekeepers and oversee the entire maintenance function of their hotels or health-care facilities. Still others see an involvement in housekeeping as an entry into the hospitality or health-care field. Regardless of position, all should have the freedom to communicate within channels to every level of the enterprise.

For all illustrative purposes in this text, we presume that our newly assigned executive housekeeper will operate from the department head level and will report to the hotel **resident manager**.

The Model Hotel

Recognizing that the major hotel market in the United States is the corporate transient market, we selected a commercial transient hotel with resort flair—the Radisson Hotel at Star Plaza in Merrillville, Indiana (Figure 2.1)—as a **model hotel** to illustrate the systems and procedures that you will study.

THE RADISSON HOTEL AT STAR PLAZA

Located in the northwest corner of Indiana at the intersection of Interstate Highway 65 and U.S. 30, this Radisson originated as a typical roadside Holiday Inn, a franchised operation, located 6 miles south of the heart of the Midwest steel-producing region near Gary, Indiana. Strategically located on the main southern interstate highway south of the Chicago area, the Radisson at Star Plaza is the result of the vision of its owner and founder, Dean V. White. In 1969, he constructed the first increment of this property as a typical 120-room Holiday Inn, with a small restaurant, a cocktail lounge, and several small meeting rooms. In 1972, the property underwent its first enlargement with the addition of 128 rooms and 6700 square feet of ballroom space.

In 1979, the property's second enlargement took place, adding 105 guestrooms, more than doubling the size of meeting and convention space, adding an indoor pool and recreation area (Holidome), renovating all older guestrooms and food facilities, and joining a

FIGURE 2.1 The Radisson Hotel at Star Plaza. *(Rendering courtesy of Whiteco Hospitality Corporation.)*

3,400-seat performing arts theater to the hotel. As a result of the 1979 expansion, the property became a system award winner, and in 1983 changed its name from Holiday Inn, Merrillville, to Holiday Star Resort and Conference Center. In early 1990, the hotel franchise was changed from Holiday Inn to Radisson. The theater is now known as the Star Plaza Theatre. Today the facility has 353 deluxe guestrooms, including 20 suites and 2 bilevel suites, 7 restaurants and lounges, and 18,000 square feet of convention space. The conference center is owned and operated by White Lodging Services, a subsidiary of Whiteco Industries in Merrillville. Unless otherwise noted, we use this 353-room commercial and resort hotel to show you the basis for housekeeping department planning and systems development.

Reporting for Work

Assume that you are in the position of the newly assigned executive housekeeper of the model hotel and have been told to report for work only six weeks before first opening. It is necessary for you to set priorities for your first activities. Recognizing that the housekeeping department consists of only one person (the executive housekeeper), you readily see that planning, organizing, and staffing functions are of first importance, and the efficient use of time is paramount. Not only is the planning of people functions important, but the design of systems, the establishment of procedures, the determination of supply and equipment needs, and reporting and coordinating relationships must be considered.

The executive housekeeper's experience usually begins by having the person to whom he or she will report (resident manager) introduce him or her to other members of the hotel staff who have been hired. These people are usually located in temporary hotel quarters such as a nearby office building.

It is at this time that the executive housekeeper will most likely be given the tentative chart of hotel organization, showing the positions of principal assistants to department heads. Figure 2.2 is an example of a hotel **organization chart** for our model hotel, showing the executive housekeeper position as that of department head in middle management.

Note the positions of the **executive committee** members at the top of the chart; this is the policymaking body of the hotel organization. Pay special attention to the positions of chief engineer and human resources director, which appear to be above the department heads and below the other members of the executive committee. The incumbents of these two positions are actually department heads, but by virtue of the fact that

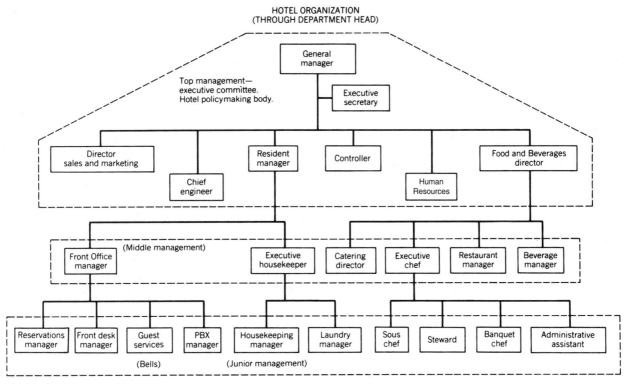

FIGURE 2.2 A hotel organization chart that might be presented to the executive housekeeper of our model hotel six weeks before opening.

their staff functions cross all departments to which they will provide a staff service, they are (ex officio) members of the executive committee. They are, in fact, middle managers with department head status.

The executive housekeeper is on equal rank with the front office manager, with both reporting to the resident manager. The executive housekeeper will have an assistant, tentatively titled **housekeeping manager**. In addition, operation of the property's laundry will be placed under the direction of the executive housekeeper, requiring another junior manager, the **laundry manager**, to report to the executive housekeeper.

Considering that we have a new property under construction that has not yet begun hotel operations, it is important to note the probable advance time when different members of the hotel organization may have reported. The director of sales and marketing is usually the first major manager on the site, being there since groundbreaking because advanced group room sales were begun at that time. The next major manager on site would probably be the chief engineer. This manager reports about the time the new building's foundation is completed and the first electrical and plumbing development has started. The chief engineer must monitor the birth of the mechanical systems, because this person will be expected to know these systems with great thoroughness. Sometimes the chief engineer will work as an assistant to the construction manager until construction is near completion. The third manager to report will probably be the general manager (six months before opening), followed by the resident manager and director of food and beverage (four months before opening), and the rest of the department heads (between six and eight weeks before opening). Junior management will report about four weeks before opening.

The significance of knowing who reports when becomes evident when we realize that the executive housekeeper must learn in six weeks what several others have been exposed to for a far greater time. For example, the executive housekeeper has to learn about available supply, storage, and security spaces before distribution of these spaces is undertaken to make sure that the housekeeping department is not slighted in the assignment of such space.

Reporting relationships also are significant. Coordination between housekeeping and front office personnel requires the respect and understanding of each of the department managers for the others' responsibilities. In addition, the executive housekeeper will have many occasions to relate to other members of the total hotel organization. It is therefore important to know and become known to each of these managers, and develop a respect and understanding for each of them and for their functions. Others should in turn develop an understanding and respect for the functions of the housekeeping department and its significance in the total operation.

Becoming acquainted with the new surroundings includes obtaining a set of working architectural drawings of the rooms portion of the hotel. Such drawings will allow the executive housekeeper to study the physical layout of the facility and will provide the basis for determining the scope of involvement and delineation of responsibilities of the various managers' areas. In addition, working drawings will assist the executive housekeeper when on-site inspections are begun.

Once the executive housekeeper has an understanding of who is who in the organization, has a knowledge of how long each person has been on site, how knowledgeable certain managers are and how helpful they can be; has met all the members of the management team thus far assembled, and has a copy of the working architect's drawings of the rooms department and related areas, he or she is ready to be shown the temporary working area in which departmental planning may begin.

Early Priority Activities

Given the various activities that make up the functions of planning, organizing, and staffing, there will be a mixture of activities that take place at the same time. Whereas there is an obvious need to determine what is to be done and how to go about doing it, there is an equal and urgent need to define the need for, establish the requisite qualifications of, and recruit the housekeeper's two principal assistants as soon as possible—the housekeeping manager and the laundry manager. Until these two managers are present, the entire planning, organizing, and staffing function rests on the shoulders of the executive housekeeper. Thus, we see the immediate need to specify the qualifications of these two managers to the personnel director in order that advertisements may be placed and recruitment begun. Recruitment is an immediate concern and will remain a part of the daily concern of the executive housekeeper until these people are hired, usually within ten days to two weeks.

DIVISION OF WORK DOCUMENT

The work that must actually be accomplished for the entire property needs to be recognized and identified as soon as possible. The executive housekeeper should make regular daily tours of the property under construction and, as soon as possible, draw up what is known as the **Division of Work Document**. This document is a recognition of what will be required in cleaning the property; all departments must become aware of this.

The Division of Work Document should include, but not necessarily be limited to, the care and maintenance of the following:

Rooms Department: Includes guestrooms, room corridors, elevators, elevator landings, stairwells, storage areas

Public Areas: Associated with the sale of guestrooms; the front desk, main entrance, public thoroughfares, public restrooms, storage areas, and similar locations

Recreation Areas: Indoor and outdoor pools, health clubs, saunas, game rooms, public restrooms, storage areas

Restaurants: Dining areas and service areas

Cocktail Lounges: Bar area, service areas, liquor storage areas

Meeting Rooms: Each by name, indicating the number of square feet in service and storage areas

Banquet and Ballrooms: Each by name, indicating the number of square feet in service and storage areas

Kitchen Areas: Main kitchen, banquet kitchens, salad preparation areas, refrigerators, freezers, holding boxes, food storerooms

Employee Areas: Includes locker rooms, employee restrooms, employee cafeteria

Offices: All offices, such as sales, reservations, and executive offices, that the public might be expected to frequent

Maintenance Shops: Main engineering work area; TV workshops; electrical, plumbing, refrigeration, and paint shops

Building Exterior
Landscaping
Lighting
Laundry
Other

Once it is completed, the executive housekeeper should present the Division of Work Document to the executive committee for review, listing the areas by name, noting anything unusual about expected cleaning requirements, and offering a recommendation as to who should be responsible for cleaning and maintaining each area.

Whereas most executive housekeepers are involved only in the guestroom portion of the hotel and related public areas, it is not unusual to be assigned the responsibility for nightly cleaning of kitchens, after-event ballroom cleaning, swimming pool maintenance, and similar tasks. There is essentially nothing wrong with inheriting such responsibilities *provided* sufficient funds and staff are allocated to compensate for the additional workload. Many times trade-offs are reasonable, such as the food and beverage department maintaining the employees' cafeteria at no cost to other departments, and the housekeeping departments maintaining all public restrooms regardless of where they are. However, if the housekeeping department is expected to clean an area foreign to the rooms department, such as kitchens, banquet space, restaurants, or cocktail lounges, then budgetary compensation and personnel must be provided to the housekeeping department and charged to the department receiving the service. It is always proper that costs be levied against the revenue generated in each of the various departments.

A Recommendation for Clean-as-You-Go

It might seem most efficient to place all cleaning responsibilities under one manager for control, but employees are inclined to be more careful and make less mess if they are required to clean up after themselves. Thus, departments charged with cleaning their own facilities create their own cost category for cleaning expense, which is to be charged against revenue generated rather than to another department. At any rate, if the housekeeping department is to be responsible for cleaning any area aside from the actual rooms department, monetary and personnel compensation is in order.

AREA RESPONSIBILITY PLAN

Once the Division of Work Document has been submitted to the executive committee for review, and the executive housekeeper has made recommendations to the resident manager (member of the executive committee), the **Area Responsibility Plan** can be drawn up by the executive committee. This plan is an assignment of responsibility of the various areas mentioned in the Division of Work Document and shows various cleaning area boundaries on a copy of a floor plan blueprint. Such boundary lines are important to ensure that no space is left unassigned and that no overlaps in cleaning responsibilities occur. An equitable Area Responsibility Plan is usually the result of the advance thinking and planning by an experienced executive housekeeper who has made multiple tours of the property when preparing the Division of Work Document. The plan should be forthcoming from the executive committee within the first week of the housekeeper's tenure.

CONTINUOUS PROPERTY TOURS

An important reason for regular and frequent tours of the property before opening is to learn the various locations of storerooms and service areas. There is little question regarding the main linen room, the laundry, and major storage areas. However, most hotels have small storage or service areas located in secluded places throughout the facility. It is important that the executive housekeeper note these out-of-the-way areas in order that enlightened negotiations for their use can take place when the time comes. For example, the executive housekeeper will need satellite (floor) linen rooms, and the chief engineer will need storage areas and TV repair space. Joint tours with the chief engineer and other department heads are highly recommended so all of those involved can reason with one another and reach an equitable agreement about the use of such space.

HOUSEKEEPING DEPARTMENT ORGANIZATION

The next task of the executive housekeeper is to develop the **housekeeping department organization**. Let us assume that the Area Responsibility Plan indicates that the housekeeping department personnel will be responsible for cleaning the rooms and associated public facilities areas, the offices, the recreation facilities, and all public restrooms. Figure 2.3 sets forth an organization chart that indicates the assignment of such responsibility.

Note that a portion of the organization devoted to cleaning rooms is not yet firm and may undergo considerable change before the final departmental organization is arrived at. However, assistant managers are clearly in place, and the task of organizing the

laundry will be delegated to the laundry manager as soon as he or she is selected. The first-line hourly supervisory structure provides for evening operations (3:30 P.M. to midnight), linen room operations (communication central), public area and utility personnel supervision, and supervision of recreation areas (two swimming pools, whirlpool, game room, sauna, and associated public restrooms). The actual size of the largest part of the organization (that which is associated with pure guestroom cleaning and servicing) is accommodated by applying a technique known as **zero-base budgeting**. Zero-base budgeting refers to worker use that takes into account actual occupancy on a specific day or for a specified period of time. Worker staffing and eventual scheduling are limited on a daily basis to the service of that specified occupancy and no more.

House Breakout Plan

The next major planning step that the executive housekeeper must undertake is the development of the **House Breakout Plan**. In order to ensure maximum familiarity with the facility, it is highly recommended

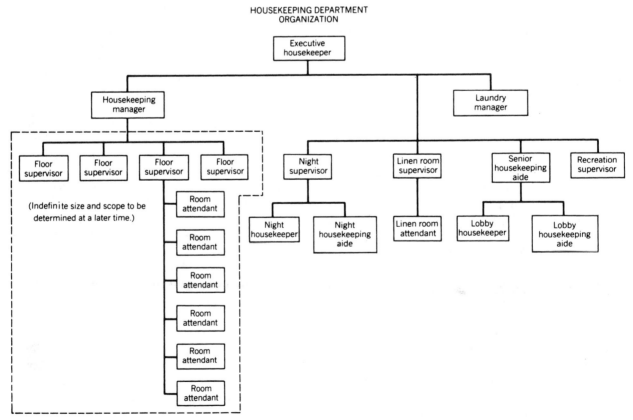

FIGURE 2.3 The executive housekeeper's first conception of department organization. Note the separation or tasks to be performed under various supervisors.

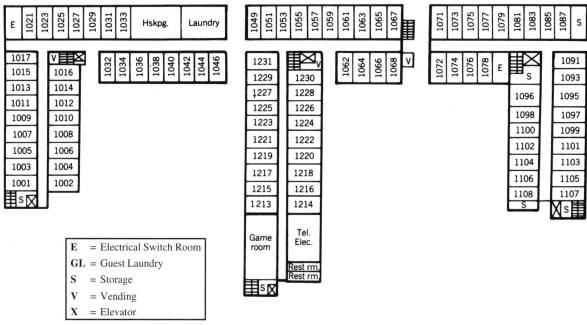

FIGURE 2.4 Floor plan layout of the model hotel; 94 first-floor rooms.

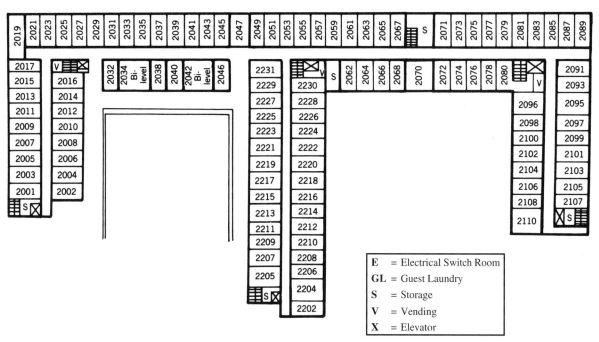

FIGURE 2.5 Floor plan layout of the model hotel; 114 second-floor rooms.

that the executive housekeeper personally develop this pictorial representation of every guestroom as it is located within the hotel. This is done by making a line drawing of the guestroom portion of the hotel, showing the relative positions of guestrooms, corridors, service areas, and other areas significant to guestroom cleaning. Figures 2.4 through 2.7 are examples of such drawings for our model hotel.

CRITERIA FOR WORKLOADS

As the House Breakout Plan is being created, certain criteria must be established: specifically, the workload of room attendants. The U.S. national average for rooms cleaned per day by one person ranges from 14 to 16 rooms, but the actual number may range from 13 rooms per day (8-hour shift) to a high of 20 rooms per day,

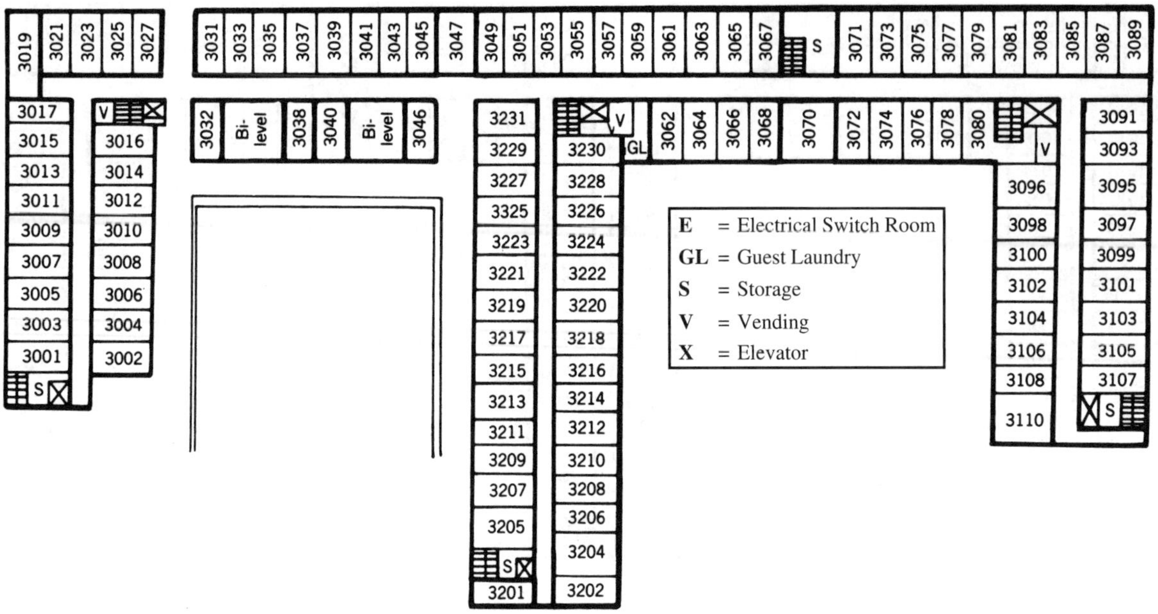

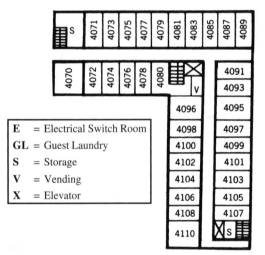

FIGURE 2.6 Floor plan layout of the model hotel; 112 third-floor rooms.

FIGURE 2.7 Floor plan layout of the model hotel; 33 fourth-floor rooms.

depending upon the type and nature of hotel activity. In resort hotels with many metal surfaces to polish, mirrors to clean, and multiple-occupancy guests who sleep in late, the workload of a room attendant may be only 13 rooms per day. In transient operations of standard-size rooms, where room occupancy consists primarily of business people (usually single occupancy) who arise and vacate early each day, room attendants can clean as many as 18 rooms per day—and clean them well if properly equipped and trained for efficient operation. (It is not a matter of working harder, just smarter.) However, recent trends in guest room design, including more pillows on beds, triple sheeting, duvet covers, thicker towels, and more guest amenities have added to the workload of the **guestroom attendant (GRA)**. If the hotel

has not planned out how these new time-consuming activities should be handled (working smarter), they should expect their GRA room productivity levels to diminish.

In our model hotel, experience dictates that approximately 18 rooms per day would not be unreasonable, taking into account special areas of the hotel in which cleaning loads might be dropped to 17 rooms per day.

A recent trend in some forward-thinking hotels is to assign room attendants "points." These points represent a standard daily workload. Then each room is evaluated and receives a point assignment by the executive housekeeper. Larger rooms, rooms with kitchens, and other rooms with special cleaning concerns, have more points assigned to them. Thus, some rooms may be equivalent to $1\frac{1}{2}$ or even $2\frac{1}{2}$ standard rooms. The purpose of this approach is to ensure that individual workloads are comparable.

Whether rooms or points are used to set workload criteria, management must remain flexible. When the condition of a room left by a guest is beyond the norm, this must also be factored into a room attendant's workload for the day.

It seems that every time the union contract for room attendants expires, this author receives a call from representatives of management asking for a study showing that room attendants can clean more rooms than they are presently required to do. At the same time, the union circulates press releases arguing that room attendants are overworked and underpaid. Typically, slight concessions are won by one side or the other and no real improvements to productivity and working conditions are made. Would it not be in both parties' interests if they concentrated on how to make the occupation of cleaning safer, healthier, and less stressful to the workers? This focus would not only improve productivity, but would also help to improve worker satisfaction. In the chapters ahead, new tools, chemicals, and methods of cleaning are presented, which may serve to revolutionize the way cleaning is conducted.

ROOM SECTIONS AND HOUSE DIVISIONS

Based on the workload criteria, the House Breakout Plan can now show the facility divided into room sections. A **room section** is a group of 13 to 20 guestrooms, reasonably contiguous to each other, that may normally be cleaned and serviced by one person in one 8-hour shift. The room section will normally be assigned a number and, for purposes of illustration, will be cleaned by the GRA.

In order for the room sections to be grouped into logical units for supervisory and control needs, **house divisions** will be used. A house division is a group of four to six room sections with associated and/or specified corridors, elevators, stairwells, service areas, and storage areas. It may be assigned a color or letter designation and placed under the charge of a supervisor. For demonstration purposes with our model hotel, house divisions will be color-coded and placed under a supervisor known as a **senior GRA** or **supervisor**.

We can use the pictorial drawings in Figures 2.4–2.7 to determine the room sections and house divisions in the model hotel. We have the 18-room-per-day criteria and 353 rooms that must be cleaned under 100 percent occupancy conditions. If we divide 353 rooms by 18 rooms per day, we get 19.6 room sections. Because a partial section is not practical or economical, we divide the house into 20 sections of either 17 or 18 rooms each. In addition, five GRAs will form a house division for supervisory and control purposes.

The House Breakout Plan may now be completed by considering the size of sections, assembly of house divisions, location of contiguous rooms, position of elevators, and transportation from room to room.

Figure 2.8 shows how the first floor of the model hotel in Figure 2.4 has been divided into room sections 1 to 5, of 18 rooms each. In addition, the rooms of entire first floor of the model hotel have been combined to form the red division, which contains a total of 90 rooms for supervision and control by the senior housekeeper. Note the four excess rooms on the first floor (rooms 1023, 1025, 4027, and 1029). At 100 percent occupancy, these rooms are not a part of the red division but will be cleaned by a section housekeeper from the second floor, who will pick up these rooms as part of another section. Figures 2.9, 2.10, and 2.11 show the same planning procedure used in Figure 2.8 for Figures 2.5, 2.6, and 2.7, respectively.

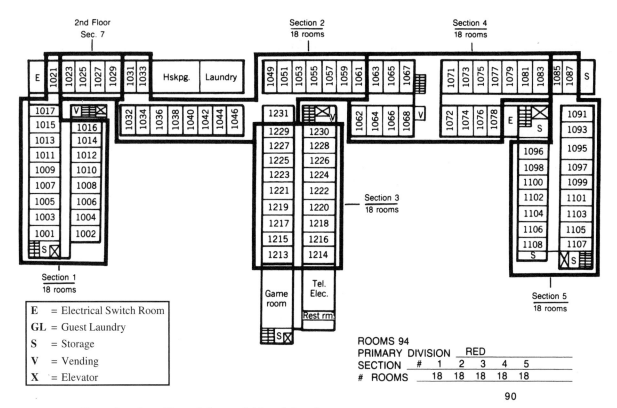

FIGURE 2.8 House Breakout Plan of the model hotel; first floor.

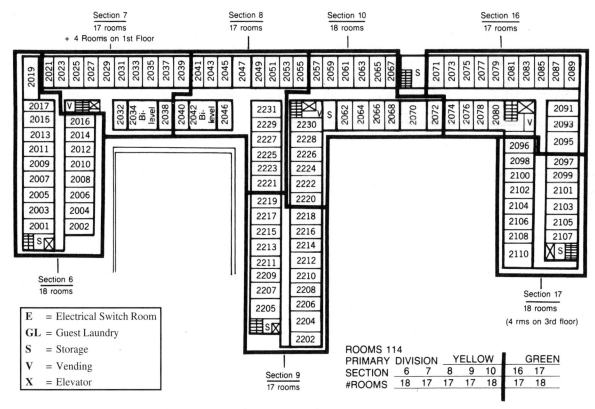

FIGURE 2.9 House Breakout Plan of the model hotel; second floor.

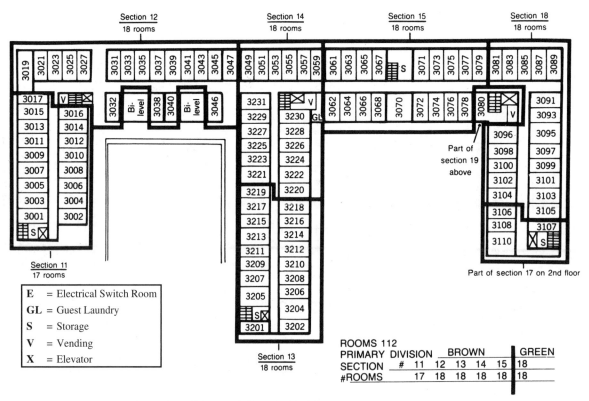

FIGURE 2.10 House Breakout Plan of the model hotel; third floor.

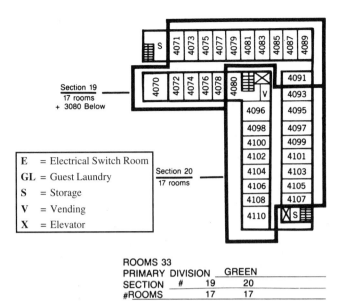

E = Electrical Switch Room
GL = Guest Laundry
S = Storage
V = Vending
X = Elevator

Section 19
17 rooms
+ 3080 Below

Section 20
17 rooms

ROOMS 33
PRIMARY DIVISION ___GREEN___
SECTION   #   19   20
#ROOMS   17   17

FIGURE 2.11 House Breakout Plan of the model hotel; fourth floor.

Note that the number of rooms on the second and third floors is much greater than that on the first floor. This requires consideration when forming the remaining house divisions. Figures 2.9, 2.10, and 2.11 show the creation of the yellow division on the second floor (composed of sections 6 through 10 on the west end of the second floor), the brown division on the third floor (composed of sections 11 through 15 on the west end of the third floor), and the green division on the second, third, and fourth floors on the east end of the building. Section 7 is completed by including the four rooms on the first floor that are not a part of the red division. Note the proximity of these rooms to section 7 (directly below and adjacent to an elevator).

The House Breakout Plan developed in this chapter is by no means the only way the model hotel can be broken into logical work units. It does, however, reflect an efficient method of division of the workload. This particular technique also lends itself to a form of work scheduling (known as team scheduling, which will be dealt with in Chapter 3).

Staffing Considerations
❧

Most hotel housekeeping departments will hire and individually schedule section housekeepers on an as-needed basis depending on occupancy. Whereas union operations may require the guarantee of a 40-hour workweek for **regular employees**, most union houses have few such regular employees. Union operations have considerably more people, referred to as **steady extras**, who can be called upon on an as-needed basis (when occupancy exceeds 25 to 40 percent).

Nonunion operations seldom guarantee a 40-hour workweek but will staff in such a way (based on expected occupancy) so as to provide between 35 and 40 hours of work each week for their regular employees. Recognizing that labor costs within a housekeeping department are the highest recurring costs in a rooms department budget, it is highly inefficient to guarantee a set number of regular employees 40 hours when occupancy is low. For this reason a practical number of employees will be hired based on expected occupancy for a given period of time.

Section housekeepers are scheduled on an individual but rotating basis to ensure a fair and equal spread of the available hours. Sometimes the size of the hotel might warrant the scheduling of several hundred such employees on a daily basis. Such scheduling techniques are time-consuming and tedious. As a result, we will use a different scheduling concept that has been tested and proven to have many advantages over individual housekeeper scheduling.

TEAM CONCEPT IN STAFFING

Rather than scheduling housekeepers on an individual basis, **housekeeping teams** may be formed. A housekeeping team consists of one supervisor (senior GRA) who is in charge and one section GRA for each section within a division. Because a house division includes the cleaning and care of corridors, stairwells, elevators, and designated service areas, as well as associated guestrooms, the additional position of **section housekeeping aide** is required on a team. (This is the nonsexist term for *houseman*.) This position may be filled by any person capable of performing the work set forth in the job description (see job description of the section housekeeping aide in Appendix A). Teams consisting of one senior GRA, five guestroom attendants (GRAs), and one housekeeping aide can now be formed, identified by a corresponding color designation, and assigned to corresponding house divisions (for instance, red team to the red division; yellow team to the yellow division). Recall that the team system of organization thus far deals only with the subject of staffing. The actual day-to-day scheduling within teams will be based on actual occupancy, as discussed in Chapter 3.

SWING TEAMS

The assignment of regular teams to house divisions for staffing purposes satisfies the need for division coverage, but it becomes obvious that the hotel operating on a seven-days-per-week basis will require additional personnel to work when regular teams have days off. To accommodate days off, **swing teams** may be formed.

Consider the requirement that no employee may work more than a 40-hour week without the provision of overtime. It becomes prudent to assume that a 40-hour week consisting of five regular 8-hour days will be the standard and that the sixth and seventh day of work in a house division must be accomplished by using additional employees.

Recall that the housekeeping department in the model situation will also operate a laundry. The laundry has about the same staffing requirements and will face the same situation of a seven-day operation, with employees requiring two days off each week. By combining the total workforce of the GRAs and laundry attendants (20 GRAs, 5 laundry attendants, supervisor, and aides for each group), a relief situation can be developed as follows:

20 GRAs + 5 laundry attendants = 25 employees
25 employees × 7 days/week
requires 175 man-days of effort
175 man-days/5 maximum number of days allowed
    = 35 employees needed

This same formula can be applied to supervisors and section housekeeping aides.

The original 25 employees will require an additional 10 employees to relieve them if a five-day workweek is to be adhered to. By forming two extra teams from the 10 extra employees, with each team having a supervisor and a housekeeping aide, a staffing rationale may be created as follows:

Regular Assigned Employees	Relief
Red team	Swing team 1 relieves two days per week
Yellow team	Swing team 1 relieves two days per week
Brown team	Swing team 2 relieves two days per week
Green team	Swing team 2 relieves two days per week
Laundry team	Each swing team relieves in the laundry one day per week

As you can see, not only are the four regular teams and the laundry staff now regulated to five days each week for staffing purposes, each swing team is also staffed for a five-day week. It should be remembered that the development of these criteria pertains to staffing only. The actual day-to-day scheduling and employee needs based on occupancy considerations are discussed in Chapter 3.

Completion of the Department Organization

❧

The staffing requirement of the housekeeping department may now be completely defined. The incomplete department organization shown in Figure 2.3 may be completed by the addition of six teams—four regular teams (identified as red, yellow, brown, and green), each having one supervisor, one section housekeeping aide, five GRAs, and two swing teams (identified as swing teams 1 and 2). The swing teams will each work four days in the rooms section of the hotel and one day in the laundry.

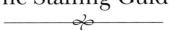

The Staffing Guide

A major phase of human resources planning may now be completed by formulation of the **Department Staffing Guide**. Table 2.1 sets forth a staffing guide showing each and every position that must be filled within the department, using the team concept of staffing.

TABLE 2.1 Department Staffing Guide

Position No.	Title	Name Assigned
Management Team		
1	Executive housekeeper	_____
2	Housekeeping manager	_____
3	Laundry manager	_____
Fixed Team		
4	Linen room supervisor	_____
5	Linen room attendant	_____
6	Senior housekeeping aide (public area supervisor)	_____
7	Public area housekeeper 1 (male)	_____
8	Public area housekeeper 2 (female)	_____
9	Public area housekeeper (relief)	_____
Evening Team		
10	Night supervisor	_____
11	Night GRA	_____
12	Night housekeeping aide	_____
13	Night (public area) housekeeper 1 (male)	_____
14	Night (public area) housekeeper 2 (female)	_____
15	Night (public area) housekeeper (relief)	_____
Regular Rooms Cleaning Teams: Red Team		
16	Senior GRA (supervisor)	_____
17	Section housekeeping aide	_____
18	GRA 1	_____
19	GRA 2	_____
20	GRA 3	_____
21	GRA 4	_____
22	GRA 5	_____
Yellow Team		
23	Senior GRA (supervisor)	_____
24	Section housekeeping aide	_____
25	GRA 6	_____
26	GRA 7	_____
27	GRA 8	_____
28	GRA 9	_____
29	GRA 10	_____
Brown Team		
30	Senior GRA (supervisor)	_____
31	Section housekeeping aide	_____
32	GRA 11	_____
33	GRA 12	_____
34	GRA 13	_____
35	GRA 14	_____
36	GRA 15	_____
Green Team		
37	Senior GRA (supervisor)	_____
38	Section housekeeping aide	_____
39	GRA 16	_____
40	GRA 17	_____
41	GRA 18	_____
42	GRA 19	_____
43	GRA 20	_____
Laundry		
44	Laundry supervisor (washer)	_____
45	Laundry helper/sorter	_____
46	Laundry attendant (ironer)	_____
47	Laundry attendant (ironer)	_____
48	Laundry attendant (folder/stacker)	_____
49	Laundry attendant (folder/stacker)	_____
50	Laundry attendant (folder/stacker)	_____
Swing Team 1		
51	Senior GRA (swing supervisor)	_____
52	Section housekeeping aide (ST-A)	_____
53	GRA A-1	_____
54	GRA A-2	_____
55	GRA A-3	_____
56	GRA A-4	_____
57	GRA A-5	_____
Swing Team 2		
58	Senior GRA (swing supervisor)	_____
59	Section housekeeping aide (ST-B)	_____
60	GRA B-1	_____
61	GRA B-2	_____
62	GRA B-3	_____
63	GRA B-4	_____
64	GRA B-5	_____

The Department Staffing Guide provides for personal and numerical identification of every person who must be hired for the department. A copy may be given to the human resources department and the resident manager for review and critique of staffing plans. Note that space is provided for writing in the employees' names opposite the position numbers. When vacancies occur, they will occur by position numbers and may be readily identified. Should projected occupancy be less than 90 percent for the upcoming year, certain established positions may be left unfilled until such time as increased occupancy is forecast.

Table of Personnel Requirements

✷

After developing the House Breakout Plan and the Staffing Guide, the executive housekeeper can develop one of the most important day-to-day tools for effective management of the housekeeping department—the **Table of Personnel Requirements**—illustrated in Table 2.2. This table has been developed for the model hotel, in which there are 353 rooms and in which each section housekeeper will clean an average of 18 rooms per day.

At each percent of occupancy, the table establishes the number of rooms that will require service, the number of housekeepers required at the rate of 18 rooms cleaned per day each working 8 hours a day, the number of housekeeper-hours required in an 8-hour workday, the number of housekeeper-hours per week, and the number of housekeeper-hours per 28-day period.

Construction of the table starts at zero base (see end of table), noting that at zero occupancy no GRAs are required. Occupancy through 18 rooms requires one section housekeeper working an 8-hour day, occupancy through 36 rooms requires the addition of the second section housekeeper, and so on until occupancy above 96 percent requires the addition of the 20th section housekeeper.

Every executive housekeeper must have a table of personnel requirements in order that the number of GRAs and the number of GRAs hours per day, per week, and per period may be determined quickly for every given occupancy. Such information becomes vital to the efficient scheduling and administration of any housekeeping department.

Job Descriptions

✷

Along with the development of the Table of Personnel Requirements, a set of **job descriptions** and/or **position descriptions** must also be developed. This is done by developing a sequence of individual tasks for operations that may be grouped and then assigned to a single person. The grouping of such tasks is the creation of the position and job description.

If one is to take full advantage of the **motivators of achievement**—growth, responsibility, and recognition—one must examine every job very closely in order to see to it that the factors that make up the job itself will form the **satisfiers** referred to by Herzberg in Chapter 1. All too often, jobs are designed around people of special ability. This is not necessarily unprofessional, provided there is *no* possibility of losing the person for whom the job was designed. In most situations, however, this is not possible. When a person of special quality leaves or is transferred, we hope to fill the position with someone of equal capability. If no one can be found with the same abilities, the job must be redefined. This is often time-consuming and may cause some reorganizing. It is a much wiser course of action first to specify the tasks that must be accomplished and then to group these tasks into logical units that have the lowest per unit cost.

When there is a choice about which tasks should be combined into a single job, the criterion of *lowest per unit cost* is applied. Because cost is to be minimized, it is logical to design tasks and combine them in such a fashion that the lowest level of skill is required. For example, we would not want to combine the task performed by a guestroom attendant with those of a supervisor, because different skill levels are required. Similarly, the tasks involved in the job of a guestroom attendant should not be combined with those involved in the job of a lobby housekeeper. The rationale is that it would not be cost-effective to have people cleaning rooms one minute and fulfilling other maintenance tasks in the lobby the next.

The objectives of a study of job descriptions must therefore be:

1. To find out what the individual tasks of operations are that make up the work of a housekeeping or environmental services department
2. To see how these tasks are grouped into positions and job descriptions
3. To understand the difference between position descriptions and job descriptions, and how each is used
4. To see what goes into writing such documents

Appendix A contains a set of job descriptions for a hotel housekeeping department.

Even though job descriptions may be written for unskilled, semiskilled, and skilled employees, they may also be written for supervisors, managers, and executives.

TABLE 2.2 Table of Personnel Requirements[a]

Percent of Occupancy	Number of Rooms	Number of GRAs per Day	GRA Hours/Day	GRA Hours/Week	GRA Hours/ 28-Day Period
100	353	20	160	1120	4480
99	350	20	160	1120	4480
98	346	20	160	1120	4480
97	343	20	160	1120	4480
96	339	19	152	1064	4256
95	336	19	152	1064	4256
94	332	19	152	1064	4256
93	329	19	152	1064	4256
92	325	19	152	1064	4256
91	322	18	144	1008	4032
90	318	18	144	1008	4032
89	315	18	144	1008	4032
88	311	18	144	1008	4032
87	308	18	144	1008	4032
86	304	17	136	952	3808
85	300	17	136	952	3808
84	297	17	136	952	3808
83	293	17	136	952	3808
82	290	17	136	952	3808
81	286	16	128	896	3584
80	283	16	128	896	3584
79	279	16	128	896	3584
78	276	16	128	896	3584
77	272	16	128	896	3584
76	269	15	120	840	3360
75	265	15	120	840	3360
74	262	15	120	840	3360
73	258	15	120	840	3360
72	255	15	120	840	3360
71	251	14	112	784	3136
70	248	14	112	784	3136
69	244	14	112	784	313
68	241	14	112	784	3136
67	237	14	112	784	3136
66	234	13	104	728	2912
65	230	13	104	728	2912
64	227	13	104	728	2912
63	223	13	104	728	2912
62	220	13	104	728	2912
61	216	12	96	672	2688
60	212	12	96	672	2688
59	209	12	96	672	2688
58	205	12	96	672	2688
57	203	12	96	672	2688
56	199	12	96	672	2688
55	195	11	88	616	2464
54	191	11	88	616	2464
53	187	11	88	616	2464
52	184	11	88	616	2464
51	181	11	88	616	2464
50	177	10	80	560	2240

TABLE 2.2 (Continued)

Percent of Occupancy	Number of Rooms	Number of GRAs per Day	GRA Hours/Day	GRA Hours/Week	GRA Hours/ 28-Day Period
49	173	10	80	560	2240
48	169	10	80	560	2240
47	166	10	80	560	2240
46	162	9	72	504	2016
45	159	9	72	504	2016
44	156	9	72	504	2016
43	152	9	72	504	2016
42	149	9	72	504	2016
41	145	9	72	504	2016
40	142	8	64	448	1792
39	138	8	64	448	1792
38	135	8	64	448	1792
37	131	8	64	448	1792
36	127	8	64	448	1792
35	124	7	56	392	1568
34	121	7	56	392	1568
33	117	7	56	392	1568
32	114	7	56	392	1568
31	110	7	56	392	1568
30	106	6	48	336	1344
29	103	6	48	336	1344
28	99	6	48	336	1344
27	96	6	48	336	1344
26	91	6	48	336	1344
25	89	5	40	280	1120
24	85	5	40	280	1120
23	82	5	40	280	1120
22	78	5	40	280	1120
21	75	5	40	280	1120
20	71	4	32	224	896
19	67	4	32	224	896
18	64	4	32	224	896
17	60	4	32	224	896
16	57	4	32	224	896
15	53	3	24	168	672
14	50	3	24	168	672
13	46	3	24	168	672
12	43	3	24	168	672
11	39	3	24	168	672
10	36	2	16	112	448
9	32	2	16	112	448
8	29	2	16	112	448
7	25	2	16	112	448
6	22	2	16	112	448
5	18	1	8	56	224
4	15	1	8	56	224
3	11	1	8	56	224
2	7	1	8	56	224
1	4	1	8	56	224
0	0	0	0	0	0 base

[a]This table is for a 353-room hotel with a work criterion of 18 rooms per day to be cleaned by one GRA.

HOTEL HOUSEKEEPING DEPARTMENTS

Position descriptions are sometimes written for managers, or for those who have management prerogatives. Such people hire, fire, set wages, and make policy. The position description type of document sets forth the **basic function** of the manager and defines the **scope** of the manager's responsibilities and authority. **Specific responsibilities** that have been created for the manager and the **reporting relationships** they have with other members of the organization are listed. There is usually a statement, referred to as a **work emphasis**, about how a manager should allot his or her time and efforts.

In the position description for an executive housekeeper in Appendix A, note that the basic function listed in the position description is a simple statement of overall responsibility. The scope helps the manager define the limits of managerial authority. What usually follows the scope is a group of specific responsibilities (actual tasks that must be accomplished). Note that the terms "coordinate," "administer control," and "be responsible for" are used frequently. They imply that the specific tasks have been delegated to someone who is working for the manager. Note also the *standard form*, first of the position descriptions for the department manager, then

of the job descriptions for the working line personnel of the housekeeping department.

HOSPITAL ENVIRONMENTAL SERVICES DEPARTMENTS

The **environmental services department** has similar requirements for job descriptions. The same form for the job description (JD) is used whether for manager or for worker. The documents remain an essential ingredient for all departments within the hospital and all departments will use the same format. The JD provides a synopsis of the requirements for each job classification. It is used by the human resources department when it recruits to fill an open position, as reference for a current employee, and as a resource in conducting performance evaluations.

The structure and number of job descriptions depend on the individual facility. The human resources department often has a preferred format for job assignments; the number needed will depend on the size and structure of the department. Departments that are structured differently may require more, fewer, or have differing types of job descriptions. The uniqueness within each facility must be taken into consideration when developing a job description.

CONCLUSION

Although the day-to-day operation of a hotel housekeeping department can be interesting and rewarding, it also has its limitations. Many of the systems and procedures used in day-to-day operations are already developed. For this reason, we began from the point of view of a newly assigned executive housekeeper for a soon-to-open hotel. This situation required that planning be started from the beginning.

In this chapter, we selected a model hotel and showed many of the first plans that must be established. We also saw that priorities for activities become paramount. The executive housekeeper must quickly become familiar with the hotel organization, which has been created before his or her arrival; making the acquaintance of staff members already present can ensure valuable sources of information, including where future roadblocks may occur. The executive housekeeper must quickly obtain a set of architect's drawings and begin planning staffing requirements and methods of operation. Daily property tours are a must so that the executive housekeeper can quickly learn every space that may be encountered in the future. Departmental organization must be started, a Division of Work Document created, an Area Responsibility Plan recommended and approved, and the House Breakout Plan created.

First personnel planning is finished when the staffing guide is complete and a Table of Personnel Requirements

has been constructed. At this time the executive housekeeper is in a position to provide first labor budgets and actual staffing requirements. Immediate steps can be taken to acquire the two junior managers noted in the organization and to make the department ready to hire personnel at least two weeks before opening.

In this chapter, you were also introduced to the team system of staffing. Much more will be said about this method of staffing when you study scheduling, supervisory direction of effort, and morale-building environments. The scenarios presented here should in no way detract from other techniques that are workable and have been proven efficient and effective. Conversely, other departments outside of housekeeping, which must schedule in a manner sensitive to occupancy changes, would do well to consider team staffing as explained herein.

The third activity of Mackenzie's sequential functions of getting organized involves the creation of position and job descriptions. In order to take full advantage of Herzberg's satisfiers (see Chapter 1), position and job descriptions need to be designed based on the job, and not on the talents of specific people.

Job descriptions are written for unskilled, semiskilled, and skilled employees, as well as for supervisors, managers, and executives. The job descriptions in this chapter are for hourly employees; included here are first-line workers and supervisors who perform hands-on work.

Position descriptions are written for employees with management prerogatives who hire, fire, and set wages. Each position description gives the basic function, scope, specific responsibilities, relationship to responsibilities, and work emphasis. Examples were presented.

Appendix A contains a partial set of job and position descriptions for a hotel housekeeping department.

KEY TERMS AND CONCEPTS

Executive housekeeper	Zero-base budgeting	Table of Personnel Requirements
Department head	House Breakout Plan	Job descriptions
Resident manager	Guestroom attendant (GRA)	Position descriptions
Model hotel	Room section	Motivators of achievement
Organization chart	House divisions	Satisfiers
Executive committee	Senior GRA/supervisor	Basic function
Housekeeping manager	Regular employees	Scope
Laundry manager	Steady extras	Specific responsibilities
Division of Work Document	Housekeeping teams	Reporting relationships
Area Responsibility Plan	Section housekeeping aide	Work emphasis
Housekeeping department organization	Swing teams	Environmental services department
	Department Staffing Guide	

DISCUSSION AND REVIEW QUESTIONS

1. Assume you are a newly assigned executive housekeeper for a soon-to-open hotel. Develop a priority list of action items to be completed before opening. How would you modify this list if the operation were already in progress?
2. Define zero-based staffing.
3. Discuss reasons why the executive housekeeper should develop a Division of Work Document. What is its relation to an Area Responsibility Plan?
4. The House Breakout Plan is developed from a line drawing of a floor plan for the guestroom portion of a hotel. Why should the executive housekeeper *personally* prepare this drawing?
5. List four reasons why the executive housekeeper should make daily tours of a new facility before opening. Should these tours be made alone? If not, who should accompany the executive housekeeper?
6. Preparing a set of job descriptions is part of which sequential function of management?
7. Once the Table of Personnel Requirments and Department Staffing Guide have been drawn up, the next step is to estimate the cost of labor for the department. Since labor is a primary expense, it is essential that the executive housekeeper have an accurate estimate of department labor cost when preparing the annual operating budget as presented in later in this text in Chapter 11. The following are projections for a large full-service hotel due to open. Develop an Annual Labor Cost Estimate projection from this data. *Note:* There are no perfectly correct answers for this problem. Begin by discussing how many personnel are needed in these positions for each shift and in total with your instructor and your fellow students. When complete, compare your cost estimates with those of your fellow students:

Number of Rooms: 3152
Forecasted Occupancy: 75%
Number of Rooms Cleaned per Day: 15
Eight Hour Day-5 Day Work Week
No Overtime Should Be Considered
Open Seven Days a Week, 365 Days a Year
Turndown Service for All Guests
Housekeeping Dept. Open for Three Shifts
Housekeeping Dept. Cleans 28,000 sq. ft. of Public Space (lobby, 6 public restrooms, convention space)
Housekeeping Dept. Cleans 3,000 sq. ft. of Office Space
Housekeeping Dept. Does Not Clean the Restaurants or Kitchens
House Porters (Housekeeping Aides) vacuum, sweep, hall trash and linens
Utility Porters operate scrubbers, floor machines, and other heavy equipment, climb ladders, and are generally more highly skilled
No on-premise laundry
Everyone gets two weeks vacation

Annual Labor Cost Estimate (A.L.C.E.)

Position	Salary/Wage Rate	Day Shift	Swing Shift	Grave Shift	Total	Person/Hours	Extension $
Ex. Hskpr.	$70,000/yr						
Asst. Ex. Hskpr.	$45,000/yr						
Other Mgrs.	$37,000/yr						
L.R. Supervisors	$12.00/hr						
Night Supervisors	$14.00/hr						
Division Supr.	$11.00/hr						
Section GRAs	$9.00/hr						
House Porters	$9.00/hr						
Utility Porters	$11.00/hr						
Seamstress	$9.00/hr						
Total	XXXXXXXXXX						

First Year Annual Payroll Estimate _____

Total Person Hours _____

Number of Housekeeping Teams: Regular _____ Swing _____

Grave _____

NAME _____

NOTE

1. John Bozarth, C.E.H., ''Leadership Styles: Where Do You Fit In?'' *Executive Housekeeping Today*, May 1983, p. 20.

CHAPTER 3

Planning to Schedule Workers: A Major Advantage of Housekeeper Team Staffing

LEARNING OBJECTIVES

After studying the chapter, students should be able to:

1. Describe the use of conventional individual worker scheduling, and list its negative and positive aspects.
2. Describe the use of team scheduling and its negative and positive aspects.
3. Construct a standing rotational schedule for a housekeeping department, given the necessary information.
4. Construct a tight schedule, given the necessary information.
5. Differentiate between team scheduling and team cleaning.

Not many hotels or hospitals close on Saturdays, Sundays, and holidays. **Worker scheduling** would be greatly simplified if such were the case. Everyone would have weekends and holidays off, and when the doors of the department were closed, workers and managers alike could relax, knowing that nothing was happening at the office.

In hotels, hospitals, restaurants, and other seven-day operations, however, worker scheduling is a major task that must be performed with absolute regularity. Not only must the manager and supervisor devote time and forethought to the task of scheduling, but they must also take into account the needs of people whom they schedule. For example, some workers may not be able to work on Tuesdays and others want weekends off; family demands and illness must also be recognized and accommodated. Add to these concerns the problem of fluctuating occupancy, which has the greatest effect on housekeeper scheduling, and the manager has a full-time task that may not allow time for other less repetitive but more creative tasks.

The manager who schedules a group of individual workers on a weekly basis and who must adjust schedules on a daily basis may well earn the label "tied down." In order to improve this routine of scheduling and in so doing greatly reduce the time that management has to spend performing these tasks; you should try the team system of organization and scheduling.

A Word about Team Staffing

The **team system of organization** presented in Chapter 2 has many advantages. A principal advantage to the manager is in being able to schedule a group of people as though it were one entity. It is true that not every person in the department can be handled in such a manner, but the majority of employees in a housekeeping department can be grouped for scheduling purposes. Another advantage of the team system of organization is that cooperation and workers' morale will be higher when they are part of a small unit than when they perform as individuals in a large group of people. A worker who is a member of a seven-person team is much more likely to relate to team performance where the impact of a personal contribution can be seen than to a large organization where he or she is but one of many.

The system of **team scheduling** and **staffing** also embraces the idea that the team will work together and will regularly be off together. Having assigned teams to work in specific areas of the hotel (red team in the red division, yellow team in the yellow division, and so on), the teams become responsible for the entire cleaning function in their areas. The team—which has a supervisor (senior GRA) in charge, several guestroom attendants (GRAs) who clean guestrooms, and a section housekeeping aide who assists and also cleans other areas of the division such as corridors, stairwells, and elevators—becomes totally responsible for the entire division of the hotel. Cleaning performance within the division becomes a primary responsibility of the entire team under the supervisor, and performance is measured on a team basis rather than an individual basis.

If the premise that each individual worker wants to be a part of a worthwhile operation is true, team spirit will cause the entire group to excel. There will always be a few above-average GRAs who excel in room cleaning and take personal pride in their individual work; however, in the eyes of the guest, the reputation of the best housekeeper will never be better than the reputation of the poorest GRAs in the entire group. GRAs, once they understand that their individual reputations are judged by the performance of the poorest in the team, will become more willing to help the poorer performers to improve. It should not be surprising, therefore, to find many small disciplinary problems such as absenteeism and tardiness resolved at the team level, because to be absent or late could have a negative effect on the team's reputation.

PROMOTING TEAMWORK

Even though the entire department is one team, and teamwork must be fostered at every turn, promoting teamwork within each individual team requires special effort. Susan C. Bakos[1] offers the following observation:

> Most people, management and employees alike, pay lip service to the teamwork concept. "Teamwork" looks good in company slogans and fits nicely into speeches. But the word usually means getting someone else to cooperate with you. Unfortunately, everyone on the "team" feels the same way!

Individuals work for the achievement of personal goals; promotions, raises, benefits, and recognition. Today's economy has made competition for these goals fiercer, with the obvious result that workers are even less willing to be team players than ever before. And managers often contribute to this situation by espousing "teamwork" yet rewarding individual performance.

Bakos continues by saying that managers who follow a teamwork approach should reward cooperation, and suggests a Manager's Teamwork Checklist, which includes the following:

- Rewarding teamwork through (team) praise, choice assignments, raises, and promotions, just as we would reward individual performance
- Including teamwork as a part of performance appraisals
- Rotating special assignments, allowing everyone an opportunity to shine as an individual occasionally
- Considering team ideas as well as individual ideas
- Sharing information, decision making, and credit for jobs well done
- Setting an example by cooperating with others

Bakos concludes by indicating that such a **Manager's Teamwork Checklist** helps make competitive individuals part of a goal-oriented group and helps individuals put self-interest aside and make company goals the first priority.

TEAMWORK AND SWING TEAMS

Swing (or **relief**) **teams**, although not assigned to a regular division of the hotel, are as accountable as regular teams for performance and for the condition of jointly used equipment on the days they are scheduled to work in a given division. This helps resolve problems that come up. For example, GRAs on occasion complain about the condition of "their" section after returning from scheduled days off, or about the condition of "their" maid's cart, vacuum cleaner, or other equipment. Such complaints are often resolved when the regular GRA knows exactly who will be cleaning in the section when the regular team is off. Problems are much easier to talk out when the same workers face each other and are held accountable for the condition of jointly used equipment.

CHANGE AGENTS

David Frank

President
Knowledge Worx

David Frank is known as "the high-impact speaker who motivates." Every year he presents more than 100 seminars specifically designed for manufacturers and distributors. He is a nationally recognized authority with over 25 years of experience in distribution, manufacturing, motivation, leadership, facility management, indoor air quality, and numerous other areas. He is the president of Knowledge Worx, a consulting and training firm dedicated to developing leaders at all levels of the sanitary supply industry. A visionary and leader, he has worked with the foremost cleaning organizations, manufacturers, and distributors, gathering experience with all levels of the industry.

Frank is an active member of the International Sanitary Supply Association (ISSA) and has served on Indoor Air Quality committees for the Carpet and Rug Institute and Underwriters Laboratories. During his tenure on these committees, he has helped to establish standards for healthy building designs, cleaning practices, and environmental remediation.

Mr. Frank also serves as the President of the American Institute for Cleaning Sciences (AICS) and in that role has contributed significantly to the establishment of ISSA's The Cleaning Industry Management Standard (CIMS 1101) which he considers to be one of his proudest accomplishments. The ISSA's Cleaning Industry Management Standard describes the procedures and principles to be considered in designing and implementing quality management programs for cleaning organizations. This standard applies to both cleaning organizations that perform cleaning and to building service contractors regardless of the size of the organization.

As another example, let's consider the regular GRA on the red team who works in section 1 five days each week. When the red team is off, swing team 1 works in the red division, and Jane from that swing team regularly works in Mary's section. On a different day, swing team 1 relieves the yellow team, and Mary and Jane both work in the hotel. Both of them, as well as their supervisor, thus have the opportunity to talk about section 1 and to discuss and resolve any problems. Also, when plaudits are offered for the condition of section 1, the red team and swing team 1 receive equal praise.

Other advantages of team staffing and scheduling will be discussed later in the text. Of primary concern at this time is the scheduling of the staff for work. You can see that scheduling four regular teams, two swing teams, and the laundry team as a group is simpler than scheduling 49 individual workers. In our model hotel, team scheduling will take care of the scheduling of 49

workers' positions. Twelve workers' positions, however, will still require individual scheduling.

Team Scheduling Is Not Team Cleaning

Team cleaning, as opposed to **zone cleaning**, is not a synonym for team scheduling. There are very few hotels that have embraced the concept of team cleaning, but those who have, have found the approach extremely promising. Traditionally, hotels have used zone cleaning, which assigns a block of rooms or an area to an individual cleaner and then makes that cleaner responsible for all aspects of cleaning in that area or block of rooms. For example, a GRA is responsible for cleaning the bathroom, dusting furniture, polishing mirrors and window, making the bed, and vacuuming. The GRA cleans everything within the assigned zone.

This approach was also standard in the cleaning of other facilities, as well, including hospitals, schools, and offices. Then, about a decade ago some operators began the practice of team cleaning. Team cleaning involves the use of specialist cleaners.

So, instead of one person cleaning the floor of an office building; you have a specialist who cleans the restrooms, a specialist who does nothing but vacuum, and another specialist who takes out the trash for the entire facility. This practice has reduced cleaning labor costs in some facilities by as much as 30 percent over the traditional zone cleaning approach.

Some executive housekeepers in hotels have tried a variation of this approach. One member of the team may make the beds while another is cleaning the bathroom, and a third does all of the team's vacuuming for the rooms and the hallway. Typically, the traditional push-pull vacuum is traded in for a backpack vacuum, and only one vacuum is required where previously five were needed, saving significant equipment costs.

Not everyone is convinced that team cleaning is right for the hotel industry. Some point to the difficulty of finding personnel who would be content to do the same functions day in and day out, such as cleaning restrooms. Others would argue that with the right tools and training, these functions are no more difficult or unpleasant than other positions on the team.

When applied to the lodging industry, the concept of team cleaning holds tremendous promise for increasing productivity and lowering equipment costs at the same time. However, more research needs to be conducted on this procedure.

Standing Rotational Scheduling and Tight Scheduling

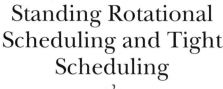

Two major tasks must be accomplished in order for the following complete scheduling system to work. The first task is constructing a system for **standing rotational scheduling**. (The word "standing" is used to denote a continuous system, and the word "rotational" to denote the cyclical nature of the system that provides for two regular days off for people each week and for staff to cover a full seven-day workweek at 100 percent occupancy.) The second task is that of providing **tight scheduling**, which is a modification of the rotational system to account for reduced occupancy. This will be accomplished by assigning extra days off when occupancy is low. The tight schedule is actually a daily modification of the standing rotational schedule based on occupancy.

In new operations, these two systems are designed before opening and are then easily implemented on a given start date. In ongoing operations, these systems may be used, but they require a thorough briefing of staff and an understanding by employees before they are implemented. Usually several weeks must pass after training employees on the scheduling system so that the one-time shock of shifting from one system to another can be accommodated. Once the system is designed and employees are properly prepared, the standing rotational system is implemented on a given start date, which usually falls on the first day of the property workweek.

STANDING ROTATIONAL SYSTEM

Using the model hotel, assume the following work situation:

1. The hotel workweek has been established as beginning on Saturdays and ending on Fridays.

2. Workers may work no more than five days in any workweek without drawing overtime pay.
3. Days off will be consecutive unless the employee can be shown an advantage for having split days off.
4. All team employees must be willing to work their share of weekends. (This can be a condition of employment, provided it is specified at the time of employment.)

The Work Calendar

The **work calendar** is divided into seven distinct workweeks. In each week, teams (or individual employees) will be assigned two regular days off. Each following week, the days that are assigned off will rotate forward one day. For example, if the red team is scheduled to be off on Friday and Saturday of workweek 1, then it will be off Saturday and Sunday of workweek 2, and Sunday and Monday of workweek 3. This form of rotation (off days moving forward) continues through the seventh workweek. The eighth workweek is a repetition of the first workweek, creating a cycle of workweek schedules that repeats every seventh week. Figure 3.1 is an illustration of this system.

Note the seven workweeks, with each day of the week indicated (workweeks are separated by a vertical line). Note also the horizontal bar under the regularly assigned days that the worker is scheduled off. As the weeks progress, the bar moves to the next succeeding days until the days off are Friday and Saturday. Here the days off split to the opposite ends of the week. Although days off are split in a particular week, each of these split days joins the two adjacent days off in the prior week or the succeeding week, allowing the worker to have three days off in a row. This will happen twice in seven weeks and is a strong selling point for the system. When the employee's days off are on the weekend, there are three days off in a row, yet only two days off in any one workweek, allowing for a full 40 hours of work in each week. Note that there are never more or fewer than two days off in any workweek, even though in most cases the worker is working six days straight. Now that we have explained the cyclical method of days off, we can construct workweek 1.

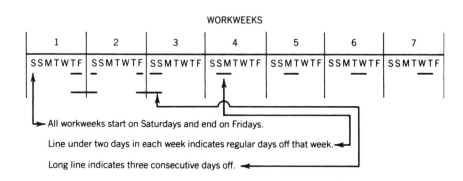

WORKWEEKS

All workweeks start on Saturdays and end on Fridays.

Line under two days in each week indicates regular days off that week.

Long line indicates three consecutive days off.

FIGURE 3.1 The standing rotational scheduling system. The eighth workweek is a repeat of workweek 1, hence the cyclical character of the system.

HOUSEKEEPING STANDING SCHEDULE
WEEK _____

TEAM/POSITION PERSON	SATURDAY	SUNDAY	MONDAY	TUESDAY	WEDNESDAY	THURSDAY	FRIDAY
RED							
YELLOW							
BROWN							
GREEN							
LAUNDRY							
SWING TEAM 1							
SWING TEAM 2							
LINEN ROOM SUPERVISOR							
LINEN ROOM ATTENDANT							
SENIOR HSKPG. AIDE							
PUBLIC AREA HOUSEKEEPER #1							
PUBLIC AREA HOUSEKEEPER #2							
A.M. PUB AREA (RELIEF)							
NIGHT SUPERVISOR							
NIGHT HOUSEKEEPER							
NIGHT P.A. HOUSEKEEPER #1							
NIGHT P.A. HOUSEKEEPER #2							
NIGHT P.A. (RELIEF)							

FIGURE 3.2 Housekeeping standing rotational schedule form.

Construction of Workweek 1

First, let us look at Figure 3.2, the **Housekeeping Standing Schedule Form** that has been specifically designed for the model hotel. The four regular teams, laundry staff, two swing teams, and individual positions that must be staffed are listed. Note that it is the **position** that is scheduled, not a specific person.

The color designations—red, yellow, brown, and green—in the column "Team Position Person" correspond with the divisions of the hotel described in the House Breakout Plan. If there is *no* indication in a schedule block, it means that the team designated by a specific color is working in the division of that same color designation; for example, the red team working in the red division will be indicated by a blank schedule block. For the swing teams, it is necessary to specify, in the appropriate schedule block, exactly where the swing team is to work. In the standing rotational system, all members of a given team will be considered as scheduled to work if the team schedule block is left blank.

We can now construct workweek 1, using Figure 3.2 as the scheduling form.

Step 1. As a starting point, assume that in workweek 1 the red team will work in the red division on Saturday, Sunday, Monday, Tuesday, and Wednesday, and will be off on Thursday and Friday. On the days off, swing team 1 will work in place of the red team. This is indicated on the schedule sheet in Figure 3.3.

In the Thursday and Friday schedule blocks, note the "off" and the "ST-1," indicating that swing team 1 is working in place of the red team when the red team is

off on Thursday and Friday. Note also that "red" must be placed opposite the Thursday and Friday schedule blocks for swing team 1.

Step 2. Now that swing team 1 has been scheduled to work on Thursday and Friday for the red team, it is necessary that the team be *kept working* five consecutive days. Given that swing team 1 also relieves the yellow team two days and works in the laundry one day, its schedule may now be completed as shown in Figure 3.4.

At this point the scheduling of the red team, yellow team, and swing team 1 has been completed, and one day off for the laundry personnel has been designated.

Step 3. Swing team 2 is next introduced to give the laundry team its second day off. The team will also work two days for the brown team and two days for the green team, giving it five consecutive workdays. (Note that the off days for both swing teams are now established.) Figure 3.5 shows the completion of the scheduling for all regular teams, the laundry, and both swing teams.

Step 4. The next step is to schedule individual positions for workweek 1. Note that individual positions are normally referred to as **fixed positions**, since their scheduling does not fluctuate based on occupancy. It is logical for the linen room supervisor and the linen room attendant to be off on different days. It is also reasonable to have one day in between their days off to facilitate routine communication and continuity between the two positions. Similarly, the senior housekeeping aide should not be scheduled off on the same day as the linen room supervisor. (Even though management positions do not show on the hourly worker schedule, it is illogical

HOUSEKEEPING STANDING SCHEDULE
WEEK ___ONE___

TEAM/POSITION PERSON	SATURDAY	SUNDAY	MONDAY	TUESDAY	WEDNESDAY	THURSDAY	FRIDAY
RED						Off / ST-1	Off / ST-1
YELLOW							
BROWN							
GREEN							
LAUNDRY							
SWING TEAM 1						Red	Red
SWING TEAM 2							

FIGURE 3.3 Beginning of preparation of the standing rotational schedule for workweek 1.

HOUSEKEEPING STANDING SCHEDULE
WEEK ___ONE___

TEAM/POSITION PERSON	SATURDAY	SUNDAY	MONDAY	TUESDAY	WEDNESDAY	THURSDAY	FRIDAY
RED						Off / ST-1	Off / ST-1
YELLOW	Off / ST-1	Off / ST-1					
BROWN							
GREEN							
LAUNDRY			Off / ST-1				
SWING TEAM 1	Yellow	Yellow	Laundry	Off	Off	Red	Red
SWING TEAM 2							
LINEN ROOM SUPERVISOR							

FIGURE 3.4 Continuation of scheduling system preparation for workweek 1. Swing team 1 is kept working five days straight by swinging in for the yellow team on Saturday and Sunday and for the laundry on Monday.

HOUSEKEEPING STANDING SCHEDULE
WEEK ___ONE___

TEAM/POSITION PERSON	SATURDAY	SUNDAY	MONDAY	TUESDAY	WEDNESDAY	THURSDAY	FRIDAY
RED						Off / ST-1	Off / ST-1
YELLOW	Off / ST-1	Off / ST-1					
BROWN					Off / ST-2	Off / ST-2	
GREEN	Off / ST-2						Off / ST-2
LAUNDRY			Off / ST-1	Off / ST-2			
SWING TEAM 1	Yellow	Yellow	Laundry	Off	Off	Red	Red
SWING TEAM 2	Green	Off	Off	Laundry	Brown	Brown	Green
LINEN ROOM SUPERVISOR							
LINEN ROOM ATTENDANT							
SENIOR HSKPG. AIDE							
PUBLIC AREA HOUSEKEEPER #1							
PUBLIC AREA HOUSEKEEPER #2							
A.M. PUB AREA (RELIEF)							
NIGHT SUPERVISOR							
NIGHT HOUSEKEEPER							
NIGHT P.A. HOUSEKEEPER #1							
NIGHT P.A. HOUSEKEEPER #2							
NIGHT P.A. (RELIEF)							

FIGURE 3.5 Completion of team scheduling for workweek 1. After five consecutive days of work in relief for several teams, swing team 2 is then off for two days.

to schedule them off at the same time. Management positions are therefore assigned two consecutive days off in such a way that either manager can cover for the one who is off or who has important obligations for part of each workday.) Note also that in the case of public area (PA) housekeepers, the third position provides a relief for the first two positions, provided the relief is not scheduled off on the same day as public area housekeepers 1 and 2. There will be one day out of seven when all three public area housekeepers are on duty. On this particular day, many special projects can be scheduled and completed that would otherwise require the hiring of additional personnel. Figure 3.6 is a logical completion of the design of workweek 1.

Even though the total staff may be reduced at times, cross-training and overseeing by other supervisors is used to keep staffing at an optimum. For example, on days that the night supervisor is off, the head housekeeping aide or the linen room supervisor might be scheduled to come in late, thereby being available to take over part of the night supervisor's duties. Another possibility is that management might be scheduled to cover for the night supervisor. The rest of the scheduling for workweek 1 as indicated is therefore one of several logical arrangements.

Construction of Workweeks 2 through 7

Recalling the standing rotational system illustrated in Figure 3.1, we can now construct the rest of the

workweeks. By using the identical form shown in Figure 3.2, the days off expressed in workweek 1 are, in every case, advanced one day on each of the six remaining workweeks. Similarly to how Figure 3.6 shows the complete workweek 1, Figure 3.7 represents the complete workweek 2. Once again, in cases where days off are Friday and Saturday, they are at opposite ends of the schedule.

System Posting and Initiation

After the standing rotational system has been designed, all that remains is posting and initiation. The schedules should be posted on a bulletin board next to a copy of the **Department Staffing Guide** on which the incumbents to all positions are indicated. Remember, these schedule forms are to become permanent and should therefore be typed and protected with coverings. The worker needs to know only what position he or she is filling and what workweek is in effect to know his or her regular days off. Figure 3.8 shows how a Department Staffing Guide and seven weeks of standing rotational schedules might be displayed on an employee bulletin board within a housekeeping department.

System initiation is begun on any upcoming day that is designated by management as the beginning of the workweek (it is Saturday in our example). Once initiated, the system is in perpetual rotation, requiring only that someone move a marker every week to indicate what workweek is in effect.

HOUSEKEEPING STANDING SCHEDULE

WEEK ___*TWO*___

TEAM/POSITION PERSON	SATURDAY	SUNDAY	MONDAY	TUESDAY	WEDNESDAY	THURSDAY	FRIDAY
RED	Off ST-1						Off ST-1
YELLOW		Off ST-1	Off ST-1				
BROWN						Off ST-2	Off ST-2
GREEN	Off ST-2	Off ST-2					
LAUNDRY				Off ST-1	Off ST-2		
SWING TEAM 1	Red	Yellow	Yellow	Laundry	Off	Off	Red
SWING TEAM 2	Green	Green	Off	Off	Laundry	Brown	Brown
LINEN ROOM SUPERVISOR		Off	Off				
LINEN ROOM ATTENDANT					Off ·	Off	
SENIOR HSKPG. AIDE	Off						Off
PUBLIC AREA HOUSEKEEPER #1		Off	Off				
PUBLIC AREA HOUSEKEEPER #2				Off	Off		
A.M. PUB AREA (RELIEF)						Off	Off
NIGHT SUPERVISOR				Off	Off		
NIGHT HOUSEKEEPER						Off	Off
NIGHT P.A. HOUSEKEEPER #1	Off	Off					
NIGHT P.A. HOUSEKEEPER #2				Off	Off		
NIGHT P.A. (RELIEF)						Off	Off

FIGURE 3.6 Completed standing rotational scheduling system for workweek 1. Days off have been assigned to individual workers not considered part of housekeeping teams.

HOUSEKEEPING STANDING SCHEDULE
WEEK _TWO_

TEAM/POSITION PERSON	SATURDAY	SUNDAY	MONDAY	TUESDAY	WEDNESDAY	THURSDAY	FRIDAY
RED	Off / ST-1						Off / ST-1
YELLOW		Off / ST-1	Off / ST-1				
BROWN						Off / ST-2	Off / ST-2
GREEN	Off / ST-2	Off / ST-2					
LAUNDRY				Off / ST-1	Off / ST-2		
SWING TEAM 1	Red	Yellow	Yellow	Laundry	Off	Off	Red
SWING TEAM 2	Green	Green	Off	Off	Laundry	Brown	Brown
LINEN ROOM SUPERVISOR		Off	Off				
LINEN ROOM ATTENDANT					Off	Off	
SENIOR HSKPG. AIDE	Off						Off
PUBLIC AREA HOUSEKEEPER #1		Off	Off				
PUBLIC AREA HOUSEKEEPER #2				Off	Off		
A.M. PUB AREA (RELIEF)						Off	Off
NIGHT SUPERVISOR				Off	Off		
NIGHT HOUSEKEEPER						Off	Off
NIGHT P.A. HOUSEKEEPER #1	Off	Off					
NIGHT P.A. HOUSEKEEPER #2			Off	Off			
NIGHT P.A. (RELIEF)					Off	Off	

FIGURE 3.7 Workweek 2 of the standing rotational system. Note how, for each entity to be scheduled, regular days off rotate forward one day from one workweek to the next.

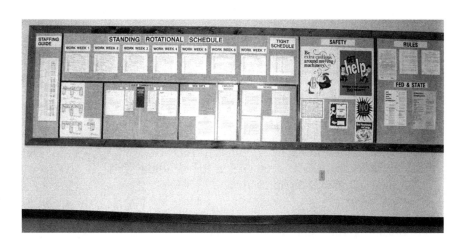

FIGURE 3.8 Bulletin board display of the standing rotational scheduling system and the department staffing guide.

In a new operation, the system should be initiated several days before opening. In an ongoing operation, the system should be explained several weeks before changing to it because of the effect the change may have on day-off rotation.

TIGHT SCHEDULING SYSTEM

Whereas the standing rotational schedule is a *permanent* system that, once established and initiated, continues to cycle on its own, the tight scheduling system is an *operational* system. It provides simple day-by-day modifications of the standing rotational schedule that are needed because of fluctuations in occupancy. The tight schedule pertains only to team scheduling; it has

no effect on the individual positions scheduled (bottom portion of the standing rotational schedule), inasmuch as all positions other than teams are considered fixed and are not affected by occupancy.

Figure 3.9 is a form especially designed for the model hotel on which the tight schedule modifications will be shown. Note especially the space for tomorrow's date, day, and workweek; and the columns labeled "area" (division), to which tomorrow's schedule refers; "team scheduled," indicating which team is to work; and "bring in," which is for a directive issued to the appropriate supervisor as to how many section housekeepers within the indicated team are to be used. In this way, management is *delegating* to the team supervisor the task of determining which people within

TIGHT SCHEDULE FOR _____ / _____ / _____
                          (date)   (day)   (workweek)
EXPECTED OCCUPANCY % _____   # ROOMS _____

AREA	TEAM SCHEDULED	BRING IN	SUPERVISOR ASSIGNMENT	EXTRA DAY OFF	OTHERS ON CALL
RED	SUPERVISOR:		1. _____ 2. _____ 3. _____ 4. _____ 5. _____	1. _____ 2. _____ 3. _____ 4. _____ 5. _____	
YELLOW	SUPERVISOR:		6. _____ 7. _____ 8. _____ 9. _____ 10. _____	6. _____ 7. _____ 8. _____ 9. _____ 10. _____	
BROWN	SUPERVISOR:		11. _____ 12. _____ 13. _____ 14. _____ 15. _____	11. _____ 12. _____ 13. _____ 14. _____ 15. _____	
GREEN	SUPERVISOR:		16. _____ 17. _____ 18. _____ 19. _____ 20. _____	16. _____ 17. _____ 18. _____ 19. _____ 20. _____	
LAUNDRY	SUPERVISOR		1. _____ 2. _____ 3. _____ 4. _____ 5. _____	1. _____ 2. _____ 3. _____ 4. _____ 5. _____	

FIGURE 3.9 Form used for the model hotel to prepare the tight schedule.

the team are to be brought in; said another way, it indicates which team members are to be scheduled for an extra day off.

Developing the Tight Schedule for a Typical Day

For illustrative purposes, assume that the following hypothetical situation exists regarding the 353-room model hotel:

1. Tomorrow's day and date are Thursday, June 16.
2. Tomorrow's date falls at a time when the standing rotational schedule is cycling through workweek 2 (Figure 3.7).
3. Today's occupancy was 95 percent, and tomorrow's occupancy is forecasted to be 76 percent (268 rooms expected to be occupied tonight; see Table 2.2, Table of Personnel Requirements).

The following steps are required operationally to develop a tight schedule for tomorrow.

Step 1. At about 4:00 P.M. on the afternoon of Wednesday, June 15, one of the managers of the housekeeping department refers to the standing rotational schedule (Figure 3.7) and notes the following teams scheduled to work on that date (in workweek 2): red team in red division, yellow team in yellow division, swing team 2 in brown division, and green team in green division (the brown team and swing team 1 are scheduled for a regular day off, and the laundry crew is scheduled to work in the laundry). This

information is then transferred to a copy of the form for tight scheduling (Figure 3.9).

Step 2. The manager contacts the front desk manager and asks for an estimate of tonight's occupancy (tomorrow's workload for the housekeeping department). The manager is informed that 268 of the hotel's 353 rooms are expected to be occupied.

Step 3. The housekeeping manager refers to the Table of Personnel Requirements (Table 2.2) and notes that 268 rooms reflects a 76 percent occupancy, requiring the use of 15 housekeepers.

Step 4. In the "Bring In" column on the tight schedule, the housekeeping manager indicates as close to an equal distribution as possible of the 15 housekeepers required to service tomorrow's occupancy. For example, three teams bring in four, and one team brings in three of the five section housekeepers who are permanent members of the indicated teams.

Step 5. The laundry will be working to service the soiled linen workload created by *today's* occupancy (95 percent), requiring a full laundry staff of all five members.

Step 6. Within a period of about 5 minutes, the housekeeping manager has developed the directive portion of tomorrow's tight schedule, which is now posted in a specially designed place adjacent to the standing rotational schedule. Figure 3.10 is a copy of the tight schedule prepared for tomorrow's workday.

Step 7. Within the next 10 or 15 minutes, each senior housekeeper (supervisor) will note the bring-in requirement for tomorrow and will, on a fair

TIGHT SCHEDULE FOR __6/16/__ , __Thursday__ , __2__
(date) (day) (work week)

EXPECTED OCCUPANCY % ____76%____ # ROOMS ____268____

AREA	TEAM SCHEDULED	BRING IN	SUPERVISOR ASSIGNMENT	EXTRA DAY OFF	OTHERS ON CALL
RED	Red SUPERVISOR: Miller	4	1. ___ 2. ___ 3. ___ 4. ___ 5. ___	1. ___ 2. ___ 3. ___ 4. ___ 5. ___	
YELLOW	Yellow SUPERVISOR: Jones	4	6. ___ 7. ___ 8. ___ 9. ___ 10. ___	6. ___ 7. ___ 8. ___ 9. ___ 10. ___	
BROWN	Swing Team 2 SUPERVISOR: Foster	3	11. ___ 12. ___ 13. ___ 14. ___ 15. ___	11. ___ 12. ___ 13. ___ 14. ___ 15. ___	
GREEN	Green SUPERVISOR: Smith	4	16. ___ 17. ___ 18. ___ 19. ___ 20. ___	16. ___ 17. ___ 18. ___ 19. ___ 20. ___	
LAUNDRY	Laundry SUPERVISOR Thomas	5	1. ___ 2. ___ 3. ___ 4. ___ 5. ___	1. ___ 2. ___ 3. ___ 4. ___ 5. ___	

FIGURE 3.10 Tight schedule form based on tomorrow's forecast occupancy for our hypothetical situation.

and equitable basis, determine who (by name) among the team members will be assigned to work. Similarly, he or she will indicate who will be assigned an extra day off. Such indications are made on the tight schedule (Figure 3.11), which all employees may refer to for tomorrow's staffing needs before the end of today's workday.

Tight scheduling is now complete for Thursday's workday and is available for all to see. (Note that the regular laundry staff was off the previous day.) It will be necessary for the laundry supervisor to call in and ask about tomorrow's requirement for workers. The supervisor will specify by phone how many laundry employees will work from among the members of the laundry team. The supervisor will then call the team members and specify tomorrow's requirement for workers.

When it is known that an annual occupancy of less than about 90 percent is forecast, 100 percent staffing is not required; that is, teams need not be staffed to capacity and may be reduced in size to provide more scheduled workdays for the staff. If staffing is reduced and occupancy exceeds the capabilities of the staff, people who are regularly scheduled off may be offered overtime to fill the gaps.

Control over the Tight Schedule

Recall that the task of specific designation as to who works within each team has been delegated to each team supervisor. Although this delegation is job enriching to each supervisor, control must be maintained to ensure equitable and fair rotation of the assignment of extra days

off for team members. For this reason, each supervisor should be required to maintain a notebook indicating rotational assignment of extra days off for each member of the specified team. If questioned by any employee regarding fairness of assignment, the supervisor must be able to produce a record of fairness in the designation of extra days off. In many cases, if a team is to be scheduled down, a request for volunteers to accept an extra day off is usually all that is needed; in other cases, the extra day off must be assigned. Records must be kept to indicate that this assignment has been performed in a fair manner.

Equipment Use Related to the Tight Schedule

Two major pieces of equipment are associated with each room section: the maid's cart and vacuum cleaner. This equipment should be identified by a number corresponding to the section to which it belongs. At 100 percent occupancy, each of the GRAs working in one of the 20 assigned sections will have the exclusive use of the specified equipment. In this manner, a specific GRA from a regular team and a swing team may be held accountable for the condition and care of the equipment. At less than 100 percent occupancy, however, several sections will not have a GRA assigned. Note that in Figure 3.11, sections 2, 9, 12, 15, and 16 have no one assigned. This does not mean that there will be no work to perform in those sections, only that the workers scheduled are to use their assigned equipment. At a later time, the actual placement of the GRA in a specific work area will be covered by a procedure known as *opening the house.*

EXECUTIVE PROFILE
Larry Morgan *Making the Team Investment*

By Andi M. Vance, Editor, *Executive Housekeeping Today*

(This article first appeared in the February 2003 issue of *Executive Housekeeping Today*, the official publication of the International Executive Housekeepers Association, Inc.)

His canter is slow and easy, revealing his confidence and satisfaction with life. His mouth opens often into broad smiles directed toward those who cross his path. A natural manager, Larry Morgan is similar to many other I.E.H.A. managers in the sense that he just kind of landed in Environmental Services. His childhood aspiration wasn't to work in a hospital; however, now he couldn't imagine being anywhere else.

The best attributes of southern hospitality fill the disposition of Larry Morgan, who was born and raised in Savannah, Georgia. A "people person" through and through, Morgan has worked to achieve a great balance between his public and private lives. Oftentimes, people find it difficult to enjoy their work as much as they enjoy their leisure time, or vice versa. Larry Morgan has developed a blend of activities to keep his mind and body stimulated and in shape. This results in a good-natured administrator who engages in work with a clear mind and an easy spirit.

IN THE BEGINNING

Larry Morgan has worked since he was old enough to pick up a shovel. His grandmother had him doing household chores before he started working at a local restaurant where he made his introduction to the workforce in Savannah. His next job was at a local plywood mill where he worked until the economy went

sour and the plant was forced to close. In search for employment elsewhere, Morgan found himself on the steps of a local hospital. He knew he was qualified for a position in Maintenance and Engineering, but found that there were no available positions in that department. When a position in housekeeping was suggested, Morgan embraced it without any preconceived notions or biases.

"I had never done anything in housekeeping before," Morgan admits, "so I decided to give it a try."

When he began as a floor tech, Morgan had no clue he'd be spending the next 21 years developing his career at the facility.

NEW BEGINNINGS

When corporate downsizing swallowed Morgan's position as Operations Manager over a year ago, he contacted a director who suggested he apply at St. Joseph's/Candler. Immediately after he filled out his application, he was interviewed and hired as the Night System Operations Manager. Approximately six months ago, he was promoted to Site Manager. He is responsible for 55 staff members, running operations, training, recruiting, quality improvement procedures, accessing chemicals and equipment. Quality improvement is a key focus area for the department at the moment, as department administrators work to involve all staff in procedures.

Morgan has introduced a program in its initial stages of implementation called the Seven Step Cleaning Process. He learned it while working for a contract cleaner at a former facility.

"The Seven Step Cleaning Process is a standardized method where you make rounds in the room," explains Morgan. "Each round entails a specific task. The final step in the process is for the staff member to go in and do a thorough check to assure the room has been thoroughly cleaned. Recently, the frontline staff became involved. No longer does the supervisor regulate the quality checks; staff members are responsible for their own work."

Quality scores are accessed through checklists and rating systems. "We have a checklist developed for the supervisor or manager to inspect the room," Morgan details. "We have a way of aggregating the information to get a quality score or percentage of clean in a particular area. We have a set goal for cleanliness in a room, so if we don't meet that standard, then we come back to access the staff members and see if they need training and/or other development."

JCAHO

Last year, JCAHO (the Joint Commission of Accreditation of Health Care Organizations) made a much anticipated visit to the facility. While the staff strives to keep the hospital immaculate on a day-to-day, minute-to-minute basis, when JCAHO is coming, the staff works a little harder to ensure the hospital and one another are prepared for the survey. Morgan recounts everything they underwent in preparation.

Close to the time when the JCAHO survey team was ready to arrive, the staff double-checked everything to make sure the facility was spotless. "It seemed as though everyone wanted us to clean everything at one time. We don't often have the staff clean all areas simultaneously, so you have to stagger and schedule those duties as you go."

"In regard to my own responsibilities," says Morgan, "I started about 90 days prior to JCAHO's arrival. I wanted to make sure all the floors had been stripped, carpets extracted, walls washed and things of that nature. I also checked to make sure my staff was completely educated on chemicals, processes, MSDS sheets, etc. They also have to have a general knowledge of procedures like biomedical waste disposal. Really, it's anything and everything that has to do with regulations."

"Extensive maintenance of paperwork is another responsibility of Environmental Services Managers. All the cleaning records, orientation checklists, infection control training and refrigerator cleaning logs should be together and in place for a JCAHO inspection," says Morgan. "As far as I'm concerned, it's all ongoing. Have your processes in place and then follow through on a day-to-day basis. My philosophy is that once you get into JCAHO mode, you need to stay in that mode for the rest of the time, rather than relaxing until the next JCAHO visit."

BEST INVESTMENTS

As an administrator, Morgan doesn't look at his equipment or type of flooring as his best investment, he looks to his staff. In a time when obtaining qualified and diligent workers poses somewhat of a challenge, Morgan puts a lot of time and energy into recognizing his staff and showing his appreciation for their labors. When Morgan first started at the facility, high turnover plagued the facility. With a recent salary increase, more qualified individuals are staying on the job longer.

To reduce turnover, the management staff is continually brainstorming and looking for ways and ideas to help employees and build loyalty within their first year. They've found that if they stay with Environmental Services for the first year, then they'll be less likely to leave if they have a job offer with a similar salary elsewhere. After that first year, they're entitled to a variety of benefits including a 403B pension plan, healthcare benefits and access to an onsite credit union.

"One thing I've come to recognize when working with people is that human resources is your most valuable asset," professes Morgan. "You can bring in all the state-of-the-art equipment, new chemicals, robots, anything you want. But if you don't have good, competent people to utilize these things, then you don't have anything."

To recognize loyal employees, Morgan continually shows them appreciation and recognition. His boss, Peter Schenk, Vice President of Clinical Services, has also been extremely supportive of the staff. Funding is provided for staff recognition functions such as International Housekeepers Week and a holiday reception.

"Every day, I make rounds and tell them how much I appreciate their great work. At staff meetings, I always thank them for the job they're doing," acknowledges Morgan. "I try to instill that in my management staff as well. Whenever I can say thank you, I do. A simple thank you helps a lot."

ASSOCIATION INVOLVEMENT

Larry Morgan has been participating in IEHA since 1986, when he was introduced to the Association by Olli Gaskin, who was President of the Georgia Coastal Chapter at the time. Serving as a mentor to Morgan, Gaskin retired and later handed over the presidential ropes to Morgan, who is currently serving his third term as the President of the Georgia Coastal Chapter.

Under his leadership, the Chapter continues to flourish. At convention last year, Morgan accepted the Father Hindel award on behalf of the Georgia Coastal Chapter for having the largest percentage increase of certified and registered members.

To maintain chapter meeting attendance, the Chapter's leadership works diligently to provide resourceful education and limited business sessions. Next year, they will sponsor a large seminar and workshop that will provide continuing education units for the members while helping generate revenue for the Chapter treasury.

Morgan's excited about the direction of the Chapter as some new blood has been introduced. He looks forward to handing over the reins of leadership to someone with new ideas and resources. Arthur Coleman has played an active role in Chapter activity, providing a venue for meetings at his facility, Savannah

State University. With increased direction and resources, they hope to overcome obstacles they encounter, such as the distance between members. Some members are located as far North as Hilton Head and others reside in Atlanta.

WINDING DOWN

Larry Morgan is not any different from other managers in that he does feel stress from his work. He identifies customers as a source of his stress. Unrealistic expectations place demands on his job that are sometimes impossible to fulfill.

"Sometimes, you have customers who will give you accolades and recognition," Morgan acknowledges. "Other times, you have those who only accentuate the negative. The only time they're ever going to call you is when something's wrong. If they're not calling you, then you're doing a good job. You just have to take it all in stride."

To Morgan, the key is finding the right way to relax from a stressful day. To stay in shape and release the physical effects of stress on his body, Morgan runs a couple of miles a day. On extremely stressful days, he runs up to four or five miles.

His other hobbies include freshwater and saltwater fishing, gardening, reading, playing basketball, bicycling—essentially anything that he can get his hands upon. Last year, his gardens were filled with various species of berry plants, including strawberries, blackberries and blueberries. He laughs as he recalls the birds in his backyard. "They just had a feast," he says. "They all got so fat."

CONCLUSION

Similar to the birds in his backyard, Larry Morgan feeds his employees with the berries of recognition and acknowledgment. He recognizes that the people who work on his staff are his best investment, and that without them, he'd be unable to direct the daily operations at St. Joseph's Hospital. Through the implementation of programs and procedures, he provides his staff with goals to reach, and measures their productivity along the way. Morgan's relaxed demeanor and attentiveness to his staff are a result of his own personal satisfaction in life. He's able to separate work and pleasure, which makes Larry Morgan a "berry" good manager.

DISCUSSION QUESTIONS

1. What do you think of Larry Morgan's attempts to build loyalty among his staff? What do you consider is the single best strategy Morgan is employing to reduce turnover? Is there anything else you would do to instill loyalty among a housekeeping staff?
2. Morgan's use of forms (e.g., checklists and rating systems) is related to which of the sequential functions of management?

FIGURE 3.11 Supervisors complete the tight schedule by indicating who from among the indicated teams will be working and who will be scheduled for an extra day off. The completed tight schedule is posted daily next to the standing rotation scheduling system (see Figure 3.8, far right).

TIGHT SCHEDULE FOR 6 / 18 / | Thursday | 2
(date) (day) (work week)
EXPECTED OCCUPANCY % 76 % # ROOMS 268

AREA	TEAM SCHEDULED	BRING IN	SUPERVISOR ASSIGNMENT	EXTRA DAY OFF	OTHERS ON CALL
RED	Red SUPERVISOR: Miller	4	1. Julia 2. 3. Yvonne 4. Billie 5. Margaret	1. 2. Gladys 3. 4. 5.	
YELLOW	Yellow SUPERVISOR: Jones	4	6. Dianne 7. Vivian 8. Marie 9. 10. Mildred	6. 7. 8. 9. Janice 10.	
BROWN	Swing Team 2 SUPERVISOR: Foster	3	11. Harriet 12. 13. Mannie 14. Jane 15.	11. 12. Elvira 13. 14. 15. Mary	
GREEN	Green SUPERVISOR:	4	16. 17. Georgia 18. Tommy 19. Donna 20. Louise	16. Lillian 17. 18. 19. 20.	
LAUNDRY	Laundry SUPERVISOR Thomas	5	1. Jane 2. Marie 3. Wilma 4. Helen 5. Laura	1. 2. 3. 4. 5.	

Union Contracts and Their Effects on Scheduling

We have shown you one of the most efficient scheduling techniques available to executive housekeepers. In real-life situations, however, **union contracts** can have an overwhelming effect on scheduling techniques. They may insist on a guaranteed 40-hour week and the requirement of additional positions on the labor force rather than cross-trained employees to perform more than one type of task (e.g., housekeeping and laundry).

Executive housekeepers thus have the challenge of presenting to unions plans that guarantee fairness to current employees as opposed to plans that pad staffs with unnecessary workers. In most cases, the best argument in favor of cross-training and scheduling of employees is that a 40-hour job does not exist and the company will not hire a full-time employee to work where only 8 or 16 hours of work actually exist. Many union houses are able to deal with this problem by having a very small cadre of full-time employees and a majority of workers who are considered **steady extras** (workers who are not guaranteed 40 hours).

Where union contracts are in force, the executive housekeeper should work to ensure fairness to employees. If union contracts are not in force, executive housekeepers should do everything possible to ensure that workers receive fair treatment and adequate wages and benefits.

CONCLUSION

Although there are several ways to schedule workers in seven-day operations, the best techniques are simple methods that use managers' time wisely, ensure fairness to workers, provide adequate coverage, and are understandable. This chapter presented a combination of two systems: the standing rotational system, which, once initiated, operates in a cyclic manner for an indefinite time, and a tight scheduling system, which modifies the standing system daily to accommodate hotel occupancy. The model hotel provided the vehicle by which these systems have been demonstrated.

The standing system defines regular days off from scheduled positions, and the tight system defines extra days off due to hotel occupancy being reduced below 100 percent. Both systems are displayed on the department bulletin board next to a copy of the Department Staffing Guide.

Both systems are adaptable to hotels of 100 rooms or more. The systems are, in fact, adaptable to any departments in which scheduling is based on a fluctuating occupancy or workload. The team method of staffing and scheduling allows for friendly competition and the delegation of more tasks to supervisors.

The executive housekeeper of the soon-to-open hotel should consider the type of scheduling presented in this chapter during the planning stage. If scheduling techniques are dealt with after opening, many overtime hours could result and workers and management will be adversely affected by the lack of a good scheduling system. In an existing operation, the system should be introduced, the staff trained, and a specific date chosen on which to institute the system. The best plan is to develop scheduling techniques before hiring the first employee.

KEY TERMS AND CONCEPTS

Worker scheduling
Team system of organization
Team scheduling
Team staffing
Manager's Teamwork Checklist
Swing teams
Relief teams

Team cleaning
Zone cleaning
Standing rotational scheduling
Tight scheduling
Work calendar
Housekeeping Standing Schedule Form

Position
Fixed positions
Department Staffing Guide
System initiation
Union contracts
Steady extras

DISCUSSION AND REVIEW QUESTIONS

1. Assume that a state law will not allow a worker to work more than five consecutive days without paying the person overtime. Design a standing rotational system (similar to the one described in Figure 3.1) that will meet the criteria of working five days in a row but will not require paying the overtime premium.
2. How does a tight scheduling system take advantage of the directional activity of delegation?
3. Assume that a standing rotational system and a tight scheduling system have been designed for an ongoing operation. What must be done before they can be initiated? Why?
4. Consider an ongoing operation that is currently cycling through workweek 3. A new employee has been hired to fill a vacancy in a housekeeping team. How would you explain the system to the new employee?
5. Are standing rotational and tight scheduling systems feasible in a union environment?
6. If your answer to question 5 is yes, how would you go about justifying the system to union officials?

NOTE

1. Susan C. Bakos, "Promoting Teamwork," *Executive Housekeeping Today*, September 1982, p. 26.

CHAPTER 4

Material Planning: Administration of Equipment and Supplies

After studying the chapter, students should be able to:

1. Describe the role of the executive housekeeper as a materials administrator.
2. Differentiate between capital expenditure budgets and operating budgets.
3. Describe the use of the preopening budget.
4. Describe the management function of inventory controls.
5. Describe classification of materials in the hotel.
6. Describe the handling of materials in the opening of a property.
7. List and describe criteria for the selection of mattresses and beds.
8. List and describe criteria for the selection of furniture.
9. Describe the recent developments in lighting for the guestroom.
10. Describe developments in guestroom safes, in-room refreshment centers, and audiovisual equipment.
11. Describe the intent of the Americans with Disabilities Act as it pertains to the lodging industry.

The executive housekeeper's time appears thus far to have been occupied only with people matters, giving the impression that other forms of planning are of no consequence. Although staff planning may require great human engineering and is assuredly the most costly part of housekeeping operations, it is also necessary to plan for and become organized in material administration. **Administration** refers to the selection, purchasing, use, and control of items; **material** refers to the various product items that will be used by the department, all of which must be properly classified and categorized.

Planning for material acquisition and use parallels staff planning and must also be initiated when the new executive housekeeper joins the organization. In the case of linen and **software items**, it would be expected that some initial planning and procurement might already have taken place due to long lead times required for acquiring such material. In this chapter, we will continue planning for the opening of the model hotel. However, all knowledge gained through understanding these procedures and concepts is applicable to ongoing operations. We will begin with a discussion about budgeting and inventory control and will then present a complete analysis of materials.

Material Budgets

Budgets are the plans by which resources required to generate revenues are allocated. There are many different types of budgets. Some allocate personnel; others deal with person-hours or with dollars. Plans that allocate material resources associated with generating revenue are a significant part of many budgets.

Two types of budgets most commonly used in hotel operations are capital expenditure budgets and operating budgets. When new properties are opened, preopening budgets are designed to guide the expenditure of resources through the event. Budgets should be prepared by the management of the departments to which they will apply. A review procedure normally takes place whereby upper levels of management comment, return for revision, and finally endorse departmental budgets for top management's approval. Once budgets are approved, they are used to guide departments to successful operations over the course of the year or period of time to which they apply.

CAPITAL EXPENDITURE BUDGETS

Capital expenditure budgets allocate the use of capital assets that have a life span considerably in excess of one year; these are assets that are not normally used up in day-to-day operations. Because such items of material are capital in nature, they are considered to add to the capital investment of the company and are therefore subject to some form of **depreciation**. The hotel building is a capital asset that may be depreciated over a period of 25 or 30 years. **Furniture, fixtures, and equipment (FFE)** are capital assets whose depreciation schedules are somewhat shorter (3, 5, or 7 years) but are nonetheless depreciable. In hotel operations, the term **software** is sometimes used to describe certain types of depreciable fixtures.

In ongoing operations, once each fiscal year there is a call for capital expenditure budgets from the various departments. At this time the housekeeping department management is required to specify needs for funds to purchase FFE. Capital expenditure budgets might also include requests for funds to support renovation and modernization programs, since both add to the asset value of the property. Once budgets are approved and funds are made available, capital expenditure budgets are implemented by the various departments.

If unexpected needs arise for FFE during the budget year, the general manager usually must submit supplementary justification to ownership before making such expenditures. Depending on company policy, some general managers have authority to spend a finite amount of money in excess of capital expenditure budgets, but such spending is quite constrained. As an example, for one major hotel corporation whose capital expenditure budget may range in the millions of dollars for a given property, the authority of its general managers for excess spending without approval from higher authority is limited to $500.

Before a specific item of equipment may be **capitalized**, there could be a requirement that the item have a life expectancy in excess of one year and that the cost be in excess of $100. Should a specific item not meet these criteria, it would be **expensed** (converted into the cost of doing business) rather than capitalized.

OPERATING BUDGETS

Operating budgets are prepared annually for a fiscal-year period. Operating budgets relate day-to-day **operating costs** to the **revenue** resulting therefrom. **Labor costs** (salaries and wages), **employee costs** (health, welfare, and benefit programs), and **controllable costs** make up the total expenditure relating to specific revenue being generated; **control profit** (or **loss**) is the result of the comparison.

Revenue is generated by a hotel rooms department, and costs are incurred by two subdepartments, front office and housekeeping. The front office manager and the executive housekeeper are therefore responsible for controlling the costs associated with revenue generated from the sale of guestrooms. That portion of controllable cost administered by the executive housekeeper includes but is not limited to items such as cleaning supplies, guest supplies, linen expense, uniform costs (for staff), and laundry costs. A detailed analysis of an operating budget for a rooms department is given in Chapter 11.

Because department managers are charged with holding operating costs in check in order that profit may be maximized, the purchase of small items of equipment on a one-at-a-time basis should be curtailed. Foresight in planning can and will maximize departmental control profit.

PREOPENING BUDGETS

Preopening budgets are usually thought of as allocating money and resources to opening parties, advertising, and initial goodwill. Preopening expenses actually go far beyond such expenditures and usually include initial cost of employee salaries and wages and supplies, food, china, glass, silver, and similar items. Recall that in our hypothetical opening, many managers have been on the payroll for several months. Other employees will soon be on the payroll for training and orientation. Preopening budgets normally include the cash and inventory requirements to meet these needs, along with others for getting the property open and operating. Preopening budgets are quite sizable and as a result are usually amortized over a three-year period from the date of opening. Preopening expenses are therefore not quite so devastating to corporate profits in the first year of operation. Most professionally sound hotel companies understand the need for substantial preopening budgets and plan such expenses into **pro formas**. Hotel companies that do not plan ahead are plagued with unplanned-for last-minute costs, and departments end up undersupplied and underequipped. The preopening budget forces the planning necessary for a smooth opening. The executive housekeeper can play a major role in establishing sound preopening budgets.

Inventory Control

Inventory control is the management function of classifying, ordering, receiving, storing, issuing, and accounting for items of value. The executive housekeeper for new and ongoing operations must not only perform tasks in controlling various classifications of inventories but must also be technically competent in the selection, use, and maintenance of material items such as textiles, sleep equipment, furnishings, department equipment, and supplies. In addition, top management might dictate the degree of quality of certain material items to be used in the hotel guestroom. In some cases, for example, the room rate charged will be an indicator of expected quality of items such as bath towels or of the number and type of bars of soap to be found in each guestroom.

As initial planning for opening takes place, systems and procedures must be designed to facilitate inventory control, and personnel training plans must be generated to familiarize the staff with how to care for equipment, use supplies, and account for items of value. Storage must be organized and allotted to the various categories of material; **pars** (required on-hand amounts) must be established; accounting methods must be coordinated with the controller's office; and fiscal inventory rules and procedures must be established. Most of all, organization, system, and forethought (inventory control) are needed to preclude unnecessary loss and waste. (We discuss more about inventory control in Chapter 11.)

Material Classification

BASIC APPLICATION TO PRINCIPLES OF ACCOUNTING

The **classification of material** is the first step in the process by which items of value will be accounted for and controlled. Recall the general principles of accounting where **assets** of the company are stated. Under the broad term assets, there are current and fixed assets. **Current assets** include items such as cash, accounts receivable, and inventories. **Fixed assets** include land, building, and equipment. (In the case of hotels, the broad term **equipment** also includes furniture and fixtures—FFE.) **Inventories** are assets until they are *used*, and FFE are carried as assets until they are fully depreciated. Capital expenditure budgets are the plans by which fixed (depreciable) assets are acquired; operating budgets are the plans by which inventories are acquired.

As portions of inventories are used up in day-to-day operations to generate revenue, they are expensed and will appear as subtractions from revenue on income statements.

Table 4.1 lists some material items under the control of the executive housekeeper that are normally carried on the hotel **books of account** as fixed assets. These items are listed under various depreciation categories indicating their **life expectancy**. Since these items are fixed assets, they are not charged against routine day-to-day operations.

Table 4.2 lists material items that might be found in inventory assets under the control of the executive housekeeper. These items are regularly used up in the course of generating revenue and are therefore considered cost items and are carried as period expenses on operational and financial performance statements.

As inventory items are purchased, their invoices become payables **(liabilities)** that must be paid for with cash from the asset account cash. The result is the conversion of one asset, cash, into another form of current asset, inventories. As material is requisitioned from inventories to support day-to-day operations, inventory assets are used up and period expenses are recognized through adjusting entries. We hope that revenue is being generated in the process. Even though the executive housekeeper is responsible for control and use of both fixed and current assets, it is the day-to-day expenditure of current assets (cash for wages and inventories for material) as guided by operating budgets that will have the greatest effect on the department control profit.

ONGOING OPERATIONS

Classification of material accounts for ongoing operations is similar to that for new operations. In ongoing operations, preopening budgets do not come into play, but capital expenditure budgets and operating budgets are presented on an annual basis. If the hotel has been in operation for some time, first operating budgets are planned and approved, and then capital expenditure budgets follow. The executive housekeeper should remember that income statements reflect progress toward attainment of the operating budget. Minor or small items of equipment that will be capitalized should not be purchased so as to be charged against operating costs (miscellaneous expenses). This type of purchase should be planned far enough in advance so as to be charged against capital expenditures.

Ongoing operations will include the routine and periodic purchase of all inventory items, requiring that systems for research, ordering, receipt, storage, issue, and the accounting for use of items of value be developed.

TABLE 4.1 Material Classification of Fixed Assets for the Housekeeping Department

Guestroom Furniture and Facility Equipment	Software	Department Equipment
7-Year Category	5-Year Category	7-Year Category
Carpet	Roll-away beds	Laundry equipment
Sleep equipment	Accent drapes	Permanent shelving
Box springs	Blackout drapes	Glass washer
Mattresses	Sheer curtains	
Sofa beds	Pillows (regular and nonallergenic)	5-Year Category
Studio couches	Bedspreads	Maid's carts
Chair beds		Corridor vacuums
In-wall beds	2-Year Category	Space vacuums
Furniture	Blankets	Pile lifter
Chests of drawers	Shower curtains	Wet vacuum
Tables		Rotary floor scrubbers
Chairs		High-pressure hot water carpet shampoo
Desks		equipment
Fixtures		Sewing machines
Paintings		Convertible mobile linen shelvir
Accessories		
Lamps and lighting fixtures		3-Year Category
Other equipment		Maid's vacuums
Telephones		Backpack vacuums
Radios		Electric brooms
Message equipment		Rubbish-handling conveyors
Televisions		Wheelchairs
In-room safes		Baby beds
Minibars		

Preopening Operations

TEMPORARY STORAGE

By now the executive housekeeper has been involved in selecting and purchasing items of material that are arriving daily for the opening of the hotel.

Although preopening budgets do not include the cost of fixed assets (FFE), it will be necessary to prepare to receive and temporarily store *all* materials ordered, regardless of whether they are capital items (Table 4.1) or part of inventories (Table 4.2). Some hotel companies arrange for the contractor to install guestroom furniture and equipment before acceptance of the facility by operations. In any case, furniture items are relatively easy to safeguard since they are either massive in size or are attached to the facility. Smaller movable (or removable) items are much more pilferable and should be kept in secure storage until operations is in control of the facility.*

MOVING INTO THE PROPERTY

Several days before opening (after operational personnel have moved into the facility), a **move-in day** is established for all material. The move-in day requires detailed planning for the staging of material (from warehouse to ballroom to permanent setup and storage) so that nothing is misplaced or lost. Every item of inventory or equipment that has been purchased and placed in

---

*I participated in the opening of a major 1,000-room hotel in which there was no provision for temporary storage of movable equipment items of initial inventory. As these items were received, they were stored in the open, in the hotel garage, and in hallways as arranged for by the contractor. After operations took control of the building, it was determined that material valued in excess of $60,000.00 had disappeared, far outweighing the expense of having provided temporary storage in a bonded warehouse.

TABLE 4.2 Material Classification of Inventory Assets

Cleaning Supplies	Guest Supplies	Linens	Uniforms
All-purpose cleaner	Guest Expendables	Sheets	Section housekeeper
Disinfectants	Matches	Pillowcases	Senior housekeeper
Germicidals	Laundry bags	Bath towels	Section housekeeper aide
Window cleaners	Laundry tickets	Hand towels	Other supervisors
Acid bowl cleaner	Stationery	Washcloths	
Metal polishes	Pens	Bath mats	
Furniture polish (lemon oil)	Notepads	Specialty towels	
Applicators (all kinds)	Postcards		
Spray bottles	Magazines		
Rubber gloves	Plastic utility bags		
Scrubbing pads	Disposal slippers		
Steel wool	Emery boards		
Brooms	Table tents (in-house advertising)		
Mops	Individual packs of coffee		
Cleaning buckets	Candy mints		
Mop wringers	Toilet tissue		
Floor dust mops	Toilet seat bands		
Cleaning rags	Facial tissue		
	Sanibags		
	Bath soaps (bar)		
	Facial soaps (bar)		
	Guest Essentials		
	Clothes hangers		
	Plastic trays		
	Ice buckets		
	Water pitchers		
	Fly swatters		
	Glass (or plastic) drinking cups		
	Ashtrays		
	Waste baskets		
	Shower mats (rubber)		
	Do-not-disturb signs		
	Bibles		
	Guest Loan Items		
	Ironing boards		
	Irons		
	Hair dryers		
	Heating pads		
	Hot water bottles		
	Razors		
	Electric shavers		
	Ice packs		
	Alarm clocks		
	Bed boards		

temporary storage must now be accounted for as it is transferred into the hotel. Depending on the size of the hotel, this process may take several days. The planning for move-in day will determine the efficiency and effectiveness by which the operation will take place and whether significant losses will occur.[†]

DISPOSITION OF SPARES

Because guestroom furniture fixtures and equipment will normally be put in place by the contractor, many hotel companies buy capital items with a 1 to 10 percent **spare component**. Spares are turned over to operations, and inventory responsibility must be assumed at that time. Storage is then allotted and future use controlled.

In many cases, the chief engineer of the hotel will be held accountable for inventory and storage of items such as carpet and furniture spares. The executive housekeeper is usually responsible for designating replacement of such items when the need arises in the future. Because carpet is a large bulk item, it is not uncommon for hotels to employ carpet companies for carpet repair and, in such cases, have these carpet companies hold spare carpet and provide periodic inventory of spares to the hotel for validation.

Guestroom Furniture and Fixtures

The items listed in Tables 4.1 and 4.2 are typical of those found in most hotel material inventories. Executive housekeepers in new and ongoing operations are involved in the purchase of such material inventories and are expected to research current literature, study samples, investigate sources of supply, decide characteristics and quality issues, and know the reputations of selected vendors for service and repair. The executive housekeeper must have a general knowledge of materials. The information in the rest of this chapter on guestroom

furnishings, and the information contained in the following three chapters, can be used as a reference for housekeeping related-materials and their use.

MATTRESSES AND BEDS

Most hoteliers would agree that one of the most important elements of a guest's comfort is the quality of the bed. There is little that the hotel can do to make up for a guest's discomfort caused by a sleepless night on an uncomfortable bed.

Unfortunately, there is no unanimity of thought as to what makes a comfortable bed. Although some guests might disagree, the prevailing thought holds that a comfortable bed is one that is firm on the inside but has a soft exterior.

Mattress Construction

Three types of mattresses are used in hotels today: innerspring, foam, and water. Mattresses range in size from twin to Eastern king, as shown in Table 4.3. Average-to high-quality hotels are using the oversize double as a standard in most rooms because of the extra 4-inch (10.2 centimeter) length. It is better to have a mattress that is at least 6 inches (15.2 centimeters) longer than the average height of the sleeper.

Mattresses may be medium, firm, extra firm, or super firm. Innerspring mattresses are constructed like a sandwich, with insulating material and padding on both sides of a coil unit. Each coil should give support and at the same time conform to body contours. The number of springs in a coil unit can range from 150 to as many as 2000 coils, with 400 to 600 being the standard, depending on degree of firmness desired.

Design of the coil unit is important in mattress construction. The resiliency, temper, number of turns in each coil, gauge of steel in individual springs, and the manner in which the springs are tied are of great importance in evaluating the quality of an innerspring mattress. Independent spring action and latex or baked enamel coating of coils provide longevity and noiseless operation. There should also be ventilators on the side of the mattress to ensure a fresh airflow into the coil unit.

Good mattresses have a layer of tough insulation to separate padding from springs. A layer of upholstery cotton or foam before ticking is applied provides a smooth surface and complies with government flame-spread regulations. The quantity of foam (latex or visco-elastic) applied has increased tremendously, often to the point that the innersprings are almost becoming superfluous. The current federal fire-safety standard for mattresses holds that a lighted cigarette should not be able to ignite the mattress's insulation or ticking.

[†]I participated in several move-ins while employed by Marriott Hotels. The Marriott system requires that bonded warehouses be used for temporary storage and that move-in day use hotel ballrooms to stage all movable equipment and inventory items temporarily. From ballroom staging areas, equipment is assembled, marked as necessary for identification, and, with other inventory items, moved to permanent storage. All this takes place according to detailed plans. Hundreds of thousands of items were thus controlled with an absolute minimum of loss. For example, in 1973 move-in day for the Los Angeles Marriott Hotel involved the staging of more than a million-dollar material inventory into two ballrooms of more than 20,000 square feet without the reported loss of a single corn broom, vacuum cleaner, or bed sheet.

TABLE 4.3 Mattress Sizes

	Width (in.)	Length (in.)	Width (cm)	Length (cm)
Twin	38	× 74	96.5	× 188.0
Double	54	× 74	137.2	× 188.0
Oversize double	54	× 80	137.2	× 203.2
Queen	60	× 80	152.4	× 203.2
California king	72	× 84	182.9	× 213.4
Eastern king	76	× 80	193.0	× 203.2

Mattress manufacturers have responded to the industry's and the public's concern over fire safety by developing mattresses that do not release toxic fumes when flame is applied; other manufacturers have created mattresses that will not support direct flame.

Ticking is the upholstered cover used in mattress construction. Ticking is found in all colors and patterns. It should be a tightly woven fabric that is well quilted to improve wearing qualities. Good-quality innerspring mattresses should last for more than ten years.

Foam mattresses are found in two types of materials—latex foam and urethane. Latex foam is a slab of 100 percent pure rubber, formed in one of two types of molds—pincore (small) holes or honeycomb (larger hole pattern). Polyurethane is less expensive than latex. Both are usually manufactured in $4\frac{1}{4}$- to 6-inch (10.8- to 15.2-centimeter) thickness, depending on the height of the foundation and box spring unit. The advantage of foam over regular innerspring mattresses is that foam is nonallergenic, less expensive, and easier to roll up for storage. Traditional foam mattresses, however, do not have the longevity of innerspring mattresses.

Ordinary foam mattresses should not be confused with the high-end foam mattresses. These use space age visco-elastic memory cell materials developed by NASA in the 1970s for the astronauts. This material is temperature-sensitive and will conform to the individual sleeper. Manufactured under a number of labels including the most famous, Tempur-Pedic, these mattresses are definitely not inexpensive. Initial cost can reach to well over a thousand dollars for just one mattress. However, they promise the sleeper a lack of pressure points often found in ordinary mattresses and no hammock or wave effect associated with water bed construction. These mattresses are definitely only for luxury properties. They are also sturdier than their more inexpensive cousins. Limited warranties of 10 to 20 years are now offered.

Water-filled mattresses, or water beds, made their debut on the hotel scene during the 1960s. They were not well received initially because they leaked, the water had to be heated, they required special (and costly) sheets, and they were prohibitively heavy for some multistory structures. Water beds were soon relegated to bridal suites and "theme" guestrooms.

Water beds today bear little resemblance to their 1960s' predecessors; in fact, many of them resemble the traditional innerspring mattresses in appearance. Mattress manufacturers such as Simmons have designed water beds that have water-filled cells in the center of the mattress. The cells are covered with a vinyl-covered urethane foam, and the perimeter of the mattress has a row of innerspring coils that provides support to an occupant sitting on the side of the bed. The mattress uses standard sheets, and the water-filled cells do not have to be heated because of the insulating foam layer. The ticking can be removed via a zipper on the top of the mattress so that the cells can be serviced.

All mattresses should have reinforced sides to prevent sagging caused by people sitting on the sides of the bed. Such reinforcement is formed by tape being stitched to the top and bottom edges and sides of the ticking. Even with all of these improvements, water beds are becoming increasingly scarce upon the scene. They will probably vanish entirely due to the increasing popularity of foam.

When purchasing new mattresses, the executive housekeeper should insist on viewing a cutaway model of the mattress prior to purchase.

Box Springs

Box springs and mattresses should be purchased simultaneously. Box springs are like shock absorbers. They cushion the weight and sleep movements of the sleeper and provide a large portion of the experienced sleep comfort. Box spring coils are much heavier-gauge steel than that found in mattresses. Springs are positioned on wooden or metal slats running laterally across the frame, giving fixed support to the underside of the unit. Box spring coils should be tied to the base, sides, and one another. The best test for a set of box springs is to stretch out on it and see if you experience firm support in all areas of the body.

Bed Frames

Two basic styles of bed frames are available to the housekeeper: metal and platform. The metal frame consists of four lengths of angle iron and a metal leg attached to each corner. Queen-size, king-size, and water beds will also have one or two crossbars added for extra support.

Platform frames are made from either metal or solid wood and provide the box springs and mattress with a platform or box on which to rest. The advantage to platform frames is twofold: carpet does not have to be laid under the platform, thus saving a considerable amount of carpet in a large hotel, and housekeepers need not worry about cleaning under the box frame. The sides of the frame are often carpeted to eliminate unsightly scuffing by vacuums.

Care and Maintenance of Beds

Preventive maintenance begins with mattress covers. Every bed should be covered with a moisture-proof mattress cover. The better-quality mattress covers are made of vinyl materials and are stain-resistant, nonallergenic, and flame retardant, as well as being moisture-proof. A washable mattress pad that is also nonallergenic and flame retardant is placed above the mattress cover. Its purpose is to provide the guest with a cushioning layer between the sheets and the mattress. Many mattresses, especially tufted mattresses that have buttons, need mattress pads.

Innerspring mattresses should be turned regularly; head to foot for one turn, and side to side for the next turn. Mattresses that are turned regularly may have their life expectancy extended by as much as 50 percent. To help monitor mattress rotation, labels can be affixed to the corners of the mattress. On one side, the label "January, February, and March" can be affixed to one corner with "April, May, and June" affixed to the opposite corner. On the reverse side of the mattress the label "July, August, and September" can be sewn, and on the opposite corner the label "October, November, and December" can be affixed. Inspections can then reveal whether or not a particular mattress has been rotated.

Roll-Aways, Cots, and Cribs

The demand for mobile beds will vary in proportion to guest type. Vacationing families and youth groups will generate the greatest demand for these items.

Cots or folding beds have disappeared from the scene because they are cumbersome to transport from storage to the guest's room. They have been replaced by the roll-away, a bed on wheels. The quality of roll-aways varies greatly by model and manufacturer. Standard roll-aways have a latex foam mattress that rests on flat bedsprings attached to a folding frame. The better roll-away beds have specially designed innerspring mattresses. Roll-aways should have plastic covers to protect them from dust while in storage.

Cribs should meet all federal construction guidelines. Most hotel cribs are collapsible in order to save storage space. To ensure that they do not collapse while occupied by an infant, they should be inspected regularly, and the staff should be instructed on how to prepare the crib. The lowest mattress level should always be used when setting up a crib to forestall the possibility of an overactive toddler crawling over the side and tumbling onto the floor.

Dual-Purpose Sleep Equipment

Dual-purpose sleep equipment provides extra sleeping capacity in guestrooms that otherwise would become crowded with a roll-away bed. Sofas, love seats, and formal chairs with ottomans convert into sleep equipment at night. There are basically five types of dual sleep equipment:

1. The sofa bed converts from a sofa into a bed by removal of the cushions. A small handle in the center of the seat unit releases the bed, which unfolds revealing a full (double-size) mattress. This type of equipment may be found in either sofa or love seat configuration.
2. The jackknife sofa converts to sleep configuration by dropping the back to the level of the seat.
3. The single studio couch converts by removing the bolsters and cover.
4. The chair bed and ottoman back drop to form a bed that is about 28 inches wide.
5. In-wall beds are becoming more the rule than the exception. Many hotels are now using the in-wall bed to conserve area in rooms normally used as sitting rooms and parlors during the daytime. Outstanding queen-size sleep equipment may now be found concealed in a wall, which by day gives the appearance of a paneled wall, with table and chair placed against it. Well-balanced swing equipment allows the foot of the bed to drop to the floor with a gentle pull on a handle usually concealed in a picture frame. In-wall beds provide outstanding sleeping comfort, with no possibility of retracting into the wall with the sleeper, regardless of the impression given by old comedies.

FURNITURE

Furniture must be both functional and attractive. It should be well constructed and easy to maintain. The variety of furniture available for hotel use today is as great as the number of companies manufacturing institutional furniture.

Most hotel furniture is a combination of wood and plastics made to look like wood. (Many times, close examination of the facades of what looks like French provincial carved wood will reveal a molded plastic exposure.) Hardwoods are scarce and expensive; therefore,

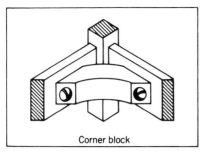

FIGURE 4.1 Corner block used in the construction of well-made chairs.

substitutes such as surfaced plywood and pressed particleboard are used extensively in the manufacture of institutional furniture. Little if any metal furniture will be found in hotels.

The executive housekeeper should examine samples to ensure that furniture is well designed, constructed with corner blocks (Figure 4.1) to withstand hard and abusive use, well finished, and refinishable. Joints are major factors in the strength and durability of well-made furniture. Figure 4.2 shows examples of various types of furniture joints. Mortise and tenon joints or double-doweled joints are used in well-made furniture. Desks, luggage racks, chests of drawers, and pieces that provide storage are known as case furniture or **case goods**, and are primarily constructed with dovetail joints. Some metal pieces will be used in the construction of case furniture for drawer guides and luggage receivers. Drawer construction in case furniture should always have concealed dovetail joints in the front piece to ensure that constant motion of the drawer will not cause the drawer front to become detached. Laminated tops are an essential element of most institutional furniture. Spilled drinks and beverage rings would quickly mar the finish and stain ordinary wood furniture.

Figures 4.3 through 4.6 are photographs of guestroom furniture at the Bellagio Hotel and Casino, Las Vegas. The furnishings here range from the merely tasteful to the sublime.

Upholstery Fabrics

Most fabrics are constructed of fibers, which are of two general classifications—natural fibers and synthetic fibers. Table 4.4 lists examples of each type of fiber. Most synthetic fabrics are made from either cellulose or coal tar derivatives.

Natural fibers are strong, long wearing, available in many finishes, and easily dyed. They must, however, be treated for insects and should not be allowed to remain wet. Natural fibers are usually expensive when woven into fabrics for upholstery. *Synthetic fabrics* are less expensive, not subject to damage by insects or moisture, and clean easily, but they are more likely to create static electricity

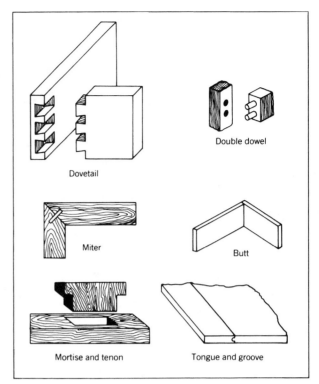

FIGURE 4.2 Methods of joining wood in furniture construction.

and are difficult to dye. Dark-color synthetics also show lint badly.

Many upholstered fabrics are blends of natural and synthetic fibers. Industrial upholstery fabrics are being woven into stretch knits that are dense, full bodied, and strong. Some are double-knit and are woven into a jacquard texture; others are woven into fine-textured materials.

Plastic fabrics have a leatherlike finish and are used in furniture construction. They may be wiped clean with a soapy cloth or sponge. Plastic fabrics may also be found in mattress ticking and blackout drapes.

Fixtures

The broad category of fixtures associated with hotel guestrooms includes decorative accessories, pictures and paintings, and lighting treatment.

Accessories, Pictures, and Paintings Most often, the designer who is responsible for the appearance of the room will have planned the accessories and paintings. The best use of accessories is to choose a few that give the desired impact. Accessories, like furniture, must be selected to conform to the size of the room and should not be overdone.

A balance of color and fundamental style is essential to achieve the proper feeling. **Formal balance** is a term used to describe a formal appearance (for example,

FIGURE 4.3 Standard junior suite furnishings with an English countryside flavor. Note the use of fabric on the end tables.

two candlesticks flanking a similar-style bowl of flowers). **Informal balance** occurs when dissimilar, unequally sized and shaped objects are assembled into groupings that appear balanced.

Framed hanging mirrors (with pronounced frames) give glamour to a room. Such a mirror might be used in place of a picture or painting. Usually the room designer will also select paintings that conform to the room decor. Most hotel paintings are lithographs, which may be purchased in volume to economize. Colors in wall hangings are used to make the room decor a pleasing experience.

The universal rule about hanging mirrors and paintings is that the geometric center of the item should be at eye level. Since viewers are of different heights, discretion must be used to balance the room properly.

LIGHTING

Proper lighting heightens the beauty of a room and adds to guest comfort. Lighting can create a desired effect by flattering the occupant as well as the room furnishings. Lighting should never be an afterthought, but should be considered in the total design of the room.

In many modern decors the source of lighting is concealed. Contemporary decors also use table, wall, and hanging lamps, which are securely fastened to the facility to reduce theft and avoid accidents. Table lamps should have their on/off switches located at their bases. This reduces the possibility of scorched fingers and the prospect of groping about in the dark for the switch. Floor lamps are seldom, if ever, used in modern hotel construction because of the space used and the tripping hazard created by unsightly cords.

Fluorescent lighting used in concealed lighting fixtures should never be of the cool variety because of the resulting harshness in the tone of light. Only warm fluorescent lighting should be used. Fluorescent lighting, like incandescent lighting, may be controlled by rheostat to create a feeling of comfort and softness. Pink incandescent bulbs provide warmth and give a rose-colored glow to skin tones. Orange or amber incandescent lighting causes an unflattering harsh gray skin tone. Warm fluorescent (approximately 2,700° Kelvin) bulbs controlled by the proper type of rheostat can be energy saving and reduce power consumption by as much as 75 percent. Furthermore, they can last up to ten times longer than ordinary incandescent bulbs. A typical compact fluorescent lamp (CFL) will have a color temperature of 2,700°K, an average rated life of 8,000 to 10,000 hours (compared with less than 1,000 in an incandescent), produce 800 to 1,000 lumens, and consume 13 to 18 watts of electricity. Compact fluorescents will screw into almost any light socket (Figure 4.7). Finally, sufficient light for reading must be provided in the room. Both hanging lamps over work tables and bed lamps for reading should have bulbs of sufficient wattage.

GUESTROOM SAFES

A recent newcomer to the guestroom fixture scene is the guestroom safe. Introduced for the first time in 1983 by Elsafe, guestroom safes are now available from companies offering dozens of models with hundreds of features. There are two main varieties available: electronic and manual. Access to many electronic safes is monitored from a panel at the front desk, and if the hotel charges a fee for their use, the system can electronically post the charge to a guest's folio. Guestroom safes

(a)

(b)

FIGURE 4.4 A far more formal sitting room in one of the Bellagio's Villa Suites. The second photo shows the same room with the entertainment center opened. *(Photos courtesy of Bellagio, MGM Mirage™, Las Vegas, Nevada.)*

come wall-mounted, floor-mounted, and hidden inside nightstands and armoires (Figure 4.8). Normal access to the safe may be through a common key, a keypad, the use of a special card, or even a standard credit card. Other features to look for when selecting guestroom safes are interior dimensions and fire ratings.

IN-ROOM REFRESHMENT CENTERS

A new and potentially very profitable fixture in the modern guestroom is the in-room refreshment center or minibar. Stocked with sodas, juices, liquor, and snacks, the minibar is a tempting convenience that few guests

can resist. As with guestroom safes, there are dozens of companies and hundreds of models from which to choose. Minibars can either be leased or purchased outright by the hotelier. A number of companies lease the equipment to the hotel for a fee and/or a share of the profits. In-room refreshment centers range from manual systems to fully automated units.

The fully automated systems can electronically sense when an item is removed from the shelf and can automatically post the charge for the item to the guest's folio (Figure 4.9). At the same time, it can print out a stock list for each room, thus letting the staff know what needs to be restocked in every room. Automated systems

FIGURE 4.5 An opulent dining room in the same suite featured in Figure 4.4. Note the Chinese influence in the furnishings. *(Photo courtesy of Bellagio, MGM Mirage™, Las Vegas, Nevada.)*

can also be electronically locked when the room is rented to minors or when the room is rented to paid-in-advance guests.

Other systems require housekeeping to take a physical inventory and relay the information via a handheld computer to the front desk. The manual systems often rely on the honor system, which may or may not be effective, depending on location and guest profile. Stories abound of guests having filled vodka bottles with water or running out to grocery stores the next day to replace used sodas and beers.

AUDIOVISUAL EQUIPMENT

Audiovisual guestroom equipment includes telephone systems, radios, televisions, videocassette recorders (VCRs), and digital videodisc (DVD) players.

The room telephone with its red message light has undergone immense technological changes at some properties over the past few years. Now the telephone serves as a communication and room control system. The television, radio, heat, lighting level, and air conditioning can be controlled from one central console. The telephone can be directly linked to the hotel's property management system, allowing housekeepers to inform the linen room and the front desk of the status of the room directly through the guest's telephone (see Figure 4.10).

Televisions have changed over the years as well. Thirty-two-inch color televisions are now considered the normal size; the television of today is commonly equipped with a guest-pay programming device that allows first-run movies to appear on the guestroom television. Gaining fast on the standard cathode-ray-tube (CRT) television are the light-emitting diode (LED) and plasma flat-screen high-definition televisions that range from 30 to over 60 inches in size. These flat-screen televisions are usually mounted on the wall of the guestroom, saving valuable square footage. Consequently, a number of hotel operators are making the guestrooms smaller, but the shrinkage is not noticed because of the flat-screen TV. This strategy is saving the owner money on construction costs of the property.

Guestroom televisions often come with no on-set secondary controls that can be broken. All tuning is done through the anchored remote on the nightstand or through a special setup transmitter that the hotel controls so that guests cannot alter the color and tint. Many guestroom TVs have AM/FM clock radio modules attached to the set, and others have installed DVD players. Many hotels rent recently released movies either from the front desk or from special cabinets located inside the guestrooms.

However, the trend is toward full automation for in-room movies. The guest selects a film from the menu on the television, and it is automatically billed to the guest's room. Such pay-per-view companies as iN DEMAND are now found in hotels and motels throughout the country.

The Americans with Disabilities Act (ADA)

All facilities, furniture, fixtures, and equipment used in public accommodations should be considered in relation to the requirements of the Americans with Disabilities Act (ADA). The **ADA** made discrimination against people with disabilities illegal in

(a)

(b)

FIGURE 4.6 Assistant Executive Housekeeper Raynette McGiness updates the status of the Villa at Bellagio. Note that the large chest at the foot of the bed is actually a large-screen TV that pops up on command from a console located on the nightstand. *(Photos courtesy of Bellagio, MGM Mirage™, Las Vegas, Nevada.)*

TABLE 4.3 Fibers Used in Upholstery

Natural Fibers	Synethetic Fibers
Cotton	Rayon
Wool	Acetate
Linen	Acrilan
Silk	Arnel
	Dacron
	Dynel
	Fiberglass
	Nylon
	Orlon
	Vicara

the United States. The ADA, signed into law July 26, 1990, is the first federal law that requires privately financed businesses to make themselves accessible to people with disabilities. There are three sections of the ADA that apply to places of lodging.

1. Title I, which deals with the equal employment opportunity for disabled persons in the workplace
2. Title III, "Nondiscrimination on the Basis of Disability by Public Accommodations and in Commercial Facilities," which requires places of lodging, and other "public accommodations," to remove barriers and provide accommodations for guests with disabilities

FIGURE 4.7 A "twist" CFL from Feit Electric. This new design fits almost any standard fixture yet consumes only one-fourth the wattage that a standard incandescent would consume. *(Photo courtesy of Feit Electric, Inc. Pico Rivera, California.)*

FIGURE 4.8 A dressing area closet with a built-in guestroom safe and a cedar lining. *(Photo courtesy of Bellagio, MGM Mirage™, Las Vegas, Nevada.)*

FIGURE 4.9 This Dometic® Auto *classic*™ refreshment center features an infrared sensing system that records each item removed that is not replaced within a preset time period. Its absorption cooling system is superquiet and has no moving parts to wear out. It can link to the front desk through existing television cables.

3. Title IV, telecommunications relay services, which addresses television and telephone access for people with hearing and speech disabilities

Architects, contractors, and building operators must comply with numerous and differing guidelines (e.g., Americans with Disabilities Act Accessibility Guidelines [ADAAG]), building codes (e.g., International Building Code), and standards (e.g., American National Standards Institute [ANSI]) that pertain to the disabled and the removal of accessibility barriers. On July 23, 2004, the U.S. Access Board (*www.access-board.gov*) announced the release of new design guidelines that cover access for people with disabilities under the landmark ADA of 1990. The guidelines update access requirements for a wide range of facilities in the public and private sectors covered by the law.

As part of this update, the board has made its guidelines more consistent with model building codes, such as the International Building Code (IBC), and industry standards. It coordinated extensively with model code groups and standard-setting bodies throughout the process so that differences could be reconciled.

As a result, the historic level of harmonization that has been achieved has brought about improvements to the guidelines as well as to counterpart provisions in the IBC and key industry standards, including those for accessible facilities issued through ANSI. The board believes that this will greatly facilitate compliance. However, these new guidelines are not enforceable standards until they are officially adopted by the U.S. Department of Justice, which has not done so as of this writing.

(a)

(b)

FIGURE 4.10 In the Villa Suites at Bellagio, a state-of-the-art communication and control system can do everything from opening the drapes to summoning the butler. These touch pads are conveniently located throughout the suite, from the night table to the wall of the dining room. *(Photos courtesy of Bellagio, MGM Mirage™, Las Vegas, Nevada.)*

CONCLUSION

The executive housekeeper must be not only a planner but also an administrator with a basic knowledge of budgeting procedure, furniture, fixtures, equipment, cleaning products, and supply inventories. Material planning for hotel operations begins with an understanding of budgeting systems by which material resources will be allocated. Capital expenditures, operating budgets, and preopening budgets were defined and discussed in this chapter. Classification of material resources must be understood. Knowledge of those material items that are part of the fixed assets and of other items that are part of inventories that will be used up in the generation of revenue is also important if costs are to be controlled. Inventory control is more than the mere counting of items; it is the entire process by which material is classified, ordered, received, stored, issued, and otherwise accounted for. The executive housekeeper involved in opening a hotel is involved not only with establishing certain material accounts and inventories, but also with arranging physical layouts to store materials, developing systems to account for supply use, making arrangements to purchase products, and establishing relationships with vendors and purveyors.

In this and the following three chapters, a complete analysis of the material inventories with which the executive housekeeper may be involved is presented. A continuation of the topic of inventory control will be presented as the management functions of direction and control are developed.

KEY TERMS AND CONCEPTS

Administration	Revenue	Fixed assets
Material	Labor costs	Equipment
Software items	Employee costs	Inventories
Budgets	Controllable costs	Books of account
Capital expenditure	Control profit	Life expectancy
Depreciation	Control loss	Liabilities
Furniture, fixtures, and equipment (FFE)	Preopening budgets	Move-in day
Software	Pro formas	Spare component
Capitalized	Inventory control	Case goods
Expensed	Pars	Formal balance
Operating budgets	Classification of material	Informal balance
Operating costs	Assets	ADA
	Current assets	

DISCUSSION AND REVIEW QUESTIONS

1. Some items of material are **capitalized**; others are **expensed**. What is the difference between these two terms?
2. Explain the difference between capital expenditure budgets and operational budgets. In an ongoing operation, how many times in a fiscal year is each prepared? Which is usually prepared first? Why?
3. Preopening budgets usually include items such as funds for opening ceremonies and parties, advertising, and public relations. List several other important items that should be funded for within a preopening budget. Why should the preopening budget be amortized, and over what period of time?
4. A disabled person wants a room on the top (suite) floor. According to ADA, must you accommodate that guest? When the first alarm sounds, elevators become inoperative. How would you evacuate this disabled person from the top floor? (Hint: Visit *http://www.evac-chair.com*.)

5. Explain the concept of using temporary storage when opening a hotel.

6. Visit a store that sells innerspring mattresses, and a store that sells foam mattresses such as Tempur-Pedic. Lie down on each one, decide which one is more comfortable, and compare your opinion with those of other students. Discuss the advantages and disadvantages of each mattress from an executive housekeeper's perspective.

CHAPTER 5

Material Planning: Floors, Walls, and Windows

LEARNING OBJECTIVES

After studying the chapter, students should be able to:

1. Identify the various types of floor coverings and describe the relative advantages and disadvantages of each type.
2. Describe standard procedures and the latest developments in floor cleaning.
3. Identify elements of carpet construction.
4. Describe and evaluate different carpet cleaning techniques.
5. Describe standard window-washing procedures.
6. Identify materials used in wall coverings and window treatments and describe the relative advantages and disadvantages of each type.
7. Describe the care and treatment of walls, windows, and floors, including the latest developments.

This chapter examines the materials used in the construction of floors and floor coverings. The specific properties of appearance, durability, cost, and ease of maintenance for each type of floor are discussed. The treatment of each floor type (methods that are used in the cleaning, sealing, and refinishing of floors) are also examined.

Particular attention is given to carpeting. Carpet composition, construction, and design are addressed, and alternative cleaning methods for carpets are evaluated.

Wall coverings and window treatments are also described. The different types of wall coverings, their durability, relative cost, ease of maintenance, and proper cleaning procedures are explored. The construction and cleaning of window treatments are presented, as well as materials used in drapes, shades, and blinds.

Cleaning for Health

For many years, when asked to consider or describe the environment, Americans would usually visualize it as being forests, mountains, lakes, and oceans. However, the indoors qualifies as the environment as well. They are interconnected—what we do in the built environment impacts the outside environment. When considering matters of human health, the built environment becomes critically important, for it is estimated that the average American spends between 90 and 95 percent of his or her time indoors. We need to choose wisely when selecting materials in the construction of floors, walls, and windows, and we also need to choose wisely when determining how we are to maintain those materials.

Cleaning for appearance is important, but it is not primary. Our primary concern as executive housekeepers is to clean for health. This entails a new perspective, not only on the chemicals used in cleaning and maintaining surfaces, but also on the methods we employ to maintain these surfaces in our properties.

For example, for many years we have "pushed the dirt around" but failed to capture it. The standard mop is a prime example of this approach. An employee pushes around a traditional mop and bucket. The mop is repeatedly dipped into the increasingly dirty water and applied to the floor. The act of mopping breaks up the dirt on the floor's surface, but does not pick up all or even most of the dirt, which is then left to dry on the floor's surface. Bacteria and viruses are transported from one area to another by the mop and the dirty water being reapplied to the floor. This is referred to as **cross contamination**, whereby pathogens are carried from one area to another by equipment and workers. The water is only changed when the worker perceives it as being too dirty to use.

The traditional mop is now being replaced by a flat mop that is made of microfiber (Figure 5.1). The mop heads collect the soil instead of redistributing it. They will even pick up as much as 98 percent of the bacteria on a surface. The mop heads are not dipped back into the cleaning solution, keeping it clean for the entire operation, and the heads can be instantly changed out when moving from room to room (e.g., from a bathroom to a hallway) to avoid cross contamination. The dirty mop heads can be washed repeatedly (i.e., an estimated 300 washings) and reused.

Consider also the cleaning system from one manufacturer, KaiVac, a "no-touch cleaning system ergonomically designed for greater employee health and productivity." The KaiVac (Figure 5.2) is a two-tank system—a clean water tank and a vacuum tank containing the wastewater. It is designed for cleaning kitchens, public restrooms, and other public areas. When cleaning public restrooms, workers do not have to touch toilet surfaces, and the prospect of cross contamination is virtually eliminated. The company also claims that restroom cleaning is done in one-third the time with its equipment.

These are only two of the new and innovative products that have appeared in recent years. The science of cleaning, which had not changed appreciably for decades, is now undergoing a tremendous revolution. So how does one become a "green cleaner"? The following article by one of the pioneers of the movement, Stephen Ashkin, gives housekeepers ten easy-to-follow tips for becoming "green." More examples of green cleaning and cleaning for health appear in this and other chapters to follow.

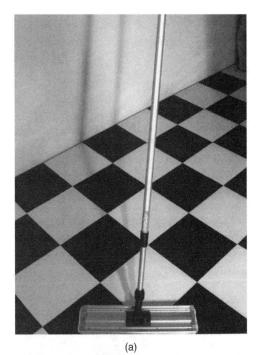

(a)

(b)

FIGURE 5.1 A Simplee Cleen™ microfiber mop with a telescoping handle has easy-to-change flat mop heads, as shown in the second photo. The heads are held on by Velcro. *(Courtesy of Newport Marketing Group, Inc.)*

Floor Types and Their Care

❧

Whether for a facility under construction or for the remodeling of an existing property, the executive housekeeper is often called upon to assist in the selection of the floor or floor coverings.

A multitude of variables must be considered when selecting the appropriate floor or floor covering. The floor must meet the aesthetic requirements of the architect and/or interior designer. Floors must coordinate with wall and window coverings as well as with the room's furnishings.

(a)

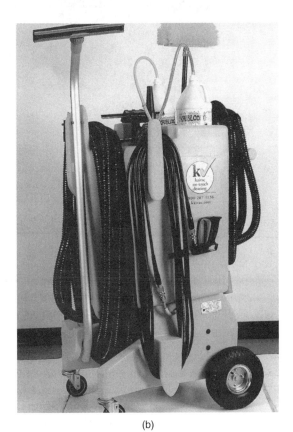

(b)

FIGURE 5.2 The KaiVac ''no-touch'' system for cleaning public areas such as bathrooms has made the traditional mop and bucket a relic. *(Copyright KaiVac, Inc., 2003.)*

Floor and floor covering selection is not predicated only upon design and aesthetic considerations, however; many other factors, such as durability, installation cost, maintenance cost, and ease of maintenance should also be considered in the selection process.

The amount and type of traffic to which a particular floor will be subjected must be determined before selecting the flooring. Next, the durability of the proposed floor materials to be subjected to the expected traffic must be considered. In other words, one must project how long each floor material under consideration can be expected to last when it is subjected to the expected wear.

The executive housekeeper should then estimate the cleaning and maintenance costs for each of the prospective floor materials over the life of the floor. These costs will include labor, chemicals, and equipment.

Installation costs should then be added to the maintenance costs. This sum should be divided by the expected life of the floor (estimated in months). The monthly costs for each of the prospective floor materials can be compared, and this comparison can be used in the decision-making process. Certainly other variables, such as how the intended flooring complements the overall design and the relative ease of maintenance, should be weighed against the cost considerations.

An Unfortunate Trend

Top management will often ask department heads to reduce costs, particularly during economically uncertain times. On the surface, deferring maintenance seems to yield an immediate savings; but does it? For example, carpet that is not regularly cleaned will for an extended period of time look none the worse for wear, but failing to clean carpet regularly can reduce its life by several years. When the cost of replacing carpet on a four-year cycle versus a six- or seven-year cycle is factored into the formula, the dollars saved through deferred maintenance disappear.

FLOOR CARE METHODS

Floor care is a four-step process, according to Bill Saunders and Rick Mazzoli of Glit Inc. (Figure 5.3). In this section we explore each phase of the Saunders and Mazzoli FPMR floor care model.[1]

Foundation

The first phase of the FPMR model is **foundation**. Floor finishes are not permanent fixtures. Periodically, a floor must be stripped of its old finish and a new finish must be applied. Saunders and Mazzoli list four reasons to strip a floor of its existing **finish**:

1. When there is a breakdown in the floor surface and there are definite worn traffic areas that are beginning to show. These areas are indicated by a worn-away finish and/or seal, and the bare floor becomes exposed.
2. A noticeable flaking or chipping of the surface of the finish from too much old finish. This mainly occurs when the wet scrubbing procedure has not been followed.
3. When the "wet look" begins to show definite dark shadowy areas as you look into the surface of the floor. This is usually blamed on burnishing the floor without wet mopping first. The result? Shiny dirt!
4. When there is a staining from spills or from inadequate pickup of the cleaning solutions while mopping the floors.[2]

Once the decision has been made to refinish the floor, the first stage is to strip the floor of its existing finish. Figure 5.4 lists the equipment required to perform this task.

The purpose of **stripping** is to remove both the old floor finish and all of the dirt that has been embedded in that finish. This is accomplished in the following way. First dust mop the floor to remove all loose dirt and dust. Then get two clean mops and two clean mop buckets and fill the buckets half full with hot water. Add the recommended amount of stripping solution to one of the buckets. Rope off the areas to be stripped and place warning signs at appropriate locations. Place mats at the exits to the area being stripped so that the stripping solution is not tracked to other floors.

Lay down a generous amount of the stripping solution in a small area of the floor and let stand for approximately five minutes. Do not allow the solution to dry. If allowed to dry, the stripping solution, mixed together with the old finish, will turn into a dirty gray paste, and the entire process must be begun again.

After the solution has stood for five minutes, start by scrubbing along the baseboards or in the corners with a scrubbing pad. Then start scrubbing with a floor machine using a black or brown pad. Use a machine that runs between 175 and 350 rpm; do not use a high-speed buffer. Be careful not to splash the walls with the stripping solution. Using the floor machine, scrub in a straight line along the baseboard; then scrub from side to side. When a section of the floor has been covered, go back over the area in the opposite direction.

Once the area has been thoroughly scrubbed, the old finish can be picked up from the floor. The best way to perform this task is to use a wet/dry pickup vacuum, but if one is not available, you must have an additional pickup bucket. The same mop that was used for laying down the solution can be used to pick up the dirty solution. Rinse that mop in the pickup bucket and change the water when it gets dirty.

10 TIPS FOR CLEANING UP "GREEN"

Create a Thorough Green Cleaning Program

A green cleaning program requires a complete overview of the cleaning program—from supply ordering to cleaning equipment and processes.

by Stephen P. Ashkin

This article first appeared in the January 2003 edition of *Cleaning and Maintenance Management* magazine and appears here through the generosity of CM B2B Trade Group, a subsidiary of National Trade Publications.

With the recent public interest in health concerns and the role cleaning plays in maintaining indoor air quality and controlling bacteria, building service contractors and facility managers who focus on cleaning for health and "green" cleaning will deliver a healthier and more productive environment for building occupants.

The following are 10 green cleaning tips to follow when cleaning commercial and institutional buildings.

1. *Work from a written plan:* Too many cleaners work without effective plans. Instead, they prioritize tasks by crisis or complaint—the bigger the crisis or louder the complaint, the more resources devoted to its solution.

    A proper cleaning plan addresses any unique requirements, such as:
    - Individual occupants with existing health conditions or sensitivities
    - Geographical settings
    - Building age
    - Changes in seasonal occurrences
    - A stewardship component to involve all building occupants
    A helpful guideline for proper cleaning plans can be found in ASTM E1971-98 (Standard Guide in Stewardship for Cleaning Commercial and Institutional Buildings).

2. *Use entryway systems:* A well-designed and maintained entryway system can have an enormous impact on both people's health and cleaning costs. Note: 80 to 90 percent of all dirt enters a building on people's feet.

    Use mats, grills, grates, etc.—covering a minimum of 12 consecutive feet—inside and outside to prevent dirt, dust, pollen and other particles from entering the building.

    Additionally, design outdoor walkways to eliminate standing water, and be rough enough to help scrape soils off shoes, but not rough enough to create slip and fall hazards.

The first set of entryway systems should be capable of capturing larger particles while the final component should be capable of capturing fine particles and drying wet/damp shoes.

3. *Use a clean, well-vented closet:* Chemical and janitorial equipment storage and mixing areas can have a serious impact on indoor air quality (IAQ) as the items off-gas volatile organic compounds (VOCs).

    To minimize the adverse effects from pollutants circulated throughout the building, operate these areas:
    - With separate outside exhaust vents
    - Without air recirculation
    - Under negative pressure
    Also, make sure areas are well organized, and hazardous products are identified and segregated, especially those that are flammable, combustible or reactive.

4. *Adopt a durable floor care system:* One-third of the entire maintenance budget ($0.35 to $0.70 per square foot) is typically devoted to the care and maintenance of floors.

    The activity of maintaining—burnishing, stripping and recoating—floors can create IAQ problems from VOCs and particles, as well as occupational hazards to custodians and huge environmental burdens.

    Using highly durable products that don't contain heavy metals, which are toxic in the environment after disposal, can limit those hazards.

    That combined with cleaning and application procedures that extend the period between stripping can reduce the long-term labor costs and liability to cleaning personnel and occupants.

    Note: The initial (upfront) cost is typically higher than traditional systems, but offer long-term savings.

5. Use environmentally preferable cleaning products. Use of green—environmentally friendly and safe-to-use—cleaning products is a natural step in switching to green cleaning procedures.

    Utilize environmentally preferable product specifications, such as those developed by Green Seal (GS 37), to ensure the green claims made by the manufacturers are verified.

6. Use biobased/renewable resource based cleaning products. Petroleum, a common building block of cleaning and other chemicals, is a non-renewable and limited resource, making use of these products not a sustainable practice.

   Biobased renewable resources—such as corn, soy, coconuts and citrus fruits, are now available in cleaning products to replace petroleum.

   Not only is their use a more sustainable practice, but generally their production is more benign then their petroleum-based counterparts.

7. Use concentrated products. Concentrated cleaning products reduce packaging—boxes, bottles, etc.—and the resulting impacts on the environment from mass transportation of large volumes of products.

   Concentrates offer good environmental savings and are a great way to reduce the cost for cleaning chemicals. However, it's important to use the appropriate dilution of the concentrated cleaning products, otherwise the environmental and costs savings can be lost.

8. Use environmentally preferable supplies. Utilizing paper containing 100 percent recycled content, a minimum of 30 percent post-consumer recycled content, and that is manufactured without elemental chlorine or chlorine compounds can help the environment significantly.

   Plastic trash can and other liners should utilize a minimum of 30 percent post-consumer recycled content to reduce the use of petroleum.

9. Use efficient equipment. Carpet care equipment should be capable of capturing 99.79 percent of particulates 0.3 microns in size.

In many applications, including hard floor care, backpack vacuums can accomplish this and save time and money.

Carpet extraction equipment should be able to heat the water, reduce the amount of water and chemicals necessary to do the job and remove sufficient moisture so that carpets can dry in less than 24 hours to minimize the potential for mold growth.

Equipment for hard floor maintenance, such as buffers and burnishers, should be equipped with active dust control systems, including:

- Skirts
- Vacuums
- Guards and other devices for capturing fine particles

Carpet and floor care equipment should be electric or battery powered and durable and should have a maximum sound level less than 70 decibels.

10. Implement an Integrated Pest Management (IPM) program. An effective integrated pest management program removes the food, moisture, nesting and entry opportunities that allow pests to enter and flourish in a building, thereby reducing or eliminating the use of pesticides.

Stephen P. Ashkin is principal of The Ashkin Group, a consulting firm specializing in greening the cleaning process. In *Environmentalism Unbound* (The MIT Press, August 2001), Robert Gottlieb, a renowned expert on the janitorial industry, describes Steve Ashkin as the "leading advocate for a stronger environmental profile among cleaning product manufacturers and suppliers" and "the most visible industry figure advancing the cause of environmentally preferable products." Stephen Ashkin can be reached at (812) 332-7950.

The next step is to completely rinse and dry the floor using a clean mop and clear hot water in the rinse bucket. Then either pick up the rinse water with the mop, or use the wet/dry vacuum to remove all rinse water from the floor.

Once the floor dries, check to see if there is a gray film on the floor by rubbing your hand over the dried floor. If a film is present, there is still old finish on the floor; the stripping procedure should then be repeated.

When finished, clean up all buckets and wringers, wash all mop heads, and wash the pad on the floor machine and all other equipment used.

The second phase involves the application of floor finish, or **sealer**. Sealers include the permanent-type, penetrating solvent-based sealers, used on concrete, marble, **terrazzo**, or other stone surfaces. Floor stripping does not remove these types of sealers. A second type is a water emulsion stripper that is placed on certain kinds of asphalt and tile floors. This type of sealer has to be replaced after floor stripping.

Today's market offers quite a variety of floor sealer/finishes, and many of them work quite well on the modern floors for which they were intended. For older floors, however, the application of a sealer, followed by a finish, is the standard approach.

A floor sealer/finish serves three purposes. First, it protects the floor from wear and staining caused by traffic, inadvertent spills, and chemicals used in the cleaning process. Second, it provides a safe surface upon which to walk. The appropriate finish should make the floor more slip-resistant. Third, the finish has an aesthetic appeal. It makes the floor shine, conveying a positive impression to both customers and employees. Today, the buzzword in floor care is the "wet look," which is an extremely high gloss on tile, wood, and stone floors. Floors of today must not only look clean enough to be noticed; they must positively shine. Interestingly,

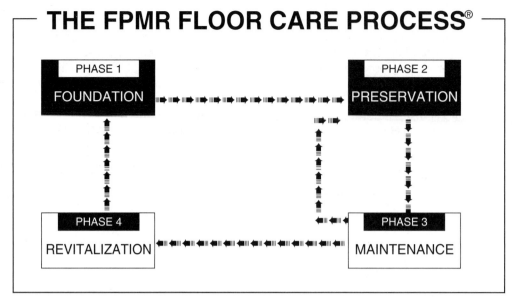

FIGURE 5.3 The FPMR Process of Floor Care. *(Used with permission of Saunders and Mazzoli.)*

Required Supplies & Equipment

Clean dust mop
Dust pan and brush
Standard speed floor machine with pad drive assembly or stripping brush
Clean floor stripping pads
Wet pick-up vacuum
Set of "Wet Floor" signs
2 clean mop buckets with clean wringers
2 wet mop handles with clean looped-end banded mops
Putty knife
Doorway mats
Hand pads and holder for edge cleaning
Floor stripping concentrate
Stripper neutralizer concentrate

FIGURE 5.4 Required floor-stripping supplies and equipment. *(Used with permission of the International Sanitary Supply Association, Inc.)*

this current trend toward the "wet look" may appear dangerous to the uninitiated, but, in reality, these floor surfaces are often less slippery than a dull surface.

Figure 5.5 lists the required supplies and equipment to seal/finish a floor. The first step is to inspect the floor and make sure that it is completely dry and clean. The International Sanitary Supply Association then recommends that the mop bucket be lined with a plastic trash liner to save cleanup time.[3]

Using either a clean nylon mop, a lamb's wool applicator, or a mechanical applicator designed for the task, first apply the finish next to the baseboard in smooth strokes (see Figure 5.5). Then apply the finish to the center area with figure-eight strokes if using the mop. Be sure that the first coat and all subsequent coats are *thin* coats. Thick coats of finish do not last as long and can make for a very slippery surface. Four thin coats are far better than two thicker coats.

After the first coat is dry to the touch, let the floor sit for at least the length of time that it took the first coat to dry before applying a second coat. Repeat this procedure for each coat.

To avoid finish buildup in corners and along the baseboards, do not apply more than two coats within 12 inches of the walls.

Finally, allow the floor to dry as long as possible before **buffing** or **burnishing**, and keep the floor closed to traffic as long as possible. Seventy-two hours is the optimal drying time for most floor finishes.

Buffing (or polishing) the floor is done with a floor machine that delivers up to $1\frac{1}{2}$ horsepower and turns at 175 to 350 rpm. Burnishing is accomplished with a different type of floor machine that places less weight

Required Supplies & Equipment

Clean mop bucket and clean wringer
Set of "Wet Floor" signs
Floor finish
Clean plastic trash bag
Clean "Floor Finish" mop

FIGURE 5.5 Required floor-sealing supplies and equipment. *(Used with permission of the International Sanitary Supply Association, Inc.)*

on the floor, which allows it to turn at speeds in excess of 1000 rpm. This higher speed, which creates more friction, creates the high-gloss "wet look" in floors that has become so popular.

Whichever type of machine is issued, the type of pad used is the same (white in color). All pad manufacturers adhere to a universal color code to ensure that the proper type of pad can be used for each application. Black and brown pads are used for stripping, blue and green pads for scrubbing, red for spray cleaning, and white for polishing.

Once the finishing process is completed, all equipment should be washed immediately. Washed mop heads should be segregated by their original use and should not be used for any other application.

A tile or terrazzo floor beginning to turn yellow indicates that too much finish has been applied to the floor, and it then becomes necessary to strip one or two of the layers off the floor in order to restore it to its original luster. One positive note is that the new polymer finishes do not yellow like the old wax finishes.

Preservation

The second phase of the FPMR model is preservation.[4] This is accomplished through three techniques: sweeping/dust mopping, spot mopping, and the use of walk-off mats.[5]

Sweeping is done only when the floor surface is too rough for a dust mop. Push brooms are used for large areas, and old-fashioned corn brooms are best for corners and tight spaces. A practiced sweeper develops a rhythm and "bounces" the push broom to avoid flattening the bristles.

Dust mopping is the preferred way to remove dust, sand, and grit from a floor. If these substances are not removed from a floor on a daily basis, they will scratch the surface of the finish, diminishing its luster, and will eventually penetrate down to the floor itself.

Use the largest dust mop that is manageable. When mopping, keep the mop head on the floor at all times and do not move it backward. When you reach the end of a corridor, swivel the mop around, and on the return pass, overlap the area that you have dusted by about 8 inches. Use a dust pan to sweep up accumulated trash, and pick up gum with a putty knife.

Clean the mop frequently by vacuuming the mop in the custodian's closet or by shaking the mop in a plastic bag. The time to treat a mop is at the end of dusting, not at the beginning, so that the mop will have a chance to dry out. Never use oil-based dust mop treatments; these can discolor a stone floor. The mop head should be periodically removed and washed when it becomes saturated with dirt.

When finished, hang the mop up with the yarn away from the wall. Do not let the mop stand on the floor or touch a wall surface because it may leave a stain.

Spot mopping is essential to the preservation of a floor's surface. Liquids and solids that are spilled on the floor's surface, if left for any length of time, may penetrate the finish and stain the floor. Even acids from fruit juices may wreak havoc on a floor if they are not immediately cleaned up. A mop and bucket should be made available to take care of these accidents.

When spot mopping, clean cold water should be used so that the finish on the floor is not softened. Detergents should be avoided unless they become a necessity; that is, when a substance has been allowed to dry on the floor. If necessary, use a pH-neutral detergent; avoid abrasives, and dilute the detergent to a level that will accomplish the task but will not harm the finish.

The use of walk-off mats is the third preservation method. Their purpose is to prevent dirt and grit from being tracked onto the floor's surface from outside sources. There are three considerations when using walk-off mats: 1) make sure that the mat is large enough so that everyone will step on the mat at least twice with the same foot; 2) select a mat that correlates to the type of soil that is being tracked into the area; and 3) change out dirty mats. A mat that is saturated with dirt and soils will be a source of floor contamination rather than a cure for that contamination.

Maintenance

The third phase of the FPMR model is maintenance.[6] This involves the periodic removal of stains, dirt, and scuffs that appear on the surface of the finish. Its purpose is to produce lustrous, shiny, clean floors. Maintenance encompasses **damp mopping**, **spray buffing**, and burnishing. These techniques are done sequentially, and each technique is often performed immediately after the preceding one.

Before the floor can be damp mopped, it must first be dust mopped. After the floor is dusted, the equipment listed in Figure 5.6 must be assembled. Add neutral or mildly alkaline detergent to the mop water. The detergent used may be the variety that needs no rinsing. If not, the floor will need to be rinsed after the detergent solution is applied. Immerse the mop in the bucket and

wring it out until it is only *damp*. Use the same pattern in the damp mopping of a floor that was used in the application of stripper to the floor.

The solution in the bucket should be changed when the water becomes dirty. A brush or a floor machine may be used for stubborn spots, and a squeegee may be used to help speed the drying of the floor. Baseboards should be wiped off immediately if solution is splashed on them.

As noted in the "Foundation" section, all equipment should be cleaned upon the completion of a task.

Spray buffing may follow the damp-mopping procedure. Spray a section of the floor (approximately 4 × 6 feet) with the buffing solution, and buff the floor with a floor machine using a red buffing pad. Buff the area with a side-to-side motion until the floor begins to shine. Allow the machine to overlap the previously buffed area and change the dirty buffing pads frequently. Figure 5.7 shows a list of the required supplies and equipment needed for spray buffing.

Burnishing, or dry buffing, uses a high-speed machine that produces 300 rpm to 1500 rpm, depending on the particular model. This machine is operated in a straight line rather than a side-to-side motion. The white floor pad is used for dry buffing and should be changed frequently. As with spray buffing, it is wise to overlap completed areas when burnishing to ensure a uniform finish.

Required Supplies & Equipment

Clean dust mop
Dust pan and brush
Automatic floor machine with pad driving assembly or brush
Clean mop bucket with clean wringer
Wet mop handle with clean looped-end banded mop
Squeegee with handle
Floor pads
Putty knife
Approved detergent solution appropriate to the area
Set of "Wet Floor" signs
Clean wipers

FIGURE 5.6 Required damp-mopping supplies and equipment. *(Used with permission of the International Sanitary Supply Association, Inc.)*

Required Supplies & Equipment

Clean dust mop
Dust pan and brush
Floor Machine (175-400 rpm) with pad drive assembly or brush
Clean floor polish pads
Clean mop bucket with clean wringer
Wet mop handle and clean looped-end banded mop
Approved detergent solution appropriate for the area
Spray buff solution in dispensing container
"Wet Floor" signs

FIGURE 5.7 Spray-buffing supplies and equipment. *(Used with permission of the International Sanitary Supply Association, Inc.)*

Revitalization

The fourth phase in the FPMR model is revitalization.[7] Revitalization, or deep scrubbing, involves removing one or more layers of the old finish and applying new finish. The first step is to combine cool water with a neutral or mildly alkaline cleaning solution, which is then applied to the floor and scrubbed with a floor machine using a black pad. The floor machine is passed over the floor once to lessen the chance of removing too much finish, and cool rather than hot water is used because hot water would soften all the layers of finish.

The dirty water is picked up with a wet vac or mop, and the floor is rinsed using a clean mop and clean rinse water. Once the floor is dry, one or two coats of finish are applied, and the floor can then be buffed to a renewed shine.[8]

In the next section we review the major varieties of floors and the floor care requirements peculiar to each variety. The following suggested floor-care techniques are meant to be only general guidelines for specific types of floors. Readers are cautioned to follow the guidelines of the manufacturer in regard to cleaning supplies and techniques.

NONRESILIENT FLOORS

Nonresilient floors are those floors that do not "give" underfoot. Their hardness ensures their durability. Dents are not a problem with these types of floors. However, the hardness of these types of floors is also a major drawback. They are extremely tiring to those who must stand on them for any length of time.

Brick

Brick is not commonly used as flooring material for interiors, except to convey a rustic theme. Brick floors are normally left in their natural unglazed state and color, but they can be sealed and finished for some interior applications.

Unglazed bricks are made of a highly porous material, and they provide a highly durable, fairly slip-resistant floor, but the mortar used between the bricks can deteriorate rapidly if it is not properly maintained. Deteriorating mortar and loose bricks can quickly become a serious hazard for slip-and-fall accidents.

Another caution is to not use bricks where there may be grease spills: Since an unglazed brick is very porous, spilled grease and oil will be absorbed into the brick and will be very hard to remove. If the floor then becomes wet, the surface of the brick will have this oil and water mixture, making for a very slippery surface.

Cleaning Procedures Brick floors create special problems in cleaning. If the bricks are specially made slip-resistant brick, they will cause cotton mop heads to fray. Also, unglazed bricks tend to become very dusty. The best approach to cleaning a brick floor is to vacuum it with a brush and, when mopping, use a bristle brush in combination with a wet/dry vacuum.

Sealing, Finishing, Stripping Although the bricks themselves are not always sealed, the mortar between the bricks needs to be sealed and maintained on a regular basis. Be sure to select a sealer that is designed for this application.

Finishes, such as waxes and acrylics, are not normally applied to brick surfaces; because of this, there is no need for stripping.

Terra-cotta and Ceramic Tiles

Like brick, ceramic and terra-cotta tiles are made from clay that is fired in a kiln. However, ceramic tile differs from brick in that a coating is first applied to one side of the tile before firing, creating a surface that is almost totally impervious to soil and liquids.

Terra-cotta tiles, typically 6 inches square, resemble bricks because they are left in their natural color, and they do not have the glaze coat that is commonly applied to ceramic tile. Terra-cotta is traditionally reddish-brown. One variety of terra-cotta is often used in kitchen floor applications because it is marketed with a rough surface that makes it slip-resistant in greasy conditions.

These tiles can also be classified as completely nonresilient surfaces, and since there is no "give" to the tile, care must be taken not to drop heavy, hard objects on the floor that could pit or crack the surface.

Ceramic tile comes in a multitude of colors and can have either a matte or glossy surface. Care must be taken when selecting ceramic tile because certain solid colors will show dirt quite easily. Ceramic tile also appears on walls and countertops, as well as on interior and exterior floors. Figure 5.8 is an example of imported ceramic tiles used to create a mosaic in a public area for a special effect.

Finally, here is one note of caution regarding ceramic tile and its use on certain types of floors: Unless a special slip-resistant surface is employed, tile surfaces that are wet, greasy, or icy make for a very dangerous floor surface.

Cleaning Procedures The tiles must be cleaned frequently to remove dust and grit that could damage the glaze on the tile. Cleaning procedures might include dust mopping, damp mopping, and light scrubbing when needed. Cotton mop heads should not be used on tiles that contain slip-resistant surfaces, because these surfaces will quickly shred a traditional mop head. Scrubbing should be done with brushes, and the water should be picked up with a wet/dry vacuum.

FIGURE 5.8 The floor of the Bellagio's Conservatory is as beautiful as the real flower gardens just a few feet away. *(Photo courtesy of Bellagio, MGM Mirage™, Las Vegas, Nevada.)*

Sealing, Finishing, and Stripping The tile does not need to be sealed because it already has a scratch- and stain-resistant surface; however, the grout between the tiles has to be sealed with a sealer that is specifically designed for ceramic tile grout.

Finishes are not normally applied to ceramic tiles, so stripping is not a concern.

Concrete

Concrete floors were once used for their utility, not for their beauty. They are composed of cement, rocks, and sand, to which water has been added to initiate a chemical reaction that changes the ingredients into a stonelike material. Today, concrete floors are showing up in hotel lobbies as well as in loading docks. Concrete is now being colored with dyes and stamped with stencils to look like tile, stone, brick, and even wood. Plain old concrete surfaces can be given a new look with concrete overlays and **epoxy** coatings. Decorative concrete that will last the life of the building is rapidly becoming a preferred material for commercial flooring. Even the mall of the sophisticated Forum Shops at Caesar's Palace in Las Vegas has decorative concrete flooring.

Cleaning Procedures The cleaning procedures that may be used on a concrete floor range from a daily dust mopping, to damp mopping, to heavy scrubbing to remove grease and soils. Since concrete, and especially unsealed concrete, is so porous, an immediate effort must be made to clean up spilled liquids before they are absorbed into the concrete and cause unsightly stains.

Sealing, Finishing, and Stripping Concrete definitely requires sealing. An unsealed concrete floor will be constantly dusty and will absorb dirt and any liquid that is spilled on it.

The sealer used on a concrete surface must be a permeable sealer. Moisture and acids in the concrete percolate to the surface as the concrete dries. A permeable sealer is one that allows moisture and acids to evaporate from the surface of the concrete. If a nonpermeable sealer is used, the moisture and acids will be trapped on the surface just under the sealer. As the acids and moisture begin to concentrate, the surface of the concrete will begin to disintegrate.

The concrete must be completely clean before a sealer is applied; if it is not, the sealer will not adhere to the surface. If the concrete is new, special sealers must be used to allow the concrete to continue to "cure."

Finishes may be applied to concrete floors, but they should be compatible with porous floors and permeable sealers. Color sealers and paints should be avoided because once they start to show wear, they become unsightly and are almost impossible to repair. However, on a cured floor, epoxy sealers and paints can be applied to help diminish the effects of heavy wear. Finishes can be buffed with a rotary floor machine.

Stripping the finish from a concrete floor normally requires an alkaline stripping agent that has been properly diluted with water. The stripping solution is then applied to the floor surface using a rotary floor machine with an abrasive pad.

After the old sealer is removed and before a new sealer is applied, the floor is often treated with a special acidic solution that will "etch" the surface of the floor, providing greater adhesion for the new sealer.

Epoxy

The epoxy floor is a compound of synthetic resins that provide an extremely durable, seamless floor. These floors are an ideal choice when a floor is required to withstand massive loads. Decorative particles can be mixed into the epoxy resin to provide an attractive, yet highly utilitarian, flooring.

Epoxy floors are ideal for trade show facilities, locker rooms, loading docks, and shower areas.

Cleaning Procedures Exotic procedures and techniques are not necessary when cleaning an epoxy floor; sweeping, mopping, and scrubbing with an alkaline cleaner diluted with water are sufficient.

Sealing, Finishing, and Stripping Epoxy floors should be sealed, and they can receive a finish; however, finishing is not necessary to the maintenance of an epoxy floor. Stripping is accomplished with commercial alkaline strippers used in conjunction with a rotary floor machine.

Stone Floors

Common types of natural stone flooring include marble, travertine, serpentine, granite, slate, and sandstone (see Figure 5.9). All natural stone products share certain properties that must be taken into consideration by the professional housekeeper to ensure the proper care of this type of flooring.

Natural stone flooring may look impervious to the elements, but it is decidedly not as resistant to damage as it looks. Acids and moisture can have disastrous effects on natural stone. Some acids are present naturally in the stone, but even the acid from spilled orange juice can have a deleterious effect on stone floors, causing pitting, cracking, and **spalling**. These floors need to have moisture-permeable sealers applied so moisture and acids do not build up under the sealer and destroy the floor's surface. Oils and grease can permanently stain untreated stone floors because these floors are extremely porous.

Cleaning Procedures To prevent the staining of stone floors, the dust mops should be free of all oil-based dusting compounds. Dusting should be carried out on a daily basis because grit, sand, and other abrasives that are tracked onto a stone floor will quickly mar the floor's finish.

A pH-neutral detergent is recommended to clean all natural stone floors. Highly alkaline cleaners, as well as acidic compounds, will damage stone floors. When mopping stone floors, do not let water or chemicals remain on the floor. A final rinse of clean water should be applied and then immediately picked up with a mop or a wet/dry vacuum.

Sealing, Finishing, and Stripping Most stone floors need to be protected with a moisture-permeable sealer. Finishes normally should be applied in one or two thin layers and buffed. Applying heavy layers of finish does not work well, because it causes stone floors to become slippery.

When stripping the finish from a stone floor, make sure that the stripping agent is either neutral or mildly alkaline. Acids and strong alkalines can damage virtually all types of stone floors.

Terrazzo

A terrazzo floor is a mosaic flooring composed of portland cement that has been embedded with marble and/or granite chips. See Figure 5.10, in which a terrazzo

FIGURE 5.9 Agglomerate marble, a fabricated marble composed of natural marble stones blended with polyester resins, from Dal Tile Corporation. *(Used with permission of Jacqueline & Associates, Las Vegas.)*

FIGURE 5.10 Burnishing a terrazzo floor. *(Used with permission of the Advance Machine Company.)*

floor is being burnished with a high-speed burnisher. Once the floor has set, it is then ground by progressively finer-grit stones until a perfectly smooth and polished surface is obtained. The chips used in a terrazzo floor can differ in both size and color, creating a variety of colorful and attractive floors.

With proper care, a terrazzo floor will hold its original luster and will last indefinitely. What destroys most terrazzo surfaces is not use, but improper maintenance.

Cleaning Procedures Terrazzo should be dusted daily to remove harmful grit and sand that can wear down the surface, but dust mops should not be treated with oil dressings because oil is the archenemy of a terrazzo floor. Once oil or grease penetrates a terrazzo floor, it is virtually impossible to remove.

Steel wool should not be used on the surface of a terrazzo floor because the steel wool may put rust stains on the marble chips.

When selecting detergents and cleaners for terrazzo floors, stay away from acid cleaners, abrasives and scrubbing powders, and preparations that have an alkalinity above pH 10. Always rinse a freshly scrubbed floor, and do not allow water or cleaners to remain on the floor surface.

Sealing, Stripping, and Finishing All terrazzo floors must be sealed with a sealer designed for this particular type of floor. The sealer must be water-permeable so that moisture can evaporate from the surface of the terrazzo but will also help to prevent the absorption of oils and chemicals into the terrazzo.

When deep scrubbing or stripping a terrazzo floor, avoid highly alkaline strippers.

Since the floor has a natural sheen, finish is often thought to be unnecessary, but if a mirrored finish is desired (often referred to as the "wet look"), one or two thin coats of finish burnished with a high-speed buffer will produce the sought-after result.

RESILIENT SURFACES

Resilient floors have various degrees of "give" to their surfaces. This degree of resiliency ranges from asphalt floors, which are almost as hard as a concrete or stone surface, to carpeted and padded floors. Under this classification we have included asphalt tile, cork, **linoleum**, rubber, vinyl, vinyl composition tile, and wood. Because the care and maintenance of carpet is such an involved and complex topic, the treatment of carpet has its own section in this chapter. Finally, some universal precautions to take with all resilient floors is to limit static loads to no more than 250 pounds per square inch, remove those little metal domes from furniture legs, and use rubber rollers on chairs.

Asphalt Tile

Asphalt tile is one of the lowest-cost resilient floor coverings available, and it is quite durable under most normal conditions. It will, however, become brittle when exposed to prolonged periods of low temperature and will also dent when heavy objects are present on its surface, particularly when the ambient air temperature is above 80° Fahrenheit.

Asphalt tile is also fire-resistant; in fact, it is one of the most mar-resistant of all floorings in regard to cigarette burns.

Cleaning Procedures Dust mopping, damp mopping, and scrubbing, as described in the "Floor Care Methods" section, will maintain and preserve the asphalt tile floor. One important item to remember when wet mopping is never to let water stand for any length of time on an asphalt tile floor. Standing water will attack the adhesive cement and will cause tiles to curl and loosen.

Sealing, Stripping, and Finishing Asphalt tile is normally given several thin coats of finish and burnished or buffed with a floor machine. Never let stripping solution remain on the floor; always pick up the dirty solution immediately after scrubbing with a floor machine to avoid curling or loose tiles.

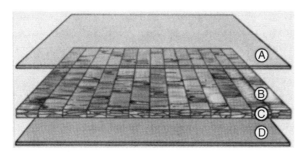

A. Pure transparent vinyl-bonded wear surface
B. Natural cork
C. Edges sealed against moisture
D. Bonded vinyl moisture barrier

FIGURE 5.11 How a vinyl-bonded cork floor from Permagrain is constructed. *(Used with permission of Jacqueline & Associates, Las Vegas.)*

Cork Tile

Cork tile is made from the outer bark of cork oak trees grown in Spain and Portugal. The cork is ground into large granules, mixed with synthetic resins, and pressed into sheets, which are then cut into tiles. Contemporary cork tiles for floors usually have a top layer of clear vinyl applied to them (Figure 5.11). This vinyl layer protects the cork from staining and wear.

Cork tiles traditionally have had limited application in industrial or institutional settings. One reason is that cork is susceptible to staining because it is one of the most porous of all floor coverings. Another limitation is that it is not durable; it is highly susceptible to abrasion. Cinders, sand, and gravel tracked on to a cork floor will severely shorten its life span. Finally, it is expensive. Cork rivals ceramic tiles in cost and does not have nearly the useful life of ceramic tile.

Although the use of cork has its drawbacks, it has three favorable properties that make it a desirable floor covering in limited settings: It absorbs sound, it is attractive, and most important, it is the most resilient of all floorings. This resilience has one drawback: Heavy objects resting on small weight-bearing surfaces will easily dent cork tile floors.

Cleaning Procedures Natural cork tile floors are among the most expensive of all floors to maintain. Cork tile floors should be swept daily, or more often, depending on usage. Natural cork tiles should only be damp mopped without detergents on infrequent occasions.

Vinyl-coated cork tiles can be wet mopped, providing that detergent solutions are not allowed to remain on the tiles for any length of time.

Stripping, Sealing, and Finishing To remove the seal from a natural cork floor and repair any staining or discoloration, a special solvent is first applied and removed along with the seal and finish. Then the floor is sanded to remove surface stains. This is followed by successive coatings of seal followed by several thin coats of finish. The floor is then buffed.

Vinyl-covered tiles need not be sealed but can be given a few thin coats of finish and buffed with a floor machine.

Rubber Floors

All modern rubber floors are made from synthetic rubber, such as **styrene butadiene rubber (SBR)**. Rubber tiles are cured or vulcanized by the application of heat. Rubber floors are nonporous, waterproof surfaces. One major advantage is that they are quite resilient and will remain resilient over a considerable temperature range.

Rubber flooring is susceptible to alkalines, oils, grease, solvents, ultraviolet light, and ozone in the air. When attacked by these components, a rubber floor will often become tacky and soft. It will then become brittle and begin to crack and powder.

Rubber tiles often have knobs on the surface or a tread pattern to improve traction, especially if liquids are frequently spilled on the surface.

Cleaning Procedures Highly alkaline cleaning solutions should be avoided; it is best to use pH-neutral detergents whenever possible. Cleaning solvents such as naphtha and turpentine should never be used on a rubber floor.

Rubber floors are fairly easy to maintain. Daily dust mopping and an occasional damp mopping are all that is needed to maintain the floor.

Stripping, Sealing, and Finishing Rubber floors need not be sealed, so the task of stripping is not necessary. A water emulsion floor polish can be applied, but it also is not necessary. The rubber floor will buff to a nice shine without the use of hard finishes. If a finish is used, it should be the type that is tolerant of a flexible floor surface and will not be susceptible to powdering. A high-speed floor burnishing system is not recommended because it may leave abrasion or burn marks on the floor.

Vinyl Floors

There are several types of vinyl floorings and tiles. The major varieties are vinyl **asbestos** tiles, vinyl composition tiles, homogeneous or flexible vinyl tiles, and laminated vinyl flooring.

Vinyl asbestos tiles are no longer made and have been removed from numerous commercial and residential settings because the asbestos in the tile is a known **carcinogen**. Improper cleaning of vinyl asbestos tile can release deadly asbestos fibers into the air and present a very real health hazard.

Laminated vinyl flooring is less expensive to manufacture than vinyl composition or **homogeneous** vinyl floors. The low initial cost may be deceiving, however, for once the top wear layer is worn through, the floor will have to be replaced. Some laminated floorings are guaranteed for only three years with moderate use. The cost of laminated vinyl flooring will vary in proportion to the thickness of the top vinyl wear layer.

In addition to the vinyl resins, vinyl composition tiles contain mineral fillers such as asphalt and pigments. Homogeneous vinyl tile may be either flexible or solid, and it has become the preferred standard for resilient tile flooring. It is practically unaffected by moisture, oils, and chemical solvents. The wearability of top-grade vinyl tile is in direct proportion to its thickness, as the colors and patterns of the tile are present throughout the thickness of the tile. Less expensive vinyl tiles will carry the pattern and color only on the surface of the tiles.

Today, vinyl tiles come in a wide variety of colors and textures. They are made to resemble wood, marble, granite, travertine, brick, and ceramic tiles. Some of these faux tiles are extremely good facsimiles, and they sell for far less than the actual product. Bruce is a flooring manufacturer that has set the stage for using different types of vinyl inlays in commercial traffic zone areas. (See Figure 5.12.)

Cleaning Procedures Modern homogenous vinyl needs only to be dusted and damp mopped to restore its luster.

Daily dusting to remove sand and grit is extremely important to the care of vinyl because most types will scratch under heavy foot traffic. Some tiles are specially treated with a scratch-resistant seal that is applied at the factory.

Modern vinyl is unaffected by alkaline detergents, but pH-neutral detergents are recommended over heavy alkaline products.

Stripping, Sealing, and Finishing Sealing, finishing, and stripping are not recommended for "no-wax" vinyl floors. Vinyl is nonporous, so sealing is not necessary and finish does not adhere well to no-wax vinyl flooring. No-wax vinyls are particularly susceptible to abrasion and should be used only in areas where the foot traffic is light to moderate. Purchasers of no-wax vinyl should look for "scratchguard" or other similar claims of protection.

On regular vinyl tile, finish is applied in thin coats and buffed. The finish is stripped by using recommended detergent strippers as described in the previous section on floor maintenance techniques.

Never allow a vinyl asbestos floor to become dry when stripping. Always keep the surface of the floor wet when operating the floor machine, and use the least abrasive strip pad possible. Also, never buff or burnish a vinyl asbestos floor that does not have a protective coat of finish. Dry stripping or buffing without a finish will release the harmful asbestos fibers into the air, which then can be inhaled and cause lung disorders.

FIGURE 5.12 Bruce vinyl flooring made to look like a stone and wood inlay in a commercial traffic area. *(Photo courtesy of Tile and Carpet Gallery, Las Vegas, Nevada.)*

Wood Floors

There is nothing quite as attractive as the warmth and richness of wood floors (see Figure 5.13). Most hardwood floors are made from oak, but other popular woods include ash, beech, birch, hickory, maple, teak, and walnut. In addition to their attractiveness, hardwood floors are extremely durable if they are properly finished and maintained.

Unfinished wood floors will quickly deteriorate under even light use, as wood is an extremely porous surface. Unfinished woods are susceptible to dirt lodging in the grains, splintering of the wood fibers, abrasions caused by normal foot traffic, and, of course, moisture, the bane of wood floors. Too much moisture will cause a wood floor to warp, and too little humidity will cause wood floors to shrink and crack.

To help forestall damage, most wood floors made today receive a factory-applied finish. In some instances the wood is heated to open its pores. **Tung oil** and **carnauba wax** are then applied to seal the wood.

In another process, **polyurethane** is used to seal the wood. One firm uses liquid **acrylics** that permeate and protect the wood. Another company even sells a wood veneer floor that is sandwiched between layers of vinyl to make it impregnable to water and as easy to install and maintain as a pure vinyl floor.

Because there is a degree of resiliency in even the hardest of hardwood floors, precautions should be taken to protect the floor from furniture legs that may dent the flooring. Wood floors are particularly susceptible to metal or hard plastic rollers and to those small metal domes that are often found on the legs of office furniture.

Cleaning Procedures　Preventive maintenance is the key to attractive and durable wood floors. One of the best prevention techniques is to use walk-off mats at exterior entrances, and rugs and carpet runners in high-traffic areas.

Wood floors should be dusted, but do not use an oily dust mop on a wood floor. The oil from the mop head may darken or stain the floor. Water is one of the most deleterious substances to a wood floor; consequently, it should not be used to clean most wood floors. Dusting, vacuuming, buffing, and, on limited occasions, a light damp mopping is all that is necessary to maintain a wood floor on a daily basis.

Stripping, Sealing, and Finishing　When a wood floor becomes badly stained or damaged, it is sanded to remove stains and marks. A sealer is then applied to the floor. There are many commercial wood sealers on the market today. Types of wood sealers include oil-modified urethane sealers, moisture-cured urethane sealers, the "Swedish-type" sealers, and water-based sealers. In most instances, the same sealer that was initially used on the floor must be used for subsequent applications. Repeated applications of certain types of sealers will darken the color of the floor over time. Sanding and sealing a floor should not be done frequently; most modern wood floors can tolerate a maximum of only three to five sandings before the entire floor must be replaced.

Surface finishes such as urethane, **varnish**, and **shellac** are not recommended for many modern wood floors. Most require only an occasional waxing and buffing, and certain modern treated wood floors may never require refinishing.

Again, it is always wise to follow the manufacturer's recommendations regarding the maintenance of any flooring or floor covering.

As we have previously stated, carpets and rugs are unquestionably the most resilient of all flooring materials and it is to this area that we now turn our attention.

Carpets and Rugs
❧

The use of carpets and rugs can be traced back three thousand years to the Middle Eastern kingdoms of Babylon, Sumeria, and Assyria.

Carpet is typically installed wall-to-wall to eliminate the maintenance of hard flooring surfaces around the edge of a carpet. Rugs, on the other hand, are often used to accentuate a tile or wood floor. In areas where there is heavy foot traffic, rugs can be used to equalize wear and to help prevent tracking onto other floor coverings.

Carpet offers a number of benefits over hard and resilient flooring materials. Carpet prevents slipping; it provides an additional source of insulation—thus making it less expensive to heat an interior in winter; it has acoustical properties that can effectively lower noise levels; and it is the most resilient of all floor coverings, which is a major benefit to individuals who must remain on their feet for extended periods.

What nature perfected, Mannington improved.

wood floors

FIGURE 5.13 A Mannington wood floor. *(Used with permission of Jacqueline and Associates, Las Vegas, Nevada.)*

CARPET COMPONENTS

Generally, carpet is composed of three elements: **pile**, **primary backing**, and **secondary backing**; it is often accompanied by a fourth element, **padding**.

Pile is the yarn that we see and can readily touch. The fibers can be either synthetic or natural in composition. Pile density is one hallmark of carpet quality; the greater the density of the pile, the better the carpet. Carpets with greater pile density hold their shape longer and are more resistant to dirt and stains. One common test of density is to bend a piece of carpet, and if the backing can readily be seen, the carpet is of an inferior quality. Density of pile is measured by the number of pile ends or tufts across a 27-inch width, called the *pitch* in woven carpets or *gauge* in tufted varieties. Another indicator of durability is the carpet's **face weight**. The face weight is the weight of the carpet's surface fibers in ounces or grams per square yard. The greater the face weight,

the higher the quality. The height of the pile is a third measure of carpet quality; longer fibers are better than shorter fibers. A fourth measure is the amount of twist the pile fibers have received. The tighter the twist, the better the carpet.

The backing is on the underside of the carpet; it secures the tufts of pile and gives additional strength and stability to the carpet. Most carpets have a double backing: a primary backing, to which the yarn is attached, and an outer backing called the secondary backing. A layer of latex adhesive is sandwiched between the two layers to seal the pile tufts to the primary backing.

Types of backing include **jute**, a natural fiber imported from India and Bangladesh, **polypropylene**, a synthetic thermoplastic resin, and foam rubber. The foam backing is often attached to the primary backing to provide a carpet with its own built-in padding, thus eliminating the need for separate padding. This is often done with less expensive carpeting. With more expensive carpeting, rubber-covered jute is the preferred material for the secondary backing. However, synthetic backings are more resistant to mildew, odor, and dry rot, and are nonallergenic.

Padding can be placed under carpet to provide extra insulation, deaden sound, add comfort, and extend the life of the carpet by serving as a "shock absorber." Common types of padding include foam rubber, urethane foam, and natural materials such as jute and hair blends. The natural paddings are firmer than the synthetic materials. The choice of padding depends on the type of carpet being used, the level of comfort sought, and the amount and type of wear that the carpet will be subjected to under normal conditions.

Some experts recommend that no padding be used and that the carpet be glued directly to the floor in high-traffic areas or where carts with heavy loads will be used. Heavy padding is thought to increase friction and cause buckling and ripping, thus prematurely wearing out the carpet.

There are three sizes of carpets available on the market. Broadloom carpets are normally 12 feet in width, but they can be ordered up to 15 feet in width. Carpet runners come in widths from 2 feet to 9 feet. Carpet squares or tiles are 18 inches square. Carpet tiles are becoming quite popular for public areas such as halls, lobbys, and meeting rooms. New adhesives for carpet tiles make tile removal less of a chore than it has been in past years. Standard rug sizes vary from 3′ × 5′ to 10′ × 12′. Custom sizes may be even larger.

Eventually, all carpets become worn and need to be replaced. However, old carpet can be recycled instead of being taken to a landfill. This is a win-win proposition for both the property and the environment. For the property, the cost associated with transportation and landfill charges can be severely reduced or eliminated entirely. For the environment, that carpet can come back in the form of a number of new products. It is estimated that 3.5 billion pounds (1.75 million tons) of carpet end up in landfills every year. This constitutes approximately 1 percent by weight (2 percent by volume) of the total municipal solid waste generated in the United States, according to the National Association of Home Builders. One use for old carpet is its manufacture into new carpet pad. Every effort should be made to reuse or recycle this valuable resource.

CARPET CONSTRUCTION

Carpet construction describes the method by which the carpet is manufactured. It involves how the face yarns are anchored in the backing and the type of backing that is used. Today, well over 90 percent of all carpet produced is tufted carpet. Tufted carpet is produced by forcing needles, threaded with pile yarn, through the primary backing (usually polypropylene) to form tufts. A coating of latex adhesive is then applied to the backing to secure the tufts. The tufting process can be used to produce a multitude of carpet textures, including:

- **Cut loop:** The carpet yarn is tufted into islands of high-cut tufts and lower-loop tufts to form a sculptured pattern.
- **Level loop:** A simple loop pile with tufts of equal height, it is appropriate for high-traffic areas.
- **Multilevel loop:** A loop pile carpet with two or three tuft levels.
- **Plush:** The loops of the pile are cut, which makes for a relatively plain, clean, and formal effect. Pile that is 1/2 inch or less in height is called Saxony plush, and pile with a height above 1/2 inch is called textured plush.
- **Frieze:** Straight tufts are mixed with tufts that are given a built-in curl. The carpet does not show footprints and can be classified as being informal in texture.
- **Random shear:** A mixture of cut and uncut loops. This approach creates a highly textured appearance.

Needle-punched carpets are produced by a manufacturing method that punches the fibers into a structural backing and then compresses the fibers into a feltlike fabric. It is used mainly in indoor-outdoor carpets.

Flocked carpets are produced by electrostatically embedding short carpet fibers into a backing, producing a velvety-look cut pile surface.

Knitted carpets are produced by a method that uses a specialized knitting machine with different sets of needles to loop together the pile, backing, and the stitching yarns.

Weaving is the traditional way of making carpet on a loom. Interlaced yarns form the backing and the pile. Lengthwise yarns are called the *warp* and the yarns going across the carpet are the *weft*. Pile is part of the warp. There are three basic types of looms: the velvet, the Axminster, and the Wilton.

Woven and knitted carpets are the two most expensive types of carpet to construct.

Carpet Fibers

Wool is the standard by which all synthetic carpet fibers are judged. Independent studies have shown that wool effectively outperforms fourth-generation nylon in soiling and appearance.[9] Wool is extremely durable and resistant to soiling, but it does have its share of negative properties. Since it is a natural material, wool provides a better breeding ground for bacteria, molds, and mildew. It is also more susceptible to damage from harsh or abrasive cleaners. Wool has very poor abrasion resistance. In low humidity, untreated wool generates more static electricity than synthetic fibers. Finally, it is quite costly. Not only is the wool itself more costly than synthetic fibers, wool carpets are normally woven or knitted, processes that are much more costly than tufting.

The most widely used carpet fiber is nylon; more than 90 percent of all carpets made today are nylon carpets. The fourth-generation nylon fibers in use today are quite resilient, fairly soil-resistant, and easy to clean, and they come in a variety of colors and textures. Nylon fibers can also be protected by fluoro-chemical treatments, as in the case of Dupont's Stain-master carpets, which are treated with Teflon to improve their soil and stain resistance.

Another synthetic in use today is polypropylene (olefin), which wears very well and is not susceptible to sun fade, but it is not as comfortable underfoot as nylon.

Other minor synthetic fibers include acetates, acrylics, polyesters, and rayons. Although each of these has outstanding positive qualities, they do not possess all of the positive features shared by wool, nylon, and Olefin.

SELECTING THE APPROPRIATE CARPET

Different settings suggest different carpet specifications. Color, texture, pattern, and padding requirements will vary from location to location. What follows is a series of carpet specifications based on aesthetic considerations.

- Solid colors magnify the effects of dirt, litter, and stains.
- If you wish to project excitement, use warm colors; if relaxation is your aim, use cool colors in the darker shades.
- Avoid precise geometric patterns in dining rooms; use organic, free-flowing designs. These hide the dirt.
- Using low-level loop pile carpet tiles with no padding is the preferred approach for high-traffic areas.
- Multilevel loop and cut loop carpets are more difficult to clean.
- Use big patterns in big rooms and small patterns in small rooms.

Figure 5.14 shows a representative sampling of modern geometric carpet patterns.

CARPET INSTALLATION

Executive housekeepers should resist all temptation to install new carpet. Laying carpet, resilient flooring, and hard floors is a job for professionals. An installation performed by amateurs often ends up costing the facility far more than was saved by not hiring professionals.

The installers should be brought back on the premises six months after the original installation to correct any buckles or bulges that have appeared in the carpet.

CARPET MAINTENANCE

Carpet maintenance is actually four related procedures that occur at intermittent times during the life cycle of the carpet.

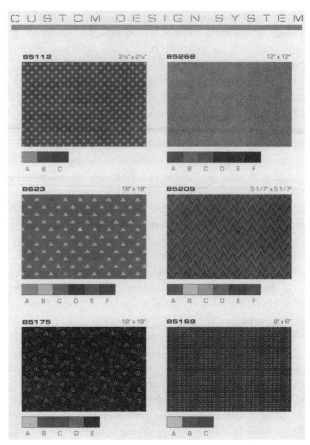

FIGURE 5.14 Modern geometric carpet patterns. *(Used with permission of Jacqueline & Associates, Las Vegas.)*

Inspection and Prevention

The most frequent activity is carpet inspection, which should occur on a continual basis. Carpets need to be inspected for spills and stains, which are far easier to remove if they are treated before they have a chance to set. Staff in all departments, from engineering to food and beverage, should be instructed to report all carpet and floor spills to housekeeping as soon as they are discovered.

Prevention includes the use of mats to absorb dirt and spills around food preparation areas and the use of grates, track-off mats, and carpet runners to absorb dirt and grit and control wear at entrances and in high-foot-traffic locations.

Interim Cleaning Methods

Interim cleaning methods include carpet sweeping, vacuuming, **bonnet cleaning**, and spot stain removal. Interim carpet care is absolutely necessary to remove gritty soil and spots before these elements become embedded in the carpet, causing the pile to wear prematurely. According to John Walker and L. Kent Fine, there are three sources of soils: tracked particulate soils from the exterior; spots, spills, and settling dust from the interior; and animal and vegetable oils, which are by-products from the dining room and kitchen areas.[10]

Soil buildup occurs at three levels of the carpet. At the top are light soils, dust, gummy sugars, and oily soils. In the middle are the heavier particles of dust and organic matter. At the base of the pile are the heaviest particles, such as sand and grit. Although the sand and grit are not necessarily seen, they do the greatest damage to the pile because they actually erode the pile fibers.[11]

It is estimated that an average of 79 percent of all soils can be removed by regular vacuuming.[12] However, the gummy and oily substances will continue to build up while binding the dry particulates to the carpet fibers, causing carpet erosion. Although vacuuming is the most critical factor in extending the life of the carpet, vacuuming alone is not enough. All carpet must be subjected to restorative cleaning methods on a periodic basis.

Standard vacuuming with an upright machine or hose vacuum is begun by plugging the cord into the electrical outlet. The plug should be a grounded three-prong plug. Inspect the cord and plug for wear. Begin vacuuming at the wall where the machine is plugged in, and work away from the plug to prevent cord entanglement. A three-foot-long push-pull stroke should be employed. Normally, only two passes over the carpet are necessary. Care should be taken not to vacuum too fast; the beater brushes and suction should be allowed to do their job. Overlap strokes slightly and vacuum so that the nap (fuzzy side) of the carpet is laid down by the pull stroke. Move furniture as little as possible, and avoid bumping both furniture and the wall.

When finished, inspect and replace worn brushes and belts if necessary, and empty the filter bag.

Vacuuming should be done after furniture has been dusted.

Traditionally, guestrooms are vacuumed daily. However, other areas in the hotel may demand different schedules. In the article "Vacuuming Carpet: Applying the Pareto Principle" (see pages 98–99), author David J. Frank explains how to set up an effective vacuuming program.

Bonnet cleaning is often categorized with other restorative cleaning methods, but it should properly be categorized as an interim cleaning method.

Figure 5.15 shows an example of bonnet cleaning using an all-purpose floor machine. Bonnet cleaning utilizes a standard floor machine equipped with carpet bonnets, bonnet shampoo, a sprayer, clean water, and a bucket and wringer.

First vacuum the area to be cleaned, and then spray a 4′ × 8′ area with the shampoo; also spray the bonnet with the solution. Then pass the machine, with the bonnet attached, over the area. Repeat this procedure until the entire carpet is cleaned. Once the bonnet begins to show dirt, it should be turned over to the clean side. When the

FIGURE 5.15 Bonnet cleaning using the "All-Purpose Matador" from Advance. *(Used with permission.)*

entire bonnet is dirty, rinse it in the bucket and wring it out with the mop wringer.

When finished, completely rinse all of the equipment, then wash the carpet bonnets and hang them up to dry. Do not replace furniture until the carpet is completely dry.

Bonnet cleaning does cause a modest amount of wear on the carpet fibers, therefore (to reiterate) it should not be viewed as a restorative cleaning method.

Finally, carpet sweepers are used to clean up dry soils and particulates on rugs before they have a chance to penetrate the surface of the carpet and lodge in the carpet's pile. They are especially handy in dining room areas where the waitstaff can use them for touch-ups under tables and in the aisles.

Restorative Cleaning Methods

Interim cleaning methods do not remove the gummy, sticky residues and the dry particulates that have become stuck to them. Deep cleaning methods must be employed to restore the carpet to a near original condition. There are four restorative carpet cleaning systems: **water extraction**, dry foam, dry powder, and rotary shampoo. There is quite a bit of disagreement in the industry as to which of these four systems is the single "best" method.

VACUUMING CARPET: APPLYING THE PARETO PRINCIPLE

ProTeam

by David J. Frank

(This article is presented through the generosity of ProTeam Inc., a Boise, Idaho, Manufacturer of backpack vacuum systems, and sponsor of Team Cleaning Seminars.)

The Pareto principle of 80/20 suggests that 80% of your vacuuming time be spent vacuuming 20% of the carpet, and 20% of your time be spent on the other 80% of the carpet. To do this intelligently means setting up an effective vacuuming program.

Applying the Pareto concept to vacuum cleaners implies that 80% of the effectiveness of a vacuum derives from 20% of its performance traits. Applying this intelligently means understanding suction and filtration—that is, how vacuum cleaners remove dirt and retain it—and how those critical factors integrate in a good vacuuming system.

According to the Carpet and Rug Institute (CRI): "Vacuuming is the most important and most cost-effective element of an efficient [carpet] maintenance program." Effective vacuuming preserves the life and appearance of carpet, while keeping the environment cleaner and healthier for building occupants. The Pareto rule suggests that 80% of carpet care planning be spent defining the vacuuming program; the 20% of carpet maintenance that produces 80% of the value. This means blueprinting vacuuming to achieve the right "architecture" or program structure to get desired results.

PLANNING STRATEGY FOR SCHEDULED MAINTENANCE

According to CRI: "Because carpet disguises soil so very well, carpet has often been cleaned in public facilities only when it shows soil. Often times, there is already damage to the carpet because embedded dirt abrades the fibers."

Since carpet tends to hide dirt and its potentially harmful effects, cleaning based on appearance is shortsighted and ineffective. Developing a good carpet cleaning strategy involves three main steps:

1. Analyze how specific areas in a facility are used.
2. Determine the frequency of vacuuming needed to prevent soil buildup in those areas.

3. Set up a vacuuming schedule that is strictly followed.

ANALYZING USAGE: DEFINING AND MAINTAINING 80/20 AREAS

Defining high-use areas for daily maintenance is not difficult, but follow-through vacuuming is often lacking since carpet in well traveled corridors can mask embedded dirt, tempting maintenance personnel to skip places that "look clean."

Setting up and following a plan based on actual use rather than appearance is vital. Pay particular attention to "20%" locations such as:

Track-off or wipe-off areas (exterior entrances, and areas where carpet and hard/resilient surfaces meet). Track off regions average 90 square feet (6 × 15 feet) at building entrances, 10 square feet (2 × 5 feet) at main internal doorways and 40 square feet (5 × 8 feet) in main corridors six feet wide.
Funnel areas or congested channels. Foot traffic often converges on a doorway or elevator, creating a soil area averaging three feet around a doorway to 10 feet around elevators. Other locations are also critical, e.g., in front of water fountains and main building directories.

CENTRAL ACTIVITY AREAS, BUSY CORRIDORS, TRAFFIC LANES

Also note the "80%" floor space, lesser used areas such as executive offices, board rooms, utility rooms, etc. These areas should be spot-checked daily, and vacuumed on a schedule that reflects actual usage. Remember, too, that dust settles on all surfaces, including carpet, and regular cleaning even in low-usage areas is important.

HOW MUCH VACUUMING?

The general recommendations for vacuuming frequency are as follows:

Heavy traffic areas: Daily
Medium traffic areas: Twice weekly
Light traffic areas: Once or twice weekly

CRI says: "Daily maintenance is the most valuable and cost-effective element in the maintenance strategy. Adequate vacuuming on a regular schedule will lessen the frequency of the more intensive cleanings and will keep soil from becoming embedded in the carpet."

PREVENTIVE MAINTENANCE

Preemptive measures that reduce or prevent soiling include:

- Walk-Off Mats: Walk-off mats placed in entry ways and elevators will collect dirt before it reaches the carpeted area.
- Keep approach areas to outside entries clean to prevent unnecessary tracking onto walk-off mats.
- Extra matting in inclement weather.
- Trash and ash receptacles located conveniently both outside and inside the building.

80/20 VACUUMING: UNDERSTANDING SUCTION AND FILTRATION

Vacuum cleaner suction and filtration are the "20%" issues that affect 80% of your ability to properly vacuum and maintain carpet. It is important to understand a little practical science to appreciate their role.

SUCTION VARIABLES

Suction is a product of several variables. Ideally, a vacuum's internal fan is powered and proportioned to create "vacuum" for moving or suctioning a desired volume of air (measured as CFM—cubic feet per minute) in relation to the size of the tool head, the diameter and length of the airflow conduit (hose and internal air channel), and the type, size, and configuration of filter media.

Of course, proper air volume and suction would be simpler to achieve and maintain if filtering the air and retaining the dirt were not necessary. Without filter media (cloth and/or paper filters, HEPA, ULPA, and secondary types) to screen and hold particles of various sizes, air passing through a vacuum cleaner would meet little resistance—suction would remain constant. The room environment would also be dirtier than ever, since dust entering one end of the vacuum would simply be blown out the exhaust end.

EFFECTIVE SUCTION—A SYSTEM APPROACH

Effective suction is a product of an intelligent system—one that permits constant airflow with practical filtration to trap particles of soil, large or small. The key component (Pareto's 20%) in a vacuuming system is the relationship between airflow and filtration—and the two are somewhat at odds.

SUCTION AND FILTRATION: TIPS FOR SUCCESS

Excellent suction and excellent filtration sometimes form an uneasy alliance.

High-efficiency filters that trap more fine particles sometimes tend to clog more rapidly, choking airflow and suction, and lowering cleaning ability. Good filters, unless *cleaned* or replaced regularly, reduce vacuum performance.

Filter efficiency, filter access, and filter maintenance are important issues related to suction. Since indoor air quality affects both health and housekeeping concerns consider four-stage filtration that captures at least 96% of dust one micron and larger—most airborne dust falls into the one to ten micron range. For more demanding applications, inexpensive high filtration disc media which increase efficiency to 99.79% at .3 micron are available. Secondly, look for a vacuum that permits easy filter maintenance (if filters are difficult to change, operators will tend to allow them to clog, reducing suction). Third, train operators to clean vacuum filters regularly (after every few hours of vacuuming, or more often as needed to maintain optimum airflow and suction).

Following the Pareto dictum, vacuuming programs succeed when operators understand that effective vacuuming is achieved through a combination of the right machine and the right scheduled carpet maintenance—that is, the right *system*—to maximize cleaning when and where it's needed most.

David J. Frank has over 12 years' experience in the sanitary supply industry. He is an active member of the International Sanitary Supply Association and the Building Service Contractors Association International. He is currently a marketing research consultant with ProTeam, Inc., Boise, Idaho, manufacturer of backpack vacuum systems and sponsor of Team Cleaning Seminars. He can be reached at (303) 770-6731.

However, all would agree that it is best to remove dry soil by vacuuming the carpet before a restorative cleaning method is attempted.

Water extraction, also referred to as hot water extraction or "steam cleaning," is a system that sprays a solution on the carpet and then picks it up with an attached wet/dry vacuum. The term *steam cleaning* is really a misnomer, as live steam is never used, only hot or cold water. The machine normally has two storage tanks, one for the solution to be sprayed on the carpet and one for the dirty picked-up solution.

Recent studies conducted by John Walker at Janitor University compared self-contained extractors with high-flow extractors. His findings showed the soil removal rate of high-water-flow extractors to be 2.5 times the rate of the conventional low-flow extractors. Of course, the unit must also remove most of the water that is applied, or mold problems are sure to follow. The operator should also use soft water if possible. Hard water leads to premature soiling and carpet wear, and prevents carpet cleaning solutions from working. The operator should overlap two to three inches on each pass. On problem spots the operator may need to presoak the area for a few minutes before using the pickup vacuum. All carpet should be totally dry before the furniture is replaced or it is opened to foot traffic.

Many experts consider this system to be the best approach to deep cleaning. However, hot water extraction can have a number of negative effects if improperly done. Wet carpet can shrink, and seams can split if the water used is too hot or if too much solution is applied. The temperature of the water should never be over 150° Fahrenheit and when cleaning wool carpet, it is best to use cold water. Most of the extractors on the market can be used with either cold or hot water. Although water extractors minimize problems associated with other wet shampooing techniques, such as mildewing and the presence of other bacteria, growth can happen in a humid environment. Use fans and the building's air-conditioning or heating system to speed carpet drying time. Ideally, carpets should be dry within one hour, and walk-off mats or furniture should never be placed on damp carpet. They form a moisture barrier that keeps the carpet from drying and gives mold an ideal environment in which to grow.

Dry foam is another method used in carpet restoration. The foam is brushed into the carpet and taken up almost immediately with a wet/dry vacuum. After the carpet is completely dry, it is vacuumed once again to remove more of the residue.

Dry foam is often used in high-traffic areas on even a daily basis to remove tracked-in soil. The biggest negative factor with dry foam is that it leaves the highest amount of detergent residue behind on the carpet, which will cause the carpet to become prematurely dirty. If the carpet is not rigorously vacuumed after laying down the foam, the carpet can, in a few days, look worse than it did before the treatment.

Dry powder (aka encapsulation technology) has the advantage of minimal downtime for a carpeted area. Once the procedure is completed, the area can reopen for use. Since water is not used, the problem of mildew, odor, carpet stretching, and seam splitting is not present.

Dry powder cleaning is done by laying down a powder or crystal on the carpet; this binds with the dirt (encapsulates), which is then removed through vacuuming while the carpet is agitated with a beater brush (Figure 5.16).

Dry powder may leave some residue behind in the carpet, and it may not remove all types of soils from the carpet.

FIGURE 5.16 The Host Dry Powder System. The powder applicator is on the right; the dry cleaning machine on the left brushes the powder into the carpet. *(Used with permission of Racine Industries.)*

Wet shampooing is accomplished through the use of a rotary floor machine, which normally has a tank attached that contains the shampoo solution. A special brush attachment agitates the carpet as the solution is dispersed onto the carpet. The carpet is then vacuumed with a wet/dry vacuum that contains a defoaming agent. Once the carpet is dry, it may be vacuumed again with a dry vacuum.

With this system, the danger exists of overwetting the carpet, causing mold, mildew, and other bacterial growth. The carpet may also stretch and then shrink, causing seams to split, and the brushes from the floor machine may damage the carpet pile if they are allowed to remain on one spot for too long. Rotary shampooing is thought by many experts to cause the most wear to a carpet.

Spot Cleaning

Spots and spills call for immediate action. If allowed to set, many substances can permanently stain a carpet, especially one that is made of nylon or wool. The following are a few general procedures that should be followed regardless of the type of stain, carpet, or cleaner:

1. Carefully scrape away excess soiling materials such as gum and tar from the carpet.
2. Blot the excess liquid that is spilled before it has a chance to soak into the carpet. Do not rub the stain; this action may actually force the stain into the fibers. Use only clean rags to blot the carpet.
3. Apply the cleansing agent to the carpet. If the spot remover is a liquid, remove the excess spot remover by blotting with clean rags or a clean sponge.
4. After the spot remover has had an opportunity to work, vacuum up the spot remover and dry the treated area.

When treating spots, it is important to identify the source of the spot and also understand the type of carpet you are trying to treat and how it was dyed. A good rule of thumb is to use the same process to remove the spot as was used to apply the spot. If a spot was cold and water-based, treat it with cold water and a water-based spot remover. If a spot was hot, you might need heat to remove the spot; and if the spot was oil-based, a solvent may be called for.

Many reputable companies have developed some remarkable spot removers that can effectively remove dozens of different types of spots.

Finally, certain harsh chemicals, such as chlorine bleaches, should not be used on spots because they will often remove the dye from the carpet along with the offending stain.

Ceilings and Wall Coverings

The selection of materials to cover walls and ceilings should be predicated on the following five considerations: cost of maintenance, appearance, fire safety, initial cost, and acoustics.

Although the product and installation cost of ceiling materials or wall covering materials must be within budgetary guidelines, consideration also must be given to the other four factors. For example, the maintenance cost of a wall covering must be part of the cost equation. Daily maintenance costs may make the product prohibitively expensive, even though the initial costs are within budget.

The ability of a wall, floor, or ceiling material to reduce sound is a major factor when considering guest comfort, whether in a conference room, dining room, or guestroom. Most commercial materials have a rating, called the noise reduction coefficient, which can be used in material selection. However, improper maintenance may adversely affect a material's acoustics, such as when acoustical ceiling panels are painted, destroying most of their noise reduction ability.

Fire safety is a major concern, especially in high-rise hospitals and hotels. Many communities have passed stringent laws concerning the use of fire-resistant materials. In fact, many fire codes specify the use of only Class A materials in hotels and hospitals. Manufacturers have responded to this fire safety concern by manufacturing wall coverings and ceiling panels that will emit harmless gases, which will trigger smoke detectors when heated to 300° Fahrenheit.

There are wall materials on the market that will emit toxic gases when burned. Many city fire codes forbid the use of these materials in guestrooms and public areas in hospitals and hotels. The National Fire Protection Association (NFPA) sets standards on fire retardancy and the toxicity of burning materials. The astute housekeeper should become familiar with these specifications.

Finally, hotels and even hospitals are concerned with the image they project. Wall coverings, ceilings, and flooring materials should be selected to enhance that image. It could be said that these materials are indeed some of the hotel's most important marketing tools.

WALL AND CEILING COVERINGS AND THEIR MAINTENANCE

The maintenance of wall and ceiling coverings resembles floor maintenance in that there are three distinct approaches: interim maintenance, restorative cleaning, and spot removal.

Interim cleaning methods include daily or weekly dusting and vacuuming. Restorative cleaning encompasses the use of detergents and solvents, which is done on a periodic basis, and spot removal, which is performed as the need arises.

The following sections examine the advantages and disadvantages of the most common wall and ceiling coverings and their specific maintenance requirements.

Cork

Cork has excellent sound-absorption properties and has a rich and luxurious appearance, but it is a delicate surface material that can be easily damaged by improper cleaning methods. Today, it is often bonded between sheets of clear vinyl, which serve to protect it from wear, but the vinyl does impair its acoustical ability. Natural cork may be vacuumed using a soft brush attachment. Natural cork walls should never be washed with water. Spot removal may require light sanding to remove stains. It is sometimes easier to replace a damaged cork tile than to attempt to restore it to its original condition.

Fabrics

Although linens, silks, and leathers may initially provide an extremely attractive wall surface, as a rule, they should not be used for wall coverings because of the difficulty involved in their cleaning, particularly in the case of spot removal. If fabrics are used, they must be fire-resistant, and it is also advisable to use only stain-resistant materials.

Fabrics are also highly susceptible to mold, mildew, and other odor-causing bacteria.

Recommended alternatives to fabrics are the new vinyl wall coverings that have fabric sandwiched between sheets of vinyl. They have the beauty of fabrics but are far easier to clean and are much more durable.

Standard fabric wall coverings may be vacuumed to remove dust. Water should never be used on fabrics because it may cause the fabric to shrink and split. Spots and stains should be removed only with chemicals recommended by the fabric's manufacturer. Some cleaning solutions will adversely affect the fire-resistant characteristics of the fabric.

Fiberglass

Fiberglass walls are often made to resemble other construction materials, such as brick. Fiberglass can be vacuumed to remove dust, and it can be deep cleaned using water and a neutral detergent.

Painted Surfaces

Paint is still one of the most popular wall coverings because of its relatively low initial cost and the wide range of colors available.

When selecting paint, the housekeeper should consider drying time, odor, and durability. The objective is to reduce costly downtime caused by these factors.

Painted surfaces can be dusted, vacuumed, and washed using a mild detergent and water. Scrubbing and use of chemicals such as trisodium phosphate will remove the paint as well as the dirt.

Plastic Laminate

One of the easiest materials to maintain, plastic laminates come in 4' × 8' panels that are nailed directly to the wall studs. Plastic laminate often has a wood-grain effect or a faux-tile appearance. All that is required to maintain its appearance is periodic vacuuming with a soft brush.

Tile

Tile walls demand the same care as the tile floors previously covered in this chapter. Most manufacturers carry two grades of tile: tile for wall applications and tile for floor applications. Tile walls are most often found in bathrooms and kitchens. Ceramic tiles are also used to accent stucco walls.

Vinyl

Next to paint, vinyl is indisputably the most popular form of wall covering. It can be purchased in a wide variety of colors and textures that can fool even the trained observer into believing that the wall covering is not vinyl, but marble, rubber, fabric, metal, or even ceramic tile.

Vinyl is easy to clean and is considered to be four times more durable than paint. It is also easy to install and remove. According to government specifications, vinyl is divided into three categories by weight per square yard. Type I is normally reserved for noncommercial applications. Type II is the category most often selected for guestrooms, halls, and lobbies. Type III is the most durable and the best choice for heavy-wear areas, such as elevators and other high-contact areas. Vinyl can tear, so it is wise to purchase extra rolls for installation. With practice, it can be restored.

The most negative aspect of vinyl has only recently been discovered. Vinyl is waterproof, and it serves as barrier to any moisture trapped between the vinyl and the drywall to which it is attached. Glue is used to attach the vinyl, and the drywall has a paper sheathing. Where there is high outside humidity and the building has an inadequate vapor barrier or a water leak, mold will start to grow between the drywall and the vinyl. The glue and the paper serve as food sources for the mold. When the vinyl is removed, thousands of mold circles can often be found growing between the vinyl and the drywall. Vinyl use is so common in some lodging properties that the mold has been given the name "Marriott's dots." Mold can lead to a host of respiratory-related illnesses and, in some extreme cases, death.

Wallpaper

Vinyl has made old-fashioned wallpaper obsolete. Vinyl wall coverings can duplicate the effect of wallpaper while providing a surface that can be easily cleaned with mild detergent and water, which is not an option with wallpaper.

Wallpaper should be vacuumed to remove dirt and dust. Some types of stains can be removed from wallpaper using dough-type cleaners, and a few wallpapers can be damp mopped with a sponge.

Wood

Wood or wood-veneered walls demand the same treatment afforded wood floors. Water should not be used on a wood-surfaced wall. Dust frequently and when needed, and oil and polish wood wall coverings according to the manufacturer's recommendations.

Glass Walls

More often, architects are now using glass walls to enrich certain areas of interior living, and to introduce light into interior spaces. Glass block used in place of masonry has the ability to introduce light while requiring little, if any, maintenance. Figure 5.17 shows a selection of glass block that may be used to construct light walls.

Windows and Window Treatments

❧

WINDOW CLEANING

Window cleaning is one of the easiest tasks to perform if the housekeeping crew has the proper tools at its disposal. What is needed is a synthetic lamb's-wool window-washing tool, a bucket that will accommodate the tool (approximately 12″ × 24″), a squeegee, and a clean lint-free cloth. The better squeegees have quick-release mechanisms and angled heads. The new microfiber cloths designed for the cleaning of windows and mirrors are simply amazing. The author witnessed a demonstration in which Vaseline was applied to a mirror, and with one wipe of a microfiber cloth (see Figure 5.18) the mirror was spotless.

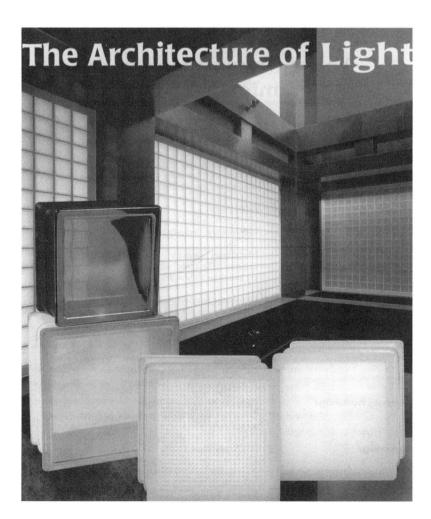

FIGURE 5.17 Glass blocks of a type used to replace other forms of masonry allow light to enter a space. *(Photo courtesy of Tile and Carpet Gallery, Las Vegas, Nevada.)*

FIGURE 5.18 A microfiber cloth designed for glass and mirrors. These may make the squeegee obsolete. *(Photo used with permission of Newport Marketing Group, Inc., Costa Mesa California.)*

A low-sudsing cleaning solution, often containing a little ammonia, is prepared with cold or warm (never hot) water. The first step is to remove all window coverings to facilitate the cleaning and to avoid the possibility of spilling cleaning solution on the drapes and curtains.

Begin by applying the cleaning solution to the top of the window, working the dirt toward the center of the window from the outside edges. Do not overwet the window and cause the excess solution to run and pool on the sill or floor. Before the window has a chance to dry, squeegee the window, starting at the top corner.

Make one pass across the glass, and angle the blade so that the dirty solution runs down onto the dirty part of the window rather than back onto the cleaned portion. Wipe the blade clean with the cloth after each pass of the blade.

Finally, never attempt to clean windows in the hot sun. The sun will cause the window to dry before it can be squeegeed, causing streaking.

Exterior window cleaning, especially on high-rise buildings, should be left to professional window washers.

WINDOW TREATMENTS

When selecting window treatments, function and appearance should both be considered. The appropriate window covering provides privacy to the guest and insulation; it is a significant design element.

Window treatments can be divided into three categories: drapery, shades, and blinds.

Drapery and curtain fabric should be fire-resistant, soil- and wear-resistant, resistant to sun damage, resistant to molds and mildew, and wrinkle-resistant. Delicate fabrics and loose weaves will quickly lose their shape, will snag and wrinkle, and will wear prematurely. One increasingly popular style of drapery is vinyl-lined fabric, because of its increased durability.

Drapery should be vacuumed daily. Dry cleaning is the preferred method of restorative cleaning. Most experts agree that dry-cleaned drapes will hold their shape better than laundered fabrics will.

Shades are available in a multitude of styles and materials. Their purpose is to provide a customized look to the window while affording privacy to the guest. Shades should also be vacuumed daily. Restorative cleaning methods will depend on the material composition of the shade.

Popular blind styles of today include the mini-horizontal blind and the vertical blind. The verticals are much easier to maintain and provide greater control of glare and light into the room. Cloth panels can even be inserted into some types of vertical blinds to add additional color and texture to the room.

CONCLUSION

The maintenance of floors, floor coverings, wall coverings, and windows consumes an overwhelmingly large portion of any housekeeping department's budget. For this reason, the astute housekeeper must develop a comprehensive understanding of these materials and how they are to be maintained. This knowledge must also be communicated to the department's staff so that they may responsibly carry out the policies of the department and see to it that standards of cleanliness and repair are maintained. Vendors who know their products will be your best experts.

KEY TERMS AND CONCEPTS

Cross contamination
Foundation
Finish
Stripping
Sealer
Terrazzo
Buffing
Burnishing
Damp mopping
Spray buffing
Nonresilient floors
Epoxy
Spalling
Resilient floors
Linoleum

Styrene butadiene rubber (SBR)
Asbestos
Carcinogen
Homogeneous
Tung oil
Carnauba wax
Polyurethane
Acrylics
Varnish
Shellac
Pile
Primary backing
Secondary backing
Padding
Face weight

Jute
Polypropylene
Cut loop
Level loop
Multilevel loop
Plush
Frieze
Random shear
Bonnet cleaning
Water extraction
Dry foam
Dry powder
Wet shampooing

DISCUSSION AND REVIEW QUESTIONS

1. When contemplating the installation of a new floor, what concerns should an executive housekeeper take into consideration?
2. Explain the relative advantages and disadvantages of the different approaches to restorative carpet care.
3. Given the following areas in a hotel—ballroom, lobby, dining room, kitchen, laundry, executive office—make recommendations for appropriate floor coverings for each area.
4. Describe the steps in the FPMR model.

5. Assume that the decision has been made to carpet the hotel's main ballroom. What suggestions would you make as to the type of carpet to use in the ballroom?
6. How would you ensure the cooperation of other departments in the hotel to report spots and spills on carpet and floors to the housekeeping department?
7. The rooms-division manager wants to install an "accent wall" in each guestroom. This wall would have a wall covering that is unlike the other painted walls in the room. What wall coverings would you suggest for this accent wall?

NOTES

1. Bill Saunders and Rick Mazzoli, "The FPMR Process of Floor Care," *Sanitary Maintenance*, October 1989, pp. 144–45.
2. Ibid., p. 144.
3. John P. Walker, *Fourteen Basic Custodial Procedures* (Lincolnwood, IL: International Sanitary Supply Association, 1989), p. 21.
4. Bill Saunders and Rick Mazzoli, "The FPMR Process of Floor Care," *Sanitary Maintenance*, November 1989, pp. 76–77.
5. Ibid., p. 76.
6. Ibid., p. 77.
7. Ibid., p. 78.
8. Ibid., p. 79.
9. Ray Draper, "Wool Performance: Better Cleanability and Soil Resistance Than Fourth-Generation Nylons," *Executive Housekeeping Today*, March 1990, pp. 8–10.
10. John Phillip Walker and L. Kent Fine, "Carpet Care," *Cleaning Team Management: Custodial Management for Increased Productivity and Safety* (Salt Lake City: Management, 1990), p. 2.
11. Ibid.
12. Ibid.

CHAPTER 6

Material Planning: Supplies and Equipment

LEARNING OBJECTIVES

After studying the chapter, students should be able to:

1. Categorize chemicals used in the housekeeping department and state their intended uses.
2. Describe recent trends in chemical use and their impact on guests, staff, and, specifically, the housekeeping department.
3. Describe the intended purposes of chemicals used in the housekeeping department and define common chemical terms presented.
4. Identify common cleaning supplies and equipment used in the housekeeping department.
5. Describe recent innovations in cleaning supplies and equipment.
6. List common guest supplies.
7. Describe recent innovations in guest bath amenities

In this chapter we continue our examination of material planning by the executive housekeeper. We now turn our attention to housekeeping supplies and equipment.

Housekeeping Chemicals

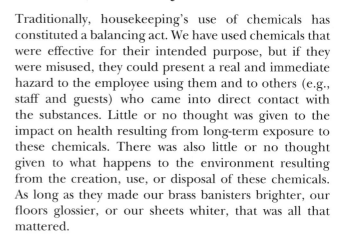

Traditionally, housekeeping's use of chemicals has constituted a balancing act. We have used chemicals that were effective for their intended purpose, but if they were misused, they could present a real and immediate hazard to the employee using them and to others (e.g., staff and guests) who came into direct contact with the substances. Little or no thought was given to the impact on health resulting from long-term exposure to these chemicals. There was also little or no thought given to what happens to the environment resulting from the creation, use, or disposal of these chemicals. As long as they made our brass banisters brighter, our floors glossier, or our sheets whiter, that was all that mattered.

Times have changed. The first priority is now health—health of our employees, our guests, our children, the planet, and the unborn generations that will follow us. The good news is that we are rapidly approaching the day when we can protect our environment, remove unwanted soil from our buildings, kill pathogenic organisms, and preserve, protect, and beautify the property. However, we have to make dramatic changes in how we clean, and we have to educate our people in these new techniques and substances. At the same time, we have to bury several myths associated with cleaning.

Unfortunately, earlier editions of this text perpetuated some of those myths by recommending chemicals that did more harm than good. These can now be replaced by chemicals that are far more environmentally benign, yet are up to the task.

The astute housekeeper knows the intended purpose of every chemical in the department's inventory. The housekeeper is also ultimately responsible for the correct handling and storage of each chemical so that it does not adversely affect the user, the public, or the environment.

CHEMICAL TERMINOLOGY

When attempting to select the proper chemical for a particular housekeeping application, the executive housekeeper is often at the mercy of the sales staff of the local chemical supply firm because he or she is not familiar with basic chemical terminology and the chemistry of cleaning.

Chapter 13 devotes an entire section to the chemistry of cleaning; the purpose of this section, however, is to acquaint the reader with a few basic terms that will aid in the proper selection and use of these chemicals.

Although there are a number of chemicals in the housekeeping department that are used to protect and beautify floors, walls, and furniture, the majority of housekeeping chemicals are intended to clean, disinfect, and sanitize the environment.

The intended use of **detergents** is to remove soil from a surface through a chemical action. Detergents dissolve solid soils and hold the soils in a suspension away from the environmental surface, thus allowing them to be easily removed from that surface. Most detergents used in housekeeping have been synthetic and were derived from a number of basic minerals, primarily sulfonated hydrocarbons. Now there are a number of green cleaning chemicals emerging that are based on soybeans, milk, citrus fruits, and hydrogen peroxide. However, executive housekeepers need to be aware of overinflated claims. There are very few recognized standards for green chemicals. Terms such as *biodegradable, safe for the environment, environmentally benign,* and even *nontoxic* are ambiguous.

There simply are no universally accepted standards for green cleaning. However, there is Green Seal According to its Web site (*www.greenseal.org*):

> Green Seal is an independent, non-profit organization that strives to achieve a healthier and cleaner environment by identifying and promoting products and services that cause less toxic pollution and waste, conserve resources and habitats, and minimize global warming and ozone depletion. Green Seal has no financial interest in the products that it certifies or recommends, or in any manufacturer or company. Green Seal's evaluations are based on state-of-the-art science and information using internationally recognized methods and procedures. Thus, Green Seal provides credible, objective, and unbiased information whose only purpose is to direct the purchaser to environmentally responsible products and services.[1]

Green Seal is a 13-year-old nonprofit environmental labeling organization operating under ISO 14020 and 14024, which are the environmental standards for

FIGURE 6.1 Green Seal logo. *(Courtesy of Green Seal, Washington, D.C.)*

ecolabeling set by the International Organization for Standardization (ISO). Green Seal is the U.S. member of the Global Ecolabeling Network (GEN), the coordinating body of the world's 27 leading ecolabeling programs, including Germany's Blue Angel and Scandinavia's Nordic Swan.

Green Seal has developed a standard for industrial and institutional cleaners (GS-37). It is very safe to assume that any cleaning product having the Green Seal logo meets the highest available standards (Figure 6.1).

EnvirOx's $H_2Orange_2$ Concentrate 117 has not only been tested and authorized to carry the Green Seal mark, but is also an EPA-registered sanitizer-virucide that has been approved for use on food preparation surfaces. $H_2Orange_2$ has also received National Sanitation Foundation (NSF) approval as a sanitizer on all surfaces in and around food-processing areas. These ratings require that a potable water rinse of cleaned surfaces in and around food processing areas be performed after using the product.

Other chemical manufacturers, such as Coastwide Laboratories of Wilsonville, Oregon, sought out other independent third parties for the certification of their green chemicals. Coastwide developed the Sustainable Earth™ product line and submitted it to Coffey Laboratories for independent review against the Sustainable Earth2 standard—the entire line passed. The standard was based on a three-part process. First a set of mandatory pass/fail criteria was established, and each chemical was compared with the criteria. Each chemical had to pass all of the criteria or be instantly rejected. The second part of the process evaluated specific environmental health and worker safety characteristics of each product. Point values were assigned to each criterion that was reflective of health and safety priorities. If a product scored more than an established threshold value, it was rejected. The third part used a reliable measurement method that established a hazard value for chemicals developed at Purdue University, entitled the Indiana Relative Chemical Hazard Score (IRCHS). A chemical product that exceeds an IRCHS threshold value is rejected as a green cleaning product. In addition, Coastwide has also sought out and received Green Seal certification for five of their products and has also received approval for six of their products from the EPA's Design for the Environment (DfE) program (*www.epa.gov/dfe/*).

Many detergents have a neutral pH, which means that they are neither an acid nor an alkaline compound. The degree of alkalinity or acidity is indicated on the pH scale. The scale runs from 0 to 14. Zero through 6 on the scale indicates acidity. Position 8 through 14 on the scale indicates alkalinity. Seven indicates a neutral compound. Alkalies are often used to enhance the cleaning power of synthetic detergents. Strong alkaline detergent cleaners should not be used on certain surfaces. (For more information on this topic, see Chapter 5.)

Disinfectants are chemical agents that have been registered by the EPA and have been proven to destroy **pathogenic microorganisms** on inanimate surfaces. The Environmental Protection Agency's categorizes disinfectants by the microorganisms they destroy and disinfectants usually do not destroy spores produced by certain microorganisms. The following definitions are from the agency's Web site:

Antimicrobial products are divided into two categories based on the type of microbial pest against which the product works.

- **Nonpublic health products** are used to control growth of algae, odor-causing bacteria, bacteria that cause spoilage, deterioration or fouling of materials and microorganisms infectious only to animals. This general category includes products used in cooling towers, jet fuel, paints, and treatments for textile and paper products.
- **Public health products** are intended to control microorganisms infectious to humans in any inanimate environment. The more commonly used public health antimicrobial products include the following:
  - *Sterilizers* (Sporicides): Used to destroy or eliminate all forms of microbial life including fungi, viruses, and all forms of bacteria and their spores. Spores are considered to be the most difficult form of microorganism to destroy. Therefore, EPA considers *sporicide* to be synonymous with s*terilizer*.
  - *Disinfectants*: Used on hard inanimate surfaces and objects to destroy or irreversibly inactivate infectious fungi and bacteria but not necessarily their spores. Disinfectant products are divided into two major types: hospital and general use.
  - *Antiseptics and Germicides*: Used to prevent inflection and decay by inhibiting the growth of microorganisms. Because these products are used in or on living humans or animals, they are considered drugs and are thus approved and regulated by the Food and Drug Administration (FDA).[2]

It is important to understand that there are no instantaneous disinfectants. Disinfectants need **dwell time** on a surface. They must remain for a prescribed number of minutes so the chemical can kill the bacteria and viruses that are present. They are said to have a bacteriostatic effect. A **bacteriostat** prevents microbes from multiplying on a surface. Disinfectants are not intended to be used directly on humans or animals. Other similar terms used to describe specific disinfectants are *bactericides, fungicides, germicides,* and *virucides.*

There are different degrees or levels of cleaning, according to Michael A. Berry. In his landmark work *Protecting the Built Environment*, he lists three different levels of cleaning: sterilization, disinfection, and sanitation. Sterilized, says Berry, means that a surface is 100 percent free from contamination; disinfected means the vast majority of pathogens have been removed; and sanitary means that a surface has some contamination, but is clean to the point that it protects health in general.[3] The purpose of disinfectants is not to remove soils from surfaces, but a number of products on the market combine a synthetic detergent with a disinfectant so that a surface can be cleaned and disinfected at the same time. The use of a disinfectant alone on a soiled surface is ineffective, as the soil serves to protect the bacteria from the germicidal action of the disinfectant.

Combined detergent-disinfectant chemicals are quite effective if they are used according to directions. In certain instances, however, particularly in a hospital environment, it is necessary to first apply a detergent to remove soil buildup and then apply a disinfectant solution after the surface has been cleaned. In most hotel applications, it is perfectly acceptable to use combined detergent-disinfectants. The great advantage to using detergent-disinfectant solutions rather than separate solutions is the labor saved by not having to wash the surface twice.

Common disinfectants include **quaternary ammonium compounds, idophors, hypochlorites, hydrogen peroxide,** and **phenolic compounds**. These compounds are discussed in greater detail in Chapter 13.

It should be noted here that a few hotel housekeepers might fail to see the relevance of disinfectants to hotel housekeeping. This attitude is based on a common misconception that only hospitals need to worry about the control of pathenogenic microorganisms. Unfortunately, hotels and restaurants provide a superb environment for the breeding and transmission of disease. For example, according to the Centers for Disease Control, 77 percent of all cases of foodborne illness originate in commercial food-service establishments. It is also estimated that hepatitis A is transmitted to thousands of restaurant customers annually from infected workers.[4] Who can forget that the dreaded Legionnaires' disease originated in the air-conditioning system of a hotel? Now we have SARS (severe acute respiratory syndrome).

There are indications that not only can this dread disease be transmitted through direct contact, but that the virus can survive for 24 hours on a surface and perhaps even longer if it is contained in fecal matter.

Bathroom fixtures in particular need to be disinfected, starting with toilets and urinals; but other areas that need special attention include door handles, soap and towel dispensers, faucets, flooring around urinals and toilets, partitions around toilets and urinals, levers to flush toilets, telephones, water fountains, and floor drains. Places where people have vomited, or where any human fluids may be found, should also be disinfected. Proper training and protective gear for the housekeeping staff must be available. According to Beth Risinger, CEO of the International Executive Housekeepers Association, hand washing by cleaners is critical every time they change environments or move from guestroom to guestroom.

In many areas of a hotel, the intention is not to maintain totally disinfected surfaces, as is required in a hospital environment, but merely to maintain sanitized surfaces. A **sanitizer** is a chemical that kills microorganisms to an accepted level, or what is generally regarded as safe. Sanitizers are not intended to provide a bacteriostatic surface. Sanitizers may be specially formulated chemicals, or they may be disinfectants that have been diluted to serve as sanitizers. Sanitizers are used on such surfaces as carpets, walls, and floors, and may also be used in conjunction with room deodorizers to sanitize the air. At the very least, the lodging industry needs to establish clearly defined standards for cleanliness in all areas of an operation. Until such standards are established, operators should develop their own high standards and follow them.

Potentially dangerous chemical reactions can take place in the housekeeper's mop bucket as well as in the chemist's laboratory. One of the most dangerous occurs when an ammoniated product is mixed with a hypochlorite (such as bleach) or when a bleach is mixed with an acid-based cleaner. In both cases, potentially deadly chlorine gases are released.

SELECTION CONSIDERATIONS

A number of variables must be considered to ensure that the most appropriate chemical product is chosen. One crucial factor is the relative hardness of the water at the site. Water hardness refers to the amount of calcium and magnesium found in the water. Most disinfectants and sanitizers that are quaternary-based are negatively affected by water hardness. Look on the product label for claims of effectiveness in hard water.

A second concern is the particular type of soil that is to be removed from the environment. Grease and oils may call for solvent cleaners that normally have a petroleum base, whereas scale and lime deposits on bathroom fixtures may require an acid-based cleaner. In the next section, we shall explore the merits of using all-purpose cleaners.

A third consideration is the initial cost of the product. Since different chemicals are diluted to different concentrations, always base your calculations on the cost per usable gallon of solution.

A fourth factor is the cost of labor and equipment. Some chemicals are much more ''labor intensive'' than others; that is, they require a greater degree of physical force in their application in order to be effective. That force requirement can translate into expensive equipment and more man-hours to effectively do the job.

A fifth factor is the relative availability of the product. Is the distributor always ready, willing, and able to provide the product? Or have there been numerous instances of **stock-outs**? If the chemical is not always available when you need it, you should seriously think of changing brands or distributors.

Sixth, does the distributor give good service? Is the vendor willing to demonstrate the proper use of the product? Is the vendor willing to conduct comparison tests of chemicals at your site? Is the company also willing to help train your staff in the proper use of the product? Also, if the product fails to meet expectations, will the distributor take back the unused product and issue a credit memo? Good service certainly adds value to the product. Sometimes this value more than compensates for an extra penny or two in cost per usable gallon. Finally, is the chemical the most environmentally sound chemical that can be obtained? Is there a third-party certification to support that claim? Does that green chemical meet your needs without becoming overkill? As Jimmy Palmer, executive housekeeper at the Four Seasons, Las Vegas, remarked, ''At the Four Seasons, we do not need a hydrochloric acid bowl cleaner to remove lime and soil buildup, because we clean our toilets every day.''

All of these variables must be carefully weighed when purchasing chemical supplies.

CHANGE AGENTS
Roger McFadden

Vice President, Technical Services, Coastwide Laboratories

Roger McFadden is Vice President of Technical Services and Product Development for Coastwide Laboratories, a position he has held since 1988. McFadden is one of five individuals in the United States appointed by Underwriters Laboratories (UL) to serve on the Industry Advisory Council on Slip Resistance Standards and has recently been appointed to a Standards Technical Panel by UL and the American National Standards Institute

(ANSI). He is a member of the ASTM D-21 Floor Polish Standards Committee and a member of the Hard Surface Inspection Task Force for the Institute of Inspection Cleaning and Restoration Certification (IICRC). McFadden is on the faculty of the Cleaning Management Institute (CMI), the chairman of Oregon governor Kitzhaber's Community Sustainability Council Workgroup for Cleaning and Coatings, and a charter member of the Unified Green Cleaning Alliance.

Holding a master's degree in chemistry, McFadden is a frequent speaker for health-care organizations, educational institutions, public agencies, and private corporations. He speaks on a variety of environmental, safety, and health topics. He has been published in several trade publications, including *Cleaning and Maintenance Management.*

He also led development of the Sustainable Earth evaluation standard and the Sustainable Earth product line at Coastwide Laboratories. "Though Sustainable Earth products met all the criteria of the leading national environmental standards, our customers were asking us to raise the bar," McFadden said. "We basically had to create a more comprehensive standard than any that has existed to date." David DiFiore, project manager for the U.S. Environmental Protection Agency's Design for the Environment program, says McFadden has been "a major change leader." DiFiore says Coastwide Laboratories worked with the Zero Waste Alliance of Portland, Oregon, to form the Unified Green Cleaning Alliance, a group of Pacific Northwest businesses working to raise standards for sustainable cleaning products. "The work he's done outlining all the ingredients used in formulations, and trying to understand the environmental and health implications of those ingredients, that's just outstanding," says DiFiore.

FIGURE 6.2 $H_2Orange_2$ 117 Concentrate has three proprietary dispensing options (lower left to right): Bucket Buddy, Spray Buddy, Blend Buddy. *(Photo courtesy of EnvirOx, L.L.C. Danville, Illinois)*

ALL-PURPOSE CLEANERS

One innovation in housekeeping chemical use has been the increasing use of **all-purpose cleaners**. Most all-purpose cleaners are pH-neutral, so they are safe for most surfaces that can be cleaned with a water-based product. All-purpose cleaners normally do not need to be rinsed, they do not leave a haze, and they do not streak. The relative cleaning effectiveness of an all-purpose cleaner is normally determined by its dilution strength, which can be set for different jobs. Figure 6.2 shows $H_2Orange_2$ 117 Concentrate, a unique all-purpose chemical that is a highly effective sanitizer-virucide and cleaner that can be used in kitchens, bathrooms, and a multitude of other applications. In different dilutions it performs various tasks, from window cleaning to mopping floors. It is also Green Seal certified.

Using an all-purpose cleaner is an effective way to reduce product inventory, and reducing inventory usually means bringing more dollars to the bottom line. Using an all-purpose cleaner can also translate to quantity buying, which can mean greater savings.

However, there are disadvantages to all-purpose cleaners. Perhaps the greatest disadvantage is that an all-purpose cleaner is inadequate for certain cleaning tasks, such as in the cleaning of bathroom equipment where a disinfectant is needed. Most all-purpose cleaners do not contain disinfectants. Another concern is whether employees are properly diluting the all-purpose cleaner for the specific task at hand. Far too often, employees will assume the attitude that "more is better" and will fail to properly dilute the detergent. This action inevitably drives up costs.

SINGLE-PURPOSE CLEANERS

There are numerous instances in which an all-purpose cleaner is inadequate. In this section, we will examine the relative merits of a variety of single-purpose cleaners.

Abrasive Cleaners

Abrasive cleaners normally contain a detergent combined with a bleach and an abrasive (usually silica, a quartz dust that can scratch glass). The abrasiveness of the cleaner is determined by the percentage of abrasive in the cleanser. Abrasive cleansers can be found in either powder or paste form. The paste is preferred because it will cling to vertical surfaces. Under no circumstances should abrasive cleaners be used on fiberglass tub and shower enclosures; furthermore, abrasives are not recommended for porcelain fixtures.

Degreasers

Degreasers or emulsifiers are usually found in most commercial kitchens. They are concentrated detergents that are formulated to remove heavy grease buildup. Figure 6.3 shows the soy-based product Soy Green 1000, from Soy Technologies, Inc., which can remove heavy kitchen grease but is nonflammable, nontoxic, and noncarcinogenic. Petroleum solvents have degreasing properties, but because of their flammability and toxicity they are rarely used on kitchen surfaces.

Deodorizers

Deodorizers, if properly used, can improve a facility's public image and improve employee morale. Some deodorizers counteract stale odors, leaving a clean, air-freshened effect through the principle of **odor-pair neutralization**. These deodorizers leave no trace of perfume cover-up. This approach is preferred in restrooms, guestrooms, and public areas. Most guests react

FIGURE 6.4 Coastwide Laboratories' Sustainable Earth Odor Eliminator safely neutralizes odors and is designed for a pump-spray container. It eliminates water- and oil-based odors. *(Photo courtesy of Coastwide Laboratories, Wilsonville, Oregon.)*

negatively to cheap cover-up deodorant perfumes in hotel lobbies or guestrooms.

However, where there are particularly strong odors, such as at a garbage dumpster or a pet kennel, a deodorant formula that contains fragrances may be appropriate. Methods of deodorant application include aerosol sprays, "stick-up" applicators, timed-release systems, liquids, powders, and hand-pump sprays (Figure 6.4).

Drain Cleaners

Drain cleaners contain harmful acids and lyes and should not be applied by the regular housekeeping staff. They should be used only by management or by staff who have been specially trained in their application. Drain cleaners are hazardous and can corrode pipes; consequently, many properties have banned their use

FIGURE 6.3 Pictured in the middle is Soy Green (SG) 1000, a nonflammable degreaser. *(Photo courtesy of Soy Technologies, Inc., Delray Beach, Florida.)*

in favor of pressurized gases or drain-cleaning augers. There is even a plastic throwaway drain auger that effectively cleans out sink drains clogged with hair.

Furniture Cleaners and Polishes

Furniture cleaners and polishes are normally wax- or oil-based products that contain antistatic compounds. The best polishes contain lemon oil, which serves to replenish the moisture that is lost from the wood.

Hand Soaps and Detergents

Hand washing is an important component of personal hygiene for all employees. One of the biggest preventatives of **nosocomial infection** in hospitals is the practice of hand washing.[5] Unfortunately, many employees do not wash their hands often enough because they believe that repeated hand washing will cause skin dryness and cracking. Since the housekeeping department is often in charge of purchasing hand soaps, the housekeeper should stock only lotion soaps that prevent dryness and cracking. An excellent waterless hand cleaner and conditioner is Soy Derm, pictured in Figure 6.3. It contains natural oils, vitamin E, aloe, and tea tree oil. It cuts through the worst grease, oils, inks, paints, and tars, and leaves hands softer than they were before application.

Laundry Chemicals

Laundry chemicals include synthetic detergents, concentrated bleaches, **antichlors**, **sours**, and fabric softeners. The detergents are often **nonionic detergents** that contain fabric brighteners and antiredeposition agents. The active ingredient in most laundry bleaches is sodium hypochlorite. Antichlors are added to remove excess chlorine from the fabric. Sours are added to lower the pH and may also contain bluing and whiteners. Suitable sours include ammonium silicofluoride, sodium silicofluoride, zinc silicofluoride, and acetic acid. Excessive use of sours may result in a sour odor remaining on the clothes. Softeners are usually **cationic** products that contain antistatic and bacteriostatic agents. Their purpose is to leave the laundered product fresh, soft, and with no static cling. When bacteriostatic agents are present, they help to reduce the growth of pathenogenic organisms on the fabric. Smart laundry managers are studying the addition of ozone to the laundry process. It increases the effectiveness of chemicals, shortens wash time, and allows for a lowering of water temperatures (saving energy and money). An article from the April 2003 edition of *Executive Housekeeping Today* on ozone in the laundry appears in Appendix D.

Metal Cleaners and Polishes

Metal cleaners and polishes are usually paste-type cleaners that contain mild acidic solutions. Some contain protective coatings that inhibit tarnishing.

Solvent Cleaners

Solvent cleaners are used to clean surfaces that are badly soiled by grease, tar, or oil. Solvents are made from pine oils, kerosene, alcohols, and now, soy. Soy Green 5000, pictured in Figure 6.3, is such a strong biosolvent that it can safely remove graffiti, paint, and varnish (Figure 6.5). Some types of solvents will not adversely affect paint, acrylics, and metals. Carbon tetrachloride

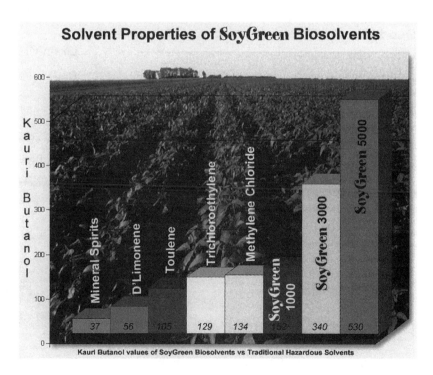

FIGURE 6.5 The Kauri Butanol scale measures the power of solvents. SG 5000 is far more powerful than traditional solvents that are toxic and often carcinogenic. *(Photo courtesy of Soy Technologies, Inc., Delray Beach, Florida.)*

and other halogenated hydrocarbons are extremely toxic and carcinogenic and should be avoided at all costs. Some **petroleum naphtha solvents** have a high **flash point**. The higher the flash point, the less chance a cleaner will ignite. The best choice for a solvent is one that will do the job and is preferably a biosolvent, versus a petroleum solvent, which is a **volatile organic compound (VOC)** that will diminish **indoor air quality (IAQ)**.

Bathroom Cleaners

To clean lime encrustations from washroom fixtures, remove rust stains, and remove organic soils, the chemical industry has produced cleaners that meet these unique needs. The emulsion toilet bowl cleaner normally contains acid, which is necessary to remove rust and corrosion, and detergents that remove fecal material, urine, and bacterial colonies. Hydrochloric acid has been the acid of choice in these cleaners, but has been replaced by the milder phosphoric acid and oxalic acid. All are corrosive and should not come into contact with metal fixtures, especially chrome, let alone people. They should also not be used on walls or floors. Now we have alternatives, such as Coastwide Laboratories' Sustainable Earth Toilet & Urinal Cleaner that effectively removes soils and mineral deposits without acids (Figure 6.6).

Jetted Hot Tub Cleaners

There are now an estimated 2 million jetted hot tubs in lodging properties and hospitals. Until now, cleaning the hot tub has been similar to the cleaning of an ordinary bathtub. However, many guests have noticed that once

FIGURE 6.6 This cleaner is formulated without fragrances and has surfactants made from rapidly renewable resources. *(Photo courtesy of Coastwide Laboratories, Wilsonville, Oregon.)*

the jets were turned on, black specs appeared in the water. In many cases these specs turned out to be algae. Up to a pint of bath water remains in the pipes and pump housing when the tub is drained. Combined with lime deposits and scale in a light-free environment, this water provides an excellent medium for the growth of algae, bacteria, and viruses. A biofilm eventually forms inside the pipes, making it extremely difficult to kill these pathogens. Organisms such as *pseudomonas, E. coli,* and *Legionella* have been found growing in these tubs. The housekeeping staff, and certainly the next guests to use these tubs, risk infection. Plainly stated, the guest who soaks in one of these tubs is soaking in some of the same water that was used by the previous guests who used the tub. Fortunately, some companies are now making chemicals designed for these tubs that will destroy the algae and pathogens that may be found in them (Figure 6.7).

CARPET CLEANERS

Carpet-cleaning chemicals, whether sprays, foams, dry powders, or shampoos, contain essentially the same types of chemicals in slightly different forms. Common chemicals include neutral water-soluble solvents, emulsifiers, **defoamers**, optical brighteners, and deodorizers. Many also contain sanitizers; however, some of these may have an adverse effect on fourth- and fifth-generation nylon carpets. Soil and stain repellents may also be included in the cleaners. When selecting a particular brand, do a comparison test between your current brand and the proposed alternatives. If the greener product works as well, consider using it (Figure 6.8).

FLOOR CARE PRODUCTS

The chemical formulation of a floor care product is dependent on the product's function.

Strippers

Strippers are used to remove the worn finish from floors. They may have an ammoniated base or may be nonammoniated products. Nonammoniated strippers may not be as effective in removing **metal cross-linked polymer finishes**, but they do not have the harsh odor associated with the ammoniated products (Figure 6.3). A neutralizing rinse is often applied after the stripper. These rinses neutralize alkaline residues left from the stripping solution that may affect the performance of the new finish.

Floor Cleaners

Floor cleaners are mild detergents that work in cool water to remove soils without affecting the existing

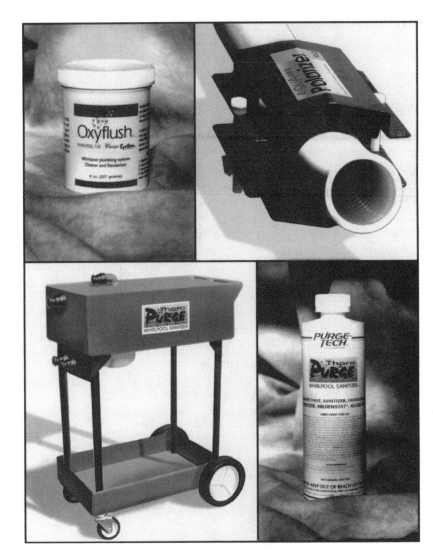

FIGURE 6.7 Purge-Tech™ offers the Jet Tub System, four products used to clean whirlpool tubs (*clockwise from upper left*): Oxyflush™, a cleaner and deodorizer for a whirlpool plumbing system; Aqua Polorizer™, a hydromagnetic suspension system for minerals in the water; ThoroPurge, a disinfectant for the whirlpool plumbing system; and the ThoroPurge Machine™, which flushes the ThoroPurge chemical through the whirlpool's piping system and down the drain. (*Courtesy of Purge-Tech, Inc.*)

FIGURE 6.8 Coastwide's Sustainable Earth Carpet Cleaner is biodegradable, contains no phosphates, and is safe on all generations of carpet. (*Photo courtesy of Coastwide Laboratories, Wilsonville, Oregon.*)

floor finish. Many floor finishes are **thermoplastic**; hot water tends to soften the finish. Most floor cleaners also have a neutral pH and many require no additional rinsing.

Sealers and Finishes

Sealers and finishes are applied to most floor surfaces to protect the flooring material from wear, cleaners, and liquid spills. The chemical composition of the sealer or finish will vary according to the type of flooring material for which it is intended. The preferred product for most resilient floors and some stone floor applications has been the metal cross-linked floor finishes (particularly zinc cross-linked polymers) because of their ability to give floors the popular "wet look." Recently, the use of these heavy metal finishes has fallen into disfavor because of environmental concerns. A number of states have prohibited their sale because of the perceived danger resulting from emptying these heavy metals into the sewer when the finishes are stripped from the floors.

Many of the same concerns are being voiced about wood sealers and finishes that have solvent bases. A water-based finish for wood is now available that is considered by many experts to be environmentally safe.

PESTICIDES

Pesticide applications should be left to the expert. Housekeeping departments are advised to seek the services of a reliable pest control company rather than attempting to control pests themselves. If there is a perceived need to keep pesticides in inventory, it is strongly suggested that only natural pyrethrins be used, if at all possible, or that you employ an integrated pest management system that encompasses predator insects. For roaches, the single best way to control them in a building is to starve them to death. Keep kitchens, storerooms, guestrooms, and offices scrupulously clean, and you will not have a roach problem.

HANDLING AND STORAGE OF CHEMICALS

Manufacturer guidelines should be strictly adhered to when storing and handling chemicals. All chemicals should be routinely kept under lock and key. A system of inventory control should be established and followed. Chemicals are expensive, and employees should be held accountable for their misuse. If bulk chemicals are used, employees should be taught how to properly dilute them.

CHEMICAL PACKAGING

Bulk Chemicals

Bulk chemicals offer the housekeeping department the greatest potential for savings, but the executive housekeeper should beware of overbuying chemicals. One problem is that large quantities of chemicals cannot always be stored properly. The cost of storing large quantities of chemicals may offset any potential cost savings from bulk purchases. Chemicals may deteriorate while in storage. The expiration dates that appear on some chemical supplies should be noted. The executive housekeeper should also compare the cost savings of bulk buying with the potential interest that would be generated if a minimal amount of chemical were purchased, and the cost difference between the minimal amount and the bulk amount invested. If the savings from buying in bulk would be greater than the amount of interest that would be generated, then the bulk purchase is a wise investment. But if the interest generated would be greater than the cost savings from buying in bulk, then the wise choice is to buy the lesser amount and invest the difference.

Another problem with bulk chemicals occurs when employees do not dilute the chemical to its appropriate level. If the dilution process is not rigorously monitored,

A MINI CASE STUDY

Pitfalls in Chemical Use

Molly Galloway, executive housekeeper at the Seacoast Pines Resort and Convention Center is in her office with her assistant, Tracy Hernandez. Anna Lopez, a guestroom attendant at the property, has just been transported to the hospital. She was found, passed out, in a guest's bathroom. She had been overcome by chlorine gas when she mixed the toilet bowl cleaner, containing hydrochloric acid, with bleach.

Galloway comments to Hernandez, "Tracy, we can't let this happen again on our watch. She could have died in that bathroom had not Randy, her supervisor, come along to check on her." Galloway pulls out the guestroom attendant (GRA) training manual. "Right here under lesson four, it states, 'under no circumstances are chemicals to be combined with other chemicals.' Didn't she go through the training?"

"Absolutely," Tracy responds, "but many of the GRAs think they know better than we do when it comes to cleaning. We have also caught some using double or triple the recommended amount of chemical concentrate. When they mix up a batch, some believe if one ounce per gallon is good, then two ounces must be better. We've even had employees bring their favorite chemicals from home to use or mix with our chemicals. Or," Tracy continues, "maybe Anna didn't get it. Her English is not that good. You know, you tell them something and they shake their head 'yes' and you come back later to find that they have completed ignored what you have told them."

"So what do we do?" Galloway responds. "Do they need more training, more supervision, more discipline? Or do we tell the top brass this just a one-in-a-million occurrence that will never happen again, and then when it happens, we lose our jobs? Tomorrow we're going to sit down at 10:00 A.M. and come up with a solution. In the meantime, I want you to put some recommendations on paper on what we should do and bring them to that meeting."

QUESTIONS

If you were Tracy Hernandez, what would you put on that list? Once you have drawn up your own list, talk it over with your fellow students and see what they have on their list. Discuss the various options and then prepare a final list from the class, with the recommendations prioritized starting with the best.

the tendency of most employees is to use too much chemical, which drives up cost. An alternative to this costly practice is the use of the new in-house chemical mixing stations, as pictured in Figure 6.9. These systems automatically mix bulk chemicals, thus eliminating guesswork and improper dilution levels.

Premeasured Chemicals

Many chemical and detergent manufacturers produce premeasured (packaged) products in filament containers that dissolve when placed in a prescribed amount of water, yielding the proper amount of chemical in solution.[6] Although these products are higher in unit price, the use of such premeasured products provides a high degree of cost control, better inventory procedures, and better quality in cleaning. In addition, housekeeping managers and hospital administrators desiring documentation on cleaning costs are more likely to accept cost documentation when premeasured chemicals and detergents are used, since exact quantities may be determined.

Aerosols

Aerosol chemicals have received considerable negative press in recent years from a variety of sources. Housekeeping managers often react negatively because of the higher net product cost associated with aerosols. Packaging and propellants drive up the cost of the product.

Environmentalists have reacted negatively to the use of aerosols for years. In the 1970s, the issue was the widespread use of chlorofluorocarbons (CFCs), which were linked to ozone depletion and global warming. Although CFCs are not used anymore, substitutes have been accused of contributing to acid rain and smog formation; and in one case, the propellant (methylene chloride) was suspected of being a carcinogen.[7] Aerosols also break the chemical into an extremely fine mist, making it much more respirable. Aerosols are a major contributor to poor indoor air quality (IAQ). It is wise to eliminate them from your inventory.

Compatibility in Chemical Product Design

One reason housekeeping managers consider the purchase of only one brand of housekeeping chemical products is chemical compatibility (Figure 6.10). Chemical manufacturers often formulate their chemicals to perform better with other chemicals in their product line than with the chemical products made by competitors. One example of this is a floor stripper that

FIGURE 6.9 A close-up of a chemical mixing station in a satellite linen and storage room. *(Courtesy of Bellagio MGM Mirage™, Las Vegas, Nevada.)*

FIGURE 6.10 Coastwide Laboratories' Sustainable Earth products are formulated to be compatible with one another. *(Photo courtesy of Coastwide Laboratories, Wilsonville, Oregon.)*

GREEN TIP

Here is a chemical to avoid if at all possible: ethylene glycol monobutyl ether (EGBE). It is often used in water-based cleaners, degreasers, wax, and finish strippers. In tests it has had negative effects on the central nervous system, kidneys, blood, hematopoietic tissues, and the liver, and it may cause lasting effects after just one exposure.

works best in removing a floor finish made by the same manufacturer.

When selecting any new chemical, a housekeeper should ask the vendor to demonstrate the product at the site where it will be used so that comparisons between brands can be drawn.

OSHA'S HAZARD COMMUNICATION STANDARD

Since 1988, hotels have been required to comply with the Occupational Safety and Health Administration's (OSHAs) Hazard Communication (**HazComm**) Standard, which applies to the handling and storage of hazardous chemical materials. Hazardous chemicals include, but are not limited to, aerosols, detergents, floor chemicals, carpet chemicals, flammable chemicals, cleaners, polishes, laundry chemicals, bathroom cleaners, and pesticides.

To be in full compliance, management must read the HazComm Standard. OSHA's Web site (*www.osha.gov*) provides extensive information on what an employer should know to be in compliance with the law. Using the search tools at this Web site, you can find the guidelines for employers on how to set up a hazard communications program. For an excellent overview, visit *www.osha.gov/ dsg/hazcom/finalmsdsreport.html* and read "Hazard Communication in the 21st Century Workplace."

The hotel must inventory and list all hazardous chemicals on the property. The Hazard Communication Standard has three elements: training, labeling of chemicals (including chemicals transferred to sprayers

and other containers), and, of course **material safety data sheets (MSDSs)** from the chemical manufacturers. These MSDSs should explain the chemicals' characteristics, recommended handling use and storage, information on flammability, ingredients, health hazards, first-aid procedures, and what to do in case of a fire or explosion. This information must be disseminated to employees and should be made available to them at all times. See Figure 6.11 for an actual Material Safety Data Sheet. The hotel must also formulate a HazComm program for the property and establish a training program for all employees who use or come in contact with hazardous chemicals. Finally, the property must provide all necessary protective equipment to its employees.[8]

A FINAL WORD ON GREEN CHEMICALS

As the demand for green chemicals is growing meteorically, led by demands of the federal and state governments, closely followed by the health-care profession, more and more chemical manufacturers are getting on the bandwagon. When choosing a green company, try to choose one that "walks the walk" as well as "talks the talk." See Figure 6.12, a statement of EnvirOx's "Corporate Environmental Commitment," for an example of a program that should be emulated throughout the entire cleaning chemical industry.

Another example is Coastwide Laboratories' recent award from the city of Portland, Oregon, for its Sustainable Earth commercial cleaning product line. The award, entitled "BEST (Businesses for an Environmentally Sustainable Tomorrow) Business Award for Environmental Product Development" was presented to Roger McFadden, vice president of technical services for Coastwide Laboratories. In a press release, David DiFore, project manager for the U.S. Environmental Protection Agency's Design for the Environment program, called McFadden "a major change leader."

Other companies of note include Oxy Company Ltd., Worx Environmental Products, Ipax Cleanogel Inc., Rochester Midland Corporation, Hillyard Industries, and 3 M, as well as the previously mentioned EnvirOx. All of these firms have cleaning products certified by Green Seal.

COASTWIDE LABORATORIES		Hazard Rating	HMIS	NFPA
Formerly Paulsen & Roles Laboratories		Health	0	0
10000 SW Commerce Circle		Flammability	0	0
Wilsonville, OR 97070		Reactivity	0	0
Office PHONE: 503-416-5300 or FAX 503-416-5304		Special	None	None
24-HR EMERGENCIES: MEDICAL 800-808-4691		DOT CHEMTREC: 800-424-9300		

MATERIAL SAFETY DATA SHEET

Complies with ANSI Z400.1 Format (All information in this document has been third party certified)

SECTION 1: PRODUCT IDENTIFICATION

Product: Sustainable Earth® 64 Neutral All Purpose Cleaner   MSDS CODE: CLSE6400.0104
This MSDS is also for Quick Mix® and Handy Mix™ Products

GENERIC DESCRIPTION	DATE ISSUED	SUPERSEDES	PREPARED BY
Concentrated General Purpose Cleaner	1-01-04	7-1-03	Regulatory Affairs Department

SECTION 2: COMPOSITION AND INFORMATION ON INGREDIENTS

Components*	% by Wt.	CAS #	Exposure Limit	LC_{50}/LD_{50}
Hydrogen Peroxide	1-3	7722-84-1	**OSHA** TWA: 1.4 mg/m3	ORAL 1518 mg/kg (rat)
			ACGIH TWA: 1.4 mg/m3	DERMAL 4060 mg/kg (rat)
				VAPOR 2000 mg/m^3 4-hrs (rat)
Alcohol Ethoxylate	08-12	68439-46-3	Not Applicable	>2,000 mg/kg (oral, rat)
Fragrance	<0.08	Mixture	None	NA
Colorant	<0.001	Mixture	None	NA
Water	60-100	7732-18-5	Not Available	Not Available

SECTION 3: HAZARD IDENTIFICATION

Primary Entry Routes: Skin Contact **Signs & Symptoms of Exposure:** Incidental skin contact is not expected to cause any significant irritation. **Effects of Overexposure:** Based on Corrositex *in vitro* testing this product is not corrosive and with prolonged skin contact or eye contact may cause slight reddening but will be non-irritating. This product has a low potential for skin absorption based upon review of the absorption information provided by individual ingredients manufacturers.

SECTION 4: FIRST AID MEASURES

Emergency First Aid Procedures: SKIN CONTACT: Rinse skin thoroughly with water. EYE CONTACT: Flush eyes with water for 15-20 minutes. If reddening occurs and persists then get prompt medical aid. INGESTION: Drink large amounts of water, consult a physician. **24-HR MEDICAL EMERGENCY PHONE: 800-808-4691**

SECTION 5: FIRE FIGHTING MEASURES

Flash Point: None-**Sustainable Earth® 64 Neutral General Purpose Cleaner** is not considered a fire hazard, nor will it support combustion. **Extinguishing Media:** Use standard firefighting measures to extinguish fires involving this material (water spray, dry chemicals or foam).

SECTION 6: ACCIDENTAL RELEASE MEASURES

Release or Spill: Recover liquid with wet mop or wet/dry vacuum. Flush residue to sanitary sewer with water. Use care, floor may become slippery. All Federal, State and Local regulations should be carefully followed. Discarded product is not a hazardous waste according to RCRA, 40 CFR 261.

SECTION 7: HANDLING AND STORAGE

Keep out of reach of children. Avoid eye and prolonged skin contact.

SECTION 8: EXPOSURE CONTROLS AND PERSONAL PROTECTION

Respiratory Protection: No special requirements under normal use conditions. **Protective Gloves:** No special requirements for normal use conditions. **Eye Protection:** No special requirements for normal use conditions.
Other Protective Measures: It is always a good practice to wear rubber, neoprene or vinyl gloves and splash proof chemical safety goggles when pouring or handling <u>any</u> liquid cleaning product.

FIGURE 6.11 Material Safety Data Sheet for a neutral pH cleaner. Note the added Hazardous Materials Identification System, HMIS, developed by the National Paint & Coatings Association (NPCA), and the National Fire Protection Association's (NFPA) Fire Protection Hazard Warning System at the top of the form. *(Courtesy of Coastwide Laboratories, Wilsonville, Oregon.)*

COASTWIDE Laboratories
Material Safety Data Sheet
Page 2 – Sustainable Earth® 64 Neutral General Purpose Cleaner   CLSE6400.0104

SECTION 9: PHYSICAL AND CHEMICAL PROPERTIES

Appearance/Odor: Yellow Liquid   **Boiling Point:** >212F   **Evap. Rate:** NA   **pH Concentrated Form:** 5-9
Vapor Density: ND   **Vapor Pressure:** <1.0   **Specific Gravity:** 1.00-1.03   **Solubility in Water:** Complete   **%Volatile:** 100

SECTION 10: STABILITY AND REACTIVITY

Sustainable Earth® 64 Neutral General Purpose Cleaner is stable and non-reactive.

SECTION 11: TOXICOLOGICAL INFORMATION

Oral Toxicity: Sustainable Earth® 64 Neutral General Purpose Cleaner is non-toxic based upon current information available to COASTWIDE and provided by all ingredient manufacturers. It exhibits acute oral LD_{50} values greater than >5g/kg for rats and acute dermal LD_{50} values greater than >2g/Kg for rabbits. **No PBTs:** This product contains none of the persistent, bioaccumulative and toxic chemicals **(PBT)** as listed by EPA: dioxins & furans, toxaphene, PCBs, Mirex, Mercury & compounds, Octachlorostyrene, alkyl-lead, DDT, Hexachlorobenzene, aldrin/dieldrin, benzo(a)pyrene and chlordane. **No Butyl:** Contains no 2-butoxyethanol (butyl). **No Endocrine Modifers:** Based upon information provided by manufacturers of all ingredients used to manufacture this product, none of the ingredients used in this product contain APE, OPE, NPE or dibutyl phthalate. **Ingredients:** All ingredients of this product are listed on TSCA 1985 Chemical Substance Inventory and 1990 Supplement. Product conforms to California Proposition 65 and meets all current VOC regulations. This product does not contain any chemical subject to the reporting requirements of CERCLA or SARA Section 302 or 313. No ingredient in this product is currently listed as a carcinogens, or reproductive toxins by NTP, IARC or OSHA.

SECTION 12: ECOLOGICAL INFORMATION

Sustainable Earth® 64 Neutral General Purpose Cleaner is readily biodegradable based upon the Modified OECD screening tests on all ingredients including the alcohol ethoxylate surfactant. This product had a test result that exceeds the 70% dissolved oxygen content requirement for classification as readily biodegradable. After this product's use, it will biodegrade in sewage systems and/or the environment. Contains no alkyphenol ethoxylates **(APE)**. No ingredients used to make this product are listed in the toxic release inventory **(TRI)** chemicals list under Superfund Amendments and Reauthorization Act (SARA) Title III, Section 313. This product contains no ozone-depleting chlorinated compounds as specified by the Montreal Protocol. This product contains no paradichlorobenzene 1,4-dioxane, sodium hypochlorite, NTA or sodium EDTA. This product contains volatile organic compounds **(VOC)** in a concentration of less than 1% of the weight of the product. This product meets the phosphate requirements of Green Seal Environmental Standard GS-37. Aquatic Toxicity: When diluted according to label directions this product is not toxic to aquatic life, as tested in an independent certified laboratory and measured by EPA Environmental Effects Testing Guidelines.

SECTION 13: DISPOSAL CONSIDERATIONS

Waste Disposal Information: Waste Disposal Information: No special method. Observe all applicable Federal, State and Local regulations, rules and/or ordinances regarding disposal of non-hazardous materials. Discarded product is not a hazardous waste according to RCRA, 40 CFR 261.This product is not considered a hazardous waste in Oregon or Washington as defined in WAC 173-303-070 or as characterized in WAC 173-303-090. Observe all applicable Federal, State and Local regulations, rules and/or ordinances regarding disposal of non-hazardous materials.

SECTION 14: TRANSPORT INFORMATION

DOT EMERGENCY 24-HR: (800) 424-9300   **DOT Class:** Not Regulated

SECTION 15: REGULATORY INFORMATION

Sustainable Earth® 64 Neutral General Purpose Cleaner is packaged in recyclable Type 2 HDPE plastic gallon containers. The plastic containers are readily refillable. And the containers are shipped in cardboard cartons that are made from 25% Post-Consumer Materials.

SECTION 16: OTHER INFORMATION

Always follow label directions carefully when using this or any other chemical product. If information about this product is required, please contact COASTWIDE Laboratories at 503-416-5300 or at Coastwide Website www.coastwidelabs.com . Keep MSDS filed and organized in an area accessible to workers according to the Hazard Communication Standards.

All information appearing herein has been third party certified and is given in good faith. No warranty is made, expressed or implied including merchantability or fitness for a particular purpose. All conditions of use are beyond the control of COASTWIDE Laboratories. Therefore, users are responsible for verifying the data under their own operating conditions to determine whether the product is suitable for their particular purposes. The data contained herein is confidential and intended solely for the user's internal use.

FIGURE 6.11 (*Continued*)

EnvirOx H₂●range₂

Corporate Environmental Commitment

EnvirOx has been implementing a program to improve our "corporate footprint profile" since January of 2002. This program has included the following completed projects:

Operations:

1) Installation of a system to eliminate all waste from our production process. In order to complete this system we have:

   a) All returned liquids are returned to the process.

   b) Installed equipment and procedures to recycle 100% of all liquids collected from blow-downs, transfers, and system clean-outs. All liquids are collected and returned to the next production batch. Even cleaning solutions produced while calibrating dispensers are recycled. All floor drains are plugged and no pipelines or hoses are preeminently or temporarily connected from the production process to sewer lines.

   c) All waste cardboard is bailed and recycled.

   d) All wasted bottles are bailed and recycled.

2) All lighting fixtures in the building have been replaced with new, high efficiency units.

3) All heating and cooling units in the building have been replaced with new high efficiency units.

Community:

EnvirOx considers support for our community an integral component of the "Corporate Footprint profile". Along with the more conventional support of local United Way initiatives, we are actively involved in supporting the local Boys and Girls Club with contributions to their building fund, participation on the Board of Directors and regular, monthly contributions to operating funds. As our company grows we remain committed to increase this support of what we consider a foundation service to our community.

M. Rebecca Melikyan, Exec. Vice President   Taylor Stewart, Vice President of Sales

Patrick Stewart, President

P.O. Box 2327 • 1938 E. Fairchild St. • Danville, IL 61832-2327 • 800-281-9604 • 217-442-8596 • Fax 217-442-2568

FIGURE 6.12 Nothing goes down the sewer from the production processes at EnvirOx. *(Courtesy of EnvirOx, L.L.C., Danville, Illinois)*

Cleaning Supplies and Equipment

Chemicals are only part of the housekeeping department's arsenal of weapons in its war against dirt. The professional housekeeper must develop standards for the equipment and supplies used by the property and must incorporate those standards into written purchase specifications. The following section is intended to aid the housekeeper in formulating those specifications.

CLEANING SUPPLIES

Nonchemical cleaning supplies include brushes, brooms, buckets, mops, pads, rags, and wringers. Although these supplies look fairly simple and straightforward, there are a number of features to look for when selecting them.

Brooms and Brushes

Common varieties of brooms include push brooms, corn brooms, and whisk brooms. The role of a broom is to remove large particles of soil from hard and resilient floors. Good push brooms will have two rows of bristles. The front row will have heavy-duty bristles designed to remove stubborn, large particles of dirt and debris. The second row will have fine, split-tip bristles designed to remove fine particles of dirt and debris. Many good push brooms have a steel brush hood that allows the operator to change worn brushes. One company even has a built-in shock absorber between the brush hood and the handle to prevent broken wooden handles.

The better scrub brushes have U-joints so that they can be used at any angle. This is particularly helpful when cleaning baseboards. Some models have rubber blades for drying surfaces.

Mop Buckets

Buckets are made of three basic materials: galvanized steel, stainless steel, and structural foamed plastic. Plastic buckets do not rust and are the most inexpensive to make, but some scratch, and dirt builds up in the scratches, making them permanently "grungy." Stainless steel buckets are typically the most expensive. The "Cadillac" of mop buckets has to be the KaiMotion SUV™. This ergonomic microfiber mopping system can be used to apply floor finishes, strippers, and degreasers; to damp mop floors; and to clean walls (Figure 6.13). With its flat mop system, you no longer have to empty dirty mop water.

Another innovative system incorporates the bucket into the mop handle. The Bucketless Mop from

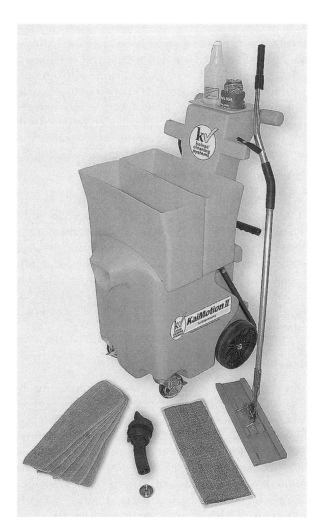

FIGURE 6.13 This bucket has an easy-lift handle that will lighten the 10-gallon load by two-thirds.

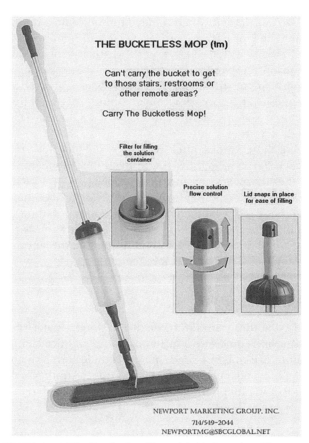

THE BUCKETLESS MOP (tm)

Can't carry the bucket to get to those stairs, restrooms or other remote areas?

Carry The Bucketless Mop!

Filter for filling the solution container

Precise solution flow control

Lid snaps in place for ease of filling

NEWPORT MARKETING GROUP, INC.
714/549-2044
NEWPORTMG@SBCGLOBAL.NET

FIGURE 6.14 The Bucketless Mop with its flat microfiber mop head is a labor-saving device that eliminates the chore of hauling a bucket upstairs.

Newport Marketing Group (Figure 6.14) is a win-win for guestroom attendants (GRAs). This system can easily attach to a housekeeper's cart and enables housekeepers to avoid having to clean the bathroom floor on their hands and knees with rags, thus avoiding stress injuries and saving time and money. The microfiber mop heads can be quickly changed out to avoid cross contamination of hospital rooms. The device can also serve as a dust mop or a floor finish applicator with only a quick change of pads. Before mopping, a quick sweep with a corn broom is still recommended, to gather up hair and large particles of soil.

Wringers

Mop wringers squeeze in one of two directions: sideways or downward. Downward wringers are better but more expensive. Wringers are made of either steel or plastic. Plastic is less expensive, but it wears out much faster than the metal wringers. Wringers can be purchased by size or in a "one-size-fits-all" size.[9]

Wet Mops

The flat microfiber mop head is destined to make all other wet mop heads obsolete. The fibers have a diameter of .01–.02 denier, which is much thinner than a human hair. The fabric is a blend of polyester (70–80 percent) and polymide (20–30 percent), which is a by-product of nylon. Appendix H contains an article originally published in the February 2003 issue of *Executive Housekeeping Today*, describing a study of microfiber flat-mop systems at the University of California–Davis Medical Center.

Wash wet mops after each use and do not apply bleach to the mop; bleach will speed the disintegration of the fibers. Wet mops can be purchased in a variety of colors for color-coding purposes. Microfiber mops can be easily changed out in a hospital setting to avoid cross contamination. Cross contamination is the transportation of germs from one area to another through such activities as mopping floors.

Mop Handles

Mop handles can be made from wood, metal, and plastic and come with a variety of features. Quick-change clamps are one welcome option. Handles are available in 54-inch, 60-inch, and 63-inch lengths.[10] Another is the telescoping mop handle, which can also be used to dust walls and ceilings.

Dust Mops and Dust Cloths

The traditional dust mop, feather duster, and lamb's wool duster are all destined for extinction, to be replaced by microfiber technology. Microfiber does not push the dust around; it picks it up and holds it until it is released by washing in soap and hot water. Figure 6.15 is a

High Quality Split Microfiber

FIGURE 6.15 Microfiber will increase worker productivity and reduce chemical costs. *(Photo courtesy of Newport Marketing Group, Inc., Costa Mesa, California.)*

cross-section photograph of a single microfiber thread (note how the microscopic thread is split to enhance pickup). Figure 6.16 shows how microfiber cloths absorb soil. Microfiber not only picks up dust, it will also pick up 97 to more than 99 percent of all bacteria on a surface.

Appendix H contains an excellent introductory article on microfiber and a companion piece that describes the maintenance of microfiber cloths. Both appeared in the February 2003 issue of *Executive Housekeeping Today*. Microfiber cloths are designed to perform specific tasks such as window and mirror cleaning, dusting, and the cleaning of bathroom fixtures. They also come in different colors and shapes (Figure 6.17) so guestroom attendants can be trained to avoid cross contamination.

Dust mops are meant to be used daily to remove dust and small particles of soil from the floor. Daily dusting helps to protect the floor's finish by removing small abrasive particles that erode the finish. Dust mops range in width from 12 to 60 inches.

Squeegees

There are two types of squeegees: floor and window. Floor squeegees have a much heavier rubber than the window variety. Window squeegees come with a number of attractive features, from telescoping handles that enable a worker to clean a third-story exterior window without the aid of scaffolding or a ladder, to U-joints that allow a worker to squeegee a window at an angle.

Pads, Bonnets, and Brushes

Floor machines and burnishers use floor pads, bonnets, and brushes. Pads are made from either natural or synthetic fibers. Floor pads have a universal color code so that users can tell at a glance if they are using the right pad for a particular application (Chapter 5). Bonnets are made of yarn and are intended to be used on a floor machine to spray clean carpets. Floor machine brushes are used to shampoo carpets. The fibers are synthetic.

Ultraviolet Lamps

Ultraviolet lamps or black lights constitute just one more small but important weapon in the executive housekeeper's war against dirt. In a dark room, an ultraviolet light will cause certain materials to fluoresce (that is, to glow in the dark). Among the substances that have been found to glow are flavins; the riboflavin vitamin B is the most well known. Other examples include soap scum and urine. Bacteria often accumulate where there are high concentrations of flavins. Hence, glowing spots in the guestroom and bathroom are considered to be unclean areas.

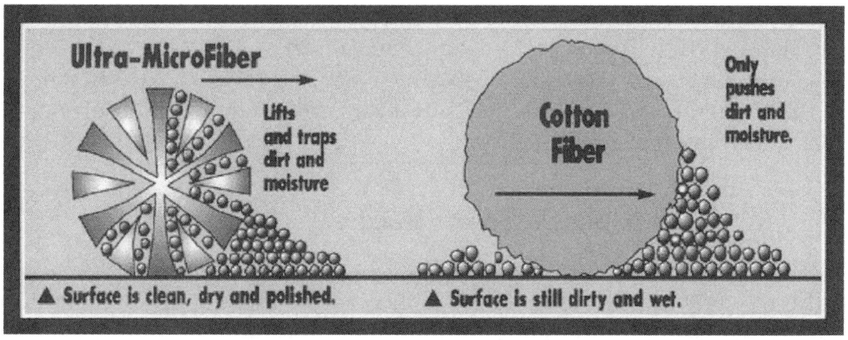

FIGURE 6.16 The split microfiber is far more effective than ordinary cotton at picking up soil. *(Photo courtesy of Newport Marketing Group, Inc., Costa Mesa, California.)*

Housekeepers should not use these lights to play "gotcha" with the staff, but as an aid to correcting problem areas. Staff can be trained to use these black lights to see where they should concentrate their efforts.

Many sophisticated travelers also carry these lights to inspect their rooms for soil and bacteria. They are often for sale in the consumer catalogs found in the pockets of airline seats.

CLEANING EQUIPMENT

When purchasing housekeeping equipment, remember that many products will seem to fulfill a requirement but will fall short of lasting needs. The challenge is to find the right piece of equipment, one that is of a quality that will withstand continuous use with limited maintenance, and that will be the most cost-effective in the use of resources.

The decision as to what equipment best meets the needs of the department is usually made as job descriptions are being written. Quality, however, becomes another issue. Some managements stress price of purchase rather than quality of product and do not consider the overall value of more substantial equipment. Other managements will demand a high quality of equipment for employees and will then expect the highest standards of cleanliness. The executive housekeeper should presume that management desires the highest level of cleanliness possible and expect that workers be supplied with the wherewithal to accomplish the task.

Many product suppliers also act as equipment representatives. When new hotels open, suppliers will seek appointments to present their products and equipment lines. A manufacturer's representative who can be depended on is an asset worth considering when purchasing equipment.

The executive housekeeper should have the final say regarding the type, quantity, and quality of equipment required for cleaning the guestrooms and public areas of the rooms department. Equipment purchases will be substantial and will therefore require the utmost care and consideration in selection. An analysis of the various items of equipment listed in Table 4.1 is appropriate for a hotel the size of our hypothetical model. General information about this equipment follows.

Housekeeper's Cart

The housekeeper's cart is an essential piece of equipment for the vast majority of hotels. There should be one cart for each section of rooms. Ideally, the cart must be large enough to carry *all* of the supplies that the GRA might readily be expected to use in the workday. However, with the trend to more linens—such as three sheets on each bed, a duvet cover that is washed every time there is a checkout,

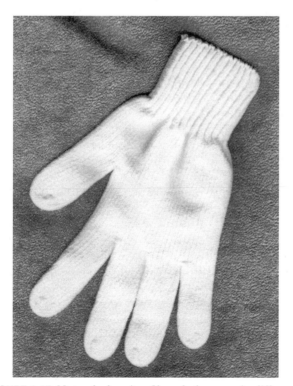

FIGURE 6.17 Not only do microfiber cloths come in different colors, but they also can be made into dusting gloves. *(Photos courtesy of Newport Marketing Group, Inc., Costa Mesa, California.)*

and six or more pillows on the same bed; it becomes physically impossible to load everything a GRA needs for the day on one cart. Bath linens may not have increased in number, but the thickness of these linens certainly has, which adds to the cart's storage limitations. Traditionally, most carts have also had two bags at either end of the cart, one for dirty linens and the other for trash. The housekeeping aide is supposed to stop by each GRA's cart several times during the shift to remove the dirty linen. However, there is now so much dirty linen out of a checkout room that one room can effectively fill the linen bag. So GRAs will often pile the dirty laundry on top of the cart, where it can cross-contaminate clean linen, glasses, and guest amenities. Either housekeeping aides must redouble their efforts to remove this dirty linen before it needs to be piled on the cart's top, or a new way must be found. Enter Dan Freeman, Vice President of Innovations Manufacturing & Distributing of Henderson, Nevada. Freeman has invented a canvas bag that comes in an assortment of colors and can even have a hotel's logo printed on its side.

The open bag is placed on the guestroom floor and the GRA loads it with dirty linen. Drawstrings close the bag, which can then be placed outside the cleaned room in the hall for the housekeeping aide to pick up. No muss, no fuss, and the dirty linen has to be touched only once on its way to the laundry. Since the bags are to be laundered too, Freeman estimates a par stock of two will suffice for most properties.

Since the cart is large and may be heavily loaded, it must be maneuverable and capable of being pushed by someone weighing less than 100 pounds. Surprisingly, such carts do exist. Quality housekeepers' carts are maneuverable, with fixed wheels at one end and castered wheels at the opposite end. The solution lies in quality caster and ball-bearing pneumatic wheels. One of Innovation's cart lines has six wheels. Two sets of wheels on either end are castered and a third set of fixed wheels in the center. This cart can almost turn on that proverbial dime.

Carts should have deep shelves, detachable linen sacks and rubbish sacks, storage for a vacuum, and a top that is partitioned for amenities, room keys, and guestroom brochures. Locking drawers are an added plus. Figure 6.18 shows a modular housekeeper's cart that comes with many options, including rolling corner bumpers to protect walls. Figure 6.19 shows some of the different modules that can be added, such as glass racks, vacuum brackets, and top amenity organizers.

At the Bellagio, the housekeepers' carts made by Innovations Manufacturing & Distributing are decorated with the same design used in the wall coverings. One of the hallmarks of a world-class property is the obsessive attention to detail (Figure 6.20).

Porters' trash and supplies carts are also available to support the work of lobby and public area housekeepers (Figure 6.21).

Housekeeper's Vacuum

There are many ways to provide vacuums for cleaning guestrooms. Some hotels have tank-type vacuums for guestroom attendants. Others have tank-type vacuums installed on the housekeeper's carts, with 24-foot vacuum hoses that will reach from the hotel corridor through the entire room. The main concern about tank vacuums being permanently installed on the housekeepers' carts, however, is the noise that permeates the hallway when one or more vacuums are in use. The vacuum most readily seen in hotel operations remains the upright vacuum with bag and belt-driven beater brush (Figure 6.22).

An improved variation of the single-motor upright vacuum pictured in Figure 6.22 is the dual-motor vacuum shown in Figure 6.23. One motor drives the beater brush, and a second motor provides the suction. These dual-motor varieties often have a convenient built-in hose for cleaning corners and upholstery.

Recent studies have called into question the need for beater brushes or beater bars and upright vacuum cleaners. A very interesting study by Robert Woellner, senior scientist for Quality Environmental Services and Technologies of Denver, Colorado, appears in Appendix I.

When shopping for a commercial-grade vacuum, consideration should be given to the rated volume of airflow in cubic feet per minute (cfm). The higher the cfm, the better. There is also *water lift*, or *static lift*, which is a measure of the vacuum's force. It is the force applied that can lift a column of water x number of inches. Again, the higher the number, the better. The third measure of performance is filtration efficiency. Little is accomplished if a vacuum with high airflow and tremendous force is spewing the dust and particles out the other end, ultimately resoiling the carpet and degrading the IAQ. Some vacuums on the market have "high-efficiency particulate air" (HEPA) filters that can effectively stop 99.8 percent of all particulates 0.3 microns or larger from passing through the filter. HEPA filters are enormously expensive, but reasonably priced filtration systems on vacuums are available with only a slightly reduced filtration capability. Other criteria are price, maintenance, and noise levels.

The Carpet and Rug Institute (CRI) now evaluates and certifies vacuums. The CRI certification carried

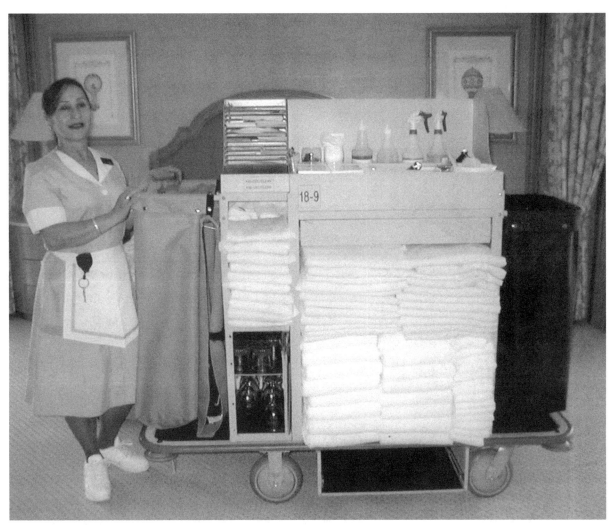

FIGURE 6.18 This modular cart has been designed to meet the special needs of the Bellagio Hotel. *(Photo courtesy of Innovations Manufacturing & Distributing, Henderson, Nevada)*

by a vacuum assures the user that the machine will remove dirt, will protect the operator and others nearby from particulate emissions, and will not harm the carpet. An article by Jennifer C. Jones in Appendix I, entitled "Raising the Bar for Vacuum Effectiveness," explains in greater detail the CRI's certification program. Appendix I also includes two articles by the president of ProTeam, Larry Shideler, entitled "What Your Customers Need to Know about Vacuum Filtration" and "The Science of Suction." These articles are all groundbreaking works on the science of vacuums and vacuuming.

Traditionally, there should be one vacuum cleaner for each GRA, one for each public-area housekeeper,

and a 10 percent complement of spare vacuums. However, there has been considerable speculation about how to reduce vacuum cleaner expenditures and, at the same time, increase the productivity of guestroom cleaning. Backpack vacuums are recognized as being much faster to use than the traditional push-pull varieties, but performing other functions, such as making the bed, while wearing a backpack vacuum would be too cumbersome. Perhaps one or two members of a housekeeping team, such as the housekeeping aide, could perform all of the vacuuming. Time-and-motion studies would have to be done, but there may be an opportunity to cut back on vacuum expenditures, increase productivity, and actually reduce

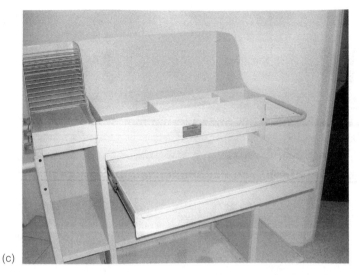

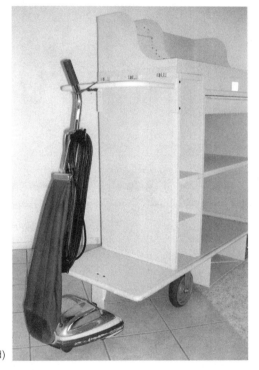

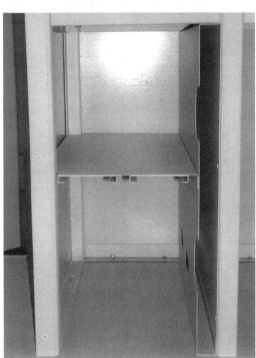

FIGURE 6.19 Optional modules for a housekeeper's cart include rotating bumpers to protect walls, glass storage, top amenity organizer with slots for room brochures and pull-out drawer, and vacuum bracket. *(Photo courtesy of Innovations Manufacturing & Distributing, Henderson, Nevada.)*

FIGURE 6.20 The Bellagio's carts are not only functional, but aesthetically appealing. Notice the neoprene bumper that protects the cart from doorknobs when pushed through a door with an automatic closer. *(Photo courtesy of Bellagio, MGM Mirage™, Las Vegas, Nevada.)*

FIGURE 6.21 A Public Area Trash/Porter Cart with choice of custom laminate or artwork on the side panels. *(Photo courtesy of Innovations Manufacturing & Distributing, Henderson, Nevada.)*

FIGURE 6.22 The Sensor XP® from Windsor Industries is a single-motor vacuum with attached wand and onboard accessories, which carries CRI certification. *(Photo courtesy of Windsor Industries, a Castle Rock Company, Englewood, Colorado.)*

FIGURE 6.23 The Versamatic® is a dual-motor unit from Windsor, with crevice tools and an attached wand. It too carries CRI certification. *(Photo courtesy of Windsor Industries, a Castle Rock Company, Englewood, Colorado.)*

FIGURE 6.24 The CRI-certified Wave® vacuum has an onboard wand and accessories, two 802-watt motors, a four-stage filtration system, and a 28-inch brush. *(Photo courtesy of Windsor Industries, a Castle Rock Company, Englewood, Colorado.)*

FIGURE 6.25 The 3640 Walk-behind Sweeper from Tennant Company adapts to a variety of users and environments and works at speeds significantly faster than hand sweeping. *(Photo courtesy of Tennant Company, Minneapolis, Minnesota.)*

some of the stress and strain associated with housekeeping activities, all at the same time.

Corridor Vacuum

Housekeeping teams have section housekeeping aides whose responsibilities include vacuuming extensive sections of hotel corridors. Such areas have open expanses of carpet that require an efficient form of vacuuming. The section housekeeping aide should have a vacuum that can do this heavy and time-consuming task. A motor-driven vacuum with an 18-inch to 28-inch foot (Figure 6.24) is appropriate for this type of work.

All manufacturers of commercial equipment make models of this type and size, and each should be investigated and compared before purchase.

Space Sweepers and Vacuums

Space vacuums and sweepers (Figure 6.25) look like lawn mowers. Vacuum/sweepers can be used on carpets and hard floors. Approximately 30 inches wide or larger, motor-driven, and capable of picking up large items of debris, space vacuums are best suited for vacuuming the large expanses of carpet found in ballrooms, meeting rooms, and corridors. In a hotel the size

of our model, both the banquet and housekeeping departments need space vacuums. On occasion, one space vacuum can substitute for the other if one is out of commission. There will be times when the catering department will need to use both space vacuums.

FIGURE 6.26 The Titan™ Wet Dry vacuums come in 8-, 16-, and 20-gallon models with attachments. *(Photo courtesy of Windsor Industries, a Castle Rock Company, Englewood, Colorado.)*

Wet Vacuums

Wet vacuums (Figure 6.26) are an absolute necessity in hotel operations. Even though wet vacuums can be used for both wet and dry vacuuming, they are usually maintained in their wet configuration and are therefore ready for any spill emergency. There should be two wet vacuums on the property, one in the banquet department and one in housekeeping, both clean and ready for use.

Wet vacuums are also required when large areas of noncarpeted floor are being stripped and cleaned. They greatly aid in water removal, making such operations more efficient.

Backpack Vacuums

Backpack vacuums (Figure 6.27) are very efficient for all types of cleaning, including floors, drapes, ceiling corners, furniture, and walls. The weight of the units has shrunk considerably, making them ergonomically viable. An excellent article on backpack vacuums by Chris Murray, entitled "Ergonomics and Backpack Vacs," appears in Appendix I. Backpacks are particularly effective on stairs and in public areas (lobbies, hallways, restaurants, meeting rooms, and other high-traffic areas).

Electric Brooms

Electric brooms are lightweight vacuums that have no motor-driven beater brush. Electric brooms are used primarily for very light vacuuming and are sometimes used in place of the housekeeper's vacuum. Electric brooms are excellent for quick touch-ups on carpet and hard floors or for sand and spills when full vacuuming is not required. They should not be relied upon to replace the housekeeper's vacuum.

Single-Disc Floor Machines

The single-disc floor machine, also known as the buffer or scrubber, is the most versatile item of equipment in the housekeeper's inventory. This machine can scrub floors, strip floor finishes, spray buff floors, sand wood floors, polish floors, and shampoo carpets. Machines are available in 17-, 18-, 19-, 20-, and 21-inch models. These machines will accommodate pads, brushes, and bonnets. As has been noted already, different pads are

FIGURE 6.27 The Super CoachVac™ from ProTeam has an impressive 150-cfm airflow and a 10-quart capacity, but weighs only 10 pounds. The unit also has CRI certification. *(Photo courtesy of ProTeam, Boise, Idaho.)*

FIGURE 6.28 The Merit™ Dual Speed Floor Machine has a 175-rpm speed for scrubbing and stripping, and a 300-rpm speed for spray buffing. *(Photo courtesy of Windsor Industries, a Castle Rock Company, Englewood, Colorado.)*

designed for different jobs, from stripping to buffing (Figure 6.28).

Brushes are used to scrub floors and shampoo carpets, and bonnets are used to "bonnet clean" carpets (described in Chapter 5). When selecting a standard single-disc scrubber, do not select too small a scrubber. A larger machine will cover an area faster, thus reducing labor costs. Depending on the model, a single-disc floor machine will operate between 175 rpm and 350 rpm.

Burnishers

Burnishers or ultrahigh-speed (UHS) buffers resemble single-disc floor machines, but they operate at between 350 rpm and 2500 rpm. They were developed to polish the new harder floor finishes now on the market. Unlike the pads of single-disc floor machines, the pad of a UHS buffer does not rest entirely upon the floor. Only the front part of the pad comes in contact with the floor; the rest of the weight is distributed to the wheels. Many models have caster wheels in the front of the machine to distribute the weight. UHS buffers operate in a straight line, whereas traditional scrubbers operate from side to side. There are battery and propane models that enable the operator to cover vast areas without the need for troublesome electric cords. Propane models are noisy, they create noxious fumes, and they present a possible fire hazard. They are illegal in some municipalities.

Recent IAQ studies have shown burnishers to be a significant source of indoor air pollution. As they grind the floor finish to a high gloss, they blow the floor finish particulates into the air. The individual at greatest risk for lung problems is the operator of the equipment, but others in the vicinity are also exposed. Only a few units come with dust-control systems. The astute housekeeper should purchase only those units that have these systems. Pictured in Figure 6.29 is an ultra-high-speed buffer with such a system.

Automatic Scrubbers

The purpose of the automatic scrubber is to scrub or strip hard and resilient floors. The units apply a cleaning or stripping solution, scrub the floor, and vacuum up the dirty floor solution in one continuous

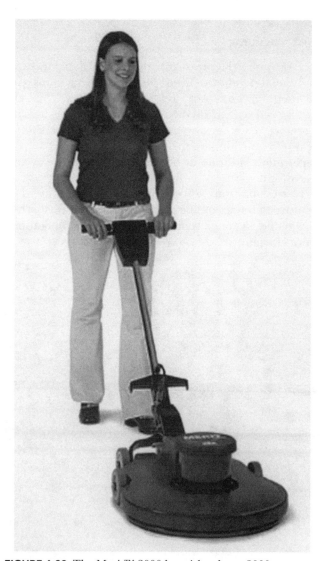

FIGURE 6.29 The Merit™ 2000 burnisher has a 2000-rpm speed and a "smart handle" that eliminates the need for a front wheel. *(Photo courtesy of Windsor Industries, a Castle Rock Company, Englewood, Colorado.)*

FIGURE 6.30 The Sabre Cutter™ with Squeeze Play has a cleaning path of 36 inches, which can be reduced to 26 inches for narrow aisles. *(Photo courtesy of Windsor Industries, a Castle Rock Company, Englewood, Colorado.)*

FIGURE 6.31 The Voyager E from Windsor® features a 40-gallon solution tank that can clean 8100 square feet of carpet per hour. *(Photo courtesy of Windsor Industries, a Castle Rock Company, Englewood, Colorado.)*

operation. Most units are self-propelled. Some have attachments that turn them into wet/dry vacuums, and others can also be used to buff dry floors. In addition to electric-cord models, there are battery-driven models. The better battery-driven models are preferred because the constant plugging and unplugging of electric cords is an inconvenience and reduces employee productivity. Automatic scrubbers come in a wide variety of sizes, from widths of 17 inches to more than 4 feet.

When purchasing a machine to clean halls and aisles, consider the number of passes necessary to clean a hall. If a machine cleans aisles in the same number of passes as a smaller machine, then there is no benefit in paying the additional cost for the larger machine. Figure 6.30 shows an automatic scrubber in action.

Wet-Extraction Systems

Wet-extraction machines are sometimes referred to as "steam" or hot-water carpet machines. These terms are actually misnomers, for these machines never produce steam, and hot water is not often used because of the shrinkage and fading risk.

There has been some recent research on wet extraction, confirming the experiences operators have had: the more water discharged and picked up, the more dirt extracted from the carpet. Most truck-mounted extraction units and the John Downey Company's Steamin Demon™ have a flow rate of more than three gallons per minute. Tank machines typically discharge only a half-gallon per minute.

However, a number of self-contained tank units have motorized beater brushes that help to dislodge dirt. The self-contained tank machines may be electric-cord or battery-powered (Figure 6.31) Figure 6.32 shows the John Downey Company's Steamin Demon™, a tankless high-flow extractor that utilizes the operator's own water supply and discharge into the sewer. Fans are often employed to help dry the carpet. A carpet should not be used, and nothing should be placed on the carpet, until it is perfectly dry. This requires taking the carpet out of commission for two to four hours. A carpet that is not properly dried may support mold growth and, if put back into use wet, will become soiled very quickly. The inconvenience of wet extraction is offset by its benefits. There is no better way to extract soil from a carpet.

Dry foam carpet cleaners brush a low-moisture foam into the carpet that is vacuumed up after it has been allowed to briefly dry. It does leave a residual amount of foam in the carpet. Units come in a variety of widths, from 12 inches to more than 28 inches. Many have attachments for upholstery.

Dry Powder Systems

Dry powder systems normally use three pieces of equipment. First, the dry powder is laid down on the carpet with an applicator. Then a brush unit works the powder into the carpet; this dislodges the soil from the carpet fibers. The powder is then vacuumed up using a standard vacuum cleaner. As mentioned in Chapter 5, the Host Dry Extraction Carpet Cleaning System (Figure 6.33) allows the carpet to be walked on immediately following cleaning.

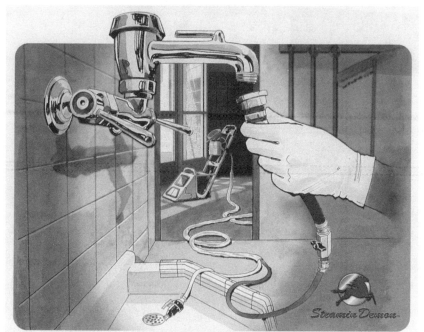

"The Steamin Demon™'s Secret Is In Your Service Closet."

FIGURE 6.32 The Steamin Demon™ by the John Downey Company. The single-pump model comes with 250 feet of supply/discharge hose. The company also makes a dual-pump model with 400 feet of hose. *(Illustration courtesy of the John Downey Company, Granville, Ohio.)*

FIGURE 6.33 The Host Dry Extraction Carpet Cleaning System. *(Photo courtesy of Racine Industries, Inc.)*

Convertible Mobile Shelving

Convertible mobile shelving is unique in its versatility and construction. (A typical convertible mobile shelving unit, shown in Figure 15.28, is discussed further in Chapter 15.)

A shelving unit in a satellite linen room, with shelves adjusted to receive soiled linen, acts as a storage hamper for used linen. At the end of the day the soiled linen is moved to the laundry in its own conveyor. In the meantime, another unit, with shelves adjusted to receive clean linen being processed in the laundry, may be moved to the satellite linen room so GRAs can load their housekeepers' carts for the next day's operation. Once emptied, the shelves are repositioned for a repeat of the cycle the next day. Mobile convertible shelving not only removes the need for permanent shelving in the laundry and satellite linen rooms, it reduces the three-step task of moving linen from shelf to conveyor to shelf to a one-step loading process. There should be at least two units for each satellite linen room.

Trash-Handling Equipment

Another piece of equipment used by the section housekeeping aide is some form of conveyor, whereby rubbish and other materials may be moved from various sections of the hotel to a disposal area.

A trash cart that looks anything but "trashy" is pictured in Figure 6.34. The cart may be used to remove soiled linen several times each day from housekeepers' carts to the satellite linen room, or it may be used to carry rubbish sacks from maid's carts for emptying. A great deal of moving of material supplies and rubbish occurs each day in each section of the hotel. Each housekeeping

FIGURE 6.34 These beauties can be used to transport trash or dirty linens and the guest will never know what is inside. *(Photo courtesy of Innovations Manufacturing & Distributing, Henderson, Nevada.)*

team (section housekeeping aide) will therefore need a conveyor for moving material.

Sewing Machines

A sewing machine of commercial quality is useful in the main linen room. This sewing machine will be used to repair drapes and bedspreads and may be used to make certain fabric items. The machine must be of commercial quality, because one item requiring repair will be heavy blackout drapes. No automatic or multiple-stitch machines are required.

Glass Washers

Depending on whether guestroom drinking glasses will be made of plastic or glass, and depending on the availability of the hotel dish room dishwasher, the housekeeping department may need its own glass washer. In hotels of major size (1000 rooms) a properly equipped linen room should have a glass washer to prevent using labor to move 15 or 20 cases of glasses to the kitchen each night.

Glass washers are expensive and are major items of equipment. The use of real glasses as opposed to plastic ones is a matter of quality as well as economics, and the multiple uses of glasses justify the expense of a glass washer.

Guest Supplies

A guest supply is any item that is conducive to the guest's material comfort and convenience. The term **amenity** is commonly used to identify luxury items that a hotel gives away to its guests at no extra charge, although the cost of those items is often hidden in the room rate.

There are also those guest supplies that are expected to be used up by the guest that cannot be classified as luxuries even at the most spartan budget property. We shall categorize those items as **guest expendables**.

Then there are items essential to the guestroom that are not normally used up or taken away by the guest. These items shall be referred to as **guest essentials**.

Guest loan items are those guest supplies that are not normally found in the guestroom, but are commonly available to the guest when requested.

These categories of guest supplies are fairly arbitrary, but they represent an attempt to distinguish those items that are necessary in every room from those items that are discretionary purchases.

Quite often the rate to be charged for each guestroom will have a bearing on the quantity and quality of these guest supplies. Although the guest supplies are not particularly expensive if considered on an item-by-item basis, their aggregate can add substantially to a hotel's costs. Today, many budget properties are scaling back on their amenity packages. Yet luxury hotels can ill afford to reduce their amenity packages. Many think that a reduction in the amenity package would seriously reduce the perceived value of many luxury hotel rooms.[11]

Guest supplies are a major storage and security concern. Some items such as guest pens, stationery, and envelopes appear in such great quantity and appear to be of such little significance that employees who are not well trained may feel that their use at home is quite acceptable. Other items of higher value (such as portion packages of guest laundry detergents and bleaches) may require even greater security in storage. In such cases, locked-cage storage (inside storage rooms) is in order. If not properly controlled, the indiscriminate use and negligent storage of guest supplies can become a costly expense.

AMENITY PACKAGES

Although amenities extend well beyond the guestroom (free breakfasts, recreation facilities, and so on), our discussion encompasses only those amenities that are found in the guestroom.

Bath Amenities

When members of the general public think of guestroom amenities, they typically think of bathroom amenity packages. Table 6.1 contains a listing of common amenity items.

There are two opposing schools of thought when it comes to bathroom amenities. One believes that the

guest appreciates seeing name-brand products on the vanity counter, whereas the other is of the opinion that the products should be "branded" with the hotel's logo. Fortunately, a number of suppliers can arrange (for a price) to print both.

What should be of even greater concern to the hotel is the cost-benefit relationship of amenities. Far too often the management of a hotel believes that customer loyalty

(a)

(b)

FIGURE 6.35 There is nothing institutional or pedestrian about the look of these dispensers, from the AVIVA™ line by Dispenser Amenities. *(Photos courtesy of Dispenser Amenities Inc., London, Ontario.)*

TABLE 6.1 Bathroom Amenity Items

Aftershave	Hair conditioner
Bath gel	Hand lotion
Bath salts	Loofah sponges
Body oils	Mouthwash
Body powder	Nail clippers
Bubble bath	Perfumes
Colognes	Razors
Cosmetics	Scissors
Deodorants	Sewing kit
Deodorant soap	Shampoo
Emery boards	Shaving cream
Fabric wash	Shoehorn
Face lotions	Shoe mitt
Face soap	Shower cap
Facial mud packs	Tanning lotion
Glycerin soap	

(a)

(b)

FIGURE 6.36 An elegant display of house-branded bath amenities at the Bellagio are shown (top) but the bottom photo shows special bath amenities found only in the "Villa Suites" at Bellagio. Look very closely and you'll see that the label says "Hermes." Only the very best will do for the highest of high rollers. *(Photos courtesy of Bellagio, MGM Mirage™, Las Vegas, Nevada.)*

can be won by throwing money into an amenity program. Management would be better served if it first analyzed what is truly important to the guests.

Another major concern in regard to amenities is the waste they create. A number of prestigious hotel chains have switched to bulk dispensers in the room, eliminating all of the thousands of small bottles from the waste stream. At the Saunders Hotels in Boston, the savings generated from buying shampoos and conditioners in bulk is reinvested in the product, giving the guest higher-quality soaps and shampoos. Dispensers need not have an institutional look (Figure 6.35), and many do have locks preventing anyone from compromising the products.

At some hotels, there is nothing but the best in bath amenities for their guests. Some, like the Bellagio, may even have different tiers of amenities (Figure 6.36).

TABLE 6.2 Guest amenities

Bathrobes	Flowers
Chocolate	Free in-room beverages
Clothes sachets	Free snacks
Coffeemaker	In-room movies
Corkscrews	Luxury stationery
Expensive pens	Quality pens

Guestroom Amenities

Guestroom amenities are items that can be found in the guest's bedroom. Table 6.2 is a list of common guestroom amenities.

GUEST ESSENTIALS

Guest essentials are intended to remain with the hotel after the guest departs. Unfortunately, this is not always the case. One particularly troublesome area for guests and the hotel is the question of the clothes hanger. Years ago, hotels eliminated the standard wooden hanger because these hangers frequently found their way into the guest's luggage. They were replaced by the knob-headed hanger, which was not stolen, but it was and continues to be a source of irritation to the guest. Enter the hanger with an undersized hook. This compromise item has a hook that is too small to fit over a standard clothes rack, but it is far easier to use.

A colleague of the author's, who is a designer by trade and a frequent business traveler, once suggested a guest essential that would warm the heart of any traveler who uses a suit bag: a small but well-anchored hook opposite the clothes rack or closet in a hotel room. These hooks would be placed approximately 6 feet 6 inches from the floor and would serve as hooks for suit bags. Unloading a suit bag from inside the closet or from the bed, contends the designer, is extremely inconvenient. Although a few hotels have recognized this need, they are an extremely small minority.

One final note on guest essentials: The hotel logo will often make these items souvenirs and, as such, will cause them to disappear at alarming rates. If it is decided that this is an effective form of "advertising," then perhaps the cost for these items should be shared with other departments in the hotel, particularly the marketing department.

A list of guest essentials appears in Table 4.2.

GUEST EXPENDABLES

Guest expendables, those items expected to be used up or taken by the guest, are sometimes supplied by organizations other than the housekeeping department. For example, laundry bags and laundry slips are usually supplied by the cleaning establishment that provides valet service. Many guest expendables (such as soaps) are not necessarily used up or taken away upon the guest's departure but are replenished when the room is made ready for a new guest. All expendable items are normally inventoried and stored by the housekeeping department.

Guest expendables are also listed in Table 4.2.

GUEST LOAN ITEMS

Guest loan items are not maintained in the guestroom but are available if requested by the guest on a receipted loan basis. Guest loan items are usually stored in the main linen room (housekeeping center of operations) and, when requested, are delivered to the guest with a receipt form. Such receipts should specify when the item may be picked up so as not to convey the idea that they are free for the taking.

CONCLUSION

The financial success of any institution is not necessarily the result of a few isolated strategic decisions. It is often accomplished through hundreds of small decisions concerning such minutiae as the selection of the right soap cake for the guestroom, the purchase of the right size of floor machine, and using a bathroom cleaner that will not harm fixtures. The professional housekeeper must stay abreast of technological developments in housekeeping supplies and equipment and must base all purchase and use decisions on objective fact finding, not on the hype of smooth-talking vendors.

KEY TERMS AND CONCEPTS

Detergents
Disinfectants
Pathogenic microorganisms
Dwell time
Bacteriostat
Quaternary ammonium
  compounds
Idophors
Hypochlorites
Hydrogen peroxide
Phenolic compounds
Sanitizer

Stock-outs
All-purpose cleaners
Odor-pair neutralization
Nosocomial infection
Antichlors
Sours
Nonionic detergent
Cationic
Petroleum naphtha solvents
Flash point
Volatile organic compound (VOC)

Indoor air quality (IAQ)
Defoamers
Metal cross-linked polymer finishes
Thermoplastic
HazComm
Material safety data sheets
  (MSDSs)
Amenity
Guest expendables
Guest essentials
Guest loan items

DISCUSSION AND REVIEW QUESTIONS

1. What amenities would you feature in a budget hotel property? In a midsized property? In a luxury property?
2. Explain the advantages and disadvantages of relying primarily on an all-purpose chemical cleaner.

3. In which areas of the hotel should a housekeeper use a disinfectant cleaner? In which areas would a sanitizer be appropriate?
4. What constitutes a "green" chemical?

NOTES

1. Green Seal, "Who We Are and What We Do," available at *www.greenseal.org/about.htm;* accessed May 20, 2003.
2. Environmental Protection Agency, "Pesticides: Topical & Chemical Fact Sheets," available at *www.epa.gov/pesticides/factsheets/antimic.htm;* accessed October 30, 2006.
3. Michael A. Berry, *Protecting the Built Environment: Cleaning for Health* (Chapel Hill, NC: Tricomm 21st Press, 1994), p. 81.
4. John J. Dykstra and Andrew R. Schwarz, "Sanitation and Disinfection Key to Infection Control," *Executive Housekeeping Today*, November 1990, p. 4.
5. "Handwashing: The Most Effective Method in Preventing Nosocomial Infection," *Executive Housekeeping Today*, May 1990, p. 12.
6. "Premeasured Detergents and Costs," *Executive Housekeeping Today*, November 1982, p. 12.
7. Ron Gillette, "Aerosols under Pressure," *Sanitary Maintenance*, June 1990, p. 22.
8. Christine O'Dwyer, "Chemical Warfare," *Lodging*, December 1990, pp. 59–60.
9. Buzz Flannigan, "Mopping Equipment," *Sanitary Maintenance*, May 1989, p. 42.
10. Buzz Flannigan, "Mopping Equipment," *Sanitary Maintenance*, May 1989, p. 80.
11. Christine O'Dwyer, "Should You Cut Amenities?" *Lodging*, October 1990, pp. 73–75.

CHAPTER 7

Material Planning: Bedding, Linens, and Uniforms

LEARNING OBJECTIVES

After studying the chapter, students should be able to:

1. Generate purchase specifications for bedding, including sheets, pillows, mattress pads, blankets, and bedspreads, for a certain class of hotel.
2. Develop purchase criteria for table linens, including proper size, fabric content, and method of construction.
3. Generate standards of selection for employee uniforms.
4. Generate criteria for bath linens for different classes of hotels.

This chapter is the fourth and final chapter devoted to the examination of material administration. In this chapter we explore **bedding**, **linens**, and **uniforms**. These are the highest-annual-cost items in hotel operational supply inventories. Initial supplies required to support operations of a commercial hotel the size of the model hotel can well exceed $200,000.

Before deciding on the requirements for an initial supply of bedding, linens, and uniforms, the professional housekeeper must have a thorough knowledge of the composition and construction of these items. The professional housekeeper must then establish purchase specifications for these items so that the purchased items complement the property rather than detract from it.

The intention of this chapter is to acquaint the housekeeper with the range of materials and manufacturing methods used to construct these textiles.

Bedding

Bedding encompasses all materials used in the making of a bed. This includes sheets, pillowcases, blankets, pillows, bedspreads, **dust ruffles**, comforters, and mattress covers.

SHEETS AND PILLOWCASES

Many small (inexpensive) hotels change linen once a week or when the guest departs, whichever occurs first.

For many years, people believed that a quality hotel should change guest linens daily, even when the guest was staying for more than one night.

Today, environmentally responsible hotels leave that choice up to the guest.

These linen reuse programs can save tremendous amounts of water and energy and can also prevent the introduction of additional laundry chemicals into the environment.

A hotel is not lowering its service standards when it gives a guest the option of reusing a towel or sleeping in the same sheets for a second night.

Fabric Materials and Construction

Although 100 percent cotton sheets are available, the overwhelming majority of hotels use a cotton/polyester (Dacron) blend. A 50/50 Dacron/cotton blend is thought to provide the optimum qualities of the natural and the synthetic fibers.

Cotton/polyester blends are more durable than straight cotton. After 100 launderings, cotton loses 35 to 40 percent of its tensile strength. Cotton/polyester blends lose 3 to 7 percent. Expected wear increases three and one-half times with a blend.

Blends do not shrink as much as cotton. If cotton is tumbled dry, it will shrink from 5 to 8 percent. A blend will shrink from 0 to 3 percent.

Blends are more economical to launder. They will retain 15 to 50 percent less water than a full cotton sheet after extraction. This feature means a faster drying time for blends.

Blends, unfortunately, are not softer. In recent years, many high-end hotels have been touting their high-thread-count, all-cotton sheets. T-250 and T-300 all-cotton sheets (see the following discussion of thread count) have replaced satin and silk sheets as a mark of luxury in many a first-class hotel. There are even T-700 Egyptian cotton sheet sets selling for more than $1000 a set. Some Ritz-Carltons advertise 300-thread-count sheets and feather beds in their rooms.

The cotton fibers in a sheet can be either combed or carded before spinning. If the fibers are carded, the fabric is rough and dull looking. Sheets that are made in this manner are called **muslin** sheets. If the fibers are combed, the fabric is much smoother and has a greater tensile strength. Sheets made from this process are called **percale** sheets.

The threads running lengthwise through the sheet are called the **warp**. The threads that run crosswise (horizontally) are called the **weft** or **filling**. The most common weave for sheets is called the plain weave. In this weave the warp and weft threads are perpendicular to each other.

Textiles are graded by the **thread count** and **tensile strength**. Housekeeping managers should specify a sheet that has a thread count of at least a T-180. This means that there are 180 threads in a one-inch-square piece of sheet. Ideally, there should be 94 threads in the warp and 86 in the weft. In any event, the numbers of warp and weft threads should be fairly close. The tensile strength is determined by the amount of weight it takes to tear a $1'' \times 3''$ piece of fabric.

Fabrics that come directly from a loom are called **gray goods**. This means that the fabric has not received a finishing treatment and is unsuitable for most purposes. *Finishing* is an all-inclusive term that is applied to a number of treatments that can be administered to a freshly woven fabric. Finishing includes washing, bleaching, and a process called **mercerizing**, in which the fabric is treated with caustic soda. Mercerizing swells the cotton fibers, increasing the strength and luster of the cloth. Fabric may also be Sanforized. **Sanforizing** preshrinks the cloth to prevent it from shrinking more than 1 percent during regular laundering. Cotton/polyester sheets are normally chemically modified during manufacturing to provide what is often called a "durable press" or "no-iron" effect. This fabric is smooth to begin with, stays smooth after laundering, and stays smooth while in use. Some finishing treatments are patented processes.

Sheets may be dyed, but white is the color choice for most hotels. If sheets are to be dyed, the best process is to dye the threads in a vat before weaving, but most of the time the completed fabric is dyed. White sheets will often have a colored thread or colored piping in the sheet to indicate the sheet's size for sorting. White sheets are preferred because they do not fade after laundering, nor do they require extra handling for sorting.

Sheets that have minor imperfections are called **seconds** and are usually marked with an "S" or have the manufacturer's tag cut off. Most seconds are perfectly acceptable in the majority of hotels.

Sheets and pillowcases are shipped in case lots. A case may have from a dozen to 12 gross in its contents, depending on the size of an order and a manageable weight per case. An example of how a linen case is marked is "2F/11 S-81 × 104." This information is translated as: 2 dozen first-quality, 11 dozen second-quality, double sheets.

Size

There are two sheet measurements. The **torn sheet** size is the size of the sheet before hemming. The **finished sheet** has a top and bottom hem. Institutional sheets normally have a 2-inch hem on the top and on the bottom. This is done so that the sheet does not require extra handling when folding or making the bed. Also, since the sheet can be reversed, it is hoped that both hems will wear evenly.

In Table 7.1 recommended sheet sizes for each mattress size are given in inches.

Fitted sheets are never used in commercial applications because they tear at their corners, they take up to three times the space in storage, and they can be used only as bottom sheets. Standard sheets, however, are more flexible, and larger standard sheets can be substituted for smaller sheets.

TABLE 7.1 Recommended Sheet Size (in inches)

Name	Mattress Size	Torn Sheet Size	Finished Sheet Size
Roll-away	33 × 76	66 × 104	66 × 99
Twin	39 × 76	66 × 104	66 × 99
Long twin	39 × 80	66 × 108	66 × 103
3/4 twin	48 × 76	66 × 104	66 × 99
Double	54 × 76	81 × 104	81 × 99
Long double	54 × 80	81 × 108	81 × 103
Queen	60 × 80	90 × 108	90 × 103
King	78 × 80	108 × 110	108 × 105
California king	72 × 80	108 × 115	108 × 110
Pillowcase	Standard	42 × 36	$20\frac{1}{2}$ × 30
Pillowcase	King	42 × 46	$20\frac{1}{2}$ × 40

Par Levels

The term **par** refers to standard, specific, or normal levels of stock. Linen pars are the standard levels of linen inventory required to support operations. "One par linen" is that quantity of each item required to completely outfit the guestrooms of the hotel one time. Since one par is hardly enough to have an efficient operation, a par number must be established to ensure adequate supply for smooth operations. (The GRA who has to wait for the laundry to finish laundering linen before a bed can be made hardly represents the efficient use of costly personnel or shows proper guest service. In addition, freshly laundered sheets should be allowed to "rest" for 24 hours before being put back into service. This will ensure their durability.)

Hotel properties having their own linen supply need to have $3\frac{1}{2}$ par linen on hand (1 par in the guestroom, 1 par soiled for tomorrow's laundry work requirement, 1 par clean for tomorrow's work in the guestrooms, and $\frac{1}{2}$ par new in storage). Hotels that must send their linen out to be laundered require 1 additional par because of out-and-in transit time.

BLANKETS

A blanket is an insulator; it keeps body heat in and cold air out. The best blanket is light in weight for comfort, but at the same time it should be a highly effective thermal insulator. Adding weight to a blanket does not necessarily make it a better insulator. The way a blanket is woven (how it traps the body heat) is what makes a blanket warm.

Fabric Materials and Construction

Although wool blankets have extremely high heat retention, they are much heavier than synthetic blankets. Synthetics such as polyester, acrylics, and nylon are the preferred fabrics for commercial blanket construction.

Another positive aspect of synthetic blankets is that they can be laundered as well as dry-cleaned. However, repeated launderings will tend to make blankets fade over time. If blankets are to be laundered, care must be taken to ensure that the blanket binding is made of the same material so that different fibers do not shrink at a different rate.

Blankets can be woven, needle-punched (similar to carpet tufting), or made through an electrostatic process. Woven blankets are normally more expensive, but they are not necessarily better insulators. One popular blanket variety is the thermal blanket. Thermal blankets are light woven blankets that have large air pockets for insulation. A regular blanket or sheet is placed on top of this blanket to increase its insulation coefficient.

Care should be taken to select blankets that are moisture permeable. A blanket that cannot transfer moisture will make the guest feel clammy and uncomfortable.

Above all, blankets should be fire retardant.

Some hotels provide electric blankets in their rooms. One school of thought holds that electric blankets are a service feature appreciated by many guests and that their use will decrease the hotel's heating costs. Other hoteliers believe that the theft rate of electric blankets is higher than that of ordinary blankets, that electric blankets are potential fire hazards, and that some of their guests hold that sleeping under an electric blanket is dangerous, unhealthy, or both.

Size

A blanket that is too short for a bed will wear prematurely from constant tugging by the guest. A blanket should be the length of the mattress, plus the thickness of the mattress, plus an additional 6 inches on each side for tucking. The width of the blanket should equal the width of the mattress, plus double the mattress thickness, plus 6 additional inches on each side for tucking.

The weight of a standard blanket will vary from $2\frac{1}{2}$ to $3\frac{1}{2}$ pounds. Lighter blankets should be used in the Southeast and Southwest, and the heavier blankets should be reserved for northern climates.

Par Levels

Blankets should be set at 1 par plus 10 percent in southern climates. In some northern climates, the par level may be as high as $2\frac{1}{2}$ par, where an extra blanket is placed in the room for each bed. This policy, however, often results in a higher theft rate.

BEDSPREADS, COMFORTERS, AND DUST RUFFLES

The bed is the focal point in most guestrooms; consequently, the bedspread is extremely important from a design perspective. The bedspread should complement the colors and other design elements in the room, but it should be durable and easy to maintain.

There are two main styles of bedspreads, throw spreads and tailored spreads. Tailored spreads fit the corners of the mattress snugly, whereas throw spreads bulge at the corners at the foot of the bed.

A bedspread may reach to the floor, covering the mattress, box springs, and the frame, or it may be a coverlet that covers only the mattress. If a coverlet is used, a dust ruffle is added to the bed to cover the box springs and the frame. A dust ruffle is a pleated cloth skirting that extends around the sides and foot of the bed. This decorative fabric is often sewn onto a muslin fabric that is placed between the mattress and box springs, thus holding the dust ruffle securely in place. The dust ruffle is normally cleaned when the bedspread is cleaned.

In a formal setting, the bed is also decorated with **shams**. Shams are pillow covers that match the fabric used in the bedspread.

In an informal setting, the bed is often covered with a quilted comforter that does double duty as a bedspread and a blanket.

Fabric Materials and Construction

Synthetic materials such as polyester have come to dominate the commercial bedspread market. Dust ruffles are often cotton/polyester blend products.

Most hotels would prefer to have a washable bedspread fabric that is guaranteed to maintain its shape through repeated washings. When purchasing new bedspreads, use one for a trial sample to ensure that it does

GREEN TIP
Replacing the hotel bedspread with a duvet is considered by many to be a "green" practice. The reason is that many hotels seldom wash those bedspreads. They are probable carriers of disease as well as extremely unappetizing items to the guest. Many guests who are "in the know" immediately throw them off the bed and into a corner of a room. A number of hotel brands switching to duvet covers have the policy of washing them every time a guest checks out.

not shrink, fade, or wrinkle. All spreads should be fire retardant.

Size

As has already been mentioned, a full-sized bedspread just touches the floor, while a **coverlet** or **duvet** covers the top of the dust ruffle. Coverlets are easier to handle and they fit better into the washer and dryer, but to place a dust ruffle on the bed requires the mattress to be removed.

Duvet covers are now preferred over any other bed covering in the better hotels. The better duvet covers are stuffed with goose down. Westin's "W" Hotels, a boutique chain, is often credited with popularizing the "overstuffed" bed look. Its bed linens have become so popular that they are available for sale to their guests.

Par Levels

The par level for bedspreads, coverlets, comforters, and dust ruffles should be 1 plus 10 percent.

PILLOWS

It seems as though everyone has a different opinion as to what is a good pillow. Some prefer soft pillows, and others prefer hard pillows. One camp holds that to be truly comfortable a pillow must be filled with goose down, whereas others contend that polyester will do just as well.

Natural Fills

The standard by which all other fills are measured is down—specifically, goose down from the European variety of goose. Goose down consists of the small, soft feathers found on a goose or duck. Duck down is considered to be inferior to goose down. Using goose down alone to fill a pillow is prohibitively expensive, so the larger down feathers from ducks are blended together with the goose down in most instances.

Down or down/feather blends are found only in the most upscale hotels.

Synthetic Fills

Synthetic fiber pillows have become the widely accepted norm throughout the United States. Polyester fibers lead the market in the synthetic category. In addition to the aforementioned cost advantage, synthetic fibers can be laundered, and fewer individuals are allergic to them as compared with down and feathers. A few rare individuals are allergic to synthetic fills, so every property should have a few down/feather pillows in its inventory.

A well-made pillow should be resilient, evenly filled (no lumps), and not too heavy (heavier pillows are an indication of inferior synthetic fibers); the fill and cover should be fire retardant, and the **ticking** should be stain- and waterproof.

The materials used in the construction of a pillow are printed on a label that is required by law.

MATTRESS COVERS

Mattress covers serve two purposes: They provide a padded layer between the guest and the mattress, making for a more restful sleep, and they protect the mattress from stains resulting from spills and from incontinent or sick guests.

Mattress covers should be changed whenever the guest checks out.

Quilted Pads

All-cotton quilted pads are very expensive. One problem associated with quilted pads is the tendency of the diagonal threads to break after a few washings, which allows the fill to shift and the pad to become lumpy.

All-cotton pads tend to shrink 15 to 20 percent, so it is imperative to allow for this shrinkage when purchasing pads.

Felt Pads

The preferred pad for hotels is the 100 percent polyester felt pad. There is less than 2 percent shrinkage with this pad. The pad does not pucker or become lumpy; it is also far less expensive than any quilted pad, and it can be moisture-proofed.

All mattress covers should meet the federal standard FF-4-72 for fire retardancy.

Vinyl

Vinyl covers are more appropriate for hospital applications. The newer generation of vinyl covers can even be washed like cloth and can be sterilized.

A MINI CASE STUDY

Pitfalls in Purchasing Bed Linens

First it was the amenity "wars," now it's the bedding "wars." In their competition for customers, hotels are offering fancier bedding, including higher-thread-count sheets. If you have ever wondered how the linen mills can fit hundreds of threads into a square inch of sheet, the simple answer is, they can't. *Consumer Reports* has actually taken the time to count the threads in those high-thread-count sheets and has found they often do not contain their stated thread count. They claim that some linen mills are counting **plies**, which are the strands of yarn that make up a thread, and are calling these plies threads. Buying sheets that claim to have a thread count in excess of approximately 350 threads per square inch means you are probably paying for "hype."

Bath and Table Linens

The quality of a hotel's bath and table linens is a remarkably accurate indicator of the hotel's class and price level. The thicker the towels, the more expensive the accommodations.

BATH LINENS

The intended purpose of a bath towel is to absorb water, but a towel is often used by the guest as a rag to wipe up spills or as a shine cloth for shoes. Considering the abuse that hotel towels receive, it really is a wonder that, according to one major linen manufacturer, the average hotel uses only 12 towels for one hotel room per year. This figure represents loss from normal wear and tear, permanent staining, and theft.

In this section we will also examine cloth bath mats and shower curtains.

Fabric Materials and Construction

The standard hotel bath linen is a white terry cloth towel that is a blend of cotton/polyester fibers.

Terry cloth towels are woven on a loom. The fibers running lengthwise in the towel (the **ground warp**) are usually a blend of two parts polyester and one part cotton. Polyester in the warp gives the towel its strength and helps to minimize shrinkage.

TABLE 7.2 Model Hotel Par Requirements

	Rooms	Rooms Breakdown		
		Furniture	Total Beds	Pillow Requirement
Suites	5	1 king bed		3/Bed
Kings	13	1 king bed		3/Bed
Parlors	15	1 queen bed		2/Bed
Double-Doubles	320	Double beds		2/Bed
Total	353	20 roll-away beds (use double sheets)		1/Bed Total pillows + 10 percent

	Bed and Bath Linen			
	1 Par	3.5 Par	Price	Cost
Sheets				
King			$12.00	
Queen			9.50	
Double			7.50	
Pillowcases			1.50	
Bath towels			3.00	
Hand towels			1.10	
Washcloths			0.40	
Bath mats			2.80	
1/Room				
Bed pads			7.70	
(1 par + 10 percent)				
Blankets			28.00	
(1 par + 10 percent)				
Pillows			7.80	
(1 par + 10 percent)				
Totals				

Pile warp is the yarn running lengthwise in the towel that makes the terry loops on both sides of the towel's surface. These fibers should be 100 percent cotton for absorbency. The filling, or weft, is the yarn that runs horizontally across the towel. The filling should be 100 percent cotton. The **selvage** is the side edge of a towel or other woven fabric. It is a flat surface with no pile warp.

Towels, like sheets, can be sold as either firsts or seconds. Seconds are usually caused by a thick filling thread, a dropped warp or filling thread, or an uneven hem or border. These types of defects in no way impair the absorbency or durability of a towel. Therefore, many hotels willingly use towel seconds.

Bath mats are made in the same way as a terry towel, but the material is much heavier.

The best type of shower curtain for a commercial operation is a curtain made of 260 **denier** nylon. This type of curtain is better than any plastic curtain because it is easier to maintain, it resists mildew, it does not become stiff or brittle over time, it does not show soap stains as readily, and it is available in a multitude of colors.

The best protection against soap stains and mildew is to use a vinyl liner with a curtain. Do not use clear vinyl liners because these will show soap stains. Use a white or pastel-colored vinyl. The vinyl should be a minimum 6-gauge thickness. Plastic snap hooks are better than other types of plastic hooks or metal hooks.

Size

The standard size for a good-quality towel is 25″ × 50″. An average size for a face towel is 16″ × 27″. A good bath mat will measure 22″ × 34″, and decent size for a washcloth is 12″× 12″.

Towels and washcloths can be found in larger or smaller sizes than the above recommendations. The selection of a particular towel size should be based on marketing considerations.

Par Levels

A reasonable bath linen par level for a hotel with its own laundry is $3\frac{1}{2}$. If the laundry must be sent off the premises, the par level should be increased to $4\frac{1}{2}$.

The information given in Table 7.2 refers to the model hotel. Room configuration and other criteria, including approximate prices per item, are given. Use this information as an exercise to determine linen pars and to develop an approximate cost of initial supplies.

TABLE LINENS

In the food business, first impressions are lasting ones. Because success in this business depends so heavily on repeat business, the astute operator wants to make a first-time impression that will cause customers to come back again and again.

The focal point in most food service operations is the tabletop. It should look as pleasing as the menu, and nothing adds to this scene more than crisp, clean **napery** (table linens).

Fabric Materials and Construction

There are two dominant types of materials used for tablecloths and napkins: momie cloth and damask.

Momie cloth is normally a 50/50 cotton/polyester plain weave cloth that is relatively inexpensive, durable, and fairly colorfast, and does not pill or attract lint.

Damask is made using a twill weave. It can be divided into three categories: linen damask, cotton damask, and cotton/polyester damask blend. Linen is superior in appearance to the other two, but it is considerably more expensive. The cotton/polyester damask has the same advantages of the 50/50 momie cloth, but it has a better appearance and looks better after laundering.

Cotton/polyester blends are expected to shrink an average of 3 percent, as compared with cotton alone, which will shrink an average of 12 percent. Blended napery is expected to last up to four times as long as cotton alone. Ordinary cotton napkins should last for 34 launderings, and cotton tablecloths should last for 32 launderings on the average. Blends dry faster and are easier to iron.

Size

The drape of a tablecloth should be a minimum of 8 inches all around the table. Table 7.3 is a listing of some of the standard sizes for tables and tablecloths. This table is meant merely to serve as a guide; only a designer or table manufacturer can give you a plan that you can depend upon.

TABLE 7.3 Tabletop and Tablecloth Sizes

Seating	Top Size	Cloth Size
Table for 2	36″ × 36″	54″ × 54″
Table for 4	45″ × 45″	64″ × 64″
Table for 6	54″ × 54″	72″ × 72″
Table for 8	60″ round	90″ × 90″
Table for 10	66″ round	90″ × 90″

speaker, radio personality, and author, Ashkin has written more than 75 articles on green cleaning, indoor air quality, sick building syndrome, protecting health, and more. He was selected to the Power 50 by the Indoor Environment Review as one of the 50 most influential people in the indoor environment industry.

His other related activities include serving as technical advisor to the Center for the New American Dream, Vermont Public Interest Research Group (VPIRG), member of EPA's Working Group on Healthy Schools, and lead author for Green Seal's environmentally preferable cleaning program, and assisting in developing several green product standards. Ashkin is the founder of the not-for-profit Internet Initiative for Children's Health and the Environment, which brings together children's environmental health professionals and advocates, such as the EPA, with major mainstream Internet firms such as AOL, WebMD, and Medscape to disseminate critical information necessary to protect children from environmental threats. He was the 2006 Excellence Award winner from the EPA's Office of Children's Health Protection for his work to protect children from environmental risk and he received the 2006 Willam D. Joyner Achievement Award from the International Executive Housekeepers Association for an outstanding contribution to the success of the organization.

He feels that his most important achievement is figuring out how to begin the transformation of the cleaning industry. Without the use of government regulations, he has learned how to work with industry, end users, labor unions, trade associations, environmentalists, children's health advocates, policy makers, media, academia, and more to use the marketplace to drive the demand for products and services that reduce impacts on health and the environment.

Par Levels

Par levels will vary depending on the number of covers forecasted, hours of operation, number of meal periods open, and frequency of the launderings.

However, as a rule of thumb in a new operation, there should be a par of 4 tablecloths per table and nine to 12 napkins per table. These par levels should do if the restaurant is open for two meals, and a 24-hour laundry service is available.

Uniforms

Many hotel departments have uniformed employees. In some cases, each department maintains its own individual supply inventories of uniforms; in other cases, the housekeeping department is custodian of uniforms used throughout the hotel. If the housekeeping department is custodian of all uniforms, a large secure storage space, along with worktables and repair capability, are necessary.

Uniforms may be processed in the laundry daily and be issued each workday as the employees report to work. Some uniforms may be subcustodied to specific employees who maintain their own uniforms. Some hotels have uniform services provided by companies that purchase, launder or dry clean, and provide 5 par of uniforms for each employee on a weekly basis. The hotel must pay a premium for this service, since the servicing company must purchase 11 uniforms for each new employee when hired.

The simplest, most cost-effective method of administering a uniform program is for each department to maintain its own uniforms and to subcustody them to employees at the time of employment, allowing each employee to care for the uniforms issued.

Housekeeping uniforms need not be unattractive or uncomfortable. They should fit well and allow for freedom of movement, since much reaching and bending is involved in housekeeping work. A sleeveless dress with a short-sleeved blouse or shirt is a must, and a pocket or two is always helpful. Cotton is best for comfort, but polyester fabrics are the most plentiful. The quality of the GRA's and the senior housekeeper's uniforms should be similar, but color distinctions may be made. An inventory of four different uniforms is appropriate for housekeeping personnel: GRA (female), housekeeping aide (male), supervisor (female), supervisor (male).

A reasonable uniform program would allow for the issue of two uniforms to each employee upon employment and an issue of a third uniform after completion of a probationary work period. Should uniforms become damaged or worn out as a result of work, they should be replaced. Carelessness that causes destruction of uniforms should be the subject of counseling or disciplinary action.

The law requires that employees who are required to clean their own uniforms be compensated. The law suggests that laundry service in the hotel laundry might be a reasonable alternative to an outlay of cash. A total inventory of uniforms should include about 5 par, the rest being available to fit new employees or to provide replacements for the staff. Sizes range from very small (4, 6, 8) to very large (22, 24). It is a difficult task, however, to maintain a correctly sized inventory.

EXECUTIVE PROFILE
Mary Ann Washington *Team of Olympians*

by Andi M. Vance, Editor, *Executive Housekeeping Today*

(This article first appeared in the May 2002 issue of *Executive Housekeeping Today*, the official publication of the International Executive Housekeepers Association, Inc.)

This winter, much of the world's attention was focused upon the city that Mary Ann Washington has grown to love: Salt Lake City, Utah. Just as Olympic athletes spend countless hours of their days training, Mary Ann Washington has worked her way through the ranks to provide similar resources for her employees at the four hospitals throughout the Urban Central District of the IHC system.

A pilgrim in many respects, Washington initiated her career in Jackson, Mississippi. She started as a housekeeper at St. Dominic's Hospital in 1970, and it only took a few months for her manager, Jessie Richardson, to recognize Washington's potential. Richardson promoted Washington to a supervisory position only six months later, despite the protest of her staff. Those with seniority in the department felt that Washington was too young to be a supervisor. Washington strove to prove them wrong.

Richardson, a member of N.E.H.A. (now I.E.H.A.), harnessed Washington's aptitude and guided her in the right direction. "She [Richardson] saw my potential before I did," remembers Washington. "I knew that she really liked the spirit of the housekeeping department, but she became my mentor. She helped introduce me to things I wouldn't have been aware of otherwise."

During this period, Richardson introduced Washington to I.E.H.A.

Since then, Washington hasn't looked back.

Already immersed up to her waist in work both day and night, Washington decided to embrace more responsibility by taking N.E.H.A. certification classes offered at Hinds Jr. College in Jackson. "I started my Certified Executive Housekeeper (CEH) certification in 1977," she remembers. "It was not an easy task, as all classes were not readily available. Back then, things weren't as organized as they are today. During this time, I would have to travel to various locations to attend classes at night. As I reflect on those times, it was difficult, but it was all worth it."

Ten years later, Washington packed up her bags and left many of her good friends and family in search of a change. While she loved the familiarity and hometown feel of Jackson, she yearned to experience life elsewhere. Landing in Salt Lake City, Utah, in January of 1980, she took one look at the surrounding mountains and discovered a sense of peace. "Moving from the South to Utah was a tremendous culture shock," she remembers of her arrival. "This city was so clean. The mountains took my breath away and the people were so relaxed and laid back. I soon felt comfortable and right at home."

Only a month later, Washington returned to her career in housekeeping at LDS Hospital (Latter Day Saints). At the time, ServiceMaster managed the housekeeping services. Once again, it took only a few months for her supervisor to recognize her potential. Soon after, she accepted a position as a supervisor, which switched her employer from LDS to ServiceMaster.

In 1986, Washington was promoted to a managerial position at Cottonwood Hospital, another hospital in the IHC system. She worked at this 220-bed hospital until 1989, when housekeeping management returned to an in-house department. While she was required to reapply for her own position, Washington remained at Cottonwood in a management capacity.

That same year, the position for Manager of Housekeeping operations opened at LDS hospital. Since she'd last worked at the hospital, refurbishment had enhanced the overall appearance of the 520-bed facility. Eager to accept the challenge of changing the image of the department, Washington applied for the position.

"I now know that I am at my best when challenged," Washington says with a laugh. "I had come full circle, having worked at LDS Hospital, then leaving, and finally returning to where I first began. This time, however, everything had changed—new people, flooring, walls and fabrics. It was a whole new ballgame."

THE FRAMEWORK FOR SUCCESS

One of Washington's primary goals in accepting the new position was to help develop a sense of pride amongst her staff. With high turnover rates, something needed to be done in order to maintain staffing levels. Changing the image of the Environmental Services (ES) department meant a complete restructuring of current methodologies. First, Washington worked with her assistants to assure that everything was in place according to IHC's policies and guidelines. Next, she worked with others within the system to develop a training program to devise schedules that were equitable for all employees.

"It was a measurement tool for us," she comments. "We feel that if you can show employees that their schedules are similar to other persons' schedules, then you'll have more buy-in to getting them to perform other functions throughout the department. They need to know it's a team effort."

Standardizing all of the uniforms was another initiative taken in the restructuring. Washington worked with administrators and staff to enhance the workers' image by providing them with new professional attire. This also worked to create a sense of unity amongst the staff. In conjunction with the new uniforms, the staff provided input for a new department logo, slogan, and mission statement. Their new mission statement reads as follows: "Environmental Services is dedicated to providing all customers with responsible and dependable services, and a clean and safe environment."

Another key program developed to reduce turnover levels at LDS was a career-pathing system. While turnover plagued the entire nation, Washington worked with other managers to address the problem. A training program was developed, which provided staff with cross-training knowledge so they could perform numerous functions throughout the department. Specific levels were instituted, which carried specific job titles. Titles ranged from housekeeper to housekeeping specialist. Floor care specialists were designated, as were team leaders. In order to ascend to the next level upon recommendation, testing was given in order to assess the individual's skill level. When an employee passed all the requirements, a five-percent wage increase was distributed.

THE EVOLUTION OF A SYSTEM

In three years much changed in the world of environmental services. The IHC system restructured to keep in line with the developments in the healthcare industry change in direction with HMO's and hospital consolidations. The staff was gathered and the name of the department changed to Urban Central Region Environmental Services. Three hospitals existed in the new consortium: AltaView, Cottonwood and LDS. Recently, Wasatch Canyons Hospital was added to the list. Washington maintains ES operations over these four facilities.

"Housekeeping is always an area everyone feels can accept cuts. As managers, we must cut costs and upgrade quality. Thanks to high morale, proper ownership and training, we were in a position to go another level," Washington remarks.

Through the Corvo computer program (trademark for Enterprise Responsibility Management), supervisors at all three facilities in the Urban Central Region maintain a network of instant data and information. Washington is able to instantly gain information regarding discharges, inventory and more.

"Corvo provides a single point of contact for the customer to reach the ES, Security or Engineering. It efficiently distributes workload to available and responsible parties," says Washington. These are the types of programs that will gain prominence in the future. Then you can track how many discharges you have in a day. It's LIVE data. So when you're asking for more full-time equivalents (FTE's), you need data to show what the workloads are. That's the kind of information that managers are going to need in order to provide for their employees and the administration."

Use of robotic technology is another way that IHC has kept abreast of industry trends. After extensive research, Washington recommended to system administration the purchase of a floor care robot. She found that use of the robot would save time and money.

"It was a big leap of faith to recommend going with it," Washington admits. "But now, years later, we still have it here. We find it to be very productive and efficient."

STEP PROGRAM

Washington sincerely cares about the development of her employees. While she initiated the career-pathing program at LDS, she has since worked with a task force to enhance some of its attributes. The result was the STEP Rate Program employed throughout the Urban Central region. According to Washington, the program encourages appropriate performance and on-the-job education by providing participants with the opportunity for supervisor/employee review of performance. Various criteria are evaluated in regard to an employee's performance: attendance, adherence to procedures, dress code, public relations skills, assuring compliance, educational requirements, etc. Once every three months, each employee sits down with either his or her immediate supervisor or Washington. If he or she doesn't meet each set of criteria established, the employee will not receive a wage increase.

"The program holds everyone accountable, but it is definitely rewarding for the employees. There's a lot of paperwork involved, particularly initially. But now, if the employees aren't called down for their three-month meeting, they're asking, "What's going on?" They really look forward to it now.

"I think the employees need to have their performance recognized regularly. They need to receive that feedback and be recognized and rewarded for the things they contribute. We want to keep our people here."

I.E.H.A. also plays a role in the development of department supervisors. "One requirement for all supervisors in the Urban Central is that they must be certified with I.E.H.A.," Washington acknowledges. "Even if they have degrees, they must attend certain classes and there is a particular curriculum that they must complete before becoming a supervisor. So now, all of our eight full-time supervisors are Certified Executive Housekeepers."

She continues, "I try to mentor my supervisors. Housekeeping is a career. You can advance yourself if you apply yourself. That's what I try to encourage in my staff as well. Go and take classes, go to night school, try to get into something you really like. If you're going to be in it, try and apply yourself to be whatever you can be."

By promoting within, Washington displays her dedication to each employee's development. At the moment, her entire staff is composed of employees who have worked their way up through the ranks. "We hire people into our department, we tell them about I.E.H.A. and give them ESL (English as a Second Language) classes, and we try to really promote our staff. This is reiterated throughout the entire department, from supervisors to frontline staff."

CONCLUSION

In her over 20 years in the industry, Washington has gained a wealth of experience and knowledge. She's served on both local and district levels of the Association, which has helped further advance her knowledge and skill level. By paying close attention to the development of her team mates and instituting programs with proven success, Washington has helped develop a team with Olympic potential.

DISCUSSION QUESTIONS

1. Mary Ann Washington is certainly ahead of the curve with her employment of robotic floor care technology. Do you think this is going to become a prevailing trend in cleaning industry? What other areas of housekeeping do you think could become automated?

2. Washington has done much to encourage her employees to succeed (e.g., new professional uniforms, establishment of proper policies and guidelines, training programs, a career-path system, the STEP Rate Program, ESL classes, etc.). Of all of her initiatives, which do you think have done the most good, and why?

CONCLUSION

Decisions that are made regarding the purchase and use of assets without a sufficient investigation into the characteristics and qualities of those assets can seriously affect the profit picture.

Costs for linens and their maintenance need to be continually assessed in order to determine if the right decisions were reached and to avoid the repetition of costly mistakes. In addition, the costs for linens should always be evaluated on a cost-per-room-per-day basis, never on a cost-per-pound-basis. If linen costs are evaluated on a cost-per-room-per-day basis, the level of consumption by the guest can also be addressed in the formula.

Linen maintenance and replacement is an ongoing cost of doing business. It is the housekeeping manager's responsibility to ensure that these costs remain reasonable while continuing to meet the guest's expectations.

KEY TERMS AND CONCEPTS

Bedding	Tensile strength	Duvet
Linens	Gray goods	Ticking
Uniforms	Mercerizing	Plies
Dust ruffles	Sanforizing	Ground warp
Muslin	Seconds	Pile warp
Percale	Torn sheet	Selvage
Warp	Finished sheet	Denier
Weft	Par	Napery
Filling	Shams	
Thread count	Coverlet	

DISCUSSION AND REVIEW QUESTIONS

1. Draw up a list of specifications for a guest-room attendant's uniform.
2. Explain the criteria that you would use to evaluate the performance of bedding materials for a hotel.
3. What are the advantages to all-white bath linens that have no logo? Can you see any disadvantages to this type of product?
4. How would you establish a par level for the napery in a new dining room? What criteria would you use to set the same par level for an existing operation?

CHAPTER 8

Staffing for Housekeeping Operations

LEARNING OBJECTIVES

After studying the chapter, students should be able to:

1. Describe the proper methodology to use when staffing housekeeping positions.
2. Describe the elements of a job specification and an employee requisition.
3. Identify proper selection and interview techniques.
4. Describe the important elements of an orientation program.
5. Describe different techniques used to train newly hired employees.
6. Describe how to maintain training and development records.
7. Describe how to conduct an objective performance evaluation.

Staffing is the third sequential function of management. Until now the executive housekeeper has been concerned with planning and organizing the housekeeping department for the impending opening and operations. Now the executive housekeeper must think about hiring employees within sufficient time to ensure that three of the activities of staffing—selection (including interviewing), orientation, and training—may be completed before opening. Staffing will be a major task of the last two weeks before opening.

The development of the Area Responsibility Plan and the House Breakout Plan before opening led to preparation of the Department Staffing Guide, which will be a major tool in determining the need for employees in various categories. The housekeeping manager and laundry manager should now be onboard and assisting in the development of various job descriptions. (These are described in Appendix A.) The hotel human resources department would also have been preparing for the hiring event. They would have advertised a mass hiring for all categories of personnel to begin on a certain date about two weeks before opening.

Even though this chapter reflects a continuation of the executive housekeeper's planning for opening operations, the techniques described apply to any ongoing operation, except that the magnitude of selection, orientation, and training activities will not be as intense. Also, the fourth activity—development of existing employees—is normally missing in opening operations but is highly visible in ongoing operations.

Job Specifications

Job specifications should be written as job descriptions (see Appendix A) are prepared. Job specifications are simple statements of what the various incumbents to positions will be expected to do. An example of a job specification for a section housekeeper is as follows:

Section Housekeeper (hotels) [often Guestroom Attendant, or GRA] The incumbent will work as a member of a housekeeping team, cleaning and servicing for occupancy of approximately 18 hotel guestrooms each day. Work will generally include the tasks of bed making, vacuuming, dusting, and bathroom cleaning. Incumbent will also be expected to maintain equipment provided for work and load housekeeper's cart before the end of each day's operation. Section housekeepers must be willing to work their share of weekends and be dependable in coming to work each day scheduled.

Any special qualifications, such as ability to speak a foreign language, might also be listed.

Employee Requisition

Once job specifications have been developed for every position, **employee requisitions** are prepared for first hirings (and for any follow-up needs for the human resources department). Figure 8.1 is an example of an employee requisition. Note the designation as to whether the requisition is for a new or a replacement position and the number of employees required for a specific requisition number. The human resources

---

department will advertise, take applications, and screen to fill each requisition by number until all positions are filled. For example, the first requisition for GRAs may be for 20 GRAs. The human resources department will continue to advertise, take applications, and screen employees for the housekeeping department and will provide candidates for interview by department managers until 20 GRAs are hired. Should any be hired and require replacing, a new employee requisition will be required.

Staffing Housekeeping Positions

Several activities are involved in staffing a housekeeping operation. Executive housekeepers must select and interview employees, participate in an orientation program, train newly hired employees, and develop employees for future growth. Each of these activities will now be discussed.

SELECTING EMPLOYEES

Sources of Employees

Each area of the United States has its own demographic situations that affect the availability of suitable employees for involvement in housekeeping or environmental service operations. For example, in one area, an exceptionally high response rate from people seeking food service work may occur and a low response rate from people seeking housekeeping positions may occur. In another area, the reverse may be true, and people interested in housekeeping work may far outnumber those interested in food service.

Surveys among hotels or hospitals in your area will indicate the best source for various classifications of employees. Advertising campaigns that will reach these employees are the best method of locating suitable people. Major classified ads associated with mass hirings will specify the need for food service personnel, front desk clerks, food servers, housekeeping personnel, and maintenance people. Such ads may yield surprising results.

If the volume of response for housekeeping personnel is insufficient to provide a suitable hiring base, the following *sources* may be investigated:

1. Local employment agencies
2. Flyers posted on community bulletin boards
3. Local church organizations
4. Neighborhood canvass for friends of recently hired employees
5. Direct radio appeals to local homemakers

EMPLOYEE REQUISITION

Requisition no. _____

Date _____   Department _____

Position _____
(Number and Title)

New _____   Replacement _____   Number required _____

Classification _____
(Full-time, Part-time, Temporary, Pool)

Working hours _____   Estimated no. of hours/week _____

Desired starting date _____

Starting rate of pay _____   Base rate _____

Specification (General description of duties)

_____
_____
_____
_____
_____

Special qualifications (desired or required)

_____
_____
_____
_____

_____ Department Manager

FIGURE 8.1 Employee requisition, used to ask for one or more employees for a specific job.

6. Organizations for underprivileged ethnic minorities, and mentally disabled people (It should be noted that many mentally disabled persons are completely capable of performing simple housekeeping tasks and are dependable and responsible people seeking an opportunity to perform in a productive capacity.)

If these sources do not produce the volume of applicants necessary to develop a staff, it may become necessary to search for employees in distant areas and to provide regular transportation for them to and from work.

If aliens are hired, the department manager must take great care to ensure that they are legal residents of this country and that their green cards are valid. More than one hotel department manager has had an entire staff swept away by the Department of Immigration after hiring people who were illegal aliens. Such unfortunate action has required the immediate assistance of all available employees (including management) to fill in.

Processing Applicants

Whether you are involved in a mass hiring or in the recruiting of a single employee, a systematic and courteous procedure for **processing applicants** is essential. For example, in the opening of the Los Angeles Airport Marriott, 11,000 applicants were processed to fill approximately 850 positions in a period of about two weeks. The magnitude of such an operation required a near assembly-line technique, but a personable and positive experience for the applicants still had to be maintained.

The efficient handling of lines of employees, courteous attendance, personal concern for employee desires, and reference to suitable departments for those unfamiliar with what the hotel or hospital has to offer all become earmarks for how the company will treat its employees. The key to proper handling of applicants is the use of a **control system** whereby employees are conducted through the steps of **application**, **prescreening**, and, if qualified, **reference to a department** for interview. Figure 8.2 is a typical **processing record** that helps ensure fair and efficient handling of each applicant.

Note the opportunity for employees to express their desires for a specific type of employment. Even though an employee may desire involvement in one classification of work, he or she may be hired for employment in a different department. Also, employees might not be aware of the possibilities available in a particular department at the time of application or may be unable to locate in desired departments at the time of mass hirings. Employees who perform well should therefore be given the opportunity to transfer to other departments when the opportunities arise.

PROCESSING RECORD FOR EMPLOYEE CANDIDATE

Name ____________ Position desired
Address ____________ ____________
Phone ____________ Date of application
Hours when can be reached ____________ ____________

Record of human resources department prescreening

Date ______ By ______ Recommended for ______ (Position)

Screening code ______

Department interview endorsement

Date interviewed ______ Interviewed by ______
Comments ____________

Recommendation ____________
Hire ______ Refer to ______ Department—File
References checked by interviewing department ______ (Yes/No)

Who was contacted?
1. ____________
2. ____________
3. ____________

Note: References will be checked on all people offered employment. The human resources department will make reference checks on all candidates before making offers *if requested by the interviewing departments.* No offers will be extended before completion of satisfactory reference checks.

Disposition

Offer extended ______ (Date) Accepted/Denied ______
Will report to work on ______
Application filed ______ (Date/By)

FIGURE 8.2 This form is used to track an applicant's progress through the employment process.

According to laws regulated by federal and state Fair Employment Practices Agencies (FEPA), no person may be denied the opportunity to submit application for employment for a position of his or her choosing. Not only is the law strict on this point, but companies in any way benefiting from interstate commerce (such as hotels and hospitals) may not discriminate in the hiring of people based on race, color, national origin, or religious preference. Although particular hours and days of the week may be specified, it is a generally accepted fact that hotels and hospitals must maintain personnel operations that provide the opportunity for people to submit applications without prejudice.

Prescreening Applicants

The **prescreening interview** is a staff function normally provided to all hotel or hospital departments by the *human resources* section of the organization. Prescreening is a preliminary interview process in which unqualified applicants—those applicants who do not meet the criteria for a job as specified in the job specification/special qualifications—are selected (or screened) out. For example, an applicant for a secretarial job that requires the incumbent to take shorthand and be able to type 60 words a minute may be screened out if the applicant is not able to pass a relevant typing and shorthand test. The results of prescreening are usually coded for internal use and are indicated on the applicant processing record (Figure 8.2).

If human resources screens out a candidate, he or she should be told the reason immediately and thanked for applying for employment.

Applicants who are not screened out should either be referred to a specific department for interview or, if all immediate positions are filled, have their applications placed in a department pending file for future reference. All applicants should be told that hiring decisions will be made by individual department managers based on the best qualifications from among those interviewed.

A suggested agenda for a prescreening interview is as follows:

1. The initial contact should be cordial and helpful. Many employees are lost at this stage because of inefficient systems established for handling applicants.
2. During the prescreening interview, try to determine what the employee is seeking, whether such a position is available, or, if not, when such a position might become available.
3. Review the work history as stated on the application to determine whether the applicant meets the obvious physical and mental qualifications, as well as important human qualifications such as emotional stability, personality, honesty, integrity, and reliability.
4. Do not waste time if the applicant is obviously not qualified or if no immediate position is available. When potential vacancies or a backlog of applicants exists, inform the candidate. Be efficient in stating this to the applicant. Always make sure that the applicant gives you a phone number in order that he or she may be called at some future date. Because most applicants seeking employment are actively seeking immediate work, applications more than 30 days old are usually worthless.
5. If at all possible, an immediate interview by the department manager should be held after screening. If this is not possible, a definite appointment should be made for the candidate's interview as soon as possible.

THE INTERVIEW

An **interview** should be conducted by a manager of the department to which the applicant has been referred. In ongoing operations, it is often wise to also allow the supervisor for whom the new employee will work to visit with the candidate in order that the supervisor may gain a feel for how it would be to work together. The supervisor's view should be considered, since a harmonious relationship at the working level is important. Although the acceptance of an employee remains a prerogative of management, it would be unwise to accept an employee into a position when the supervisor has reservations about the applicant.

Certain personal characteristics should be explored when interviewing an employee. Some of these characteristics are native skills, stability, reliability, experience, attitude toward employment, personality, physical traits, stamina, age, sex, education, previous training, initiative, alertness, appearance, and personal cleanliness. Although employers may not discriminate against race, sex, age, religion, and nationality, overall considerations may involve the capability to lift heavy objects, enter men's or women's restrooms, and so on. In a housekeeping (or environmental services) department, people should be employed who find enjoyment in housework at home. Remember that character and personality cannot be completely judged from a person's appearance. Also, it should be expected that a person's appearance will never be better than when that person is applying for a job.

Letters of recommendation and references should be carefully considered. Seldom will a letter of recommendation be adverse, whereas a telephone call might be most revealing.

If it were necessary to select the most important step in the selection process, interviewing would be it. Interviewing is *the* step that separates those who will be employed from those who will not. Poor **interviewing techniques** can make the process more difficult and may produce a result that can be frustrating and damaging for both parties. In addition, inadequate interviewing will result in gaining incorrect information, being confused about what has been said, suppression of information, and, in some circumstances, the candidate's complete withdrawal from the process.

A well-accepted list of the steps for a successful interview process is as follows:

1. *Be prepared:* Have a checklist of significant questions ready to ask the candidate. Such questions may be prepared from the body of the job description. This preparation will allow the interviewer to assume the initiative in the interview.
2. *Find a proper place to conduct the interview:* The applicant should be made to feel comfortable. The interview should be conducted in a quiet, relaxing atmosphere where there is privacy that will bring about a confidential conversation.
3. *Practice:* People who conduct interviews should practice interviewing skills periodically. Several

managers may get together and discuss interviewing techniques that are to be used.

4. *Be tactful and courteous:* Put the applicant at ease, but also control the discussion and lead to important questions.

5. *Be knowledgeable:* Be thoroughly familiar with the position for which the applicant is interviewing in order that all of the applicant's questions may be answered. Also, have significant background knowledge in order that general information about the company may be given.

6. *Listen:* Encourage the applicant to talk. This may be done by asking questions that are not likely to be answered by a yes or no. If people are comfortable and are asked questions about themselves, they will usually speak freely and give information that specific questions will not always bring out. Applicants will usually talk if there is a feeling that they are not being misunderstood.

7. *Observe:* Much can be learned about an applicant just by observing reactions to questions, attitudes about work, and, specifically, attitudes about providing service to others. Observation is a vital step in the interviewing process.

Interview Pitfalls

Perhaps of equal importance to the interviewing technique are the following **pitfalls**, which should be avoided while interviewing.

1. Having a feeling that the employee will be just right based on a few outstanding characteristics rather than on the sum of all characteristics noted.

2. Being influenced by neatness, grooming, expensive clothes, and an extroverted personality, none of which has much to do with housekeeping competency.

3. Overgeneralizing, whereby interviewers assume too much from a single remark (for instance, an applicant's assurance that he or she "really wants to work").

4. Hiring the "boomer," that is, the person who always wants to work in a new property; unfortunately, this type of person changes jobs whenever a new property opens.

5. Projecting your own background and social status into the job requirement. Which school the applicant attended or whether the applicant has the "proper look" is beside the point. It is job performance that is going to count.

6. Confusing strengths with weaknesses, and vice versa. What is construed by one person to be over-aggressiveness might be interpreted by another as confidence, ambition, and potential for leadership, the last two traits being in chronic short

supply in most housekeeping departments. These are the very characteristics that make it possible for management to promote from within and develop new supervisors and managers.

7. Being impressed by a smooth talker—or the reverse: assuming that silence reflects strength and wisdom. The interviewer should concentrate on what the applicant is saying rather than on how it is being said, then decide whether his or her personality will fit into the organization.

8. Being tempted by overqualified applicants. People with experience and education that far exceed the job requirements may be unable for some reason to get jobs commensurate with their backgrounds. Even if such applicants are not concealing skeletons in the closet, they still tend to become frustrated and dissatisfied with jobs far below their level of abilities.

The application of the techniques and avoidance of the pitfalls will be valuable tools in the selection of competent personnel for the housekeeping and environmental service departments.

For many years, the approach of many managers was to write a job description and then fill it by attempting to find the perfect person. This approach may overlook many qualified people, such as disadvantaged people or slow learners. Job descriptions may be analyzed in two ways when filling positions: 1) what is actually required to do the work, and 2) what is desirable. Is the ability to read or write really necessary for the job? Is the ability to learn quickly really necessary? A person who does not read or write or who is a slow learner can be trained and can make an excellent employee. True, it may take additional time, but the reward will be a loyal employee as well as less turnover. It has been proven many times that those who are disadvantaged or slightly learning disabled, once trained, will perform consistently well for longer periods. There are agencies that seek out companies that will try to hire such people.

Results of the Interview

If the results of an interview are negative and rejection is indicated, the candidate should be informed as soon as possible. A pleasant statement, such as "Others interviewed appear to be more qualified," is usually sufficient. This information can be handled in a straightforward and courteous manner and in such a way that the candidate will appreciate the time that has been taken during the interview.

When the results of the interview are positive, a statement indicating a favorable impression is most encouraging. However, no commitment should be made until a *reference check* has been conducted.

Reference Checks

In many cases, **reference checks** are made only to verify that what has been said in the application and interview is in fact true. Many times applicants are reluctant to explain in detail why previous employment situations have come to an end. It is more important to hear the actual truth about a prior termination from the applicant than it is to hear that they simply have been terminated. Reference checks, in order of desirability, are as follows:

1. Personal (face-to-face) meetings with previous employers are the least available but provide the most accurate information when they can be arranged.
2. Telephone discussions are the next best and most often used approach. For all positions, an in-depth conversation by telephone between the potential new manager and the prior manager is most desirable; otherwise a simple verification of data is sufficient to ensure honesty.
3. The least desirable reference is the written recommendation, because managers are extremely reluctant to state a frank and honest opinion that may later be used against them in court.

Applicants who are rated successful at an interview should be told that a check of their references will be conducted, and, pending favorable responses, the personnel department will contact them within two days. Applicants who are currently employed normally ask that their current employer not be contacted for a reference check. This request should be honored at all times. Applicants who are currently working usually want to give proper notice to their current employers. If the applicant chooses not to give notice, chances are no notice will be given at the time he or she leaves your hotel.

In some cases, the applicant gives notice and, upon doing so, is "cut loose" immediately. If such is the case, the applicant should be told to contact the department manager immediately in order that the employee may be put to work as soon as possible.

Interview Skills versus Turnover

There is no perfect interviewer, interviewee, or resultant hiring or rejection decision in regard to an applicant. We can only hope to improve our interviewing skills in order that the greatest degree of success in employee retention can be obtained. The executive housekeeper should expect that 25 percent of initial hires into a housekeeping department will not be employed for more than three months. (This is primarily because the housekeeping skills are easily learned and the position is paid at or near minimum wage.) Some new housekeeping departments have as much as a 75 percent turnover rate in the first three months of

operation. Certainly this figure can be improved upon with adequate attention to the interviewing and selection processes. However, regardless of the outcome of the interview, the processing record (Figure 8.2) should be properly endorsed and returned to the personnel department for processing.

ORIENTATION

A carefully planned, concerned, and informational **orientation program** is significant to the first impressions that a new employee will have about the hospital or hotel in general and the housekeeping department in particular. Too often, a new employee is told where the work area and restroom are, given a cursory explanation of the job, then put to work. It is not uncommon to find managers putting employees to work who have not even been processed into the organization, an unfortunate situation that is usually discovered on payday when there is no paycheck for the new employee. Such blatant disregard for the concerns of the employee can only lead to a poor perception of the company. A planned orientation program will eliminate this type of activity and will bring the employee into the company with personal concern and with a greater possibility for a successful relationship.

A good orientation program is usually made up of four phases: employee acquisition, receipt of an employee's handbook, tour of the facility, and an orientation meeting.

Employee Acquisition

Once a person is accepted for employment, the applicant is told to report for work at a given time and place, and that place should be the personnel department. Preemployment procedures can take as much as one-half day, and department managers eager to start new employees to work should allow time for a proper **employee acquisition** into the organization. Figure 8.3 is an **Employment checklist** similar to those used by most personnel offices to ensure that nothing is overlooked in assimilating a new person into the organization. Once an applicant has been prescreened and interviewed, has had references checked, and has received an offer of employment, the checklist is used to ensure completion of data required to place the employee on the payroll.

At this time it should be ensured that the application is complete and any additional information pertaining to employment history that may be necessary to obtain the necessary work permits and credentials is on hand. Usually the security department records the entry of a new employee into the staff and provides instructions regarding use of employee entrances, removing parcels from the premises, and employee parking areas. Application for work permits and drug testing will be scheduled

```
                    EMPLOYMENT CHECKLIST

  Name _____  Social Security number _____

  Address _____

  City _____  State _____  Zip _____

  Item                              Complete

  Application                       _____
  Employment history                _____
  Security identification           _____
     (Health card/Work permit)
  Health and welfare documents      _____
  W-4 forms submitted               _____
  Deductions from pay (if any)      _____
     (union, state income tax)
  Hotel employee handbook issued    _____
     (acknowledgment received)
  Data processing
     Personnel action form filled out  _____
     Employee payroll number assigned  _____
     Wage dept. classification number  _____
  Application for name tag
     (First name only except for management)  _____

  Employee has been turned over to _____
  in the _____ department for training and department
  orientation.

  Property orientation meeting has been scheduled for this employee on
  _____.

  Personnel supervisor              Receiving department

  _____           _____
  Signature                         Supervisor signature
```

FIGURE 8.3 Employment checklist.

where applicable. All documents required by the hotel's health and welfare insurer should be completed, and instructions should be given about immediately reporting accidents, no matter how slight, to supervisors. The federal government requires that every employer submit a W-4 (withholding statement) for each employee on the payroll. The employee must complete this document and give it to the company. Mandatory deductions from pay should be explained (federal and state income tax and Social Security FICA), as should other deductions that may be required or desired. At this time, some form of personnel action document is usually initiated for the new employee and is placed in the employee's permanent record.

A computer-printed document called a **Personnel Action Form (PAF)** (Figure 8.4) collects all data that are required about the new employee. Note the permanent information that will be carried on file. The PAF is serially numbered, is created from data stored on magnetic discs, and is maintained in the employee's personnel file. When a change has to be made, such as job title, marital status, or rate of pay, the PAF is retrieved from the employee's record, changes are made *under* the item to be changed, and the corrected PAF is used to change the data in the computer storage. Once new information is stored, a new PAF is created and placed in the employee's record to await the next need for processing. A long-time employee might have many PAFs stored in the personnel file.

When either regular or special **performance appraisals** are given, the last (most current) PAF will be used to record the appraisal (Figure 8.5), as well as written warnings and matters involving terminations. These forms are usually found on the reverse side of the PAF. Since performance appraisals may signify a raise in pay, the appropriate pay increase information would be indicated on the front of the PAF (Figure 8.4). All recordings on PAFs, whether on one side or both, require the submission of data, storage of information, and creation of a new PAF to be stored in the employee's record.

The PAF and performance appraisal system should be thoroughly explained to the new employee, along with assignment of a payroll number. The employer should also explain how and when the staff is paid and when the first paycheck may be expected.

The Employee Handbook

The new employee should be provided with a copy of the **hotel** or **hospital employee's handbook** and should be told to read it thoroughly. Since the new housekeeping employee is not working just for the housekeeping department but is to become integrated as a member of the entire staff, reading this handbook is extremely important to ensure that proper instructions in the rules and regulations of the hotel are presented. The handbook should be developed in such a way as to inspire the new employee to become a fully participating member of the organization. As an example, a generic employee's handbook is presented in Appendix B. Note the tone of the welcoming letter and the manner in which the rules and regulations are presented.

Familiarization Tour of the Facilities

Upon completion of the acquisition phase, a **facility tour** should be conducted for all new employees. For new facilities, access to the property should be gained within about one week before opening, and many new employees can be taken on a tour simultaneously. It is possible for employees to work in the hotel housekeeping department for years and never to have visited the showroom, dining rooms, ballrooms, or even the executive office areas. A tour of the complete facility melds employees into the total organization, and a complete informative tour should *never* be neglected.

For ongoing operations, after acquisition, the new employee may be turned over to a department supervisor, who becomes the tour director. An appreciation of the total involvement of each employee is strengthened when a facilities tour is complete and thorough. If necessary, the property tour might be postponed until after the orientation meeting; however, the orientation activity of staffing is not complete until a property tour is conducted.

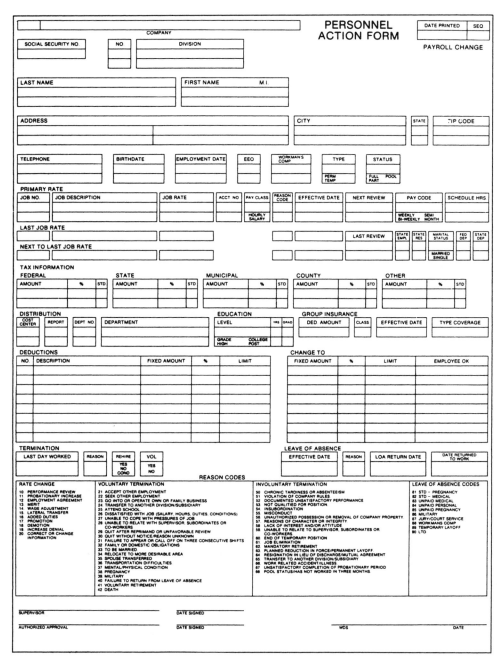

FIGURE 8.4 Personnel Action Form (PAF) is a data-processing form used to collect and store various types of information about an employee. *(Courtesy of White Lodging Services.)*

Orientation Meeting

The **orientation meeting** should not be conducted until the employee has had an opportunity to become at least partially familiar with the surroundings. After approximately two weeks, the employee will have many questions about experiences, the new job, training, and the rules and regulations listed in the Property and Department Handbooks (see the following section on training). Employee orientation meetings that are scheduled too soon fail to answer many questions that will develop within the first two weeks of employment.

The meeting should be held in a comfortable setting, with refreshments provided. It is usually conducted by the director of human resources and is attended by as many of the facility managers as possible. Most certainly, the general manager or hospital administration members of the executive committee, the security director, and the new employees' department heads should attend. Each of these managers should have an

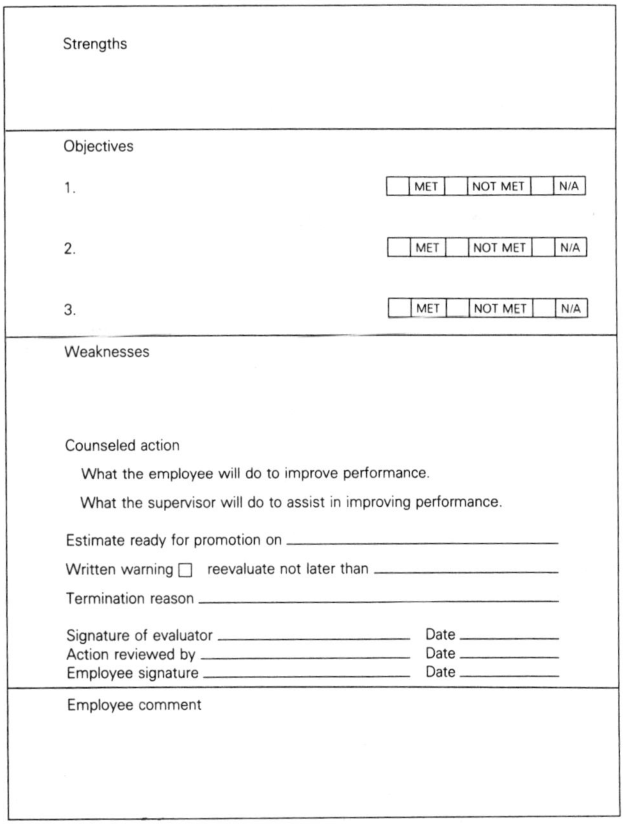

Strengths			

Objectives			
1.	MET	NOT MET	N/A
2.	MET	NOT MET	N/A
3.	MET	NOT MET	N/A

Weaknesses

Counseled action

What the employee will do to improve performance.

What the supervisor will do to assist in improving performance.

Estimate ready for promotion on _____

Written warning ☐ reevaluate not later than _____

Termination reason _____

Signature of evaluator _____ Date _____
Action reviewed by _____ Date _____
Employee signature _____ Date _____

Employee comment

FIGURE 8.5 The reverse of the PAF may be used to record performance appraisals, written warnings, or matters involving terminations.

opportunity to welcome the new employees and give them a chance to associate names with faces. All managers and new employees should wear name tags. In orientation meetings, a brief history of the company and company goals should be presented.

A planned orientation meeting should not be concluded without someones' stressing the importance of each position. Every position must have a purpose behind it and is therefore important to the overall functioning of the facility. An excellent statement of this philosophy was once offered by a general manager who said, "The person mopping a floor in the kitchen at 3:00 A.M. is just as valuable to this operation as I am—we just do different things."

The orientation meeting should be scheduled to allow for many questions. And there should be someone in attendance who can answer *all of them.*

Although the new employee will be gaining confidence and security in the position as training ends and work is actually performed, informal orientation may continue for quite some time. The formal orientation, however, ends with the orientation meeting (although the facility tour may be conducted after the meeting). Finally, it should be remembered that good orientation procedures lead to worker satisfaction and help quiet

the anxieties and fears that a new employee may have. When a good orientation is neglected, the seeds of dissatisfaction are planted.

TRAINING

General

The efficiency and economy with which any department will operate will depend on the ability of each member of the organization to do his or her job. Such ability will depend in part on past experiences, but more commonly it can be credited to the type and quality of **training** offered. Employees, regardless of past experiences, always need some degree of training before starting a new job.

Small institutions may try to avoid training by hiring people who are already trained in the general functions with which they will be involved. However, most institutions recognize the need for training that is specifically oriented toward the new experience, and will have a documented training program.

Some employers of housekeeping personnel find it easier to train completely unskilled and untrained personnel. In such cases, bad or undesirable practices do not have to be trained out of an employee. Previous experience and education should, however, be analyzed and considered in the training of each new employee in order that efficiencies in training can be recognized. If a new employee can demonstrate an understanding of department standards and policies, that portion of training may be shortened or modified. However, skill and ability must be demonstrated before training can be altered. Finally, training is the best method to communicate the company's way of doing things, without which the new employee may do work contrary to company policy.

First Training

First training of a new employee actually starts with a continuation of *department* orientation. When a new employee is turned over to the housekeeping or environmental services department, orientation usually continues by familiarizing the employee with *department rules and regulations.* Many housekeeping departments have their own **department employee handbooks.** For an example, see Appendix C, which contains the housekeeping department rules and regulations for Bally's Casino Resort in Las Vegas, Nevada. Compare this handbook with that of the generic handbook (Appendix B). Although these handbooks are for completely different types of organizations, the substance of their publications is essentially the same: both are designed to familiarize each new employee with his or her surroundings. Handbooks should be written in such a way as to inspire employees to become team members, committed to company objectives.

A Systematic Approach to Training

Training may be defined as those activities that are designed to help an employee begin performing tasks for which he or she is hired or to help the employee improve performance in a job already assigned. The purpose of training is to enable an employee to begin an assigned job or to improve upon techniques already in use.

In hotel or hospital housekeeping operations, there are three basic areas in which training activity should take place: **skills**, **attitudes**, and **knowledge**.

Skills Training　A sample list of skills in which a basic housekeeping employee must be trained follows:

1. *Bed making:* Specific techniques; company policy
2. *Vacuuming:* Techniques; use and care of equipment
3. *Dusting:* Techniques; use of products
4. *Window and mirror cleaning:* Techniques and products
5. *Setup awareness:* Room setups; what a properly serviced room should look like
6. *Bathroom cleaning:* Tub and toilet sanitation; appearance; methods of cleaning and results desired
7. *Daily routine:* An orderly procedure for the conduct of the day's work; daily communications
8. *Caring for and using equipment:* Housekeeper cart; loading
9. *Industrial safety:* Product use; guest safety; fire and other emergencies

The best reference for the skills that require training is the job description for which the person is being trained.

Attitude Guidance　Employees need guidance in their attitudes about the work that must be done. They need to be guided in their thinking about rooms that may present a unique problem in cleaning. Attitudes among section housekeepers need to be such that, occasionally, when rooms require extra effort to be brought back to standard, it is viewed as being a part of rendering service to the guest who paid to enjoy the room. Carol Mondesir,[1] director of housekeeping, Sheraton Centre, Toronto, states:

> A hotel is meant to be enjoyed and, occasionally, the rooms are left quite messed up. However, as long as they're not vandalized, it's part of the territory. The whole idea of being in the hospitality business is to make the guest's stay as pleasant as possible. The rooms are there to be enjoyed.

Positive relationships with various agencies and people also need to be developed.

The following are areas in which attitude guidance is important:

1. The guest/patient
2. The department manager and immediate supervisor
3. A guestroom that is in a state of great disarray
4. The hotel and company
5. The uniform
6. Appearance
7. Personal hygiene

Meeting Standards　The most important task of the trainer is to prepare new employees to **meet standards**. With this aim in mind, sequence of performance in cleaning a guestroom is most important in order that efficiency in accomplishing day-to-day tasks may be developed. In addition, the *best method* of accomplishing a task should be presented to the new trainee. Once the task has been learned, the next thing is to meet standards, which may not necessarily mean doing the job the way the person has been trained. Setting standards of performance is discussed in Chapter 11 under "Operational Controls."

Knowledge Training　Areas of knowledge in which the employee needs to be trained are as follows:

1. Thorough knowledge of the hotel layout; employee must be able to give directions and to tell the guest about the hotel, restaurants, and other facilities
2. Knowledge of employee rights and benefits
3. Understanding of grievance procedure
4. Knowing top managers by sight and by name

Ongoing Training

There is a need to conduct **ongoing training** for all employees, regardless of how long they have been members of the department. There are two instances when additional training is needed: 1) the purchase of new equipment, and 2) change in or unusual employee behavior while on the job.

When new equipment is purchased, employees need to know how the new equipment differs from present equipment, what new skills or knowledge are required to operate the equipment, who will need this knowledge, and when. New equipment may also require new attitudes about work habits.

Employee behavior while on the job that is seen as an indicator for additional training may be divided into two categories: events that the manager witnesses and events that the manager is told about by the employees.

Events that the manager witnesses that indicate a need for training are frequent employee absence, considerable spoilage of products, carelessness, a high rate of accidents, and resisting direction by supervisors.

Events that the manager might be told about that indicate a need for training are that something doesn't work right (product isn't any good), something is dangerous to work with, or something is making work harder.

Although training is vital for any organization to function at top efficiency, it is expensive. The money and man-hours expended must therefore be worth the investment. There must be a balance between the dollars spent training employees and the benefits of productivity and high-efficiency performance. A simple method of determining the need for training is to measure performance of workers: Find out what is going on at present on the job, and match this performance with what should be happening. The difference, if any, describes how much training is needed.

In conducting **performance analysis**, the following question should be asked: Could the employee do the job or task if his or her life depended on the result? If the employee *could not* do the job even if his or her life depended on the outcome, there is a **deficiency of knowledge (DK)**. If the employee could have done the job if his or her life depended on the outcome, but did not, there is a **deficiency of execution (DE)**. Some of the causes of deficiencies of execution include task interference, lack of feedback (employee doesn't know when the job is being performed correctly or incorrectly), and the balance of consequences (some employees like doing certain tasks better than others).

If either deficiency of knowledge or deficiency of execution exists, training must be conducted. The approach or the method of training may differ, however. Deficiencies of knowledge can be corrected by training the employee to do the job, then observing and correcting as necessary until the task is proficiently performed. Deficiency of execution is usually corrected by searching for the underlying cause of lack of performance, not by teaching the actual task.

Training Methods

There are numerous methods or ways to conduct training. Each method has its own advantages and disadvantages, which must be weighed in the light of benefits to be gained. Some methods are more expensive than others but are also more effective in terms of time required for comprehension and proficiency that must be developed. Several useful methods of training housekeeping personnel are listed and discussed.

On-the-Job Training   Using **on-the-job training (OJT)**, a technique in which "learning by doing" is the advantage, the instructor demonstrates the procedure and then watches the students perform it. With this technique, one instructor can handle several students. In housekeeping operations, the instructor is usually a GRA who is doing the instructing in the rooms that have been assigned for cleaning that day. The OJT method is not operationally productive until the student is proficient enough in the training tasks to absorb part of the operational load.

Simulation Training   With **simulation training**, a model room (unrented) is set up and used to train several employees. Whereas OJT requires progress toward daily production of ready rooms, simulation requires that the model room not be rented. In addition, the trainer is not productive in cleaning ready rooms. The advantages of simulation training are that it allows the training process to be stopped, discussed, and repeated if necessary. Simulation is an excellent method, provided the trainer's time is paid for out of training funds, and clean room production is not necessary during the workday.

Coach-Pupil Method   The **coach-pupil method** is similar to OJT except that each instructor has only one student (a one-to-one relationship). This method is desired, provided that there are enough qualified instructors to have several training units in progress at the same time.

Lectures   The **lecture method** reaches the largest number of students per instructor. Practically all training programs use this type of instruction for certain segments. Unfortunately, the lecture method can be the dullest training technique, and therefore requires instructors who are gifted in presentation capabilities. In addition, space for lectures may be difficult to obtain and may require special facilities.

Conferences   The **conference method** of instruction is often referred to as **workshop training**. This technique involves a group of students who formulate ideas, do problem solving, and report on projects. The conference or workshop technique is excellent for supervisory training.

Demonstrations   When new products or equipment are being introduced, **demonstrations** are excellent. Many demonstrations may be conducted by vendors and purveyors as a part of the sale of equipment and products. Difficulties may arise when language barriers exist. It is also important that no more information be presented than can be absorbed in a reasonable period of time; otherwise, misunderstandings may arise.

Training Aids

Many hotels use **training aids** in a conference room, or post messages on an employee bulletin board. Aside from the usual training aids such as chalkboards, bulletin boards, charts, graphs, and diagrams, photographs can supply clear and accurate references for how rooms should be set up, maids' carts loaded, and routines accomplished. Most housekeeping operations have films on guest contact and courtesy that may also be used in training. Motion pictures speak directly to many people who may not understand proper procedures from reading about them. Many training techniques may be combined to develop a well-rounded training plan.

Development

It is possible to have two students sitting side by side in a classroom, with one being trained and the other being developed. Recall that the definition of training is preparing a person to do a job for which he or she is hired or to improve upon performance of a current job. **Development** is preparing a person for advancement or to assume greater responsibility. The techniques are the same, but the end result is quite different. Whereas training begins after orientation of an employee who is hired to do a specific job, upon introduction of new equipment, or upon observation and communication with employees indicating a need for training, development begins with the identification of a specific employee who has shown potential for advancement. Training for promotion or to improve potential is in fact development and must always include a much-neglected type of training: **supervisory training**.

Many forms of developmental training may be given on the property; other forms might include sending candidates to schools and seminars. Developmental training is associated primarily with supervisors and managerial development and may encompass many types of experiences.

Figure 8.6 is an example of a **developmental training program** for a junior manager who will soon become involved in housekeeping department management. Note the various developmental tasks that the trainee must perform over a period of 12 months. Also note the position of the person who will coach the development in the various skills, and the time expected to be spent in each area.

Development of individuals within the organization looks to future potential and promotion of employees. Specifically, those employees who demonstrate leadership potential should be developed through supervisory training for advancement to positions of greater responsibility. Unfortunately, many outstanding workers have their performance rewarded by promotion but are given no development training. The excellent section housekeeper who is advanced to the position of senior housekeeper without the benefit of supervisory training is quickly seen to be unhappy and frustrated and may possibly become a loss to the department. It is therefore most essential that individual potential be developed in

an orderly and systematic manner, or else this potential may never be recognized.

While undergoing managerial development as specified in Figure 8.6, student and management alike should not lose sight of the primary aim of the program, which is the learning and potential development of the trainee, not departmental production. Even though there will be times that the trainee may be given specific responsibilities to oversee operations, clean guestrooms, or service public areas, advantage should not be taken of the trainee or the situation to the detriment of the development function. Development of new growth in the trainee becomes difficult when the training instructor or coordinator is not only developing a new manager but is also being held responsible for the production of some aspect of housekeeping operations.

RECORDS AND REPORTS

Whether you are conducting a training or a development program, suitable **records** of training progress should be maintained both by the training supervisor and the student. Periodic evaluations of the student's progress should be conducted, and successful completion of the program should be recognized. Public recognition of achievement will inspire the newly trained or developed employee to achieve standards of performance and to strive for advancement.

Once an employee is trained or developed and his or her satisfactory performance has been recognized and recorded, the person should perform satisfactorily to standards. Future performance may be based on beginning performance after training. If an employee's performance begins to fall short of standards and expectations, there has to be a reason other than lack of skills. The reason for unsatisfactory performance must then be sought out and addressed. This type of follow-up is not possible unless suitable records of training and development are maintained and used for comparison.

EVALUATION AND PERFORMANCE APPRAISAL

Although **evaluation and performance appraisal** for employees will occur as work progresses, it is not uncommon to find the design of systems for appraisal as part of organization and staffing functions. This is true because first appraisal and evaluation occurs during training, which is an activity of staffing. Once trainees begin to have their performance appraised, the methods used will continue throughout employment. As a part of training, new employees should be told how, when, and by whom their performances will be evaluated, and should be advised that questions regarding their performance will be regularly answered.

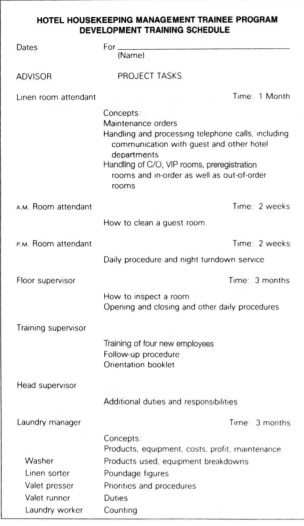

(a)

(b)

FIGURE 8.6 Hotel Housekeeping Management Trainee Program Development Training Schedule, used to cycle the trainee through the various functions involved in a hotel housekeeping department.

Probationary Period

Initial employment should be probationary in nature, allowing the new employee to improve efficiency to where the designated number of rooms cleaned per day can be achieved in a **probationary period** (about three months). Should a large number of employees be unable to achieve the standard within that time, the standard should be investigated. Should only one or two employees be unable to meet the standard of rooms cleaned per day, an evaluation of the employee in training should either reveal the reason why or indicate the employee as unsuitable for further retention. An employee who, after suitable training, cannot meet a reasonable performance standard should not be allowed to continue employment. Similarly, an employee who has met required performance standards in the specified

probationary period should be continued into regular employment status and thus achieve a reasonable degree of security in employment.

Evaluation

Evaluation of personnel is an attempt to measure selected traits, characteristics, and productivity. Unfortunately, evaluations are generally objective in nature, and raters are seldom trained in the art of subjective evaluation. Initiative, self-control, and leadership ability do not lend themselves to measurement; therefore such characteristics are estimated. How well they are estimated depends to a great extent on the person doing the estimating. Two raters using the same form and rating the same person will probably arrive at different conclusions.

EXECUTIVE PROFILE

Cigdem Duygulu *Spanning the Globe*

by Andi M. Vance, Editor, *Executive Housekeeping Today*

This article first appeared in the February 2002 issue of *Executive Housekeeping Today*, the official publication of the International Executive Housekeepers Association, Inc.

The golden palace surrounded by waving palm trees, vast green plains and the ocean's surf is her home. A gracious hostess, she welcomes her guests with open arms, a warm smile and impeccably clean rooms. Throughout her entire life, Cigdem Duygulu has been completely immersed in the hospitality industry. However, like the many immigrants who come to the U.S. in search of opportunity, she's made a long voyage to get where she is today.

THE GREAT JOURNEY

As a small child, Cigdem Duygulu would wander throughout her grandparents' bed and breakfast in Golcuk, Turkey, each summer. She'd make friends with the guests and assist with small tasks, while her parents worked in the kitchen and other areas of the hotel. Her blood runs thick with the hospitality gene; luckily, she recognized this at an extremely early age.

The bed and breakfast welcomed a regular guest each summer, a gentleman from Switzerland who pampered Cigdem with gifts of soap and cookies from his country. He related tales from faraway places, opening her eyes to the world beyond the small city and village in Turkey where she lived with her family. "He showed me that there were so many things in the world to see," Duygulu recalls. "My dream was to get out of the country. I wanted to leave Turkey and travel as much as possible."

Taking her collection of soaps with her, Duygulu left high school to pursue her Bachelor's degree in Tourism and Hospitality management at Gazi University in Ankara, Turkey. Her superior performance and efforts were recognized by the University and rewarded with a six-month internship at the Bade Hotel Baren in Zurich, Switzerland. She went on the internship to gain experience in the hotel industry, but she received much more of an education than she had expected.

"I was on the German-speaking side of the country," she reminisces. "On my first day, the General Manager approached me and told me to go here and there and do this. I didn't know what he said, so I asked the assistant, 'Do you speak English?' She said, 'No.' I said to myself, 'Oh no! What am I going to do? No one speaks English or Turkish!' Later, I found out that the assistant spoke five languages. She just didn't communicate with me in English so I would learn German."

From that point, Duygulu began taking classes so she would learn the language. Already, she was relatively fluent in English and French, but was most familiar with her native tongue of Turkish. As a child, her two aunts would read her stories from America and Europe and assist her in the translation as she went. "They were very fluent in English and French," she relates. "They would teach me a lot and help me with my education."

While she continued learning the language, her eyes were opened to many other things throughout the six-month period, which helped her realize many things about herself and her interests. It was here that she discovered her love for housekeeping. She enjoyed the interactions with the guests and providing them with a warm environment for them to stay. Her attachment to the guests grew stronger, and when she found one of her favorite guests dead from a heart attack one day, she recognized just how attached she had become. "She was from the French side of Switzerland," Duygulu fondly recalls. "She would always make me speak French to her; she was so nice. One morning, I knocked on her door and there was no answer. As I knew her routine, I laid her breakfast trays by the table, but still she didn't awake. When I returned to get the trays, I saw the food was still there and she appeared to be sleeping. I said to myself, 'Oh my gosh! I hope not!' But she was!"

When Duygulu ran downstairs to find the Executive Housekeeper, she found the hotel lobby busy with guests scurrying everywhere. She approached her manager and tried to tell her in broken German that she needed to show her something immediately, while attempting not to portray her dismay to the guests. The Executive Housekeeper brushed her off, telling her she was busy and didn't have the time to go up to the room. When she finally was able to get the Executive Housekeeper to the woman's room, Duygulu found herself in tears, shocked at her death.

"That was my first really traumatic experience in the business," she recalls.

But Duygulu didn't let that dissuade her from continuing her life in hotels. She wanted to pursue her career in housekeeping; she loves housekeeping. "In the housekeeping department," she says, "I feel like I'm the hostess of the hotel. Guests are coming to my hotel, my home, and I want to welcome them. If I'm working in the housekeeping area, I feel I can welcome them more than if I were working in other departments."

Following the conclusion of the internship, she returned to Turkey to finish her degree.

"At the end of it, my general manager wanted me to stay," she acknowledges, "but I went back to Turkey. My country needed me at that time. I put my resume in at a couple of places, and they called me back immediately. As soon as I finished my degree, I became the Assistant Executive Housekeeper at the Golden Dolphin Holiday Resort on the West Coast of Turkey."

Duygulu climbed her way up the ranks, working a variety of positions until becoming the Executive Housekeeper at the Golden Dolphin. After five years of service, her general manager told her he was relocating to Switzerland, and invited her to join him.

She agreed. While waiting on her work papers to arrive, she worked odd jobs throughout the country before growing impatient. "At that time," she says with a grin, "my brother was living in New York City. He said to me, 'Cigdem, why don't you just come here and wait on your papers instead of returning to Turkey and waiting?'

"I thought to myself, it's only a three-hour flight back to Turkey, and a nine-hour flight to the States, but why not? I'd like to see the United States too!"

After arriving in the U.S., Duygulu obtained her green card. She found it difficult to get a job, as many American hotel managers seemed not to recognize the dedication and extensive training required in earning a degree in hotel management in Europe. "I knew that in time I would get the job I wanted," she remembers. "After all, housekeeping basics remain the same no matter where you are: provide quality service to your guests."

Soon thereafter, she found a job and worked for a brief time at the New York Hilton at Rockefeller Center, "It was a great job and everyone was wonderful! Rockefeller Center was just amazing at Christmas time; guests came from everywhere to come and see it."

While in New York, Duygulu married a man she knew from Turkey. The two complement one another well, as he also works in the hospitality industry—in food service. "I'm a terrible cook," she admits with a laugh, "so food and beverage is not my deal."

When her husband opened a restaurant with some of his friends in Coral Springs, Florida, Cigdem accompanied him. She was anxious to continue her travels. After obtaining a position with Prime Hospitality Corporation, she moved throughout the Southern states, opening new hotels for the company. "I like the idea of working in a new hotel," she relates. So, I would keep opening the new hotels and training everyone. I loved it! They were opening new hotels everywhere. I loved traveling and learned a lot of things. I even got to watch a Dallas Cowboys football game!"

After she opened nearly 15 hotels for the company, she took an employment opportunity with John Q, Hammons Hotels, where she opened up more hotels in Oklahoma, North Carolina and Florida, which led her to where she is today. After opening the Radisson Resort-Coral Springs, Duygulu found her palace by the ocean. Not far from the Everglades, the hotel also features over 17,000 square feet of meeting space, a 30,000-square-foot conference center and an 18-hole golf course designed by PGA tour player, Mark McCumber.

SATISFACTION GUARANTEED

With 224 rooms, Cigdem Duygulu services her guests with a continual smile and dedication that is continually acknowledged by her management and guests. She believes that quality service is a "result of training room attendants to provide more than what is expected." She concentrates on training and educating herself, as well as her staff. Many individuals on her staff come from Haiti. She finds them anxious to learn English, as well as other areas in the Housekeeping department. Just as she was expected to learn German in Switzerland, she tries to help members on her staff learn English by turning on American radio stations for them to listen to as they work in the laundry room. She teaches staff by actually demonstrating what she'd like them to do. "Before I tell them what to do, I have to do it, or do it with them," advises Duygulu. "Particularly those things that they don't necessarily like doing. You have to take the action right away, 'Come on, we'll do it together!' I tell them."

She keeps her staff motivated by constantly recognizing their efforts, "It's the little things that are important for all of us," she says. "You have to communicate with them. You have to give them recognition, appreciation and training. Cross-training is also very important. You have to be positive and always take the action with them. That way, they will go the extra mile to make the guests happy too!"

"TRAINING IS KNOWING WHAT YOU DO; EDUCATION IS KNOWING WHY YOU DO IT!"

For Duygulu, I.E.H.A. is her family. As a charter member of the Florida Intercoastal Chapter, she continually pursues prospective members, sharing her excitement about the Association, "You have to know the Association, so you can sell the Association," she says. "Before I became a member, I was in the country for almost six months before finding I.E.H.A. At that time, there was no 800 number. I knew I.E.H.A. existed because my college books in Turkey told me there was an Association for Executive Housekeepers in the U.S., but no one seemed to know how to contact I.E.H.A. I asked everyone: my general manager, assistant managers,

hotel owners, even people on the street. I asked, 'Where is this Association?!'

"I asked a vendor, and he told me of an Association he knew of in Palm Beach. I went to the meeting, and found the Florida Gold Coast Chapter. That's how I became a member!

"Now, when I call prospective members in the area, I say to them, 'You know what, you don't have to look for I.E.H.A., I'm calling you and telling you! We have an 800 number now, so everyone can find it! Come on!' It's a big thing, like the airlines, 'Call us on our 800-number and make your reservations now!' I wish all Executive Housekeepers would become members of I.E.H.A. If any company is really looking at the education or degrees, then you won't go wrong being a member. Our conventions are like big reunions for me, because I get to see everyone. So, I have a huge family!"

This past Spring concluded Duygulu's four-year tenure as President of the Florida Intercoastal Chapter. While she's maintained a variety of positions within the Chapter, she's recently stepped up to become the Assistant District Director for the Florida International District.

ALL IN THE FAMILY

Cigdem Duygulu has passed down her passion for the hospitality industry to her son, who currently works at the Radisson Resort Coral Springs in room service. "He's following in my family's footsteps, and I'm so happy for that," she relates excitedly. "My family just loves the tourism and hotel business! We love the people! The hotel business is a

service business, and not everyone can do it. You have to really love it; otherwise, you can't do it. You have to love the people and love your job.

"People are always complaining, 'Oh, I don't like this, I don't want to be here.' I tell them if you don't like it, then find another job. You'll make the guests miserable with that attitude. You have to give 100% of yourself and sacrifice. When everyone's having fun during holidays and weekends, and you are working, you have to love it."

But then again, when you live in a *palace* off the coast of Florida with a lifetime of hospitality in your blood, how could you not love it?

DISCUSSION QUESTIONS

1. Cigdem Duygulu exhibits an extremely positive attitude toward the hospitality industry in general and the housekeeping department in particular. Unfortunately, not everyone shares this same positive attitude, particularly with regard to the profession of cleaning. Why do you think many feel housekeeping is a demeaning occupation? If you were an executive housekeeper, how would you improve the esteem of your employees?

2. Cigdem Duygulu speaks several languages. Should all executive housekeepers be multilingual? In addition to English, what are the most important languages an executive housekeeper should learn? Why? Is it necessary to have an absolute mastery of a language?

Certain policies on the use of evaluations should be established so that they are understood by both the person doing the evaluating and the person being evaluated. These policies must be established and disseminated by management. In order to establish such policies, the following questions, among others, must be answered and communicated to all those involved in the evaluation: What will evaluations be used for? Will evaluations influence promotions, become a part of the employee's record, be used as periodic checks, or be used for counseling and guidance? What qualities are going to be evaluated? Who is going to be evaluated? Who will do the evaluating?

Reliable evaluations require careful planning and take considerable time, skill, and work. The employee must understand the evaluation.

Evaluation should be used at the end of a probationary period, and the employee must understand at the beginning of the period that he or she will be observed and evaluated. Each item, as well as what impact the evaluation will have on future employment, should be explained to the employee. People undergoing periodic evaluations, such as at the end of one year's employment, should also know why evaluations are being conducted and what may result from the evaluation. In both situations, the evaluation should be used for counseling and guidance so that performance may be improved upon or corrected if necessary. Certainly, strong points should be pointed out. An employee should be made aware of good as well as not-so-good evaluations.

Evaluations should be made for a purpose and not for the sake of an exercise. They should ultimately be used as management tools. Evaluations should be developed to fit the policies of the particular institution using it and the particular position being evaluated. The same evaluation may not be suitable for every position.

An example of an evaluation—a performance appraisal form—is presented in Figure 8.5 (the back-side of the PAF in Figure 8.4). More is mentioned on the subject of performance appraisal in Chapter 11 when we discuss subroutines in the housekeeping department.

OUTSOURCING

In certain locales, such as isolated resorts, hotels are tempted to use contract labor because the local market does not support the necessary number of workers, particularly in housekeeping. Advocates of **outsourcing** are quick to point out the advantages of the practice. Scarce workers are provided to the property, and there is no need to provide expensive employee benefits. The entire staffing function is assumed by the contractor. There are no worries regarding

A MINI CASE STUDY

Pitfalls in Outsourcing

Molly Galloway has called a meeting with her assistant manager, Tracy Hernandez. "I don't know if this is a problem or an opportunity. Since we are in a remote location, finding an adequate number of housekeeping personnel has been a perpetual problem. Starting this season we have a new competitor opening its doors only three miles from our property line and we have already lost 20 percent of our guestroom attendants and porters to this new property. I just don't know what we are going to do to replace that number.

Hernandez leans forward in her chair as if she is going to reveal a secret that she doesn't want anyone else to hear. "I have this friend, see, who is going with this guy who is starting a new business out of his home. He is starting an outsourcing agency for cleaning personnel. He will deliver housekeepers and porters to us and the charge is only $3.00 more an hour than what we are currently paying our own people," says Hernandez.

"That sounds great," responds Galloway. "But where does he expect to find these people? I have combed the entire county looking for people. We have ads every Sunday in the paper; we have standing requests with the state employment bureau; and we offer our employees bonuses if they can bring us a friend or relative who is willing to clean rooms."

"Well," says Hernandez, "He is bringing them from out of town, way out of town." Hernandez continues, "He has some connections and some of his people, well; let's just say their papers may not be all that accurate. But we are not their employer; he is. If anything were to happen, we could just claim we were duped. Besides, I have seen some of the documents he's got and I couldn't tell the difference from the real stuff! He's got Russians, Ethiopians, and, of course he's got lots of Mexican nationals, too."

"I really don't want to tell Belcher (Tony Belcher, the hotel manager) he's got to clean 15 rooms every day in addition to his regular job," exclaims Galloway. "Let me think on it for a couple of days. I don't know if I have any other way out of this mess."

recruiting, selecting, hiring, orienting, or even training the employees. Merely issue them uniforms and send them off to clean rooms. Some employers may even be willing to relax their responsibilities regarding employment law such as immigration and naturalization requirements.

Management should never forget that once a contracted employee dons a company uniform, the guest believes (and has no reason not to) that person is an employee of the hotel. The guest also believes the hotel has made every reasonable effort to screen that person in the hiring process to ensure that he or she is of good moral character, who has the best interests of the guest at heart.

Unfortunately, there have been several incidents in which the outsourced employees did not quite have the best interests of the guest at heart. There have been more than a few cases in which outsourced workers were wanted felons who inflicted considerable bodily harm on guests during the performance of their duties. A number of these incidents have resulted in lawsuits, with awards against the hotel in the millions of dollars.

This author does not recommend outsourcing in housekeeping, and cautions operators who ignore this advice to keep their guard up and continue to meet their legal and ethical responsibilities regarding employees and employment law.

CONCLUSION

Staffing for both hospital and hotel housekeeping operations involves the activities of selecting, interviewing, orienting, training, and developing personnel to carry out specific functions in the organization for which they are hired. Each activity should be performed with consistency, dispatch, and individual concern for each employee brought into the organization. Whereas the major presentation of staffing in this text has been developed for the model hotel where a mass hiring has been performed, each and every aspect of selecting, orienting, and training new employees applies equally to situations in which replacement employees (perhaps only one) are brought into the organization.

Job specifications are the documents that indicate qualifications, characteristics, and abilities inherently needed in applicants. The employee requisition is the instrument by which the human resources department seeks specific numbers and types of candidates for employment for each of the operating departments.

The next step is interviewing, which should be done by people from various departments. Actual selection, however, should only be performed by the department manager for whom the employee will work.

The employee acquisition phase is vital to the successful orientation of a new employee and should not be omitted. Upon acquisition of the new employee, presentation of an employee's handbook (Appendixes B and C) is appropriate. This handbook should contain major company rules, procedures, and regulations, along with relevant facts for the employee. Orientation is the basis for allowing the new employee to become accustomed to new surroundings. The quality of orientation will determine whether the new employee will feel secure in a new setting, and it will set the stage for the relationship that is to follow.

As training begins, orientation continues but is now conducted by the specific department in which the new employee will work. There are several methods of training, each of which should be used so as to gain the best effect for the least cost. Employee performance in training should be evaluated by methods similar to those used in evaluating operational performance that will follow. After new employees receive approximately 24 hours of on-the-job training in the cleaning of rooms, they should become productive and be able to clean a reasonable number of rooms (at about 60 percent efficiency). Continued application of skills will develop greater productivity as the new employee spends each day working at the new skills.

As preliminary training ends, orientation should be completed by ensuring that an employee orientation meeting and a tour of the entire facility have taken place. Failure to complete an orientation or to provide sufficient training can plant the seeds of employee unrest, discontent, and possible failure of the employee's relationship with the company that might well have been prevented.

Whether conducting training or development, adequate records of employee progress should be maintained. Records of training that have been successfully completed establish a base for future performance appraisal. Measurement of growth in skills and promotion potential may not be recalled if training records and evaluations are not initiated and continued. Employees have a right to expect evaluations, and usually consider objectively prepared statements about their performance a mark of management's caring about employees.

KEY TERMS AND CONCEPTS

Staffing
Job specifications
Employee requisitions
Processing applicants
Control system
Application
Prescreening
Reference to a department
Processing record
Prescreening interview
Interview
Interviewing techniques
Pitfalls
Reference checks
Orientation program
Employee acquisition
Employment checklist

Personnel Action Form (PAF)
Performance appraisal
Hotel or hospital employee's handbook
Facility tour
Orientation meeting
Training
First training
Department employee handbooks
Skills
Attitudes
Knowledge
Meet standards
Ongoing training
Performance analysis
Deficiency of knowledge (DK)
Deficiency of execution (DE)

On-the-job training (OJT)
Simulation training
Coach-pupil method
Lecture method
Conference method
Workshop training
Demonstrations
Training aids
Development
Supervisory training
Developmental training program
Records
Evaluation and performance appraisal
Probationary period
Outsourcing

DISCUSSION AND REVIEW QUESTIONS

1. When should a job specification be prepared? What should it contain?
2. What services should the human resources department of an organization perform in the hiring process? What services should department managers for whom employees will be working perform?
3. Draw up an interview plan. What questions would you ask? What questions should be avoided?
4. After reviewing the hotel handbook in Appendix B and the departmental handbook in Appendix C, discuss the differences in approach in these two documents.
5. What are the three basic areas in which housekeeping employees should receive training? List the elements found in each area.

NOTE

1. Dan Wilton, ''Housekeeping: Cleaning Up Your Hotel's Image,'' in an interview with Carol Mondesir, *Canadian Hotel and Restaurant*, March 1984, pp. 36–37.

Operational Planning

The subject of planning for the opening of a hotel has thus far included staffing; scheduling; preparing job descriptions; using materials; and hiring, orienting, and training employees. Even though the who, what, and when may have been decided, procedures for the *how* of operations still remain to be established. The executive housekeeper may have, through past experience, established a mental plan of daily operations as they should be conducted. Much remains to be done, however, in standardizing specific procedures and routines for the new property. This chapter deals primarily with procedures for direction and control of housekeeping operations in hotels.

Recall Mackenzie's three-dimensional management chart (Chapter 1), which includes the sequential management functions of direction and control. Certain activities of direction and control must be planned for in advance of opening. These are delegating work (an activity of direction) and establishing reporting systems, developing performance standards, measuring results, and taking corrective action (activities of control). These activities cannot take place without having procedures designed and communicated to employees. Since most of the work of the housekeeping department is a routine that recurs on a daily basis, communication for direction and control is best done with **forms**.

The day-to-day delegation of tasks as to which rooms require service and who will actually service them is performed through a routine commonly known as opening the house. This delegation takes place through the creation and use of several forms that are developed in advance of opening and are made available in sufficient quantity as to provide this communication on a daily basis. Additional forms relating to communication, control of information about progress, and timely reporting of information are also necessary. Such forms are usually explained via documents known as **standard operating procedures (SOPs)**. The SOPs not only establish and describe routines for normal daily operations, but they cover a variety of other procedures such as key control, room inspections, inventory procedures, standards of performance, and lost-and-found operations. Several procedures associated with housekeeping operations are presented in this chapter, including examples of the SOPs that control the operations.

Procedures for Opening the House

Opening the house is a procedure by which the following events take place:

1. Front desk provides information to housekeeping as to which rooms will require service on a given day.
2. Information received by housekeeping is transferred to **working and control documents** for senior GRAs (team leaders or supervisors) to use that day to control work progress.
3. Information is provided showing room sections with specific GRAs assigned and any **open sections** (sections with no GRAs assigned as a result of occupancy being less than 100 percent).
4. If occupancy is less than 100 percent, the information is used to establish **18-room workloads** for those GRAs who are scheduled to work on the specific day. This is accomplished by taking occupied rooms from open sections and marking them as **pickup rooms** for GRAs whose regular sections are less than fully occupied. Total pickup rooms combined with the regular rooms of sections that are occupied form the 18-room workloads. (With 100 percent occupancy, all sections have GRAs assigned and there are no pickup rooms.)
5. After all occupied rooms have been assigned to a specific GRA, and information is cross-checked on all team leader documents, the daily planning is transferred to documents whereby GRAs are informed of individual work assigned.
6. Because the House Breakout Plan (Chapter 2) divided the model hotel into four divisions of five sections each, daily opening-the-house exercises require the preparation of 24 documents (forms) to convey information from the front desk to the workers and supervisors who will be responsible for performing the work.
7. Once all forms are properly filled out, placed on a clipboard, and positioned on the main linen room counter, room keys associated with appropriate work areas are prepared for issue. When this is done, opening-the-house planning for that specific day is considered complete.

Note: It is important to recognize that all planning relating to opening the house may be computerized, and the specific documents referred to in this section can be obtained through hotel computers.

A detailed look at forms and how they are to be used will now be presented. All forms relate specifically to the 353-room model hotel.

NIGHT CLERK'S REPORT TO HOUSEKEEPING

The document whereby early morning information is passed from the front desk to housekeeping is called the **Night Clerk's Report to Housekeeping**. Figure 9.1 shows an example of this form, completed with information from the hotel room rack at the front desk. The position of room numbers on the form is identical to the order in which rooms appear on the front desk room rack.

Note the columns next to the ones with room numbers. Checkmarks in columns "OCC" indicate rooms that were **occupied** last night with an expected stay-over guest; these rooms will require service during the upcoming day. Checkmarks in columns "C/O" will not only require service, but occupants of these rooms are expected to **check out** of the hotel sometime during the day. If there are no checkmarks in any of the columns next to a room number, the rooms are considered **ready rooms (R)** and will not require the services of a GRA that day. Rooms marked "OOO" are **out of order** and will also not require service until the engineering department reports their status as being ready for cleaning.

At the top of the report is the date and a summary of total rooms occupied, total rooms vacant, checkouts expected, rooms in which guests are expected to stay over, and rooms that are out of order. In Figure 9.1 note that stayovers (176) plus checkouts (72) equal total rooms occupied (248); and that total rooms occupied (248) plus total rooms vacant (102) plus out-of-order rooms (3) equal total rooms in the hotel (353).

This summary information is provided as a backup check and must agree with the totals of the individual marks. The report is usually available at about 6:30 each morning and is picked up by a housekeeping supervisor or manager, who then proceeds to the housekeeping department to open the house. The Night Clerk's Report to Housekeeping is one of several forms referring to today's specific date that will later be collected and filed as a permanent record of work performed today.

After the supervisor has the Night Clerk's Report, the first task is to compare the actual rooms occupied with the Table of Personnel Requirements (Table 2.2) and to determine the number of GRAs needed to clean the 248 rooms requiring service. From the table we see that 14 GRAs are required to service 248 rooms; the next immediate concern is to determine whether 14 GRAs were told to report to work that day. Quick reference to

**NIGHT CLERK'S REPORT
TO HOUSEKEEPING
(Rooms Requiring Service)**

Total Rooms Occupied 248 Date 10/1

Total Rooms Vacant 102 Prepared By A.B. Clark

Checkouts 72

Stayovers 176

Out of Order 3

Room	Occ	R	C/O	Room	Occ	R	C/O	Room	Occ	R	C/O	Room	Occ	R	C/O	Room	Occ	R	C/O	Room	Occ	R	C/O	Room	Occ	R	C/O	Room	Occ	R	C/O
1001	✓			1068	✓			1228	✓			2051	✓			2110	✓			3015	✓			3079	✓			3222			
1002				1071	✓			1229			✓	2053	✓							3016				3080				3223	✓		
1003	✓			1072			✓	1230			✓	2055			✓	2202	✓			3017	✓			3081				3224	✓		
1004	✓			1073			✓	1231			✓	2057			✓	2204	✓			3019				3083				3225			
1005				1074			✓					2059			✓	2205	✓			3021	✓			3085	✓			3226			
1006	✓			1075	✓			2001	✓			2061	✓			2206				3023				3087				3227			
1007	✓			1076	✓			2002	✓			2062	✓			2207				3025				3089				3228	✓		
1008	✓			1077	✓			2003				2063				2208	✓			3027				3091	✓			3229	✓		
1009	✓			1078	✓			2004	OOO			2064	✓			2209	✓			3031	✓			3093				3230			
1010	✓			1079	OOO			2005	✓			2065	✓			2210				3032				3095	✓			3231			✓
1011				1081			✓	2006	✓			2066				2211	✓			3033	✓			3096				4070			
1012	✓			1083			✓	2007	✓			2067				2212				3035			✓	3097	✓			4071			✓
1013	✓			1085				2008				2068	✓			2213	✓			3037			✓	3098	✓			4072			
1014	✓			1087	✓			2009			✓	2070	✓			2214	✓			3038	✓			3099				4073			✓
1015				1091			✓	2010	✓			2071	✓			2215	✓			3039				3100	✓			4074			✓
1016				1093				2011	✓			2072	✓			2216	✓			3040				3101	✓			4075			
1017	✓			1095	✓			2012	✓			2073				2217	✓			3041	✓			3102	✓			4076	✓		
1021	✓			1096	✓			2013			✓	2074			✓	2218	✓			3043	✓			3103	✓			4077			✓
1023	✓			1097			✓	2014	✓			2075			✓	2219	✓			3045	✓			3104				4078			✓
1025	✓			1098	✓			2015	✓			2076				2220			✓	3046	✓			3105				4079			✓
1027			✓	1099	✓			2016	✓			2077	✓			2221			✓	3047				3106				4080	✓		
1029	✓			1100	✓			2017	✓			2078	✓			2222	✓			3049	✓			3107				4081	✓		
1031			✓	1101	✓			2019				2079			✓	2223			✓	3051	OOO			3108				4083	✓		
1032	✓			1102	✓			2021			✓	2080				2224	✓			3053	✓			3110	✓			4085	✓		
1033			✓	1103			✓	2023	✓			2081	✓			2225				3055	✓			3201				4087	✓		
1034	✓			1104			✓	2025	✓			2083			✓	2226			✓	3057				3202				4089			✓
1036	✓			1105	✓			2027				2085	✓			2227				3059	✓			3204	✓			4091	✓		
1038			✓	1106				2029	OOO			2087				2228			✓	2061	✓			3205	✓			4093			✓
1040			✓	1107	✓			2031			✓	2089	✓			2229				3062				3206	✓			4095	✓		
1042	✓			1108				2032			✓	2091				2230	✓			3063	✓			3207				4096			
1044	✓			1213				2033			✓	2093	✓			2231			✓	3064			✓	3208				4097			✓
1046	✓			1214	✓			2034				2095				3001	✓			3065	✓			3209	✓			4098	✓		
1049	✓			1215				2035	✓			2096	✓			3002	✓			3066	✓			3210	✓			4099			
1051				1216				2037	✓			2097				3003	✓			3067				3211				4100			✓
1053				1217	✓			2038			✓	2098				3004	✓			3068	✓			3212	✓			4101	✓		✓
1055	✓			1218				2039	✓			2099	✓			3005	✓			3070				3213				4102	✓		
1057	✓			1219				2040			✓	2100				3006	✓			3071	✓			3214				4103			✓
1059				1220	✓			2041	✓			2101			✓	3007			✓	3072				3215	✓			4104			✓
1061	✓			1221			✓	2042			✓	2102				3008			✓	3073	✓			3216				4105			✓
1062	✓			1222			✓	2043	✓			2103				3009	✓			3074	✓			3217				4106	✓		
1063	✓			1223				2045	✓			2104	✓			3010				3075				3218	✓			4107	✓		
1064	✓			1224		✓		2046			✓	2105			✓	3011	✓			3076	✓			3219				4108	✓		
1065	✓			1225			✓	2047	✓			2106			✓	3012	✓			3077				3220	✓			4110	✓		
1066			✓	1226			✓	2049				2107				3013				3078	✓			3221							
1067			✓	1227			✓					2108	✓			3014	✓														

FIGURE 9.1 The Night Clerk's Report to Housekeeping indicates which rooms will require service as a result of being occupied or being vacated and not being serviced.

the tight schedule (Chapter 3) will answer this question. If not enough GRAs are expected in, phone calls are made to standby workers telling them to come to work. If there is an excess of workers indicated on the tight schedule, workers may be called early and told not to report that day, preventing an unnecessary trip. If scheduled workers call to say they will not be in while the supervisor is in the process of opening the house, standby workers may be called to work.

SUPERVISOR'S DAILY WORK REPORT

The information contained on the Night Clerk's Report to Housekeeping is transferred to the **Supervisor's Daily Work Report**. Figures 9.2 through 9.5 show this report for the four divisions of the model hotel—red, yellow, brown, and green. The four forms are created by reference to the House Breakout Plan that was developed in Chapter 2.

SUPERVISOR'S DAILY WORK REPORT

RED — Division (90)

Senior GRA _Georgia_   Day _Wednesday_   Date _11/4_

Section 1 GRA _Julia_		Section 2 GRA _(Open)_		Section 3 GRA _Yvonne_		Section 4 GRA _Billie_		Section 5 GRA _Marjorie_	
1001	✓	1031	✓ CO	1213		1062		1091	✓ CO
1002		1032	✓	1214	✓	1063	✓	1093	
1003	✓	1033	✓ CO	1215		1064	✓	1095	✓
1004	✓	1034	✓	1216		1065	✓	1096	✓
1005		1036	✓	1217	✓	1066	✓ CO	1097	✓ CO
1006	✓	1038	✓ CO	1218		1067	✓ CO	1098	
1007	✓	1040	✓ CO	1219		1068	✓	1099	✓
1008	✓	1042	✓	1220	✓	1071	✓	1100	✓
1009	✓ CO	1044	✓	1221	✓ CO	1072	✓ CO	1101	✓
1010		1046	✓	1222	✓ CO	1073	✓ CO	1102	✓
1011	✓ CO	1049	✓	1223		1074	✓ CO	1103	✓ CO
1012	✓	1051		1224	✓	1075	✓	1104	✓ CO
1013	✓	1053		1225	✓ CO	1076	✓	1105	
1014	✓	1055	✓	1226	✓ CO	1077		1106	
1015		1057	✓	1227		1078	✓	1107	✓
1016		1059		1228	✓	1079	OOO	1108	
1017	✓	1061	✓	1229	✓ CO	1081	✓ CO	1085	
1021	✓	1231	✓ CO	1230	✓ CO	1083	✓ CO	1087	✓

FIGURE 9.2 Supervisor's Daily Work Report: red division. This report contains the transferred information from the Night Clerk's Report to Housekeeping regarding rooms that are part of the five sections of the red division.

SUPERVISOR'S DAILY WORK REPORT

YELLOW — Division (87)

Senior GRA _Katy_   Day _Wednesday_   Date _11/4_

Section 6 GRA _Dianne_		Section 7 GRA _(Open)_		Section 8 GRA _(Open)_		Section 9 GRA _Janice_		Section 10 GRA _Mildred_	
2001	✓	2021		2040	✓ CO	2202		2220	✓ CO
2002	✓	2023	✓	2041	✓	2204	✓	2222	✓
2003		2025	✓	2042	✓ CO	2205	✓	2224	✓
2004		2027		2043	✓	2206		2226	✓
2005	✓	2029	OOO	2045	✓	2207		2228	✓ CO
2006	✓	2031	✓ CO	2046	✓ CO	2208	✓	2230	✓
2007	✓	2032	✓ CO	2047	✓	2209	✓	2057	✓ CO
2008		2033	✓ CO	2049		2210		2059	✓ CO
2009		2034		2051	✓	2211	✓	2061	✓
2010	✓	2035	✓	2053	✓	2212		2062	
2011	✓	2037	✓	2055	✓ CO	2213	✓	2063	
2012		2038	✓ CO	2221	✓ CO	2214	✓	2064	✓
2013		2039	✓	2223	✓ CO	2215	✓	2065	✓
2014	✓	1023	✓	2225		2216	✓	2066	
2015	✓	1025	✓	2227		2217	✓	2067	
2016	✓	1027	✓ CO	2229		2218	✓	2068	✓
2017	✓	1029	✓	2231	✓ CO	2219	✓	2070	✓
2019								2072	✓

FIGURE 9.3 Supervisor's Daily Work Report: yellow division.

SUPERVISOR'S DAILY WORK REPORT

BROWN Division (89)

Senior GRA: Jesse — Day Wednesday — Date 11/4

Section 11 GRA Florence		Section 12 GRA Wilma		Section 13 GRA Marilyn		Section 14 GRA (Open)		Section 15 GRA Susie	
3001	✓	3019		3201		3220	✓	3061	✓
3002	✓	3021	✓	3202	✓ CO	3221		3062	
3003	✓	3023		3204	✓	3222		3063	✓
3004	✓	3025		3205	✓ CO	3223	✓	3064	
3005	✓ CO	3027		3206	✓	3224	✓	3065	✓
3006	✓	3031	✓	3207		3225		3066	✓
3007	✓ CO	3032		3208	✓ CO	3226		3067	
3008	✓ CO	3033	✓	3209	✓ CO	3227		3068	✓
3009	✓	3035	✓ CO	3210	✓	3228	✓	3070	
3010		3037	✓ CO	3211		3229	✓	2071	✓
3011	✓	3038	✓	3212	✓ CO	3230		3072	
3012	✓	3039	✓ CO	3213	✓	3231	✓ CO	3073	✓
3013		3040	✓ CO	3214		3049	✓	3074	✓
3014	✓	3041	✓	3215	✓	3051	o-o-o	3075	
3015	✓	3043	✓	3216	✓ CO	3053	✓	3076	✓
3016		3045	✓	3217	✓ CO	3055	✓	3077	
3017	✓	3046	✓	3218	✓	3057		3078	✓
		3047		3219		3059	✓	3079	✓

FIGURE 9.4 Supervisor's Daily Work Report: brown division.

SUPERVISOR'S DAILY WORK REPORT

GREEN Division (87)

Senior GRA: Heidi — Day Wednesday — Date 11/4

Section 16 GRA Harriet		Section 17 GRA (open)		Section 18 GRA (open)		Section 19 GRA Jane		Section 20 GRA Mary	
2071	✓	2096	✓	3081		3080		4080	✓
2073		2097		3083		4070		4093	✓ CO
2074	✓ CO	2098		3085	✓	4071	✓	4095	✓
2075	✓ CO	2099	✓	3087		4072		4096	
2076		2100		3089		4073	✓	4097	✓ CO
2077	✓	2101		3091	✓	4074	✓	4098	✓
2078	✓	2102		3093		4075		4099	
2079	✓ CO	2103		3095	✓	4076	✓	4100	✓ CO
2080		2104	✓	3096		4077	✓ CO	4101	✓
2081	✓	2105	✓ CO	3097		4078	✓ CO	4102	✓
2083	✓ CO	2106	✓ CO	3098	✓	4079	✓ CO	4103	✓ CO
2085	✓	2107		3099		4081	✓	4104	✓ CO
2087		2108	✓	3100	✓	4083	✓	4105	✓ CO
2089	✓	2110	✓	3101	✓	4085	✓	4106	✓
2091		3106		3102	✓	4087	✓	4107	✓
2093	✓	3107		3103	✓	4089		4108	✓
2095		3108	✓ CO	3104	✓ CO	4091	✓	4110	✓
		3110	✓	3105	✓ CO				

FIGURE 9.5 Supervisor's Daily Work Report: green division.

Next to each division name is the total number of rooms in that division. Note also that there are five room sections in each division and that there are either 17 or 18 rooms in each section. At the top of the report there are spaces for the name of the senior housekeeper, day, and date. There is also a space for the name of the GRA who will be assigned to each section. The checkmarks next to certain rooms, along with an indication of which rooms are expected to be vacated that day (CO), are transferred information from the Night Clerk's Report. This transfer of information can be a tedious task until the opening supervisor is familiar with the two reports and how they relate to each other. The organization of numbers on one form does not necessary relate to the organization of numbers on the other. (The Night Clerk's Report is a reflection of the room rack, which is based on data collected by the front desk, and the Supervisor's Daily Work Report is designed around the House Breakout Plan.)

After the transfer of information is made, GRAs' names from the tight schedule are now placed against specific section numbers. In most cases, housekeepers reporting to work should be assigned their regular sections according to the staffing guide so that they will be working with their regularly assigned equipment. Because occupancy requires only 14 GRAs, six sections will not have a GRA assigned. These six sections will be listed as open sections even though they contain rooms that will require service.

The next step in the process requires a thorough knowledge of the hotel layout—positioning of rooms in relation to each other and elevator location. The best written reference for this information is, again, the House Breakout Plan shown in Chapter 2. At this step, occupied rooms in open sections are assigned to GRAs who have been assigned to regular but partially unoccupied sections. Rooms so assigned are referred to as pickup rooms.

The technique of assigning pickup rooms will be illustrated for the red division and will involve the readjustment of sections 1 through 5 only. (In some cases, the reassignment of workload rooms may require the transfer of occupied rooms from a section in which a GRA is assigned to a section in which another housekeeper is assigned. This is due to the proximity of certain rooms in one section to those of another and to a desire to balance the workload. Refer to Figure 9.6, which is a continuation of the opening process for the red division (Figure 9.2). Note the small circled number to the left of the GRA's name. This is the number of rooms in the regular section that require service and is a reference for the opening supervisor.

Assignment of Pickup Rooms

The assignment of pickup rooms requires specific reference to the House Breakout Plan. Note in Figure 9.6

that sections 1 and 2 are adjacent. Section 1 has a GRA (Julia) assigned; section 2 is open. Also note that at 100 percent occupancy, rooms 1023, 1025, 1027, and 1029 are located in section 7 (directly above on the second floor). Since occupancy is less than 100 percent, and since section 1 is not a full section, first consideration should be to remove the need for an elevator trip by anyone assigned to section 7. Hence, the four rooms mentioned (if in need of service) are assigned as pickup rooms for Julia. This is indicated by writing the four room numbers at the bottom of the column marked section 1. The workload for Julia has now increased from 13 to 17 rooms. Note also that room 1031 in section 2 is adjacent to room 1029, making it a logical pickup choice to complete the workload of 18 rooms for section 1.

Section 2 has been listed as an open section; therefore, all occupied rooms in section 2 must be reassigned for service. Remember that we moved 1031 in section 2 into the workload for section 1. Rooms 1032, 1033, 1034, 1036, 1038, 1040, and 1231 have been transferred to section 3, where Yvonne is assigned, since the House Breakout Plan shows that these rooms are contiguous to section 3. The remaining rooms in section 2 (1042, 1044, 1046, 1049, 1055, 1057, and 1061) are more closely associated with section 4, where Billie is assigned, and are transferred there. Note the techniques for showing how the movement of the rooms into the various sections is indicated. The supervisor must remember to write the room numbers of pickup rooms in both the original and new sections.

All rooms in the open sections have now been reassigned. However, in doing so, Billie in section 4 has been given an overload. To remedy this, rooms 1076, 1077, 1078, 1081, and 1083 are taken out of Billie's regular section and reassigned as pickups for Marjorie in section 5. The planning for the red division workload is now complete. The numbers in parentheses to the right of each GRA's name refer to the final number of rooms assigned to each employee. Note the even distribution of work: three sections with 18 rooms and one section with 17.

Planning the workload of the other three divisions proceeds as with the red division. There is no one correct answer to the placement of pickup rooms. There is, however, "the best" answer, which can be arrived at only through practice. The best indication that planning for opening has been satisfactory is the lack of complaints from employees who have to work according to the plan.

GRA'S DAILY REPORT

Figures 9.7 through 9.11 are the **GRA's Daily Report** forms for the five sections of the red division. These particular forms will serve two functions: 1) to pass the workload information about pickups to each GRA, and 2) to provide a duplicate copy of the blank form to each GRA in order that a **P.M. Report** of the regular section

SUPERVISOR'S DAILY WORK REPORT

_____ **R E D** _____ Division (90)

Senior GRA _____ *Georgia* _____ Day _*Wednesday*_ Date _*11 / 4*_

Section 1 (13) GRA *Julia* (18)		Section 2 (15) GRA *(open)* (0)		Section 3 (11) GRA *Yvonne* (18)		Section 4 (16) GRA *Billie* (18)		Section 5 (12) GRA *Marjorie* (17)	
1001	✓ ←	1031	✓CO	1213		1062		1091	✓
1002		1032	✓ →3	1214	✓	1063	✓	1093	
1003	✓	1033	✓CO →3	1215		1064	✓	1095	✓
1004	✓	1034	✓ →3	1216		1065	✓	1096	✓
1005		1036	✓ →3	1217	✓	1066	✓ CO	1097	✓
1006	✓	1038	✓CO →3	1218		1067	✓ CO	1098	
1007	✓	1040	✓CO →3	1219		1068	✓	1099	✓
1008	✓	1042	✓ ↗4	1220	✓	1071	✓	1100	✓
1009	✓ Co	1044	✓ ↗4	1221	✓CO	1072	✓ CO	1101	✓
1010		1046	✓ ↗4	1222	✓CO	1073	✓ CO	1102	✓
1011	✓ Co	1049	✓ ↗4	1223		1074	✓ CO	1103	✓ CO
1012	✓	1051		1224	✓	1075	✓	1104	✓ CO
1013	✓	1053		1225	✓CO	1076	✓ →5	1105	
1014	✓	1055	✓ ↗4	1226	✓CO	1077	✓ →5	1106	
1015		1057	✓ ↗4	1227		1078	✓ →5	1107	✓
1016		1059		1228	✓	1079	ooo	1108	
1017	✓	1061	✓ ↗4	1229	✓	1081	✓ →5	1085	
1021	✓	1231	✓ CO →3	1230	✓	1083	✓ →5	1087	✓
1023,1025,1027,1029 *1031*				*1231,1032,1033,1034,1036* *1038, 1040*		*1042,1044,1046,1049, 1055* *1057,1061*		*1076,1077,1078,1079* *1081,1083*	

FIGURE 9.6 Supervisor's Daily Work Report: red division. The supervisor has added specific room-scheduling information during opening operations for that day. Similar information is also added to the supervisor's reports for the other divisions.

rooms (rooms whose numbers are printed) may be performed in the afternoon. Note that on copy number 1 of the form, nothing is given except pickup rooms and special notes or remarks. Note also that in Figure 9.10, section 4, Billie is informed that Marjorie will do rooms 1076, 1077, 1078, 1081, and 1083. In this particular case, regular rooms in section 4 would have normally been done by the assigned GRA. However, there was an overload in this section due to pickups being assigned; therefore, rooms at the opposite end of section 4 were passed to the GRA in section 5.

The form has columns headed "C/O," "OCC," and "R." These columns become significant as the second use of the form develops (covered in detail in Chapter 10). The significant point to remember at this time is that a duplicate blank copy of the form with the GRA's name and date are provided in the morning as a part of opening the house.

PREPARING FOR ARRIVAL OF EMPLOYEES

Planning the workload distribution for the day has now been completed. Note that the forms used are in fact routine directives for the accomplishment of work for the day. They are the delegation of tasks to employees based upon the specific occupancy requirements for the servicing of guestrooms on a specific day. All that remains to be done now is to prepare for the arrival of employees.

Copies of the four senior GRAs' work schedules are made and displayed on the linen room counter near the telephone and the computer that transmits and receives messages between housekeeping, front office, and engineering. Original Supervisors' Daily Work Reports are attached to clipboards and placed on the linen room counter to await employee arrivals at about 8:00 A.M.

A copy of the GRAs' Daily Report for *open* sections is also attached to the senior housekeepers' clipboards. All other GRAs' Daily Reports with pickups assigned are attached to smaller clipboards, along with a blank copy of the same form (to be used later in the day for a room report). Passkeys associated with work areas are put next to the clipboards on the linen room counter. Opening-the-house operations are now considered complete, and the department awaits 8:00 A.M. and the arrival of employees for work.

GRA's DAILY REPORT						
SECTION __1__ (18) RMS. AM. PM.						
GRA __Julia__ Day __Wednesday__ Date __11/4__						
ROOM #	C/O	OCC	R	REMARKS	PICKUP	
1001					1023	
1002					1025	
1003					1027	
1004					1029	
1005					1031	
1006						
1007						
1008						
1009						
1010						
1011						
1012						
1013						
1014						
1015						
1016						
1017						
1021						

FIGURE 9.7 GRA's Daily Report for section 1, which has been assigned to Julia. Julia will be expected to clean all guestrooms requiring service from the list of rooms printed in the left column, plus rooms specifically listed as pickup rooms. The fact that 5 rooms have been listed as pickup rooms is an indication to Julia that 5 of the 18 rooms listed in the left column will not require service. Julia will also be given a blank copy of the Section Report for use later in the day when the P.M. room check is conducted.

GRA's DAILY REPORT						
SECTION __2__ (18) RMS. AM. PM.						
GRA __(Open)__ Day __Wednesday__ Date __11/4__						
ROOM #	C/O	OCC	R	REMARKS	PICKUP	
1031						
1032						
1033						
1034						
1036						
1038						
1040						
1042						
1044						
1046						
1049						
1051						
1053						
1055						
1057						
1059						
1061						
1231						

FIGURE 9.8 GRA's Daily Report for section 2. This is an open section, indicating that no GRA has been assigned on this day. The form, however, will be given to the senior GRA, red division, in order that a P.M. room check can be performed later in the day. All occupied rooms in section 2 have been reassigned to other GRAs working in the vicinity of section 2 and are referred to as pickup rooms for other GRAs.

Other Forms for Direction and Control: Standard Operating Procedures

STANDARDIZATION

Standard operating procedures (SOPs) are written instruments that set forth specific recurring actions. They are the devices by which procedures are standardized and are the basis for ready reference as to how to accomplish specific tasks. The opening-the-house procedure just described is a prime example of a procedure requiring documentation. The existence of an SOP on a given subject tacitly prevents deviation from standard activities

until such time as a controlled change takes place. At that time a new or revised SOP may be promulgated. SOPs are similar in form, are numbered, and are usually kept in a reference journal (manual) available to anyone who will have any responsibility regarding a specific procedure. SOPs are coded into various departments of the hotel and may be collected into a master SOP notebook available to the general manager and others interested in reviewing operational techniques. All SOPs usually begin with a simple statement of policy, followed by paragraphs indicating directives, procedures, explanation of forms, records to be kept, positional responsibilities, and coordinating relationships.

STRUCTURED VERSUS UNSTRUCTURED OPERATIONS

Some managers feel that large numbers of controlled SOPs form an organization that is too highly structured,

GRA's DAILY REPORT					
SECTION __3__ (18) RMS. AM. PM.					
GRA _Yvonne_ Day _Wednesday_ Date _11/4_					
ROOM #	C/O	OCC	R	REMARKS	PICKUP
1213					1231
1214					1032
1215					1033
1216					1034
1217					1036
1218					1038
1219					1040
1220					
1221					
1222					
1223					
1224					
1225					
1226					
1227					
1228					
1229					
1230					

FIGURE 9.9 GRA's Daily Report for section 3, which has been assigned to Yvonne, who will have seven pickup rooms.

GRA's DAILY REPORT					
SECTION __4__ (18) RMS. AM. PM.					
GRA _Billie (18)_ Day _Wednesday_ Date _11/4_					
ROOM #	C/O	OCC	R	REMARKS	PICKUP
1062					1042
1063					1044
1064					1046
1065					1049
1066					1055
1067					1057
1068					1061
1071					
1072					
1073					
1074					
1075					
1076					Marjorie will do
1077					" " "
1078					" " "
1079					
1081					" " "
1083					" " "

FIGURE 9.10 GRA's Daily Report for section 4, which has been assigned to Billie, who has seven pickup rooms. The supervisor opening the house recognizes that the pickup rooms given to Billie create an overload. Rooms 1076, 1077, 1081, and 1083 have therefore been reassigned to Marjorie, working in section 5, because they are adjacent to Marjorie's regular section.

creating an environment that stifles initiative. On the contrary, organizations that do not have controlled processes and procedures usually have as many ways to perform an operation as there are people working at the tasks. Some employees may present better ways of accomplishing a task than the manner prescribed in an SOP. If such is the case, testing of a new procedure may well warrant the promulgation of a change in procedure, again standardizing to the better way. SOPs can therefore present a challenge to employees to find better ways to accomplish tasks. If such participation results, employees may be given credit for their participation in improving operations.

SUITABLE SUBJECTS FOR STANDARD OPERATING PROCEDURES IN HOTELS

The following procedural items are suitable for presentation by SOPs. Note that these procedures recur regularly, are suitable for delegation of tasks, allow for communication by forms, and are the foundation upon which change may be made if warranted.

Opening the house
Daily routine
Night activities

GREEN TIP

If you have not already heard, traditional floor finishes are not very good for the environment. They contain heavy metals (i.e., zinc) and nasty hydrocarbons, volatile organic compounds (VOCs), which we do not want in our lungs or in the atmosphere. So how do you keep your floors shiny and respect the planet? Look into UV floors. The floor finish resins are cured by shining an ultraviolet light on them. No more VOCs, no more costly and nasty stripping and waxing, and you are doing your part to save the planet at the same time. They are not for every floor, but they may be just right for yours.

GRA's DAILY REPORT

SECTION _____5_____ (18) RMS.   AM.   PM.

GRA _Marjorie_ (17) Day _Wednesday_ Date _11/4_

ROOM #	C/O	OCC	R	REMARKS	PICKUP
1085					1076
1087					1077
1091					1078
1093					1081
1095					1083
1096					
1097					
1098					
1099					
1100					
1101					
1102					
1103					
1104					
1105					
1106					
1107					
1108					

FIGURE 9.11 GRA's Daily Report for section 5, which has been assigned to Marjorie, who has five pickup rooms.

Key control
Lost-and-found operations
Inventory control procedures
Linen-handling procedures
Time card control
Dilution control for chemicals used in cleaning
Inspection checklists
Standards of performance
Maintenance work-order program
Control of guest loan items

Examples of Standard Operating Procedures for Hotels

There are many procedures that may warrant the publication of an SOP. As examples we present three typical procedures that are standard in almost all housekeeping departments.

LOST-AND-FOUND OPERATIONS

Hskpg Dept SOP-1 6/91

Your Hotel
Anywhere, USA
Standard Operating Procedure 1
Lost-and-Found Operations

Responsibility

A hotel lost-and-found will be operated by the housekeeping department. No department other than the housekeeping department will maintain a collection of found items. Any employee finding an item anywhere in the hotel that appears to be of value will follow his or her supervisor's instructions regarding lost items, and each departmental supervisory staff will ensure that its internal procedures provide for the orderly flow of found items to the housekeeping department for proper storage and disposal. The housekeeping department has also been assigned the task of controlling and coordinating the return of found property to rightful owners, *if such property is inquired about.* Under no circumstances will any employee of the hotel attempt to contact who they think might be a rightful owner for the return of the property. (For property to be returned, it must be inquired about.) Nor will any employee admit to seeing an item or suggesting that such an item may be in the lost-and-found unless the employee has the item in his or her hand.

Procedure (Items Found)

1. When an item is found during day-shift operations (8:00 A.M.–4:00 P.M.), it will be taken to the linen room office for logging and custody control.
2. At other times, items will be turned in to the front desk for custody control.
3. The linen room supervisor will take any item left at the front desk booth during the swing or grave shift to the linen room for proper storage and logging.
4. If a purse or wallet is found, it will be inventoried by two (2) managers, the contents noted in the Log Book (described in the next section), and the book signed by both managers.

The Lost-and-Found Log

All property turned into the housekeeping department for safekeeping will be logged in a Lost-and-Found Log Book containing the following columnar entries: Date/Serial Number/Description of Item/Where Found/By Whom/Department/Disposition/Cross-Reference/ Signature/Remarks.

1. Each item turned in to the housekeeping department will be logged with the information indicated earlier, noting the date found. The entry will be assigned a serial number, and a description of the item will be recorded, along with where it was found, by whom, and in what department the finder may be located.
2. The item will then be placed in an opaque bag, if possible, and the bag marked with the *Log Book serial number only.*
3. The item will then be placed in the lost-and-found storeroom, using a sequential numbering system to make for easy location.
4. The linen room supervisor or linen room attendant will be responsible for making all log entries and for maintaining the Log Book and the lost-and-found storeroom.
5. The linen room supervisor or attendant will ensure that at the close of the day shift, the Lost-and-Found Log Book is locked *inside the lost-and-found.*

Lost-and-Found Inquiries

1. All inquiries about items lost or missing will be referred to the housekeeping department linen room supervisor or attendant for processing. Any inquiry made to any employee in the hotel about a lost item will be referred to the housekeeping office. The business hours of the lost-and-found will be from 9:00 A.M. to 5:00 P.M., Monday through Friday.
2. Upon the inquiry by a guest about a lost item during day operations, the linen room supervisor will first check the Lost-and-Found Log Book. If the item is recorded, he or she will proceed to the lost-and-found and actually locate the item. Once the supervisor has the item in hand, he or she may then tell the guest that the item is in the lost-and-found. If the guest is in the hotel, he or she will be told how to come to the lost-and-found. Upon presenting him- or herself, and after properly describing the item, the guest will be required to sign the Lost-and-Found Log Book under the column marked "Disposition." A name, address, and phone number will be recorded in the "Disposition" column. The guest may then

be given the item. A reward should *never* be sought; however, if a reward is offered, it will be noted in the "Remarks" column of the Log Book. (The finder may then be called to the housekeeping office to receive the reward.) Under no condition will a person be told that the item is in the lost-and-found solely on the strength that it is noted in the lost-and-found Log. The item must be personally in hand before an acknowledgment is made that the item is in the lost-and-found.
3. Any inquiries during swing and grave shift operations will be noted on a lost-and-found inquiry form and left for the linen room supervisor. If the property is located, the linen room supervisor will mail the item(s) to the rightful owner.

Items to Be Mailed

When a lost item has been positively identified by an inquirer and the item must be mailed, the item will be packaged for mailing by the housekeeping department linen room attendant. The mail room will then be requested to pick up the package for mailing. The person taking the package for mailing will sign the Lost-and-Found Log Book, assuming temporary custody of the item.

Control of the Lost-and-Found Storeroom

Strict control of the lost-and-found storeroom will be maintained. The executive housekeeper or assistant and the linen room supervisor or attendant will be the only people permitted in the lost-and-found storeroom. These people will be the only ones permitted to release property from the lost-and-found storeroom. At the end of each day shift, the linen room supervisor will ensure that the lost-and-found door is locked.

Disposition of Items Not Claimed

Any item maintained in the lost-and-found will be held for 90 days. If at the end of this time period the item has not been properly claimed by its rightful owner, it will be offered to the finder as his or her personal property. If the finder desires the item, he or she will be issued a hotel property pass by the housekeeping department authorizing the removal of the property from the hotel. Should the person not desire the item, it will be given to a charitable organization such as Opportunity Village or any other charity that may be designated by the management. Disposition will be so noted in the Lost-and-Found Log.

Proper Guest Relations

Proper handling of lost-and-found matters for our guests is one of our best opportunities to further our public image. Every effort should be made to recognize the concern of our guests and grant them that concern by offering prompt and efficient service regarding lost items.

CHANGING DOOR LOCKS

Hskpg Dept SOP-2 6/91

Your Hotel
Anywhere, USA
Standard Operating Procedure 2
Procedure for Changing Door Locks

Procedure

Whenever the need arises to request a room lock change, the following procedure will be followed:

1. The manager requesting the lock change will fill out the new Lock Change Request Form, indicating the room number, the lock cylinder number, the date, time, and a housekeeper's name.
2. A security officer will also date and approve the request on the line provided.
3. If request is made on the day shift, the Lock Change Request Form will be hand-carried to the locksmith, who will sign and receipt for same. The pink copy will then be left with the locksmith.
4. If request is made on swing or grave shift, the request form will be brought to the security office. The secretaries will be responsible for taking the form to the locksmith's office the next day.

A notation will be made on the report indicating that a lock change request has been made.

The Lock Change Request Form is a three-part form, and the distribution is as follows:

White copy: Retained by security office
Yellow copy: Forwarded to front desk and housekeeping
Pink copy: Given to locksmith

There will be occasions when the maintenance of proper security will require the changing of door locks.

KEY CONTROL

Hskpg Dept SOP-3 6/91

Your Hotel
Anywhere, USA
Standard Operating Procedure 3
Key Control

General

The control of keys is basic to the security of the hotel and to the safety of the employees and guests. The security department holds a number of emergency keys, master keys, and special keys that are subcustodied to employees authorized to use them on specific occasions. Tight security of these keys is required, and the security department will establish procedures for the maintenance of security of these keys.

Procedure

1. The housekeeping department will maintain floor master keys in a locked key control cabinet.
2. Each of these keys will be identified by a stamping and a tag as to their use and level of entry and will be listed on the Master Key Control Chart in the security office.
3. People who have a legitimate need or those involved in an emergency that warrants the use of such keys will contact the housekeeping linen room supervisor for assistance.
4. Keys must be signed for on the Master Key Control Chart.
5. Keys returned will be receipted for on the Master Key Control Log Sheet.

Found Keys

Employees finding keys on the premises must turn them in to the security department. Employees having knowledge of an unauthorized person in possession of any key must report such information to the security department. Employees in possession of an unauthorized key will be subject to disciplinary action.

Key Assistance for Guests

1. If a guest is locked out of his or her room, has no key, and asks for assistance, a security officer or manager should be notified.
2. Upon arrival at the guest's room, the security officer should ask the guest his or her name and home residence.
3. The security officer may then enter the room, leaving the door open and asking

the guest to remain outside until positive identification may be obtained.

4. The security officer will then call the front desk and ask *the name and hometown of the guest in the designated room.*

5. If the information received by the security officer over the phone from the front desk coincides with what the security officer was told by the guest, then the guest may be allowed to enter the room.

There should be no exceptions to this policy. Security officers will write an incident report any time they are required to let a guest into a room.

Examples of Standard Operating Procedures for Hospitals

✂

The following pages show the SOP in a different format. Three examples of hospital SOPs are shown to illustrate the changed format. The examples provided in this chapter were provided by Janice Kurth, author of *Environmental Services Policy and Procedure Manual*, published by Aspen Publishers, Inc. Grateful appreciation is extended to both author and publisher for allowing this work to be reprinted.

GENERAL PROCEDURES

SUBJECT: **Cart Setup** _____
DEPARTMENT: **Environmental Services** _____ DATE ISSUED: _____
APPROVED BY: _____ DATE EFFECTIVE: _____
ORIGINATED BY: _____ SUPERSEDES DATE: _____

Page 1 of 1.

Purpose: To provide the Environmental Technician with a checklist of equipment and supplies that will be needed to complete a routine job assignment. (Project work assignments will require different and/or additional equipment and supplies.)

The following items should appear on a properly equipped cleaning cart:

1 dust mop handle
1 wet mop handle
5 (or more) wet mop heads
1 (or more) dust mop head
An adequate supply of 23″ plastic bags
An adequate supply of 15″ bags
1 plastic bottle equipped with trigger sprayer
1 bottle liquid abrasive cleaner
1 bottle toilet bowl cleaner

1 toilet swab
1 high duster
1 dust pan
1 small broom
1 5-gallon mop bucket
1 small wringer
1 10-quart plastic bucket
6 containers liquid hand soap
An adequate supply of toilet tissue
An adequate supply of paper towels
1 gallon of disinfectant with pump dispenser or measuring device
Rags
Environmental Technicians are expected to keep cleaning carts clean and orderly at all times.
All cleaning solutions and chemicals must be labeled clearly as to contents.

USE OF MACHINES

SUBJECT: **Use and Care of Wet Vacuums** _____
DEPARTMENT: **Environmental Services** _____ DATE ISSUED:_____
APPROVED BY: _____ DATE EFFECTIVE: _____
ORIGINATED BY: _____ SUPERSEDES DATE: _____

Page 1 of 1.

Purpose: To provide supplemental instruction to the employee on using and caring for a wet pickup vacuum safely and efficiently.

The Environmental Services Department has several models of vacuums designed for wet pickup. They have stainless steel tanks and are mounted on wheels.

Procedure:

1. Place the motor onto the tank and fasten securely; if the motor is not fastened properly, the machine will not operate properly.
2. Place a section of hose (not to exceed 50 feet) into the opening at the front of the machine and fit securely; the hose will fall out if not fastened properly.
3. Fit the metal extension into the hose at one end and the squeegee attachment to the other end below the curved section.
4. Plug the machine in, turn on the on/off switch, and place the squeegee onto the floor extended in front of you.
5. Pull the hose toward you for maximum effect; lift, extend, and pull toward you; repeat.
6. Be alert as to when the machine is full; the automatic float valve will operate and the machine will not pick up any more liquid. There also will be a change in the sound of the motor when the tank is full.
7. Turn off the machine, disconnect the hose, unplug (be careful not to lay plug on a wet surface), and empty the tank.
8. Clean and dry the inside of the machine to prevent rust before returning it to its proper storage area.
9. Run clear water through the hose to clean it out.
10. Damp wipe the hose, cord, squeegee, and outside of the tank and motor.
11. Report any irregularities or maintenance problems to your Area Manager.
12. Store properly.

CARPET AND UPHOLSTERY CARE

SUBJECT: **Carpet Cleaning—Using a Bonnet***

DEPARTMENT: **Environmental Services**	DATE ISSUED: _____
APPROVED BY: _____	DATE EFFECTIVE: _____
ORIGINATED BY: _____	SUPERSEDES DATE: _____

Page 1 of 1.

Purpose: To clean the surface of a carpeted area quickly with little interference in the operation of the area, with minimum wetting and minimum drying time.

Assemble needed equipment:
Vacuum cleaner
Rotary floor machine
Spin yarn pads
Carpet shampoo
Pressure sprayer and/or 2 large buckets with one wringer

Procedure:

1. Vacuum area to be cleaned thoroughly, first across width of the room, then lengthwise; this is a crucial step—do not omit.
2. Mix shampoo solution in large bucket following label directions carefully for proper dilution ratios.

Method A:

1. Pour solution into the pressure sprayer.
2. Work 4-foot squares, spraying the area thoroughly, but avoid overwetting.
3. Soak the yarn pad in clear water and wring out thoroughly. Place on carpet and center floor machine over it.
4. Move the machine across the square widthwise, then lengthwise, taking care to agitate the entire area.
5. Repeat this procedure in overlapping 4-foot sections until completed, turning the pad when soiled; for large areas, you may need to rinse the pad to remove excess soil and/or use several pads.
6. Allow to dry before allowing foot traffic.
7. Clean equipment and store properly.

Method B:
This differs from A only in application of solution.

1. Prepare solution in a large bucket.
2. Fill a second large bucket with clear water.
3. Soak the yarn pad in the detergent solution and wring thoroughly.
4. Follow the procedure outlined above to clean the carpet, rewetting and turning the pad frequently.
5. Rinse pad in the clear water to remove excess soil and prolong its use.

---

*A bonnet, also called a spin yarn pad, is a thick yarn pad made of cotton or cotton polyester that fits onto the pad holder of a standard floor machine.

EXECUTIVE PROFILE
Janet Marletto *A Dream Realized: A Life from Childhood Playhouses to Luxury Hotels*

by Andi M. Vance, Editor, *Executive Housekeeping Today*

(This article first appeared in the October 2001 issue of *Executive Housekeeping Today*, the official publication of the International Executive Housekeepers Association, Inc.)

It all started one Christmas Eve in the early 1950s when a special gift was brought to young Janet Marletto. Throughout the night, her father and his friends worked diligently by the light of flood lamps, erecting a structure that would catalyze Janet's passion for housekeeping. In the morning when she awoke, she went to the living room to see what Santa had brought for her: a single key under the Christmas tree. Running outside to see what the key would unlock, her mouth gaped in awe at the elaborate playhouse with a large Dutch door, two side windows and a plate glass window overlooking the San Francisco Bay. A miniature palace—in her backyard! Janet spent many years playing house and school in this special place where her imagination had free rein. Since then, Janet has gone on to make her dreams realities: her playhouse became luxury hotels.

"Classic" is the way Marletto describes her upbringing. A child well versed in the arts, etiquette, food, travel and culture, her mother and maternal grandmother served as major role models in her life. "My mother was Martha Stewart before there was a Martha Stewart," she fondly recalls. "She and my grandmother were both excellent homekeepers. My training was always very

formal. By four years old, I knew how to use a finger bowl. My parents regularly took me to the symphony and art galleries. We always gathered for dinner and had interesting conversation based on world events or the philosophy of life. These standards have stayed with me throughout my life.

"When I was 10, my mother said something to me as I was doing my chores that was rather prophetic," Marletto remembers. "She told me that it was important for me to know how to do things properly. She continued to say that even if I was to direct a staff when I grew up I needed to be able to show them how I wanted things done."

Since her days of playing house in her backyard, Marletto's chosen profession reflects these childhood interests and influences. But she didn't delve into the hospitality industry immediately. Early in her career, she worked as a middle and high school French, English and history teacher in Santa Barbara. She exposed her students to every opportunity within her reach. For example, her French students experienced the finest in French culture and cuisine through field trips and dinners.

After seven years of teaching, Marletto decided that she needed a change. She wanted a venue where she could continue creating change and influencing others, but she was unsure of where she'd be most effective. She'd volunteered at the

DeYoung Museum in San Francisco's Golden Gate Park on days off from school. She enjoyed it so much that she entered the extensive training program from docents of the Avery Brundage Asian Art Collection at the DeYoung. This involved classes taught by UC Berkeley art historians and research in the museum's library, culminating in the right to give tours in the Asian collection.

Her appetite whetted, she went on to explore Chinese calligraphy character by character and still presents friends and colleagues with samples of her brush work. Her developing sensitivity to Asian culture served as a natural lead into her study of Feng Shui (see February 2001 *EHT* article by Marletto on the basics of Feng Shui) and subsequent role as an active Feng Shui consultant which continues today.

She explored interior design as another potential occupation, considering her knowledge of European and Chinese art and interest in Feng Shui. "Then I realized that everything I had done as odd jobs (e.g., house cleaning in college, payroll, retail, etc.), served as training to the hotel field," she says. "It only seemed natural for me to become involved with luxury hotels."

Since she made that decision in 1975 and completed the management training program at the Westin St. Francis in San Francisco, Janet has directed the housekeeping departments in a number of luxury establishments: the Broadmoor in Colorado Springs, the Registry Resort in Naples and Walt Disney World Swan in Orlando, just to name a few. At the time of this article, Marletto works as a consultant at the St. Regis Beach Monarch Resort in California.

With already a wealth of knowledge beneath her belt, Marletto has an unbelievable zest for acquiring as much information as possible—and not just within the realm of housekeeping. She pursues each endeavor with a childlike earnestness, keeping her eyes open to all opportunities. While her interests may not be directly related to housekeeping, all contribute to her expertise in the field. Her vast experiences make her a valuable resource to all departments within the hotel.

CULTURAL DISPARITIES

Since she's been in the business, Marletto has cross-trained at the Dolder Grand in Zurich, Switzerland, and at the Sonesta in Amsterdam. The differences between housekeeping in Europe and the U.S. spiral off of distinct differences in procedural principle. In the U.S., housekeeping is based upon room occupancy, whereas in Europe, this is not the case. Instead, housekeepers are assigned their sections daily whether occupied or not. Although European hotel owners charge more for luxury accommodation than their counterparts in the U.S., they can provide additional services for their guests using this approach. "There [in

Europe] additional training is possible," she mentions. "Detail work is possible and service levels can be met more easily. The staff is salaried so the budget is not a question."

Another difference is regarding storage space. In the U.S., the lack of secured storage space often presents an obstacle for Executive Housekeepers. Marletto discovered that in Europe, almost everything had a space for safekeeping. "The old cliché of doing things right the first time is probably the most economical way of doing anything," she advises. "You need to know that what you need is where you thought it was and is in good condition. Then you don't need to handle things more than once. This is one of the keys to good housekeeping."

The lack of secured storage space is one of the vexations of "value-engineering" in hotel design. "Most every space needs to have an income," she contests. "I understand all of that, but it makes running a housekeeping operation very difficult." She advises Executive Housekeepers to look at their resources through a creative lens for procuring a safe storage space. At a hotel where she worked in Florida, a cage was designed from an old trash chute. After having the length of the chute professionally cleaned, it was painted and sealed. "The room attendants brought their vacuums down every day for checkout before each vacuum was locked in the cage for safekeeping. This prevented loss or damage to the equipment."

THE MENTOR

To those who work with Marletto, her role extends far beyond that of a typical director. "When I worked with Janet at the Walt Disney World Swan Hotel,"

says Beverly Morris, a previous co-worker of Marletto, "she was a jewel. She really knew how to get people motivated. Janet Marletto's the best person I've ever had the privilege to work with anywhere." Marletto demands five-star excellence from all of her staff, but she encourages her staff in all spheres of development and provides them with guidance. This is a value-added resource for them; housekeeping is only the beginning of the many opportunities that will become available to them if they choose to open the right doors.

She's also interested in developing her staff physically. Prior to the start of every shift, Marletto leads her staff through a few minutes of stretching exercises. A proper breathing technique is essential in this ritual which yields both physical and mental benefits for those who choose to participate. "It's relaxing and it's proven to lower blood pressure," she advises. "It helps everyone start the day smiling and even laughing." Once, she was unable to lead the staff through the morning routine and was delighted to find a group stretching even in her absence.

For those who step up to the plate, Marletto also offers opportunities for mentoring programs. Of the approximately 1,000 people she's directed, she's taken more than 12 under her wing and developed them into upper-level managers. While this opportunity is open to all of her staff, she only considers those with a personal vision. Through the mentoring process, she develops individuals in a systematic way so that they can move up in their careers. She provides a solid knowledge base grounded in all aspects in a Director's basic responsibilities. By presenting information in steps, students are able to backtrack through the process if expected results are not achieved. "When I train people to do a budget," she advises, they must first know (and be comfortable with) all of the supplies. They must be able to do inventory and order the supplies. When they become comfortable with the supply end and begin to get a feel of usage amounts, they can then start the process of ordering. When they do projections, they can tell if something's out of line. We can then talk about what we can do for the orders and they begin to assist with other areas of the budget. I do it in those steps because I find that it works and that it's easy to understand. If you've done the steps and arrived at a result you may be unsure of, you can always retrace your steps and check the results. I guess you'd call it old-fashioned training, but you really need it. If you know how to do it, the stress of inaccuracy is taken away."

THE MENTORED

Throughout her life, Marletto has widened her spheres of influence to broaden her experiences. Through opportunities she creates, she at times comes into contact with individuals who serve as mentors to her. Once when she was between jobs, she served as a relief cook to the matriarch of the John Deere tractor family, Mrs. Charles Deere Wiman, in Montecito, CA. "Everything in the home was museum quality," Marletto recalls. "Much of the decor was Sung Dynasty porcelain and the only paper in the house was toilet paper in the bathrooms and paper towels in the kitchen. She had monogrammed linen made by nuns in Madeira, Portugal. It was amazing."

Mrs. Wiman was the first person to teach Marletto how to inspect a guest's room—a technique Marletto still employs

today. "Sit in a chair," she instructs, "extend your arms and think, What would a guest need in this chair?' You wouldn't place the tissue box two inches further from your reach. You want to go around the room and sit in the various positions to see and feel what the guest is experiencing. You'll catch things you wouldn't have normally seen—like a cobweb hanging in the corner."

On a personal development level, Marletto considers her chiropractor, Dr. Lee Blackwood, as a mentor, "I find him very inspiring, knowledgeable and stimulating," she says. "He has strength. Being that kind of person, I've always provided that for others but never had that type of person myself. When I hit a wall or am contemplating how I should handle a particular situation, he's a person I can turn to and ask for guidance. He puts a spotlight on a particular aspect of the situation and helps me move forward. It's an honor to have someone of his caliber (he is a success coach for Nightingale Conant and has mentored major executives) in my corner at this point in my life."

"When I first met Janet," recalls Dr. Blackwood, "she was in a period of transition. She had an abundance of options available to her, but nothing really stood out. I was instantly able to see where her paradigms and emotional areas were located and helped her by focusing on those. Janet's very intuitive and lives her life actively; she just goes out and gets what she wants once she determines what she wants."

CHALLENGES

Dispelling the stigma attached to the Executive Housekeeper's position is a major challenge she strives to achieve. As she puts it, "I see the role of a director as *director*. There are too many

people who think that a director should be doing the cleaning. But that's not our role."

She also aims to defeat the judgments and stereotypes associated with frontline workers. Marletto identifies what she calls the "Coolie Concept," wherein people who aren't in the housekeeping field feel that the job is not being completed unless the room attendants are down on their hands and knees scrubbing. She sees this as one of the biggest challenges to the industry, particularly during a period when excessive staffing shortages plague the field. "My search has always been to utilize technology and knowledge to make things as simple as possible," she advises. "I find tools and equipment to make things easier for those doing the cleaning like backpack vacuums, etc. There's nothing mystical about it. We're in the 21st Century, and we should come up with ways that are as labor saving and as easy and pleasant as possible for the people doing the job."

DREAMS REALIZED

Since the Christmas morning when Janet Marletto awoke to find the playhouse in her backyard, her career as an Executive Housekeeper has taken her throughout many larger "playhouses." By keeping abreast of opportunities and developments around her and maintaining five-star standards, Marletto stays in the upper tier of her chosen profession. She readily shares the knowledge she's acquired.

No matter what, she keeps posterity in the back of her mind and keeps in touch with her niece and nephews so that she can be sure to share family traditions with them and build new ones. "One of the highlights of my life was to teach my nephew, Christopher, how to blow bubbles. Sharing the little joys in life means more to me than anything else."

In the near future, Marletto hopes to publish a few books and possibly have her own unique radio program. "Success is a journey," she says. "It's getting to the point in your life when you're satisfying your soul and creating wonderful memories. When you're comfortable with who, what and where you are in life, then you are a success ... and a happy person!"

DISCUSSION QUESTIONS

1. Repetitive stress injuries among housekeepers are viewed by many occupational health authorities as a major problem in housekeeping departments. What is Janet Marletto doing to lessen the possibility of stress injuries to her staff?

2. Many people equate success with large salaries, but not Janet Marletto. What do think of her philosophy that "Success is a journey"?

Standard Operating Procedures Are Not to Restrict Initiative

The extent to which housekeeping department managers choose to document procedures for reference, standardization, and use in training is a matter of personal preference and, in most cases, company policy.

Most companies requiring the promulgation of SOPs are usually quick to emphasize that such SOPs are to be used primarily as guidelines for operations and should not stifle **initiative** in the investigation of ways and means to improve operations. Many hotels are quick to reward employees who find better ways of performing tasks; some even offer incentive awards for improvement of procedures. The SOPs may very well become the framework for operations and, simultaneously, the tool whereby controlled change may take place.

CONCLUSION

In this chapter we saw how preparation for opening the new hotel moves into the operational planning phase. Although the hotel is not yet in operation, preliminary techniques for routines, delegation, and control have been constructed, as were other systems involving concept development, organizing, staffing, and material planning. Although direction of operations has not yet begun, preparation for the routine communication of daily activities must be conceptually developed and standardized.

One of the first routines by which daily activities are directed—opening the house—has been developed in detail, as have the necessary forms by which this direction is communicated. In addition, a system of standard operating procedures has been presented, with examples, by which the opening the house and other routines may be standardized. Topics for the SOP approach are listed, but are only the beginning of such a list.

KEY TERMS AND CONCEPTS

Forms
Standard operating procedures (SOPs)
Opening the house
Working and control documents
Open sections

18-room workload
Pickup rooms
Night Clerk's Report to Housekeeping
Occupied
Check out

Ready rooms (R)
Out of order
Supervisor's Daily Work Report
GRA's Daily Report
P.M. Report
Initiative

DISCUSSION AND REVIEW QUESTIONS

1. Discuss how operational planning is related to delegation and why preplanning an operation is so important.
2. Explain why forms are important in the operation of a housekeeping department. Explain how these forms are used in opening the house: Night Clerk's Report to Housekeeping, Supervisor's Daily Work Report, GRA's Daily Report.
3. Define the following terms and give their symbols if appropriate:

   Ready room
   Occupied
   Checkout
   Out of order
   Pickup room
   Open section

4. Explain the meaning of "controlled change."

PART THREE

DIRECTING AND CONTROLLING ONGOING HOUSEKEEPING OPERATIONS

In Part Two, the planning, organizing, and staffing principles of management discussed earlier were applied before the opening of a new hotel or similar operation. Part Three concentrates on the direction and control functions as applied to ongoing operations of housekeeping management. It begins by discussing the hotel housekeeper's daily routine of department management. It then presents "subroutines," that is, other functions of hotel housekeeping management that are not necessarily daily routines but are essential routines nonetheless. Part Four addresses swimming pool operations, housekeeping in other venues, protection of assets, and linen and laundries, and presents a conclusion.

CHAPTER 10

The Hotel Housekeeping Daily Routine of Department Management

LEARNING OBJECTIVES

After studying the chapter, students should be able to:

1. Describe the steps involved in the daily routine of cleaning guestrooms.
2. Describe the priority for cleaning guest-rooms.
3. Identify communication symbols used on the daily work report.
4. Identify in chronological order the specific steps taken by a GRA in the cleaning of a guestroom.
5. Describe the coordination that must take place between the housekeeping department's first and second shifts.
6. Identify in chronological order the evening activities of the housekeeping department.

In Part Two we opened the house. The stage is now set for presentation of the primary daily routine that occurs in ongoing operations. In fact, opening the house is the first step of the daily routine in the ongoing cycle known as the housekeeping day.

The Housekeeping Day

The chronology of the **housekeeping day** may be divided into several distinct parts. This chronology differs depending on the type of property to which it is related and whether a computer application is in effect. For the purpose of illustration, the model hotel (commercial transient type; noncomputerized in housekeeping communication to the front desk) will continue to be the basis for system development. You should recognize, however, that destination resorts and resorts that are located in the center of activities may present different chronologies due to different types of markets.

A **daily routine chronology** for the model hotel housekeeping department might be as follows:

6:30 A.M. to 8:00 A.M.	Opening the house
8:00 A.M. to 1:00 P.M.	Morning activities (also, cleaning the guestroom)
1:00 P.M. to 3:00 P.M.	Resolution of Do Not Disturbs (DNDs)
3:00 P.M. to 3:30 P.M.	The P.M. room check
3:30 P.M. to 4:30 P.M.	Shift overlap: first and second shift coordination
At 4:30 P.M.	Housekeeper's Report is transmitted to the front desk

4:30 P.M. to 6:00 P.M.	Discrepancies generated (identification of those rooms in which front desk status is different from that noted on the Housekeeper's Report). Many discrepancies will be resolved by close investigation of guest accounts at the front desk. Rechecks generated (unresolved discrepancies published to housekeeping). Rooms on recheck list are again viewed to ensure correct status. P.M. housekeeping workload is finalized.
6:00 P.M. to midnight	Evening activities (until housekeeping closes)

OPENING THE HOUSE (6:30 A.M. TO 8:00 A.M.)

Opening the house is the first step in the chronology of the housekeeping department day. Information communicated from the front desk to housekeeping via the Night Clerk's Report to Housekeeping is transcribed onto working forms for the housekeeping department. Adequate staffing is ensured, and preparation is made for the arrival of workers. Figures 9.6 through 9.11 are examples of the means by which the direction and delegation of daily tasks for the routine conduct of work by a portion of a housekeeping staff (red team for our model) might normally be conveyed on a typical day. The conveyance of direction and delegation to other segments of the housekeeping staff (yellow, brown, and green teams) occur in a similar manner. As we discuss the daily chronology of events, the forms used in Figures 9.6 through 9.11 for direction to the red team will continue to be used.

MORNING ACTIVITIES (8:00 A.M. TO 1:00 P.M.)

Most housekeeping departments start their daily routine at about 8:00 A.M. The time for the start of **morning activities** may vary based on the ability of guestroom attendants (GRAs) to gain access to guestrooms. In commercial transient properties in which weekend packages might be offered to families, the start of work may be delayed until 9:00 A.M. or even 10:00 A.M., depending on how late guests are known to sleep in. In hotels in which businesspeople are the major occupants, however, there are sufficient numbers of early risers to allow GRAs to start work at about 8:00 A.M. Such will be assumed for the morning activities in the model hotel, which commence at 8:00 A.M. (The examples of communication that follow will again relate to the red team as presented in Chapter 9.)

In small properties, employees simply clock in for work and proceed directly to their central housekeeping area to pick up their assignments. Frequently, employees come to work in their uniforms and are essentially ready to pick up their assignments and proceed directly to their floors.

Some hotels, however, do not allow their employees to take uniforms off the property. Others do not even have locker rooms where street clothing can be stored during working hours. In these latter cases, **changing rooms** are provided adjacent to **wardrobe departments**, which help facilitate large numbers of employees reporting to work at the same time.

For example, at the Bellagio, MGM Mirage Resort in Las Vegas, Nevada, employees clock in at a time clock area as they enter the building. They then proceed some distance to a wardrobe department, where they pick up preassigned **plastic hang-up bags**. The hang-up bag has one of four or five uniforms (costumes) that have been purchased for each employee. The wardrobe department at the Bellagio is seen in Figure 10.1 (note the admonitions to employees in the third photo). The suit bags with the fresh uniforms are then checked out by the employees (Figure 10.2), who proceed to the changing room. Upon changing into the **costumes**, the employees put their street clothing into the hang-up bags, then return the bags to the wardrobe department for storage while the employees are at work. At the end of the workday, the procedure is reversed and the soiled costumes are returned to the wardrobe department. The employees will be resupplied with fresh costumes for the next workday.

Figure 10.3 shows Mirage GRAs arriving at the floor linen room on their assigned floor where they are actually "reporting for work in uniform." According to the work rules at that hotel, it is at this time that the eight-hour workday will commence.

As workers arrive, GRAs and senior GRAs pick up work assignments and sign for keys on the Passkey/Beeper Control Sheet (Figure 10.4). All issues and turn-in receipts of communication beepers and passkeys should be recorded as they occur.

The Supervisor's Daily Work Report (Figure 9.6) had notations of rooms expected to be checked out on that day. The question now is this: Have any of these or other rooms actually been vacated as of 8:00 A.M.? (Figure 10.5.) If checkouts have actually occurred, the front desk would have conveyed this information as soon as possible to housekeeping central. This type of information (rooms actually vacated) will flow all during the day from the front desk, through housekeeping central, to the satellite linen rooms, where it will be picked up by the floor supervisors. They in turn will pass this information to the GRAs in order that the latter may clean the rooms as soon as it can be done.

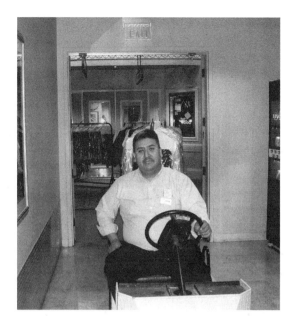

(a)

(b)

(c)

FIGURE 10.1 A housekeeping aide arrives with a "trainload" of clean uniforms for the wardrobe department. The automated conveyor racks contain thousands of uniforms. *(Photographs courtesy of Bellagio, MGM Mirage, Las Vegas, Nevada.)*

FIGURE 10.2 One attendant signs for a costume as another electrically calls it forward from storage. *(Photo taken with permission of MGM Mirage.)*

FIGURE 10.3 Guestroom attendants and a housekeeping aide check in with their supervisor on their assigned floor for the day. *(Photo taken with permission of MGM Mirage.)*

Early in the shift, the executive housekeeper reviews the hotel's status before communicating with the scheduling clerk to ensure that there are sufficient staff members to cover the day's activities (Figure 10.6).

Figure 10.7 shows how the Supervisor's Daily Work Report (Figure 9.6) is used to record *actual* checkouts against those rooms that had heretofore only been *expected* to check out. Note that some rooms that had been expected to remain occupied (such as Rooms 1228 and 1096) are now showing checkout status. These guests were early and unexpected departures, resulting

in additional checkout rooms. In either event, the actual checkout is recorded by circles around the C/O notation. This information is passed to the GRA to immediately enter the rooms to service them for reoccupancy.

Upon arriving at the satellite linen room (Figure 10.8), the supervisor ensures that members of the team are properly prepared and move toward their assigned workstations as soon as possible. The sheets hanging on the wall in the photo are actually locking cloth bags that the GRAs place over their housekeeping carts at the end of the shift after stocking them for the

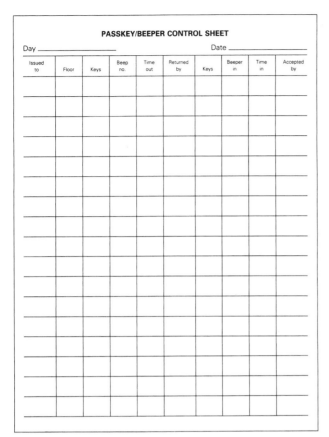

FIGURE 10.4 Passkey/Beeper Control Sheet. Such records keep close control over these objects. *(Form courtesy of MGM Mirage, Las Vegas.)*

FIGURE 10.5 Bellagio central status operator Danielle Kelly passes needed information to the floor supervisor regarding last-minute morning status. *(Photo taken with permission of MGM Mirage.)*

(a)

(b)

FIGURE 10.6 Bellagio Executive Housekeeper Kevin Holloway (a) reviews room status reports before contacting Scheduling Clerk and UNLV hotel graduate Jennifer Kambegian (b). *(Photo taken with permission of MGM Mirage.)*

next day to prevent other shifts from helping themselves to sheets, towels, and amenities. With GRAs' carts properly loaded the day before, they should require only slight attention before being completely in order for work (Figure 10.9). Each GRA now moves toward the assigned area of room-cleaning responsibility.

The section housekeeping aide begins a routine inspection of corridors, elevators, stairwells, and other public areas to determine if any place needs emergency attention as a result of some accident during the night (spills, cigarette urns turned over, and so on). The section housekeeping aide records on the inspection

SUPERVISOR'S DAILY WORK REPORT

RED Division (90)

Senior GRA _Georgia_   Day _Wednesday_   Date _11/4_

Section ___1___ (13) GRA _Julia_	Section ___2___ (15) GRA _(Open) (0)_	Section ___3___ (11) GRA _Yvonne (18)_	Section ___4___ (16) GRA _Billie (18)_	Section ___5___ (12) GRA _Marjorie (17)_
1001 ✓	1031 ✓ CO	1213	1062	1091 ✓
1002	1032 ✓ →3	1214 ✓	1063 ✓	1093
1003 ✓	1033 ✓ CO →3	1215	1064 ✓	1095 ✓
1004 ✓	1034 ✓ →3	1216	1065 ✓	1096 ✓ (CO)
1005	1036 ✓ →3	1217 ✓	1066 ✓ CO	1097 ✓
1006 ✓	1038 ✓ CO →3	1218	1067 ✓ CO	1098
1007 ✓	1040 ✓ (CO) →3	1219	1068 ✓	1099 ✓
1008 ✓	1042 ✓ ↗4	1220 ✓	1071 ✓	1100 ✓
1009 ✓ (CO)	1044 ✓ ↗4	1221 ✓ CO	1072 ✓ (CO)	1101 ✓
1010	1046 ✓ ↗4	1222 ✓ (CO)	1073 ✓ CO	1102 ✓
1011 ✓ CO	1049 ✓ ↗4	1223	1074 ✓ CO	1103 ✓ CO
1012 ✓	1051	1224 ✓	1075 ✓	1104 ✓ CO
1013 ✓	1053	1225 ✓ CO	1076 ✓ →5	1105
1014 ✓	1055 ✓ ↗4	1226 ✓ (CO)	1077 ✓ →5	1106
1015 ✓	1057 ✓ ↗4	1227	1078 ✓ →5	1107 ✓
1016	1059	1228 ✓ (CO)	1079 ○○○	1108
1017 ✓	1061 ✓ ↗4	1229 ✓	1081 ✓ →5	1085
1021 ✓	1231 ✓ CO →3	1230 ✓	1083 ✓ →5	1087 ✓
_1023,1025,1027,1029, 1031_		_1231,1032,1033,1034,1036 1038, 1040_	_1042,1044,1046,1049,1055 1057 1061_	_1076,1077,1078, 1079 1081, 1083_

FIGURE 10.7 Supervisor's Daily Work Report, red division, as it may appear at 8.00 A.M. Note circles around COs, indicating that rooms expected to be vacated have in fact now been vacated.

form what, if any, attention is needed in the public areas of the guestroom section of the hotel (Figure 10.10). The aide also notes any project work that will become a part of the regular day's cleaning assignment or of a future plan. Figure 10.11 shows a Mirage housekeeping aide (houseman) cleaning up a previous night's spill, which was discovered in an elevator lobby during morning inspection of an assigned area. Otherwise, the section housekeeping aide commences work in accordance with the job description, as noted in Appendix A. The senior GRA (supervisor) begins a morning room check.

A.M. Room Check

Daily **A.M. room checks** are performed to determine whether the status of rooms reported by the front desk is in fact the correct status from the preceding night. For example, if the front desk reports certain rooms as **occupied** (with guest or with luggage) and in need of service, the A.M. room check determines if these rooms are actually occupied or the status is

incorrect. The report verifies rooms reported as **ready to rent** or **on change** (in the process of being serviced for reoccupancy); sometimes called checkouts or simply C/O) are as reported. Are these rooms in fact ready to rent and vacant? Or has a **discrepancy** been uncovered in the status held by the front desk?

Since this information is needed and must be accurate, room checks are conducted in the early morning in most hotels. GRAs knock on doors and, where necessary, enter rooms. Some hotels do not even use an opening-the-house routine. Daily routine simply starts with someone in the housekeeping department entering every room to determine if service is needed.

A.M. Housekeeper's Report In some cases an A.M. room check is conducted, and the results are assembled into an A.M. Housekeeper's Report. The report is submitted to the accounting department as a cross-reference and audit check on the revenues reported by the front desk from occupied rooms. The primary function of an

(a)

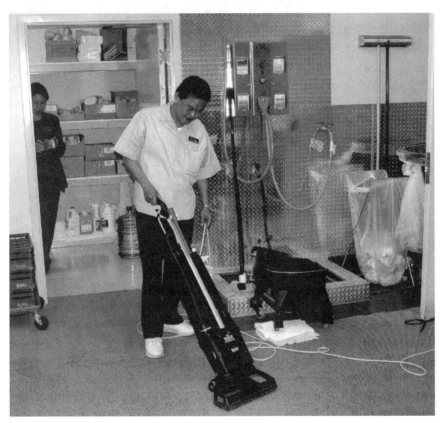

(b)

FIGURE 10.8 A typical satellite linen room at the Bellagio (a). In the same room, housekeeping aide William vacuums while housekeeping supervisor Teresita Arenas inspects the amenities closet (b). *(Photo taken with permission of MGM Mirage.)*

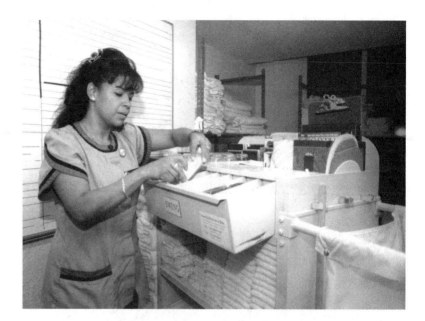

FIGURE 10.9 Meanwhile, the GRA makes a final check of her loaded cart to ensure that she will be able to stay at her worksite without having to return to her storage room for more supplies later in the day. *(Photo taken with permission of MGM Mirage.™)*

HOUSEKEEPING AIDE—EARLY A.M. CHECK	
Date: _____	
Area	Location and Condition
Satellite Linen Rooms	
Stairwells	
Hallways	
Elevators	
Vending areas	

FIGURE 10.10 Housekeeping Aide—Early A.M. This report will form the basis for special work that must be performed.

A.M. Housekeeper's Report, then, is to ascertain that revenue is reported for every room that was occupied last night.

Quick Discrepancy Check There is a simpler way to ascertain the status of rooms for which revenue should be reported than to disturb every guest in the hotel every morning. Rooms that are thought to be occupied have been scheduled for service. Rooms that are thought to be vacant and ready to rent have not been scheduled for service and their boxes are blank on the Supervisor's Daily Work Report (Figure 10.7). Since the primary concern is whether there are rooms

FIGURE 10.11 A housekeeping aide (houseman) cleans a spill discovered on an early-morning inspection. *(Photo taken with permission of MGM Mirage.)*

occupied for which no revenue is being received, there is no need to check rooms known to be occupied; senior housekeepers need to inspect only those rooms thought to be vacant and/or ready to rent. Such rooms in this category that are found occupied (or obviously not ready) need to be investigated immediately to determine why their statuses are incorrectly held by the front desk. A discrepancy report may therefore be generated from the inspection of ready rooms only.

There are several reasons why discrepancies occur:

1. A guest was to have been in room 2204 but was inadvertently handed the key to room 2206. A simple error in key selection went unnoticed by the clerk, and the guest went to the address (2206) found on the key. At this point the front desk thought that room 2204 was to have been occupied when it will actually be discovered at morning room check that 2206, thought to be vacant, is the one that is occupied. This type of error is of no major consequence involving revenue; however, the possibility of inadvertently **double rooming** another person into room 2206 can occur, which may prove embarrassing to both hotel and guest.
2. Another and more major concern is the possibility that the room may have been given away by someone who did not have the authority to do so. (No records kept, therefore no questions asked!)
3. Finally, there is the possibility that some member of the hotel staff (bellperson, night security watch, desk clerk) who had access to guestrooms keys did, without proper authority, use a guestroom for an unauthorized night's rest—or whatever.

Regardless of the reasons for rooms that have been used and not recorded for revenue, they must be uncovered, and corrective measures taken to prevent such happenings in the future.

A Matter of Quality Service It is indeed unfortunate that many hotels cling to the notion that it is necessary to knock on every guestroom door at 8:00 A.M. in order to conduct an accurate room check. Other hotels recognize that it is not necessary to disturb a guest in a room thought to be occupied in order to determine whether a room thought to be vacant is in fact vacant. It is not necessary to disturb a guest only to conduct a room check; A.M. room checks should be confined to rooms thought to be vacant and ready or vacant and on change (checked out of). If this procedure is followed, GRAs need not approach any room in the morning until they are ready to clean that room. The A.M. room checks may then be left to the senior GRA; who will open every door of guestrooms thought to be vacant to ensure their status.

Techniques of Keeping Track Figure 10.12 illustrates a technique of recording A.M. room check information. Note the R placed opposite each room found to be ready, thus verifying correct status (for example, see rooms 1002, 1005, and 1010). A line is drawn through

the room number and the space next to it, indicating that there is no further service required from the housekeeping department in that room for that day. Also note how discrepancies uncovered during A.M. room check are recorded. Circles are drawn around the room numbers for rooms 1216 and 1098, indicating these discrepancies. An immediate call is then made to the front desk, pointing out the discrepancies so that the front desk personnel might resolve the matter immediately. The only action required of housekeeping department personnel is recognition by the supervisor that an additional room in the division will require service. This room may then be assigned to one of the GRAs, or the room may be "sold" to any GRA desiring to work an overload, or the supervisor may actually do the room.

The A.M. room check is normally completed in about 30 minutes, depending on the number of unoccupied (ready or checkout) rooms listed. Once morning room check is completed, the supervisor is free to resume his or her supervisory responsibilities with the team.

Communication and Supervision The supervisor circulates throughout the assigned division, communicating with GRAs and section housekeeping aides and monitors work progress during the day. The supervisor is constantly receiving information and conveying it to GRAs. The supervisor receives information about rooms having been vacated by communicating with the status-board operators. This information is passed on to GRAs so that these rooms may be cleaned as soon as possible. Also, information—about rooms that are cleaned and ready for reoccupancy—that is received from GRAs is conveyed back to the status-board operators, who in turn pass it on to front desk personnel.

In Figure 10.12, room 1222 has been reported to the supervisor as having been cleaned by the GRA and is now ready to be reported to the front desk. The supervisor places an R after the circled CO indication, thereby keeping track of all rooms reported as having been cleaned (whether occupied or checked out). The supervisor may make an inspection of the room or, if confident that the room will meet standards, simply mark the Supervisor's Daily Work Report as indicated by room 1222 on Figure 10.12. Since the room is *actually reported* to status-board operators as a ready room, the supervisor draws a line through the entire entry opposite the room number. This has been done for room 1226, noting that all routine interest in that particular room has now been completed for that day.

Similar action may be applied to occupied rooms in which there are stayover guests. Room 1224 required service as a result of a stayover guest (Figure 10.12; the room did not have a CO indication and therefore was not expected to be vacated). Since the room did require service, the GRA should report when service has been

SUPERVISOR'S DAILY WORK REPORT
R E D Division (90)

Senior GRA *Georgia*   Day *Wednesday*   Date *11/4*

Section 1 — (13) GRA Julia (18)	Section 2 — (15) GRA (Open) (0)	Section 3 — (11) GRA Yvonne (18)	Section 4 — (16) GRA Billie (18)	Section 5 — (12) GRA Marjorie (17)
1001 ✓	1031 ✓ CO	1213 R ———	1062 R ———	1091 ✓
1002 R ———	1032 ✓ →3	1214 ✓	1063 ✓	1093 R ———
1003 ✓	1033 ✓ CO →3	1215 R ———	1064 ✓	1095 ✓
1004 ✓	1034 ✓ →3	(1216) DISC (CO)	1065 ✓	1096 ✓ (CO)
1005 R ———	1036 ✓ →3	1217 ✓	1066 ✓ CO	1097 ✓
1006 ✓	1038 ✓ CO →3	1218 R ———	1067 ✓ CO	(1098) DISC (✓)
1007 ✓	1040 ✓ (CO) →3	1219 R ———	1068 ✓	1099 ✓
1008 ✓	1042 ✓ ↗4	1220 ✓	1071 ✓	1100 ✓
1009 ✓ (CO)	1044 ✓ ↗4	1221 ✓ CO	1072 ✓ (CO)	1101 ✓
1010 R ———	1046 ✓ ↗4	1222 ✓ (CO) R	1073 ✓ CO	1102 ✓
1011 ✓ CO	1049 ✓ ↗4	1223 R ———	1074 ✓ CO	1103 ✓ CO
1012 ✓	1051 R ———	1224 ✓ R ———	1075 ✓	1104 ✓ CO
1013 ✓	1053 R ———	1225 ✓ CO	1076 ✓ →5	1105 R ———
1014 ✓	1055 ↗4	1226 ✓ (CO) R ———	1077 ✓ →5	1106 R ———
1015 R ———	1057 ✓ ↗4	1227 R ———	1078 ✓ →5	1107 ✓
1016 R ———	1059 R ———	1228 ✓ (CO)	1079 ooo	1108 R ———
1017 ✓	1061 ✓ ↗4	1229 ✓	1081 ✓ →5	1085 R ———
1021 ✓	1231 ✓ CO →3	1230 ✓	1083 ✓ →5	1087 ✓
1023,1025,1027,1029, 1031		1231,1032,1033,1034,1036 1038,1040	1042,1044,1046,1049,1055 1057,1061	1076,1077,1078,1079 1081,1083

FIGURE 10.12 Supervisor's Daily Work Report for the red division, indicating results of the morning room check.

completed. The R also indicates that an occupied room has been serviced, and the line drawn through the entry indicates that no further routine service is necessary.

Communication Symbols The following list is a summary of the **communication symbols** regarding the progress of work for each room on the Supervisor's Daily Work Report.

1. A checkmark indicates a room that requires service.
2. The symbol CO indicates that the room is expected to be vacated at some time today.
3. A circle around the CO indicates that the room has actually been vacated (GRA notified).
4. The symbol R indicates that the room has been reported as serviced by the GRA to the supervisor.
5. A line drawn through the entire entry indicates that the room has been reported to the status-board operator as a ready room (no further routine action required in that particular room that day).

The supervisor is capable of progressing a large number of rooms each day and can keep up with this progress by a simple system of symbols used to indicate varying degrees of status change. When every room has a line drawn through its entry, all routine services have been concluded.

Progressing Work in the Status System (sometimes referred to as "Housekeeping Central") A copy of each of the four divisions of the Supervisor's Daily Work Report has been displayed in the main linen room on the counter (or may be viewed on video monitors, where computer status boards are in operation). Therefore, the status operator, who is in contact with the front desk, can forward relayed information concerning recently cleaned ready rooms. (If the hotel has an electrowriter, it transmits a facsimile of the sender's handwriting. The numerous communications sent in both directions by housekeeping and the front desk are thereby preserved. This may also be done in a computer system.) As ready rooms are reported to the status-board operators by each supervisor, the status operator also marks a copy of the Daily Work Report with a symbol R. As these rooms are reported to the front desk, a line is drawn through the room number and a completed record of work is therefore available in housekeeping central for all departmental managers to review any time during the day.

Priority for Cleaning Rooms

In what order should rooms be cleaned by each GRA? It would seem that nothing could be more convenient for each GRA than to begin cleaning rooms at one end of an assigned section and proceed from room to room down the corridor until reaching the other end, at which time all rooms in the assigned section are completed. Although this may seem to be the most efficient way of proceeding through the workday, it does not take into consideration concern for guests who do not want to be disturbed or who may want their rooms cleaned first or last.

As the GRAs first move into their work areas each day, they should survey each room assigned for cleaning (both regular and pickup rooms) to determine rooms in which the guest has indicated "Do Not Disturb" and rooms in which the guest has indicated "Please make up ASAP." (Rooms in which the guest has put the night latch on the door will normally be in evidence by a small pin that will protrude through the doorknob. This small pin is easily discerned by feeling the center of the doorknob. When the pin is out, the GRA should consider the room occupied and not to be disturbed until the night latch is taken off or until a later time of the day.)

A priority for cleaning rooms can be established as follows:

1. Rooms in which the guest has requested early service
2. Early-morning checkouts that are specially requested by the front desk (usually required for preblocking of preregistered guests expected to arrive)
3. Other checkouts
4. The rest of the occupied rooms requiring service
5. Requests for late service

A proper priority for cleaning rooms provides the greatest concern for the guest's needs and desires. Although it is true that some occupied rooms (stayovers) will be the last to be cleaned each day (about 4:00 P.M.), the guests who wonder why their rooms are not serviced until the afternoon need only be reminded that a phone call to housekeeping or a sign on the door requesting early service will be accommodated as soon as possible. Otherwise, a room occupied by a stay-over guest might indeed be the last room cleaned that day in a particular section.

Occasionally, especially on weekends and holidays, many guests will indicate that they do not wish to be disturbed until late in the morning. A large number of such rooms could interfere with a particular GRAs being able to enter *any* of the assigned rooms. If such is the case, a notification to the supervisor may warrant the GRAs helping another housekeeper in a different part of the division until such time as rooms begin to open up. At the later time the "favor" can be returned. This is another example of the significance of teamwork and team operation within the division.

Many times during the morning the GRA may visibly notice rooms being vacated. When this is the case, such a room immediately becomes a checkout and can be entered next, provided there are no rooms of a higher priority (guest requests or front desk requests) that have yet to be serviced.

Cleaning the Guestroom

At this point the "housekeeping day" scenario will be suspended temporarily and the specific techniques and systems on how to clean a guestroom will be addressed. We will first look at the large hotel where all guestrooms are quite similar in size and furnishings. Then we will investigate the "suite-type" hotel, where more than one room may be involved in an individual unit.

As mentioned in an earlier chapter, the national standard for numbers of rooms cleaned in one eight-hour shift by one person can vary from 13 to 20 rooms per day. This is usually dependent on the type of market being served, the type of furniture and bathroom involved, and the facility itself. The numbers of rooms cleaned each day will not, therefore, be at issue in this section.

Most hotels have set routines for guestroom cleaning based on their own objectives and experiences. There are many hotel corporations that have had years of experience to build upon in their procedures. Through experience they have developed and honed their procedures until they become quite unique. Other hotels take a different approach by letting their executive housekeepers start from scratch and develop new room cleaning procedures based on their own individual experience.

What follows, then, is not necessarily unique or generic, but an example of the systematizing of routines that must take place in any individual hotel if the operations are to become systematic, effective, and efficient. Although the following procedural examples are specific, they do not rule out the possibility that other examples can be offered as to the best way to clean a guestroom.

FIGURE 10.13 This Bellagio GRA begins her day at her first room to be cleaned with a friendly knock as she calls out, "Housekeeper." *(Photo taken with permission of MGM Mirage.)*

FIGURE 10.14 After the Bellagio GRA has knocked and waited for an answer, she prepares to enter the room by inserting her key (in this case a "smart" key, similar to a key card). *(Photo taken with permission of MGM Mirage.)*

Special thanks are extended to the MGM Mirage and Mandalay Resort Group for allowing the use of their hotels as examples for this section on room cleaning.

ENTERING THE GUESTROOM

The GRA should knock softly with the knuckles, not with a key (Figure 10.13). (Over a period of time, a key can damage the door finish.) An attendant should announce "Housekeeper," "Room Attendant," or simply "Housekeeping." If there is no response after about fifteen seconds, the GRA should repeat the procedure and insert the key or card-entering device into the door lock (Figure 10.14). If there is still no answer after another five seconds, the GRA should open the door, announcing, "Housekeeper, may I come in please?" If there is a guest in the room who failed to answer the door previously, then the guest should be addressed as follows: "I am sorry I disturbed you. When would it be convenient for me to service your room? I will be glad to come back at a later time if you wish."

The guest's answer should prevail as to whether the room is to be cleaned now or the attendant should come back at a later time. If the guest indicates it is all right to service the room now (while the guest remains in the room), the attendant should excuse him- or herself for a moment and report to the housekeeping supervisor, informing the supervisor that he or she will be cleaning that room and that a guest is currently inside the room. This is done to protect both the housekeeper and the guest from possible harm. The GRA should then return to the room, prop open the door with a rubber door wedge, and place the housekeeper's cart with its wheels firmly locked in front of the door. Under no circumstance should a GRA be in a guestroom with a guest behind a closed door.

There are now male as well as female guestroom attendants in American hotels and motels. Even if nothing untoward happens in that room, one does not want to give a disturbed or malicious guest an opportunity to falsely accuse a hotel employee of attempted molestation.

In recent years, GRAs and guests have both been assaulted in guestrooms. If a housekeeper is seen to enter a room and close the door, and a guest is known to be in the room, other hotel employees should be trained to immediately report that GRA's behavior to their supervisor. There have been cases where this has happened, and the other employees did not report the incident. In one instance, the male GRA proceeded to forcibly rape the guest repeatedly.

After the GRA has returned to the room, he or she might start a conversation by asking, "Did you have a nice sleep last evening?" or offer any other pleasant remark.

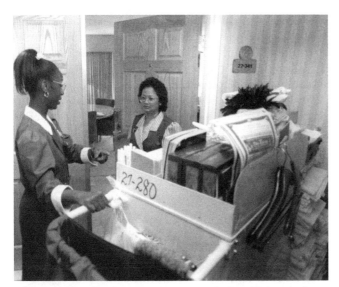

FIGURE 10.15 The floor supervisor reminds a GRA to make sure her cart completely blocks the door. *(Photo taken with permission of MGM Mirage.)*

The GRA might also ask, "Will you be staying another night with us, or will you be leaving later today?" The answer to this question will determine whether only the bed should be made and the room **tidied**, with the intent of returning later to finish the work for a new guest. The GRA might also conclude this remark by saying (if the guest is leaving later today), "All right, I will just make the beds and tidy the room and bathroom for you now, and I'll return later to finish after you have departed."

If the guest is staying another night, simply continue with a complete servicing of the room. If there is no guest in the room at the time of entry, continue with the cleaning procedure.

Leave the door wide open. The attendant should pull the housekeeping cart across the doorway, positioning the linen side toward the room and as close to the wall as possible. Figure 10.15 shows a supervisor admonishing the housekeeper to cover the entire door with her cart. The cart should be positioned in such a way that no one can enter the room without being discovered.

The vacuum cleaner should be taken into the room, not left in the hallway. As the GRA enters the room, he or she should turn on all lights and open all drapes for proper light. If the TV was left on, it should be turned off.

The GRA should check around the room for items missing, damaged, or broken. If noticed, he or she should call the room status operator and notify a supervisor so an engineer or security person can be dispatched immediately.

The GRA should be sure to inspect the following items in every room, regardless of whether the room is a checkout or a stay-over. The GRA should report immediately to the **room status operator** any discrepancies found with the following items that cannot be immediately attended to:

1. Check all lights in the room; replace burned-out bulbs in the **swag lamp**, dresser lamp, or nightstand lamp. Report any other burned-out lamps to the room status operator.
2. Check drapes, cords, and pulleys.
3. Check shower doors or shower curtains for serviceability.
4. Check shower, toilet, and sink for leakage or other problems.
5. Check TV for proper sound and picture.

If any room service or bar items need to be returned, remove them to an assigned location or to the hallway and notify a housekeeping aide so that they can be further positioned for retrieval by the appropriate department. The supervisor should see to their quick removal from the hallway since they are unsightly and can begin to smell. If these items are not removed in a reasonable period of time, notify housekeeping central by phone.

If the room is an occupied room, pick up magazines and newspapers, fold them neatly, and place them on the table or dresser. Never recycle these items unless they are in the wastebasket.

SUGGESTED CLEANING METHODS

Before actually entering into the servicing of a guestroom, a list of cleaning methods should be reviewed. All dusting should be done with a damp cloth or a cloth treated with an Endust-type chemical. Here are several suggested methods of cleaning specific items:

Mirror—Rinse with hot water and finish with a microfiber cloth.
Lamp shades—Brush lightly with a microfiber cloth.
Shower stalls—Use an **all-purpose cleaner** and dry with a microfiber cloth.
Bath floor—Sweep with a broom, and damp mop with a sanitizer and an all-purpose cleaner.
Shower doors—Scrub with all-purpose cleaner, rinse, and dry with a microfiber cloth.
Sinks—Use an all-purpose sanitizer-cleaner, rinse, and dry with a microfiber cloth.
Tubs—Scrub with all-purpose cleaner, rinse, and dry with a microfiber cloth.
Chrome—Use all-purpose cleaner, rinse, and dry with a microfiber cloth; make sure there are no water spots.
Toilet Bowl—Wash the toilet inside and out. Wash the inside of the bowl with a Johnny Mop and the outside with a red microfiber cloth. (Red

is the cloth color reserved for toilets so there is no cross contamination.) Use a disinfectant cleaner on the toilet, and never, ever use the cloth used to clean the outside of the toilet for any other purpose, including the cleaning of other toilets. Wash the cloth before reuse..

A colleague reported to me that he once observed a GRA clean his hotel room. She started in the bathroom with the toilet. Once she finished the toilet, she proceeded to clean the tub, sink, and mirror with the same cloth. From there she moved into the bedroom, where she used the cloth to dust the furniture and wipe down the telephone. Needless to say, my colleague felt compelled to report this activity to the executive housekeeper. The executive housekeeper replied that he just could not get good help anymore. My colleague replied that it might be a training rather than a hiring issue.

The following items should be dusted with a damp, or treated, microfiber cloth: luggage rack, drawers and shelves, wastebaskets, lamp bulbs, air conditioner, thermostat, pipes under sink, tables and chairs, TV and stand, headboards, nightstands, picture frames, and windowsills.

Special considerations in cleaning may require special products. When this happens, the supervisor should closely control the use of **special cleaning compounds**. All employees should be cautioned against "becoming chemists" and mixing chemicals, thinking a better solution can be attained if a few products are mixed together. For example, **acid bowl cleaner** used to remove spots and buildups in toilet bowls, when mixed with bleach, can create deadly chlorine gas. In addition, some people may be allergic to certain kinds of products in concentrated form. All-purpose cleaners are supposed to be used at **specified dilution ratios** for specific cleaning jobs. Employees should be trained in this area and should be required to comply with the manufacturer's specifications for dilution.

For protection, it is advised that rubber gloves be worn for all cleaning duties to guard against germs, infection, and possible chemical reaction. Although few products are used that can cause harm in cleaning, as mentioned elsewhere in the text, **HazComm requirements** direct that the dangers of each product used should be clearly labeled on each container. This information must be made available to the users of such products.

THE BEDROOM

Get all trash out of the room. The GRA should collect all waste and trash, remove it, and empty it into the trash receptacle bag on the cart. Take trash receptacles into the bathroom for cleaning. Collect all ashtrays in smoking rooms, empty them into the toilet, and flush; then wash all ashtrays and wipe dry. Damp wipe

all trash receptacles, then replace ashtrays and trash receptacles.

Bring clean linen and any other supplies needed to service the room into the room. Do not place clean linen on the floor while preparing to make the bed.

Shake all bed linen carefully when stripping the bed. Guests tend to leave articles and valuables in and under the bed and in pillowcases. Notify the floor supervisor and follow **lost-and-found procedures** for any item left behind by the guest.

Check mattresses and box springs for soiled or torn spots. Also check for wires that may be sticking outside of the box springs. The mattress and box springs should be straight on top of each other and should be placed firmly against the headboard. Check bed frames where used (dangerous items if out of place). If adjustment is needed, notify the floor supervisor. Any bedding in need of replacement (wet mattresses; soiled bed pads; torn or soiled bedspreads; damaged or soiled pillows; soiled, damaged, or torn blankets) should be reported to the floor supervisor and replacement items secured immediately in order that work can continue efficiently.

Fresh linen should be placed on every bed that was used or turned down the night before. Do not use torn or spotted linens. Place any rejected linen in the reject linen bag in the linen locker (satellite linen room).

The bottom sheet should now be placed on the mattress so as to facilitate tucking in the top at the head of bed with a **mitered corner** (Figure 10.16). The bottom sheet should also be tucked in on both sides of the bed, but not necessarily at the foot.

The second sheet should be placed on the bottom sheet with the smooth fabric finish down (so as to be next to the body), with the major hem (if any) placed "jam-up" against the headboard. This should leave plenty of top sheet at the foot of the bed to perform another mitered fold after the blanket is placed in the proper position.

The blanket should now be placed on top of the second sheet, nine inches from the head of the bed. When the blanket is properly squared on the bed, the top sheet should be folded back across the top of the blanket. The top sheet and the blanket should now be tucked in together at the foot of the bed, and a mitered fold (Figure 10.16) made on both sides of the foot of the bed.

Many hotels employ a **snooze sheet** (a third sheet placed precisely on top of the blanket). This step also gives a quality application to the appearance of the bed if the spread is turned back or removed, but it is primarily done to protect the blanket from spills and spots. If a snooze sheet is employed, it will be tucked in at the foot of the bed simultaneously with both the blanket and the second sheet before the mitered corner is made.

Some hotels now *tuck in* the second sheet, blanket, and snooze sheet on both sides of the bed. Other hotels

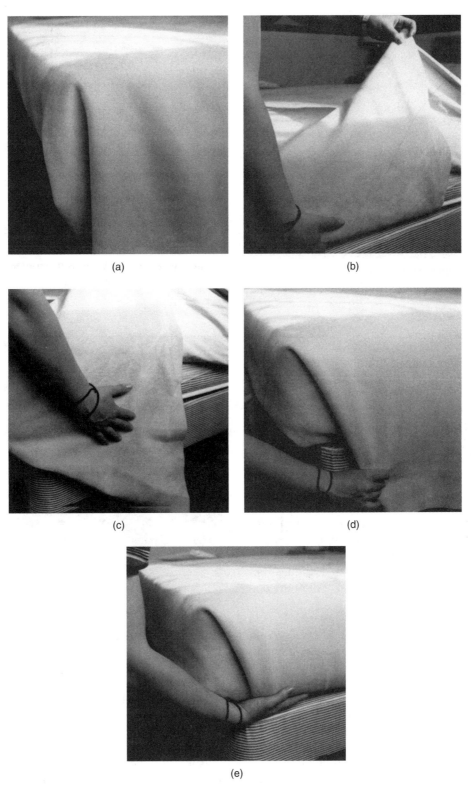

(a)

(b)

(c)

(d)

(e)

FIGURE 10.16 Making a bed using the mitered corner. Tuck in the top sheet and blanket across the foot of the bed with the sides hanging free (a). Pick up the sheet and blanket together at about a 45-degree angle and place tight against the side of the bed (b). Tuck the bottom selvage under the mattress while still holding up the top at a 45-degree angle (c). Allow the top to fall and then smooth it (d). Tuck the side under the mattress (e). Depending on company policy, the sides could be left hanging down. The bottom sheet should also be mitered by itself at the head of the bed.

FIGURE 10.17 The GRA turns the spread back about 10 inches. *(Photo taken with permission of MGM Mirage.)*

FIGURE 10.18 The GRA now rolls three pillows and the bedspread toward the headboard. *(Photo taken with permission of MGM Mirage.)*

leave both sides untucked. When sides are tucked in, the guests will more than likely "unmake" the bed when they try to get into it. As top sheet and blanket are pulled back, the bottom sheet becomes untucked also.

This writer suggests the best of both methods. Tuck in the top sheet and blanket on the side of the bed opposite to the side the guest is more likely to use when entering the bed. Leave the side that the guest will most likely use to enter the bed untucked.

The bedspread. Because the bed is most often the major focal point of the guestroom, the bedspread must be properly positioned, smoothed, and without lumps upon completion of the makeup. Assuming the spread is properly fitted, it should just miss touching the floor on three sides and be properly tucked in at the head of the bed. The corners of the spread at the foot of the bed should either be tucked or pleated.

The spread at the head of the bed is easily dressed by first turning the spread back about 12 inches from the headboard. The pillows should be placed about 15 inches from the headboard on top of the turned-back spread. Once done, the front edge of the spread can be carried back over the pillows on both sides of the bed, and then the entire unit can be rolled together toward the headboard. Figure 10.17 shows the GRA turning back the spread about 10 inches from the head of the bed in preparation for rolling the pillows as a unit.

In Figure 10.18, she has placed three pillows on the turned-back spread and is now turning the spread back over the pillows. Once done on the other side of the bed, the entire unit can be "rolled" toward the head of the bed. This is an efficient way for one person to handle three pillows.

The spread should then be smoothed as necessary for a complete and dressed look. This technique of making the head of the bed is easily mastered with practice and

FIGURE 10.19 This Bellagio GRA uses a specially prepared and properly diluted product for damp wiping. *(Photo taken with permission of MGM Mirage.)*

is especially useful when one person is making up a king bed with three pillows.

Portable beds are to be made with clean linen and, unless otherwise instructed, no bedspread is used. Most are made with a snooze sheet, which will act as a bedspread. If the room is a "checkout," the bed is to be made up, pillow strapped vertically under the retaining strap, and stood up on its rollers. Once standing upright, the bed can be replenished under the retaining strap with one bath towel, one hand towel, one washcloth, and two fresh bars of soap neatly tucked in with the pillow. A housekeeping aide can now be called to remove the bed from the room and have it properly stored. Remember, portable beds are to be made up before being moved into the hallway.

Clean (**damp wipe**) chairs, tables, dresser tops, windowsills and tracks, headboards, air conditioner, thermostats, hanging swag lamps, pictures, luggage racks, and closet shelves. Figure 10.19 shows a GRA using a solution diluted and prepared especially for damp wiping furniture. Also dust all light bulbs and lamp shades. Properly adjust lamp shades and move the shade so that the shade seam is located in the rear of the light as would be seen by the guest. Dust bar areas (if applicable) and clean all mirrors in the bedroom.

Replace and/or reposition all literature, ashtrays, and hotel guest service directories or public relations (PR) items. Matches should be carefully *placed* in ashtrays (not thrown into them) striker side up, with advertisement facing the front of the table or desk where they are supposed to be located according to hotel specifications.

Drawers should be opened in "checkout" rooms and damp-wiped. Check carefully for any items the previous guest may have left behind. Do not go into drawers of **stay-over rooms.**

Dust the desk area, including lamp and chairs. Check the phone directory. If the cover is torn or is marked or bent, replace it. All literature on and in the desk drawer should be checked for completeness, and writing items should be clean and unmarked.

Check all drawers and closet shelves. Also check safes (if provided) and check underneath beds for items left behind. If any item is found, complete a lost-and-found slip, place the item and the slip into a plastic bag, and turn in to the lost-and-found at the end of the shift. Remove any clothes hangers not belonging to the hotel; replace hotel clothes hangers as necessary.

FIGURE 10.21 The Bellagio GRA damp wipes all telephone receivers with a germicidal disinfectant. *(Photo taken with permission of MGM Mirage.)*

Clean the guestroom TV. Figure 10.20 shows the GRA using an all-purpose product that has been properly diluted for cleaning glass. (This dilution is also correct for all glass, mirrors, and clear plastics.) The final wipe should always be with a dry cloth. The GRA should check to see that all telephone books have been returned to their proper place, then damp wipe all telephone receivers and remote controls with a germicidal disinfectant (Figure 10.21).

Adjust as necessary all drapes, light fixtures, and any other item that may be moved out of position.

For the *final dusting* step, if the room is a connecting room, open the connecting door and damp wipe the inside of the door and wipe the door sill. Damp wipe inside the entrance door around the lock area. Damp wipe the doorsill. Clean the entire area and damp wipe plastic covers (if applicable) on any signs on the back of the room door.

Vacuuming is the final step to cleaning the guestroom (Figure 10.22). Some hotels require that every room be *vacuumed* every day. Others call upon the judgment of the GRA to make this decision based on a standard set of appearance criteria and a critical look at the floor by the GRA. Most times the GRA's judgment is well founded and time can be saved in the room-cleaning routine. If the GRA's judgment is not good, the supervisor must work to help with his or her power of observation.

CLEANING THE BATHROOM

Turn on all lights and flush the toilet. What may seem like a waste of water is done as a precaution in case a guest has emptied chemicals into the toilet that might react

FIGURE 10.20 The GRA uses a properly diluted all-purpose cleaner for damp wiping the glass face of the TV. *(Photo taken with permission of MGM Mirage.)*

FIGURE 10.22 A GRA vacuums the bedroom portion of the guestroom. *(Photo taken with permission of MGM Mirage.)*

FIGURE 10.24 A GRA demonstrates the proper way to clean inside a shower. *(Photo taken with permission of MGM Mirage.)*

FIGURE 10.23 The GRA is properly gloved while cleaning the bathroom commode with a Johnny Mop. *(Photo courtesy of the Excalibur Hotel, Las Vegas.)*

with the cleaning chemicals. It also ensures that any remaining human effluent is evacuated and the toilet is not plugged. A plugged toilet will require a visit from the engineering department *before* cleaning chemicals are added to the toilet. The toilet should be cleaned with a germicide cleaner inside and out. Clean the outside of the toilet tank, the toilet lid, seat, and base with the cleaner and a red microfiber cloth as mentioned earlier, or use paper towels. With a **Johnny Mop**, clean the inside of the bowl. Make sure to clean under the rim where the flushing water emerges (Figure 10.23). Flush and rinse the Johnny Mop carefully so as not to drip on the floor, and return it to the housekeeper's cart.

To clean the tub/shower area, first place a soiled but dry towel inside the tub/shower to keep from slipping or from scratching the floor surface (Figure 10.24). Then, with the designated cleaner, clean the shower walls, soap dish, and shower doors inside and out. Wipe chrome fixtures clean, including the showerhead. Use a sanitizing cleaner to clean the inside of the tub. Pull the tub stopper out of the tub and clean it thoroughly. Replace. Dry all surfaces and wipe all water spots from chrome fixtures.

Clean the sink with the designated product and a microfiber cloth. Pull the sink stopper and clean thoroughly. Wipe clean and dry all faucets.

FIGURE 10.25 The GRA checks the amenity package for completeness and placement in accordance with her hotel's standards. *(Photo taken with permission of MGM Mirage.)*

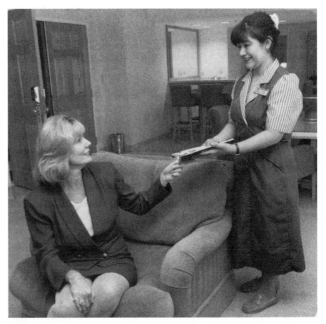

FIGURE 10.26 Although GRAs should not be overly conversational with the guests, they should welcome the opportunity to provide simple amenities with a smile. *(Photo taken with permission of MGM Mirage.)*

Check other chrome fixtures, including the toilet tissue and facial tissue holders and chrome towel rods. Damp wipe and ensure they are free from water spots. "Repoint" the toilet tissue and facial tissue (the first extended sheet of paper from each fixture should be folded so as to present a neat triangle-pointed tip for the next user of the bathroom).

Clean the mirror and damp wipe the sides of the mirror frame (if applicable). The mirror should be spotless. A damp microfiber cloth with no cleaner will usually give the best results. Wipe all chrome plumbing fixtures underneath the sink and behind the toilet.

The floor should first be swept with a small corn broom to remove hair and large particles of dirt. Wipe the floor (using a sanitizing cleaner), including all corners, and behind the toilet and the door. Damp wipe the wastebasket and reposition.

Check the supplies. Replace as needed. Most guestrooms should be equipped with one bath towel, one hand towel, and one washcloth for every pillow in the guestroom.) Also include at least one bar of bath soap and one bar of facial soap. Some hotels use two bars of each kind of soap in every guestroom. Still others are using the **amenity package** (Figure 10.25) for soaps, shampoos, softeners, and powders. Additional rolls of toilet paper and boxes of facial tissue are also included. Do not replace the toilet tissue in the fixture until the roll is less than one-fourth full. Fold towels properly and set up the bathroom as instructed.

For the *final bathroom check*, recheck all lights in the bathroom. Check the room once more before leaving and lightly spray with air freshener. Turn off all lights in the bathroom.

For the *final inspection of the bedroom*, the guestroom attendant should move to the front of the room next to the entrance door and observe the entire room. Remember, what is now seen is what the guests will see as they enter the room. The attendants should also be prideful about their work. They should leave behind what they would be willing to enter upon if they were paying what the guest is going to be paying.

In general, the GRA will come into more contact with the guest than will the department head or even the general manager. For this reason, the GRA should remember to wish guests a "happy visit with us" and invite them back again. After all, the guest pays everyone's salary.

Should the guest be present when the room is being serviced, the GRA should act the way a host or hostess would in his or her own home. After all, it is the first-line employee (in this case, the GRA) who delivers hospitality in our industry. In Figure 10.26, at the request of the guest, the GRA locates a magazine suitable for relaxing entertainment. (Employees must remember that the guest is the reason for our work, not an interruption to it.) The GRA should now back out of the room, ensuring that the door is completely locked, and either move to the next room to be cleaned or, when finished with the shift, move to the satellite linen room and restock the housekeeper's cart for the next day.

If this had been a *room made ready* (after the prior guest had checked out), the supervisor would have been

FIGURE 10.27 A supervisor checks the interior of a window for smudges. *(Photo taken with permission of MGM Mirage.)*

FIGURE 10.29 The supervisor checks the bathroom for correct towel setup. *(Photo taken with permission of MGM Mirage.)*

FIGURE 10.28 As a form of quality control, Teresita Arenas, Housekeeping Supervisor at Bellagio, checks a drawer to ensure it is empty and dust-free. *(Photo taken with permission of MGM Mirage.)*

FIGURE 10.30 The final touch—fluffing the sofa pillows. *(Photo taken with permission of MGM Mirage.)*

notified that the room is properly serviced. In this case, he or she may choose to inspect the work for completeness and standardization of setup. In Figure 10.27, the supervisor checks to ensure that windows on the inside are dust and smudge-free. Drawers are inspected to be sure they are damp wiped, dust-free, and have

no extraneous articles in them (Figure 10.28). The supervisor makes sure that towels are properly counted, folded, and shelved in the bathroom (Figure 10.29). Finally, a last-minute tidying of a pillow on the sofa is in order (Figure 10.30). Then the supervisor automatically reports the suite as "ready for occupancy" by

FIGURE 10.31 The supervisor calls the computer to report that the suite is ready for occupancy. *(Photo taken with permission of MGM Mirage)*

FIGURE 10.32 The GRA is reminded that tags on guest bathrobes should show price information in case the guest would like to purchase one. *(Photo courtesy of MGM Mirage)*

dialing the rooms management computer system (Figure 10.31). Status-board operators in housekeeping central and front desk are notified of the availability of a ready room.

A housekeeping manager stops by to add his input. After praise, he indicates that price information on bathrobes (available for guests to buy should they choose to do so) should be visible (Figure 10.32).

Suite Hotels (with Kitchens, Fireplaces, and Patios)

Many different types of hotel offerings involve standard but, in their own way, unique routines. A good example of this type of hotel is a **suite hotel**, where more than the standard bedroom and bath are offered. Such facilities might include a formal sitting room or parlor, bedroom, kitchen and dining area, fireplace, and formal patio. A good example of such a facility is the chain of hotels known as Marriott's Residence Inns.

The Marriott Corporation reaches into several market areas of the hotel industry: the Full Service Hotels are at the top of the line; Residence Inns are upper-scale apartment-type accommodations for guests expecting to stay anywhere from one night to six months. This type of operation is designed to reach the guest who might be moving into a community or someone working in a community for a limited period of time. Because this operation caters more to the individual who is having to maintain a home away from home, it is not unreasonable to find that linen would not be changed as often as in a full-scale hotel, where guests are expected to come and go almost daily.

What follows is the daily routine of the guestroom attendant (GRA) for this unique type of hotel. The reader should assume that the GRA is equipped as before with the necessary cleaning equipment and supplies. Specific details on how to clean or make beds will not be repeated.

Grateful appreciation is extended to Marriott's Residence Inn, Las Vegas, Nevada, for allowing part of its systems to appear in this text.

CLEANING THE SUITE AREAS

Daily cleaning (vacant and ready rooms) is begun as before, by observing the proper protocol for entering the room. The **suite attendant** will then turn on all lights to check for burned-out bulbs; replace as necessary, then clean all light switches, lamps, and lamp shades.

Treat any carpet stains present.

Empty wastebaskets, trash containers, and ashtrays, then clean and damp wipe all wastebaskets as necessary, and wipe and dry ashtrays. Replace liners in wastebaskets, if applicable, and reposition.

Damp wipe furniture and shelves, and vacuum the carpet as necessary. Make sure that all furniture out of place is restored to its proper position.

Check patio doors and the outside door. Make sure they are locked and the **security bar** is set with **security chain** in place.

Check for finger smears or dirt on the sliding glass doors or windows; clean as needed.

Clean all windowsills, windows, curtain rods, and doors, including the door tracks.

Ensure that the telephone is restored to its proper place and that the phone cord is not tangled.

Blot, rinse, and dry all pretreated spots on carpets as necessary.

ENTRANCE AREA AND CLOSETS

Using a damp cloth, wipe the inside and outside of the entrance door, door facing, the threshold plate, door knob, and all door hardware. (Do not use abrasive cleanser on hardware.) Clean and vacuum the entrance mat.

Ensure that a flyswatter is positioned on the closet shelf. Check also that the proper type and number of clothes hangers are in the closet. Foyer closet has four hangers, main closet has four to six regular/skirt hangers. Vacuum interior of closet. Ensure that the **room rate card** is properly in place.

LIVING AREA

If the fireplace has been used, notify a housekeeping aide to come and clean the residue. Clean all fireplace tile, the black faceplate, flue handle, screen, and poker. Close the flue and clean the picture above the fireplace. Such routines become instinctive after repeatedly following the prescribed procedures (Figure 10.33).

Ensure that all reading and PR materials are in place. The radio should be tuned to an "easy listening" station.

Dry wipe the TV screen. Damp wipe the TV stand and faceplate. All cords to standing lamps should be dust free and placed safely out of the way.

Ensure that the candy jar is clean and has the required candy pieces. Make sure that the live plant is in its proper place.

BEDS

Empty and clean the bed bench and nightstand drawers. Return all phone books to their proper place.

Check the spread for stains, topside and underside. Replace with a clean spread if necessary.

Check blankets for holes, stains, and tears. If a hole is smaller than two fingers, triple sheet the bed.

Mattress pads should be stain-free. Make the bed.

Sheets should be changed at least twice a week in stay-over rooms. All checkout rooms must have linen changed.

Check the alarm clock and ensure that the time is accurately set.

FIGURE 10.33 A suite attendant damp wipes the picture frame above the fireplace as part of her servicing routine. *(Photo taken with permission, Marriott's Residence Inn of Las Vegas.)*

BATHROOM

Wipe and dry the shower curtain and rod with a cloth dampened with all-purpose cleaner. Clean the tub enclosure with the assigned product.

Clean all mirrors and polish chrome with glass cleaner.

Clean the toilet bowl. Check holes under the rim. Disinfect weekly or upon checkout. Clean the toilet seat/lid hinges, base, and caps with all-purpose cleaner.

Clean sinks with all-purpose cleaner. Remove any burn marks.

Reset the shower area with clean bathmat and fresh soap (Figure 10.34).

Replace other soaps and tissues as necessary. If facial tissues are low, leave extra supplies on the vanity. Always leave an extra roll of toilet tissue.

Place clean bath towels, hand towels, and washcloths in the bathrooms according to placement standards.

KITCHEN

Wipe clean the front, controls, and crevices of the dishwasher. Check inside the dishwasher for objects left behind by the guest, or for any small items that may have fallen into the bottom. If dirty dishes have been left by the guest, load them in the dishwasher (Figure 10.35) and turn on; or, if the dishes do not make a full load, wash them by hand.

FIGURE 10.34 The tub/shower area; clean, dry, and properly set up with a cloth bath mat and fresh soap. *(Photo taken with permission.)*

FIGURE 10.35 In cleaning the kitchen of an occupied suite, the suite attendant loads all soiled dishes into the dishwasher and turns it on. *(Photo taken with Residence Inn permission.)*

Place any clean dishes and utensils in their proper place according to the **Quest for Quality Standards Placement Guide**. (This is a small publication of photographs indicating the proper setup of every item in the kitchen and other parts of the suite. Every dish, pot, pan, knife, fork, and spoon has its place.)

Pots and pans should be cleaned daily; make sure that any black marks or stains are removed.

Check the inside of the refrigerator and freezer:

- Wipe up any spills.
- Remove any items left behind.

Clean the outside, top, hinges, and the door gaskets of the refrigerator door. Clean and leave dry.

Check oven burners for operation; check inside the oven for spills; clean as necessary. Damp wipe the oven front and control panel as necessary. Clean the oven hood and air cleaner.

Cupboards: Wipe all shelves. Ensure that all dishes and glasses are clean and free of water spots. Wipe the fire extinguisher and store properly.

If small appliances have been used (toaster, coffeemaker, popcorn popper), clean and/or polish the exteriors or wash as needed. Replace in appropriate positions. Wipe any crumbs off the bottom of the toaster tray.

Wash down countertops and behind sinks and ledge. Clean sink and polish chrome.

Check dishwasher soap supply. Replenish as needed; no less than one-third of a small box is to be left.

Replace the **first-nighter kit**, which contains small amounts of kitchen soaps and small packets of coffee, creamers, sugar, and sweeteners (Figure 10.36). Set the dining area properly for a newly arriving guest.

Gather dirty napkins and replenish the clean napkin supply as necessary.

Place a clean kitchen towel and dishcloth by the sink according to standards.

Replace all ashtrays in their proper position. Figure 10.37 shows the suite attendant checking a final setup in the desk area of the suite.

BEFORE LEAVING THE ROOM

On checkouts, set the thermostat: air-conditioning at 75 degrees, heat at 65 degrees. Ensure that the fan is left on "auto."

Turn off all lights except over the kitchen sink.

When completed, stand back and observe your work. Complete any maintenance request forms and turn in to the supervisor.

When servicing suites where guests are present, experience has shown that guests will more than likely

FIGURE 10.36 A suite attendant checks the "first-nighter kit" for an incoming guest. *(Photo taken with permission, Marriott's Residence Inn.)*

FIGURE 10.37 A suite attendant places a clean ashtray in its proper place at the desk. *(Photo taken with permission, Marriott's Residence Inn.)*

remain out of your way, allowing you to get on with the work. This does not rule out the opportunity to be pleasant and extend hospitality to the guest. All suite attendants are encouraged to participate in friendly conversation when the opportunity presents itself.

The daily cleaning guide for stay-overs is essentially the same, except that, in the kitchen, soiled dishes are placed in the dishwasher and the machine started.

Check the refrigerator and freezer for any spills. Clean as necessary.

THE HOMES MANUAL

The preceding steps involving suite hotels are contained in one of the Marriott's Residence Inn's *Hospitality Operations Manual for Excellent Service (HOMES)*. There are other **HOMES manuals** for procedures involving the Front Office, Maintenance Department, Hotel and Housekeeping Management, Uniform and Grooming, and **Commitment to Quality**. There is also a "Quest for Quality Placement Standard Guide" for every item in a suite. Additional guidance is offered when working in guest contact areas.

As should now be evident in the scenarios just presented, there is great detail in the step-by-step procedures involved in cleaning the guestroom. At first glance, what has been shown might seem almost insurmountable. What appears to be overwhelming becomes quite instinctive, however, with training and practice. At the Residence Inn, the experienced GRA cleans more than 16 rooms a day.

Let us now return to the scenario of the "daily routine."

The Housekeeping Day Continued

As the GRAs complete each room, they should make a written record of each room cleaned in order to know when the daily work assignments have been completed. In addition, the GRAs should reevaluate the priority of cleaning rooms after each room is finished. A new request for early service may have appeared, or checkouts may have been noticed while cleaning a particular room; these situations can cause a small change in the order in which the work schedule should be progressed.

Suppose, during "opening of the house" the supervisor was notified on the Daily Work Report which rooms were expected to check out that date. However, the GRA was not so notified. When the GRA is told about expected checkouts, it is important to know whether to wait for those rooms to be vacated before rendering service. What if a room is scheduled to be vacated and the outgoing guest requests early service? The room might have to be serviced twice in the same day: once by special request of the guest for early service and then again after the guest departs. A reasonable compromise can be reached, provided the early service request is honored. The GRA asks all guests requesting early service, "Will you be staying another night with us?" Then expected departures will be noted, and the GRA may say, "Very well then, I will just spread up your bed and tidy the bathroom until after you have left, then I will come back and completely service the room. In this way, your room will be straight and I need not disturb you for any great length at this time." Such an answer is usually well received by any guests expecting to have visitors in their rooms and who are departing later.

The GRA continues throughout the day cleaning each room assigned in a priority order, as described here, until the last room on the schedule has been serviced. Likewise, the section housekeeping aide and the supervisor continue with their functions as described here and as further set forth in their job descriptions.

The working team takes a 15-minute break from work in the morning, a 30-minute lunch break, and a 15-minute break in the afternoon. Most housekeeping departments operate in such a way that lunch breaks are on employee time—that is, employees punch out for lunch and are on their own time—and the 15-minute morning and afternoon breaks are on company time. During the rest breaks and lunch periods, it is advisable that some member of the team stay behind in the general work area until the main portion of the work team returns. This staggering of break time allows for someone always to be present in the event of some emergency or priority of work requirement. The priority of work and chronology of the day continue very much as described until 1:00 P.M., at which time the status of those rooms heretofore noted as "do not disturb" must be resolved.)

RESOLUTION OF DO NOT DISTURBS (1:00 P.M. to 3:00 P.M.)

Let us assume that no prior specific notification has been received by the housekeeping department regarding a known late sleeper and that no specific request for late service has been received. (If such had been the case, a specific time would have been arrived at for the receipt of daily room cleaning service.) It then becomes necessary to resolve the status of those rooms that have heretofore been noted as **do not disturb (DND)**. This also involves determining the status of rooms in which pins have been out on doors. It would not be uncommon for GRAs to have several such rooms in their sections each day.

Because 1:00 P.M. is checkout time, this is a reasonable time to resolve the DND status of such rooms. Room doors with pins out are simply knocked on. Since it is difficult to knock on a door in the face of a sign indicating "do not disturb," a more practical method of resolving this dilemma is to call the room. This call may be made from a vacant room, possibly as close as across the hall. Before actually making the call, it is appropriate to consider all of the possibilities you could face by making such a call:

1. Case 1: The answering guest is either asleep, or is awake but not aware that the DND sign is on the door.
2. Case 2: The guest does not answer.

In Case 1 it would be appropriate to open the conversation as follows: "Good afternoon, this is Mary from the housekeeping department. I am calling to find out at what time you would like to have your room serviced today." Most answers to such a question asked over the telephone fully resolve what is to be accomplished in the DND rooms. Such answers as "You may come now" or "Come in about one hour" or "Do not come until 6:00 P.M." or even "I do not want service today" resolve the problem. However, any guest not desiring service today should prompt the following type of reply: "Very well; however, I have an attendant on her way up to your room with some fresh towels. She will be there in just a moment."

What has been accomplished with such a scenario is that someone will be able to evaluate the situation. Even though the guest has paid for a room that comes with daily service, including a change of bed linen, you cannot force service on a guest. It is imperative, however, that someone get a peek into the room in question to verify that nothing illegal is happening in the room. (Most illegal acts being performed in hotel rooms are covered by a DND sign and a statement that no service is desired that day.) The peek will be obtained under the guise of delivering the fresh towels into the room. In every case in which service is being refused, the supervisor and a housekeeping manager should be notified. The supervisor or manager might deliver the towels to verify that service was in fact being refused, as well as to engage the guest in conversation to ensure that no illegal activity is taking place within the room.

In Case 2, in which there is no answer to the phone call, the GRA should go immediately to the room, knock on the door, and enter the room. In most cases in which a phone call has received no answer, entering the room will reveal only that the guest is out of the room or has checked out. In either case, the guest has usually left the room and forgot to remove the DND sign from the door.

If the door pin is out and the guest has failed to answer a knock on the door or a phone call, immediate management attention is warranted. The main concern in this case is that someone in the room has locked him- or herself in and is now incapacitated to the extent that he or she cannot answer the door. Without delay, this room requires a manager with an emergency key that will allow immediate entry.

A similar situation exists if the GRA attempts to enter a room with the floor master key after a phone call to a room and, as the door is opened slightly, the chain lock is found to be on the door. Concern in this situation is great enough to warrant calling a manager and an engineer with a bolt cutter in preparation for cutting the chain on the door.

There are two specific exceptions to the concerns stated, both of which should be considered before using the emergency master key or the bolt cutter. The room may have been sold as a part of a suite that adjoins the adjacent room. Quite often when guests have two rooms, they will chain lock and/or bolt latch one room and enter the locked room through the internal door of the adjacent room. A quick check at the front desk will reveal whether or not this has happened. The other exception occurs when the room is on the first floor and is capable of being vacated through a sliding glass door. It is not unusual to find that guests have chain locked and placed the latch bolt on the hall door, left a DND sign on the door, and checked out, departing through the sliding glass door to the street. This possibility should always be investigated before cutting chains and using emergency keys on first-floor room doors.

Although the possibility might seem remote, guests have been found dead in hotel guestrooms, and this possibility will always confront the GRA when access to guestrooms cannot be immediately gained. The fact that a deceased person could be discovered in a guestroom should be covered well in training sessions.

Having resolved the status of all rooms previously seen as DNDs, the GRA continues cleaning guestrooms, following the same priority as in the morning. The first part of afternoon cleaning of guestrooms will find heavier involvement with checkout rooms, since most checkouts would have departed by 1:00 P.M. The overload of vacant and checkout rooms will be eliminated within about two hours, leaving mostly occupied stay-over rooms to be finished in late afternoon. Afternoon room cleaning will be interrupted only by the necessity to make a P.M. room check.

THE P.M. ROOM CHECK

Unlike the A.M. room check during the morning activities, there is now a need to obtain a factual "look" at the status of *every* room in the hotel and to report this status in order that the front desk may purify the room rack in preparation to selling out the house each night. The **P.M. room check** is carried out by each GRA, at a specific time and as quickly as possible, checking every room in the normally assigned section.

There are exceptions to the need to knock on every door. Should the GRA see a guest vacate a room a short time before the room check, there is no need to open that door since the room is known to be vacant. Likewise, should the GRA see a guest check in just a short time before room check, the room will obviously be occupied. Sometimes stay-over guests make themselves known to their GRAs. Again, known occupancies do not require the guest to be unnecessarily disturbed.

However, accuracy must take precedence over bypassing a room at the P.M. status inspection.

Recall from Chapter 9 that the GRAs were given a blank copy of their section reports and that the supervisors were given a blank copy of the open section reports. Thus, in the model hotel there are 20 section P.M. Report sheets available in the house each day upon which to record the results of the P.M. Report. At approximately 3:00 P.M., most expected checkouts have departed (there could be exceptions) and a majority of today's arrivals have not yet arrived. Therefore, 3:00 P.M. is an appropriate time to conduct the P.M. room check and prepare the report. The P.M. inspection is conducted in such a way as to ensure accuracy. Except for the situations mentioned earlier, every door in each section will be opened between 3:00 P.M. and 3:10 P.M.

There are many different ways of knocking on room doors and announcing the GRA's presence. The worst possible situation occurs when the GRA knocks on the door with the key (thus damaging the woodwork finish on the door) and yells, "Maid," thereby disturbing everyone within hearing distance. There is a much more professional manner in which to proceed.

It should be standard practice that the GRA knock on guestroom doors only with the knuckles, never with an object of any kind that could damage the door with repeated abuse. The term *housekeeper* should be used in place of *maid*. The following is a professional procedure that may be followed:

1. Knock on the door with the knuckles.
2. Announce yourself as "Housekeeper." If there is an answer, say; "Please excuse the knock, I am conducting a room status check. Thank you, have a nice stay with us." Then go to the next room. If there is no answer, continue the procedure.
3. Knock on the door again.
4. Insert the key in the door.
5. Announce again, "Housekeeper."
6. Open the door and, as the room is entered, say, "May I come in, please?"

Someone who may not have heard the first knock usually hears the key enter the door. At any time there is a reply, simply apologize and indicate that a room status check is being conducted. When no one answers, enter the room to determine the room status.

The person conducting the room check observes the room to determine the following:

Ready rooms (R): Rooms that are clean and ready to rent

Occupied (OCC): Rooms that have a guest in residence (rooms that contain luggage are also considered to be occupied)

Checkout (C/O) or on change: Rooms that have been vacated and have not yet been made ready for a new occupant

GRA DAILY REPORT					

SECTION _____1_____ (18) RMS.   AM.   (PM.)
GRA _____Julia_____   Day _Wednesday_ Date _11/4_

ROOM #	C/O	OCC	R	REMARKS	PICK-UP
1001		✓			
1002	✓				
1003		✓			
1004		✓			
1005			✓		
1006			✓		
1007		✓			
1008		✓			
1009	✓			Engineer working on A/C	
1010	✓				
1011			✓	Request 8:00 P.M. late service	
1012			✓		
1013			✓		
1014		✓			
1015			✓	L & F item removed	
1016		✓			
1017		✓			
1021	✓				

FIGURE 10.38 GRA's Daily Report for section 1. Form used to record results of the 3:00 P.M. room check.

GRA DAILY REPORT					

SECTION _____2_____ (18) RMS.   AM.   (PM.)
GRA _____Open_____   Day _Wednesday_ Date _11/4_

ROOM #	C/O	OCC	R	REMARKS	PICK-UP
1031			✓		
1032	✓				
1033			✓		
1034		✓		Luggage Only	
1036		✓			
1038			✓		
1040		✓			
1042			✓		
1044		✓			
1046	—	—	—	ooo	
1049		✓			
1051			✓		
1053		✓			
1055	✓				
1057			✓		
1059		✓		Request 10:00 P.M. late Service	
1061			✓		
1231			✓		

FIGURE 10.39 GRA's Daily Report for section 2, which was an open section and was therefore inspected by the senior GRA for tile red division.

Figures 10.38 and 10.39 show the GRA's Daily Report for the P.M. for sections 1 and 2, respectively. Julia was assigned to section 1 and she therefore conducts the inspection for that section. Section 2 was an open section, so the supervisor will conduct the room inspection. One of the three defined statuses—C/O, OCC, R—will be indicated for each room by placing a checkmark in the appropriate column. Any special remarks that need to be forwarded will be noted. Those rooms provided to Julia in the morning as pickup rooms are not checked by Julia since they will appear on another section sheet. It is therefore only the printed room numbers (left column) that need to be checked. Each room should always have *one* of the three statuses marked next to it—*never more than one.*

After each GRA has completed a room check for the section and filled in the P.M. Report, the report is placed on the GRA's cart to await pickup. After the supervisors have completed checking all open sections within the division, they circulate among their teams and pick up the completed room reports. In the four divisions in the model hotel there will be 20 reports, all of which should be brought to the main linen room by about 3:30 P.M.

It is at about this time that the second, or evening, shift will be reporting for work; there will be a shift overlap of about one hour.

OTHER ACTIVITIES DURING THE SHIFT

There are many other activities associated with cleaning guestrooms that are not as obvious as those done by the room attendant.

The GRA is assisted by someone keeping soiled linen and trash off the housekeeper's cart. That person is a **section housekeeping aide** and is usually a member of the team working in the area.

Other matters of resupply are also significant. Having the necessary linen to resupply the housekeeper's cart along with the other supplies needed to service the guestroom requires a whole new army of support personnel involved in total linen handling, especially when linen must be sent out from large hotels to commercial laundries.

There is the resupply of major cleaning chemicals, most of which must be diluted to **specified dilution ratios**. To maintain control of dilution, it is usually

FIGURE 10.40 During the day shift, the floor housekeeping aide provides linen and trash removal services to all GRAs on the team and is also responsible for guestroom public area cleaning. Here the housekeeping aide is vacuuming a hotel hallway per schedule. *(Photo courtesy of MGM Mirage.)*

accomplished in a separate place by one person qualified to do so.

Figures 10.40 through 10.47 depict some of these activities.

SHIFT OVERLAP: FIRST AND SECOND SHIFT COORDINATION (3:30 P.M. to 4:30 P.M.)

When the night supervisor and night housekeeper report to work at about 3:30 P.M. their first task will be to accept the 20 GRAs Daily Reports. They will then transcribe the information from each of these 20 reports onto the **Housekeeper's Report** for later forwarding to the front desk and the controller's office. This report is somewhat tedious to transcribe because of the different order in which rooms will be arranged on the Housekeeper's Report (which follows a pattern laid out on the front desk room rack). Figure 10.48 is a Housekeeper's Report consolidated from the information received from each of the Section Reports. (Rooms that are first indicated as C/O and then changed to R are explained later.) Note that, where applicable, the information received from Julia in section 1 and from the supervisor in the red division coincides with the information contained in the Housekeeper's Report. Note also that the form on which the Housekeeper's Report is prepared is identical to the form on which the night clerk prepared the report early in the morning that was used to open the house. However, on the Housekeeper's Report, every room will

have an indication next to the printed room number of the status in which it was seen over a time span of about 10 minutes (between 3:00 and about 3:10).

The report will normally take about 30 minutes to transcribe. No sooner than the transcription is completed will the report need to be updated before forwarding. Between 3:00 and 4:00 P.M. many things happen to cause the status reported at 3:00 P.M. to change. Guests are checking into ready rooms; a few guests will be departing after 3:00 P.M.; but most significant is that the rooms reported as checkout rooms will now have been made ready. (It is quite possible that a GRA who had reported three rooms as checkouts would have been able to service all of them between 3:00 and 4:00 P.M.) As each GRA leaves the floor at 4:00 P.M., he or she notifies the supervisor of the rooms previously reported as checkouts that are now ready. As the GRA moves to the satellite linen room to resupply the cart with linen for tomorrow's work effort, each senior housekeeper carries the updated information to the main linen room. The night supervisor uses this information to update the Housekeeper's Report.

In Figure 10.48 update corrections have been made to many of the rooms originally showing checkout status. There is also an update recap at the top of the page. What had been originally noted as 45 checkout rooms has now been reduced to 13. Also, the vacant and ready rooms have been increased from 158 to 190. It is not uncommon to erase the original indications and replace them with the correct indications. However, passing the updated information on to the front desk in both its original and corrected forms may help front desk personnel resolve discrepancies, since they will know which rooms were rented or vacated between 3:00 and 4:00 P.M.

At 4:30 P.M.

The Housekeeper's Report should be completed *no later than 4:30 P.M.* It is reviewed by a manager (and signed), a copy is made and retained, then the original is taken immediately to the supervisor or manager at the front desk.

In the meantime, GRAs should have finished loading carts for tomorrow's work schedule. There is a fresh supply of linen that the section housekeeping aide brought from the laundry and placed in the satellite linen room before 4:00 P.M. The section housekeeping aide collects all soiled glasses in cases, places them on rolling dollies, and moves them to the main linen room for washing and rebagging by the night crew. The supervisor returns to the satellite linen room to see that all carts are properly loaded and stowed for the night. Finally, all linen rooms are checked to ensure that trash has been removed and the linen room has been left in an orderly and locked condition. If top caddies

(a)

(b)

FIGURE 10.41 In the linen chute room at the Bellagio (a), a utility person gathers all soiled linen and packs it into large rolling hampers to transport it to a commercial laundry. The work is grueling, but it has been made into a badge of honor. These T-shirts (b) are only for "snake eaters." *(Photos courtesy of MGM Mirage.)*

are used on carts, they are returned to the main linen room for restocking. All workers who started work at 8:00 A.M. clock out at 4:30 P.M., having concluded an eight-hour workday in $8\frac{1}{2}$ hours lapsed time. (Recall that each employee was not on the clock during a 30-minute lunch break.) Before leaving the facility, each employee checks the Tight Schedule (see Chapter 3) to see if he or she is scheduled to work on the next day.

DISCREPANCIES AND RECHECKS GENERATED (4:30 P.M. TO 6:00 P.M.)

After the A.M. shift has departed, some member of department management or one of the day supervisors inspects all corridors and service areas to ensure that no piece of equipment, soiled linen, trash, or debris of any kind has been left in any hallway. Satellite linen rooms are spot checked to ensure that no trash cans

FIGURE 10.42 A clean supply of blankets and bedspreads is being returned to a satellite linen room from a commercial laundry. *(Photo courtesy of MGM Mirage.)*

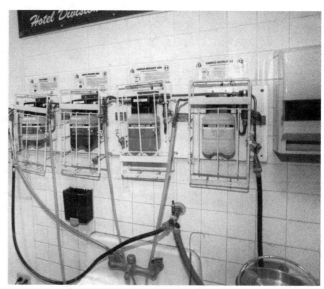

FIGURE 10.44 A chemical mixing station, where spray bottles are filled with tomorrow's supply of products for GRAs to use. *(Photo courtesy of MGM Mirage.)*

FIGURE 10.43 The GRA loads her cart with a fresh supply of linen. Some hotels require that carts be loaded at the end of the work shift; others reload in the morning. Usually this depends on whether or a clean supply is available at the end of the shift. Large properties that send their linen out to commercial laundries usually have to wait until satellite linen supply rooms have been restocked during the night. *(Photo courtesy of the Excalibur Hotel, Las Vegas.)*

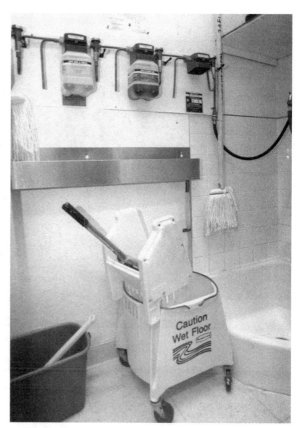

FIGURE 10.45 Another chemical mixing station located near a mop sink in a satellite storeroom, allowing users easy access. Note the labeling of containers, required by Hazardous Communications Laws (HazComm). Information regarding hazards connected with a product must be clearly specified on the container. Products in smaller containers must carry the same precautions as the container from which the product was drawn. *(Photo courtesy of MGM Mirage.)*

FIGURE 10.46 Other supplies needed by the guestroom attendant are made available in storerooms where carts are loaded. *(Photo courtesy of the Excalibur Hotel, Las Vegas.)*

FIGURE 10.47 Issuing storekeeper utility person checks on inventory or dry storage supplies, which are drawn daily by floor housekeeping aides. *(Photo courtesy of MGM Mirage.)*

(fire hazard) have been left unemptied and that all service doors are properly locked. Before the departure of the last department manager, the lost-and-found is chain locked (see the section on the lost-and-found, SOP, Chapter 9).

Barring any late administrative work or the need to remain behind to visit and/or work with the night crew, management's day can now be considered at an end. Evening operation of the department is now left in the control of the night supervisor, who will direct the activities of the night GRA, night section housekeeping aide, and night public area housekeepers.

A short time after the Housekeepers' Report is delivered to the front desk, the night supervisor would have transcribed all checkouts remaining on the Housekeeper's Report to the **Night Supervisor's Report of Evening Activities** (Figure 10.49), which is used to record the activities of the evening crew. The report specifies checkout rooms not finished as of 4:00 P.M., the results of rechecks, rooms requiring a light tidying, the fulfillment of guest requests during the evening, and any special project work completed during the evening.

Recall that there were 13 rooms indicating checkout status on the Housekeeper's Report. These room numbers are transferred into the first column of the Night Supervisor's Report. Rooms 1011 and 1059, which had been listed on Section Housekeepers' P.M. Reports for sections 1 and 2 as requesting late service, are inserted on the Night Supervisor's Report with the time that they should be cleaned.

Note the column marked "Turn down." This information is received from the front desk and refers to rooms that are to have one or more beds turned back for night use. Turn-down service is usually begun when guests are out of their rooms during the evening dinner hour and continues until all rooms are completed. It is a service once reserved for VIP guests but is now provided in many higher-priced hotels as a routine function in all guestrooms. During turn-down, the bedspread may be removed or folded down with the top sheet and blanket, exposing pillows (Figure 10.50). A touch of elegance includes placing a candy mint on the pillow with a small card saying, "Have a pleasant night's sleep, and a good day tomorrow."

The last column of the Night Supervisor's Report, **Guest request**, indicates services specifically requested by guests during the evening hours; room numbers and the services needed are recorded. If a guest loan item is needed, a receipt should be made out for the guest to

HOUSEKEEPER'S REPORT

Total Rooms Occupied ___147___
Total Rooms Vacant ___~~158~~ 190___
Check Outs ___45 13___
Stayovers _____
Out of Order ___3___

Date ___11/4___
Prepared By ___R. J. Housekeeper___

Room	OCC	R	C/O	Room	OCC	R	C/O	Room	OCC	R	C/O	Room	OCC	R	C/O	Room	OCC	R	C/O	Room	OCC	R	C/O	Room	OCC	R	C/O	Room	OCC	R	C/O
1001	✓			1068			✓	1228			✓	2051			✓	2110		✓		3015		✓		3079		✓	✓	3222	✓		
1002			✓	1071	✓			1229	✓			2053	✓			2202		✓		3016	✓			3080	✓			3223	✓		
1003	✓			1072		✓		1230	✓			2055		✓		2204		✓		3017		✓		3081	✓			3224	✓		
1004	✓			1073			✓	1231			✓	2057			✓	2205	✓			3019		✓		3083	✓			3225	✓		✗
1005		✓		1074	✓							2059	✓			2206		✓	✗	3021	✓			3085		✓		3226	✓		
1006		✓		1075	✓							2061	✓			2207	✓			3023	✓			3087	✓			3227		✓	✗
1007	✓			1076		✓		2001			✓	2062		✓		2208		✓		3025	✓			3089		✓		3228	✓		
1008	✓			1077		✓		2002			✓	2063		✓		2209	✓			3027		✓		3091	✓			3229	✓		
1009		✓	✗	1078		✓		2003			✓	2064	✓			2210	✓			3031		✓		3093	✓			3230	✓		
1010		✓	✗	1079	OOO			2004			✓	2065		✓		2211	✓			3032	✓			3095	✓			3231	✓		
1011	✓			1081		✓		2005	✓			2066		✓	✗	2212	✓			3033		✓	✗	3096		✓		4070	✓		
1012		✓		1083	✓			2006	✓			2067		✓	✗	2213	✓			3035	✓			3097	✓			4071	✓		
1013		✓		1085	✓			2007		✓		2068	✓			2214		✓		3037	✓			3098		✓	✗	4072	✓		
1014	✓			1087	✓			2008		✓		2070	✓			2215	✓			3038		✓	✗	3099		✓	✗	4073		✓	✗
1015		✓		1091		✓	✗	2009	✓			2071	✓			2216	✓			3039	✓			3100	✓			4074	✓		
1016	✓			1093	✓			2010		✓	✗	2072			✓	2217	✓			3040	✓			3101	✓			4075	✓		
1017	✓			1095		✓	✗	2011			✓	2073	✓			2218		✓		3041	✓			3102		✓		4076	✓		
1021		✓	✗	1096	✓			2012	✓			2074	✓			2219	✓			3043	✓			3103	✓			4077	✓		
1023		✓		1097	✓			2013	✓			2075	✓			2220	✓			3045	✓			3104		✓	✗	4078	✓		
1025		✓		1098		✓		2014		✓	✗	2076		✓		2221		✓	✗	3046	✓			3105	✓			4079	✓		
1027			✓	1099	✓			2015	✓			2077	✓			2222	✓			3047	✓			3106		✓		4080	✓		
1029		✓		1100		✓		2016	✓			2078	✓			2223	✓			3049	✓			3107		✓		4081	✓		
1031		✓		1101	✓			2017		✓		2079		✓		2224	✓			3051		✓	✗	3108		✓		4083	✓		
1032		✓	✗	1102	✓			2019	OOO			2080	✓			2225	✓			3053	✓			3110		✓		4085	✓		
1033		✓		1103		✓		2021	✓			2081		✓		2226	✓			3055	✓			3201	✓			4087	✓		
1034	✓			1104		✓	✗	2023	✓			2083	✓			2227	✓			3057		✓		3202		✓		4089	✓		
1036	✓			1105		✓		2025		✓		2085	✓			2228	✓			3059		✓		3204		✓		4091	✓		
1038	✓			1106	✓			2027	✓			2087	✓			2229			✓	3061	✓			3205	✓			4093			✓
1040	✓			1107	✓			2029	✓			2089	✓			2230	✓			3062	✓			3206		✓		4095	✓		
1042		✓		1108		✓		2031		✓		2091	✓			2231	✓			3063		✓		3207		✓		4096	✓		
1044	✓			1213		✓		2032	✓			2093	✓			3001	✓			3064	✓			3208		✓		4097	✓		
1046	OOO			1214		✓	✗	2033		✓	✗	2095		✓		3002	✓			3065		✓		3209	✓			4098	✓		
1049		✓		1215		✓		2034	✓			2096	✓			3003		✓	✗	3066		✓		3210	✓			4099		✓	✗
1051		✓		1216		✓		2035		✓		2097		✓	✗	3004	✓			3067		✓		3211		✓		4100	✓		
1053	✓			1217	✓			2037		✓		2098	✓			3005	✓			3068		✓		3212	✓			4101	✓		
1055		✓	✗	1218	✓			2038	✓			2099	✓			3006	✓			3070	✓			3213		✓		4102	✓		
1057		✓		1219		✓		2039		✓		2100	✓			3007			✓	3071		✓		3214		✓		4103	✓		
1059	✓			1220		✓		2040	✓			2101	✓			3008	✓			3072			✓	3215	✓			4104	✓		
1061		✓		1221			✓	2041	✓			2102	✓			3009	✓			3073		✓		3216		✓		4105	✓		
1062	✓			1222		✓		2042	✓			2103	✓			3010		✓	✗	3074	✓			3217		✓		4106	✓		
1063	✓			1223		✓		2043	✓			2104	✓			3011	✓			3075		✓	✗	3218		✓		4107		✓	✗
1064	✓			1224	✓			2045		✓		2105	✓			3012	✓			3076		✓		3219		✓		4108	✓		
1065		✓		1225		✓		2046	✓			2106	✓			3013			✓	3077		✓		3220	✓			4110		✓	✗
1066		✓		1226	✓			2047	✓			2107		✓		3014	✓			3078		✓		3221		✓					
1067			✓	1227			✓	2049			✓	2108		✓																		

FIGURE 10.48 In the Housekeeper's Report, changes in original recordings reflect what happened between 3:00 P.M., when the original data were collected, and 4:00 P.M..

sign, and the item logged out of the linen room in the Guest Log Book to ensure proper return of the item.

By 6:00 P.M. the front desk would have had the opportunity to use the Housekeeper's Report to **purify the room rack**. This is a procedure in which the status of each room as reported on the Housekeeper's Report is compared with the status of each room as indicated on the room rack. There will be numerous discrepancies, primarily because of the changing of room status that has been occurring between 3:00 and 6:00 P.M.

Most discrepancies can be resolved at the front desk by comparing arrival times of those guests for whom the front desk is showing the room as occupied (OCC) and the Housekeeper's Report is showing the room as ready (R). What might have happened is that at 3:00 P.M. the GRA saw a ready room (R); however, at 6:00 P.M. the front desk room rack showed an occupied (OCC) room.

Discrepancies may also show the opposite condition. The front desk can show a checkout, whereas the Housekeeper's Report shows an occupied room. This type of discrepancy may have occurred as a result of a late checkout or of a departure *after* the room had been cleaned. Such discrepancies must be **rechecked**.

All discrepancies that cannot be reconciled by the front desk, and all rooms that the front desk indicates are checkouts, must be physically rechecked. The room numbers of guestrooms to be rechecked are sent to housekeeping via the computer or in writing. Each recheck is listed on the Night Supervisor's Report of Evening Activities in the first half of column three. The evening supervisor or night GRA should immediately recheck the status (take another look) of each of the rooms so listed and record the results of the recheck in the second half of the column.

NIGHT SUPERVISOR'S REPORT
OF
EVENING ACTIVITIES

DAY _____ DATE _____ SUPERVISOR _____

C/O	Make-up late	Recheck		Tidies		Turn down		Guest request	
Rm no.	Rm no.	Rm no.	Stat	Rm no.	Stat	Rm no.	Comp	Rm no.	Item
1002	1011 8pm	1007	C/O/T	1007	MR	1005		1034	Iron Ret
1027	1059 10pm	2013	c/o	2083	MR	1067		2217	Foam Pillows
1067		2083	C/O/T	3055	MR	1103		2064	Bed Board
1073		3055	C/O/T	4105	MR	2040		3067	Iron Ret
1221		3068	R			2059		3225	Hair Dryer Ret
2004		3207	C/O			3018		3051	Sewing Kit
2057		3214	R			3108		2012	Bed Board
2072		4072	C/O			3222		1021	Roll-Away Bed
2229		4099	OCC			4080		2105	Crib
3007		4105	C/O/T			4107		2224	Roll-Away Bed
3066								1023	Razor Ret
3218								3067	Crib
4093								4075	Sick Guest
2013									
3207									
4072									

Other nightly duties	Completed
Vacuum front office, reservations, res. mgr's office, exec office	
Shampoo site entry carpet	
Shampoo soft furniture in Div F&B office	

FIGURE 10.49 Night Supervisor Report of Evening Activities; codes: R, ready; C/O, checkout; T, tidy; MR, made ready; OCC, occupied; RET, returned; COMP, completed; STAT, status.

As an example, refer to the Housekeeper's Report (Figure 10.48) to note the first status listed for each room in which there is a discrepancy. Rooms 1007, 2083, 3055, and 4105 were first listed as OCC but upon recheck were found to be CO/T; the T refers to a condition requiring a tidying. A **tidy** is a room that had been serviced earlier in the day when it was occupied but has now been vacated. Tidies require only a very light service; removal of small amounts of litter, replacing a glass, cleaning an ashtray, or perhaps smoothing a bed. A change of linen is required if a bed has been turned back and slept in or on. Night GRAs must check to make sure that the departing guest did not remake the bed after sleeping on what had been clean linen, leaving an unwelcome surprise for the next guest. The bathroom might also require a light touch-up. A tidy requires two to five minutes of service, provided the guest did not get back into bed before departing.

All rooms listed in the recheck column that are showing checkout and tidy (CO/T) are also listed in the tidies column. As soon as they are **made ready (M/R)**, they are so listed and phoned to the front desk as ready rooms in order that they may be sold as soon as possible.

Rooms 2013, 3207, and 4072 were simply listed as CO in the recheck column. These rooms will require a complete makeup, similar to those rooms originally listed in the C/O column. They are therefore added to the C/O column if they were not already listed.

Rooms 3068 and 3214 were originally listed as R and upon recheck were found in that same status. The front desk must continue to research these two rooms to determine why the front desk status remains in error, since on two occasions both rooms were viewed by housekeeping as ready rooms. Possibly a **room found vacant (RFV)** has occurred, which happens when a customer intends to pay the account with a credit card and expects the hotel to find the room vacant, total the bill, and send through a voucher for what is owed. The other possibility is that someone has **skipped** without

FIGURE 10.50 Night GRA provides turn-down service for guestroom at the Los Angeles Airport Marriott Hotel. *(Photo taken with permission of the Los Angeles Airport Marriott Hotel.)*

FIGURE 10.51 At the Bellagio, high rollers do not get an ordinary foil-covered, mass-produced mint on their pillows. Instead they receive a lovely wood-grained package of handmade chocolates from the Bellagio kitchens. *(Photo taken with permission of MGM Mirage.)*

paying the account. Room 4099 was originally reported as R and is now found to be occupied. The front desk shows this room vacant, and must continue researching until the discrepancy is resolved.

In the manner prescribed earlier, all rechecks will have their status determined for the day. Most rechecks will need a light tidy. On many occasions, these tidies can be completed as they are discovered and the room reported as a ready room immediately by phone to the front desk. The final status of all rechecks is recorded and sent back to the front desk in writing or on the computer.

EVENING ACTIVITIES (6:00 P.M. TO MIDNIGHT)

The workload of the evening crew can be summarized as follows:

1. To transcribe the Housekeeper's Report and then update the report.
2. To transcribe the remaining checkouts to the Night Supervisor's Report of Evening Activities and the night GRA to begin cleaning these checkouts.
3. Public area housekeepers to assume responsibility for public area cleaning and servicing.
4. Evening crew to begin providing special services as requested by the guests and to note each service on the report.
5. At about 6:00 P.M., to receive rechecks and to check the statuses of rooms listed for recheck to determine what, if anything, must be done by the housekeeping department to service these rooms. Many rechecks will require a light tidy; some rooms will require a complete makeup; others require only the verification of correct status. Rooms tidied and any other special projects required of the night crew are noted on the report.
6. Turn-downs are begun at about 7:00 P.M. and are continued until completed (Figure 10.51).
7. The night housekeeping aide usually washes all guestroom drinking glasses and helps repackage them in sanitary containers for use during the next day. These glasses are delivered to satellite linen rooms at night.
8. The night supervisor, assisted by other members of the night crew, may restock cart-top baskets with the proper par of guest supplies; these baskets will be picked up the next day by GRAs as they proceed to work.

Of greatest significance is the fact that the night supervisor is *in charge* and must *take charge* of the evening activities of the housekeeping department. He or she must therefore wear a beeper and not be confined to an office. Computer messages are reviewed upon return to the office, and telephone messages are intercepted and relayed by the PBX operator. The supervisor works closely with the night supervisor at the front desk to ensure that all rechecks are properly resolved and that every room is left clean and saleable. The hotel should *never* lose room revenue because the housekeeping department failed to clean a room.

The night supervisor must also make inspections of public restrooms to ensure that they are being properly maintained. A night guestroom attendant may service ten or fifteen rooms each night to ensure their availability for guests who arrive late (Figure 10.52). The night supervisor should see to it that the main linen room is cleaned and properly prepared for the oncoming supervisor who will be opening the house the next morning.

Of greatest importance is that the night supervisor keep an eye out for the unexpected. A change in the weather at 10:00 P.M. can have a surprising effect on tomorrow's schedule. Any unusual change in expected occupancy may warrant notification to the executive housekeeper in order that special direction may be forthcoming for the unusual occasion.

When all vacant rooms are clean and ready to rent, turn-downs are completed, linen room is clean and ready for the oncoming shift, glasses washed and packaged for use the following day, and cart-top caddies replenished for GRAs to pick up in the morning, the evening activities are essentially finished. The final step in each evening's activity is for the supervisor to assemble all reports, records, forms, and paperwork associated with the day's activities for filing chronologically according to date. The following is a list of documents that should be filed:

1. Night Clerk's Report to Housekeeping (used to open the house that day)
2. Original and copies of all Supervisor's Daily Work Reports (original was given to each senior housekeeper; copy was placed on the linen room counter to monitor work progress of each division)
3. All GRA's P.M. Reports

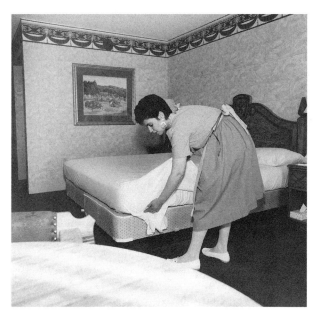

FIGURE 10.52 The night GRA services a late checkout to make the room ready for a late-arriving guest. *(Photo taken with permission Excalibur Hotel & Casino.)*

4. Copy of the Housekeeper's Report
5. Completed passkey/beeper control sheet
6. Night Supervisor's Report of Evening Activities

There will be numerous occasions when this information will need to be researched. It is therefore imperative that it be retained for at least one year.

Computers Come of Age in the World of Housekeeping

The subject of **computers** and their application to the techniques of rooms management in hotel operations has at last come of age. Once confined to the realm of top management, statistical analysis, corporate planning payroll, and the like, state-of-the-art development of computer application to property management systems is now commonplace. The race to devise and provide economical information-handling and reporting systems has been nothing short of spectacular. Although the race goes on, **hardware** (input terminals, microprocessors, disk drive components, and printers) and hotel **software packages** (programs by which computers assimilate information), once thought to be out of reach of housekeeping personnel, have become part of the daily routine of housekeeping operations. Computers are now just another tool to help housekeeping departments become more efficient in handling management information.

The development of computers is currently seen to be in its fifth generation. With each step into the future, computers have become less expensive, allowing even the smallest hotel the opportunity to modernize the efficient handling of information.

Although the hotel industry seems as ageless as history, the 1980s introduced not only the computer into housekeeping information handling, but also the **telephone switch** (system) as the vehicle by which computer technology is applied. Since every guestroom has one, the telephone has become the chief instrument for housekeeping to use in accessing the computer. This technique greatly reduces the cost of updating existing facilities since major expenses can be avoided in adding wiring to each individual room.

For example, an **interface** is created between the telephone system and the **central processing unit (CPU)** of the computer network. This is accomplished by the guestroom attendants dialing a specific sequence of numbers on the phone from a specific guestroom. Once connected, the computer immediately recognizes the room number to which it is being connected. After the connection, a specific list of **dial-up codes** becomes available to the GRA by which he or she can now transmit information. Figure 10.53 shows the GRA dialing the special code from a room.

Assume the following scenario:

1. The GRA in Housekeeping Section 54 currently is in room 2025 and she wants to communicate with the computer. The special phone number of the computer is 71555.
2. GRA dials 71555 and hears a new and different dial tone. This tells her that she is connected to the computer.
3. The following list of three-digit codes is now available by which she can input information:

Status Code	Information Transmitted
111	Room is a *ON CHANGE* (A Checkout—C/O)
112	Room is *Occupied* (Clean)
113	Room is *Occupied* (Dirty)
114	Room is *Vacant* READY (Ready to Rent)
115	Room is *OUT OF SERVICE* (Maintenance) (This code can be read and acknowledged in the Maintenance Department and a maintenance person dispatched immediately.)
116	Room is Out-of-Order (OOO) (This code is available only to the Maintenance Department to ensure that the Chief Engineer, who is ultimately responsible for returning [OOO] back to a service status, is aware of the situation.)
117	Room is returned to operative status—Needs Housekeeping. (This code is available only to the Maintenance Department. It does *not* return the room to rentable status. Only Housekeeping can do that after checking the room following whatever had to be done by Maintenance.)

4. After dialing one of the codes (111–15), the GRA then dials his or her three-digit section number (027), which identifies him or her as the initiator of the message. If the message is a Code 116 or 117, a **special initiator code** must be assigned to a maintenance person before a code will be accepted by the computer.

After inputting information, room 2025 is identified as being in a specific **Rooms Inventory**. For example, this specific room now becomes identified in numerical order with other rooms in the same category, such as ROOMS READY FOR SALE, OCCUPIED ROOMS NOT

FIGURE 10.53 Preparing to input information into the computer about a room ready for occupancy. *(Photo taken with permission Excalibur Hotel & Casino.)*

AVAILABLE FOR SALE, ROOMS THAT ARE ON CHANGE. (between departing and newly arriving guest, not yet serviced—C/O).

The GRA is not the only person who can make a status change entry for a guestroom. When the front desk clerk rents a room, a selection is made from the inventory of rooms identified as being READY FOR SALE. In the process of inputting check-in information for a guest, the desk clerk, through a **computer terminal**, changes the status of the room to OCCUPIED NOT (no longer) AVAILABLE FOR SALE. The front desk clerk can also put rooms into a special status, such as RUSH. Rooms in this status are rooms that have been **preassigned** and have guests waiting for them. These rooms are given priority attention by housekeeping from among other ON CHANGE rooms.

Housekeeping central operations can also make inputs into the system. Many times a status change needs to be reported that cannot be directly inputted from a guestroom (guest might be using the telephone, or is a *do not disturb*). Status changes can be phoned into the *status-board operator* in housekeeping. This information can then be inputted by the status-board operator (Figure 10.54). Status-board operators take calls from guests for services and check input information from

FIGURE 10.54 Housekeeping central—the hub of operations for more than 600 employees. *(Photo courtesy of MGM Mirage.)*

floor supervisors throughout the hotel regarding the status of rooms. Two-way radios are also used in the transfer of information.

At different times during the day, or on call, the status-board operator can print out the status of all guestrooms at a given instant and provide floor supervisors information regarding their particular sections. Also, management can review total rooms status at any time by calling for a printout.

This is an example of only one of many ways a computer can be employed in the management of guestroom information. New hotels can be wired for different types of systems that can give housekeeping information, and also can turn on air-conditioning systems and lights when a room becomes rented, tell whether or not the GRA is currently in a specific room, and, through the door-locking system, tell who were the last 24 persons to enter the room.

The *Night Clerk's Report*, opening the house, and the scheduling of work for supervisors and GRAs are now available through computers. Information about rooms not to be disturbed, rooms out of order, and late checkouts are updated and available, and P.M. Reports and information about rooms requiring immediate service or about turn-down requirements on specific rooms are created instantly. Room status discrepancies are handled efficiently, allowing for the cleaning of questionable rooms for reoccupancy earlier in the day.

As for spectacular advancement in the realm of computers for housekeeping, consider the following scenario:

A supervisor or manager inspects a guestroom and records the findings vocally into a handheld tape-recorder. Upon completion of the inspection, the recorder is *plugged into* a receptacle located in the guestroom. The inspection information is immediately transmitted to a **microprocessor**, where it is voice-read into a data memory bank. At any time from that moment on, a printout of inspection results for all rooms inspected is immediately available to the manager. Microprocessors have the capability to sort, codify, and classify information in such a fashion that inspection comments containing a maintenance work request would be immediately transmitted to the engineering department. As work is completed, additional input from the guestroom would cause reports to be updated. Should rooms be necessarily held in out-of-order status, information would be available indicating the nature of the problem, corrective action being taken, and expected time the room will be back in service.

This is only one of many possible uses of computer applications in the housekeeping department. As you read Chapter 11, you will see many places in which computer application will also be beneficial. Remember, however, that before computer application becomes a reality, a thorough understanding of systems as they might be conducted *by hand* is most important; otherwise, extraneous capability might be purchased when what might have been needed can only be found installed in the hotel across the street.

EXECUTIVE PROFILE
Della Gras   *The "Gras" Is Greener at the Rosen Plaza*

by Andi M. Vance, Editor, *Executive Housekeeping Today*

This article first appeared in the September 2001 issue of *Executive Housekeeping Today*, the official publication of the International Executive Housekeepers Association, Inc.

The Rosen Plaza Hotel in Orlando, Florida, opens doors for people. In October it'll open doors for many I.E.H.A. members who attend I.E.H.A.'s Educational Conference and Convention in conjunction with ISSA/INTERCLEAN®–USA '01. Della Gras, Executive Housekeeper of the hotel, is excited about the event and will be prepared. "I've already advised my staff of the event," Gras explains. "This place will be immaculate for our members at the time of the convention."

The hotel also opens doors for its staff. Gras is living proof of the opportunities available to Rosen Plaza employees. "This is a great place for advancement," she says over the phone. "We have quite a few people who have been here for quite some time. Many have moved from room attendant, to a supervisory position, and then to management."

Prior to the hotel's opening 10 years ago, Gras assisted in the housekeeping department by ordering supplies and setting up the computer systems. While she had no prior experience in the hospitality industry, the hotel's management recognized her ambition and offered her a position wherever she felt she was qualified.

Knowing that housekeeping was her niche, she learned more about procedures and operations of the entire department rather than focusing upon one particular aspect. As an administrative assistant, she gained the needed experience and skill to become an assistant. Two years ago Gras reached a milestone when she was promoted to Executive Housekeeper at the Rosen Plaza. Just as many doors were opened to Gras, she opens doors for her 150 staff.

Currently, Gras is responsible for overseeing the activities of the entire department. By providing the final approval for labor schedules, inventory and payroll, she enables the supervisors to be responsible for the construction of these schedules. "If I do everything, then they don't learn," Gras advises. "One of my biggest responsibilities is keeping up the morale within the department. We all have to come to work, but if they enjoy the atmosphere, that's one of the things that keep them returning."

DOORS TO RESPECT

Of all the individuals under Gras' direction, many are long-standing employees of the hotel. Their loyalty can be partially attributed to the respect they receive from all levels of the administration. "They [room attendants] can absolutely see that they are cared for from the top down," says Gras. "You'll see them just beaming when you notice that they have a new hairdo, or ask them about their family. If there's a problem at home, we do our best to accommodate their needs. You just can't hassle them. If I had a serious personal problem within my family, that would be my priority. I love my job, but family is family. You can't place a bigger burden on their shoulders than the one they may already carry. I think that really makes a difference."

By paying close attention to each employee's needs (both personal and professional), the administration and hotel owners display their respect and appreciation for the housekeeping staff. "If one of the room attendants were to stop the owner in the hallway, he would make time for them," she says. "The administration really nurtures their relationship with the staff in order to maintain a comfortable atmosphere here."

Once a month, staff members have the opportunity of dining with either the general manager, Gary Hudson, or the owner, Harris Rosen. This provides a forum for the discussion of any problems either party may be experiencing. "The open flow of communication really makes it a family at the Rosen Plaza," Gras admits.

DOORS TO NEW LANGUAGES

With over 60% of non-English speaking room attendants, you would think that communication within the department would be difficult. Creole is the predominant language of the group with Spanish and Filipino also represented. For Gras, a smile transcends communication barriers. "Everyone understands a smile," she reiterates to her staff every morning.

Throughout the school year, representatives from Florida Tech University provide language classes at the hotel. Non-English speaking personnel can attend the class for one hour on Monday and Wednesdays. While this not only helps to bridge the language divide, it also serves to build esteem and unity amongst the staff. Over 40% of Gras' staff takes advantage of this resource. At the conclusion of the course, a ceremony is held for the graduates where they are presented with a certificate for completion.

DOORS TO INCENTIVES

While longevity and detail yields great returns at the Rosen Plaza, other incentives are offered to keep morale high. Within the housekeeping department, Gras has organized the attendants into teams of nine for a monthly competition. While they do not use team-cleaning at the hotel, this competition also helps to establish unity amongst the group. Points accumulated by each team are tracked on a board in the office so that everyone can see where they stand in comparison to other teams. Teams can earn or lose points in such areas as: attendance, energy conservation and accidents. For example, if an attendant forgets to turn off the lights in one of the rooms he or she has cleaned, points are deducted from the team's final score. At the end of the month, the team with the most points wins $25 each.

The PM Program (Preventative Maintenance) also provides an incentive for detailed work. Each day of the week, a particular area is designated to assure that no part of the room is dirty (e.g.: Mondays are window ledges). Room attendants who participate in the program are required to focus upon that particular area. With a free lunch for one randomly chosen individual as an incentive, many of the staff regularly participate. "They really respond to these programs," Gras mentions. "Each morning at line up, they are made aware of their responsibilities for the day. The more you tell them over and over, the more it's in their heads and the less likely they'll be to forget."

The owners and management provide monetary incentives for long-time employees. Christmas and yearly bonuses are multiplied by the number of years the individual has been with the hotel. This can amount to a large sum for those who have been with the Rosen Plaza for more than a few years! Supervisors can also earn monetary benefits from exemplary performance on the job. Each month, a supervisor is chosen for commendation based upon general clean rooms and guest comment cards.

DOORS OF LOYALTY

When many hotels occupy a particular area, competition for staff can be fierce. When a room attendant is offered a slight increase in hourly wage by a neighboring hotel, he or she generally jumps at the opportunity. But Gras doesn't experience a problem with retention, even though the Rosen Plaza doesn't provide the highest wages in the area. By keeping morale high within the department and the doors of opportunity open for her staff, this Executive Housekeeper assures that the "gras" stays greener at the Rosen Plaza Hotel.

DISCUSSION QUESTIONS

1. As Della Gras observes, loyalty of the staff is based on more than the size of the paycheck they receive. However, others have observed that often employees will "go down the street" for relatively small wage increases. Why is this so? Might both views be correct? Is it possible to quantify the price of loyalty?

2. The Gras profile points out many "doors to incentives." Can you come up with others that might work for a housekeeping department? Have you ever heard of incentives in any other departments that might be tailored to work in a housekeeping department?

CONCLUSION

Recognizing that direction and control requires the communication of directive instructions and the accomplishment of many procedures, the simplest method of accomplishing direction of routine tasks is to communicate through forms. In this chapter, the principal daily routine for the housekeeping department associated with the model hotel has been segmented and presented in a chronological manner. This is the major routine of the department that *recurs on a daily basis.*

First, routine information regarding which rooms would require service was communicated by a form to the housekeeping department. This information was then converted into meaningful information according to the plan of work established for the housekeeping department. Workers were then specifically assigned to work tasks according to the volume of work that had to be accomplished. This too was done through the use of forms in a procedure called opening the house.

In the afternoon the P.M. Report was conducted, which formed a basis for the executive housekeeper's report to the front desk as to the current and up-to-the-minute status of all guestrooms in the hotel as of about 3:00 P.M. This report was assembled under the direction of the supervisor of the second work shift, who would later be required to recheck the status discrepancies of certain rooms that could not be resolved by the front desk. As these discrepancies were resolved, the balance of the workload for the day was finalized for the housekeeping department, and the second shift completed the workday about 11:00 P.M.

All of this was accomplished before workers reported for work. The workday was then segmented into several parts.

Morning activities included an explanation of the various activities of each member of the housekeeping team, the A.M. Report and how the morning room inspection generated discrepancies in room status that had to be resolved with the front desk, the priority of room cleaning by the GRA, and a technique of using forms and symbols for keeping up with the constantly changing status of rooms during the day. There are also fairly standardized procedures on how to clean a guestroom and their rationale should be understood.

Then, early afternoon presented a need to resolve the status of rooms that had been tagged do not disturb (DND) in the morning. A technique was presented to accomplish this task that gave primary consideration to the guest and guest safety.

Other evening activities were presented, including turn-down service, servicing guest requests, and the collecting of all the day's paperwork into a package for filing.

There are many other procedures, known as subroutines, that are equally important but do not necessarily occur on a daily basis. Several of these subroutines will be addressed in Chapter 11. Once the routines are understood, any and all of them are capable of being adapted to computer operation.

KEY TERMS AND CONCEPTS

Housekeeping day	Tidied	Amenity package
Daily routine chronology	Room status operator	Suite hotel
Opening the house	Swag lamp	Suite attendant
Morning activities	All-purpose cleaner	Security bar
Changing rooms	Special cleaning compounds	Security chain
Wardrobe departments	Acid bowl cleaner	Room rate card
Plastic hang-up bags	Specified dilutions ratios	Quest for Quality Standards
Costumes	HazComm requirements	Placement Guide
A.M. room checks	Lost-and-found procedures	First-nighter kit
Occupied	Mitered corner	HOMES manuals
Ready to rent	Snooze sheet	Commitment to Quality
On change	Portable beds	Do not disturb (DND)
Discrepancy	Damp wipe	P.M. room check
Double rooming	Stay-over rooms	Section housekeeping aide
Communication symbols	Johnny Mop	Specified dilution ratios

Housekeeper's Report
Night Supervisor's Report of
  Evening Activities
Guest request
Purify the room rack
Rechecked
Tidy
Made ready (M/R)

Room found vacant (RFV)
Skipped
Computers
Hardware
Software packages
Telephone switch
Interface
Central processing unit (CPU)

Dial-up codes
Special initiator code
Rooms Inventory
Computer terminal
Preassigned
Microprocessor

DISCUSSION AND REVIEW QUESTIONS

1. Explain the different purposes of the A.M. and P.M. room checks. How can A.M. room checks be conducted so as to show maximum concern for guests?
2. Why are forms and symbols so important to the progress of the daily routine in housekeeping departments?
3. Explain the term *discrepancy*. Is there any difference between a discrepancy and a recheck?
4. What are the reasons for maintaining a Night Supervisor's Report of Evening Activities?

5. During an A.M. room check, a supervisor discovers two rooms thought to be ready rooms that have actually been occupied. What alternatives are available to facilitate this unexpected and additional workload?
6. List as many tasks as you can that are a part of the evening crew's responsibility. What is the last function normally performed by the night supervisor before securing the housekeeping department for the night? As part of the daily routine, what is the primary objective of the evening?

CHAPTER 11

Hotel Housekeeping Subroutines

LEARNING OBJECTIVES

After studying the chapter, students should be able to:

1. List and describe other vital functions of the hotel housekeeping department—subroutines.
2. Define the term subroutine.
3. Generate a standard operating procedure for a subroutine.
4. Describe the importance of preplanning subroutines.

In Chapter 10 the primary housekeeping function of the department was presented as a chronology of events that normally constitutes the daily routine. There are many other functions, however, with which the housekeeping department may become involved. They are also best presented as routines, even though they do not all occur on a daily basis. These routines, which we call **subroutines**, are vital to total operations and should be given equal planning attention with the daily routine.

Subroutines can be presented through standard operating procedures (SOPs), several of which have been shown in Chapter 9 (lost-and-found procedures, key control, and procedures for changing door locks). It may appear that much of what will be described in this chapter cannot be delegated without abdication of responsibilities. This is not a correct assumption, as the astute professional manager will realize. Budgeting, for example, occurs so seldom (once a year) that junior managers may never have an opportunity to become involved before they are transferred and/or promoted. Every manager within the department therefore must become involved at every opportunity if professional development is to take place.

Table 11.1 contains topical areas and associated routines that will be encountered in most housekeeping operations from time to time, and, rather than be considered exceptions to the daily routine, should be thought of as subroutines. A detailed analysis of each of the subroutines in Table 11.1 is worthy of the executive housekeeper's time and effort in order that they also become routines rather than exceptions to the daily routine.

As with the daily routine, subroutines lend themselves to control by forms. Some require only limited planning and policy formulation regarding their substance, whereas others need detailed planning and careful implementation. We will now look at each of these subroutines, keeping in mind the importance of proper delegation to overall department morale, effectiveness, and efficiency of operation.

TABLE 11.1 Topical Areas and Routines

Topical Area	Subroutine
Cleaning and maintenance	Public area cleaning
	General cleaning of guestrooms
	Projects
	Maintenance work-request programs
Operation controls	Room inspections
	Total property inspections
	Inventories
	Personnel use (forecasting and analysis)
	Period statement critiques
Purchasing	Cleaning and guest supplies
Personnel administration	Linens
	Time card control
	Payroll administration
	Performance appraisals
Communication and training	Departmental meetings
Long-range planning	Budget formulation

Cleaning and Maintenance
❧

PUBLIC AREA CLEANING

Guestroom attendants (GRAs) are efficiently used when their efforts are confined to the guestroom areas of the hotel. The section housekeeping aide provides support to the housekeeping team and performs certain duties related to the maintenance of guestroom corridors, stairwells, elevators, vending areas, and satellite linen room stocking and maintenance. There are, however, other areas that require cleaning and maintenance throughout a facility and for which the executive housekeeper is often responsible. In very large hotels, such as hotel/casinos, that have an enormous amount of public space, there may be a need for an entirely separate department devoted to cleaning, often referred to as a **public areas department**. The administrator of that department often goes by the title of **director of public areas** and is considered to be on the same level as the executive housekeeper. In a full-service hotel, there is often one other department whose primary mission is to clean, and that is the **stewards department** in the kitchens. This department is usually administered by an individual with the title **chief steward**.

However, in smaller properties, the organizational structure will be similar to what we saw in the Division of Work Document presented in Chapter 2. We saw that there may be many **public areas** under the executive housekeeper's umbrella of responsibility that require daily if not hourly attention. Hotel lobbies, public restrooms, lobby thoroughfares, offices, banquet area restrooms, employee locker rooms, and assorted service areas require scheduled cleaning and maintenance.

Such functions normally fall under the supervisory responsibility of the *senior housekeeping aide*, who should be a specialist in unique cleaning and maintenance tasks. Recalling the established organization for the model hotel, the lobby housekeepers, housekeeping aides, and utility housekeeping personnel normally report to the senior housekeeping aide and are available for the large number of specialized tasks that must be performed. Such personnel should be uniquely uniformed and temperamentally suited for work among members of the general public.

Cleaning and **maintenance circuits (rounds)** need to be established in order that all areas of concern are kept under control. The straightening and repositioning of furniture, the emptying of ash urns and ashtrays, the cleaning of smudges from glass doors and mirrors, and the servicing of public restrooms can require attention as little as once every eight hours and as often as once every 15 minutes, depending upon the circumstances. Figures 11.1 through 11.13 are examples of special cleaning requirements in the public areas at the Bellagio, Las Vegas. Director of Public Areas Donald G. Trujillo has a staff of 439 employees in his department, including 281 casino porters and 129 utility porters.

Employees functioning under the senior housekeeping aide or the director of public areas must be trained to respond to these needs without immediate and direct supervision.

Special initiative might be expected of the lobby housekeeper to modify the cleaning circuit based on observations of crowds as they migrate through the hotel. For example, lack of activity in the lobby during certain hours of the day would indicate that less attention is required once an area has been properly serviced. Times of heavy check-in may warrant the prolonged and

FIGURE 11.1 Donald Trujillo, Director of Public Areas at Bellagio, poses for the camera—not in the lobby, but in a back-of-the-house corridor with a colorful mural and marble floors. At Bellagio it is difficult to tell where the front of the house begins and the back of the house ends. *(Photo courtesy of Bellagio, MGM Mirage™, Las Vegas, Nevada.)*

FIGURE 11.3 A public area housekeeping aide (porter) may work on a cleaning circuit. Here such an aide is touching up a public restroom sink at Bellagio. The public bathrooms use an average of 39,264 rolls of toilet paper each month! *(Photo courtesy of Bellagio, MGM Mirage™, Las Vegas, Nevada.)*

FIGURE 11.2 Here a Bellagio public area housekeeping aide (casino porter) puts away a vacuum. In a large casino/hotel there is an immense amount of money invested in supplies and equipment. There were more than 20 vacuums in this storeroom. *(Photo courtesy of Bellagio, Las Vegas, an MGM Mirage™, property.)*

continued attention of the lobby housekeeper to the point that this person cannot leave the specific lobby area until the crowd subsides.

Supplies and equipment must be suitable and, where necessary, specialized for the tasks. Standard equipment for lobby personnel is a specially designed cart that is stocked with necessary supplies. Microfiber floor mops, vacuum cleaners, and dusting materials are carried on carts with good trash-handling capability and paper supply transport. The lobby housekeeper and aide should not only be equipped to handle routine tasks, but they should have specialized equipment on hand, such as paint scrapers to keep ahead of (or behind) those who deposit chewing gum on concrete walks, hard

FIGURE 11.4 Yes, the modesty panels in this men's room are made of marble, as are the floors. Exquisite furnishings and fixtures like these present a real challenge to the public areas department. As an added touch, the staff embosses the ends of the toilet paper in the restrooms whenever they enter to touch up the facility. *(Photo courtesy of Bellagio, MGM Mirage™, Las Vegas, Nevada.)*

FIGURE 11.5 Here Guerardo Sanchez puts a shine on a drinking fountain. The plants behind him are real, as are all of the plants in the hotel. *(Photo courtesy of Bellagio, MGM Mirage™, Las Vegas, Nevada.)*

FIGURE 11.6 Vronny Bartor makes certain there are no blemishes on the floor in her lobby at the Bellagio. If you need directions to the high-limit gaming area, she will point you in the right direction. *(Photo courtesy of Bellagio, MGM Mirage™, Las Vegas, Nevada.)*

FIGURE 11.7 Even the ashtrays are made of marble at the Bellagio. It is difficult to see in the photo, but the black sand in each ashtray is imprinted with the Bellagio crest. *(Photo courtesy of Bellagio, MGM Mirage™, Las Vegas, Nevada.)*

FIGURE 11.8 There is always a need to replace worn furnishings, such as the carpet, but it all cannot be done overnight. Here is an example of old and new carpet side by side in the main casino. Because a casino never closes, the refurbishment is done in small stages late on the graveyard shift. *(Photo courtesy of Bellagio, MGM Mirage™, Las Vegas, Nevada.)*

FIGURE 11.9 Here an elevator foyer absolutely gleams at Bellagio. *(Photo courtesy of Bellagio, MGM Mirage™, Las Vegas, Nevada.)*

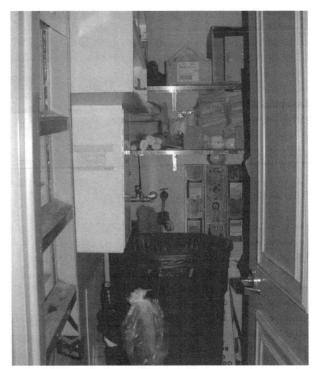

FIGURE 11.11 A typical public area utility closet at the Bellagio. Note the chemical mixing station at the rear of the closet. *(Photo courtesy of Bellagio, MGM Mirage™, Las Vegas, Nevada.)*

FIGURE 11.10 One of the hallways in the convention area. Most of the flooring is either wool carpet or marble. On an average day at Bellagio there are 25 people who do nothing but clean carpets and 24 people who spend their entire time maintaining the marble. *(Photo courtesy of Bellagio, MGM Mirage™, Las Vegas, Nevada.)*

FIGURE 11.12 A unique property poses some unique challenges in cleaning, such as the Dale Chihuly chandelier in the lobby. It takes two workers two days just to clean the top of the chandelier/sculpture. *(Photo courtesy of Bellagio, MGM Mirage™, Las Vegas, Nevada.)*

floors, or even carpets. Indoor hard surfaces such as decorative Mexican clay tile or terrazzo floors require specialized equipment for cleaning and maintenance. In most cases, carpet shampooing requires the use of special equipment and skills in equipment maintenance. Normally, specially trained employees who perform work such as carpet shampooing will be under the direction of the senior housekeeping aide.

After the day shift has been relieved by the second shift, the night supervisor is responsible for public area cleaning and maintenance, as well as guestroom cleaning. The senior housekeeping aide and the night supervisor are therefore vital to the success of the overall housekeeping operation. The executive housekeeper should work to establish, then strengthen, the technical and supervisory skills of these two employees. Most

(a)

(b)

(c)

FIGURE 11.13 Another unique public area to clean is the Conservatory at Bellagio with its romantic grand staircase (A) and the challenge of keeping all of these giant butterflies tidy (B, C). "Now, if they would only hold still!" *(Photo courtesy of Bellagio, MGM Mirage™, Las Vegas, Nevada.)*

of all, the executive housekeeper should delegate properly and then allow these supervisors the opportunity to do their jobs and not interfere, other than to coach and counsel in the performance of assigned tasks.

Both the senior housekeeping aide and the night supervisor should be involved in establishing the standard operating procedures for performance of public area housekeeping and in developing job descriptions for employees under their control. Although actual employment is a management decision, these two supervisors should be allowed to question and give indication of their approval of any employee considered for assignment to areas under their supervisory control.

GENERAL CLEANING OF GUESTROOMS

The routine servicing of guestrooms normally includes removing rubbish, changing linens, thoroughly cleaning bathrooms, vacuuming floors (when necessary), lightly dusting or damp wiping flat surfaces, and setting up and supplying the room for the next stay-over guest. Guestrooms also need a periodic **general** or **deep cleaning**.

Tasks such as high dusting, vacuuming drapes and casements, wiping down walls, cleaning carpet edges and vent filters, moving beds and furniture, and turning mattresses must be performed on a regular but not daily basis. The frequency of such general cleanings depends on heaviness of use, weather conditions, and quality of routine maintenance.

General cleaning can be performed by the GRA or by a special team of employees who do nothing other than general cleaning of rooms. I have been involved with operations in which guestrooms were general cleaned by GRAs assisted by section housekeeping aides, as well as with operations in which a specialized team was used to do nothing but general clean guestrooms. My experience strongly favors general cleaning by regular personnel; the added workload is not necessarily so difficult that additional personnel must be added to the staff for this task.

A good general cleaning should take approximately twice as long as a routine room servicing. For example, consider a typical day of $8\frac{1}{2}$ hours. Remember that each employee has 30 minutes for lunch and two 15-minute breaks, leaving $7\frac{1}{2}$ hours for work. Let us assume that a GRA can service three rooms routinely in 1 hour and needs $\frac{1}{2}$ hour to service the housekeeping cart at the end of the day. Depending on the nature of the hotel and its clientele, each GRA can service from 14 to 20 rooms per day. This leaves 15 minutes to add to one room for deep cleaning. If each GRA general cleans one assigned room each day, each room will receive a deep cleaning once every 15–20 days.

The section housekeeping aide also becomes involved in general cleaning because of the need to move furniture and perform high dusting of several rooms.

A section housekeeping aide may be required to help more than one GRA. If the section housekeeping aide becomes overloaded, a utility housekeeping aide might be employed to assist in the general cleaning of guestrooms. Supervisors should keep records of rooms that have received general cleaning in order that each room receive such cleaning on a regular basis.

CHANGE AGENTS

Larry Shideler

President, ProTeam, Inc.

The concept of backpack vacuums began in the 1970s at Western Building Maintenance (WBM), which Larry Shideler founded in 1962. At the time Larry had used some of the old metal units made by Clarke, but they were square, very heavy, and uncomfortable. It was then that Shideler decided to make his own units out of PVC pipe.

This invention turned out to work very well, and Shideler learned that he could clean buildings much faster, reducing labor costs significantly. Backpacks turned out to be a major factor in making WBM the largest contract cleaner in the state of Idaho.

Building WBM into a large successful company was rewarding, but dealing with hundreds of employees and the multiple problems that go with running a service business led Shideler to sell WBM and move onto something new.

In December of 1987, Shideler incorporated ProTeam, Inc. and introduced the first modern backpack vacuum, the QuarterVac. At that time, ProTeam had three employees: Shideler, a secretary, and the secretary's husband, who manufactured the units in his garage.

Yes, ProTeam was literally started from the garage up. To say that things took off from there would be a lie. Finding sales representatives and distributors to sell a new product proved to be very difficult, and in 1990, ProTeam almost closed the doors for good.

Instead of giving up, Shideler, got a few investors and gave it one last push. Sale by sale, ProTeam started to gain more distributors, and in 1991, ProTeam posted its first profit and has never looked back. In 1993, the company sold more than 10,000 vacuums. In 1997, nearly 27,000 vacuums and 60,000 packages were shipped out of the Boise warehouse, and ProTeam had grown to nearly 40 employees, 60 sales reps, and more than 600 distributors.

Shideler has created a progressive culture within ProTeam and does his best to eliminate turnover by paying very competitive wages, offering the best benefits, and promoting from within. The corporate philosophy is "Happy people know no limits."

In 1997, ProTeam, Inc. won the Boise Chamber's Small Business of the Year Award for medium-sized companies. ProTeam, Inc. was recently notified by *Industry Week* magazine that it had been named one of the winners of the Growing Companies 25 Award. The magazine highlights America's most successful small manufacturers.

Larry Shideler is a recognized industry leader in JanSan education. Through his sponsorship of research on cleaning and his Team Cleaning Seminars, he has taught the industry how to become more efficient and effective in its approach to cleaning.

His concern for occupant health, including the health of the housekeeping staff, is clearly demonstrated by his concern over particulate matter released by ordinary vacuums. ProTeam vacuums possess an elaborate Four Level Filtration system that ensures there is no adverse impact on indoor air quality. Finally, unlike some other manufacturers, Shideler has welcomed and supported the efforts of the Carpet and Rug Institute in developing its certification program for vacuums.

Larry Shideler's biggest contribution to the JanSan industry is certainly in the evolution of the backpack vacuum. Larry's incredible knack and unwavering commitment to finding a better and more effective way to clean buildings has moved the entire cleaning industry out of the Dark Ages and into the 21st century. His insistence that vacuums produced by ProTeam be focused on Cleaning for Health and offering cleaning workers the ability to minimize reintroduction of particulates back into the environment has truly defined a high-filtration vacuum system. Leaders come and go but true innovators leave a lasting impression. Shideler's impression will continue to be an inspiration on product development for generations to come.

PROJECTS

The management of every housekeeping department requires the performance of occasional special **projects**. Periodic shampooing of a specific carpeted area, stripping and refinishing a hard-surfaced floor, removing scuff marks on a seldom-used but accountable space, and cleaning and sanitizing rubbish-handling equipment are projects that must be scheduled from time to time based on someone's observation during an inspection. These projects are usually the purview of the senior housekeeping aide. The results of an early-morning

inspection conducted by the senior housekeeping aide (Figure 10.10) may lead to such projects.

Special projects are performed by utility personnel under supervision. Records of projects should be maintained and reviewed periodically to determine the extent of man-hours being expended on this type of work. Many projects can be eliminated in the future by making them part of routine work. In addition, projects justify the maintenance of man-hour expenditure records that can later be used to substantiate the need for additional budgeted hours in the staffing of the department.

MAINTENANCE WORK-REQUEST PROGRAMS

Many times the quality and condition of a facility can be assessed by investigating the relationship that exists between the executive housekeeper and the chief engineer. When this relationship is positive and the people are mutually respectful of each other's responsibilities and workload, the physical appearance of a hotel will be excellent. When such positive relationships do not exist, property inspections will reveal little in addition to what might be expected—a substandard facility.

I recall a philosophy told to me by a ruddy up-through-the-ranks chief during my initial housekeeping training:

> You keep the place clean, and if you can't clean it like it was new, let me know and I'll replace it or repair it so you can; but I need your *eyes* in the hotel because I can't be everywhere at one time and I don't have the staff to look for problems.

Specifically, the chief engineer is charged with the **repair and physical maintenance** of a hotel facility (maintenance does not refer to guestroom servicing). The executive housekeeper is responsible for cleanliness and maintenance (servicing) of specific areas. The housekeeping department staff is much larger than the engineering department and is therefore in a better position to look for and find areas in need of repair and maintenance. The major concern is to have a reporting and follow-up system between the two departments that allows for the orderly flow of information. Figure 11.14 is a standard form used for requesting repair and maintenance services not available through normal cleaning.

The **Maintenance Work Request Form** is composed of two soft copies and one hard copy and is serialized for easy reference when communicating about a reported discrepancy. The top copy (usually soft white) is filled out and kept by the department initiating the report; the other two copies are forwarded to engineering, where the request is logged in so that materials can be

```
┌─────────────────────────────────────────────┐
│                                               │
│              YOUR HOTEL                        │
│                  ○                             │
│                                                │
│   Maintenance          Serial no. 0261248     │
│   work                                         │
│   request                                      │
│                                                │
│   Requested by _____  Date _____        │
│   Dept _____       │
│   Location _____     │
│   Problem _____     │
│           _____     │
│           _____     │
│           _____     │
│           _____     │
│           _____     │
│                                                │
│   Assigned to _____     │
│   Date completed _____     │
│   Completed by _____     │
│   Work time required   Hrs.      /Min.        │
│   Remarks _____     │
│           _____     │
│           _____     │
│           _____     │
│                                                │
└─────────────────────────────────────────────┘
```

FIGURE 11.14 A typical Maintenance Work Request Form, which is used to record the disposition of all problems and discrepancies.

ordered and work scheduled. When work is completed, the rest of the form is filled in and the second (soft blue) copy is returned to the initiating department for comparison and progressing of the original request. Work is then inspected, and, if completed satisfactorily, the soft (white and blue) Work Request Forms may be destroyed. The hard (bottom) copy remains with the engineering department as a record of time and materials expended.

The system is simple, but in many cases it is not used in a manner that will ensure that repair and maintenance are properly accomplished. The secret to a successful maintenance and repair program stems from understanding two important precepts: 1) the executive housekeeper will not be allowed to dictate the priorities of the chief engineer's workload, and 2) paper is cheap.

If the discrepancy is not corrected in a reasonable period of time, write it out again and mark it **second request**. Should there be a parts or material problem, the chief engineer may communicate this fact to the executive housekeeper and indicate that further Maintenance Work Request Forms will be unnecessary. In addition, second requests might indicate that the priority of the engineer's workload precludes the immediate response to certain types of requests, or that the engineering department will schedule certain service requests with others of a similar nature (such as vinyl

repairs, furniture repairs, and painting). Items that will cause a guestroom to be out of order should be given the highest priority by the chief engineer.

If a property is to be kept in a proper state of repair, there will be an abundance of Maintenance Work Requests, many of which will be repeated. The age of a property will determine how many requests from the housekeeping department might be in the pipeline at any given time. The prime consideration is remembering that personnel in the housekeeping department are the "eyes" of the engineering department in areas under the responsibility of the executive housekeeper and that *everything not in order and not cleanable must be repaired* if the property is to be maintained in a like-new condition.

The executive housekeeper must develop a system that fosters the writing of Maintenance Work Requests. It is best to *require* that a certain number of Maintenance Work Requests be written by the department each week. Such specific requirements help ensure that every defect has a chance of being reported. Examples of what should be reported are minor tears in hallway and room vinyl, chips and scratches in furniture, leaky faucets, broken lamp switches, and burned-out lightbulbs (not under the purview of housekeeping). Areas in need of paint, noisy air-conditioners, bad TV reception, minor carpet repair problems (seams coming unglued), doors that rattle when closed, and unsightly tile caulking in bathtubs are also subject to Maintenance Work Requests.

I recall systems whereby all supervisors and department managers were required to write a minimum of 10 work orders each week. Such a requirement forced the "look" so greatly needed by the engineering department. When I was an executive housekeeper, I wrote 40 work orders each week. Those 40, in addition to ones written by other department managers and supervisors, totaled over 100 work orders each week. The property was six years old but looked new because the systems described here were meticulously followed.

Another system whereby the executive housekeeper and chief engineer cooperate is in combining the general cleaning program with the maintenance program. Clarence R. Johnson[1] suggests that each month 25 percent of the rooms receiving a general deep cleaning should also receive a thorough **maintenance inspection**. Every room would therefore be completely checked three times a year and maintained in a near-perfect condition. Johnson proposed a **Maintenance Checklist** (Figure 11.15) that could be used in such a program to keep track of repairs to furniture, fixtures, and equipment in the guestroom.

Proper relationships inspiring mutual cooperation between the executive housekeeper and the chief engineer may at times be difficult to maintain. This usually stems from differences in background. This fact, however, should in no way detract from the *professional effort* necessary to make a relationship work for the good

MAINTENANCE CHECKLIST

☐ **CHECKED**   ☐ **NEEDS REPAIR**   ■ **REPAIR COMPLETED**

Room No. _____

AIR CONDITIONERS

☐ 1. Switches/controls/valves—check operation
☐ 2. Thermostat dial positioned, works correctly
☐ 3. Thermostat probe secure, calibrated, working
☐ 4. Filter—clean
☐ 5. Fan & fan motor—clean, lubricated, secure
☐ 6. Evaporator and condenser—clean
☐ 7. Condensation pan & drain—clean
☐ 8. Exterior grill—clean, maintained to complement building exterior
☐ 9. Compressor—clean
☐ 10. Check for leaks in refrigeration system
☐ 11. Check electric plug, receptacles, cord
☐ 12. Heating unit, clean & operating correctly

ELECTRICAL

☐ 13. Lamp switches on/off—3 way working correctly
☐ 14. Lamp sockets & swivels, tight, in good repair
☐ 15. Lampshades, clean, no holes, secure
☐ 16. Light bulb—replace burned, check wattage
☐ 17. Plugs, cords, & connections, repair as needed
☐ 18. Lamp base/body in good repair
☐ 19. Light switches on/off—working and in good repair
☐ 20. Switch & outlet wallplates—good repair and match in color
☐ 21. Wall sockets/receptacles operate, no shorts
☐ 22. Timer switches work correctly, knob secure
☐ 23. Heat lamps, correct wattage, clean, good repair
☐ 24. All light fixtures are clean, dust free, complementary to room decor

TELEVISION

☐ 25. Audio—clear (radio and television)
☐ 26. Visual—in focus (check each channel)
☐ 27. Knobs—replace, if necessary
☐ 28. Fine tune—color contrast, horizontal, vertical
☐ 29. Antenna—cable connections secure
☐ 30. Chassis/screen—clean, dust-free, no apparent damage—security mounts secure

TELEPHONE

☐ 31. Overall appearance & condition—clean, good repair
☐ 32. Dialing instructions—replace if faded
☐ 33. Defects (good connections, audio good, bell works, etc.) report to telephone company

FURNITURE

☐ 34. Drawer handles, knobs tight, good repair and drawer guides lubricated
☐ 35. Mattresses and box springs, good repair, turned clean, etc.
☐ 36. All furniture surfaces—stains, scratches, damages, repair
☐ 37. Chairs (cushions, legs, brace springs) repair/replace as needed
☐ 38. Tables/desks—tops and bases tight, stable and in good repair
☐ 39. Headboards—secure, clean top and front
☐ 40. Nightstands—stable, stain and scratch-free
☐ 41. Bedbox/bedrails and castors clean and in good repair
☐ 42. Pictures secure, clean, good condition, color coordinated with room

WINDOW AND MIRRORS

☐ 43. Window guides and latches clean, work easily
☐ 44. Window trim clean, caulk in good repair
☐ 45. Drapery hardware (rod, pulls, cord, mounting, pin, hooks) all in good repair
☐ 46. Mirror(s) good condition, hangers secure, no scratches or mars

SLIDING DOORS/WINDOWS

☐ 47. Tracks clean and in good repair
☐ 48. Guides, wheels are clean to slide freely
☐ 49. Doorstop and bumpers present so doors close quietly and securely

(a)

FIGURE 11.15 Maintenance Checklist records should be kept of the date the room is checked and work completed. *(Reprinted from Stan Gottlieb, "Maintenance: A Workable Program for the Smaller Property," Lodging, May 1984, based on an interview with Clarence R. Johnson, Melcor. American Hotel Association Directory Corporation.)*

☐ 50. Latches—primary and secondary security—are effective

DOORS, ENTRANCES

☐ 51. Handles—check and secure
☐ 52. Lock cylinder, keyhole, condition & operation
☐ 53. Hinges, hinge pins lubricated, secure
☐ 54. Door chain/deadbolt, securely attached, and working correctly
☐ 55. Lock striker and check plates secure to prevent unauthorized entry
☐ 56. Door frame, bumpers, replace as necessary
☐ 57. Weatherstripping in good repair, replace as needed
☐ 58. Threshold is secure, replace rubber inserts if needed
☐ 59. Door fit (security, energy and noise control) smooth and tight
☐ 60. Peepholes correctly installed, clean
☐ 61. Door condition—check for holes, need of cleaning, repair
☐ 62. Door stops in place to prevent damage to handle or wall

BATHROOM/VANITIES

☐ 63. Bathtub safety strips, clean and in good condition
☐ 64. Tub and lavatory drain, plugs, popups, strainer clean and working
☐ 65. Shower head secure, clean, has correct spray pattern
☐ 66. Bath tile and walls—check for loose tiles, grout holes, need for caulking
☐ 67. Toilet flush and drain—no excess noise, leaks
☐ 68. Toilet tank, tank top, clean, no cracks, secure to base
☐ 69. Seat, hinges, bumpers all in good repair—replace if in doubt
☐ 70. Toilet seal—check evidence of leaks
☐ 71. Hot, cold faucets—check for leaks.
☐ 72. Shower/mixing valve doesn't leak
☐ 73. Chrome fixture appearance is bright—clean/replace if needed
☐ 74. Shower rod, curtain, clean, chrome or plastic sleeve
☐ 75. Basin ''P'' trap is clean, no leaks
☐ 76. Tub and basin appearance is free of scratches
☐ 77. Toilet paper holder, properly mounted, clean

☐ 78. Facial tissue holder secure and clean
☐ 79. Soap dish & grab bars are secure, good repair
☐ 80. Towel racks—fastened securely, good repair
☐ 81. Vanity top/cabinet not marred, clean, attractive
☐ 82. Floor(s) clean & in good repair
☐ 83. Light switches, heat lamp & timer switch work correctly
☐ 84. Bath privacy lock works correctly
☐ 85. Exhaust fan is clean, lubricated, operating correctly and efficiently

GENERAL ITEMS

☐ 86. Coat racks/hangers clean, secure, sufficient number
☐ 87. Baseboards, secure to wall, clean, free of scratches
☐ 88. Carpets—no stains, holes repaired, no ripples or loose curls
☐ 89. Wall covering/paint condition— all holes, scratches, tears repaired
☐ 90. Ceiling—check if clean; no cracks, peeling paint, stains
☐ 91. Smoke detectors checked, batteries replaced
☐ 92. Air leaks or insulation effectively repaired
☐ 93. Hot water set at correct temperature (120°)

GENERAL AREAS

☐ 94. Emergency exit lights, signs in good condition
☐ 95. Fire extinguishers in place, fully charged
☐ 96. Automatic door closers working properly
☐ 97. Luggage carts clean & in good repair
☐ 98. Stairway handrails are secure
☐ 99. Sidewalk, exterior walkways, good repair, clean
☐ 100. Interior hallways—well lighted, carpet clean and in good repair
☐ 101. Stairs free of debris, no loose treads, handrails, etc.
☐ 102. Emergency lighting system— checked & operating
☐ 103. Background music/public address system is effective
☐ 104. Emergency exits kept clear of hazards, panic bars work correctly

FIGURE 11.15 (*Continued*)

(b)

of the property. Gentle persistence and persuasion are usually the keys that can foster strong relationships.

Operational Controls

ROOM INSPECTIONS

Methods of conducting **room inspections** of guestrooms may take many forms. In addition, room inspections may be given great, varied, or no emphasis, depending on the management style of the hotel's department heads and general managers. Some hotels employ **inspectors**—people whose only operational function is to inspect guestrooms and report their findings. Other hotels never inspect guestrooms, and still others have sophisticated inspection procedures.

A project for students in a senior housekeeping management class in the Las Vegas area was for them to survey inspection techniques of several hotels. Students had to describe the results and effectiveness of the inspection programs they surveyed. Certain hotels employed inspectors, others used floor supervisors to inspect every room before its being reported ready for occupancy, others had periodic room inspections by a general manager, and some had no inspection programs at all.

Results were measured by the appearance and cleanliness of guestrooms inspected. Surprisingly, those hotels employing inspectors did not fare well in the surveys; nor did hotels with elaborate inspection forms used regularly by supervisors. Hotels with well-maintained and very clean rooms were those that were intermittently inspected, or **spot-checked**, by people in the operational supervisory chain (floor supervisors, section managers, the executive housekeeper, sometimes GRAs, occasionally someone outside the department, and especially the hotel general manager). Inspection forms that stated simple and reasonable standards of performance were also in evidence in these hotels. (Refer to Figure 1.2, noting a guestroom inspection form whereby *standards* are indicated for the several areas of concern that might be encountered in a guestroom. A simple checkmark indicates that the standard is being met, that items need improvement, or that an item is unsatisfactory. An indication of "unsatisfactory" must be corrected before the room is rented.)

Inspectors outside the operational framework for cleaning guestrooms (floor supervisors and GRAs) risk nothing if they complain heavily about substandard items or conditions, since they would not be held accountable for correcting them. These inspectors are therefore resented by those having to do the work. Human dynamics dictates that the inspectors would be better liked if they did not complain heavily about discrepancies. Floor supervisors who spot-check employees assigned to operational control are much more likely to find solutions to substandard performance and, as a result, improve the performance of employees. Spot-checking two or three rooms each day from each section seems to give all the indication needed to bring about top-quality performance from each employee. Such action also allows each GRA to report his or her own rooms ready for reoccupancy, thus enriching the job and improving efficiency of communication between housekeeping and the front desk.

There is also much to be said about displaying trust and confidence in employees, which is a great motivator for proper performance. In addition, most section housekeepers are proud of their work and look forward to exposing the results of their efforts to those in authority. It is for this reason that the executive housekeeper and the resident and/or general manager should regularly inspect guestrooms. The importance of managers inspecting guestrooms regularly cannot be overemphasized. Not only is the inspection of the room paramount, but the opportunity for the manager to associate with his or her employees on the job is of great importance.

There are more than 600 employees in the housekeeping organization at the Excalibur Hotel in Las Vegas. Such a large number of employees can present a layering problem within the organization that might be hard to overcome. There will always be a few problem employees, but those who are outstanding need the "positive stroke" of the manager who cares about employees as individuals. When the work is well done, some well-placed humor helps to express warmth and acknowledge the value of a good employee (Figure 11.16).

FIGURE 11.16 Executive Housekeeper Sonja Beaton-Wiker adds a touch of humor to her comment to one of her GRAs during a room inspection at the Excalibur Hotel in Las Vegas, saying, "I see the nice 'Crown Turndown'; now how many jewels did you put in that crown?" *(Photo courtesy of Excalibur Hotel & Casino, a member of Mandalay Resort Group™.)*

Such expectation of inspections by higher authority usually brings about an added emphasis on total work quality on **inspection day** and, as a result, tends to improve the appearance of each room cleaned.

A technique of inspection that has merit in areas in which specific employees are not performing up to standard is to let the GRA conduct the inspection in the presence of the designated inspector and supervisor. Specifically, the person inspecting invites the person who cleaned the room to inspect and report while the manager or supervisor writes notes on the inspection form. This technique has proved enlightening to many GRAs who must, in the presence of their supervisor and manager, expose not only their questionable work but also their quality work.

Inspection programs for guestrooms should be conducted in such a way that quality performance is amply noted and publicized. Programs involving "the housekeeper of the week," who earns points toward a meaningful prize over some given time period, are effective in motivating employees to excel. A GRA must understand that his or her reputation as a GRA will never be better than the weakest of all GRAs in the department. This information reminds each of them that they need and must support one another to accomplish quality work, and fosters commitment to standards.

Another technique whereby room appearance and cleanliness can be made to flourish is with a team system of reward. In earlier chapters the team system of scheduling for guestroom maintenance was presented for the model hotel. Performance systems were designed whereby each GRA was expected to clean 18 guestrooms in each eight-hour shift. There are programs whereby each team that properly finishes its work has rooms spot-checked by an outside supervisor or manager and, given proper results, is provided with an added incentive of leaving early and receiving credit for the full eight-hour shift. (This would be allowed only on a team basis, never on an individual basis; otherwise the team aspect of performance could be destroyed.)

In summary, room inspections are essential to quality guestroom cleanliness and servicing and should be conducted regularly. The more efficient systems do not involve the total inspection of every guestroom cleaned. Spot inspections, properly recorded by floor supervisors, department managers, and the general manager, have proven to be the most effective form of room inspection program. Recognition should be given for quality work, and work incentives should be created to encourage high-quality performances, especially team performance.

TOTAL PROPERTY INSPECTIONS

If hotels are to be maintained as top-quality facilities, it is not enough that the executive housekeeper inspect only

guestrooms or, for that matter, be the only one who does inspect rooms. Not only does the entire property require a thorough, regular, and carefully orchestrated **property inspection program**, but guestrooms need to be looked at by more than one management person. A **fresh look** is needed to ensure that items viewed but not seen are eventually picked up for correction. Managers above the executive housekeeper in the table of organization may delegate the task of rooms maintenance to the executive housekeeper but may not abdicate their own responsibility of ensuring that the hotel is properly maintained.

Other departments also have cleaning responsibilities. The restaurant manager, bar manager, chef, and catering manager have large areas for which they are held accountable for proper cleaning, maintenance, and safe operation. The chief engineer may be held accountable for the entire outside area of the facility, including shrubs, grounds, and parking areas.

In the Division of Work Document in Chapter 2, the executive housekeeper is instrumental in ensuring that each part of the property is permanently assigned to a specific department manager for upkeep. Thus, there should be a manager responsible for every square foot, corner, and crack of the hotel. The Division of Work Document should in fact be used to establish a zone inspection program (see the following section) whereby every part of the property is identified and periodically looked at to ensure that proper maintenance, cleanliness, and safety of both space and operation are being maintained.

Finally, the fresh look we mentioned not only brings another pair of eyes into an area, it also allows for orientation and development of management personnel in areas in which they may not normally be operationally involved. A property inspection that uses the front office manager to inspect housekeeping and the executive housekeeper to inspect kitchens is good training for future growth and development of managers for promotion and greater responsibilities.

Zone Inspection

There are many inspections that might be conducted on a subroutine basis, but none should be more thorough and, as a result, more beneficial to total property maintenance than the **zone inspection program**. **Zones** are usually created by dividing the entire facility into equal parts, whereby each inspector is responsible for an equal workload in a given period of time. Zone inspections should be conducted in not more than three hours, otherwise they lose effectiveness.

The inspection should be **documented**, and a technique must be developed whereby the person or persons responsible for each zone of the inspection may react to items found deficient and corrective measures may be

SENIOR HOUSEKEEPING AIDE
WEEKLY MAINTENANCE INSPECTION

Date ______ Time ______
Inspected by ______

Linen Room		Vending	
Linen carts—well supplied	____	Waste cans (clean, not full)	____
Floor	____	Floor	____
Shelves—neat	____	Vending machine (top, side, front)	____
No extras—Wire hangers	____	Ice machine	____
Glasses		Elevator	
Trays		Door (inside and out)	____
Trash		Walls	____
Neat general appearance	____	Stainless steel	____
Hallway		Carpet	____
Carpet edges	____	Ceiling	____
Carpet	____		
Baseboards	____		
Fire extinguisher	____		
Fire boxes and bells	____		
Ashtrays	____		
Wall guards	____		
Windows (inside)	____		
Windowsills	____		
Air conditioner	____		
No cobwebs	____		
Neat general appearance	____		
Stairway/Stairwell			
Handrails and pipes	____		
Floor	____		
Corners	____		
Doors	____		
Neat general appearance	____	Total points ______	

FIGURE 11.17 The senior housekeeping aide's Weekly Maintenance Inspection form has a place to record quality points so that housekeeping aides may be included in performance competition.

taken before the next inspection. Documentation about unsafe conditions is also important. Liability in claims regarding negligence may be greatly reduced if it can be shown through documentation that regular, thorough, and controlled inspections of an entire property are conducted and that there is adequate follow-up on significant items.

Weekly Maintenance Inspections

Although zone inspections are all encompassing for the entire property, there may be times when a particular zone is not inspected because of prior superior condition. This does not preclude public area portions of the rooms department from receiving a regular **weekly maintenance inspection** that is conducted by the senior housekeeping aide or a department manager. The Weekly Maintenance Inspection Form (Figure 11.17) provides a checklist of areas to be surveyed during an inspection and can be used by the rooms department supervisor at the end of each week, usually on Friday evenings, to ensure that the property was in proper condition before the weekend.

Figure 11.17 can also be used to record "quality points" for work well done. People assigned to clean public areas in a rooms department can thus be included in an incentive program with other housekeeping department personnel.

INVENTORIES

In Chapters 4 through 7, we listed various categories of **inventories** with which the executive housekeeper might become involved. There are some subroutines related to ordering and keeping track of these inventories. Items of furniture, fixtures, and equipment (identified as FFE), along with software items (bedspreads and so on), form the basis of capital expenditures. These items have limited useful lives and are depreciated over several years. Other material items are operational in nature and are expended over much shorter business cycles (usually a four-week or monthly period); they are part of the cost of doing business in the production of revenue over the same period of time. Items such as cleaning supplies, guest supplies, and the amortized cost of basic bed and bath linens are among costs that occur monthly. Not only must the expenditure of such supplies and linens be expensed against revenue produced, such items that are on hand form the basis of balance sheet assets and must be periodically accounted for. Thus, use balances on hand, and supply levels are critical **control information** that must be routinely maintained to ensure availability of materials when needed.

Figure 11.18 is a **Cleaning and Guest Supply Inventory** for a typical property. Note the units by which certain supply items are purchased and/or shipped. Note also the column marked "Par stock." This column might also be marked "Minimum on hand," allowing the manager to review counts and determine if stock levels are falling too low. According to this example, ice buckets are normally shipped in case lots (CS), each case containing six dozen items (6 DZ). It has a .5 par, which indicates that supply on hand should not fall below one-half case before reordering.

Figure 11.18 can also be used as a **count sheet** when conducting a routine inventory. The last column would be used to indicate how many of an item should be ordered at the next available opportunity.

Figure 11.19 is an **Inventory Record Log** that can be used to record information in an inventory logbook or journal. This type of log describes usage during a given period, how supplies were used, current pricing information, and the value of supplies on hand. Hotel **controllers** expect that these types of records are maintained and that inventories are conducted on a regular and routine basis.

The cost of operations should include only that portion of inventory that has been used up during the period. Such costs should not include the value of amounts purchased but still on hand. Most hotel controllers agree that unopened cases of supplies

CLEANING AND GUEST SUPPLY INVENTORY (a)

Date _____   Inventoried by _____

Item	Units	Units on hand	Par stock	Reorder (X)
Laundry bags	BDL/500		2	
Laundry lists	EA/250		250	
Room service menus	EA		500	
Stationery bags	CS/1000		1	
Stationery	CS/10 PK		1	
Envelopes	CS/1000		1	
Postcards	CS/10 BX		1	
"Tell us" forms	CS/500		1.5	
Sanitary bags	CS/1000		1	
Utility bags	CS/1000		1.5	
Guest services directory	EA/		500	
"Choose your credit"	EA/		500	
Advance reg. forms	EA/		1000	
Hotel maps	CS/		1000	
Facial tissue	CS/36 BX		3	
Toilet tissue	CS/96 RL		2	
Bath soap	CS/500		5	
Toilet seat strips	CS/10,000		.5	
Name cards	CS/		1	
AM EX. Applications	CS/		.5	
Light bulbs 100W	CS/		.5	
Light bulbs 60W	CS/		.5	
Phone books	EA/		25	
Bibles	EA/		12	
Hangers (wood)	CS/50		.5	

CLEANING AND GUEST SUPPLY INVENTORY (b)

Date _____   Inventoried by _____

Item	Units	Units on hand	Par stock	Reorder (X)
Hangers (plastic)	CS/50		.5	
Ashtrays	CS/48		2	
Ashtrays (gold)	CS/6		.5	
Ice buckets	CS/6 DZ		.5	
Trays	CS/12		2	
Waste baskets	CS/12		1.5	
Matches	CS/50 BX		1	
Phone pads	CS/500		.5	
Do-not-disturb signs	PK/100		.5	
Garbage bags	CS/100		2	
Glass wrap	CS/12 RL		2 RL	
Dust mop treatment	GAL/		.25	
Bathroom cleaner	DRUM/55 G		.25	
Tablecloths	EA/		12	
Glasses	CS/36		24	
Scrubbing sponge	CS/40		.5	
Brooms	CS/12		.5	
Vinegar	CS/6 G		.5	
Trigger sprayers	CS/12		1.5	
Pint spray bottles	CS/12		1	
Stock solution btls.	EA		6	
Portion pac 202	CS/4 BX		4 BX	
Portion par 265	CS/4 BX		4 BX	
Vacuum bags (paper)	CS/250		25 BAGS	

FIGURE 11.18 Cleaning and Guest Supply Inventory form, indicating units by which items are ordered and shipped, par stock, units on hand, and quantities to be reordered.

FIGURE 11.18 (*Continued*)

on hand will be valued at full price in inventory. Once a case is opened, however, items are considered expended. There may be exceptions to this rule, allowing departments to account for individual items remaining in storage in opened cases at full price. Individual items out of the main storeroom that can be sited in satellite linen rooms may also be considered in inventory. Once established, whatever accounting systems are specified by the controller must be followed.

Storage

Operational supply storage rooms must be closely controlled, and access to storerooms limited only to personnel in charge. Certain items of high unit cost or high usage such as specialty soaps might even warrant cage storage to prevent pilferage. Operations in which storage rooms are thrown open for the day usually have inordinate supply costs, and profits are proportionally affected. Tight storeroom controls are usually evidenced

by cleaning supply costs that do not exceed $\frac{3}{10}$ of 1 percent of revenues and guestroom supply costs that are within $\frac{6}{10}$ of 1 percent.

PERSONNEL UTILIZATION

Another important subroutine is the weekly (or sometimes daily) **forecasting of man-hour requirements**—the most expensive operational cost in the entire rooms department. Executive housekeepers should be involved in the annual budgeting process (discussed later) whereby they help determine man-hour requirements based on budgeted occupancies. Once the budget has been established, it is imperative that a weekly forecast of expected man-hour utilization be developed and substantiated based on the weekly forecast of occupancy. Forecasts must be in line with expected occupancies and workload, or higher management must be notified.

Figure 11.20 is an example of a **Weekly Wage Forecast** form based on occupancies expected during the third week of the fourth period in the model hotel. **Forecast occupancy** refers to the expected percentage and number of occupied rooms out of the 353 rooms in the model

INVENTORY RECORD LOG

1	2	3	4	5	6	7	8	9	10	11	12
Item	Par	Prior inventory	Purchases	Issues	Condemned	Due on hand	Actual count	Variance	Price	Inventory valuation	Reorder

FIGURE 11.19 The Inventory Record Log is a means of recording information about each item of inventory carried. Due on hand = prior inventory + purchases − issues − condemned. Variance = due on hand − actual count. Inventory valuation = actual count × price.

WEEKLY WAGE FORECAST

Period __4__   Week of period __3__   Week Ending __4/18__
(date)

Forecast occupancy	91%/322	89%/297	97%/343	94%/332	100%/353	100%/353	78%/276	92.1%/2276
Wage Department	Saturday	Sunday	Monday	Tuesday	Wednesday	Thursday	Friday	Total
02	40	48	48	40	48	40	32	296
06	56	56	56	56	56	56	56	392
07	144	136	160	152	160	160	128	1040
08	32	32	32	32	32	32	24	216
Total	272	272	296	280	296	288	240	1944

Submitted by:

Richard J Martin

Executive Housekeeper

Estimated revenue __227,600__ ($100.00 average rate forecast.)

Estimated sales/man-hour __117.08__

Budgeted sales/man-hour __116.77__

Section Housekeeper's hrs/occupied room: Budget __.46__ Actual __.45__

FIGURE 11.20 A Weekly Wage Forecast used for forecasting man-hours in various wage departments during the upcoming week.

WEEKLY WAGE ANALYSIS

Period ___4___ Week of period ___3___ Week Ending __4/18__
(date)

Actual occupancy	347	306	242	319	285	353	270	2122
Wage Department	Saturday	Sunday	Monday	Tuesday	Wednesday	Thursday	Friday	Total
02	42.1	47.9	48.1	40.2	40.2	40.4	30.8	289.7
06	56.0	54.5	55.6	56.2	50.4	56.1	56.0	384.8
07	162.4	137.5	113.4	144.9	136.6	164.6	126.1	985.5
08	32.1	32.1	32.3	30.8	30.9	32.1	32.2	222.5
Total	292.6	272.0	249.4	272.1	258.1	293.2	245.1	1882.5

	Budget	Forecast	Actual
Revenue	227,000.00	227,600.00	220,121.67
Sales/man-hour	116.77	117.08	116.93
Section Housekeeper's hours/occupied rm	0.46	0.45	0.46

Explanation of major variances _Forecast Sales/MH were missed slightly but both Sls/MH and Section Housekeeper Hr/Occ Rm were within tolerance of budget. No significant variations_

Submitted by: _Housekeeper_
Executive Housekeeper

FIGURE 11.21 The Weekly Wage Analysis for the concluded week, along with a forecast for the upcoming week, are submitted to higher management.

hotel. For example, on Tuesday, 94 percent, or 332 rooms, are expected to be occupied. **Wage departments** refer to the accounting classifications assigned to various types of labor. In Figure 11.20, department 02 is for supervisors, 06 is for fixed-hour employees such as lobby housekeepers and utility housekeeping aides, 07 is for GRAs, and 08 is for section housekeeping aides. Forecast includes statistical targets (sales per man-hour and GRA hours per occupied room), indicating comparisons of what was budgeted against what is being forecast.

The man-hours for supervisors in the model hotel are the total hours of the four team leaders, the linen room supervisor, the night supervisor, and the senior housekeeping aide (minus hours of those scheduled off). The man-hours for GRAs are obtained from the Table of Personnel Requirements in Chapter 2.

The planned numbers of hours for each day are listed. Hours are totaled both for the seven-day week for each wage department and for the four wage departments for each day. Revenue for the expected 2276 rooms (see seven-day forecast in Figure 11.20) is predicted for the week, and **target statistics** are developed involving sales

per man-hour and GRA hours per expected number of occupied rooms. Forecast statistics are then compared with those budgeted to determine whether man-hour forecasts are **in control**. Once the forecast is prepared, it is submitted to top management, who evaluates whether planned operations for the upcoming week appear to be in control.

Weekly Wage Analysis

Not only should wages be forecast, but actual expenditures of man-hours should be analyzed after the week has been completed. The **Weekly Wage Analysis** (Figure 11.21) is a near replica of Figure 11.20; however, the information reflects **actual expenditures**, which should now be compared with the same week's forecast to evaluate forecast accuracy and to determine where variances may be occurring that may need adjusting.

Note the variations between Figures 11.20 and 11.21. In situations in which occupancies were not as predicted, the executive housekeeper would have made the necessary adjustments during the week through the *Tight Schedule*, which would compensate for actual occupancies being less than or more than expected. Note that Wednesday had been expected to be a 100 percent day but was not, by a considerable amount. Adjustments were made to accommodate the lower occupancy, and GRA man-hours were adjusted to keep labor utilization in line, thereby keeping statistical targets in line. Executive housekeepers who do not forecast and analyze man-hour utilization run the risk of having uncontrollable wage costs telegraph the department into an unfavorable labor-cost situation for the year that cannot be recuperated.

STATEMENT CRITIQUES

Period statements provide results of period operations, especially results in attempts to control costs during these operating periods. Efficient hotel organizations require that costs be kept in line with revenues and that statements be analyzed to determine where unacceptable variations may be occurring. Many hotel organizations require that statements be **critiqued** to determine where revenues and cost are out of prescribed tolerances.

Critiques are usually required by top management within five days after statements are received. Typical standards for cost control may require that a critique be made at any time a cost variance is greater than $\frac{1}{10}$th of 1 percent of revenue. Such critiques must explain why costs are out of tolerance and what will be done to bring them back into tolerance. (A period statement will be analyzed in detail in relation to Figure 11.33.)

Purchasing

CLEANING AND GUEST SUPPLIES

Purchasing is a subroutine that can take up a part of each day for the executive housekeeper. Even though some hotel chains have centralized national purchasing of items that bring quantity discounts, for the most part cleaning and guest supplies will be purchased either by the **purchasing agent** in the hotel (if there is one) or by the department heads for their respective departments.

Considering the size and variability of the housekeeping cleaning and guest supply inventory, there will be many suppliers and purveyors who will do their best to obtain the business from the executive housekeeper. Suppliers can be outstanding allies in the conduct of services within the housekeeping department, or they can be outstanding nuisances. Competitively shopping for suppliers or vendors will simplify the question as to who will be used and for what products. The **Competitive Shopping Form** (Figure 11.22) can be used to determine

COMPETITIVE SHOPPING FORM							
Item	Qt/size	Price	Vendors				Remarks

FIGURE 11.22 A Competitive Shopping Form used to compare vendor prices for a given item of supply inventory.

the various attributes of vendors. Vendors should be evaluated periodically to ensure that the best price is being paid for items purchased. Serious thought should also be given to evaluating vendors on their environmental practices.

A separate shopping form should be maintained for each and every product that is used in the cleaning and guest supply inventory. Product prices should be reviewed at least once every six months. Comments such as how well the vendor or purveyor services the account and how well products are understood and demonstrated by the vendor are significant when selecting vendors. Price, although important, should not be the only criterion for selecting a product. Quality, suitability, storage requirements, and lot sizes each play an important part in making the right selection.

It is not unusual to find that one vendor will be selected for all paper products, another vendor for cleaning chemicals, and another for mops, brooms, and the various and sundry items used in day-to-day cleaning. If the number of salespeople being dealt with can be limited, more efficient use of time is possible. Some suppliers call on the executive housekeeper on a weekly basis; others will call less often. Orders might be placed by phone, whereby suppliers will visit only occasionally to ensure that the account is being properly maintained. Periodic or drop shipments might be arranged, whereby the supplier rather than the hotel retains the storage problem.

Two major areas of caution need be mentioned at this point. Most suppliers budget funds to service the customer. Some will offer prizes and personal discounts to executive housekeepers for allowing them to have the hotel's account. Great caution is necessary to ensure that it is the hotel that is receiving the discount, not the executive housekeeper. Said more simply, watch out for offers of kickback. Every executive housekeeper should know and thoroughly understand company policy about accepting gifts during the holiday season or other periods of benevolence when suppliers are generous with their clients. Usually, hotel organizations have set guidelines about what should or should not be accepted.

On one particular occasion when I was executive housekeeper, I received a long-distance phone call from a supplier who indicated that its new all-purpose cleaner was meeting with spectacular success and that if I would allow the product to be tested on my property, I would receive *at my home address* a complete home entertainment center with stereo and TV. Of significant note was the fact that this new product was $7.80 a gallon to be purchased in 55-gallon drums. The product currently being used, and with satisfactory results, had been purchased on a national contract for $1.20 a gallon. You should immediately recognize who would be paying for the home entertainment set.

LINENS

As you will recall from Chapter 7, in housekeeping operations "linens" normally refers to items associated with guestroom beds and bathrooms—sheets, pillowcases, bath towels, hand towels, washcloths, and fabric bathmats. Several subroutines concerning linens might be developed. Some might warrant simple policies and standard operating policies describing the movement of linens to and from the laundry and floor areas each day, whereas others might relate to routines involving condemnation, storage, repair, and normal care of linens. Linens rank second, next to wages, in departmental costs. For this reason, particular interest must be taken in the subroutines associated with the inventory and ordering of linens.

Linen Inventories

The initial supply of house linens might be a part of preopening expenses, whereby initial requirements would be placed in position for operational use and amortized over an extended period. Replacement of this initial supply, however, is an operational expense. Because of relative costs (labor versus linens) the total supply of linens should never be so small as to cause employees to have to wait for linens to service rooms. Overall linen supplies therefore should be in amounts several times those required to cover all rooms one time (one par).

If the hotel has an on-premises laundry, an initial supply of linens includes the following:

1 par	*To cover all beds* and baths (after daily service is complete)
1 par	*Soiled* or just removed from beds and baths after daily service (tomorrow's workload for the laundry)
1 par	*Clean* and ready to use in servicing guestrooms the next day
$3\frac{1}{2}$ par	*New*, in storage to be used as replacements when necessary
$3\frac{1}{2}$ par	Total

If the property does not have an on-premises laundry, add one par for linen in transit to and from a commercial laundry.

Because an unnoticed reduction in the supply of linens can cause a reduction in efficient service to guestrooms, **physical linen inventories** should be conducted regularly, and accurate records should be maintained to ensure forewarning of additional needs. Many hotels inventory linens monthly. In situations in which inventories are under good control and count systems are accurate, inventories may be conducted on a quarterly basis.

Let us assume that a 3.5 par is to be maintained for the model hotel and that linen usage and control are stabilized, allowing for a quarterly inventory. A linen inventory log book should be maintained, with headings similar to the Inventory Record Log described in Figure 11.19. Periodic needs for resupply are determined upon the completion of each physical inventory.

On days when inventories are conducted, special care must be taken to ensure that every piece of linen can be located for counting. Inventories should be conducted at the end of the normal workday when linen movement is at a minimum. (After the laundry has completed work, usually all guestroom regular servicing has been completed and each section housekeeper's linen cart has been loaded for the next day's routine.) Figure 11.23 is an example of a **Linen Count Sheet** used by employees taking the inventory.

The more employees involved in counting linens, the faster the inventory process can be completed. In addition, when employees are involved in the actual count, they become more aware of the significance, importance, and value of the linen. Each GRA counts linens loaded on his or her cart; supervisors count linens found on mobile linen trucks and shelves in satellite linen rooms. The linen room supervisor and assistant count all items found in the main linen room. Section housekeeping aides count linens on made-up roll-away beds. Laundry workers count soiled linen in the laundry, which will make up the next day's laundry workload, as well as any clean linen that might be lingering after the day's workload has been completed. The senior housekeeping aide and assistants count new linen in storage.

LINEN COUNT SHEET

Count Location: Cart 14 Counted by: Marie
Date: 5-17-

Item	Number Counted
Sheets King	6
Queen	4
Double	26
Twin	0
Pillowcases	39
Bath Towels	35
Hand Towels	35
Wash Cloths	35
Bath Mats	18
Bed Pads	—
Blankets (optional)	—
Pillows (optional)	

FIGURE 11.23 A Linen Count Sheet used by employees counting linen in various locations of the hotel.

PERIOD LINEN INVENTORY COUNT RECORD

1 Item	2 Beds	3 Laundry soiled	4 Laundry clean	5 Housekeeping soiled	6 Main linen room	7 Satellite linen rooms	8 Housekeeper carts	9 Roll beds	10 Total in use	11 New in storage	12 Grand total

FIGURE 11.24 Period Linen Inventory Count Record used to record the results of linen inventories, which are transferred to a Linen Inventory Record Log so that comparisons can be made with prior inventories to determine usage and variances.

When counting bed sheets, differentiation must be made in sizes of sheets (Figure 11.23). For convenience, other items not necessarily a part of linens, such as pillows, blankets, bed pads, and bedspreads, might also be counted at this time.

Where items were located when counted and who counted them at that location should be noted on the Count Sheet so managers can audit certain counts. (It would not be unusual for the hotel controller to participate in the inventory by auditing certain count sheets.)

When counts have been completed, Count Sheets are collected and recorded in a **Period Linen Inventory Count Record** (Figure 11.24), which is used to compile all count sheets and record **total linen in use** and **total new linen on hand**. Columns 2 through 9 equal column 10. Columns 10 plus 11 equal column 12. Once total counts have been determined, they are compared with the prior inventory to determine usages (as in Figure 11.18). The separation of linen in use from new linen is done to assign a proper value to the inventory. Most hotel operations will value new linen (linen in unopened boxes) at full price and linen in use at half price. Total **linen valuation** is thus determined as follows:

$$\left(\frac{\text{Linen in use} \times \text{price}}{2}\right) + \text{new linen} \times \text{price} = \text{linen valuation}$$

Care should be taken in counting linen to ensure that unexplained increases do not occur in specific items. For example, a prior inventory indicates 1000 double sheets on hand. Between inventory periods there were 500 double sheets purchased. Total availability of double sheets thus should not exceed 1500. A current inventory, however, reveals that 1724 double sheets are now on hand, giving an unexplained increase of 224 sheets. When such as increase occurs, either the prior inventory or the current inventory is suspect, requiring that a recount be made. When such unexplained increases occur, inventories need to be conducted more frequently until inventory subsystems are under control.

Linen Purchases

Linen inventories reveal the need for purchases, and there are many **linen brokers** who gladly service this type of need. When linen must be purchased from a linen broker, however, it should be expected that a premium will be paid. Savings of up to one-third may be available when the services of a linen broker are not used and linens are purchased directly from **linen mills**. Direct purchases from mills require long-range planning and purchase arrangements contracted up to $1\frac{1}{2}$ years in advance, allowing the mill to produce ordered linens at its convenience.

Such planning may seem impossible, but the **annual linen reorder plan** (Figure 11.25) is quite feasible. Note how quarterly inventories are conducted and compared with an on-hand requirement of 3.5 par. Appropriate replenishment orders for quarters 1, 2, 3, and 4 for the upcoming year may be determined at the beginning of the third quarter of the current year. Linen orders may be made up for a one-year period, one-half year before the effective date of the order; the order is then drop-shipped on a quarterly basis.

The vertical axis in Figure 11.25 indicates the number of a particular item of inventory. Heavy black vertical lines indicate the increase of linen inventory caused by the receipt of drop shipments. The horizontal axis indicates the passage of time from one quarter to the next. Diagonal lines between quarters indicate the linen shortage generated as a result of linen loss, use, and condemnation that might occur between inventories. The shortages determined in each of four quarterly inventories generate annual linen usage that must be replaced each year. A horizontal line at some given value indicates the count of a given item when being maintained at 3.5 par. The count levels are then seen to vary equally above and below 3.5 par value.

As an example, let us assume that a linen order for double sheets (DS) is to be developed on 30 June and will be initiated on 1 January for the upcoming year, and that this order is to be drop-shipped on a quarterly basis during the year the order is in effect. The 3.5 par value of DS is given at 2000. On 30 June, inventory counts reveal 1750 DS on hand (250 short of 3.5 par). Shortly after the 30 June inventory, a drop shipment (prior order) of 500 DS is expected to arrive that will raise the count of DS to 2250. Prior quarterly shortages indicate that a forecast shortage in September may be expected, but a second drop shipment of 250 DS (already ordered) will again arrive that will return the inventory count on 1 October to a value of about 1950 DS. A similar quarterly usage is then forecast for the final quarter of the year, creating a forecast shortage on 31 December of 225 sheets. An order may now be created on 30 June, which will include annual usage (four prior quarterly shortages) plus the shortage forecast to exist on 31 December. This annual order may then be divided into four quarterly drop shipments and the order placed directly with a mill a full six months before the effective commencement of the order. Hence the formula:

Shortage (expected at the end of the current order) + Annual Usage = Future Order

Order/4 = expected quarterly drop shipments to commence six months hence

As has been shown, the preplanned purchase of linens for future use can produce great economies of operation. Whereas linen brokers are available and willing to fill linen needs, the profits made by such brokers represent

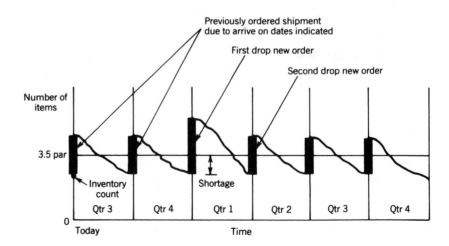

FIGURE 11.25 Annual linen reorder plan shows the supply and replenishment of a given item of linen inventory.

Ethical Dilemmas in Purchasing

Molly Galloway, executive housekeeper at the Seacoast Pines Resort & Convention Center, made a change in her chemical inventory this past year. She switched to Viroban, a disinfectant cleaner that is proven to eliminate most of the harmful bacteria and viruses in guestrooms. It is EPA registered and its material safety data sheet reads like a baby's formula, not a disinfectant cleaner. It is also biodegradable and 20 percent less expensive than her prior guestroom disinfectant cleaner. On top of everything else, the guestroom attendants love the product.

One Saturday, just before the winter holidays, Molly's doorbell rings. It is UPS with a big, big package for her. Excitedly, she opens it to find a 42″ LCD television and a note from the manufacturer of Viroban thanking her for her business over the past year. "Wow, now I get to see the Pasadena Rose Parade on New Year's as if I was there in person," thinks Molly. "Considering Viroban is clearly the best product and I'm saving the company money, what would it hurt if I quietly accept this television?"

Questions
How would you respond to Molly? Is this a "win-win" situation for her and the hotel? Is there a downside? Discuss with your fellow students and instructor what Molly should do.

true cost savings for housekeeping departments who order linens directly from mills. Linen brokers should therefore be used only in an emergency.

Personnel Administration

TIME CARD CONTROL

Another subroutine requiring the daily attention of management is **time card control**. Employees should be counseled at the time of employment as to how many hours constitute the work shift each day. Some organizations specify an 8-hour shift, including time off for work breaks and lunch. Others require that employees clock out for lunch, thus leaving them on their own time for lunch. A housekeeping operation may be arranged in such a way as to have employees on

the property for $8\frac{1}{2}$ hours, including two work breaks of 15 minutes each on company time, but require the employee to clock out for lunch, creating a net 8-hour workday. This arrangement is specified; however, employees are still required to punch a time clock at the beginning and end of each shift, as well as to clock out for lunch and back in after lunch. Federal regulations require that time card records be maintained for each employee to guarantee fair wage administration.

Some employees, although understanding that their shifts begin at 8:00 A.M., may clock in early (7:45) and then expect to be paid for all time worked as indicated on the time card. Employees must not be allowed to enter times on a time card indiscriminately and expect to be paid for these times. It therefore behooves department managers to set specific ground rules about overtime and the time spread in which employees may punch in and out each day. Then, should employees be available and needed before the normal working day, they may be asked to clock in early and can expect to be paid for this early time; otherwise, clock-ins between 7:55 and 8:05 A.M. will be considered 8:00 A.M. clock-ins. Similar policies apply to clock-out times.

Many hotels have two time card racks for each employee; one is for time cards when employees are off the property, and the other is for time cards when employees are on the clock. In large operations, quick note of where the time card is located can determine whether or not an employee is actually at work.

While the employee is on the property, there should be a record of a clock-in with no clock-out yet showing. During this time, managers can audit clock times on cards from the previous day and indicate the number of hours that are to be paid based on the punched indications. This allows employees to note exactly how many hours they may expect to be paid for the previous day. Any questions that arise may then be immediately resolved. Also, indications of overtime authorization can be noted.

Figure 11.26 shows an example of a time card upon which several days of clock time have been recorded. Note the penciled indications wherein the manager has audited the card and indicated the amount of time for which the employee will be paid. This type of audit of time worked by employees is a subroutine that should be done on a daily basis. It is easier to audit time cards using a 24-hour time clock that records hours and hundredths of hours than in A.M. and P.M. hours and minutes. Note that the audit of time on Tuesday indicates a total of 8.5 hours because of an early clock-in time. This early time was not authorized; therefore, only the normal 8-hour shift will be allowed. John Smith would have noticed this reduction on Wednesday during the normal work shift. If there were any questions about the audited reduction, John would have been counseled not to clock in early unless requested to do so. On Wednesday, overtime was

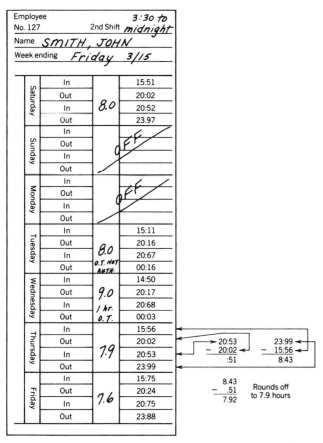

FIGURE 11.26 The daily time card audit. Note the example for Thursday: The first clock-in time is registered as 15.56 (or about 3:34 P.M.—56/100 of an hour past 3:00 P.M.). The last clock-out is 23:99 (1/100 of an hour before midnight). Subtracting the smaller time from the larger yields the total time the employee was on the property. The two intermediate times register out and in times for the dinner break. Subtracting the smaller from the larger time determines the amount of time taken for dinner. Finally, subtracting the dinner break time from the overall time determines actual time on the clock for pay purposes.

authorized; hence the 9 hours were allowed. Some states require that overtime be paid after the 8th hour worked on any given day; others require the payment of overtime only after 40 hours have been worked in one workweek. In the first instance, John worked 39.5 regular hours and 1 overtime hour. In the second instance John worked a total of 40.5 hours; hence only the excess over 40 hours should have been paid at the overtime rate.

PAYROLL ADMINISTRATION

The proper payment of wages due an employee is a matter requiring great attention to detail by the department manager. Employees have a right to expect to be paid for work performed. It is therefore vital that department managers ensure that hours worked during a given workweek be properly recorded on **time sheets** from which actual pay will be calculated.

Time sheets are normally given to department managers by the payroll department before the end of each workweek. Time sheets contain an alphabetical listing of all employees on the payroll. Employees hired after time sheets are originated may be added. Assuming there has been a daily audit of time cards at the conclusion of the workweek, the time cards must be totaled and their values entered on time sheets (Figure 11.27), which will be submitted to the personnel department timekeeper or paymaster.

Weekly time sheets indicate the number of hours for which employees will be paid. Days off are also indicated so that no blanks are noted for any day; special forms of pay are entered where appropriate. Items such as sick pay, vacation pay, total regular time, overtime, and wage rates are entered, as are the wage department classification under which the employee is to be paid. Some employees may have a secondary job code for which they may be paid at a secondary rate. For example, the section housekeeper in wage department (07) may work one day during the week as a relief for a senior housekeeper in wage department (02). The employee should then be paid at the higher wage rate for that particular day. After all time has been correctly recorded, summaries of information are included on Weekly Wage Analysis reports (Figure 11.21).

Proper wage administration includes orientation of the employee in understanding when wages will be paid. Given a workweek that runs from Saturday through Friday, time sheets would normally be prepared at the end of work on Friday. Lapse time, which ranges from five to ten days, is required to prepare checks. Depending on methods of payroll preparation, pay due an employee for the week ending Friday, June 5, for example, may not be presented until Wednesday, June 10, creating what is known as **time in the hole**.

The employee must be counseled at the onset of employment that pay for work completed on the upcoming Friday of the first week worked will not be received until Wednesday, five days hence. Even though this procedure may be burdensome for some employees, it is better to have a payday far enough delayed to guarantee that paychecks will be available on the stated payday than have earlier stated paydays that are *not* met due to late arrival of paychecks. Late paychecks tend to produce major uproars and should be avoided.

Employees need to understand that upon termination of employment, pay owed will be received and termination will not affect amounts owed. Employees who quit their jobs should expect to wait for scheduled paydays to receive their pay. It is best if employees who are terminated by the company are paid off immediately with a special paycheck in order that they need not return to the property after termination.

WEEKLY TIME SHEET

Week Ending ___5/17___

Name (Primary Wage Dept) (Secondary Wage Dept)	Rate	Hours							Total Hours	Earnings			
		SAT	SUN	MON	TUE	WED	THU	FRI		Reg	OT	SPEC	Total
ADAMS, Sarah (07)	9.90	8.0	8.0	8.1	7.9	OFF	OFF	8.0	40.0	396.00			
													396.00
BROWN, Betty (07)	10.15	9.0			8.0	7.9	OFF	OFF	24.9	242.59	15.23		
(02)	10.65		8.0	8.0					16.0			170.40	428.21
CARTER, Louis (06)	9.90	9.0	8.0	OFF	OFF	8V	8V	8V	41.0	158.40	14.85	237.60	
													410.85
GREEN, Martha (02)	10.90	OFF	EDO	8S	8.0	8.0	8.0	OFF	32.0	261.60		87.20	
													348.80
JONES, Thomas (08)	9.90	LOA					▶	LOA					
(02)													0.00
KING, Mary (07)	9.40	8.2	8.1	8S	8S	OFF	OFF	8.0	40.3	225.60	4.23	150.40	
													380.23
SMITH, John (08)	9.65	8.0	OFF	OFF	8.0	9.0	7.9	7.6	40.5	390.83	7.24		
													398.06
THOMAS, William (08)	9.40	8.0	8.0	OFF	OFF	T	T	T	16.0	112.00			
													112.00
WHITE, Jane (06)	9.90	8.0	8.0	8.0	7.4	8A	OFF	OFF	39.4	310.86		79.20	
(02)	10.40												390.06
Totals (Primary)		58.2	40.1	32.1	47.3	40.9	23.9	31.6	274.1	2097.87	41.54	724.80	
(Secondary)			8.0	8.0					16.0				2864.21

Special Codes

S-Sick Pay	LOA - Leave of Absence
V-Vacation Pay	OFF - Regular day off (without pay)
J-Jury Duty	EDO - Extra day off (without pay)
A-Administrative pay	T - Terminated

Prepared by: _Annette Moccio_

Approved by: _____

FIGURE 11.27 A weekly time sheet prepared by the payroll department illustrating a computer-printed page of an alphabetical listing of employees on the payroll. An entire department payroll may be made up of many such pages. Explanations for entries on the weekly time sheet are as follows:

Adams: Worked five regular days as a section housekeeper (07); was off on Wednesday and Thursday. A total of 40 hours worked that week at a pay rate of $9.90/hour for total weekly earnings of $396.00.

Brown: A GRA; worked three regular days under a primary job classification (07) and two days under a secondary job classification (02) (a supervisor). Also worked nine-tenths of an hour overtime, for which she will be paid time and a half.

Carter: Worked two regular days as a public area housekeeper; had two regular scheduled days off, had requested and was granted three days' vacation pay.

Green: Worked three regular days, was scheduled off for an extra day, and was granted eight hours sick leave.

Jones: Has been on a leave of absence for several weeks. (Leave was authorized, therefore benefits continue to accrue.)

King: Worked three regular days; requested and was granted two days sick leave. Also worked three-tenths of an hour overtime.

Smith: Similar schedule to Adams; off Sunday and Monday.

Thomas: Worked two regular days, was off two days, and then failed to return to work. Thomas was terminated. He will be paid monies due on the next regular payday. Had Thomas been fired, he would have been paid off immediately and a cross-reference made on the time sheet that he had already been paid.

White: Worked four regular days, asked for and was granted one day administrative leave (without pay). Also had a secondary job classification but did not work in that capacity during the workweek.

Because the department manager is controlling the employee's working time and pay, the passing out of paychecks is the department manager's responsibility, which should not be passed on to any other department (such as the personnel department).

Employees whose names appear on time sheets for which no pay is entered constitute two categories of personnel; those on legal and granted **leaves of absence (LOA)** and those who have been terminated but for which no terminating paperwork has been received by the payroll division. This latter category requires the immediate attention of the department manager to ensure that time sheets do not contain the names of employees who no longer work for the company.

The subroutine of **time sheet preparation** is a tedious and time-consuming one requiring great attention to detail. With proper training, however, the task can be delegated on a rotating basis to all department supervisory personnel. An authenticating signature of the department manager (or acting manager) should be required on all time sheets.

PERFORMANCE APPRAISALS

One subroutine that must never be neglected is **performance appraisals** of all employees within the department. Every employee has a right to know management's expectations and to receive appraisals of how well responsibilities and tasks are being carried out. Performance appraisals should be conducted at stated intervals and at other times when appropriate.

The first regular appraisal occurs at the end of a **probationary period of employment**. Employees are usually hired for probationary periods, which may last from three to six months. An employee should be notified at the end of a probationary period that his or her performance has been satisfactory and that he or she is now considered a full-time permanent, temporary, or pool employee in good standing. Or the employee should have been advised well in advance of the end of the probationary period that the performance was lacking. Managers who wait until the end of a probationary period to inform an employee that performance has been unacceptable are being insensitive to the human dynamics of supervisory responsibilities.

Routine performance appraisals should occur at stated intervals. After successfully completing a period of probationary performance, the time of the next performance appraisal should be made known to the employee (usually one year hence). When a probationary period is successfully concluded, it should be presumed that the employee is capable of performing the task assigned properly. Failure to continue to perform in a like manner is an indication of unsatisfactory performance and becomes worthy of a special performance evaluation.

When performance is noted as being routinely outstanding, it should also be made the subject of a special performance evaluation.

Satisfactory and outstanding performance evaluations should offer consideration of **pay increases** in accordance with company policy. Assuming that an employee has successfully passed from a probationary status, a raise in pay is appropriate. One year later, given satisfactory performance, another pay increase might be expected.

Many companies have **pay scales** that allow for a start rate, base rate, one-year rate, and maximum rate for each job classification. For example, for the GRA the following rates might apply:

Start rate	$9.50/hour
Base rate	$10.00/hour
One-year rate	$10.50/hour
Maximum rate	$12.50/hour

The start rate is applied when the person begins employment. Given satisfactory performance at the end of a three-month probationary period, pay will be increased to the base rate. Satisfactory performance throughout the year warrants an additional pay increase at the end of the year if for no other reason than inflation. The same might occur for the next three years. Upon reaching the maximum rate, no further increases may be obtained, other than for changes in wage scales due to cost-of-living increases or promotion increases.

Essentially satisfactory performances warrant standard increases to the limit specified by the type of work performed, not years in service in a specific job category. The wage scale might be expected to increase each year due to cost-of-living increases, not seniority. To achieve better-than-standard wage increases, the worker must be above average or be promoted to the next higher classification.

Technique of Performance Appraisal

Performance appraisals should be personal between the manager and the employee. The manager may consult with other supervisors, but the actual appraisal should come from only one of the department managers.

In Chapter 8, a Personnel Action Form (PAF) was instituted for each employee who was hired. The front side of the PAF (Figure 8.4) contains all pertinent identifying data on the employee, and the back (Figure 8.5) is used for performance appraisal. Longtime employees might have several PAFs in their personnel jackets, which had been completed any time the employees had significant personal data changed or when performance was appraised. The front side of the most recent PAF contains the most current data on the employee, with the back page blank awaiting the next needed action (change of data or performance appraisal).

The human resources department helps the executive housekeeper recall when performance appraisals are due for each employee by pulling the most recent PAF and sending it to the housekeeping department. The subroutine of performance appraisal requires action when such appraisals are sent to the department (usually within one week). A set time each week might be scheduled for writing and presenting these appraisals to employees.

As Figure 8.5 shows, the appraisal form requires the following:

1. A statement of observed strengths.
2. An indication of whether objectives assigned have been met.
3. A statement of observed weaknesses. (It is highly doubtful that an employee's performance will be perfect. Weaknesses therefore should be noted in order that the employees know where they need improvement. A performance appraisal indicating no weaknesses is an implied statement that improvement cannot be made in any aspect of performance.)
4. A statement of counseled action—what the employee should do to improve performance and what the employer will do to assist.
5. An estimate of when the employee should be ready for promotion (does not guarantee that promotion will be gained).

Once the appraisal has been prepared, a conference with the employee should be scheduled. The written appraisal is used to discuss the employee's performance. After discussion and ensured understanding, the employee should sign the appraisal as an acknowledgment that he or she has in fact received the appraisal and is aware of the meaning of its contents. The signature is not an acknowledgment of the accuracy of the contents of the appraisal, only that it has been received and understood as the appraiser's view. The employee should then be allowed to comment in writing in the space provided on the appraisal. Should the appraisal warrant an increase in pay, such notation would be made on the front side of the PAF, as should a notation as to when the next appraisal is due.

SPECIAL APPRAISALS

Special appraisals should be conducted in a similar manner as regular appraisals, except that the occasion would be to note either routinely outstanding performance or substandard performance. Poor performance should be appraised *before* the employee's performance becomes unsatisfactory. This allows for corrective action before

the possibility of termination. The PAF may be used to document that a verbal warning has been issued or to document an official written warning. When poor or questionable performance must be appraised, a technique known as leveling should be used. The **leveling technique** is carried out as follows:

1. Conduct leveling sessions on a one-to-one basis. There are rare exceptions when a third person should be present to validate conditions or observations; one-on-one is usually more open and conducive to agreement and future commitment.
2. Be completely honest and straightforward. Do not use the leveling technique if less than total honesty is contemplated.
3. Deal with the problem as soon as possible. Immediate action is much better than delayed action. Delays in dealing with a problem imply a weakness on the part of management and a lack of willingness to deal with unpleasant issues when they occur in hopes that problems will go away. They usually do not.
4. Set up the room so that nothing is between the evaluator and the employee. Move out from behind a desk and sit as an equal with the employee. Do not stand while the employee sits, or vice versa.
5. Go immediately to the problem. No small talk or jokes are appropriate.
6. Send "I" messages. "I" messages show concern without implying that the employee is necessarily a bad person. Statements such as "I am concerned about your repeated tardiness for work" or "I am troubled because you are having difficulty adjusting to your fellow workers" are not so likely to put the employee on the defensive but will likely cause the person to open up and talk about problem areas.
7. Give honest positive reinforcement when deserved, but never patronize.
8. Listen. Half of communication requires listening, understanding meanings, and determining where people are coming from when they talk.
9. Avoid references to past mistakes if they are not relevant to current issues. (Past mistakes should have been dealt with in the past. *It is now that counts.*)
10. Arrive at a mutual decision or understanding as to what future actions or behavior may be expected.
11. Reconfirm understandings by providing written notes of discussions and decided actions; do this for the record and provide a copy of such notes to the employee (may be a copy of a written warning).
12. Keep the entire encounter professional and free of emotion on the part of the evaluator. Should

the employee become emotional, allow the employee to calm down before proceeding with the appraisal.

Employee performance appraisal is one of the most important aspects of personnel administration in which the executive housekeeper will become involved. A manager gets things done through people. To understand this requires a commitment to the understanding of human dynamics and a desire to be a professional in the task of supervision.

Communication and Training

Good management requires an absolute understanding of proper delegation and how such delegation brings about commitment and involvement on the part of employees. Successful commitment cannot be attained by being secretive about matters that employees have a *need to know* out of concern for jobs to be performed or about matters that they *want to know*, which indicate that employee performance is contributing to the success of the company. Commitment and involvement stem from thorough orientation, individualized training, and regular meetings through which the employees get the word.

DEPARTMENTAL MEETINGS

On a regular basis (at least monthly), **departmental meetings** should be scheduled. They should be interesting, informative, and productive. Praise for jobs well done is always appropriate in departmental meetings where individual praiseworthy performances may be recognized in front of others.

Announcements about upcoming events and the success (or failure) of past events are appropriate, as well as management observations about certain happenings. A portion of meetings should be devoted to the presentation and discussion of new hotel policies, as well as the regular and periodic review of existing policies.

Guest comments as to service (both good and bad) need to be presented; however, specific comments about poor individual performance are best presented in private. Meetings should allow time for questions from employees, whereby management may learn about matters concerning employees.

The executive housekeeper should allow junior managers and supervisors to chair meetings but should always be present to convey management's control over meetings. Team leaders should conduct regular (simplified) meetings with team members, keep notes of such meetings, and discuss the results with the executive housekeeper.

Long-Range Planning

THE ONCE-A-YEAR SUBROUTINE: BUDGET FORMULATION

There are many cases in which budgets are presented to executive housekeepers that dictate how much in the way of labor and supplies will be expended in the performance of tasks. Such budgets, which originate with top management and are handed down, seldom draw the commitment of operational managers, because little or no planning was contributed at the department level. The participation of the executive housekeeper in formulating the **operational budget for the housekeeping department** is essential if managers are to commit themselves to successful accomplishment of the long-range plan known as the budget.

Top Management's Input to the Budget

Top management must be involved in the budgeting process: Company expectations should be stated and national trends analyzed; criteria should be established regarding standards to be met in the use of supplies; marketing plans must be finalized for the upcoming year; and budget guidance is essential. Once these tasks are done, however, each department of the hotel should begin the task of assembling, from a zero base, requirements for the expenditure of man-hours, materials, and money to produce the service or product that will be creating revenue. After identifying expected sales and related costs, top management should critique the budget, indicating where adjustments must be made in order that company or corporate objectives will be met. If modification of the budget is necessary, it should be revised by the operating departments until agreement is reached.

The Budget Cycle

The **operational budget cycle** usually requires several months from the onset of planning until critiques and adjustments are finalized. The budgeting process must therefore be begun well in advance of the beginning of the budget (fiscal) year.

Operational budgets usually reflect **periods** of the fiscal year. Some hotel operating budgets are constructed with each of the 12 months reflecting a period. Other systems reflect 13 (28-day) periods, each of which is made up of four consecutive weeks. The 13-period system seems most appropriate because periods will start on the first day of a scheduled workweek and will end on the last day of the following fourth workweek. It allows for the comparison of revenues and costs on a consistent basis each period.

		%OCC	# Rooms	Ave Rate	Sales Dollars	% Inc. in Rooms	% Inc. in Dollars
Current Year	1	73	7215	101.21	730,230		
Actual	2	74	7314	101.43	741,859		
	3	77	7611	101.39	771,679		
	4	73	7215	104.04	750,649		
	5	82	8105	104.08	843,568		
	6	79	7808	103.95	811,642		
	7	85	8401	103.99	873,620		
	8	89	8797	104.02	915,064		
	9	83	8203	104.10	853,932		
(Forecast)	10	82	8105	103.94	842,434		
(Forecast)	11	81	8006	104.06	833,104		
(Forecast)	12	69	6820	104.04	709,553		
(Forecast)	13	60	5931	104.13	617,595		
Total		77.5	99531	103.43	10,294,929		
Budget Year	1	75	7413	105	778,365	2.7	6.6
Budget	2	78	7709	105	809,445	5.4	9.1
	3	86	8500	105	892,500	11.7	15.7
	4	86	8500	105	892,500	17.8	18.9
	5	88	8697	105	913,185	7.3	8.3
	6	92	9093	107	972,951	16.5	19.9
	7	93	9192	107	983,544	9.4	12.6
	8	93	9192	107	983,544	4.5	7.5
	9	92	9093	107	972,951	10.8	13.9
	10	89	8797	107	941,279	8.5	11.7
	11	89	8797	107	941,279	9.9	13.0
	12	80	7907	107	846,049	15.9	19.2
	13	63	6227	107	666,289	5.0	7.9
Total		84.9	109117	106.25	11,593,881	9.7	12.6

FIGURE 11.28 A Consolidated Room Sales Summary presents the expected room sales, percent occupancy, average room rate, and sales dollars to be generated by the annual budget. Current statistics are provided for comparison, and percent increases in number of rooms to be sold and revenue dollars are given in relation to the current year.

Budget periods based on calendar months create 2 months out of 12 in which an extra payday will occur, causing a distorted comparison of wage cost against revenues. Such distortion will not occur in 13-period systems. In addition, set days of each period will always occur on the same days of the week in each period, allowing for systematic comparisons of similar days. For example, assume that workweeks begin on Saturdays and end on Fridays. The first day of every period will then occur on a Saturday. The sixteenth day of every period will similarly always be the third Sunday of each period. Except for special holiday periods, hotel revenues and resultant costs of operations will more likely reflect similarity by days of the week than any other statistical criteria.

The Budgeting Subroutine

Each budget planning cycle is commenced by those involved in budgeting room sales. Schedules indicating the volume of room sales to be expected on each day of the upcoming year are prepared and finalized before operational cost budgeting is begun by any department affected by fluctuating occupancy (such as housekeeping). Most schedules of expected room sales will also show a comparison of the upcoming budget year with the existing year in order that growth can be analyzed. Not only will growth in the sale of guestrooms be significant, but changes in average room rate and expected period revenues will later prove significant in the development of statistical targets for the housekeeping department. Figure 11.28 is an example of a typical **Consolidated Room Sales Summary** which will serve as a basis for the formulation of the housekeeping department's budget. The summary must be developed and distributed to all departments before cost budgeting can be initiated. Since the budget cycle must be begun about the tenth period of the active year in progress, figures listed as "actuals" for the tenth through thirteenth periods are "forecast" since they have not yet occurred. As the budget process continues, these last-period forecasts of the active year will be updated. For illustrative purposes, however, assume that all periods of the current year have been completed.

Wage Classification

Because man-hour utilization represents the highest housekeeping cost of operation, the greatest detail in justification will be required in the development of man-hours to be expended. Recall that man-hours for the various types of work performed within the

Wage department no.	Wage category
00 •	Management
01 ••	Front office supervisory
02 •••	Housekeeping supervisory
03 ••	Front office/reservations clerks
04 ••	Front office cashiers
05 ••	Bell staff
06 •••	Housekeeping (fixed)
07 •••	GRAs
08 •••	Section housekeeping aides
09 ••••	Recreation attendants

FIGURE 11.29 A wage classification system for budgeting and accounting purposes is necessary so that man-hours in specific wage categories may be budgeted, collected, and analyzed.

housekeeping department are classified for accounting purposes. In our earlier example, man-hours worked by GRAs were classification (07), hours worked by section housekeeping aides were (08), those worked by supervisory personnel were (02), and those worked by public area, linen room, and utility personnel do not fluctuate and are therefore classified as fixed hours (06). Other classifications of man-hours to be performed in a rooms department include front office personnel (01, 03, 05), which would be under the control of the front office manager. Figure 11.29 illustrates a system whereby man-hours are classified into **wage departments**.

Budget Justification

The executive housekeeper needs to explain how man-hour requirements are established for each wage department. Usually a standard form for **man-hour justification** is prepared and included as part of the budget submission package. Figure 11.30 is an example of a budget justification of man-hour form explaining utilization of GRA man-hours (wage department 07), which is one wage department for which the executive housekeeper in our example was responsible. The method of department operation is written out and then summarized in tabular form for each period of the budget year. This form becomes a part of the budget submission package.

Considering the expected occupancies noted in Figure 11.28, the executive housekeeper refers to the Table of Personnel Requirements (Table 2.2) to determine exactly how many man-hours will be required to service this occupancy for the model hotel. Statements about method of operation as related to the GRA wage department (07) are based on the least number of man-hours that will accomplish the servicing of budgeted occupied guestrooms.

Figure 11.30 illustrates the detail of the budget justification, although justification sheets for other wage departments may not be so detailed. Note that night operations are identified separately; training costs are also identified separately but are not included at

this point. Training cost will be added with other property training costs and summarized separately. In the example, it is estimated that four employees will be replaced each period at a training cost of 24 nonproductive hours per employee replaced per period.

If a critique challenge is made by top management to the detail expressed in the budget justification, a clear statement as to what service will be discarded or downgraded before hours can be reduced must be made. If profits must be increased but services maintained at the level specified in budget justifications, average room rates would have to be increased to improve revenues and resultant profits. Such may be the topic of discussion during budget critiques.

Wage Summaries

Figure 11.31 is a summary statement of all man-hour and wage cost information for the entire rooms department. At the bottom is the calculation of the **sales per man-hour**. This is an efficiency calculation referring to the number of wage department (07) man-hours to be expended for each dollar of sales revenue generated. Once the statistic is accepted, it becomes an efficiency target to be maintained or bettered in each period. Later, comparisons of sales per man-hour for the budget year with that for the current year indicate whether efficiencies are being maintained, exceeded, or lessened over the prior year.

In our Figure 11.32 revenue for the budget year is given as $11,624,451. GRA hours (Wage Department 07) required to service the occupancy that generates this revenue will be 53,088 man-hours. Sales per man-hour then becomes $11,624,451/53,088 = $218.97. Upon acceptance of this statistic, revenue may be compared each period with GRA hours to determine whether the statistic is achieved or is more or less than budgeted. If the current year sales-per-man-hour figure is more than what is budgeted for the year, it indicates improved efficiencies for the department.

Budgeting Supplies and Other Controllables

The budgeting of other **controllable items**, although not as detailed as man-hours, will require the same effort. Figure 11.32 shows the entire rooms department budget, which combines all sales budgeting that will generate revenues for the rooms department and includes related costs from the front office and housekeeping. Note the format by which current year actuals and projections through the end of the current year are compared with next year's budget. Certain key budget items have been compared with revenues as a percent of revenue to provide performance targets. Dollars, as well as man-hours, are budgeted. Department control profit is established, as are statistical targets generated from

BUDGET JUSTIFICATION
FOR
MANPOWER UTILIZATION

Department _Rooms_   Cost Center _Housekeeping_   Wage dept. _07_

Position Title _Section Housekeepers_

Staffing rationale

Hours of Operation   _1st Shift 8:00Am to 4:30 pm._
               2nd Shift 3:30pm to Midnight

Shifts per day: _2_   Managers assigned _2_   Hourly Supervisors _6_

Explanation of operation:

Section Housekeepers to be scheduled in accordance with Table of Personnel Requirements (attached). Each Section Housekeeper is expected to service 18 rooms/day. Hours are based on 7 days/week operations. Department is staffed by "Swing team" personnel to cover days off for regular teams.

Summary

Per	OCC	Avg pers day/night	Hrs/Day	Days/wk	Hrs/Wk Total	Hrs/Prd Total	Avg Rate	Cost
1		15/1	128	7	896	3,584	9.76	34,967
2		16/1	136	7	952	3,808	9.78	37,229
3		17/1	144	7	1,008	4,032	9.80	39,500
4		17/1	144	7	1,008	4,032	9.81	39,580
5		18/1	152	7	1,064	4,256	9.83	41,822
6		19/1	160	7	1,120	4,480	9.84	44,068
7		19/1	160	7	1,120	4,480	9.85	44,112
8		19/1	160	7	1,120	4,480	9.87	44,202
9		19/1	160	7	1,120	4,480	9.89	44,292
10		18/1	152	7	1,064	4,256	9.91	42,162
11		18/1	152	7	1,064	4,256	9.92	42,205
12		16/1	136	7	952	3,808	9.93	37,800
13		13/1	112	7	784	3,136	9.94	31,161
Tot yr		17/1	146		13,272	53,088	9.85	523,100

Comment on wage increases:

Training man-hours _not included_ Cost _____

Night Operations _2912_   Cost _____

Total mh __53,088__
Total Cost __523,100__

(Submitted)

FIGURE 11.30 Budget justification for man-hour utilization is used to support requirements for man-hours in various wage categories. A specific justification document is needed for each wage category. (This particular form with position title "Section Housekeeper" refers to GRAs.)

which performance can be measured. Other supporting data (Figures 11.28, 11.30, and 11.31) form a part of the budget package that will be presented to top management for review and approval. Once approved, the budget is spread into 13 period budgets, which will be used to compare actual happenings when they occur in each period.

The final budget is divided into six parts: total sales, total salaries and wages, total employee costs, total controllables, control profit, and statistics. The presentation of wage cost is by wage department, the balance of which has now been added for the entire rooms department. The total employee costs refer to costs over and above salaries and wages, including benefits averaging about 20 percent of salary and wage cost. Controllables refer to the various supply cost accounts where monies will be needed. Not all cost accounts fall under the purview of the executive housekeeper, but those that do are obvious. They include cleaning supplies, guest supplies, laundry expenses, linen costs, and parts of several other accounts, including general expense. Each controllable cost may also be expressed as a percentage of revenue. For example, cleaning supplies might approximate $\frac{3}{10}$ of 1 percent of revenue and guest supplies approximate $\frac{6}{10}$ of 1 percent of revenue. Such statistics have a tendency to vary with type of hotel, type of market, expectations for excellence, and other specific factors.

Rooms Budget Worksheet

SALARY AND WAGE SUMMARY

Period	% OCC	Period Total Amount	Rate / Man-Hours	Dept Amount	01 Rate / Man-Hours	Dept Amount	02 Rate / Man-Hours	Dept Amount	03 Rate / Man-Hours	Dept Amount	04 Rate / Man-Hours	Dept Amount	05 Rate / Man-Hours	Dept Amount	06 Rate / Man-Hours	Dept Amount	07 Rate / Man-Hours	Dept Amount	08 Rate / Man-Hours	Dept Amount	09 Rate / Man-Hours
1																34,967	9.76 / 3584				
2																37,229	9.78 / 3808				
3																39,500	9.8 / 4032				
4																39,580	9.82 / 4032				
5																41,822	9.83 / 4256				
6																44,068	9.84 / 4480				
7																44,112	9.85 / 4480				
8																44,202	9.87 / 4480				
9																44,292	9.89 / 4480				
10																42,162	9.91 / 4256				
11																42,205	9.92 / 4256				
12																37,800	9.93 / 3808				
13																31,161	9.94 / 3136				
Year Total		1,543,366	11.54 / 133,728	61,226	12.25 / 5,000	211,936	11.77 / 18000	147,048	10.36 / 14,192	27,851	10.36 / 2,688			138,465	9.89 / 14,000	523,100	9.85 / 53,088	178,027	9.89 / 18,000	66,011	7.54 / 8760
		Sales Per Man-Hour	Average Rate	Sales Per Man-Hour	Average Rate	Sales Per Man-Hour	Average Rate	Sales Per Man-Hour	Average Rate	Sales Per Man-Hour	Average Rate	Sales Per Man-Hour	Average Rate	Sales Per Man-Hour	Average Rate	Sales Per Man-Hour	Average Rate	Sales Per Man-Hour	Average Rate	Sales Per Man-Hour	Average Rate
Budget																218.97					
Last Year																210.77					

FIGURE 11.31 A Salary and Wage Summary on which total hours, wage rates, and dollar wage cost for each wage department within the rooms department are totaled. For simplicity, only wage department (07) and department totals are shown.

Budget in Operation

Once the budget has been developed, it will be critiqued as we described earlier. Once approved, the major long-range operational plan is now in place for the upcoming year. As the budgeted year progresses, period statements will be produced by the accounting department in a form almost identical to that expressed in the budget (Figure 11.33).

New actual costs are next to what has been budgeted. The executive housekeeper is expected to explain any serious negative deviations from the plan and how these deviations will be corrected. This type of control is one of the major challenges to expert professional housekeeping. The executive housekeeper, having been a part of the budget process, should look forward to the management challenge afforded by budget planning, analysis, and control.

To understand budgets and the related processes, carefully analyze the explanations given in Figures 11.32 and 11.33. For Figure 11.33, a period critique of questionable items directly under the control of the executive housekeeper might appear as follows.

Critique notes

1. Wage cost for supervisor remains high in the third period and continues a trend established in the first two periods.

2. GRA wage costs appear inordinately low, considering occupancies slightly above budget (line 30, page 2).

3. Major purchases of all-purpose cleaner were paid in periods one and two. These purchases will not recur for six months. Area will be under control and will be on budget by the fifth period.

4. Completed contract with AJAX Exterminator Company and paid balance of contract due. A major cost reduction will accrue upon commencement of contract with GETTABUG Company.

5. General expense purchases over budget by $1241.00 in the third period and are $2963.00 YTD. Purchases have involved the expensing of new shelving for the main linen room, as opposed to the inclusion of these items in last year's capital expenditure budget. Controller indicates that approval is forthcoming to transfer these cost items to capital expenditures. Item is already over budget for the year. If this transfer is not made, additional funds need to be budgeted in this area.

6. Guest supplies for third period are now under control after being well over budget for periods one and two due to payment of invoices for annual supplies of guestroom stationery. Item will remain in control for the remainder of the fiscal year.

ROOMS DEPARTMENT
<u>BUDGET</u>

Page 1

Performance Budget
Year

	Year	Actual $	%	1998 Budget $	%	1997 Projected $	%
1	Total Room Sales			$ 11,606,264		$ 10,308,686	
2	Rebate Allowance			(12,383)		(13,757)	
3	Net Room Sales			11,593,881		10,294,929	
4	Other Sales			65,015		55,748	
5	Cost of Sales			(34,445)		(29,251)	
6	TOTAL SALES			11,624,451	100.0%	10,321,427	100%
7	Wage Dept. 01			61,226		60,515	
8	02			211,936		216,072	
9	03			147,048		148,708	
10	04			27,851		28,423	
11	06			138,465		140,251	
12	07			523,100	4.5%	481,219	4.7%
13	08			178,027		182,772	
14	09			66,011		60,676	
15	TOTAL WAGES			1,346,504	11.6%	1,318,636	12.8%
16	Overtime Prem.			2,449		2,790	
17	Holiday Pay			43,702		44,455	
18	Management Salaries			131,872		108,606	
19	Bonuses			18,839		13,208	
20	TOTAL SALARIES & WAGES			1,543,366	13.3%	1,487,696	14.4%
21	Vacation Management			4,898		2,840	
22	Vacation Hourly			10,361		6,671	
23	Payroll Taxes			54,908		48,054	
24	H & W Insurance			11,974		7,636	
25	Employee Relations			942		1,367	
26	Employee Food			42,442		36,097	
27	TOTAL EMPLOYEE COSTS			125,525	1.1%	102,666	1.0%
28	CONTROLLABLES						
29	Bad Debts Provision					948	
30	Corp. Public Relations					533	
31	Cleaning Supplies			34,782	0.3%	41,179	0.4%
32	Commission Exp.			2,449		2,433	
33	Contract Services			5,652		8,067	
34	Decoration & Plants			2,449		1,519	
35	Entertainment			1,225		1,778	
36	Equipment Rental			2,543		2,800	
37	General Expense			2,449		6,698	
38	Guest Supplies			69,564	0.6%	72,065	0.7%
39	Holidex Rental			16,955		17,377	
40	Laundry Expense			78,530		86,152	

(a)

FIGURE 11.32 The rooms department budget is annualized and displayed side by side with the current year in order that comparisons can be made.

Page 2

Year	Actual $	%	1998 Budget $	%	1997 Projected $	%
1 Linen Expense			$ 81,372	0.7%	$ 85,447	0.83%
2 Linen Rental						
3 Office Print and Post.			15,071		18,010	
4 Telephone Exp.			2,449		7,628	
5 Uniforms			3,768		9,503	
6 Walked guest			942		1,558	
7 Xerox Costs			3,768		3,305	
8 TOTAL CONTROLLABLES			323,752	2.8%	368,997	3.6%
9						
10 CONTROL PROFIT			$ 9,631,808	82.9%	$ 8,362,067	81.0%
11						
12 HOURS						
13 Wage Dept. 01			5,000		5,141	
14 02			18,000		17,984	
15 03			14,192		14,297	
16 04			2,688		2,543	
17 05						
18 06			14,000		13,591	
19 07			53,088		48,969	
20 08			18,000		18,721	
21 09			8,760		7,623	
22 TOTAL HOURS			133,728		128,869	
23						
24 Average Wage Rate			11.54		11.54	
25 Sales/Manhour			$ 86.93		$ 80.09	
07 Sales/Manhour			$ 218.97		$ 210.77	
26 Hskpg MH/Occ. Room			0.49		0.49	
27 Wage Cost/Sales Dollar (%)			11.58%		12.78%	
28						
29 % Occupancy			85%		77.5%	
30 Room Nights			109,117		99,531	
31 Average Room Rate			$ 106.25		$ 103.43	
32						
33						
34						
35						
36						
37						
38						
39						
40						

(b)

FIGURE 11.32 (*Continued*)

ROOMS DEPARTMENT
Period Statement

Monthly Income Statement
For 3rd Period, 1997

		Year	Period Actual $	%	Period Budget $	%	YTD Budget $	%	YTD Actual $	%
	1	Total Room Sales	893,771		893,455		$ 2,483,175		2,473,982	
	2	Rebate Allowance	(544)		(955)		(2,865)		(2,187)	
	3	Net Room Sales	893,227		892,500		2,480,310		2,471,795	
	4	Other Sales	4,857		5,074		15,324		15,415	
	5	Cost of Sales	(2,663)		(2,684)		(8,115)		(8,369)	
	6	TOTAL SALES	895,421	100%	894,890	100%	2,487,519	100%	2,478,841	100%
	7	Wage Dept. 01	4,750		4,773		13,929		11,593	
(1)	8	02	19,495		16,521		49,447		48,178	
	9	03	11,482		11,462		34,156		31,961	
	10	04	2,377		2,171		6,064		13,938	
	11	06	10,795		10,794		32,134		29,845	
(2)	12	07	36,746		39,500		111,696		108,143	
	13	08	12,514		12,409		37,017		34,287	
	14	09	5,195		5,145		15,057		16,202	
	15	TOTAL WAGES	103,353	11.5%	102,775	11.5%	299,500	12.0%	294,147	11.9%
	16	Overtime Prem.	431		191		577		989	
	17	Holiday Pay	932		3,406		10,299		4,619	
	18	Management Salaries	9,853		10,280		31,079		31,188	
	19	Bonuses	-		1,468		4,440			
	20	TOTAL SALARIES & WAGES	114,569	12.8%	118,120	13.2%	345,896	13.9%	330,943	13.4%
	21	Vacation Management	-		382		1,154			
	22	Vacation Hourly	1,250		808		2,434		2,830	
	23	Payroll Taxes	4,177		4,280		12,940		11,392	
	24	H & W Insurance	361		382		2,822		2,643	
	25	Employee Relations			808		221		-	
	26	Employee Food	3,947		4,280		10,003		9,704	
	27	TOTAL EMPLOYEE COSTS	9,735	1.1%	10,939	1.2%	29,575	1.2%	26,569	1.1%
	28	CONTROLLABLES								
	29	Bad Debts Provision	325						1,150	
	30	Corp. Public Relations							325	
(3)	31	Cleaning Supplies	3,169		2,711		8,198		10,949	
	32	Commission Exp.	269		191		1,539		618	
(4)	33	Contract Services	859		441		1,331		1,962	
	34	Decoration & Plants			191		577			
	35	Entertainment			95		289		231	
	36	Equipment Rental			199		600			
(5)	37	General Expense	1,432		191		577		2,963	
(6)	38	Guest Supplies	5,386		5,422		16,394		22,418	
	39	Holidex Rental	1,321		1,321		3,994		3,994	
(7)	40	Laundry Expense	5,622		6,122		18,506		19,222	

(a)

FIGURE 11.33 Rooms Department Period Statement indicating progress toward the budget for the third of thirteen periods in the fiscal year. (The statement refers to Figure 11.34, which is based on the model hotel.) Note that the third period is compared with the spread budget for the third period, and that year-to-date (YTD) comparisons (totals of periods one, two, and three) are also made. Look closely to see if performance for the third period reflects improvement toward the overall year or a deterioration of performance.

Monthly Income Statement
For 3rd Period, 1997

		Year	Period Actual $	%	Period Budget $	%	YTD Budget $	%	YTD Actual $	%
(8)	1	Linen Expense	8,631		6,327		19,128		8,631	
	2	Linen Rental								
	3	Office Print and Post.	1,149		1,174		3,540		3,338	
	4	Telephone Exp.	283		191		577			
(9)	5	Uniforms	4,622		294		887		4,658	
	6	Walked guest	168		73		221		568	
	7	Xerox Costs	168		294		887		721	
(10)	8	TOTAL CONTROLLABLES	33,404	3.7%	25,236	2.8%	77,246	3.1%	81,747	3.3%
	9									
(11)	10	CONTROL PROFIT	$ 737,713	82.4%	$ 740,595	82.8%	$ 2,034,803	81.8%	2,039,581	82.3%
	11									
	12	HOURS								
	13	Wage Dept. 01	379		385		1,155		1,131	
(12)	14	02	1,632		1,385		4,154		4,280	
	15	03	1,088		1,092		3,275		3,198	
	16	04	205		207		621		626	
	17	05								
	18	06	1,045		1,077		3,231		3,166	
(13)	19	07	3,525		4,032		11,424		10,609	
	20	08	1,839		1,874		4,154		3,594	
	21	09	670		674		2,022		1,554	
	22	TOTAL HOURS	10,383		10,726		30,036		28,158	
	23									
(14)	24	Average Wage Rate	11.03		11.01		11.52		11.75	
(15)	25	Sales/Manhour	$ 86.24		$ 83.43		$ 82.82		$ 88.03	
	26	07 Sales/Manhour	$ 254.02		$ 221.95		$ 217.75		$ 233.65	
(16)	27	Hskpg MH/Occ. Room	0.41		0.47		0.48		0.45	
	28	Wage Cost/Sales Dollar (%)	11.5%		11.5%		12.0%		11.9%	
	29									
	30	% Occupancy	86.6%		85.9%		77.5%		77.5%	
	31	Room Nights	8,563		8,500		23,883		23,622	
	32	Average Room Rate	$ 104.31		$ 105.00		$ 103.85		$ 104.64	

(b)

FIGURE 11.33 (*Continued*)

7. Laundry expense now under control after major breakdown in second period required the use of outside laundry services.
8. Period linen expense reflects payment of invoice for drop shipment. Expense well under control for the year.
9. Uniform cost well over budget due to direction from top management to change senior housekeeper's uniform (not budgeted). Cost savings during the year should bring this item near control by the end of the fiscal year.
10. Total controllables 32.4 percent over budget for the period but only 5.8 percent for YTD. Controls and management decisions as indicated will make annual budget attainable and on target by the fifth period.
11. Control profit requires no comment since it is under control.
12. The trend noted on lines 1 and 2 is also reflected in supervisor and GRA hour use. [What appears to be happening is that supervisors are cleaning guestrooms in the absence of sufficient GRAs on daily staff. This problem will persist if (07) staffing remains low or if there is an attendance problem with GRAs.] Management attention to this area of personnel administration will be forthcoming. Staffing and call-off problems will be resolved and under control by the beginning of the fifth period.
13. Same as No. 12 above.
14. Average wage rate being high may be a reflection from another department. In addition, low turnover can keep a wage rate high.
15. Rooms department sales per man-hour is in excellent condition.
16. GRA hours per occupied room is too low (.41 as opposed to .47 budgeted—and getting worse). This is another indication that rooms are being cleaned by supervisors at a higher wage rate.

The use of supervisors to clean guestrooms is the most glaring problem revealed when analyzing the period statement. Immediate attention is needed here. Other areas out of control have been recognized and intentions for corrective measures have been given. Analyze other portions of the statement to ensure understanding.

CONCLUSION

Subroutines are as much a part of the executive housekeeper's daily concerns as the housekeeping daily routine. Although the subroutines mentioned in this chapter do not directly relate to one another, the tie between them is the need to make each one a *routine* rather than an exception to the daily routine.

Because all routines recur periodically, they are subject to standardization and procedural specification through the use of forms. Numerous forms were introduced, all of which could be modified to fit any hotel, hospital, or health-care operation of any size or complexity.

Participation in the subroutines by junior managers and supervisors serves two important functions: It adds to personnel development, and it frees the executive housekeeper to become more involved in solving unique problems and in thinking creatively. Although many subroutines are handed down by top management, a well-informed and progressive executive housekeeper can be very influential in presenting and fostering the development of subroutine ideas that could become company-wide standards of practice.

For organizational purposes, subroutines were presented under five major headings: cleaning and maintenance, operational controls, purchasing, personnel administration, communication and training, and long-range planning.

KEY TERMS AND CONCEPTS

Subroutines	General cleaning	Room inspections
Public areas department	Deep cleaning	Inspectors
Director of public areas	Projects	Spot-checked
Stewards department	Repair and physical maintenance	Inspection day
Chief steward	Maintenance Work Request Form	Inspection programs
Public areas	Second request	Property inspection program
Cleaning and maintenance circuits (rounds)	Maintenance inspection	Fresh look
	Maintenance Checklist	Zone inspection program

Zones
Documented
Weekly maintenance inspection
Inventories
Control information
Cleaning and Guest
   Supply Inventory
Count sheet
Inventory Record Log
Controllers
Forecasting of man-hour
   requirements
Weekly Wage Forecast
Forecast occupancy
Wage departments
Target statistics
In control
Weekly Wage Analysis
Actual expenditures

Period statements
Critiqued
Purchasing
Purchasing agent
Competitive Shopping Form
Physical linen inventories
Linen Count Sheet
Period Linen Inventory
   Count Record
Total linen in use
Total new linen on hand
Linen valuation
Linen brokers
Linen mills
Annual linen reorder plan
Time card control
Time sheets
Time in the hole
Leaves of absence (LOA)

Time sheet preparation
Performance appraisals
Probationary period of
   employment
Pay increases
Pay scales
Leveling technique
Departmental meetings
Operational budget for the
   housekeeping department
Operational budget cycle
Periods
Consolidated Room Sales
   Summary
Wage departments
Man-hour justification
Sales per man-hour
Controllable items

DISCUSSION AND REVIEW QUESTIONS

1. Name three subroutines not mentioned in this chapter. In a new operation, why is it so important to identify as many routines as possible and to prepare SOPs as quickly as possible? What major role do SOPs play in the operation of a department?

2. Describe the concept of zone inspection. How is it related to the Division of Work Document and the Area Responsibility Plan? In what way does a zone inspection program facilitate the development of junior managers?

3. Explain a maintenance work request system. Describe the flow of information required to ensure proper control.

4. Who should inspect guestrooms? Develop a plan around each person listed, indicating how many rooms should be inspected by each person, how often, and why.

5. Prepare a department meeting agenda. How would you go about gaining maximum participation from attendees?

6. Explain what is meant by the 13-period system. What are advantages and disadvantages of using this system for operational reporting? For financial reporting?

7. List the parts of a budget submission package. Explain the use of each part. How would you justify expenditures for additional GRA man-hours during the evening shift after being told that room rates would be increasing?

NOTE

1. Based on an interview with Clarence R. Johnson, MELCOR. Reprinted from Stan Gottlieb, "Maintenance: A Workable Program for the Smaller Property," *Lodging*, May 1984, American Hotel Association Directory Corporation.

PART FOUR

SPECIAL TOPICS: SWIMMING POOL OPERATIONS AND MANAGEMENT, HOUSEKEEPING IN OTHER VENUES, SAFEGUARDING OF ASSETS, IN-HOUSE LAUNDRIES, AND THE FULL CIRCLE OF MANAGEMENT

In Part Three, the management functions of direction and control were applied to the ''Daily Routine of Housekeeping'' and to various ''subroutines'' that may be encountered by members of a housekeeping team during daily operations. In this final part, the specific topics of swimming pool operations and management, housekeeping in other venues, concerns for the safeguarding of assets (security and safety), and on-premises laundries are covered. In conclusion, problem solving, management styles, and the future of housekeeping as a management profession are also discussed.

CHAPTER 12

Swimming Pool Operations and Management

LEARNING OBJECTIVES

After studying the chapter, students should be able to:

1. Identify terms and their definitions related to swimming pool and spa operations, including the components of a pool system.
2. Describe the process of pool water filtration, the different types of filters, and the tests for water purity and clarity.
3. Describe the various chemicals used to maintain swimming pools and spas.
4. Describe how to control algae growth in pools and spas.
5. Describe staffing concerns for pools, including selection and training criteria for pool attendants.
6. List and describe the duties and responsibilities of pool attendants.

Some may wonder why it is necessary to have a discussion of swimming pools in a book on housekeeping. Shouldn't the pool be under the purview of the maintenance department? It should be remembered that the classical **matching principle** of accounting requires that expenses be related to the revenue being generated by a specific department. The maintenance department is normally responsible, and is budgeted for, the **repair** and **maintenance** of a facility, not the management of an operating department. Should there be a breakdown in the physical operation of the pool system, water leaks, or mechanical breakdowns of the filtering or chlorinating systems, such repairs should be made by the maintenance department. Otherwise, the day-to-day **operation** of the pool should come under some operational subdepartment associated with rooms operations and revenue. Because the main task demanding most of the employee **wage dollar-hours** is generated by keeping the pool area clean and supplying guest services, operation and management of the pool and pool area will usually come under the domain of the housekeeping department.

In very large pool systems it is possible that an **operating engineer** be assigned to nothing else but the mechanical systems of the swimming pool, but this is usually an exception. Most pool operating functions are organized under the overall responsibility of the executive housekeeper, assisted by a **senior lifeguard** or **pool supervisor** who will oversee the total operation of the pool and surroundings as further assisted by a staff of **lifeguards** or **pool attendants**. The difference between the lifeguard and the pool attendant is explained later in this chapter.

Components of a Swimming Pool System

❦

Although no two swimming pool systems are exactly alike, most are designed with certain generic operating requirements. The following 13 components are usually present in any system, and understanding their purpose and operation can help the reader visualize how the first three objectives mentioned earlier are attained. To do this, the components are named and their functions fully described.

The layout of the pool system is shown in Figure 12.1 (plan view) and Figure 12.2 (profile view). It includes the various components listed here:

Water Inlets—Plumbing jets where filtered water enters the pool. **Inlet jets** direct the water in a counterclockwise motion around the pool.

Skimmers—Water-level basket holders with plumbing leading water out of the pool into the **internal piping system** leading back to the filters. **Fill water** must be regulated to keep the pool water at the optimum level; otherwise, a low water level will cause air to be drawn into the **closed liquid loop** and the circulating system will cease to operate.

Skimmer Baskets—These are catch baskets (4 are shown) designed to fit into skimmers where surface debris can be caught and removed from water. The counterclockwise circulation of the surface water will cause most debris to pass into one or more of the skimmer baskets. Baskets holding the debris can be lifted out and emptied periodically.

Main Drain—Located at the bottom of the deepest point in the pool, drains debris off the bottom of the pool, or can be used to drain the pool entirely, if necessary.

Drain Manifold—Collects water from all drain lines returning water from the pool to the filter. Manifold has a **regulating valve** on each line for controlling the

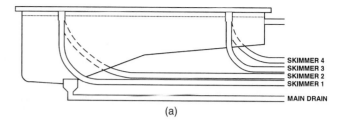
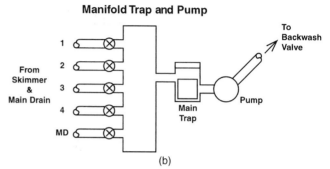

(a)

Manifold Trap and Pump

(b)

FIGURE 12.2 Profile view of pool shows shallow and deep ends of pool with plumbing for *main drain* and four skimmer lines (a). Water from these five lines is collected in a manifold with regulating valves on each line to control the flow of water. (b) Water is then collected and sent through the main trap. This trap should be opened periodically, and the basket removed and emptied. Water is then drawn into the pump due to vacuum pressure from the pump when it is running.

volume of flow from each returning line. Valves are usually adjusted to regulate an even flow through each skimmer with a partial flow through the main drain.

Main Trap—May be opened and the **trap basket** emptied of any debris that was missed by the skimmer baskets (small rocks, etc.), before water enters the pump.

Pump—Creates the **positive** pressure that forces water through the filter and back through **return lines** to the pool. The pump also creates the **negative** (vacuum) pressure on the circulation system that brings water through the skimmers and drain from the pool. This **vacuum pressure** can also be used to facilitate vacuuming the pool, mentioned later.

Backwash Valve—This valve, operated by a push-pull handle, directs water under normal operations, into the top of the filter, forcing the water down through the filtering material from where the filtered water returns to the pool. When the position of the backwash valve is reversed, flow through the filter is reversed and water levitates the filtering agents so that debris caught in the filter is moved to the top of the **filter tank**, where it can be carried off into the sewer system.

Sight Glass—A tubular piece of glass or clear plastic pipe through which the clarity of the water being discharged from the filter can be observed. Water being backwashed usually appears brown until the

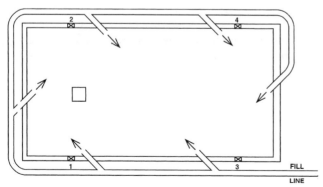

FIGURE 12.1 Plan view of pool and fill line with water jets directing the flow of water counterclockwise around the pool, allowing surface water to pass by four skimmers.

filter is cleared, after which the backwash valve can be readjusted to the normal operating position.

Pressure Gauge—A combination pressure gauge and relief valve; sits on the top of the filter, which is the highest point in the **circulating system**. A pressure reading, taken at the time of installation when the system is clean, is identified as the **normal operating pressure**. As the filter continues to filter **particulate matter** from the water, the pressure will tend to increase, giving an indication that it is becoming harder to push water through the filter and that the system should be backwashed. (For example, if the normal operating pressure is 16 psi and the pressure rises to 20 psi, backwashing would be indicated. After the discarded water clears, as noted, through the sight glass, and the filter is returned to normal operation, pressure should return to a normal reading of 16 psi.)

The system should also be maintained as a **liquid loop** (free of air to prevent hydraulic loss of vacuum and pressure). Air trapped in the system will rise to the top of the filter. This trapped air can be removed by turning on the pump and opening the valve on the pressure gauge. This will cause the air to be forced from the system, making the circulation totally liquid again.

Pool Heater—Pools in the southern part of the country will not be comfortable enough to swim in (78°F) until after late May. Most pools will be provided with a heater to warm the water about 5 to 10° in order to gain usage of the pool earlier in the season. In the northern part of the country, outdoor pools are usually heated, except in July or August. Usually in smaller pools, the heater is a 100,000 **Btu** heater, capable of heating either the main pool or a spa if one is available. Water is heated just before it is returned to the pool.

Chlorinator—A controllable device used to feed a **Chlorinating Agent**—(chlorine or similar product such as **bromine**) into the pool circulation prior to the water returning to the pool.

Pool Vacuum—A **vacuum foot** with two connections—one for a pole that gives the user access to the bottom of the pool in deep water, and the other that connects to a length of hose that can reach the surface of the water and fit into one of the skimmers. By adjusting the valves at the manifold, all vacuum pressure may be directed to only one skimmer to which the vacuum hose is connected. This provides a total vacuum capability to the location where the vacuum foot is directed at the bottom or side of the pool. This procedure should be done when needed or at least once a week. CAUTION: When attaching a vacuum hose to the skimmer inlet, the pump should be turned off. If the pump is running, the force of the vacuum in the skimmer is strong enough to capture and break fingers.

FIGURE 12.3 Mirage Resort main pool with hotel and waterfall in the background. Notice the three lap lines in the foreground. *(Photo taken with permission of MGM Mirage™.)*

Pool Sizes and Shapes

Swimming pools can be found in all sizes and shapes. The average 300-room hotel will probably have a heated pool about 25′ × 60′, rectangular in shape, with a shallow end at 3 feet and a deep end at 6 feet. It will hold about 30,000 gallons of water and will have a plumbing system as described earlier. Some have diving boards and some do not. In cold climates, pools are usually indoors. Most have *spa* hot tubs associated with the main pool.

The major resorts have much larger pools that can handle several thousand people at one time. Figure 12.3 shows the Mirage Resort in Las Vegas. There are two pools in the cabana area. The two pool decks have 1150 lounge chairs and can accommodate about 6000 guests per day. There are also two waterfalls that have about 7000 gallons of water running through them at the same time, and three water slides. On a busy day there are 12–14 lifeguards watching the water, and an additional 10 pool attendants seating people and handing out towels. The main pool has a water surface area of 17,780 feet, 486,000 gallons of water, 1033 feet of perimeter, 53 bottom returns, 35 inlet jets, 46 skimmers, and 6 drain covers that are 2′ × 56′ in length. There are also 555 feet of expansion joints built into the pool.

Water Clarity

Water clarity refers to a measure of the proper **degree of filtration**. Pool water must be properly filtered if it is to be as clear as it should be. Water will be clear if all **solid particulates** are removed and kept out of the water. This is more difficult for outdoor pools because the greatest source of particulates in the water are dust, leaves, and other debris.

Water that is free of particulates appears blue in color and completely transparent. Water that is green is not being properly filtered and is usually the product of **airborne spores** blooming into algae. This will not only appear green but will also make the water appear cloudy. Water can become so cloudy because of this type of problem that the pool bottom cannot be seen. If this happens, the pool should be considered unsafe to swim in, not because the water is chemically unsafe, but because you would not be able to see a swimmer on the bottom of the pool who might be in distress. Therefore, we believe that the correct test for the proper degree of filtration is as follows:

> Toss a dime into the deepest part of the pool, and after it reaches bottom, can it be seen well enough to determine whether it is heads or tails? If the answer is yes, then the water has the proper degree of clarity. If not, then filtration must be improved.

Types of Filters and How They Work

After passing the backwash valve, water enters the filter. There are two basic types of filters found in hotel-type swimming pool installations. One is the *earth sand (ES) filter* and the other is called a *diatomaceous earth (DE) filter*. These two filters are usually distinguished by their size.

The ES filter (Figure 12.4) is the larger of the two and is filled with graduating sizes of sand to coarse aggregate rock, over which the pool water will be pumped under pressure. This filter must be periodically backwashed thoroughly; otherwise it will become *caked* with debris and require opening and replacement of all sand and earth. This is a tedious and labor-intensive procedure. Figure 12.5 is an example of the much smaller DE filter. Note the internal structure of the DE filter in which **filter vanes** are present. These several vanes are constructed of a microscopic-size nylon mesh screen, over which a coating of **diatomaceous earth** (a white powder made from the skeletal remains of microscopic sea creatures) is evenly distributed.

Over a period of time, particulate matter will also cause a pressure rise as it becomes harder to force water through the filter. A backwashing process must then take place. With this type of filter, the DE coating on the vanes will also be flushed out of the system and will require that fresh DE again be entered into the system when backwashing has been completed. This is done by mixing a **slurry** of water and DE and placing it into the

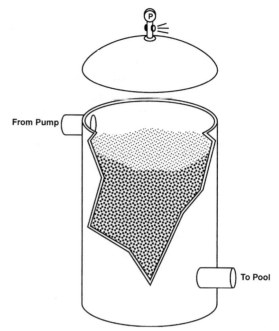

FIGURE 12.4 In the ES filter, water enters the top and is forced down through the filter under pressure. Water is then returned through a heater (if present), a chlorinator, and finally to the pool under pressure.

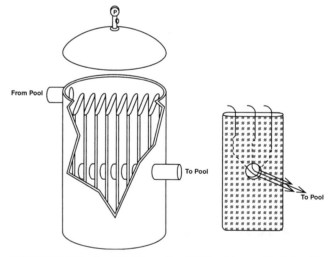

FIGURE 12.5 In the DE filter, after DE has been added, it will coat all filter vanes with a slurry. Water enters at the top of the filter, surrounds the vanes, and is forced through the DE slurry and surface of each vane. Water is then collected from the center of each filter vane and returned to the pool.

system by pouring the slurry into one of the skimmers with the pump running. This slurry will eventually reach the filter vanes and coat them for proper operation. The amount of DE required is determined by the square foot surface area of the filter vanes in the filter. This amount is usually posted on the filter case (e.g., "This filter contains 57 square feet of filter area and requires four pounds of DE for proper coating."). Failure to properly

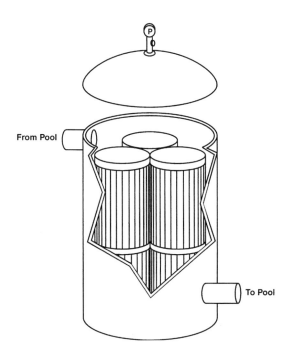

FIGURE 12.6 A cartridge filter usually contains six cartridges, as shown. The water surrounds each cartridge, made of heavy filter paper, and is forced through the filter to the inside. Water is then collected at the bottom of the filter and returned to the pool. The filters must be opened periodically and the cartridges removed, hosed off, and acid washed.

filter cartridge thoroughly cleaned and **acid washed**. (Replacing these filter cartridges can be very expensive).

A Note of Caution Regarding Filter Maintenance

Recent findings have shown that bacteria can grow and thrive on dirty pool filters even though the pool water has the proper levels of disinfectants. Evidently the biomass on a dirty filter offers protection to the bacteria from the chlorine or bromine. In one case, *Legionella bacteria* broke loose from a spa filter and were inhaled by a guest sitting in the spa. The guest developed legionellosis, was permanently incapacitated, and sued the property, winning an $8 million settlement. Properties would be wise to regularly clean and treat their filters with a disinfectant.

The Backwashing Cycle

coat DE filters may cause improper operation and early breakdown of filter vanes.

A third type of filter available but seldom seen in hotels is the **cartridge filter**. This filter's construction is similar to that of the others, but it contains six or more paper cartridges that are stacked inside (see Figure 12.6). Although no backwashing is required, this filter must be opened periodically and each

As indicated earlier, both the ES and the DE filters must be backwashed when system pressure indicates the need. Both systems have some form of backwashing valves (Figure 12.7) that indicate how a **reversed water flow** is created, which in turn forces the discharge of the residue into the sewer system. Figure 12.7 shows how this reversal is made to occur.

A. Setup for Normal Operations

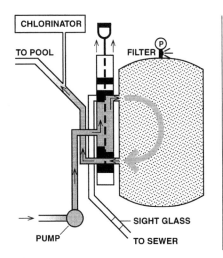

B. Setup for Backwash

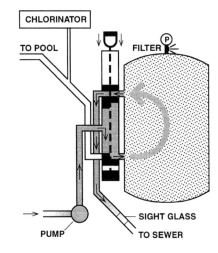

FIGURE 12.7 The backwashing cycle. The backwash valve has the capability to reverse the flow of water through the filter. When backwashing is in operation, water does not return to the pool but is pumped to the sewer, passing the sight glass. Backwash continues until the water passing the sight glass is clear.

TABLE 12.1   pH Levels

			Acidic					Neutral		Alkaline					
pH	5.6	5.8	6.0	6.2	6.4	6.6	6.8	7.0	7.2	7.4	7.6	7.8	8.0	8.2	8.4

Best Range for
Chlorine Function

The Spa

A spa is nothing more than a small pool with no skimmer. Water usually flows over a **spa dam** into the main pool if they are connected. And if not, they have two separate plumbing systems. Otherwise, plumbing valves allow the main drain and the water inlet to be directed either at the main pool or the spa. Temperatures should not be allowed to exceed 103°F, and warning signs should be present, advising guests about overexposure to the heat and recommending that another person be present when someone is in the spa.

Water Chemistry

Although keeping the pool water clear and inviting is part of the challenge, water chemistry is quite another matter and certainly of equal importance. The chemical safety of water for swimming purposes requires the control of harmful bacteria that may be present in the water.

Chlorine is one of two agents that can be used for the purpose of sanitizing the water, and bromine is the other. Both agents do relatively the same thing, but chlorine is more apt to have a distinctive odor at times, which can annoy some bathers. Bromine has less odor but is considerably more expensive to use. Proportions of each may also be relatively different, therefore the rest of this discussion will relate to the use of chlorine. To be **bacterially safe**, pool water must contain at least two parts per million (2 ppm) of free (dissolved) chlorine (**by volume**) if harmful bacteria are to be rendered harmless.

THE GOOD AND BAD EFFECTS OF CHLORINE

The solution of chlorine in water is not hard to attain, but it is extremely hard to maintain without close attention to detail. The good effects of chlorine cannot be attained without also assuming some of its bad effects.

The good effect gained by 2 ppm of **free chlorine** is easily lost as a result of *light*, *heat*, and *agitation*. Direct sunlight, air temperature of about 85°F, and people splashing around in the water can quickly lower the chlorine to an unacceptable level. Therefore, chlorine levels should be elevated to 6 ppm at the beginning of the day. The water should then be monitored throughout the day and more chlorine should be added to ensure a minimal level of 2 ppm at all times.

THE UPS AND DOWNS OF THE (PH) OF WATER

The neutral pH of water is 7. At less than 7, water is acidic; at greater than 7, the water is **alkaline** (a base). Adding a gallon of chlorine to the pool water has the effect of adding a pound of salt, which tends to raise its pH, making the water more alkaline. The bad effect of adding chlorine to water occurs when we continue to add chlorine and the pH continues to climb.

Table 12.1 shows the pH of **chemically pure water** with a value of 7, and indicates the ideal range at which the pH should be for chlorine to work its greatest good (7.4 to 7.6). As the pH increases above 7.6, and the optimum working range of chlorine is exceeded, acid must be added to reduce the pH. There are tables that indicate how much acid to add, based on the pH differential and the size of the pool in gallons of water. The significance of this balancing act is that the right 2 ppm of chlorine must be maintained along with the proper pH of 7.4 to 7.6. This is difficult to do when correction of one value throws off the other.

MAINTAINING PROPER RECORDS

The aforementioned difficulties with pool water chemistry indicate the need for measurements to be taken and recorded at several times of the day. At the end of the swim day (9:00 P.M.) the chlorine count will probably be low, and so will agitation and lighting. A measured amount of chlorine should be added through the night. At the 8:00 A.M. reading, the chlorine count should have recovered well above 2 ppm, but acid will probably now be required. This acid (**muriatic** or **hydrochloric**) should be added by pouring alongside the deep end of the pool. No one should be in the pool when acid is being added. This acid should become well dispersed in about 30 minutes and definitely before the pool opens at about 10:00 A.M.

Health inspectors normally inspect the records maintained by the personnel of the pool department. When they see that people are having trouble trying to maintain balance in their water chemistry, they will usually lend a hand in achieving the proper balance. Should such records not be found, your pool will probably be closed, which would be embarrassing.

Other telltale characteristics of the chemical condition of the water are:

Sides and bottom slimy (people slip and can't stand up in the pool)—water is too alkaline, and prone to form black algae.

Sides and bottom feel rough—water is too acidic; pool finish is being etched away. Look for possible pump damage because of acid action.

POOL TEST KITS

These are small test kits that can be purchased in any supermarket or pool supply store, are self-explanatory as to their use, and provide the user with a small amount of **reagents (orthotolodine** and **phenol red)**, which can test for chlorine content in the water and for proper pH. A test can also be made for the **total hardness** of the water. This test measures the increasing hardness of water as you continue to add chlorine. As total hardness approaches 1000 gm/mL, it may become necessary to drain the pool halfway, then refill the remaining half with fresh (less hardened water). High total hardness can herald the formation of "rock" in pipes and on corners and fixtures in the pool and a possible onset of black algae. High total hardness and black algae are the only two reasons that a pool should ever have to be drained.

About Algae

Algae is an **organic growth**, unpleasant to look at but not harmful to humans. Usually there are three types of algae that can attack the pool, commonly known as green, brown, and black algae. Conditions that must exist before algae can exist are **spores** in the water, light, heat (temperature above 85°F), and pH (above 8.5). But where do the spores come from? They are in the air and are carried on the wind. If there is a rainshower, just consider that those raindrops have gathered spores and dumped them into your pool. They will remain there and never be seen until the mentioned conditions are right, at which point the spores will **bloom**. This is not a pretty sight and can occur before your eyes in a moment's time. Usually the water will **flash green** and become cloudy as

you watch it happen. These algae will adhere to the sides of an alkaline pool and may later turn brown. This is prevented by using an **algicide** *before* it happens. If you did not prevent it, add an algicide immediately, stabilize your water chemistry, and commence brushing the sides of the pool. Green and brown algae are easily removed by brushing, but the residue must be filtered and vacuumed out of the pool. To quickly stabilize the water, you can **shock** the pool with a concentrated treatment of chlorine (65[per] **calcium hypochlorite**), but you must close the pool for several days after this treatment to allow the shock treatment to do its job. The water will cloud up heavily, then clear, after which you must vacuum the residue off the bottom of the pool.

Black algae is the worst enemy. It tends to form in cracks and small pits in the finish of the pool when everything else seems under control. It is extremely difficult to remove and keep out of the pool. It may require that you drain the pool and acid wash the sides, but in the long run, this is detrimental to the pool finish. Early detection of black algae is a must, and concentrated localized shock treatment can keep it in check. Usually it must be *dug out* of its nesting place.

Chloramines

Sometimes guests may complain about the "amount of chlorine" in the water and that their eyes burn because it is so bad. In a clean pool, chlorine dissolves in water and has no odor. What the guest is smelling is not free chlorine in the water, but chloramines. Chloramine is a chemical combination of chlorine and organic material. Leaves, skin oils, urine, and other organic material combine with chlorine to cause the heavy smell of chlorine. The solution, again, is the shock treatment—65 percent calcium hypochlorite. This will cause the closing of the pool until the level of chlorine recedes to no more than 6 ppm.

Pool Equipment

As opposed to pool components, the following is a list of *equipment* that should be available at poolside:

Brush (with pole)
Surface skimmer net (with pole)
Vacuum (with pole and hose)
Garden hose (for washing down pool decks)
Shepherd's hook (for safety)
Life ring (use caution if it is thrown)
Pool rules and regulations (usually a state requirement)
Fencing around pool (in accordance with state codes)

About Diving Boards

❧

Most diving boards are being removed from small hotel pools because they are considered a hazard. Prudent operators studying the law can easily note negligence cases brought against hotel operators in which guests have been injured because of diving accidents. The depth of water at major resorts with sizable pools and attending lifeguards may be able to preclude this hazard, but in general the trend is increasingly toward the pool without the diving board.

Staffing (Using Lifeguards or Pool Attendants)

❧

A lifeguard or pool attendant should be qualified as a **Senior Red Cross Life Saver** and/or **Water Safety Instructor**. There should be no person identified with the pool activity who is not qualified to save a life or perform **CPR**. As to the job title of this person, there is some concern. This writer believes that hotel swimming pools are for the relaxation of guests, who should not be led to believe that the swimming pool area is a place to abdicate responsibility for their own safety. Signage such

as "Pool Open—No Lifeguard on Duty—Swim at Your Own Risk" is reasonable. If you announce that you have a lifeguard on duty, then you must have a person who does nothing but sit on the perch and wait for someone to get in trouble. If, however, you have no lifeguard on duty, but you do have one or more pool attendants, they can perform as lifesavers if necessary, but they can also be performing other duties such as keeping the pool deck neat, orderly, and free of glasses; providing towels and plastic containers where necessary; and being good hosts. An advertised lifeguard on duty increases the hotel's liability in the event of a drowning or severe accident.

Major resorts with large pools, diving activities, sliding boards, and other games have little choice but to provide lifeguards. It is generally expected at a resort, but not in small hotels.

Staffing of a pool should be sufficient to carry out morning preactivities before the pool opens (water testing and adjusting) and to maintain the proper balance during the day, maintaining log entries on water chemistry. The log should also note any unusual circumstances or activities.

It should be remembered that swimming pools have been the basis of many accidental happenings for which the hotel has been found negligent in its operations. It is hoped that this caveat will be valuable in future pool operations.

CONCLUSION

On many occasions, swimming pools are brought under the purview of the executive housekeeper. When breakdowns occur, the maintenance department must repair or replace as necessary. However, the operation and management of the pool and recreation areas are usually part of the housekeeping operations because they primarily represent a cleaning and servicing type of operation.

The objectives of pool operation must include water clarity, water chemistry control, zero algae growth, and being properly equipped and properly staffed for safe operations. The pool nomenclature was discussed, as were the various components of the pool itself. Control of the safety of the water (chemistry) is considered

an operational function and must be maintained and recorded several times daily to ensure that the water is kept chemically safe to swim in and that the pH balance is maintained in a specified, limited range.

Algae must be foreseen and properly controlled, as should the condition of the pool areas in general. The use of diving boards at small hotel pools is questionable and should be considered a safety hazard.

Pools should be properly equipped for the work that must be done. Staffing should favor the use of pool attendants as opposed to lifeguards. Lifeguards are to be expected at major resort pools that are equipped with diving boards, slides, and other play equipment.

KEY TERMS AND CONCEPTS

Matching Principle	Wage dollar-hours	Pool Supervisor
Repair	Operating engineer	Lifeguards
Maintenance	Senior lifeguard	Inlet jets
Operation	Pool attendants	Internal piping system

Fill water	Degree of filtration	Reagents
Closed liquid loop	Solid particulates	Orthotolodine
Regulating valve	Airborne spores	Phenol red
Trap basket	Filter vanes	Total hardness
Positive	Diatomaceous earth	Organic growth
Return lines	Slurry	Spores
Negative	Cartridge filter	Bloom
Vacuum pressure	Acid washed	Flash green
Filter tank	Reversed water flow	Algicide
Circulating system	Spa dam	Shock
Normal operating pressure	Bacterially safe	Calcium hypochlorite
Particulate matter	By volume	Black algae
Liquid loop	Free chlorine	Shepherd's hook
Btu	Alkaline	Senior Red Cross Life Saver
Chlorinating agent	Chemically pure water	Water Safety Instructor
Bromine	Muriatic	CPR
Vacuum foot	Hydrochloric	

DISCUSSION AND REVIEW QUESTIONS

1. Explain the need for, and the technique for, backwashing a pool. What is the purpose of the sight glass in the backwashing procedure?
2. Pool water looks great, chlorine content is good, pH is balanced, but total hardness is exceeding 1,000 g/mL. What is happening? What do you do about it?
3. Discuss the pros and cons of having lifeguards versus pool attendants on the pool staff.

CHAPTER 13

Housekeeping in Other Venues

After studying the chapter, students should be able to:

1. Identify all terms and definitions related to hospital and nursing home housekeeping.
2. Identify common pathogenic organisms, types of soil, and common disinfectants.
3. Describe methods of handling infectious linen and other contaminated articles, and how to dispose of infectious waste.
4. Describe how to properly administer pest control operations.
5. Describe the role the Joint Commission on Accreditation of Health Care Organizations in the establishment of standards for environmental services departments.
6. Describe the role of housekeeping in meeting environmental challenges in the twenty-first century.
7. List and describe other employment and business opportunities for executive housekeepers.

Environmental Services: Nature of the Profession

The **International Executive Housekeepers Association (IEHA)** has long recognized the similarity in responsibilities of persons performing housekeeping functions in hospitals, hotels, and nursing homes. The association draws its membership not only from hotels, retirement centers, and contract cleaning establishments, but also from hospitals and nursing homes. In addition, the movement of management personnel between these fields is well documented.

When asked how difficult it is for a manager to make the transition in either direction, Don Richie, **Director of Environmental Services**, University Medical Center, Las Vegas, Nevada, stated, "The main function of housekeeping in both areas is to clean rooms and public areas, and to dispose of trash and rubbish. There is only one major difference, however, and that is in hospitals we know exactly what we are walking into, and in hotels, we don't know what we may be dealing with." Herein lies the primary difference in technical training between the executive housekeeper and the environmental services director of a hospital or nursing home.

Although the environmental services director may benefit equally with the hotel executive housekeeper by understanding the principles of planning, organizing, staffing, directing, and controlling set forth in the earlier chapters of this book, the **Joint Commission on Accreditation of Health Care Organizations (JCAHO)** has stringent requirements that must be met in the field of environmental services for hospitals and nursing homes. This chapter is devoted to the terminology and definitions encountered in this unique environment and to the requirements set forth by the various agencies that control these issues.

Grateful appreciation is extended to Ms. Janice M. Kurth, vice president of operations, Metropolitan Hospital, New York City, and to Aspen Publications for allowing the use of its publication *Hospital Environmental*

Services Policy and Procedure Manual as a framework for this chapter. Thanks also to the Desert Springs Hospital of Las Vegas, Nevada, for its assistance and access to its procedural manuals.

HOSPITALS AND HOTELS REQUIRE SIMILAR PROFESSIONAL SKILLS

In most cases, the actions required of persons working in hospital environmental service departments are very much the same as the actions required of persons working in hotel housekeeping. After studies are made of the work that must be performed, job descriptions are prepared, indicating the proper divisions of work; then step-by-step guidelines are prepared in the form of *standard operating procedures (SOPs)*. These documents *formalize* procedures that must be performed by workers assigned to specific routines. The uniqueness of hospitals and health-care institutions becomes evident, however, when one investigates the special care and consideration that must be taken when dealing with the following:

- The daily and terminal **disinfection** of patient rooms
- The **terminal cleaning** of hospital surgical suites (operating rooms)
- The disposition of used **needles**, **syringes**, and **sharps**
- The disposal of infectious waste

Each of these procedural tasks will be dealt with in detail; but first a proper groundwork must be laid regarding basic knowledge of **microbiology** and the **chemistry of cleaning and disinfecting**.

"BLOODBORNE PATHOGENS": THE NEWEST CONNECTING LINK

In December 1991, the lodging and hospital professions were brought closer together when the Occupational Safety and Health Administration (OSHA) published a new standard relating to "Occupational Exposure to Bloodborne Pathogens." What at one time had been primarily a concern of hospitals and health-care institutions had now entered the lodging industry as well.

First, some basic definitions: *blood* refers to human blood, blood components such as plasma and transfusional blood, and products made from human blood. *Bloodborne pathogens* are microorganisms present in blood that can cause disease. Other potentially infectious substances may be other human body fluids, such as semen, amniotic fluids, and other body fluids that may be hard to differentiate, and HIV and HBV cultures.

Other governmental agencies have been involved with the issue of employee exposure to infectious materials for some time. For a number of years, the Department of Health and Human Services has written and published *Guidelines for Prevention of Transmission of Human Immunodeficiency Virus and Hepatitis B Virus, That Could Affect Health Care and Public Safety Workers.* Concerns have been varied. First, the publicity of recent years regarding the HIV virus and AIDS awakened concerns among the public and legislators alike regarding the transmission of infectious diseases. In addition, increased attention to employee safety and health has caused the concern regarding exposure to hepatitis B to increase. Finally, OSHA began work preparing a Bloodborne Pathogen Standard. This *standard* became law in 1991, and regulations for industries and professions that might become exposed to HIV and HBV viruses were to have been in compliance with the law by March 1992. The law (29 CFR 1910.1030), since revised, has defined certain words in the lexicon, as follows:

Contaminated: having potentially infectious materials on an item or surface
Regulated Waste: liquid or semiliquid blood or other potentially infectious materials; contaminated items that would release infectious materials if compacted; items that are caked with dried infectious material; contaminated sharps (needles); waste containing infectious materials
Source Individual: an individual whose potentially infectious materials may be a source of exposure
Universal Precaution: the practice of approaching all human blood and other body fluids as if they contain bloodborne pathogens
HIV (human immunodeficiency virus): spreads rapidly; has no known cure and no vaccine; generally leads to the development of AIDS; symptoms may not show for some time
HBV (hepatitis B): the most prevalent form of liver disease; results in inflammation of the liver, cirrhosis, and liver cancer; a vaccine exists that prevents infection
Parenteral Exposure: infectious material entering the body through cuts or abrasions, needle sticks, or bites

All lodging facilities that have departments with a propensity for exposure (housekeeping departments through soiled linen), engineering departments (cuts and abrasions), and security departments are required by law to have an *exposure control program*. This program must address limiting/eliminating exposure through *Universal Precautions* (use of equipment and handling of contaminated waste), *personal work practices*, the use of *protective equipment*, and good housekeeping practices. The program must also deal with the use of warning labels/signs and exposure procedures, and must also establish an HBV vaccination program (which is free to employees). Finally, compliance with the law must be substantiated through good record keeping. As of this writing, the effects of AIDS have been reduced through certain medications, but the basic problems are still with us.

Basic Microbiology*

Microbiology* is a natural science that began with the discovery of the microscope, which led in the seventeenth century to the dramatic realization that living forms exist that are invisible to the naked eye. It had been suggested as early as the thirteenth century that "invisible" organisms were responsible for decay and disease. The word *microbe* was coined in the last quarter of the nineteenth century to describe these organisms, all of which were thought to be related. As microbiology eventually developed into a separate science, microbes (small living things) were found to constitute a very large group of extremely diverse organisms—thus the subdivision of the discipline into three parts, known today as bacteriology, protozoology, and virology.

Microbiology, therefore, is the study and identification of **microorganisms**. Such study encompasses the study of bacteria, rickettsiae, small fungi (such as yeasts and molds), algae, and protozoans, as well as problematical forms of life such as viruses. Because of the difficulty in assigning plant or animal status to some microorganisms—some are plantlike, others animal-like—they are sometimes considered to be a separate group called **protists**. Microbes can also be divided into prokaryotes, which have a primitive and dispersed kind of nuclear material—such as the blue-green algae, bacteria, and rickettsiae—and eukaryotes, which display a distinct nucleus bounded by a membrane. These are the small algae other than the blue-greens, yeasts and molds, and protozoans. (All higher organisms are eukaryotes.)

The daily life of humans is interwoven with microorganisms. They are found in the soil, in the sea, and in the air. Although unnoticed, they are abundant everywhere and provide ample evidence of their presence, sometimes unfavorably, as when they cause decay in objects valued by humans or generate disease, and sometimes favorably, as when they ferment alcohol to wine and beer, raise bread, flavor cheeses, and create other dairy products. Microorganisms are of incalculable value in nature, causing the disintegration of animal and plant remains and converting them into gases and minerals that can be recycled in other organisms.

It might be said that approximately 90 percent of all microorganisms are good and essential to nature and humankind. Our concern in this text, however, is the 10 percent that are not.

---

*Adapted with permission from the introduction to "Microbiology," *Encyclopaedia Britannica*, 15th edition, 1979, by Encyclopaedia Britannica.

TERMINOLOGY APPROPRIATE TO THE SUBJECT OF MICROBIOLOGY

What follows is a list of specific microorganisms worthy of our concern. Some are represented here as if they were properly stained and seen under a microscope at 500 × magnification.

Bacteria: used to refer to microorganisms in general; also, the same as germs and/or microbes

Bacillus: a rod-shaped bacterium

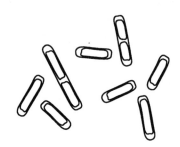

Coccus: a round bacterium

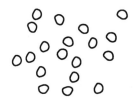

Fungi: simple plants lacking chlorophyll; bread mold is an example.

Spirochete: corkscrew-shaped microorganism

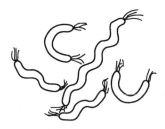

Spores: microorganisms that are in a restive, protective shell

Staphylococcus: agrapelike cluster organism that can cause boils, skin infections, purulent discharge, and/or peritonitis

Streptococcus: a chainlike round organism that causes the strep throat infection

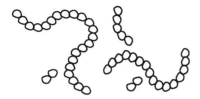

Virus: the smallest of all microorganisms

Other words significant to the study of microbiology include the following:

Aerobic: bacteria that must be exposed to, and require, air (oxygen) to survive and grow

Anaerobic: bacteria that can live without exposure to air (oxygen)

Antisepsis: a process whereby chemicals are used on the skin for bacteriostatic and germicidal purposes

Asepsis: to be free from germs and infection

Asepsis *(medical):* a method used to prevent the spread of a communicable disease; hand washing and isolation are examples.

Asepsis *(surgical):* a method using sterile equipment, supplies, and procedures when entering the sterile interior of the body

Autoclave: an ovenlike machine, using steam under pressure, in which supplies are subjected to intense heat for a specified period of time; also called a sterilizer

Chemical agent: a chemical added to a solution in the correct dosage that will kill bacteria, or at least stop their growth

Disinfection: process whereby chemicals are used on floors and equipment for bacteriostatic and germicidal purposes

Disinfection *(concurrent):* process used while disease is still in progress

Disinfection *(terminal):* process used when disease is ended

Gram(positive/negative): refers to the color staining of test samples for certain bacteria. *Gram positive* is a "blue" test result when certain bacteria are treated with testing reagents. *Gram negative* is a "red" test indication.

Intermediate host: one who transmits a disease but is not affected by it; also known as an "immune carrier." An example is the anopheles mosquito, which bites a person infected with malaria, then bites another person, thus transmitting the disease.

Micron: a unit of measure, 1/25,000 of 1 inch. (Bacteria are usually found in the range of 1 to 300 microns.)

Pathogenic: disease-causing or disease-producing

Physical agents: nonchemical agents that will affect the growth of bacteria or will destroy them.

Examples of nonchemical agents are sunlight, temperature, heat, moisture, and pressure.

Reagents: a group of testing solutions used to identify certain bacteria and their properties. Such tests can help determine which chemicals should be used to kill certain bacteria.

Sterilization: a process whereby all bacteria are killed by heat

SEVERAL SPECIFIC MICROORGANISMS AND THEIR CHARACTERISTICS

The following is a list of 11 common microorganisms with which one might come in contact while working in a hospital, nursing home, or hotel. The phonetic pronunciation of the name and several characteristics are also given.

1. *Clostridium perfringens* (clos-TRID-ee-um per-FRIN-gins): no gram stain; an anaerobic spore.;"botulism"; found in feces, sewers, improperly sterilized milk, or sealed foods; also found in untreated wounds (gaseous gangrene)

2. *Diplococcus pneumoniae* (dip-lo-COCK-us new-MOAN-ee-a): gram positive lobar (lung) pneumonia. Also walking pneumonia. Treatable with antibiotics.

3. *Escherichia coli* (ee-shear-EEK-ee-ah COAL-i): gram negative; can grow in soap; never use bar soap in a public washroom. Bacteria can be spread through animal droppings.

4. *Mycobacterium* diphtheria (my-co-back-TEER-ee-um dif-THEE-ree-ah): gram positive; transmitted in milk; not very prevalent because of vaccination

5. *Mycobacterium tuberculosis* (my-co-back-TEER-ee-um too-BER-cue-LOW-sis): gram negative (red stain); acid-fast (cannot be killed with acid)

6. *Pseudomonas aeruginosa* (sue-doe-MOAN-us air-o-gin-O-sa): gram negative; very resistant to disinfectants; bacteria will grow in standing water; major problems are public restrooms; disease is more prevalent in women

7. *Salmonella choleraesuis* (sal-moe-NELL-a coll-er-ah-SUE-iss): gram negative; a form of food poisoning; body can usually tolerate and throw off; the bacteria are used to test germicides.

8. *Streptococcus pyogenes* (strep-tow-COCK-us pie-O-jeans): gram positive; Bacteria found in public places; cause wound and throat infections. Also associated with scarlet fever and rheumatic fever.

9. *Staphylococcus aureus* (staff-ill-i-COCK-us OAR-ea-us): gram positive (blue stain); size: 0.8 to 1 micron; major cause of infections (boils, carbuncles, ear infections), food poisoning; resistant to antibiotics; best cure is heat

10. *Tricophyton interdigitale* (tri-CO-fi-ton inter-digit-ALL-ee): no gram stain; a fungus (athlete's foot). The fungus can be used to evaluate a germicidal.
11. *Virus*: A part of the protist kingdom; includes influenza (flu virus), herpes simplex, vaccinia (cowpox), adenovirus type 2, Norovirus, SARS, HBV, and HIV

The Five Types of Soil

There are five types of soil that present the environmental service manager, or anyone with the responsibility to "clean," with a challenge. Not all soils are directly and solely bacteria-related, but we shall keep bacteria on the list. Each soil, regardless of whether it is organic or inorganic, is a compound capable of being altered by chemical reaction.

The following are the five types of soil:

1. **Mineral:** A solid homogeneous crystalline chemical element or compound, having a specific chemical composition, that results from the inorganic processes of nature.
2. **Organic:** A substance consisting only of matter or products of plant or animal origin. Chemically, such substances are compounds containing strings of carbon molecules attached to one or more hydrogen molecules.
3. **Osmological:** Relating to soils of organic or inorganic matter that emit an (unpleasant) odor.
4. **Bacterial:** Soils or compounds containing active (live) bacteria.
5. **Entomological:** Soils involving insects, especially those that can cause or carry diseases.

The Chemistry of Cleaning*

To understand the chemistry of cleaning, the student must first accept the fact that he or she need *not* become a chemist to do a cleaning job well. Having a layperson's understanding of what is happening as we apply a disinfectant or detergent can give us respect for the value of using products for the purposes for which they are designed. Too often, employees "assume" that something *red* will clean better than something *blue*, that a *thick* solution must be better than a *watery* one, or, most often, that *more* is *better*. This section, although presenting no **chemical formulas**, does require the student to master a new group of terms and, it is hoped, to develop a respect for what has gone into the several products currently

---

*Adapted with permission of the Administration, Desert Springs Hospital, Las Vegas, Nevada.

in use in the world of cleaning and disinfecting. The chemistry of cleaning is most appropriate in this section because we are not only cleaning (i.e., removing soil), we are also killing bacteria (disinfecting).

What follows is a brief discussion of lay chemistry for the professional, who might then better understand the history and significance of product development.

Atom According to the Periodic Table of Elements, an **atom** is the smallest combination of nucleus (center core of protons and neutrons) and surrounding electrons associated with a given named element. For example, an atom of sulfur (S), oxygen (O), hydrogen (H), or carbon (C) is the smallest particle that is recognizable by that name. All atoms have different "weights," hydrogen being the lightest and uranium one of the heaviest, because of their respective atomic structures. More than 106 elements have been discovered in the universe. Some of them do not even occur naturally but have been created by humans in only the last century.

Molecule A **molecule** is a compound created by combining a certain group of atoms. Many of the atoms described here when found in nature are seen as molecules that will combine with other molecules to form more complex chemical compounds. For example, chemically speaking, atoms of hydrogen (H) or oxygen (O), in nature are found as gaseous molecules of hydrogen (H_2) oxygen (O_2). The associated suffix number or describes certain characteristics as to how they react chemically when combined with each other or with other elements. Their "chemical" reactions are based on many different phenomena, but primarily on how many free electrons are found in their outer rings of electrons. A molecule having the same number of protons in its nucleus as it has electrons in orbit around the nucleus would have an electrical charge of 0 (zero **valence**). If there is an excess of protons in the nucleus, a positive charge of $+1$ or $+2$ exists (positive valence); if there are more electrons than protons, then the charge would be negative (-1 or -2, negative valence). The combination of valence plus the "type" of atom being considered determines how difficult, easy, violent, or modest the reaction will be as we try to combine molecules of atoms with other molecules to form more elaborate compounds. Each single molecule of water is made up of two atoms of hydrogen and one atom of oxygen. The smallest atom of hydrogen found in nature is a gaseous molecule of hydrogen (H_2). The smallest molecule of oxygen found in nature is gaseous oxygen (O_2). Under certain conditions, igniting hydrogen in the presence of oxygen causes a violent explosion, with a by-product of water. To keep the accounting correct, one molecular formula is mentioned to show that things do balance. For example, two molecules of gaseous hydrogen, $2H_2(g)$, will chemically combine with one molecule of gaseous oxygen O2(g), to form two molecules of liquid water, 2H2O(l).

Some molecules, particularly those in biological systems and plastics, are very large and contain thousands of atoms.

CHEMICAL COMPOUNDS

Chemical reactions are also called chemical transformations. They entail the conversion of one or more substances into one or more different substances called **compounds**. The substances that react are called **reactants**, and the results of the reaction are called **products**.

In a chemical reaction, atoms are regrouped to form different substances; atoms are not destroyed or converted into atoms of other elements (as one might find in **atomic reactions**). Cleaning chemicals are designed to chemically combine with specific types of soil. The chemical products are then removed chemically, clinging to the soil to be removed.

The following is a list of some basic terms relevant to chemical reactions:

Acid: a compound in which a majority of anions, either atoms or radicals, are combined with the cation hydrogen ($H^+ +$)

Alcohols: methanol, ethanol, isopropanol; function similarly to quaternary ammonium compounds in method of action.

Alkali: a catonic metal combined with the anionic hydroxyl (OH) radical known chemically as a hydroxide of the metal. Alkalis combine with acids to form *water* and *salts*.

Anion: an atom containing a negative electrical charge

Antiseptics: substances that slow bacterial growth; includes both iodine and **alcohols**

Bacteriostat: prevents bacteria from multiplying; an antibiotic (not for consumption, but for use in such places as laundries)

Cation: an atom containing a positive electrical charge

Detergent: a synthetic organic soap, either oil or water soluble, derived from hydrocarbons, petroleum, alcohols, amines, sulfonates, or other organic compounds

Disinfectant: compound that kills bacteria. Most chemical agents that have been created for use in cleaning *and* disinfecting fall into the *quaternary ammonium* or the **phenolic** category. They both destroy pathogenic bacteria.

Hydrogen peroxide: an unstable compound, H_2O_2, used as an oxidizing and bleaching agent, an antiseptic, and a propellant. It breaks down into water and oxygen, making it a very environmentally friendly product.

Iodine: a highly reactive element, which makes it a highly effective disinfectant with a broad spectrum of efficiency

Ion: an atom or group of atoms that has acquired an electrical charge by a gain or loss of electrons

Organic compounds: compounds made up of carbon, hydrogen, and oxygen

pH: a measure of the acidity or alkalinity of a substance. A scale from 0 to 14 is used, with 7 as the neutral point. All substances with a measured pH more than 7 are *alkaline*; less than 7, and the product is *acidic*.

Phenol: carbolic acid

Phenolic: derivations of phenol widely used as disinfectants. Long carbon chains are attached to a precise position on the phenol molecule; one thousand times more active than pure phenol.

Preservatives: used in foods to inhibit bacterial growth

Quaternary ammonium compounds: A class of disinfectants that are cationic surface-active agents containing nitrogen, long carbon chains (Rs), and an anion, usually chlorine

R: the letter used to identify a long carbon group of some known chain length or configuration of a chemical compound

Radical: a group of atoms that do not dissociate during a chemical reaction but stay together. The following are common radicals:

(OH) Hydroxide	(NO_3) Nitrate
(SO_4) Sulfate	(PO_4) Phosphate
(NH_4) Ammonium	(CO_3) Carbonate

Salts: result when the hydrogen ion of an acid is replaced with a metal

Sanitizer: normally used in food areas and to chemically treat filters in air-handling units

Water: the **universal solvent** (usually the first liquid tried when testing a substance to see if it can be dissolved into a solution)

Familiarization with the various aspects of chemical usage in both health-care institutions and hotels requires a basic understanding of chemicals and of the chemical process. The wise director of environmental services knows and understands the chemical products being used at his or her facility and how to use them.

PRODUCT TESTING

There are several tests that can determine the efficiency and effectiveness of a product. The Association of Analytical Chemists (AOAC) can also test products both for the manufacturer and the user.

A typical test is to prepare several **Petri test dishes** (small flat, round dishes with a nourishing gelatin [host]), which can be daubed with a swab containing the bacteria to be tested. First the bacteria are given a period of time to grow. Then the bacteria are treated with differing dilutions of a germicidal product. The goal of the test is to determine at what **dilution ratio** the product kills a bacterium. Further tests might be done to determine how long it takes for a given germicidal to kill bacteria at a set dilution, or to determine the effects of adding certain products to increase the efficiency of a certain germicidal.

The Product Manufacturer and the Chemical Challenge

The challenge to the product manufacturer becomes obvious: to determine what product can first clean, then disinfect. Inorganic cleaning can be as simple as sweeping dust from the floor, picking it up, and disposing of it in such a way that it will not find its way back into a space. The products available in supermarkets most often exploit certain chemicals that will loosen "soil," hold it in **chemical suspension**, and then pick up the suspension by a number of different means and dispose of it.

A disinfectant, however, adds an additional challenge: not only to clean, but to enter the membrane of the bacterial cell and kill the bacterial nucleus.

CARBOLIC ACID (PHENOL)

Carbolic acid (phenol) was, for years, the best killer of bacteria available for disinfecting an area. However, the compound required extended periods of contact with the area to be disinfected. In addition, whereas phenol would kill bacteria, it was not a good cleaning agent.

With the development of phenolic (a derivative of phenol), the disinfectant became 1000 times more effective at entering the protective membranes of bacteria and killing them. However, it continues to be a poor cleaning agent, and it is a highly **toxic** material. The normal dilution ratio for this product is 256 to 1 ($\frac{1}{2}$ ounce in one gallon of water).

QUATERNARY AMMONIUM COMPOUNDS

In addition to being effective antibacterial agents, quaternary ammonium compounds are good cleaning agents. They are also highly toxic, however, and for years these compounds had one additional drawback as a disinfectant: they were ineffective against the tuberculosis bacteria. Recent progress in the development of quaternaries has conquered the tuberculosis problem, and these compounds have since become the disinfectants of choice in hospitals. However, when diluted, they have been shown to support certain bacterial growth, such as Pseudomonas.

HYDROGEN PEROXIDE

Hydrogen peroxide, or H_2O_2, has long been recognized as an effective oxidant and has occupied a place in almost every home's bathroom as a hair bleaching agent and a topical antiseptic. Recent research has significantly improved its stability and disinfectant properties. In high concentrations, hydrogen peroxide can be toxic, but the beauty of hydrogen peroxide is that it will eventually break down to harmless water and oxygen. One day, this may be the chemical of choice for sanitizing and disinfecting surfaces.

Nonchemical Agents That Kill or Slow Bacterial Growth

Light is an excellent killer of bacteria as long as they are on the surface of an object or on the skin. Sunlight and ultraviolet light are excellent sanitizers but do not penetrate beyond the surface of an object or the skin.

Cold does not kill but slows and inhibits growth; in some cases bacteria will go dormant because of cold.

Heat kills bacteria. A steam sterilizer is vital for sterilizing equipment. In cases where human tissue is involved, contact time of heat is important.

Physical removal by use of air filters and electrostatic filters is significant. Also, vacuuming and simply wiping can remove bacteria.

A Controlled Bacterial Environment

A controlled bacterial environment is an environment that is kept clean and bug-free and has garbage properly disposed of. In addition, covered storage is needed, garbage handlers should wear gloves, and steps should be taken to prevent all forms of pollution.

To prevent the spread of infection, facilities must be kept clean and healthy. Disease is spread through **bacteria trails**. The following chain of events is seen as the bacteria trail. The **chain of infection** starts with a *pathogenic causative agent*. Next is the *reservoir*, or place for the **pathogen** to live, followed by the *mode of escape, method of transmission*, and *mode of entry into the host*. The person is the host who passes the pathogen, and the chain continues. Break the chain of events at any point, and the infection is stopped.

THE ISOLATION UNIT

Figure 13.1 shows the layout of an **isolation unit** in a major hospital. Note how the isolation cart contains a

The Isolation Unit

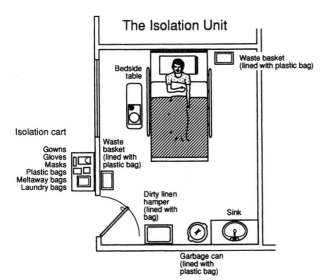

FIGURE 13.1 Layout of an isolation unit.

supply of gowns, gloves, masks, plastic bags, meltaway bags, and laundry bags. Inside the unit are various methods and locations to dispose of isolation clothing prior to coming out of the room.

CONTAMINATED ARTICLES AND EXCRETA

For some patients in isolation, it is necessary to take special precautions with articles contaminated by urine or feces. For example, it may be necessary to disinfect (or discard) a bedpan with the excreta.

Terminal Cleaning and Disinfecting the Surgical Suite

✂

The purpose of cleaning and disinfecting a surgical suite is to reduce the number of microorganisms present and thereby maintain a clean, safe environment for patients, staff, and visitors.

The necessary equipment must first be assembled:

A 10-quart plastic bucket for washing furniture
Cloths for damp wiping, wet and dry
Disinfectant/detergent
Spray tanks for applying solution to floors
Water vacuums to pick up solution
Floor machine with scrub pad
Wall-washing equipment (includes bucket, wringer, mop handle, and mop heads)

The suite-cleaning procedure would then include the following:

1. Prepare, clean, and check all equipment.
2. Prepare disinfectant solution and place in the spray tank, wall-washing unit, and 10-quart bucket.

3. Proceed to the first assigned surgical suite; clean and disinfect the bed/table and damp wipe every surface with the disinfecting/cleaning agent.
4. Using a similar technique, disinfect all furniture (ring stands, kick buckets, tables, and other pieces of rolling equipment), moving them to the middle of the room around the table/bed. Rinse each item with a hand cloth after damp wiping.
5. Disinfect all wall-hanging fixtures, being careful not to get solution inside or behind humistats, thermostats, X-ray screens, sterile cabinet doors, or electrical outlets.
6. Spray disinfectant solution on the floor; use a water vacuum to pick up solution. Leave a 12-inch wet strip close to and around the furniture that is still in the middle of the room.
7. Replace the furniture, being sure to roll the wheels through the 12-inch wet strip to disinfect them. Then roll the bed/table through the solution to one side of the room.
8. Clean the light fixture in the same way the furniture was cleaned.
9. Spray solution on the floor in the middle of the suite. Use the wet vacuum to pick up all remaining solution.
10. Return the table/bed to its proper place.
11. Retire from the suite and thoroughly clean all equipment with disinfectant/detergent. Store equipment properly or proceed to the next surgical suite and repeat the procedure.

SPECIAL CONCERNS

1. There should be no spraying of solutions close to sterile carts.
2. Corridors, ceilings, and walls should be disinfected monthly. Spot wash as needed.
3. Cubicle curtains in the recovery area or elsewhere in the surgical theater should be changed monthly, or sooner as needed.

In the following article, David Holsinger offers two simple steps that are necessary to ensure a successful infection control program in a number of different environments, ranging from hospitals to schools.

Disposition of Used Needles, Syringes, and "Sharps"

✂

It is essential to ensure that used sharp objects such as needles, syringes, and sharps (i.e., sharp plastic cases in which needles and disposable scalpels are placed for disposal) are carefully and safely removed from

TWO STEPS TO A SAFE WORK ENVIRONMENT

by David Holsinger

This article is presented through the generosity of ProTeam Inc., a Boise, Idaho, manufacturer of backpack vacuum systems and sponsor of Team Cleaning Seminars.

Accumulation of microbial contaminants on environmental surfaces is a major concern in maintaining a safe environment in hospitals, clinics, dental offices, nursing homes, child day-care centers, and schools. The build up of microorganisms on desktops, phones, chairs, door knobs, light switch plates, beds, and bedside tables creates a potential source of nosocomial infections (an infection that was not present or incubating at the time of admission to a health-care facility).

A crucial tool in any cleaning program is a hospital approved germicidal detergent. The primary purposes of this product is to disinfectant and stop the spread of microbes that cause life-threatening disease such as HIV (human immunodeficiency virus), hepatitis, MRSA (methicillin-resistant *Staphylococcus aureus*) and VRE (vancomycin-resistant enterococcus).

Two steps are vital to a successful infection control program:

1. Following appropriate guidelines in selecting a germicidal detergent
2. Ensuring an environment that does not inactivate the disinfecting process or contribute to the spread of microorganisms

When selecting a germicidal detergent consider its use, efficacy, acceptability, and safety for the intended environment. The following guidelines will help you in this process:

1. Ensure the product has been Registered with the Environmental Protection Agency (EPA) and has a registration number on the label.
2. The product must be germicidal or effective against *Staphylococcus aureus*, *Salmonella choleraesuis*, *Pseudomonas aeruginosa*, VRE, and MRSA; fungicidal or effective against *Trichophyton entagrophytes*; mycobactericidal, or effective against *M. tuberculosis*; and virucidal or effective against influenza, herpes simplex, and vaccinia.
3. It must be effective against stated organisms when diluted with hard water to a level of 400 ppm calcium carbonate. The product must also work in either hot or cold water.
4. The germicide must be effective against target organisms in the presence of some organic matter, specifically 5 percent blood serum (organic substances tend to deactivate disinfectants).
5. It should have a pH factor between 7 and 9. A pH of 10.5 or more is highly alkaline and may damage floor finishes and other surfaces.
6. Determine the safety of the product by reading the Material Safety Data Sheet (MSDS) for the following information:
   a. Name of chemical
   b. Health and other hazards
   c. Exposure cautions
   d. What to do when exposure occurs
   e. How to safely handle and store
   f. What to do if a spill occurs
   g. What personal protective equipment (PPE) to wear
   h. How to properly dispose of the chemical

After selecting an appropriate germicidal detergent, consider the environment in which it will be used. Do facility cleaning methods and frequencies prevent the build up of dust and soil on environmental surfaces? This is extremely important for proper disinfection. Dust and soil particles can shield microbes from contact with disinfectants and react with (i.e., inactivate) the cleaning agents. Failure to remove foreign (especially organic) matter from a surface before attempting to disinfect can render germicides ineffective. Plainly, successful disinfecting requires an efficient *cleaning* program.

Of the many cleaning systems utilized in the cleaning industry today, team cleaning (cleaning using specialists) is one to consider. It has proven to work extremely well under intense regulatory scrutiny and meets industry expectations for cost effectiveness. Using specialized cleaning positions focused on specific tasks, team cleaning yields consistent daily cleaning and disinfecting of offices, exam rooms, classrooms, play rooms, restrooms, carpets, and tile floors. Team cleaning uses carefully selected tools to optimize the specialist approach. For example, backpack vacuum cleaners raise productivity, and units with four-stage filtration help facilitate the disinfecting process.

An efficient vacuum filtration system is extremely important in removing dust, soil, and microorganisms from the environment. A vacuum equipped with a HEPA filter (99.97 percent efficient in filtering particles .3 micron and larger in size) in a four-stage configuration will minimize the dispersal of fine dust from the vacuum exhaust. Why is this important? Dust contains dirt, textile fibers, pollen, hair, skin flakes, residue from cleaning chemicals, decaying organic matter, dust mites, bacteria, fungi, and viruses. Microorganisms can travel through the air on dust particles. The removal of airborne fungal spores such as Aspergillus is especially important because they can cause fatal infections in patients with weakened immunity.

Proper vacuum systems will reduce the potential for cross contamination and also minimize allergic reaction to dust in sensitive individuals. Powerful suction-only units such as backpacks not only clean carpet but also allow cleaning hard and resilient floors without using dust mops or brooms, which tend to stir contaminated dust into the air.

Effectively managing the modern cleaning function positively affects the health and well-being of all building occupants. It's very easy to wrongly assume your current germicidal detergent and cleaning program is doing its job. To assure you are meeting customer needs, use appropriate guidelines in selecting a germicidal detergent and review your cleaning program to assure consistent daily cleaning by the environmental services staff. You will be two steps closer to a safer, healthier environment for your employees and customers.

(David Holsinger and Michael Wilford are cofounders of Midas Consulting in Redlands, California. They have 37 years of experience in the health-care industry and pioneered the seven-specialist team cleaning model at a large southern California medical center.
Resources: Association of Professionals in Infection Control and Epidemiology.

the hospital and safely disposed of in such a manner that unsuspecting persons coming in contact with them run little risk of becoming contaminated. The hospital nursing service has primary responsibility in preparing such objects for disposal.

The following procedures should be used:

1. Nursing service personnel—place used syringes found in patient floor-care areas into the plastic disposal containers designated by Nursing Service as "for sharps disposal."
2. Sterilize all sharps containers from patient floor care areas and send to Central Service for collection and disposal.
3. Sterilize containers from Surgery, Emergency Room, Isolations, Respiratory Care, Pulmonary Function, and Nuclear Medicine, and send to Central Service for collection and disposal.
4. Central service personnel—send all sterilized sharps to the laboratory for final disposition.
5. Laboratory personnel—place all needles and syringes into the proper containers; seal them, place in a red plastic bag, and sterilize before final disposal.
6. The laboratory must then ensure that Environmental Services personnel pick up the sterilized sharps and dispose of them with normal refuse.

OSHA announced changes to its Bloodborne Pathogens Standard 29 CFR 1910.1030, which took effect April 18, 2001. These changes were mandated by the Needlestick Safety and Prevention Act. The revisions clarify the need for employers to select safer needle devices as they become available and to involve employees in identifying and choosing the devices. The updated standard also requires employers to maintain a log of injuries from contaminated sharps.

Disposal of Refuse from Antineoplastic Agents

The purpose of safe removal and disposal of waste associated with the preparation and disposal of **antineoplastic agents** is to ensure that unauthorized or unsuspecting personnel will not become contaminated by coming in contact with such agents.

The following procedures should be used:

1. Environmental Services will be responsible for the removal of the sealed trash receptacles marked with a green label as **chemotherapy drugs**. These containers are usually found in the soiled utility rooms on floors where antineoplastic agents are administered.
2. The environmental technician, aide, nurse, or unit secretary will notify Environmental Services when containers are full.
3. A full container will be sealed before it is removed from the soiled utility room by the assigned environmental services technician, who will replace it with an empty container.
4. The full container will be taken to the temporary storage area designated for antineoplastic agents refuse.
5. Containers will be removed periodically by a properly licensed firm authorized to remove such waste.

These procedures are subject to review and periodic inspection by an agent of the Joint Commission.

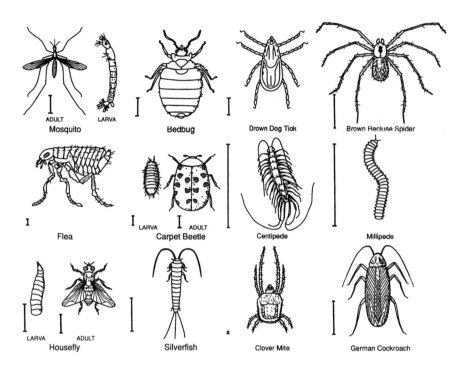

FIGURE 13.2 Twelve common household pests. The line adjacent to each illustration indicates approximate size.

GREEN TIP

Disinfectants kill germs, but if they are not used properly, they can harm people too. When selecting a disinfectant, read the precautionary statements and the Material Safety Data Sheet first. Make sure it is safe to humans if used as directed and will not harm the surfaces you intend to clean. It should be soluble, stable (bleach is not), non-toxic, hypoallergenic, and not a skin or mucous membrane irritant. It should not smell bad, and it should work fairly quickly at low concentrations. It should continue killing pathogens for a reasonable time after it has been applied.

The bad news is that nothing on the market will meet all these requirements, but some are better than others.

Unsatisfactory results of such inspections could form the basis of a "Warning," with notification of action required to maintain "Certification." Unheeded warnings or lack of action to correct may ultimately lead to the suspension of certification.

Pest Control

❧

Insects have been on this earth for millions of years, and most have "weathered the storm" better than any other species. Most have short life spans; they propagate over short spans of time and die, yet the species live on and on.

Figure 13.2 shows 12 of the "garden variety" pests that should be kept under control as much as possible, but not all necessarily for the same reasons. Some insects sting; others live in damp contaminated areas or in human and food waste and can contaminate the human environment. All insects are capable of transmitting bacteria by picking them up on their bodies and legs and then traveling through their domains and infecting everything they touch, whether human or otherwise.

A TRUE SCENARIO

The ordinary wood tick provides a good example of all the elements of the chain of infection. The tick normally originates (propagates) in damp, heavily wooded or vegetated areas. It lies in wait for a warm-blooded animal to pass close enough for it to sense body heat. It then hops (and/or flies) 10 to 15 feet and firmly attaches itself to the animal and begins to siphon blood. This activity continues over a period of several days, during which time the host animal may travel long distances. While a passenger, the tick is exposed to areas heavily contaminated with bacteria through contact with feces and other decomposing tissue (**causative agent**). After several days the tick grows to the size of a human thumbnail (**the reservoir**). The wound area created by the tick's attachment now grows purulent and weak, allowing the weight of the tick to cause it to drop to the ground (**mode of escape**), possibly thousands of miles from its initial location. It winds up carrying not only its supply of blood, which it digests over a period of several days, but also a plethora of bacteria on its body shell (**immune carrier**).

Eventually the tick returns to its original size and again takes up the stalk, lying in wait for the next exposure to the heat of animal warmth (**method of transmission**). Suppose that this time it is a human who becomes the target for the bite of the long-jumping tick (mode of entry into the new **host**). Ten days to two weeks later, the human notices a rash developing on the extremities and commencing to radiate inward to the torso, giving the appearance of measles. What appeared to be measles, however, is not, inasmuch as the recovery time for measles is within ten days from the onset of the rash. Suppose further that upon close examination, a tick is discovered in the hair of the human and the diagnosis is changed to Rocky Mountain spotted fever (tick fever). One day later, the young girl dies in her home in Florida. This true scenario clearly demonstrates how the first animal and the tick may both be immune carriers, and the chain of infection may be discovered thousands of miles from where the sickness is readily suspected—discovered too late for effective treatment.

KEEPING PESTS UNDER CONTROL MEANS MANIPULATING THE ENVIRONMENT

Persons working in environmental services must set goals regarding tasks related to pest control:

1. Keep the area clean.
2. Remove and dispose of all trash frequently and completely.
3. Use screens in areas where insects are prevalent.
4. Keep facilities in a good state of repair.
5. Have a program of chemical pest control to rid *all* the property of all insects.

Using multiple approaches to pest control instead of relying entirely on chemicals is referred to as **Integrated Pest Management**. Several hotels have recently been experiencing a resurgence of bedbugs due to their importation in luggage by international visitors. Typical room eradication can result in the loss of thousands of dollars to the hotel due to the practice of throwing out mattresses, carpets, and upholstered furniture in the infested room and the corresponding heavy use of pesticides. A new approach that uses heat can completely eradicate bedbugs and their eggs in the room without having to remove any furniture. The room is sealed and the temperature is raised to approximately 150°F for four hours. There is no need to use pesticides and the room can back in service on the same day.

APPLICATION OF PESTICIDES

The application of pesticides must be closely monitored and controlled. Only those personnel properly trained in the storage, dilution, and application of pesticides, and properly licensed by the appropriate state agency should be authorized to apply pesticides. Records should be maintained as to the licensing of specific personnel.

When outside agencies are contracted to do pest-control work, credentials should be checked and contracts let for no more than a one-year time period. This will allow the facility manager to have quick access to a new outside contractor if pests are not being kept under control.

TYPES OF PESTICIDES

Pesticides may be classified in a number of ways:

1. By their effectiveness against certain kinds of pests:
   insecticides versus insects
   herbicides versus weeds
2. By how they are formulated and applied:
   dusts
   fogging oils
   granular powders
   wettable powders
3. By the chemistry of the pesticide:
   chlorinated hydrocarbons (chlordane)
   organic phosphates (Malathion)
   natural organic insecticides (Pyrethrum)

Effectiveness against a particular pest species, safety, clinical hazard to property, type of formulations available, equipment required, and cost of material must all be taken into account when choosing a pesticide for a particular job. Recommendations change with experience, the development of new materials, and new governmental regulations. It should be kept in mind, however, that these are not the only materials that will work, but they are standard products that will work if properly used.

Malathion is an organophosphate-type, broad-spectrum insecticide that has a very low hazard threshold when used according to directions. Although only slightly toxic to humans and other mammals, it is highly toxic to fish and birds. It is effective against the two-spotted spider mite. Premium-grade 2 to 3 percent Malathion residual sprays can be used against most household pests; there is less chance of an odor problem with the premium rather than the regular grade. Malathion may be purchased as a 57 percent emulsion concentrate or a 25 percent wettable powder. It is recommended for use by nonprofessionals.

Methoxychlor (Marlate) is a chlorinated hydrocarbon-type, slightly toxic insecticide that is being used as a replacement for DDT. Methoxychlor is not accumulated in human body fat and does not contaminate the environment as does DDT. It is available as a 50 percent wettable powder and is commonly sold as Marlate. It is safe for use by nonprofessionals.

There are many other pesticides available. In commercial, hospital, or nursing home settings, however, pest control is best left to competent experts in the field, properly licensed and experienced to do the job of pest control. Contracting out pest control also removes the necessity of storing pest-control products and equipment.

The environmental concern with insects (pests) is primarily **preventive** in nature. Clean-out and cleanup will probably do more to control insects in areas where they are not wanted than any other prevention that can be adopted.

Waste Disposal and Control

There are nine classifications of **waste**, each presenting a slightly different disposal requirement. The term *waste* is associated with that which is useless, unused, unwanted, or discarded. Classifications are as follows:

Type 0—Trash. Primarily paper. After incineration there is less than 5 percent residual solid remaining.

Type 1—Rubbish. 80 percent type 0, 20 percent restaurant waste; 10 percent is incombustible. This term includes all nonputrescible refuse except ashes. There are two categories of rubbish: combustible and noncombustible.
  a. *Combustible.* This material is primarily inorganic—it includes items such as paper, plastics, cardboard, wood, rubber, and bedding.
  b. *Noncombustible.* This material is primarily inorganic and includes tin cans, metals, glass, ceramics, and other mineral refuse.

Type 2—Refuse. 50 percent type 0, 50 percent type 1. Has a residual moisture content of 50 percent. Requires firing at a higher heat. Leaves 10 percent solids after firing.

Type 3—Garbage. All food waste. 70 percent water. Designates putrescible wastes resulting from handling, preparing, cooking, and serving food.

Type 4—Residue. Includes all solid wastes. In practice this category includes garbage, rubbish, ashes, and dead animals.

Type 5—Ashes. Residue from fires used for cooking, heating, and on-site incineration.

Type 6—Biologic wastes. (includes human and animal remains). Wastes resulting directly from patient diagnosis and treatment procedures; includes materials of medical, surgical, autopsy, and laboratory origin.
  a. *Medical wastes.* These wastes are usually produced in patient rooms, treatment rooms, and nursing stations. The operating room may

also be a contributor. Items include soiled dressings, bandages, catheters, swabs, plaster casts, receptacles, and masks.
  b. *Surgical and autopsy wastes (pathologic wastes).* These wastes may be produced in surgical suites or autopsy rooms. Items that may be included are placentas, tissues and organs, amputated limbs, and similar material.
  c. *Laboratory wastes.* These wastes are produced in diagnostic or research laboratories. Items that may be included are cultures, spinal fluid samples, dead animals, and animal bedding. Eighty-five percent of this type of waste is released to morticians for incineration.

Type 7—Liquid by-product wastes. Usually toxic and hazardous. Must be treated with germicidal/disinfectant prior to disposal in sanitary sewers.

Type 8—Solid by-product wastes. Toxic, hazardous; capable of being sterilized, packaged, and discarded with normal trash.

Any of the preceding categories can produce **infectious waste**. It is the method of handling, however, that allows for safe disposal. Each environmental service center will develop its own procedures for disposal of all types of waste. (See procedures previously mentioned for disposal of "needles, syringes, and sharps" and for "antineoplastic agents.")

GREEN TIP

Cleaning with less-caustic chemicals is more than just a health and safety issue. It's a matter of protecting a company's investment.

So says Kaivac Inc. President Bob Robinson Sr., who noted that the restroom is the highest-priced-per-square foot room to construct in most facilities, taking into account the cost of fixtures, ventilation, pipes, ceramic walls, and other related accompaniments.

Using chemicals, such as "standard" toilet bowl cleaners with a high hydrochloric acid base, can damage not only the fixtures they are applied to, but other restroom fixtures, said Robinson.

When a "standard" acid-based cleaner is sprayed on a fixture, it creates a mist that seeks out moisture, notably the condensation on restroom fixtures and even the privacy dividers.

"This eats away at the metals. Once it gets past the chrome, it rusts away the pipes," said Robinson.

Robinson recommends a "one-stop" restroom cleaner that combines mild acids that together won't corrode fixtures, and at the same time clean tough stains such as mineral buildup.

The Joint Commission (JCAHO)

The Joint Commission on Accreditation of Health Care Organizations (JCAHO) is the prime **certifying authority** for hospitals and nursing homes in this country. This organization sets the standards for hospital and health-care administration and for housekeeping standards within the institutions.

Each institution is initially and annually surveyed to ensure that departments are organized to carry out their functions properly and that standards of operations and cleanliness are being maintained.

THE FACILITY SURVEY IN HOUSEKEEPING

In its survey of a facility's housekeeping, the JCAHO usually begins with a review of all written policies and procedures. Documentation of a continuing education program for housekeeping personnel is required. Contracts or written agreements with any outside sources providing such documentation are also required.

The individual who has primary responsibility for the environmental services department as designated by the chief facility administrator must complete certain sections of a written facility survey questionnaire.

The following conditions must be met in the survey:

1. The director's responsibilities must include participation in the development of department procedures, training and supervising personnel, scheduling and assigning personnel, and maintaining communications with other department heads.
2. Written departmental procedures must relate to the use, cleaning, and care of equipment; the cleaning of specialized areas; the selection, measurement, and proper use of housekeeping and cleaning supplies; the maintenance of cleaning schedules; infection control; and personal hygiene.
3. Participation of housekeeping personnel in a relevant continuing education program must be documented.
4. The extent to which outside housekeeping services are used must be documented. (If housekeeping services are provided by outside sources, a written agreement must require that the company meet JCAHO standards of such services. If such services have been terminated in the past year, the reasons for such termination must be stated.)

LINEN AND LAUNDRY

There are also strict controls and procedures associated with collection, processing, and distribution of linen and laundry. The **JCAHO standards** in this regard require the following:

GREEN TIP

If you choose to work with hazardous chemical products, then be sure to follow all the safety requirements and recommendations.

Workers should NEVER apply or use an aggressive acid toilet bowl cleaner without wearing appropriate gloves and goggles.

Corrosive acids and alkalis can produce acute and/or chronic injury to eyes and skin.

Some volatile solvents and glycol ethers can absorb through the skin or cause respiratory problems.

It is important to wear the appropriate personal protection equipment required or recommended on the product label and/or the MSDS.

This tip by Roger McFadden first appeared in *Cleaning and Maintenance Management*, May 2002, and is presented here through the generosity of CM B2B Trade Group, a subsidiary of National Trade Publications.

---

1. A statement is made as to which organization (internal or external) is responsible for linen and laundry.
2. There is an adequate supply of clean linen.
3. Clean linen is handled and stored so that the possibility of its contamination is minimized.
4. Soiled linen is placed in bags or containers of sufficient quality to functionally contain wet/soiled linen during the time required to collect it and remove it from the patient care area.
5. Linen is placed in bags or containers that, when filled, are properly closed prior to further transport.
6. Linen is identified when originating from isolation and septic surgical cases.
7. Soiled linen is kept separated from clean linen.
8. Functionally separate containers are used for the transportation of clean and soiled linen.
9. The hospital laundry is functionally separate from the patient care facility.
10. The laundry ventilation system has an adequate intake, filtration, exchange, and exhaust system.
11. Quality assurance procedures are in effect for both outside services and in-house laundries.
12. The participation of linen and laundry personnel in relevant continuing education programs is documented.

Environmental Pollution

It would be improper to dissociate the topic of environmental services from a discussion of the topic of pollution; it is a major concern of all mankind, especially for those of us in the profession where so much pollution is generated. First, here is a layman's look at the environment.

ELEMENTS OF THE ENVIRONMENT

The **Earth's crust** is composed of **oxides** of the following elements:

Silicon	SiO_2	66.4
Aluminum	Al_2O_2	15.5
Calcium	CaO	3.8
Sodium	Na_2O	3.5
Potassium	K_2O	3.3
Iron	FeO	2.8
Magnesium	MgO	2.0
Iron	Fe_2O_3	1.8
Manganese	MnO	0.1
Phosphorus	P_2O_3	0.3
All other elements	(rare earth)	0.5

Water (oceanic) is composed of the combination of hydrogen and oxygen (H_2O), sodium chloride ($NaCl$, common table salt), and numerous trace minerals. The *fresh water element* of total water is derived from seawater evaporating and condensing into clouds and precipitation and thereafter finding its way into underground water tables, lakes, and rivers.

The *Earth's atmosphere*, commonly called air, consists of layers of gases, water vapor, and solid and liquid particles.

The air near the earth's surface (0 to 15 kilometers [km] is known as the troposphere. This is an area of well-defined gases of two different groups, as follows:

Principal		
Nitrogen	N_2	78%
Oxygen	O_2	21%
Argon	Ar	1%
MINOR		
Carbon dioxide	CO_2	
Nitrous oxide	N_2O	
Carbon monoxide	CO	
Ozone	O_3	
Methane	CH_4	
Nitrogen monoxide	NO_2	
Hydrogen	H_2	
Helium	He	

The *middle layer* (15 to 500 km) is known as the stratosphere. This is where a mixing of atomic gases is taking place, forming the molecular gases.

The *ionosphere* (greater than 500 km) is a part of the atmosphere where free atoms of oxygen (O), helium (He), and hydrogen (H) exist in a free state, hydrogen (H) being the lightest and most distant layer of gas in the atmosphere.

THE EARTH'S PROTECTIVE SHIELD

The Earth is constantly being bombarded by **ultraviolet radiation** from the sun. Molecular oxygen (O_2) is being photodissociated into atoms of oxygen (O), immediately leading to the production of ozone($O + O_2 = O_3$). Ozone (O_3) restricts the amount of ultraviolet radiation reaching the earth's surface. This barrier protects land and plant and animal life from ultraviolet destruction. Because ultraviolet radiation has little penetrating effect, plant and animal life in the oceans is readily protected; this explains why such life was the first to occur on earth. Life on land, however, could not occur until oxygen that was created from the sea ultimately became a part of the creation of ozone in the atmosphere, which then protected life on the land.

Ecology

Ecology, as a branch of biology, is a study that is concerned with the relationship of plants and animals to their environment and to each other. It is our interest in ecology that, it is hoped, will bring about a major concern for what we are doing to ourselves by abusing our environment. The pollution we are generating today must be recognized and stopped if life as we know it on this planet is to continue. The time of life of humankind on earth in relation to the time of life on the earth is so infinitesimally small, it is difficult to realize how foreshortened the human life span can become unless we realize in the very near future what we are doing to our planet. The aim here is not "to save the planet"; the planet will survive and adapt—it is to save ourselves.

AIR POLLUTION

Air pollution occurs both naturally and unnaturally. Natural air pollution includes volcanic ash, blowing dust, and smoke from forest fires. These forms of air pollution have existed for millions of years and are not a major concern.

Unnatural air pollution, however, consists of filling the atmosphere with carbon monoxide, hydrocarbons containing sulfurs such as sulfur dioxide, nitrous oxide, **chlorofluorocarbons**, carbon dioxide, and particulates.

Most of this pollution results from the burning of fossil fuels (e.g., coal, oil, natural gas, and so on); energy conservation and the reduction of air pollution go hand in hand.

The two most significant problems associated with the burning of fossil fuels are 1) the **photochemical reaction** that takes place in the atmosphere that leads to **smog** and **acid rain** and 2) **global warming**, which is caused by the release of too much carbon dioxide and other **greenhouse gases** (e.g., methane, nitrous oxide, ozone, perfluorocarbons, hydrofluorocarbons, and sulfur hexafluoride) into the air.

Smog occurs in bright sunlight when nitrogen oxides, hydrocarbons, and oxygen interact chemically to produce powerful oxidants like ozone (O_3) and peroxyacetyl nitrate (PAN). These secondary pollutants are damaging to plant life and lead to the formation of photochemical smog. PAN is primarily responsible for the eye irritation so characteristic of this type of smog. Smog has caused lung ailments and even death in some metropolitan areas. The catalytic converter in automobile exhaust systems reduces air pollution by oxidizing hydrocarbons to CO_2 and H_2O and, to a lesser extent, converting nitrogen oxides to N_2 and O_2.

Global warming occurs when greenhouse gases absorb and send infrared radiation back to the earth, causing the "greenhouse effect." This condition will ultimately change climatic conditions and weather patterns.

Chloroflourocarbons chemically react with ozone in the stratosphere, creating **holes in the ozone layer**, increasing ultraviolet radiation. Since the signing of the Montreal Protocol in 1987 that banned the production of these chemicals, much progress has been made, showing the world that governments and corporations can positively impact the environment.

WATER POLLUTION

There are an incredible number of pollutants and sources of pollution that negatively affect the world's oceans, lakes, rivers, and aquifers. Mine runoffs, oil leaks, factory wastes, pesticides, even the chemicals we pour down the sewers in housekeeping have an adverse impact on water supplies. In many areas of the world, nature's ability to process these toxins has been overwhelmed, resulting in the loss of our natural resources and human life.

SOLID WASTE

Hotels and hospitals are tremendous generators of solid waste. Not only is waste an environmental concern, it is also a cost to the operation. Even the word *waste* connotes a loss. Waste must be collected at the property (a cost), it must transported from the property (another cost), and it must be disposed of in some manner (a third cost). For years, we had only one solution for the problem of solid wastes—**landfills**. Some waste must be

GREEN TIP

Bleach is a less than perfect solution (pun intended) to our housekeeping needs. It loses its strength quickly. A bleach/water solution left on a shelf for any period of time will lose its effectiveness. It also "gases off" quickly when applied, losing its strength. It can damage floor finishes, textile fibers, and carpets. It will corrode and discolor hard surfaces such as metals. It will even hide soil. The bleach can make some soil transparent, leading a cleaner to think he or she has actually cleaned a surface when, in fact, the soil remains. Finally, and most important, it can harm the health of your staff and the occupants of the building.

landfilled, but we have come to realize that landfills are problematic. Landfills can contribute to the pollution of underground aquifers that are the only source of water for some communities. Landfill space is rapidly being depleted in many areas of the country, thus driving up waste disposal costs.

Given that some of our waste must be landfilled, what are the other options open to us? What can we do in our operations to diminish our dependence on landfilling?

The Environmental Protection Agency (EPA) has developed a strategy called **integrated waste management**, which incorporates the use of landfills plus the following: **source reduction, reuse, recycling**, and **waste transformation**. By incorporating all of these in an organization's waste management program, the EPA contends, we can effectively reduce our dependence on landfills.

Source reduction is the most compelling strategy. It reduces the waste stream by preventing items from entering it in the first place. Buying in bulk to reduce packaging, or simply deciding to do without something that isn't really necessary to the enterprise, are examples of source reduction. Source reduction generates the greatest savings and should be practiced whenever it is practical to do so.

Reuse is the next best strategy. By giving an item a second life (sometimes even more lives), it can significantly reduce our waste stream. Recycling implies that a product will be broken down to its elements and remade into another product—sometimes the same product, sometimes not. This is far better than burying an item in a landfill, but it isn't without costs. There is the cost of collecting the item, the cost of transporting it, and, of course, the cost of making the item into a new product. However, the cost of recycling for most items is usually less than the cost of burying it in a landfill.

Waste transformation includes several options. Items can be compacted, using less space in the dumpster and the landfill; they can be turned into energy in a waste-to-energy plant, and they can be processed by shredders and pulpers that reduce the mass of the waste. However, these are considered by many to be less than desirable options, for either they create new forms of pollution (e.g., air pollution) or the product's ultimate destination is still the landfill.

OTHER FORMS OF POLLUTION

Other forms of pollution include radioactive waste, noise, and even light pollution.

The Housekeeper's Role in Environmental Management

A sound waste management and pollution reduction program should be a major goal for all of those involved in housekeeping operations. Regardless of the type of facility, all must make the environment a part of their professional concern.

Some of the specific activities a housekeeping department may employ include buying their guest amenities in bulk and putting up dispensers in the guestrooms. They should also buy their supplies in bulk whenever possible and instruct vendors to omit needless packaging.

As discussed earlier, housekeepers should buy the most environmentally benign chemicals that will still do the intended job, and they should eliminate chemical use whenever possible. Buying microfiber cleaning products and softening the facility's water will both serve to reduce chemical use.

Avoid polluting the air in your facility by eliminating aerosols; have dust collectors on the burnishers; and purchase only those vacuums that meet Carpet and Rug Institute certification requirements.

Set up a linen reuse program for your guests; give them the option of using their sheets for more than one night and using their bath linen for more than one service. You will save labor, chemicals, water, energy, and linens.

Appendix J includes several fine articles on housekeeping and the environment from National Trade Publications, Inc. There is an article on chemicals in the restroom by Roger McFadden. Pay close attention to the Hazard Value Chart in the article. There is an interview with Stephen Ashkin on the subject of mold, a very topical subject. There is also an interview with Michael Berry on indoor art quality (IAQ). Odors can be a vexing problem in any building, particularly in bathrooms; for possible solutions look to the article from Cleaning and Maintenance Distribution Online. A third article on IAQ, by Stephen Ashkin, contains some sound advice for all housekeepers. Finally, a letter from a reader of Cleaning and Maintenance Distribution Online, Arthur

B. Weissman, president of Green Seal, explains the role of his organization in assisting housekeepers everywhere in their efforts to improve the environment.

Other Opportunities for Housekeepers

The executive housekeeper rarely makes it into the general manager's suite. Advancement in this profession is often through relocation to larger and more prestigious properties. It has been shown that executive housekeepers can move into environmental services departments fairly easily, but hospitals and nursing homes are not the only options available. There are also opportunities in a host of different facilities, including schools, colleges, arenas, airports, convention centers, stadiums, malls, and office buildings, to name a few. For the entrepreneur, there is contract cleaning; with a mop in one hand and a bucket in the other, you too can become your own boss.

There are many opportunities in related areas as well. For instance, in property management, one will work with tenants and manage all aspects of the building, inside and out. Then there is the building engineer, who keeps a large facility up and running, handling everything from the air conditioning to decorating. The opportunities are tremendous; housekeeping is far from a dead-end position. The following sections explore a few of these career opportunities.

AIRPLANES

In the following article, the experts at ProTeam take us behind the scenes to glimpse a highly specialized area of cleaning: aircraft.

Behind the Scenes in Aircraft Cleaning by Pro Team

This article is presented through the generosity of ProTeam Inc., a manufacturer of backpack vacuum systems and sponsor of Team Cleaning Seminars located in Boise, Idaho.

Among commercial cleaning jobs, cleaning aircraft is surely one of the most unusual. It is performed not only under tight deadlines between flights, but also in tight quarters. There's little room for error, and no room for maneuvering cumbersome equipment.

A DEFINING TOOL

Although the original backpack vacuum was designed specifically for more conventional applications, it turns out to be ideally suited to cope with the narrow aisles and cramped underseat areas of aircraft.

"Backpack vacs are lightweight, have good suction, and are very efficient," says Michael Pulli, Manager of Contract Administration for One-Source, one of the largest service and maintenance companies in the world. The OneSource Aviation Division is one of the largest companies servicing aircraft and airports in the world.

"Backpack vacuums are versatile. The floor tools move easily between seat tracks and under aircraft seats, and the units are quiet," Pulli continues. "They do an excellent job for us."

The One Source Aviation Division is a full-service operation for ground-handling, cargo and ticketing functions, and cleaning, including hangars, offices, terminals, and aircraft. This division cleans aircraft in both the United States and Europe, including locations such as O'Hare, JFK, and Atlanta International airports.

Before Pulli joined OneSource, he was district marketing manager for Delta Airlines, where he had worked his way up the system—including a stint at the cleaning function early in his career. On the ground, turnaround is crucial in aircraft cleaning, he says. In a limited amount of time, the plane must be cleaned from stem to stern. "The plane is on the ground 35 or 40 minutes in total," Pulli says, "and we have about 20 minutes to clean the interior."

In that 20 minutes, galleys and tray tables are wiped down, trash removed, floors vacuumed, and literature restocked and properly arranged. "If the plane looks clean, the passengers feel comfortable," Pulli says.

"Cleaning is choreographed," Pulli emphasizes. A four-person cleaning team descends on the space: one specialist for the lavatories, one for galleys, and one vacuuming/detail specialist works from for-ward to the rear while another works from rear to forward, meeting in the middle. Such focused specialization increases cleaning efficiency, Pulli says.

TRYING SOMETHING NEW AND DIFFERENT

Pulli says that when his company tested the backpack unit they "liked that it was small and light. It moved easier, and the vacuum operator was in full control."

In cleaning aircraft, Pulli says, "we follow the exact specifications of each airline." Details include placing emergency cards and literature in seat pockets, crossing seat belts neatly across seats, folding blankets, placing pillows in specified compartments, and vacuuming the floors.

While airlines sometimes provide their own equipment, OneSource prefers to use backpacks extensively in three of its locations, including Little Rock. "Before the backpack vac, we used a bullet tank-type model. It was difficult to drag down the aisle of the aircraft," Pulli says. The bullet would catch on seat tracks, slowing the workers down.

Les Payne, manager of OneSource operations in Little Rock, who oversees a staff of 21, concurs. With a backpack, "we get more done in less time. It does the job as well or better than conventional vacs and can be used on hard flooring as well as on indoor/outdoor carpeting," he says. "Our workers like the portability of the backpack. They just strap it on. It's easier to use since they don't have to drag it.

"Backpacks do a good job. I know because I inspect each plane after it has been cleaned," confides the 32-year veteran airport worker, who was a ticket agent and ramp agent for 25 years before joining OneSource. Payne's crews clean 737s, 727s, and DC-9s for TWA and Southwest Airlines at Little Rock Regional Airport.

Extensive training of cleaning personnel is imperative, Pulli says, because of time constraints. Cleaning must be precise and systematic or it cannot be performed in the allotted time. OneSource's cleaning team members attend airline cleaning classes for eight hours, plus more hours provided by OneSource.

Since the favorable experience in cleaning aircraft with backpack vacuums, OneSource has adopted backpacks for additional uses in the company's worldwide Building Maintenance Division. For example, in airport concourses and other buildings, he explains, "Day porters on call use a backpack to tidy up dry material spills, such as debris from planters and accidental ashtray dumps."

IN-DEPTH CUSTOMER SERVICE

Besides on-the-ground aircraft cleaning between flights, OneSource also provides overnight aircraft cleaning in many locations. Overnight cleaning is more extensive, Pulli says, requiring about 8 to 10 personnel hours. In other words, a team of four cleans a 727 in 2.5 hours or the slightly smaller MD-80 in 2 hours. Pulli says that the backpack vac is used for overnight cleaning, too. Its portability and maneuverability make it the machine of choice. After each overnight cleaning, Pulli says, the flight crew is given a quality control postcard checklist so OneSource can receive customer feedback on the work it is performing for airlines.

Separate OneSource crews are responsible for exterior cleaning of aircraft. Typically, the exterior is washed every eight days and waxed once a month.

Contracts vary, depending on the RFP (request for proposal). For example, the Airport Authority asked for competitive bids on the entire Atlanta International Airport, OneSource was awarded the contract for the whole airport, including janitorial services at the gates, offices, and terminals. Typically, 7 to 10 major companies vie for the cleaning contract at the largest airports.

In other situations, airlines may individually request bids. And sometimes the cleaning service that performs between-flight cleaning is not the same company that cleans the aircraft overnight.

Those in the business of cleaning aircraft often have a special affinity for airport facilities. Pulli, for example, has been around planes and airports all of his life. "It's in my blood," he acknowledges. "My uncle was lead pilot and Employee #4 at California's Pacific Southwest Airlines. I would have been a pilot, too, if I didn't need to wear glasses since age six," says the 48-year-old aviation services executive.

Like the work of flying aircraft, the work of cleaning them is demanding, rewarding for those who make the grade, and no place to wing it.

ARENAS AND STADIUMS

Don Rankin, president of Facilities Maintenance Services at Houston, has a wealth of knowledge about the specialty cleaning area of arenas and stadiums. He, with the support of the staff at ProTeam, shares his considerable expertise with us.

Arena and Stadium Cleaning: The Team Specialist Approach by Pro Team

This article is presented through the generosity of ProTeam Inc. a manufacturer of backpack vacuum systems and sponsor of Team Cleaning Seminars located in Boise, Idaho.

Today's arenas and stadiums seat anywhere from 15,000 to 75,000 people and cleaning up after a concert or major sports event is no small matter. Facility Maintenance Services (FMS) of Houston, Texas, believes that using teams of cleaning specialists is the best way to optimize labor while ensuring cleaning quality and value for its clients.

MEETING THE CHALLENGES

FMS provides contract cleaning and maintenance for three major facilities: Arena Theater in Houston, Texas; Baltimore Arena in Baltimore, Maryland; and Pro Player Stadium in Miami, Florida.

In arena/stadium cleaning—unlike an office building where cleaning costs and procedures are standardized based on square footage—the size of the task, logistics, and corresponding billing are based on each day's attendance. The number of people attending an event and the time constraints dictated by the next scheduled event dictate the number of cleaning personnel needed, and the number of hours in which the job must be completed. For example, was the stadium filled or only partially filled? Were most of the people on the lower level or the upper level? How many hours are available to clean between one event and the next? If a stadium has an 8 P.M. game on Saturday night and a 2 P.M. game the next day, the facility must be thoroughly cleaned by 11 A.M. Sunday.

A well-trained maintenance supervisor is able to quickly calculate the number of specialists and number of teams needed to accomplish the cleanup in the most efficient way possible. For example, specialists may be allocated based on a predetermined ratio of cleaning workers to attendance, such as one worker per 500 seats filled, and so on, contingent on the tasks to be accomplished.

Weather, too, can be a challenge in maintaining open-air sports facilities, depending on their location and time of year. From Milwaukee County Stadium (Wisconsin), where baseball is sometimes played in the snow, to Pro Player Stadium (Florida), which hosts more than 100 events annually and hardly a day passes without a rain shower, team specialists pull on ponchos, boots, or whatever additional clothing is necessary to face the elements and complete their appointed tasks. "We work in everything but lightning and hurricanes," says Rick Elbon, FMS vice president of operations.

Arena/stadium maintenance contracts, like the job itself, are event-driven. This means contract employees may work seven consecutive days and then not work for another seven, or they may work practically nonstop from March through October and then find themselves with nothing to do the rest of the year. Under those conditions, retaining a staff of cleaning specialists isn't easy. Fortunately, using specialists means that each worker has a narrow repertoire of tasks to learn, so training replacements is simpler.

HOW DO THEY DO IT?

Between 40 and 200 workers are needed to clean an arena or stadium, and team specialists are cross-trained to provide maximum flexibility. FMS's cleaning staff is divided into three groups; those who work during an event ("event attendants"), those who clean up after ("post-event staff"), and those who provide regular maintenance ("daily staff") for the facility.

The job begins with a pre-event walk through of the facility's offices, executive suites (Pro Player Stadium has 220 of these), restrooms, and concourse by event attendants who perform needed touch-ups.

Throughout the event, attendants police the concourse for trash and spills, and monitor restrooms (Pro Player has 66) and restroom supplies. Surgical gloves and a special deodorant/disinfectant are required for cleanup of bodily fluid spills.

Once the event is over and the fans have left the facility, the post-event staff moves in. Depending on the facility's size and that day's attendance, there may be six or seven different cleaning teams—totaling approximately 40–50 people for an arena, 150 or more for a stadium. All post-event work is broken down into defined tasks. Each team handles a specific task and the bulk of the work is done in about six hours.

A team of "pickers"—allocated at a ratio of one specialist to 1000 persons attending an event—moves through the stands, picking up any large debris left behind including souvenirs, paper bags, and beverage containers. This group of specialists is followed by a team of "sweepers" who remove medium-sized trash such as candy wrappers, paper cups, and so on. Trash is first swept in a lateral direction to a set of concrete stairs and then down the stairs to a collection point at the bottom. A team of "blowers" follows, using gasoline-powered blowers to clear the area of the smallest trash.

While this is happening, a "concourse team" completes the same tasks on the arena or stadium concourse. When the initial group of specialists is about halfway finished removing large items of trash from the concourse, part of the team diverts to collect restroom trash. After all the trash has been collected, "follow-up teams" sweep and blow the concourse. Once all of this is finished, a "pressure-washing team" washes down the facility's concrete, nonskid aggregate, rubber floors, aisles, and stairwells, using hot water and a water-based degreaser to remove chewing gum, beer, and soda stains. Concourse floors are given a final deep cleaning with a walk-behind automatic scrubber.

A "restroom team" cleans the facility's restrooms, showers, locker rooms, and dressing rooms. The team divides into groups handling subspecialties such as fixtures, floors, and so on. Restroom floors and showers are pressure-washed with an odor counteractant/disinfectant. Special attention is given to floor drains where disinfectant chemicals are used to reduce bacteria and odor. Specialists keep drain/sewer traps filled with liquid to keep sewer gas traps functioning properly and to prevent the backup of sewer gases.

A special "suite crew" concentrates on the carpeted offices and glass-enclosed executive suites—dusting and wiping down surfaces, cleaning the glass and vacuuming. FMS's specialists use backpack vacuums designed to easily reach into corners and under and around furniture. Vacuums equipped with four-stage filtration systems improve indoor air quality and reduce dusting.

Detail cleaning of fabric seats and armrests, metal seating frames, and bleacher risers, along with periodic carpet extraction, is performed by the facility's regular maintenance staff between home game stints while professional athletic teams and/or performers are on the road.

SPECIALTY EQUIPMENT LEVERAGES LABOR

FMS utilizes backpack vacuums, pressure washers, and autoscrubbers to optimize labor. Vacuuming with backpack units, which have greater access and mobility in carpeted suites, has reduced cleaning times by as much as 50 percent compared to more traditional equipment. Pressure washers increase productivity in heavy-duty cleaning applications fourfold over older methods such as rotary scrubbing. Autoscrubbers are five to ten times faster than manual methods for deep cleaning floors. All of these tools make more effective use of labor, producing higher quality at lower cost to customers.

KEEPING SCORE: QUALITY

Cleaning teams—like their professional sport counterparts—tend to be self-monitoring, focused, and goal-oriented, yielding optimum performance levels more easily. With a strong quality benchmarking program in place and proper training, service excellence increases automatically.

However, quality should never be left to chance. FMS maintenance supervisors conduct regular walk-through inspections of suites, offices, and seating areas. Clients also conduct periodic formal inspections. At least once a year, FMS clients submit written evaluations that cover everything from individual job performance to the attitudes of FMS managers, to workers' uniforms and decorum issues.

Most telling—and gratifying—are personal client comments such as "This place is *clean*—your company has made a real difference." Clients are a valuable source of input. We make it a priority to utilize our clients' service comments to structure the most effective teams possible, and to determine with certainty that our cleaning program is customized to fit our clients' needs.

Don Rankin, author of this article, is president of Facility Maintenance Services (FMS), a full-service janitorial firm in Houston, Texas. FMS has extensive experience in cleaning arenas, theaters, and ballparks. The 40-year-old company employs about 1500 workers.

CONTRACT CLEANING

Contract cleaning is the entrepreneurial side of our industry. If executive housekeepers want to become their own bosses, all they have to do is run a classified ad in the newspaper and have a few business cards printed. Actually, it is a little more involved than that; there are a number of steps to be taken first. You will need a federal tax ID number and a state sales tax number. You will need licenses and permits from the state, county, and city, including commercial vehicle licenses. Then there is state unemployment tax, state withholding, and workmen's compensation insurance. Your business will need more insurance than just worker's comp, however; you will need accident and health insurance, public liability insurance, property damage insurance, and disability insurance. And then there are the unions to contend with.

If you are still interested in becoming your own boss at this point, you will have to decide what is going to be your specialty. But first you must decide whether you are going to serve the commercial or the residential market. Typically, there are higher profit margins in the residential end, but on the commercial side the contracts are much larger. Most contract cleaning businesses had their start in commercial cleaning.

The next step is to decide what will set you apart from the rest—what is your specialty. Carpet-cleaning services are very common. One estimate is that there are more than 25,000 of these services in the United States already. This does not mean that there isn't room for one more exceptional service. You will need a track (van) and a **truck mount**; this is a tank/heater/pump system that sends a cleaning solution through a hose from a van to the operator inside the residence. The solution comes out the wand and is then vacuumed up by the wand attachment and transported back to the dirty solution tank in the van.

Other specialties include disaster cleanup (e.g., floods and fires), drapery or furniture cleaning, construction cleanup, finishing and sealing floors, pest extermination, window cleaning, and swimming pool maintenance; you may even want to be a chimney sweep. One of the most specialized cleaning services around is featured in the following article from Cleaning and Maintenance Online, the **bio-recovery service**.

You may even want to be a generalist, but attempting to perform too many services may make you a "jack-of-all-trades and master of none." A final word of advice on contract cleaning: "Start small." If you start small, you may be able to get started with an investment of only a few thousand dollars. Those who start big (particularly those who purchase large cleaning businesses that are for sale) often live to regret it.

From Carpet Cleaner to Crime and Trauma/Bio Cleaning Specialist: Essential Don M. McNulty

This article first appeared in *Cleaning and Maintenance Management Online* 2003 and is presented though the generosity of CM B2B Trade Group, a subsidiary of National Trade Publications, Inc.

KANSAS CITY, MO—In most US states, just about anyone can get into bio cleaning or crime scene clean up with little or no training.

Consider, however

- The federal government through OSHA regulates the bio cleaning industry by means of the Blood-borne Pathogen Rule (1910.1030). This regulation states that each company engaging in such a service as to where the employees have a "reasonable anticipation" of coming into contact with blood or other potentially infectious material (OPIM) . . . must have a written "exposure control plan."

  That plan will set the perimeters of conduct through certain engineering controls, and training in every aspect with a thorough understanding of this plan needs to be accomplished, and documented before the technician goes into the field.

  Since there are things lurking in blood that can be fatal, the crime scene/biohazard cleaner needs to receive a Hepatitis B vaccine (at company expense for all employees). This vaccine is a series of three shots and each individual needs to have the first shot at least 10 days before entering a scene. If the employee refuses to have this vaccine, that employee needs to sign a declination form and have it further explained, through this form, that the offer for a vaccination is open to him at any time in the future, should he change his mind.

- Training in epidemiology, specifically disease transference. Knowledge of the different kinds of pathogens and bacteria that can be lying in wait for the right opportunity to set up shop in a host, namely the carpet/biohazard cleaner.

- Familiarity with waste disposal regulations. Joe (or JoAnne) Carpet Cleaner shouldn't be trying to suck up blood into a truckmount. Every state does have regulations as to how medical waste needs to be disposed of, and everyone should be familiar with and follow such state regulations. Contaminated carpet cleaning equipment can transfer disease sources into the next space to be cleaned; liabilities loom great in the bio cleaning business.

  The carpet cleaner has knowledge about cleaning processes; which is often a step above many people working in medical or first responder (police, fireman, etc.) fields who want to get into the bio cleaning industry and lack knowledge of basic cleaning techniques.

- Basic knowledge of construction. Crime scene/biohazard cleaners need to know . . . if a portion of a wall or ceiling needs to be removed, what may be on the interior of that wall or what could be above that ceiling. Cutting into a live electrical wire or cutting into a water pipe can have disastrous results.

- Deodorization techniques should be in the biohazard cleaner's knowledge base. Knowing how to deodorize from decomposing bodies is paramount.

Other pertinent regulations

- Hazard Communications Standard 1910.1200.
- Respiratory Protection Standard 1910.134.
- Confined Space standard.
- Fall Protection standard.

MARKETING STRATEGIES

Send your marketing information to coroners, funeral homes, police agencies and any other first responder groups you can think of.

Getting out and making face-to-face contact and designing appropriate mail pieces is essential.

Department policy prohibits most police officers and coroners from giving out referrals, but you can give them ways to offer help without giving a specific referral.
—D. M.

STRESS AND THE CRIME SCENE/BIOHAZARD CLEANING PRO

The cleaning pro tackling this work should not be the type of person who thinks, "I can see that stuff and never get sick."

Visual "shocks" are just one area affecting the cleaner in this specialty: The cleaner needs to know that it's going to be felt and smelled—and it isn't the same as a deer killed on a hunting trip.

Every tech I've had—including myself—has suffered from "stress dreams." These dreams have weird story lines and usually deal with blood and gore. This comes from "Critical Incident Stress Syndrome" (CISS), or what some call "Secondary Posttraumatic Syndrome." These dreams and the stress that comes from doing this work can lead to grave psychological disorders for people who can't handle these stresses.

The carpet pro turned crime scene/biohazard cleaner must learn how to defuse or debrief this stress in him/herself and employees. This stress doesn't just come from seeing and handling the physical scene, it comes while dealing with grief stricken individuals. The professional should develop the coping, emotional, and social skills necessary to help these individuals while maintaining a sense of detachment; there is a need to learn to listen while various stories are recounted, and what to say and not say in response.

Cleaners will need to explain the work order and obtain the proper signatures while people are struggling with grief and disbelief, oftentimes bursting into tears when they feel overwhelmed; "compassion" is the watchword.

There is other work within the bio cleaning field Joe may have to respond to. One would be "unsanitary dwellings." This is what some people call "pack rats." The dwelling gets so stuffed with garbage and trash you usually have to walk through the house or apartment through paths. Many times buckets and jars of human waste accumulate, sometimes drug paraphernalia, and if people die in this mess ... it can lead to quite the job.

Bio cleaning is more than death and trauma and most carpet cleaners would welcome the revenue. Most "bio cleans" bring in an 85 percent gross profit margin; it is possible to earn up to $200 per man-hour.

Bio cleaning is not the type of business Joe can just walk into and start one day, however. It takes planning, a certain amount of training, and a special kind of preparation.

Don McNulty of Bio Cleaning Services of America, Inc., based in the Kansas City area, is an author and speaker throughout the United States. McNulty wrote the *American Standard for Bio Technicians* and currently teaches a seminar called "The Basic Bio Technician Course."

CONVENTION CENTERS

The meetings and conventions industry has evolved into a tremendous business during the last 25 years. Almost every U.S. city of any size has built a convention center, and every one of them needs cleaning specialists to service them. The following article highlights some of the unique duties and responsibilities of the professional provider of services to this industry.

Convention Services by Blane Blood

We are indebted to Blane Blood, Customer Services Shift Supervisor at the Las Vegas Convention and Visitors Authority (LVCVA), for his contribution.

The cleaning of a facility that has many variables is a major challenge. Such challenges are best addressed by looking at how a facility operates. In this article, we will use the Las Vegas Convention Center as our example.

The Las Vegas Convention Center (LVCC) is a 3.2 million square foot facility with more than two million square feet of exhibit space; it also has 144 meeting rooms (more than 290,000 square feet) with seating capacities ranging from 20 to 2500. In addition, the facility has a grand lobby and registration area (more than 225,000 square feet), administrative offices, and more than 46 sets of restrooms (men's and women's) and 16 family restrooms.

So, how do you maintain a facility of this size with a visitor volume of approximately 9 million delegates per annum? In order to accomplish this, it takes many dedicated people, from the custodial staff, which does the actual cleaning, to the Board of Directors, who approves the final budget.

The cleaning and maintaining of the facility falls within the Client Services Department, which is the largest within the Facilities Division. We will focus our attention primarily on this department. The mission statement for this department is as follows:

To maintain the facilities and grounds of the LVCVA in a clean and presentable condition. Provide, in a professional manner, the highest standards of service to both our internal as well as our external customers.

With this mission in mind, we will first examine the shift supervisor position. The shift supervisor is responsible for three primary job duties: identify, assign and inspect.

IDENTIFY

The supervisor must identify what tasks need to be accomplished for that shift or within the near future. This is an ongoing duty. It is not just done at the beginning of a shift but continuously. A good supervisor will not only identify duties that are noticeable and need to be done right

TABLE 13.1

Daily Tasks	Less Frequent
• Trash and debris	• Cleaning light fixtures
• Vacuum carpets	• Stripping and waxing floors
• Cleaning windows and floors	• Extracting carpets

away, but will also identify tasks that are not done frequently and not always within public view. Table 13.1 lists basic examples of each.

There are a host of other duties too numerous to mention here such as the cleaning of doorjambs and thresholds, kick plates, and cleaning behind furniture.

ASSIGN

It is the duty of the supervisor to assign an employee to each of the identified duties. A good supervisor will ensure that job assignments are rotated among the staff to allow each staff member the opportunity to learn and be efficient in all duties to which they will be assigned and within their posted classification. It is also vital that the supervisor understands the various strengths and weaknesses of each staff member. When assignments are made, employees who may not be as adequate in some tasks should be assigned these tasks when time allows for them to be trained or coached on these tasks. However, during a critical time, it is important that the person with the greatest skills be assigned to that task. It is also important that every employee needs to be trained in all jobs since the most skilled individual might not be on duty.

INSPECT

This is probably the most critical aspect of the three. This step will ensure the work is done to the standards you have set. It sends a positive message that we are all measured on outcomes, not just good intentions. An employee's abilities and a positive attitude toward the job are important, but they are meaningless if the job does not get done correctly. Inspection should not just be done when an assignment is completed, but also during the process. The supervisor needs to determine if the job is being done safely, efficiently, and within company identified operating procedures. This also allows the supervisor to

determine an employee's strengths and weaknesses.

If a supervisor does not observe the staff performing their job duties, the supervisor will not be able to conduct a fair and proper annual evaluation. Furthermore, the supervisor will not have any credibility with the staff if the staff does not believe that the supervisor knows and understands their jobs.

These three job duties are intertwined, no single aspect can function without the others. Remember, these duties cannot be done from behind a desk, or with just a few staff members. Staff members hold their supervisor at a higher standard. A supervisor is more than a manager; a supervisor is a leader who must set an example. When staff members are working, supervisors should be working. A supervisor should always provide support and counseling for the staff. All legwork for a task or project should be done prior to the implementation. For example, if the task identified is to clean the upper windows in an area, the supervisor should determine the best time this task is to be performed, and will also make sure that the area is accessible and all tools and the needed equipment are available. It should not be up to the staff member to make these arrangements.

CUSTODIAL ACTIVITIES

Custodial tasks specific to the convention industry fall within three primary categories; they are restroom maintenance, preparation of common areas and cleaning offices. When duties are performed will be determined by the activity within the building.

Activities are defined as follows:

Pre-event: Prior to an event or tradeshow, the facility must be "show ready." Each lease agreement specifies that the client will receive its leased space in a clean and presentable condition. This means that the carpets will be clean and free of spots and debris, tables and chairs will be clean and set to specifications required for each meeting or event, restrooms will be cleaned and fully stocked with supplies, common areas will be clean and swept, and the facility will be free from hazards. In short, the building will be given to the client in a clean and safe condition and suitable for it to conduct business.

Pre-event cleaning is not as easy as it may appear; there are many factors involved. First, independent contractors who have been awarded the contract of setting up and tearing down the show have a negative effect on Client Services ability to ready the facility. For example, these contractors will utilize restrooms and common areas, which limits our ability to adequately clean these areas. It is not a good idea to clean these areas to "show ready" standards too early since they will just have to be redone. Instead, by breaking the restrooms into sections and blocking off access to portions of the area, detail cleaning can then proceed in these areas.

With regards to common areas, these areas cannot be blocked off; the subcontractor is then required to lay a protective plastic covering over the carpet and hire a subcontractor to clean up any debris that may be left behind in the areas where they are working.

Most detail cleaning is done within 24 hours prior to show opening. It is the supervisor's responsibility to inspect all common areas to ensure they are clean. Emphasis is placed on highly visible areas such as:

- Elevators
- Entrances
- Escalators
- Stairwells
- Trash receptacles
- Meeting rooms
- Windows
- Restrooms
- Phone banks
- Parking lots

How these tasks are scheduled is critical to ensure labor and materials are not wasted. For instance, restrooms were once locked down to ensure there was no activity in them during cleaning. This ensured a thorough, systematic cleaning, and eliminated any risk of accident to the client or another staff member. After the restroom had been detailed and stocked, it was ready to reopen. This was the standard method for restroom cleaning for many years.

To meet our customers' demands, we have had to rethink how we do business. We now realize that closing an entire restroom was as much for our convenience, as it was for our customer's safety. This practice is now obsolete. In addition, more events being scheduled has resulted in a commensurate increase in demand for restrooms and a shrinking window of opportunity in which to clean them. We have had to rethink and re-engineer our approach. We now cordon off sections, allowing for part of the restroom to be used while we detail clean the rest of the unit.

Event: When an event is progress, it can be very challenging to maintain a restroom. This, of course, will depend on the size of the event. Smaller events [20,000 to 60,000 attendees] can still be challenging, but the traffic is light and restocking stalls and paper products is easily accomplished. Debris on the floor can quickly be cleaned and trash is light. In an effort to maintain a clean environment, trash is removed as often as possible; this is done by placing several liners in the trash can so they can just be pulled and the next one is ready to go. During larger events [80,000 to 200,000 attendees] maintaining a restroom takes more time. Product is depleted quickly so the restroom attendants are responsible for fewer areas. Trash removal and cleanliness becomes an ongoing issue. It is not uncommon for advertisements that are not approved by show staff to be left in a restroom area. The attendant will remove the literature and give a copy to the supervisor. This is important since the authority for the display of any advertisements is solely reserved by the Las Vegas Convention and Visitors Authority.

During these heavy events break schedules are adjusted so that not all staff members are on break at the same time and all are present during peak times. This is also important during shift change. Staff members are required to stay on the show floor until just before shift change and are encouraged to apprise the next crew of the present status of the area.

Post-event: Post-event is the time for restoration of the facility to its former state. All supply closets are filled and cleaning supplies replenished. Post-event is not necessarily when the total show ends and move out begins, but when the event is done for the day. Restrooms are cleaned and everything is brought back to show ready standards, and all fixtures are sanitized.

Sanitation of fixtures is a vital aspect of the restroom function. The LVCVA is an international destination that brings delegates from across the globe to conduct business. The threat of a foreign illness is very real and taken seriously. Not only must we protect our clients from incoming foreign illnesses but we also must protect foreign clients from illnesses that are domestic to our region.

The cleaning of common areas is done on a regular basis with people in place to monitor them before, during and after events. It is the responsibility of the staff members to walk the assigned area prior to an event and make sure that everything is show ready. As the event progresses, the staff members will note problem areas where debris may have collected and make sure more trash receptacles are in place for the next day. They will also monitor for any unsafe conditions. If a problem is identified like a broken door handle, they will mark the door and take it out of service and request a supervisor to put in a work order so that it can be fixed as soon as possible. This may be done during the event if at all possible. If not, it will be done before the opening of the next show day. It is important to note that not all of the common areas are the responsibility of the staff members. If a booth or display area is present, then the show staff will contract an outside cleaner to handle these areas. This is done for security reasons.

Parking lots are monitored as well to ensure that the facility is clean on the outside as well. This is vital since this is the first impression delegates get when they enter the property. A sweeper truck is used in the evenings when all traffic has left the property and it can operate safely. The outside staff is responsible for the entrances of the facility. This includes all trash receptacles, ash urns, walk-off mats and seating areas. All the planter boxes, tree wells and grass areas are also part of their cleaning duties. The custodian position is a union position so full-time staff members are guaranteed 40 hours a week. However, during larger events it may be required to bring in staff members on overtime. Overtime is used primarily on the opening day of the show since there are many variables and this is the heaviest traffic day. As the show progresses, attendance drops and overtime is generally not needed.

Unlike the hotel industry, convention centers are not open 24 hours a day, but they are open seven days a week. The facility does have some dark periods when extensive cleaning can be done. When an event is in progress it is important that the client's needs are being met even when it may not know what its needs are. It is also extremely important that the client does not learn at the wrong time that what he or she needs most of all is toilet paper.

SCHOOLS AND COLLEGES

There is a correlation between cleanliness and learning. The education of our next generation is one of our society's greatest responsibilities. How can we expect learning to take place in an environment where there are cockroaches running under the desks, the floor is filthy, and the classroom smells of excreta? Unfortunately, these and other abysmal conditions are not isolated instances in the United States. States are operating in a crisis environment; there is simply not enough money to fund our public institutions. The worsening of the economy has exacerbated this situation. Policymakers and even educators have attempted to implement stopgap measures to see them through these difficult times. A widely practiced tactic is that of **deferred maintenance**, which has almost become a buzzword on the campus. Substantial short-term savings can be realized by not cleaning floors or emptying the trash. This shortsighted policy has two long-term results: 1) The government ends up spending more money in the long run to save a few dollars in the short run, and 2) students and their education suffer in the interim.

Deferred maintenance ultimately wears buildings out faster, dramatically increasing capital expenditures, and may also negatively impact safety, occupant health (see the Ashkin interview in Appendix J), and security. It destroys the morale and hope of the building occupants. It may also drive up costs for the institution in the form of lawsuits when building occupants sue for compensation for injuries and illnesses resulting from these cutbacks. Mold cases are now particularly common.

CHANGE AGENTS
Dan Bornholdt, President
Green Suites International

Dan Bornholdt, president and founder of Green Suites International, has more than 20 years of experience in environmental issues and equipment. As an innovative entrepreneur, he has made Green Suites International the preeminent provider of environmentally sound products and services to hotels worldwide. The company was founded in 1997 as Ecorp, Inc., a unique and dynamic environmental marketing and distribution company.

While still a student at the University of California at Berkeley, Bornholdt founded Bornholdt Transportation, Inc. in 1979, specializing in the expedited handling and transport of environmentally unsafe materials. After selling this company in early 1991, he went on to found Risk Assessment Services, an environmental consulting company, where he utilized his expertise in environmental issues to provide his clients with profitable solutions to corporate environmental problems. Bornholdt is an active member of the Association of Environmental Professionals and has served on the American Hotel and Lodging Association's Engineering Committee for the past five years. Green Suites International has introduced the hotel industry to countless environmentally responsive products through the years, including Project Planet's guestroom brochures (Figure 13.3) that encourage guests to save water and energy by reusing their bath and bed linens during their stay.

These conditions were once thought to exist only in K–12 schools. Now we have seen them spread up to the most prestigious universities in the land. The effect is the same—there is a deadening of the spirit. Tragically,

these conditions have given some unscrupulous building services managers justification for doing less than they ought. Some have seen this as an opportunity to "retire in place." As the deferred maintenance figure rises, so does the justification to do even less.

What are so desperately needed are managers who have the resolve to meet these challenges and the ability to rethink and reengineer how we conduct our business. Improved methods of operation must be found and implemented. The author once heard President Bob Suzuki of Cal Poly Pomona address this very subject. His building services department was faced with a one-third cut in operating budget. The challenge he gave his staff was how to do more than they had done in the past, but with less money. Doing less with less was not an option. His staff went to work retooling how they conducted their business, and by the end of the planning period they were able to develop a plan that would meet the challenges before them.

Managers entering this field who wish to be successful must bring with them some extraordinary talents. They must understand the complexities of the budget process. They must be aware of all of the very latest techniques and trends in the JanSan and housekeeping industries. They must be able to sell members of a workforce (often unionized) on the need to reinvent themselves. Finally, they must have, at the core of their beliefs, a love and respect for those whom they serve, their students.

Dan Bornholdt, President

FIGURE 13.3 These brochures encourage guests to participate in the hotel's linen reuse program.

Marilyn Rajski   *Embracing the Challenge of Change*

by Andi M. Vance, Editor, *Executive Housekeeping Today*

This article first appeared in the September 2002 issue of *Executive Housekeeping Today,* the official publication of the International Executive Housekeepers Association, Inc.

Place yourself in the following scenario: You're an interior decorator. Your forte lies in fabric selection and paint. One day, your boss approaches you with a hammer in hand and asks you to build a house for his son-in-law.

"A HOUSE?!" you ask him, dumbfounded at his request. You know nothing about lumber or building. The only thing you know about nails is that you (or your wife) make an appointment to get them done once every few weeks.

So how do you handle his request? Do you tell him, "Sorry, that's not my area of expertise." Or do you accept the challenge?

As a lifelong resident of South Bend, Indiana, Rajski was very familiar with Saint Mary's College. She appreciated the all-female environment at the college and was very interested in the support of its operations. That college has a reputation for its great treatment of ... faculty and staff. Saint Mary's is an all-women's liberal arts institution with a strong spiritual foundation. She started working at the college in 1975 as the Assistant to the Director of Publications, a position that was in line with her course studies. Maintaining the college's commitment to excellence for its students stayed at the top of her agenda. When she ascended into the personnel department, she was better able to execute these goals. Calling upon her education in public relations, Rajski assisted the Director of Personnel in a human resource capacity. Through the recruitment

and training of numerous employees, conduction of salary analysis and other developmental programs, Rajski's credibility spread throughout the college's administration.

In 1991, the college had decided not to renew the contract of the service organization that had maintained custodial operations for years, and wanted the services to be brought in-house. It was looking for a strong manager with a background in human resources and psychology so he/she would be capable of dealing with situations that arose. Rajski pondered the new opportunity. She then decided to pick up the metaphorical hammer by submitting her candidacy for the Director of Building Services at Saint Mary's College. She was ultimately chosen for the position.

While she tackles new challenges with earnest dedication, the decision to make a complete 180-degree turn in her career path wasn't the easiest decision of her life. "I thought about it long and hard," she recalls, "Obviously, when you change professions, it's difficult to return. But I had a really special feeling for the folks [in Building Services]. In the Human Resources department, I'd seen a lot of the situations this staff had endured with the contract cleaning company. I understood how often times, people in this industry are considered subservient to the rest of the staff. My objective became to change these notions and ideals."

When she began her new position, staff was the only tool she was provided in the construction of an entirely new department. Even more challenging was the fact that attrition had yielded a rather sparse amount for the number of FTE's [full-time employees] required at Saint Mary's. Forced to start from scratch, Rajski not only looked to acquire the skills and resources necessary for her own personal development, she had to construct a building services department from the ground up. New equipment had to be purchased, policies and procedures implemented, and staff workloads and shifts assessed in order to get things running—and that was just the framework.

She took a close look at the resources available to her before doing anything. In order to gain accountability with her staff, Rajski looked to both vendors and peers for industry knowledge. "I knew nothing about the custodial industry," she admits. "They [the staff] also knew this, but they also understood that I was anxious to learn. I think that was something they took to heart, because they were extremely helpful throughout the learning process.

"I also went to a good friend of mine who (at the time) was the Director of Facilities at a college in Ohio. I went there to work alongside the staff and obtain an independent overview of the facilities duties in a college atmosphere. To really learn the equipment, you really have to do everything hands-on. I ran scrubbers, buffers—everything that was necessary to make it work."

To acquire compliance and regulatory information through agencies such as OSHA, Rajski attended as many seminars as possible. A year after stepping into her position, she joined I.E.H.A., which also afforded her another vehicle for education and resources. She studied hard and attained her (C.E.H.) [certified executive housekeeper] status in 1995.

Upon her return to Saint Mary's, Rajski developed certain objectives for her department. Constructing a departmental mission statement, strategic plan and vision was one of her primary goals. Their mission statement now reads: To provide a clean, healthy and safe environment for students to live, learn and socialize; for faculty to teach; and staff to work. The goal of the department remains consistent with the objectives of the college: To foster the highest standard of custodial operating procedures through skilled professionalism, integrity, conduct and competence.

Developing a staff capable of executing these goals followed next on Rajski's agenda. While some workers had made it through the years under the supervision of the contract cleaning service, Rajski felt it important to foster a sense of pride and achievement amongst them.

"Before I started," she recalls, " I talked to the staff and asked them for ideas of ways I could make them feel better about their jobs."

Changing uniforms was one of the ideas brought to the table. Rajski had the uniform tops changed from the smocks that read "House-keeping," to blue and white types that proudly bear the Saint Mary's logo.

Changing the name of the department was another employee's suggestion. The department changed from "Housekeeping" to "Building Services." This has also served to enhance not only the staff's vision of themselves, but also the faculty and students' perception of the department.

Rajski strives to provide as much education as possible to her staff so they are able to communicate situations and solutions to other departments. Staff members are strongly encouraged to strengthen their work knowledge by attending a minimum of two (2) educational training sessions annually. This education comes in the form of off-campus seminars provided by vendors, or seminars and/or workshops brought in-house by the college. This is expected of all the employees, not reserved just for the supervisors. When staff members reach their educational goals, they are presented with a personal certificate that recognizes them at their annual review. Rajski also makes all industry-related trade publications available to the staff in her office, so they can keep up to date on industry trends and information.

Establishing a working staff schedule was another consideration Rajski made when she began as Director. The contractor had implemented only two shifts, which resulted in countless interruptions throughout the staff's duties. "When I took over in 1991," she notes, "I took a look at how we could best service the college by providing additional service and gaining productivity. That's when we instituted the night shift. Of course, there were some problems at first as people adjusted their biological clocks, but ultimately we have been very successful. Even today, we had some openings on the afternoon and day teams, but the night staff don't want to change their hours."

Recently, she worked with vendors to institute a program that enables Rajski and her administration to critically evaluate the department's operations. It provides factual and concise custodial reports including: total square feet by building and floor type, total labor costs and quantity of cleaning supplies, cost per square foot, routine task list by area. Most importantly, the program documents the number of FTE's needed to provide quality cleaning service.

"Everyone in our industry needs solid information to present to finance and administration when asking for additional employees," says Rajski.

One of the remaining significant challenges Rajski faced in the department's development was obtaining new equipment. "Equipment was almost nil," she remarks. "We didn't have automatic scrubbers or anything at all, really. We needed to look at ways we could make work more productive and easier for the staff. We went from mops and buckets to automatic scrubbers. We increased our fleet of equipment with carpet extractors, portable upholstery cleaners, etc. We changed over our entire cleaning system. We had a Heinz 57 of products that we were able to streamline, which enhanced the familiarity of materials amongst the staff. Ultimately, this affects their productivity.

"Aesthetics over practicality seem to have become a priority in today's architectural world," says Rajski. "It's these aesthetics that hinder an effective custodial operation. Light fixtures are being placed in unreachable areas; light, solid color carpet being installed in heavy traffic areas; lack of electric outlets; windows not reachable for cleaning, the list goes on." Because of repeated hounding by Rajski, Building Services has now been given an active role in advising on much of the new construction renovation happening around campus and a handbook she developed for architects that includes things to keep in mind during the process to keep the building sustainable and maintainable for years to come.

THE PERPETUAL VISION

Since the initial challenges she encountered in the developmental stages of the Building Services Department at Saint Mary's College, the breadth of Marilyn Rajski's knowledge has extended tenfold. And when she was last seen at a convention in Saint Paul, Minnesota, she was still smiling. However, some of the dilemmas presented when she began her position still exist today.

"I continue to stress the credibility of a service entity within any facility," she asserts. "All service entities are put at the back burner, while other departments receive new computers, etc., rather than buying other capital items such as equipment. Without that state of the art equipment, we can't provide the quality of service. We need to have people realize the importance of our department's needs."

Marilyn Rajski has gained ground in helping to develop the attitudes of both the staff and the faculty in regard to the Building Services Department at the college for the better, but the challenge remains to continue garnering respect to the profession as a whole. Not only has she taken the challenge of learning an entirely new profession, but she's found her way in a difficult and extremely visible industry. "Everything we do is seen," she remarks. "We certainly can't hide anything. One thing we always say: Secretaries can make a mistake in a letter, and only the recipient views it. In Building Services, if you forget to clean something, put out paper products or change a light ... everyone knows about it!"

DISCUSSION QUESTIONS

1. Rajski admitted that her Building Services Department does not get the respect it deserves from the staff and faculty at St. Mary's. This is a problem, not only in schools and colleges, but throughout the cleaning industry. She even changed the name of the department from "housekeeping" to "building services." Should the industry discard the "housekeeping" appellation? Even the International Executive Housekeeper Association has repeatedly considered changing its name. What do you think? Would a name change help to earn the respect of the public?
2. Although there seems to be a trend on the part of many businesses and institutions to outsource the housekeeping function, St. Mary's brought the housekeeping function "in-house." What would be the advantages of not outsourcing the cleaning function in a hotel, hospital, or school?

CONCLUSION

The work of those involved in environmental services in hospitals and health-care institutions is not unlike that of the hotel housekeeping employee. Both have policies and procedures that are documented. Both have job descriptions capable of setting forth the various jobs that must be done, and there is a hierarchy of supervision similar to that found in hotel housekeeping. The knowledge of "what one might be dealing with," however, is far more detailed for the environmental services worker. Yet it would also be wise for the hotel housekeeper to be aware of the hidden dangers that can abound in hotel housekeeping.

Diseases are caused by microorganisms. The spread of pathogens is reduced by keeping everything clean. Being extra careful to avoid contamination is a way of keeping the hospital (and hotel) environment safe.

Isolation techniques in hospitals are especially important. Each step in every isolation procedure must be done carefully and completely.

Pest control was addressed in this chapter, and examples were given of the various types of pests that can create a contamination problem. Types of insecticides were presented, along with recommendations for their use. There was a strong recommendation to use qualified contract people to perform pest control work and to use an integrated approach to the problem.

Different types of wastes were identified and categorized, and information was presented on how to dispose of the several classifications of waste.

The Joint Commission on the Accreditation of Health Care Organizations is the agency that establishes the standards whereby such institutions are maintained and operated.

The **washing of hands** before and after contact with patients is probably the most important item to remember that will serve to protect the people—personnel as well as patients.

The subject of pollution and the environment was explored. Here is a truly win-win opportunity. By paying attention to the needs of the environment both indoors and out, housekeepers can do what is right and save money at the same time. A healthier environment means greater productivity, with a corresponding decrease in costs.

Finally, other career situations for the professional housekeeper were explored, including work in such diverse areas as the airlines, arenas and stadiums, contract cleaning, convention centers, and schools and colleges. This should clearly help to reinforce the widely held belief that the housekeeping profession is one of opportunities, and not a dead-end job.

KEY TERMS AND CONCEPTS

International Executive House-
   keepers Association (IEHA)
Director of Environmental Services
Joint Commission on Accredi-
   tation of Health Care Orga-
   nizations (JCAHO)
Disinfection
Terminal cleaning
Needles
Syringes
Sharps
Microbiology
Chemistry of cleaning and
   disinfecting
Microorganisms
Protists
Bacteria
Bacillus
Coccus
Fungi
Spirochete
Spores
Staphylococcus
Streptococcus
Virus
Aerobic
Anaerobic
Antisepsis
Asepsis
Asepsis (medical)
Asepsis (surgical)
Autoclave
Chemical agent
Disinfection
Disinfection (concurrent)
Disinfection (terminal)
Gram (positive/negative)
Intermediate host

Micron
Pathogenic
Physical agents
Reagents
Sterilization
Mineral
Organic
Osmological
Bacterial
Entomological
Chemical formulas
Atom
Molecule
Valence
Compounds
Reactants
Products
Atomic reactions
Acid
Alchohol
Alkali
Anion
Antiseptics
Bacteriostat
Cation
Detergent
Disinfectant
Hydrogen peroxide
Iodine
Ion
Organic compounds
pH
Phenol
Phenolic
Preservatives
Quaternary ammonium
   compounds
R

Radical
Salts
Sanitizer
Water
Universal solvent
Petri test dishes
Dilution ratio
Carbolic acid (phenol)
Chemical suspension
Toxic
Bacteria trails
Chain of infection
Pathogen
Isolation unit
Antineoplastic Agents
Chemotherapy drugs
Causative agent
Reservoir
Mode of escape
Immune carrier
Method of transmission
Host
Integrated Pest Management
Preventive
Waste
Infectious waste
Certifying authority
JCAHO standards
Earth's crust
Oxides
Ultraviolet radiation
Chlorofluorocarbons
Photochemical reaction
Smog
Acid rain
Global warming
Greenhouse gases
Holes in the ozone layer

Landfills	Recycling	Deferred maintenance
Integrated waste management	Waste transformation	Washing of hands
Source reduction	Truck mount	
Reuse	Bio-recovery service	

DISCUSSION AND REVIEW QUESTIONS

1. Mr. James from Houston, Texas, checked into the University Inn in late afternoon. He was feeling feverish and nauseated after his flight from Los Angeles. He called the front desk and asked for some ice, drank a glass of water, and went directly to bed. He noticed a red swelling on the back of his neck, which had been draining onto his shirt collar. He used a wash cloth to rinse it off.

   When Mildred, the housekeeper, came to turn down the bed, she found Mr. James very ill. She gave him some water from his glass at the bedside and asked Mr. James, "Do you want me to call you a doctor?" to which he answered, "Yes."

   a. What kind of policy should be written that would help Mildred know what to do in this situation?

   b. What specific items in the room are contaminated?

   c. When the doctor arrives, he has Mr. James transported to the hospital. What kind of step-by-step procedure should Mildred use to clean up this room?

2. Upon admission to the hospital Mr. James's temperature was 102°F, the red swollen spot on his neck was draining, and he was having difficulty breathing.

   a. What type of isolation would be best for him?

   b. What specific steps should the housekeeper take in the isolation unit?

   c. For handling trash?

   d. For handling laundry?

   e. What articles must be cleaned, removed, or sterilized in the unit when Mr. James leaves?

3. What do you see as the pluses and minuses of contract cleaning? Make a list of positives and negatives. Now do the same for arenas and stadiums, convention centers, hospitals, nursing homes, schools, and colleges.

CHAPTER 14

The Safeguarding of Assets: Concerns for Safety and Security in Housekeeping Operations

LEARNING OBJECTIVES

After studying the chapter, students should be able to:

1. List and describe the primary concepts of risk management and the safeguarding of assets.
2. Describe the inherent problems associated with maintaining safety and security in hotels and hospitals.
3. Describe how to minimize theft in guestrooms.
4. Describe how to make guests and guestrooms secure.
5. Describe common emergencies that can occur in hospitals and hotels.
6. List actions to be taken in case of an emergency and tell how to safeguard against potential disasters.

The **body of knowledge** that is now becoming of major concern to those involved in management of the service professions is about **safeguarding assets** of an organization. This is a responsibility for which all who work within such organizations must take heed.

The **American Society of Industrial Security (ASIS,** the national association for directors of security) has now catalogued this body of knowledge into a resource that forms the basis for educating, certifying, and training not only directors of security groups but also those in charge of other organizational departments.

It is to this end that environmental services directors and hotel executive housekeepers must become involved in the analysis of risks being taken daily by their companies **(risk analysis)** and in the management of such risks **(risk management)** in such a way as to reduce the threat to a company's assets.

The Concept of Safeguarding Assets

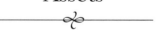

It is first necessary to understand what might be recognized as ''the assets'' of a hospitality or health-care organization, as listed in the following table.

Human	Physical	Intrinsic
Guests	Land	Goodwill
Patients	The facility	Reputation
Employees	Equipment	
	Inventory	
	Cash	
	Accounts receivable	

SECURITY VERSUS SAFETY (THE DIFFERENCE)

The concept of **security** in hospitality operations has many times been addressed in tandem with that of **safety**, even though the general thrust of each term is somewhat different. The current trend today uses the term *safety* in discussing matters such as disaster, fire prevention, fire protection devices, and conditions that provide for freedom from injury and damage to property. *Security*, however, is used more as a means to describe the need for freedom from fear, anxiety, and doubt involving ourselves, as well as the protection and defense against the loss or theft of guest, employee, and company property. Both terms are, however, more generally recognized as only parts of a greater whole. There are now new terms in the lexicon, such as *protection and safeguarding of assets, threat analysis, security surveys, risk analysis,* and *risk management.* Hospitality operations, large and small, are extremely vulnerable to security hazards. The very nature of their operation, which involves the presence of a wide diversity of people, most of whom are unknown to the proprietor, poses a considerable threat to the security of a property. Risks of fire are also serious. The incidence of hotel fires causing loss of life and serious damage to property has increased in recent years. As a result of property owners and managers being accountable for the safety and protection of guests and employees, their property, and the assets of the company, the status of security has in many cases been elevated to the executive boardroom.

Not all hotels are of the 100-room variety. Many small units (40 rooms) are operated by one or two persons in one family. And, to the contrary, 1000-room units are now being dwarfed by 5000 + rooms, resorts, and casinos. However, the small unit is confronted by the same threats as the larger establishments, and wrongdoers are aware that the small establishments do not have the same large, complete security forces as do the giant properties.

Proprietors must also be aware of a much larger volume of legal provisions than would apply to the owner of a private home. They have direct responsibility for the safety and well-being of their guests, and part of this responsibility is compliance with such laws as are in effect respecting the operations of public enterprises.

THE BASIC FUNCTION OF SECURITY

The security function in the hospitality industry today is best described as that major preventive and proactive activity used to protect the assets of the organization. But who would have thought 40 years ago that the *asset list* would evolve to include our guests and invitees, our employees, and the property of all three, in addition to supplies, equipment, and funds, as well as our reputation and goodwill.

To fulfill this function, those involved in security work must be able to foresee and assess (even predict) threats, then make recommendations to ownership and management regarding the most appropriate action to take that will safeguard both life and property. In addition, personnel of all departments must search out and alert operational management of the need to "prevent" unreasonable and imprudent operation that could result in liability for incautious action and negligent behavior.

NATURE OF THE SECURITY FUNCTION

Few facilities are more vulnerable to security hazards than hotels with restaurants, lounges, casinos, parking garages, and theme parks. The nature of a business that involves the presence of large numbers of people, most of whom are not known to the manager, poses an ever-present threat to the security of other guests, employees, and the property. The risks of fire and natural disaster, riot, theft, embezzlement, civil disturbance, or bomb threats, have increased in recent years, all of which can cause serious injury or loss of life, theft, loss or damage to property belonging to the guests, employees, or the facility itself.

WHAT SECURITY IS NOT

Security is not what was once seen to be the **plainclothes house detective** whose only functions were to keep the peace within the hotel and on occasion evict the noisy guest or the one who did not have the means to pay the bill.

Even though in most cases security officers are uniformed, badged, and sometimes armed, such persons are not members of the local metropolitan police, nor are they a part of the sheriff's posse. Seldom do members of private organizations possess police powers, only the power of an ordinary citizen to teach, observe, report, call for help, and, on occasion, perform a citizen's arrest.

It is hoped that this information will encourage all housekeeping personnel to become aware and have concerns regarding the volatility and fragility of our hospitality industry with regard to foreseeable security and safety matters.

The function of hospitality security is every *employee's responsibility.* Looking for what is "out of the ordinary" or "just doesn't look right" (JDLR), preventing, foreseeing, predicting, and removing hazards and other causes of crime, injury, and unsafe practices must be primary in the minds of every employee, regardless of the size of the establishment or the department in which one is employed. Every employee, manager, and owner must become the eyes of the security department—whether there are 100 employees assigned to security or only one employee on the property in early-morning hours.

Remember, if nothing ever happens, security is doing a good job.

Security from Theft in the Housekeeping Department

EMPLOYEE THEFT: NATURE OF THE PROBLEM

No other hotel employees have as much access to hotel assets and guest property as do members of the housekeeping department.

This writer recalls being shown a photograph taken by an employee of her children at home. In the background were drapes, a bedspread, and a lamp from the hotel in which she was employed.

Management's attitude about employee honesty runs to the extremes, as illustrated by the following commonly heard statements: "My employees would never steal," or "I don't trust any of my employees; they will all steal if given a chance." Both statements tell a story: either management is naive about people in general, or it believes that the only way to manage people is by Theory X techniques (covered in Chapter 1), and using scare tactics.

Harold Gluck,[1] a registered criminologist and a member of the American Association of Criminology, quoted reports stating that "30% of your employees will steal from you; 30% of them are honest, and the remaining 40% go with the tide and the opportunity." Gluck's conclusion provides hope that there is an unemotional and objective point from which to depart in establishing a sound program for **employee theft prevention**.

EMPLOYEE CONTAMINATION: A REAL AND PRESENT DANGER

Bob Curtis[2] talks about **contamination of employees**, stating that it may come from several causes:

1. When one employee is known to be stealing, others will tend to follow.
2. Employees who are frustrated and angry at the way they are being treated by management think nothing of talking with each other about how easy it is to rip off the firm. These employees receive the plaudits of peers for their ability to beat the system. Once an employee starts to beat the system, he or she will brag about it to companions or will even put himself or herself in a place in which companions can view the theft. When word gets around that management cannot uncover the stealing, others join in.
3. Borderline honest employees do not think it dishonest to "get even" with a greedy, impersonal, giant company that is indifferent to employee needs for recognition and support.
4. Low morale is a sickness sign that forewarns of contamination of employees regarding theft.
5. The problem of contamination is considerable in firms with a highly authoritarian management style, because authoritarian management is only successful where punishment and threats of punishment are primary controls.

THE SECTION HOUSEKEEPER AND ROOM THEFT

Not long ago, Bob Stafford of *Eyewitness News*, Channel 9, Orlando, Florida, ran a series feature story entitled "Do Not Disturb, Thief at Work." Stafford reported how more than 80 burglaries had been reported as occurring at a major small chain hotel located on International Drive in Orlando in less than one year. The hotel had been hiring inmates from a local penal institution on work release to work as guestroom attendants at the hotel. During the day they were brought by prison bus to work and were picked up at the end of the day and returned to prison at night. Stafford, with the help of a hidden camera, was able to catch several guestroom attendants stealing from people's wallets when in the room. The room attendants would not admit their theft, nor was management even interested in seeing the video of its people stealing. Stafford concluded his series by showing how easy it was to purchase a master key from a guestroom attendant (the going price was $100 to $500). Good hiring practices, thorough background investigations, and management's demand of unconditional honesty from all employees, are all essential policies and procedures in any well-run hotel.

No one is more sensitive to the problems of theft from hotel guestrooms than the honest GRA who is known to possess a floor master key to a guestroom that has just been robbed. There is the unfortunate assumption that, because the GRA has a key to the room, if anything is missing she or he is automatically the culprit. Seldom does the guest realize that the floor supervisor, bellperson, room clerk, engineer, room service waiter, executive housekeeper, and general manager also have keys, as does possibly the last guest to check out of the room, to say nothing of the professional hotel thief who may have just purchased a key to the room from some pawn shop.

In such cases, if GRAs are part of Gluck's 30 percent honest people, they may lose heart and resign. If part of the 40 percent who go with the tide, they may become a part of the Curtis sample and conclude, "Why not steal—I am going to be accused anyway, and no one will support me if I don't do it."

Even though Gluck and Curtis both present convincing arguments, an objective and professional approach to theft control can be established and maintained, provided that personnel within the department are enlisted in a practical and positive program of theft prevention similar to that which follows.

A 14-POINT PROGRAM FOR EMPLOYEE THEFT PREVENTION

Let us begin by assuming that applications will be made for positions within the department by people who are symbolic of Gluck's 30–40–30 percent sample distribution. The following **14-point theft prevention program** is a reasonable attack on the 30 percent who will steal at any price, and a positive program to keep the questionable 40 percent on the honest side of the equation.

1. *Institute and ensure professional hiring practices:* Ensure that proper screening methods are used during hiring operations. Complete applications, including follow-up of questionable information and gaps, are vital to good hiring practices. Gaps in **employment history** on applications may hide significant information.

   Every employee should understand that references will be checked before any hiring decision will be made. When making reference checks, phone calls are often better than requests in writing. It is of maximum benefit during a reference check to get as close to the truth as possible, even to the point of asking pointed questions such as whether the person giving the reference would take the applicant back if given the chance. A hesitation in an answer may be all that is needed to indicate the right go or no-go decision.

   In places in which **polygraph (lie detector) examinations** are not prohibited by law or union contract, they may be considered, especially for people who will handle company funds. Every employee, however, should understand as a condition of employment that, should a situation arise where suspicion is cast over an employee, that person may be given the opportunity to establish innocence by voluntarily undergoing a polygraph examination. In such cases, the polygraph examination is not being used to prove guilt in a court of law but to establish innocence by creating reasonable doubt as to the guilt of an employee in a given set of circumstances.

   Employees who are hired after exposure to thorough reference checks and indoctrination are usually better employees because they know that management is aware of their backgrounds, recognizes their application statements to be honest,

and is less likely to tolerate dishonesty. Applicants should also be made aware of controls such as package checks and periodic locker inspections so that they understand that management does exert reasonable theft control over employees as a routine course of doing business.

2. *Establish positive identification techniques for employees:* Large properties require identification of all employees, usually by a **badge system** that contains a photograph, signature, and a color code indicating the department or work area of the employee. Such identification systems discourage people bent on thievery from trying to pass as employees.

   Color identification of badges or even name tags identify the work areas of employees and expose employees who are out of their work areas without good explanations. Special uniforms also identify employees as to work area, provided that such uniforms are not off-the-rack uniforms that may be purchased by anyone. Photo name badges are the best means of identification, provided security personnel and supervisors are trained to observe them as a routine course of business. Close observation will not be necessary after the employee becomes known to management and security personnel. But most hotels have a few new employees every day or at least every week. Management and security personnel also change over periods of time. Therefore, constant checking of photo identification badges is necessary, and in the long run will have an effect on company profits and, ultimately, costs to guests.

3. *Conduct theft orientation and attitude training:* During employee training it is important to remind trainees that even though the vast majority of employees are completely honest, one dishonest housekeeper with a passkey can be devastating to an operation. One such person in the midst of other honest employees can cast mistrust over the entire organization. Discuss the scenario in which an honest GRA is confronted by an irate guest who thinks the housekeeper has stolen property from the guestroom. Employees should understand that it is each person's duty not only to encourage honesty among fellow workers but also to confront and bring forth those who would cause any employee to fall under suspicion of dishonesty.

   Employees should be taught that many guests will misplace items brought with them to the hotel and for an instant will assume the "simplest" explanation—that the item has been taken, and that the housekeeper is the guilty person. Employees should be taught that during such a moment, their attitude, composure, and behavior will tend to foretell future actions on the part of the guest and even management. The employee who becomes emotional, denies with force, or cannot seem to be found at that moment engenders deeper suspicion, whereas the employee who is composed, calls management or security to the scene immediately, then offers to help search for the missing item is much less likely to be suspected in the long run. Honest employees need not be thin-skinned in such a moment but should try to put themselves in the guest's place and ask themselves, "What kind of reaction would be expected from a hotel employee if situations were reversed?" Possibilities other than theft by the housekeeper are best explained to the guest by a member of management or by security personnel. Employees' actions should be helpful and cooperative.

It should be explained during training that employees are not handed over by management to accusing guests, but the name of the housekeeper who cleaned a room from which items are missing will be made available to the police should the guest actually make a formal charge against an employee, as will the record of the employee, which, it is hoped, will indicate no prior suspicious behavior. Employees should also be informed that records involving items missing from rooms cleaned by GRAs will be maintained in employee personnel files. Several such unexplained or unresolved occurrences will most certainly cast suspicion on an employee, who should then be given an opportunity to remove such suspicion by voluntarily participating in a polygraph examination.

Other important matters that should be covered in training regarding theft prevention are procedures involving the lost-and-found, what to do if illegal acts are observed while working, procedures to follow regarding the use of locker rooms, and rules about employees' handbags not being permitted in hotel guestrooms and satellite linen room areas. The fact that these procedures and rules are mentioned during training indicates to employees that the company is conscious of the ramifications of theft, that it intends to exercise reasonable controls and institute procedures that will assist people in maintaining integrity, and that the presence of temptations is recognized but need not be compelling. Finally, it shows employees that most procedures enacted to prevent theft are, if they are followed, also inclined to prevent suspicion of employees.

4. *Closely monitor behavior and adhere to company policies and procedures during employee training and probationary periods:* Too often, **probationary periods** are perfunctory and taken for granted. Probationary periods should be understood as trial periods in which the employee is to demonstrate not only worker skills, but also attitudes and perceptions about compliance with company policies.

Probationary periods are also trial periods for the company. Management and supervisors should demonstrate the organizational attitudes toward employees and the manner in which employees are to be treated, thus giving the employee an opportunity to learn about the company before employment becomes permanent.

Observations of the employees' attitudes are very important at this crucial time of employment, and employees should not be passed into permanent full-time employment without some evaluation of their attitudes toward guests, other employees, property, and company assets. All too often an employee is allowed to pass into full-time permanent status with questionable attitudes about the company and its guests, which may later prove to be grounds for termination, when all during probationary employment the evidence was present but not challenged.

5. *Inaugurate and closely administer a program of key control:* The large number of multipurpose keys maintained within the housekeeping department makes it necessary for a **key-control program** to be all-encompassing and strictly enforced. Each day keys should be subcustodied to employees who have a need for them by an acknowledging signature; they should be properly receipted for when turned in at the end of each workday. Keys must be properly accounted for at all times, either as inventory in a key locker or properly logged out.

Workers should be provided with a way to attach keys to their persons so that they need not be unattached while being used. Such a method (Figure 14.1) allows GRAs and supervisors to attach master keys to their persons. The master keys are on a lanyard with a slip O-ring that is attached to a **key pouch**. When not in use, keys can be stored in the pouch and the lanyard wrapped around the pouch. The pouch can be appropriately marked by section number and inventoried in a like manner. When the key is worn (Figure 14.2), the lanyard is placed around the waist with the pouch in back, out of the way. A pelican hook is attached to the slip O-ring, allowing the keys to be carried in the pocket until they are needed. The strap length is sufficient to allow freedom of movement.

The entire issue of department keys should be sight-inventoried at the end of each day and management notified immediately should any irregularities be noticed in the key inventory.

FIGURE 14.1 Guestroom master keys attached to a lanyard with storage pouch.

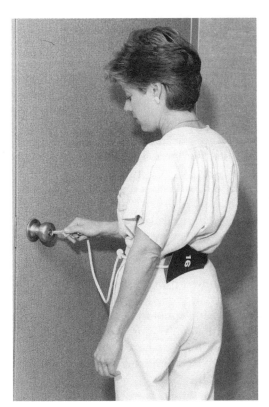

FIGURE 14.2 Master keys are worn by an attendant. Sufficient lanyard is available for easy use of the keys.

All employees must be strongly impressed with the necessity to safeguard master keys entrusted to them. The loss or misplacement of a master key must be immediately reported to management, and location of the key must take precedence over further work. Therefore, several people must become involved in finding

RED TAG

Serial No. _____

_____
(Date)

_____
(Issued to)

Has permission to remove
from the premises

_____
(Item)

Personal property ☐   Hotel property ☐

_____
(Authorizing signature)

FIGURE 14.3 Red tag used to authorize removal of personal or hotel property from the premises.

a misplaced key. Finally, employees should be made to understand that the loss of a master key may be grounds for termination, especially if negligence is determined.

Guestroom keys left by departing guests and subsequently found by GRAs who are cleaning the rooms must be safeguarded by the GRAs and not left on the top of GRAs' carts. Many hotels provide lock boxes on the tops of carts that can be used for depositing room keys. The hotel should have someone regularly pass among the working GRAs to retrieve and return such keys to the front desk. Professional hotel thieves are known to search for room keys left in sight on top of carts.

6. *Have a red tag program:* There are legitimate reasons why an employee may be allowed to remove property from the premise. Property given to an employee or awarded from the lost-and-found can be removed under the protection of a **red tag system**.

Red tags (Figure 14.3) are issued by management to employees after the manager has examined the item to be removed. The red tag contains granted authority for the removal of property and in some cases will cover the loan of company property, such as a vacuum cleaner or a roll-away bed. For such red tag programs to work, they must have the support and compliance of employees.

All red tags should be serially numbered. Tags should be attached to parcels and collected by security personnel as the parcels are removed from the premises. As a form of control, a red tag collected by an employee gate security guard should be subsequently returned to the manager who signed the tag in order that the manager may know what went out of the building over his or her signature.

7. *Have regular locker inspections:* Although regular and routine locker inspections (even though unannounced) are conducted primarily to ensure that items such as company property, drugs, alcohol, and soiled uniforms are not being allowed to accumulate in lockers, the knowledge that a locker inspection could occur at any time tacitly disqualifies the locker as a place for temporarily storing contraband or stolen items. Employees should be made aware at hiring that locker inspections will be conducted periodically by a member of management and the hourly workforce. Employees should also be informed about the purpose of locker inspections.

8. *Establish inventory control programs and conduct regular physical inventories with results (and implications) published to the entire department:* Guest supplies, cleaning supplies, linens, and other capital items should be inventoried regularly and the results and implications presented to all employees. Employees who have been counseled to be frugal with supplies need to be told when their efforts have brought about cost reductions. Special recognition should be made in front of the entire department. Yet employees must understand that situations in which inventory usage is high and out of control will have the immediate attention of management.

   Admittance to storerooms and issuance of supplies should be limited to a few employees; policies that allow help-yourself access to supplies by employees are not recommended. The issuance of supplies should not be so restrictive as to prevent efficient work procedures; a proper balance between restrictive and loose procedures should be maintained. Any sudden affluence on the part of an employee warrants concern.

9. *Keep records of missing items of guests and of the hotel:* When items are reported or found to be missing, make cross-reference files of the item by type and of the employee who could have been involved. Sometimes patterns develop that are valuable in uncovering causes for the disappearance of items.

10. *Employee parking should not be adjacent to the building:* Employee parking areas should be sufficiently far away from buildings and structures so as to make it difficult to slip in and out of an entrance several times a day and

into a parked car. Areas to and from employee parking should be well lighted.

11. *Trash handling requires special consideration:* The handling and disposal of trash is a significant part of most housekeeping department jobs. Trash collection and disposal should be monitored by different supervisors on a rotating basis. Because of the possibility that trash might be used to hide contraband, it should not be allowed to accumulate near incoming supplies and equipment.

   Employees' automobiles should be periodically observed, and any employee cars that are parked near a trash disposal site should be carefully checked.

   There are classic cases in which one or more employees have been in collusion with trash pickup personnel. Should the housekeeping department have its own loading dock, allow a truck to park at the dock only to unload; it should be moved as soon as it is unloaded. Many hotel television sets disappear in delivery trucks that are allowed to remain at the loading dock for more time than is necessary.

12. *Enlist employees as part of the security team:* Security is not a one-person job. GRAs and supervisors can be valuable in theft prevention and security by reporting suspicious behavior by guests, damage to rooms, items noted as missing from rooms, and special or unique types of belongings noted in opened luggage in guestrooms. Several large suitcases with few articles of clothing hanging in a closet may be an indication of things to come—or possibly to go—such as linens, bedspreads, and towels.

   All housekeeping personnel should know on sight all engineering personnel. The TV repair person, especially, should be well known. A TV removed from a room should be accompanied by an immediate replacement, or else suspicion should be aroused.

   Satellite linen rooms and other storage areas should always be kept locked unless attended. Satellite linen rooms should be kept clean and free of litter, and every item in the linen room should be recognized.

   Strange items or packages found adrift or in hallway corridors could spell trouble and can even be worthy of an immediate phone call to the security department.

13. *When problems are suspected, bring in an expert:* Many times inventory losses or reported thefts indicate a problem that may not easily reveal itself. When such is the case, hire an expert **snoop**. Snoops are security specialists who pass as employees, gather the evidence needed to resolve theft problems, then quietly fade out of the employee workforce.

I once hired a snoop when a department was plagued with the disappearance of linens from GRAs' carts during the daytime. The snoop applied for work as a section housekeeping aide, giving the appearance that he could neither read nor write. The actual identity of the snoop was limited only to the executive housekeeper and the resident manager. The snoop (for want of a name, John) worked as a utility employee, which allowed him presence in all areas of the property.

John was known as a talker, was well liked by all who met him, and was seen to lean on his broom and gossip quite often. In about three weeks, John appeared to come to work intoxicated and unfortunately had to be terminated. Three days later a detailed, comprehensive, and very professional report was received from the security specialist (who had been John), naming three employees who had been in collusion and had tried to enlist John into their organization. John's statement was sufficient to convict all three employees on grand larceny charges, as well as to recover about 25 percent of the stolen inventory. What was most surprising was that one of the three employees uncovered in the theft ring was a junior manager.

14. *Set the example:* The first 13 steps of this theft prevention program require positive planning and follow-through. Aside from those measures used in hiring employees and the systems used to identify employees, all other steps may appear unduly oppressive and authoritarian. To the contrary, each step is designed to help honest employees remain honest by removing temptation through known and publicized controls and by emphasizing the fact that honest employees have no problem coping. Dishonest employees, however, will find that dishonest acts meet with equal and opposite vigor.

No one step has as much effect as does management, from the top down, setting the proper example. In the case of the housekeeping department, the executive housekeeper must demonstrate that the rules and controls outlined apply to management, as well as to the most junior employee, to the fullest extent. No exceptions—not even taking a pencil or a sheet of paper for the children to do their homework—can be tolerated. Many times it is being completely trustworthy about these small items that sets the tone for what management expects or, better yet, has a right to expect. And there is nothing that generates temptation in an honest employee more than seeing the boss taking something.

A MINI CASE STUDY
Ethical Dilemmas in Security

Molly Galloway, executive housekeeper for the Seacoast Pines Resort and Convention Center, is sitting at her desk when the phone rings. It's Tony Belcher, hotel manager for the Seacoast Pines. There is a big convention in the hotel, the Western Regional Used Automobile Dealers Association (UADA). They have been holding their annual convention at the hotel for the past 12 years and theirs is one of the biggest and most profitable conventions held at the property. Belcher tells Galloway that he has just gotten off the phone with the executive director of the UAD, "Big" Bill Williams, and it's bad, very bad. It seems that the convention's special guest star entertainer, Trophy Mushro, who has been staying in the hotel, has just reported that her diamond earrings worth at least $50,000 are missing from her room. She is claiming she left them on a table in her room and went to the pool while the female housekeeper cleaned her room. When she returned, they were gone. There were no other witnesses to the incident.

Belcher tells Galloway she has to produce that GRA and she should be fired immediately. "We might even lose this convention, if we don't take immediate action on this and discipline the perpetrator," warns Belcher.

"Wait a minute," Galloway responds. "We have policies covering this. First we interview the employee and we ask the employee if she would volunteer to take a polygraph to corroborate her claim of innocence. If the employee has had no other incidents similar to this one in her file and she passes the poly, then we support the employee's claims of innocence. That's company policy!"

"And we potentially lose a half-million-dollar piece of business over this," Belcher retorts. "I say we fire her and if you think she is innocent, you can always help her find another job. If she passes the poly, we won't prosecute her. This is a 'right-to-work' state and nobody owns their job."

QUESTIONS

1. If you were Molly Galloway, what would you do? Should she do as Belcher wants, or should she argue against the action with Belcher and top management?

2. Do you think employees should even be given voluntary polygraph tests? They are not admissible in court, but are they fairly reliable?

3. Should the employee's past record and length of employment influence the decision making? Even if the GRA is innocent, would firing her be the best response in this situation? And even though the hotel's legal liability is limited, should concern for the hotel's potential economic loss dominate management's decision making?

4. How much concern should the hotel have for a single employee? Discuss these questions and your other thoughts with your fellow students and your instructor.

USEFULNESS OF EMPLOYEE PROFILES

Barbara Powers, general manager of the Branford Motor Inn, Branford, Connecticut, and officer of the Connecticut Lodging Association (C.L.A.), suggests that there is an **employee profile** by which a prospective thief among employees might be identified.[3]

Such profiles are developed on the basis of experience with people who have been proved guilty of pilferage or theft. Understand that the profile might apply to honest people. That said, here are the characteristics employees likely to be dishonest often have in common:

- They wear an air of dissatisfaction with someone or something.
- They don't identify with the hotel. The hotel is "they" rather than "we."
- They lack respect for people or property, don't tend to accept responsibility, and are self-centered.
- They resent criticism.
- They have financial difficulties.

An additional point might be added to an effective theft-prevention program by maintaining profiles on employees who display the characteristics enumerated by Powers. Such profiles may prove useful in establishing a likely list of suspects when things start to disappear and no further indication or evidence is immediately at hand, if only to know whom to watch more closely in the future.

THEFT BY GUESTS AND OTHERS

There is some question about who might be more to blame for theft losses: employees, guests, or other people bent on dishonesty. The degree of loss from each source seems to depend more on the attention paid by management to each of the sources than any other factor. Management cannot assume that theft losses will come more from one source than any other source. Guests bent on stealing linens can bring as much havoc to inventory cost as can employees or outsiders who have targeted the hotel as a source for contraband.

As mentioned earlier, employees should be enlisted into a network of security-conscious people trained to react when they observe suspicious activities. GRAs, especially, should be trained to cite each item of furniture and software as they enter a guestroom. Missing items should be immediately reported to management in order that positive action may be taken.

If GRAs report seeing a guest's suitcase loaded with towels, the executive housekeeper should notify the front desk manager to discreetly but with certainty add a specified amount to the guest's account in the form of a **miscellaneous charge**. If questioned by the guest, the clerk can say that it was assumed that the guest intended to pay for the souvenirs being removed from the hotel, and that it was customary to add appropriate charges to the guest account to cover the cost of such souvenirs when they happen to be linens. In most such cases, the guest does not press the matter further but pays the account in full. Revenues received as a result of such charges are transferred to inventory accounts so that the housekeeping department costs are kept in control.

TV THIEVES

The most expensive item that attracts the attention of thieves in hotels is the television set. This is especially true of television sets in rooms that are first-floor drive-up rooms, with sliding glass doors that open directly into parking areas. There is only one thing that can improve on this setup as far as the thief is concerned—not to have to unbolt the television to remove it.

First and foremost, all televisions *should be bolted down*, either on a pedestal, a chest top, or on a wall, so that without a key or the proper tool, removing the television is a major undertaking. Many hotels have security systems on televisions that initiate an alarm at the front desk if an antenna is disconnected. Such systems have greatly reduced the clandestine removal of televisions, especially where security personnel have been trained to respond quickly to such alarms.

The modus operandi of many television thieves is to cruise a hotel parking lot during the daytime and observe first-floor rooms that are unoccupied. After selecting several such rooms, the thief enters the hotel and, under pretense of having just checked out and inadvertently leaving an article in the room, prompts the GRA to let him or her into the room. Once in the room, the thief chains the door so as not to be immediately interrupted. The thief then goes about the business of separating the television from the premises, removing it through the sliding glass door and putting it into a van that a partner has waiting outside the room.

Housekeepers must be trained never to open a door of a guestroom for anyone claiming to be a guest unless she or he has personally observed the person to be a guest on several prior occasions; then the housekeeper is best advised to call a supervisor. If you open a door for a guest not in possession of a key, do not allow the guest to enter the room until a phone call is made to the front desk to verify the name of the party registered in the room. Legitimate guests are impressed with this type of precaution taken on their behalf.

Visibility into first-floor rooms from the outside during daylight hours must be restricted. This is easily accomplished by using a glass casement curtain in all first-floor rooms. During daylight, if there is no lamp or other light on inside a guestroom, it is impossible to see inside a room with a drawn glass curtain and to determine if the room is in fact vacant.

All employees must be trained to be suspicious of unusual happenings and report them to the proper authority. I heard of a bizarre incident in which a general manager was touring a first-floor corridor of a hotel. The general manager was confronted with a guest struggling with a television that seemed to be quite heavy; the general manager promptly offered to help the guest with his heavy load. After helping the guest load the television into a waiting automobile and wishing him a safe journey and speedy return, he overheard a GRA exclaim that a television had just been stolen from one of the guestrooms. Everyone needs training.

Security within Hotel Guestrooms

Innkeepers have a common-law responsibility to provide secure premises within which guests may abide. Security is defined as the measures that are required to promote a state of well-being relative to an establishment to protect life and property, and to minimize risks of natural disasters or crime. The protection of guests within their rooms must be paramount.

Several states have become quite specific in what constitutes adequate security for hotel guestrooms. In addition, most major hotel companies have set minimum standards relating to locking devices for guestroom doors. Holiday Inns, Inc., specifies about 16 criteria that door locks must meet or exceed before they may be used in Holiday Inns.

FIGURE 14.4 Locking device that replaces door chains at the Los Angeles Airport/Marriott Hotel. *(Photo courtesy of the Los Angeles Airport/Marriott Hotel.)*

Reasonable security for guestrooms includes the following:

- Automatic closing doors
- Automatic latching devices on latch bolts that require a key or other specialized device to open or unlock the door from the outside
- Dead bolts that are an integral part of latch bolts; set from inside the room; must be capable of being opened from outside the room with an emergency passkey
- A door chain or other mechanical locking device that may be set from inside the room, such as the mechanical locking device that has replaced door chains in the Los Angeles Airport/Marriott Hotel (Figure 14.4). When the lever attached to the door frame (on the right) is thrown across the ball attached to the door (on the left), opening the door will catch the ball up in the track slot, allowing the door to be opened only three inches.
- A peephole installed in the room door whereby the guestroom occupant may see who is on the outside of the door before opening it
- Drapes that fully close and are capable of blacking out the room in bright sunlight
- Locking latches and chain locks on all sliding glass doors

CARD ENTRY SYSTEMS

The greatest change to have come about in many years for guestroom security is the **card entry system**. The large numbers of manufacturers that are now involved in producing such systems is a testament to the need for some technique that will replace the antiquated systems of guestroom door keys.

The difficulty in making a system of guestroom keys secure, especially in hotels that have lavish key tags hanging from keys, is well known. The replacement cost for lost, misplaced, stolen, or simply carried-away keys as souvenirs is in itself a major cost problem, to say nothing of the lack of control resulting from such practices. Hotel maintenance departments usually have to establish a routine **lock cylinder** change program, whereby cylinders from locks on one floor are swapped with cylinders from locks on other floors and new keys are manufactured and stamped with new codes, if any control is to be maintained at all.

Card entry systems have simplified and greatly improved the security capability of locking systems in hotel guestrooms. Most of the systems are designed around the premise that when a guest checks into the hotel, a plastic card of some type, which has a magnetic signature impressed thereon, is presented to the guest. The card operates the assigned room door with a combination that has been set just for the new occupant. When the guest checks out, all prior memory of the card signature is wiped out of the door combination and the system to await the arrival of the new guest.

Housekeeping and other master card systems may be set or reset in an instant as the need arises, and the fear of a lost master key can be short-lived. The state of the art is such that retrofits for hotels still using regular key systems are available and warrant immediate investigation and possible conversion.

SECURITY CONSCIOUSNESS FOR GUESTS

Today's seasoned hotel traveler is much more security conscious than travelers in past years. The guest who frequently travels has been forewarned and is therefore forearmed to use all locks provided on guestroom doors when retiring for the night. All too often robberies involving guests in hotel rooms can be traced to the guest who failed to lock and chain the door properly before retiring, to say nothing of the guest who indiscriminately opened the door without looking through the peephole to see who was in the hall.

Day or night, the executive housekeeper and all members of the housekeeping staff should be trained to close every door found open within the hotel. This practice is a measure of protection for guests who may or may not be in their rooms, as well as a means of protection for hotel property.

The Los Angeles Airport/Marriott Hotel has provided a reassuring touch with its table card (Figure 14.5). The sign provides a phone number that guests may call if there is reason to believe that they need extra security attention. Such messages caution guests about security

for valuables and provide a phone number for security if assistance is needed, without causing undue alarm to guests.

CHANGE AGENTS

John Garfinkel

Executive Director, International Sanitary Supply Association

John Garfinkel is Executive Director of the International Sanitary Supply Association (ISSA), based in Chicago, and a board member of the National Association of Wholesalers and Distributors (NAW), based in Washington, D.C. ISSA conducts the largest trade show in the cleaning and maintenance industry, ISSA/INTERCLEAN. The 2002 show in Las Vegas, the 90th largest trade show in the United States, drew 16,600 attendees and featured a wide array of training programs for the cleaning industry. This trade show is one of the oldest, celebrating more than 75 years.

Garfinkel's leadership guided the ISSA board to open its show for the first time, in 1999, to the entire cleaning industry, welcoming the Facility Service Providers, also for the first time. ISSA is currently pursuing a redirection of its focus from only the distributors and manufacturers to become an association that represents the entire cleaning industry.

Garfinkel's background includes a baccalaureate degree from St. John's University in New York, with a major in accounting and a minor in economics, and a master's degree in marketing from the C. W. Post College of Long Island University. He also served as an officer in the U.S. Marine Corps.

Housekeepers should make every attempt to attend ISSA/INTERCLEAN. More can be learned about one's profession in a single afternoon at this show than can be learned in a typical year on the job.

Garfinkel has said, "Associations tend to be like fraternities and welcome only those most like themselves. Within the cleaning industry we are even more fragmented than some other industries." The change he considers most important would be to help bring the cleaning and environmental management professionals together from the many end market segments with the contracted facility services and cleaning contractors, the distributors, and the varied types of manufacturers for the benefit of all participants, organizations, and for the greater efficiency and health of all of us." Garfinkel is certainly the epitome of an agent of change in our profession.

FIGURE 14.5 Desktop display used in guestrooms at the Los Angeles Airport/ Marriott Hotel. *(Photo courtesy of the Los Angeles Airport/Marriott Hotel.)*

DUAL RESPONSIBILITY

Although it is the duty of all innkeepers to provide a secure area within which guests might abide in relaxing comfort, free from usual threats from the street, guests should never be lulled into a false sense of security so as to abdicate responsibility for their own security. Guests must be prudent and cautious. Housekeeping personnel should therefore never imply that there is nothing to worry about when staying in the hotel. To the contrary, housekeeping personnel should gently and appropriately remind guests to be cautious about leaving doors unlocked and about reasonable rules of security.

The Do-Not-Disturb Sign Competes with the "Need to Foresee"

✂

THE GUEST'S ABSOLUTE RIGHT TO PRIVACY

Most common laws affecting hotels in America stem from the English Common Laws of Innkeepers, which originated in the seventeenth century. One such law deals with the guest's right to privacy and is quoted frequently even to this day. On occasion, guests, and more to our surprise, many hotel operators, presume that the guest has an **absolute right to privacy**, and when in his or her room should *never* be disturbed. Actually, research indicates that the English Common Law was not constructed to guarantee that the guest would never be disturbed, only that he or she would be guaranteed sole occupancy of the assigned quarters. Prior to the law's being enacted, it was common practice

for the innkeeper to **dormitory** his guests; all men in one sleeping room and women in another room. The law later provided that upon issuance of the key, the guest who paid for *private* quarters had sole use of the assigned room and no one else would be moved into the room; hence the "absolute" right to privacy. It was not meant to be a guarantee that the guest would never under any circumstances be disturbed.

MANAGEMENT'S RESPONSIBILITY TO OWNERSHIP, THE LAWS OF THE LAND, AND THE GUEST

With due and proper regard for the guest's privacy, management has an important responsibility to the owner of the hotel (which happens to be private property), to state and federal laws that must be enforced on the property, and to the guest, whose safety should always be paramount to the hotel staff.

In light of this management responsibility, and with due respect for the guest's right to privacy, there must be a **reasonable time** each day that management, or its representative, enters the room to service the room and to ensure that 1) the room has not been vandalized or furniture and fixtures destroyed, 2) the law is not being broken in the room, and 3) there is no guest in distress in the room.

Without specific information to the contrary respecting the guest's right to privacy, it is considered reasonable to enter the guest's room between the hours of 8:00 A.M. and 4:00 P.M. daily to service the room. Should the guest display the do-not-disturb (DND) sign or have the door **dead-bolted** from the inside, every attempt should be made to avoid disturbing the guest, at least until normal checkout time. Also, should the guest leave a specific request for late service, this too should be honored.

A Matter of Foreseeability

Imagine the following scenario. You are the executive housekeeper in a suburban hotel catering heavily to the individual traveling businessperson. It is one hour after checkout time, and you receive a call from the guestroom attendant on the third floor who says that room 3019 has had a DND sign on the door all morning. When she checked with housekeeping and the front desk, there had been no instructions given *not* to disturb the guest until some later appointed hour. The front desk had no record of a checkout due today from room 3019. The GRA called the room to find out what time the guest would like to have the room serviced, but no one answered the phone. The GRA tried to enter the room with her passkey but found the room dead-bolted from the inside. End of scenario.

At that moment, what becomes the most foreseeable probability regarding room 3019? Would this be a proper time to respect, above all else, the guest's absolute right to privacy?

Consider another scenario that actually occurred. In November 1990, this author was certified as an expert in hotel operations in a federal court in Maryland and did testify on behalf of a plaintiff who was suing a major hotel for gross negligence. This negligence was alleged to have resulted from the hotel's not taking reasonable precaution regarding a prior visit by her husband to the hotel, during which he had suffered a diabetic coma in his guestroom. He was not discovered for a period of over 50 hours. Once discovered, he was hospitalized but died five days later. A medical doctor testified that had the victim been discovered 10 hours sooner, he would have survived.

The chronology of events was reconstructed as follows: The victim had been at the hotel for several days. His room had been last serviced on Tuesday morning about 9:00 A.M. while he was not in the room. He had returned to his room sometime before midnight on Tuesday, and chained and dead-bolted his door prior to retiring. On Wednesday, the GRA had noticed the dead bolt and had honored it until about 3:00 P.M. on Wednesday afternoon, at which time she knocked on the door but got no response. She then used her key but was stopped by the chain on the door. She followed her departmental instructions and summoned a security officer to the room. The security officer noticed that a TV was on in the room and then commented that "the guest just does not want to be disturbed," even though there had been no *coherent response* to the security officer's knock on the door.

No further check was made on the guest or the room until the following day when, at 4:00 P.M. on Thursday, the GRA again called security to report that she still had not been able to gain entry into the room. At this time the same security officer came to the room, knocked on the door, got no response, and said he would report the incident to the security office.

Finally, at about 6:00 P.M., another manager, aware of the possibilities, called for an engineer to cut the chain on the door and entered the room to find the guest unconscious in the bathroom, 56 hours after the room was last entered by a member of the hotel staff.

The hotel's insurance company, after hearing the testimony of the case, offered a settlement out of court to the plaintiff, which she accepted—in excess of $1 million.

In this case, negligence occurred because the hotel failed to follow a **reasonable procedure** whereby the guestrooms would be checked at least once each day. Respect for the guest's right to privacy was allowed to overshadow the need to ensure the guest's safety at a reasonable time during the day, at least once every 24 hours.

Not only did staff negligence contribute to the demise of the guest, the same negligence contributed to a failure to protect the assets of the hotel company, namely, cash and reputation.

Safety

NATURE OF EMERGENCIES

The two most important aspects of **emergencies** are that they are *unforeseeable* and *uncontrollable*. Both of these factors produce unwanted and unanticipated side effects, since reactions to emergencies by guests and, at times, employees are equally unanticipated and (sometimes) unwanted. It is therefore imperative that there be advance planning and that training and drills be held in combatting all types of emergencies.

In order to maintain safe premises, management must be ready to cope with four types of emergencies:

1. Fire
2. Bomb threats and bombings
3. Natural disasters
4. Riots and civil disturbances

Because property is replaceable but life is not, it is obvious where most concern must rest. The burden is first to *prevent* any occurrence that may bring about one of the aforementioned emergencies. If prevention is impossible, the burden shifts to minimizing 1) risk of death or injury, or 2) property damage.

Because housekeeping employees are usually in the vicinity of a large number of guests during daytime hours, it is imperative that they be well trained in procedures that command confidence in order that they set the best possible example for guests who may be caught in an emergency. For example, some housekeeping personnel are afraid of using handheld extinguishers because of the noise generated and the cloud of white smoke created when activated. Such fears require training and drill to quell. Drills should be regular and should not be concealed from guests. Rather, guests should be informed when drills are to take place in order that those present can see what precautions are taken to deal with emergencies.

FIRE PROTECTION AND THE HOTEL GUEST

Timothy Harper, of the *San Francisco Chronicle*, wrote the following[4]:

> Until recently, hoteliers were about as eager to talk about fire as they were to jump off the 13th floor. But with 118 people killed and hundreds injured in three disastrous hotel fires this winter [1980, when 84 were killed at the MGM Grand, Las Vegas; 26 were killed at Stouffer's Inn in White Plains, New York; and 8 were killed at the Las Vegas Hilton], it is obviously on their minds....
>
> It's no longer bad business to give guests the idea there may be a fire in their hotel. Indeed, the 14-story Red Lion Inn SEATAC near Seattle-Tacoma International Airport in Washington State, gives every guest a copy of a letter from the local fire chief, saying that the motel is one of the safest hotel-convention centers in the country.

Harper continued by quoting Michael Scherkman of the Fire Protection Association as saying:

> Despite all the improvements in hotel fire safety, people should remember two things. First, people are usually safer in hotels than in their own homes, which is where 75 percent of all fire deaths occur. Secondly, people have to be responsible for their own safety wherever they go, whether in hotels or in their own homes.

Recently, hotel guests have been bombarded with information about how safe hotels have become. Although fire protection and prevention and training have been highly upgraded, the manner in which some guests will receive and accept the information can be dangerous. Guests are inclined to let their guard down if or when someone else implies that there is nothing to worry about. It is not necessary to scare hotel guests into an early departure, but there is excellent reason to counsel guests gently about what to do in what-if situations.

An excellent **"what-if" publication** was recently created and published by the James H. Barry Company, San Francisco. This publication may be customized and made available for hotels to place in guestrooms. It is a simple yet appropriate publication that subtly reminds guests that fire can happen and, it if does, what they should do. Appendix E contains a copy of this publication.

A great concern for training in the housekeeping department is an understanding of the **panic emotion**.

Panic is defined as follows by the National Fire Protection Association:

> A sudden overpowering terror, often affecting many people at once. Panic is the product of one's imagination running wild, and panic will set in as soon as it dawns on a person that they are lost, disoriented, or without knowledge of what to do in an emergency situation. Panic is also contagious and can spread to anyone and everyone. Panic is also irreversible, and once set in, seems to grow. Panic can make a person do things that can kill. People in a state of panic are rarely able to save themselves.

Training employees and drilling them in various situations is a most effective tool to reduce the possibility of panic in a fire situation.

I have been associated with five hotels in which fires have occurred; four of them were directly associated with the rooms department. The situations causing the fires and related hotel rule violations follow.

1. *An intoxicated smoker in bed set a mattress on fire:* No one was injured. The smoker, however, was extremely lucky that he was not overcome, because the smoke was heavy enough to fill the entire rooms department on three floors and was dense enough to prevent visibility beyond 10 feet. *Rule violation:* Renting a room to an intoxicated guest without taking away all smoking materials.

2. *Late-night fire in a satellite linen room:* The direct cause of this fire was trash and rubbish left on a housekeeper's cart overnight in a satellite linen room in which the door had been left not only unlocked but also ajar. Had it not been for an alert security patrol at 2:00 A.M., this situation could have been disastrous. The fire was noticed because of a hallway filled with smoke and was found in a smoldering stage within the trash hamper. *Rule violation:* Failing to dispose of trash properly at the end of the workday and leaving a service door unlocked.

3. *Late-night fire deliberately set in an elevator:* Because of the hour, few people were up and about. The entire rooms department of the hotel became completely filled with smoke without being noticed. On this particular night the hotel was full and a large number of elderly people in a tour group were in occupancy. Outside temperatures were below freezing. The fire itself was completely contained within the elevator, and burned a section of the carpet less than three square feet. Yet because of the shaft of the elevator, smoke completely filled the hallways on all three floors. There had been no smoke in any guestroom until one panicking guest ran blindly through the hallway shouting "fire" and banging on doors. As guests became aroused, they entered the smoke-filled hallways, in many cases

leaving their rooms without their keys, thus preventing their return to a safe environment. Many of the guests quickly evacuated the building, only to become exposed to the elements in unsuitable clothing. *Rule violation:* Leaving a known safe environment when a fire is reported without protecting your ability to retrace your path.

4. *A television exploded within a guestroom:* This is a rare happening, but if it occurs, it is usually in a vacant room where the television has been left in operation. In this particular fire, maximum damage occurred within the guestroom in a very short time. The guest was at dinner, and upon returning to his room was surprised to find firefighters and hotel personnel gathered in *his* room. *Rule violation:* Leaving a television in operation in a vacant room.

Knowledge about Smoke and Fire as a Foundation for Training Programs

Contrary to what has been seen on television or in the movies, **fire** is not likely to chase people down and burn them to death. It is almost always the **by-products of fire** that kill. Smoke and panic will more likely be the cause of death long before a fire arrives, if it ever does. It is most important that all employees, especially housekeeping employees, be drilled about the effects of smoke and be taught how to avoid smoke and panic in order to set a proper example for guests.

Where there is smoke there is not necessarily a fire out of control. A smoldering mattress will produce great amounts of smoke that may be picked up in air-conditioning systems and transported over vast areas of the hotel. Since smoke is warmer than air, it will start accumulating in ceiling areas and work its way down. When a hotel hallway fills with smoke, it is too late to start looking for exit signs, since they are *always* mounted in ceilings and become obscured by the smoke, which rises to the top of the hallway. (We hope that someday building codes will require the placement of indestructible emergency exit signs near baseboards where they can be seen in a fire emergency.)

In the long run, smoke will affect your eyes. Eyes can take only so much smoke, and then they will close by reflex. As hard as you try, once your eyes are closed they will not reopen in a smoke-filled area. Finally, the only fresh air that will be available will be at or near the floor. Employees must be taught to get on their hands and knees to take advantage of what fresh air might be available.

There are articles about fire prevention and safety available through the National Fire Protection Association in Washington, D.C. This agency can provide the latest state-of-the-art information to support training programs in fire protection in hotels.

Fire drills should be conducted and should include, but not be limited to, the following:

1. Demonstration of blindfolded employee leaving a hotel from any known point within the hotel
2. Demonstration of proper action when there is reduced visibility in a hotel hallway due to smoke
3. Under the supervision of local fire department personnel, demonstration of the use of handheld extinguishers to put out an actual preset fire (Fires set in a trash can in the hotel parking lot can usually provide insights about employee behavior when using these extinguishers.)
4. Showing any of the numerous films available from local fire prevention agencies for housekeeping employees
5. Making demonstrated knowledge about fire protection and the use of fire equipment a part of performance appraisal

METHAMPHETAMINE LABORATORIES

Methamphetamine laboratories (meth labs) are simple to build, and the supplies are easy to obtain and very inexpensive. Best of all for the aspiring drug lord, the profits are enormous. The only problem is that the process of "cooking" is extremely hazardous. The chemicals are highly flammable and even explosive. Some of the by-products are so toxic that when a laboratory is discovered, the cleanup team arrives in HazMat protective gear. One of the possible by-products of a "Red P" lab is phosgene gas—the same gas that was used to gas the troops in World War I.

There are a host of very scary chemicals associated with methamphetamine production, including acetone, anhydrous ammonia, ether, red phosphorous, drain cleaner, methyl alcohol, hydrochloric acid, sulfuric acid, and strips of lithium metal removed from batteries. All of these chemicals are very toxic and highly reactive. Exposure to meth lab chemicals can cause liver disease, inflammation and scarring in the lungs, skin eruptions, profound anemia, and impaired immune function.

The really bad news is that the "tweekers" (addicts) and their labs may show up in your hotel. In Las Vegas, almost every property has found a meth lab in a guestroom, and not just the run-down traps on the periphery. Some of the biggest and fanciest hotel-casinos on the strip have had experiences with clandestine meth labs.

Why? The answer is that these criminals know of the danger, so they don't want to do their dirty business in their homes. Why not go to a nice hotel and either register under an assumed name or get someone else to register for you? By the time anything is discovered, they hope to be long gone.

What are the obvious signs of a meth lab? Tell your GRAs to be aware of rooms that refuse service. In addition, look for rooms that run the air conditioner in the winter, or rooms that have put plastic bags around the smoke detectors, chemicals in a room such as those mentioned earlier, plus empty blister packs of pseudoephedrine. Solvent smells and cat urine smells in a room (with no cats) are other signs. Look for electric cooking plates and Pyrex or even chemical beakers. Duct tape, hoses, and tubing are also common. If housekeepers find two or more of these items, management should contact the police immediately.

The cost of cleaning up after these criminals is enormous, ranging from a few hundred dollars per room, if one is lucky, to thousands of dollars. Carpets have to be ripped out, and even drywall may be contaminated and have to be removed. This is not a job for housekeeping; special hazardous cleanup crews must be hired.

The biggest cost may be in the lives of your staff and guests. One Las Vegas narcotics detective advised a group of executive housekeepers that if they ever get off an elevator and see a GRA lying by her cart down the hall, and they smell something in the air that is very unpleasant, they must be careful. By the time they reach that GRA, they might be dead as well. One good whiff of phosgene is all it takes to kill a person.

BOMB THREATS

The hotel personnel who will be involved during a **bomb threat** will probably be the PBX department and hotel management, along with the fire or police department. Whether a hotel should be evacuated is the decision of the **on-scene commander**, who is usually a member of the local police or fire department. The decision as to who will order an evacuation is not made on the spur of the moment. It is usually prearranged that the on-scene commander will order any evacuation that is considered necessary.

In most cases, selected personnel who thoroughly know the hotel will be part of search teams; the executive housekeeper, chief engineer, resident manager, and other such management personnel might become involved with property searches.

The hotel facility must always be kept clean and free of debris and unnecessary equipment and supplies. If everything is neatly stored in its proper place, suspicious-looking articles are much easier to spot, and housekeeping personnel are better able to participate in searches and make observations faster.

Housekeeping department personnel should be trained not to touch strange items when a property search for a possible explosive device is in progress; they should be trained to notice strange objects and report them to the proper authority.

NATURAL DISASTERS

Floods, hurricanes, earthquakes, and sometimes freezing temperatures and snowstorms are **natural disasters**. Each has its own set of rules. When such events happen, some hotels tend to empty, whereas others fill up, depending on the location and type of problem.

Hotels on major arteries and interstate highways fill when weather conditions prevent traffic from moving. Such unexpected heavy occupancy can cause hotels to find themselves in unpredicted circumstances. In most cases, the first conclusion of management would be to send their employees home thinking that business would become extremely slow. Then as emergency conditions start to compound, the hotel might start to fill, and 100 percent occupancy could be reached. Real problems set in when the hotel does fill and there is no one who can come to work because of the disaster.

Planning is the answer to such occurrences. At any time the hotel might fill due to a natural disaster or extreme weather, provision should be made for employees who can stay, without creating additional personal hardship, at the hotel; there are always sufficient numbers of such employees. An adequate number of guestrooms should be set aside for food and beverage and housekeeping personnel to ensure that by having employees work in relays, all guests will be accommodated in a reasonable fashion.

RIOTS AND CIVIL DISTURBANCES

Civil disturbances may originate in the hotel or may start miles away and drift into the hotel. People in an unruly crowd at a football game may return to their accommodations and continue their unruliness. Housekeeping personnel should be exposed to the possibilities that such events could take place and should be trained in techniques that will calm unruly people.

Employees can learn the principles of transactional analysis and be exposed to *Games People Play*.[5] Transactional analysis (TA) is the study of communications (transactions) between people based on theories presented in the mid-1960s. Of primary concern is for employees to treat guests properly and avoid injuries to guests. The hotel is liable for any injury that might beset a guest because of a short-tempered employee. This is another reason for close observation of the temperament of employees during probationary periods of employment.

The Spector of Terrorism

Most hotels will never experience a terrorist attack. Terrorists tend to select "high-profile" targets that will produce the most publicity and, correspondingly, public fear. However, some hotels, are on the terrorist's list of possible "soft targets" because of their symbolism. The world has witnessed attacks on hotels around the world including the JW Marriott in Jakarta, a hotel identified as a symbol of U.S. imperialism by Jemaah Islamiyah (JI), an organization allegedly affiliated with al-Qaeda. The Marriott Hotel bombing occurred on August 5, 2003, in Setiabudi, South Jakarta, Indonesia. A suicide bomber detonated a car bomb outside the lobby of the JW Marriott Hotel, killing 12 people and injuring 150.

The housekeeping department, along with all departments in the hotel, should be constantly on guard for suspicious activities. The department's major role is to act as the eyes and ears of the hotel and immediately report any out-of-the-ordinary behavior on the part of employees or guests, including the discovery of unusual equipment in the guestrooms and packages or luggage in public areas.

In the case of an attack, there should be an emergency plan in place with a well-defined role for the housekeeping department. Training of all personnel must be in place if the plan is to succeed.

The Loss Prevention Manual

InterContinental Hotels Group, as part of its **loss prevention program**, provides excellent training and training outlines for its property management in order that a proper and professional emphasis may be applied in the areas of safety and security. InterContinental's plan is presented in detail in Appendix F.

CONCLUSION

In this chapter we introduced the concept of the safeguarding of assets and explored the subjects of security and safety, emphasizing that each requires special and separate attention. We discussed how to maintain a secure housekeeping department and presented a fourteen-point program for employee theft prevention. We also talked about security within hotel guestrooms, specifically card entry systems and dual responsibility.

After a general discussion of the nature of emergencies in a hotel situation, we gave specific procedures for dealing with fires, bomb threats, natural disasters, and civil disturbances. The emphasis was on safety in all situations.

Management's responsibility in the areas of security and safety is clear and must not, under any circum-

stances, be abdicated in favor of the belief that nothing of an emergency nature could ever happen to this hotel or health-care facility or to guests, patients, or employees. Wariness, training, objectivity, and study are the keys to protection from the perils brought by lax attitudes toward security and safety within the housekeeping department of a hotel or health care institution. All planning should culminate in the creation of an emergency action plan that foresees potential problem areas and catalogs plans for swift, effective action to prevent the loss or destruction of assets. Emergency action plans should also have as their objective a quick recovery and return to a "business as usual" status as soon as possible.

KEY TERMS AND CONCEPTS

Body of knowledge
Safeguarding assets
American Society of Industrial Security (ASIS)
Risk analysis
Risk management
Security
Safety
Plainclothes house detective
Employee theft prevention
Contamination of employees
14-point theft prevention program
Employment history

Polygraph (lie detector) examinations
Badge system
Probationary periods
Key-control program
Key pouch
Red tag system
Snoop
Employee profile
Miscellaneous charge
Reasonable security for guestrooms
Card entry system
Lock cylinder
Absolute right to privacy

Dormitory
Reasonable time
Dead-bolted
Reasonable procedure
Emergencies
"What-if" publication
Panic emotion
Fire
By-products of fire
Bomb threat
On-scene commander
Natural disasters
Civil disturbances
Loss prevention program

DISCUSSION AND REVIEW QUESTIONS

1. Explain the difference between safety and security.
2. What is employee contamination? List several reasons for it.
3. What is an employee profile? How and when is it used? What characteristics of it should cause concern?
4. How would you use employees to reduce theft by employees? By guests? What points would you make during employee orientation to gain participation in a theft prevention program?
5. Explain the benefits of a card entry system over the hard key method of entry for guestrooms.

NOTES

1. Harold Gluck, "How to Reduce Loss Potential During the Hiring Process," *Motel/Motor Inn Journal*, 1979, p. 5.
2. Bob Curtis, "Tips on Keeping Employees Honest," NRN Book Excerpt, *Nation's Restaurant News*, September 1979, p. 1.
3. Barbara Powers, "Crime Shouldn't Pay: Curbing Employee Theft," from an interview conducted by *Lodging*, May 1983, p. 31.
4. Timothy Harper, "U.S. Hotels Find Guest Keen on Fire Protection," *San Francisco Chronicle*, 1981.
5. Eric Berne, *Games People Play: The Psychology of Human Relationships* (New York: Grove Press, 1961). For an excellent and more direct application of the subject to the hospitality and service industries, see Maurice F. Villere, Thomas S. O'Connor, and William J. Quain, "Games Nobody Wins," *Cornell HRA Quarterly* 24 (no. 3, November 1983): 72–79.

CHAPTER 15

The Laundry: Toward an Understanding of Basic Engineering and Operational Considerations

LEARNING OBJECTIVES

After studying the chapter, students should be able to:

1. Present a reasoned argument for or against having an on-premises laundry.
2. Describe the steps involved in setting up a laundry.
3. Describe how to properly size a laundry.
4. List the electrical and mechanical considerations in planning an on-premises laundry.

Most of the material written about **on-premises laundries** addresses the issue of whether to have such a facility. Numerous trade publications have dealt both analytically and subjectively with cost-saving considerations and with quality and inventory control, efficiency of operation, dependability of outside contracts, and linen investment costs.

This chapter presents these arguments, both for and against on-premises laundries. For those properties that decide in favor of an on-premises laundry, a proposed set of criteria is offered for their use.

A Statement in Favor of On-Premises Laundry Operations

Jack E. Scott, president of Baker Linen Company of California,[1] believes that one should strongly consider installing an on-premises laundry if outside laundry costs are in excess of $900 per month. The latest research report by the American Hotel and Lodging Association (AHLA), cited and updated by Scott, indicates the following comparisons for in-house service, outside service, and rental service for a typical 120-room unit:

Weekly in-house laundry costs	$324.00
Allowance for weekly linen depreciation	133.91
Total in-house laundry costs	$457.91
Weekly outside service	
Using owned linens—880.60 pounds at 10 cents per pound	$880.60
Allowance for weekly linen depreciation	133.91
Total outside laundry costs	1014.51
Weekly linen rental service	$1782.17

OLD CONCERNS RESOLVED

Maintaining the quality of linens has always been a deterrent to in-house laundries, but the primary problem has been resolved. Modern **no-iron linens** (50/50 polyester blends) now undergo a dual finish process that improves the molecular structure of the polyester fiber, resulting in a linen that retains its no-iron properties throughout its normal life expectancy. Refined blend sheets now last three times as long as their cotton predecessors. In fact, the polyester fiber in new-generation no-iron linens tends to relax and actually increases in elasticity with use.

The no-iron linen industry has also perfected the equipment that processes the new-generation linens. The timing of wash-and-rinse cycles, temperature control, and the automatic adding of detergents, bleaches, and softeners have eliminated the problems of human error and operator inattention and the need for extensive employee training.

In summary, for many operators, there is a very strong case for having an economical on-premises laundry.

Another View of the Efficacy of On-Premises Laundry Operations

Almost every major hotel in Las Vegas has abandoned its on-premises laundry, choosing to outsource its operations to a commercial laundry service. Why? According to Hal Hobbs, vice president of plant operations at Mission Industries, many hotels have decided that they prefer to be in the casino/hotel business—not the laundry business.

Hotel managers have confided to this author that the move to a commercial laundry has happened for two reasons: convenience and real estate costs. Convenience is an issue because many of these hotels do not want the responsibility of having yet another large department in their organization. Hobbs is certainly correct when he states that many hotel/casino operators simply do not want the added responsibility. Because of the enormous economy of scale, a commercial laundry operation can undoubtedly make its fees enticing to a hotel operator. This is probably not true in most other communities in America. When Mission Industries opened its Mayflower Avenue Plant, it was the single largest laundry operation in the world. The size of the Mission Industries operation in Las Vegas is unmatched anywhere else on the planet. So hotels in Las Vegas have relieved themselves of a major headache without substantially increasing their costs.

Second, real estate is very costly on the Strip and in downtown Las Vegas, and laundries take up a considerable amount of space in a 3000-room hotel. It has probably become too expensive to build them into the architectural plans of any new Las Vegas Strip hotel. As for the existing hotels, many have converted their former laundries to needed office space for other departments.

Many have never seen the inside of a commercial laundry, let alone one of the world's largest operations. Via Figures 15.1 through 15.23, we can take a tour of Mission Industries' Mayflower Avenue Plant, which is now the second largest laundry in the world. (Mission Industries has since built a larger operation in California.)

Planning and Preengineering

Some architects of small laundry facilities suggest that an on-premises laundry requires nothing more than installing a few washers and dryers in some remote space in the facility. Such inadequate planning usually results

FIGURE 15.1 A Mission truck pulls up to the dock with soiled laundry from a hotel. *(Photograph courtesy of Mission Industries, Las Vegas.)*

FIGURE 15.2 A mechanical arm lifts a laundry cart, dumping its contents onto a conveyor belt. An average of 1200 of these carts arrive at this plant every day. *(Photograph courtesy of Mission Industries, Las Vegas.)*

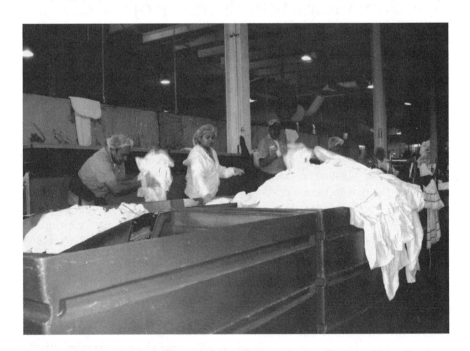

FIGURE 15.3 Workers sort the laundry by type (e.g., pillowcases, sheets, towels). *(Photograph courtesy of Mission Industries, Las Vegas.)*

in laundries that must be reengineered by qualified designers and laundry equipment contractors, resulting in costly modifications. For example, let's consider a Canadian hotel, described as a magnificent creation.[2] The location was inspiring, the architectural design was impressive, the accommodations were outstanding, and the quality and comfort standards were exemplary. It was perceived as exceptional in every respect except one. In spite of detailed planning, the laundry was poorly engineered and had less than half the space required to be efficient. What area it did have was poorly designed. The problem was more than mere engineering and design; machinery was not of the industrial caliber demanded by millions of pounds of laundry each year. In an attempt to keep up with volume, 11 shifts per week were required.

Large laundries are not the only ones that receive improper planning and initial engineering attention. Often it is the owners of small properties who, after having made the decision to have an on-premises laundry, fail to give the consideration and planning that laundry operations warrant.

FIGURE 15.4 The sorted laundry goes up a conveyor into a tunnel washer. These machines can wash up to 3,400 pounds of soiled laundry per hour. There are seven of these tunnel washers at this plant. *(Photograph courtesy of Mission Industries, Las Vegas.)*

FIGURE 15.5 After washing, the laundry is pressed to extract water from the fabric. The washer dispenses the clean laundry in the form of 110-pound cakes. The largest tunnel washer produces a 220-pound cake. *(Photograph courtesy of Mission Industries, Las Vegas.)*

For example, here is a description of what one small property owner built as an in-house laundry in the basement of a new 80-room hotel. The amount and size of equipment were basically correct, but decisions had not been based on an understanding of efficient laundry operation and mechanical requirements. There was *one* 44-inch floor drain provided to receive the effluent water from two, or possibly three, washer/extractors draining under pressure, each having a 34-inch-diameter drain line. No complementary drain trough was provided with the floor drain to handle the effluent overflow temporarily. Instant floods would occur every time two or possibly three washers discharged effluent into the undersized drain system. In addition, three 100-pound dryers each exhausted 800 cubic feet of air per minute into the laundry room, which had a low ceiling. No provision had been made to exhaust this heavily heated and moisture-laden air. Unbearable working conditions and moisture condensing on every pipe in the basement were certain to occur. In addition, a supplemental lint disposal system was not provided. The only lint removal was provided by the lint traps of each individual dryer. Lint can be a serious fire hazard in laundry operations and must be dealt with accordingly.

Small properties may not require the detailed planning needed in larger properties (between 300 and 2,500 rooms); however, planning variables apply equally to small and large hotel laundries. The AHLA can supply the names of reputable and knowledgeable **laundry consultants**, engineers, and equipment manufacturers, most of whom will engineer laundries and specify equipment within certain budgetary constraints. In addition, they oversee installation and provide management and worker training during start-up operations. One of the many companies that provides this type of service, Baring Industries,[3] has coined the term **systemeering** to represent the following 10 services it specifies in all of its contracts. These steps may be followed regardless of the specific laundry consultant used.

1. *Determination of needs:* This step involves meeting with owners, architects, interior designers, engineers, and other project consultants to obtain all the data pertinent to sizing laundries in housekeeping systems. Data include the number of rooms, number of beds, expected occupancy, variety of services, areas of services, and budgetary restrictions. From these data a report containing information about size, type, and location of facilities is composed. This report describes the basic integration and development of the laundry in the overall hotel concept and design.

FIGURE 15.6 The cake is transported automatically via a conveyor to a lift that picks up two cakes at a time and moves them to a dryer. *(Photograph courtesy of Mission Industries, Las Vegas.)*

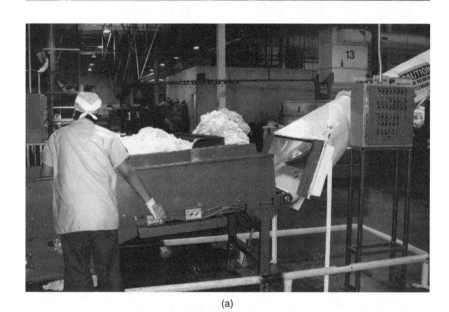

(a)

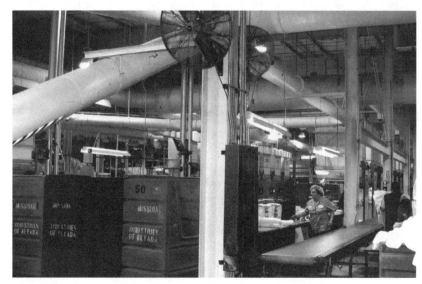

(b)

FIGURE 15.7 Dried bath linen is then transported to a negative resistance (vacuum) conveyor (a) that shoots it through tubes to the automatic folders (b). *(Photographs courtesy of Mission Industries, Las Vegas.)*

FIGURE 15.8 A worker feeds a towel into a folder. *(Photograph courtesy of Mission Industries, Las Vegas.)*

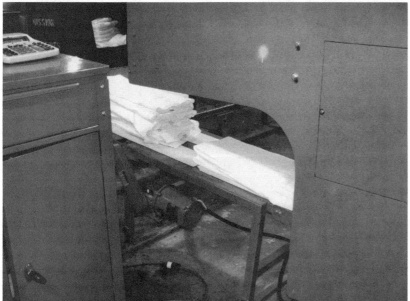

FIGURE 15.9 The towel is dispensed and automatically stacked on the other side. *(Photograph courtesy of Mission Industries, Las Vegas.)*

FIGURE 15.10 The towels proceed down a conveyor, where a worker ties them into bundles and they are stacked back into waiting carts. *(Photograph courtesy of Mission Industries, Las Vegas.)*

FIGURE 15.11 Sheets are not dried, but are taken directly from the washers to the flatwork finishers, where they are automatically ironed and folded. A worker has only to find a corner of the sheet and put it into the machine; the flatwork finisher does the rest. *(Photograph courtesy of Mission Industries, Las Vegas.)*

FIGURE 15.12 The ironed, dried, and folded sheets come out the other side, where workers bundle and place the sheets into carts for transport. *(Photograph courtesy of Mission Industries, Las Vegas.)*

FIGURE 15.13 In addition to the tunnel washers, the plant has smaller units for uniforms and smaller jobs. The plant has six 125-pound washer-extractors, six 450-pound washer-extractors, and five 900-pound washers with three separate 400-pound centrifugal extractors. *(Photograph courtesy of Mission Industries, Las Vegas.)*

FIGURE 15.14 Here one of the midsized washers is being emptied. Note how the washer tips to aid the worker in emptying the machine. *(Photograph courtesy of Mission Industries, Las Vegas.)*

FIGURE 15.15 Some of the linen is not shot through tubes, but moved in giant laundry bags on an overhead conveyor system. The linen is emptied by releasing a drawstring on the bottom. *(Photograph courtesy of Mission Industries, Las Vegas.)*

FIGURE 15.16 Not all of the linens are folded by machine. Small washcloths and towels are done by hand. *(Photograph courtesy of Mission Industries, Las Vegas.)*

FIGURE 15.17 This state-of-the-art folder can fold all sizes of towels with just a push of a button. *(Photograph courtesy of Mission Industries, Las Vegas.)*

2. *System definition and space allocation:* Once needs are defined, specialists concentrate on selecting systems and components most able to handle the project requirements. Interrelationships of those allocated spaces are analyzed from a human engineering standpoint to eliminate costly extra steps or crossed traffic patterns. Many different approaches are considered in designing a system that optimizes efficiency and, therefore, economy of operations.

3. *Equipment layouts:* Labor-saving ideas are meshed with the most efficient work-flow patterns that can be designed within the given space. Alternate system components and layouts are investigated to ensure selection of the best possible system.

4. *Equipment selection, specifications, and budgets:* The selection of quality options for equipment are presented. Costs are studied, including equipment installation and rigging equipment costs. Follow-up maintenance considerations are included, along with the expected life of the equipment. Budgets are finalized using standard specifications that allow for fast tracking to early completion of the project.

5. *Detailed drawing and specification:* Equipment connection schedules and mechanical, electrical, and ventilation details are defined, showing exact locations of all rough-in points. Such drawings enable the contractor to rough-in utilities properly before equipment arrives.

The preceding five steps expedite connection and installation of equipment. Detailed specifications for each piece of equipment are provided, reflecting every option selected.

All mechanical and electrical requirements must be coordinated with architects, engineers, and contractors throughout this phase.

The next five steps in Baring's service are as follows:

6. Equipment procurement and shipment coordination
7. Installation scheduling and supervision
8. Start-up, test, and demonstration
9. Operator training, maintenance
10. After-sale service

Regardless of the size of the laundry facility, all steps in the systemeering plan should be carried out to ensure the best possible laundry facilities.

Basic Knowledge for the Owner

It may not be economically advantageous for small property owners to use the services of a laundry consultant. In such cases, owners need to know the basic considerations in the development of a small on-premises laundry operation.

The most commonly used and technically correct way of deciding the size and composition of equipment is by analyzing **linen poundage requirements**. It is usual for laundry equipment manufacturers to design and specify equipment using this criterion. Thus, washers and/or dryers are available with load capabilities ranging from 25 to 600 pounds, allowing for the selection of

(a)

JENSEN JET TOWEL FOLDERS #19 AND #20

CUSTOMER # and NAME			TASK # and NAME		STD
0	White Rental (Blanco)	1	Bath Towels	Toallo de Bano Medida 50	1173
1	Bone Rental (Vanila)	2	Large Bath Towels	Toalla de Bano Grande	1000
2	Venetian	3	Hand Towels	Toalla de Mano	1744
3	Rio	4	Bath Mats	Tapete	1260
4	Luxor	5	Bath Sheets	Sabano de Bano	720
5	Palms	7	Pool Towels (44)	Toalla de Alberca Medida 44	1260
6	Gaughn Properties(GP)	8	Large Pool Towels	Toalla de Alberca Grande	1000
7	Alexis Park	9	Pool Sheets	Sabano de Alberca	720
8	Cancun	197	No Work	No Trabajo	DWK
		198	Maintenance	Martenimiento	DWK

1. Insert card in side of PPS box. (Insertar la tarjeta alado de la caja "PPS")

2. Select the customer using the up/down arrow buttons or press clear and enter the customer number on the keypad. Hit the enter button. (Seleccione "Customer" usando los botones de "Arriba/Abajo" o apriete el boton "Clear" y marque los numberos del "Customer" en el teclada. Apriete el boton "Enter")

3. Select the task using the up/down arrow buttons or press clear and enter the task number on the keypad. Hit the enter button. (Seleccione "Task" usando los botones de "Arriba/Abajo" o apriete el boton "Clear" y marque los numberos del "Task" en el teclada. Apriete el boton "Enter")

4. Begin work. Hit the change customer/task button to change customers or tasks and follow the steps as above. (Empieze a trabajar. Apriete el boton "Task/Customer" para cambiar el "Task" o/y "Customer", siga los pasos de arriba "2" & "3")

5. The operator must hit the "Mend" or "Stain" buttons on the folder or PPS box for each reject piece. (El operator debe apretar los botones de "Mend"(Costura) o "Stain"(Mancha) el el folder o en la caja de "PPS" por cada piesa que sea recharzada)

6. Remove card when leaving station for lunch, end of the day or when moved to another work area. (Quite la tarjeta cuando salga de la estacion para ir almorzar, al final del dia o, cuando se mueva de estacion)

(b)

FIGURE 15.18 Here is a closer look at the controls. Employees enter information about what type of job they are doing and which hotel they are servicing (a). They also enter information about themselves so their time on the job can be electronically recorded. Bilingual instructions are also included (b). *(Photographs courtesy of Mission Industries, Las Vegas.)*

FIGURE 15.19 Laundered uniforms enter a large steamer; when they come out, the wrinkles are gone. *(Photograph courtesy of Mission Industries, Las Vegas.)*

FIGURE 15.20 The finished uniforms are transported on a conveyor system far above the plant floor, saving valuable floor space. *(Photograph courtesy of Mission Industries, Las Vegas.)*

the most reasonably sized equipment for a given set of requirements. Most washers extract their own wash and rinse water; therefore, separate extractors are not necessary. Recognizing that labor costs will normally be the highest of all operating costs, it is desirable to specify the optimum-sized equipment that will minimize these costs.

Another consideration is that **washing capacity, drying capacity,** or **handling capacity** can provide the primary constraint for the laundry, and therefore these three constraints should be balanced. For example, a laundry

with 400 pounds of washing capacity operating on a 30-minute cycle, 150 pounds of drying capacity operating on a 50-minute cycle, with adequate space for handling, storing, and folding linen, would be dryer limited. However, a laundry with one 50-pound washing machine operating on a 30-minute cycle and one 100-pound dryer operating on a 1-hour cycle with adequate handling capacity would be properly sized.

In small operations, the number of dryers is normally related to the number of washers in a 2-to-1 ratio; for example, two 50-pound dryers to one 50-pound washer.

FIGURE 15.21 Finished products are weighed before being sent out to the trucks. *(Photograph courtesy of Mission Industries, Las Vegas.)*

FIGURE 15.22 Trucks are loaded for return trips to the hotels. The hotels expect and need deliveries every day. Note the lift that raises the carts up to the level of the truck. *(Photograph courtesy of Mission Industries, Las Vegas.)*

FIGURE 15.23 We leave through the front door of one of the largest laundry facilities in the world. This is only one of four plants that Mission Industries has in Las Vegas. *(Photograph courtesy of Mission Industries, Las Vegas.)*

This rule is based on the fact that a standard drying cycle is likely to be twice as long as a standard washing cycle.

Laundries equipped with **ironers** do not require that sheets and pillowcases pass through dryers. In such operations, dryers are used only for terry linen. All of these factors enter into the planning of how much and what type of equipment needs to be installed.

Major Equipment Requirements

WASHERS

Consider a hotel with 100 guestrooms and linen requirements (Table 15.1).

The approximately 1000 pounds of daily laundered linen in this 100-room hotel will be used as a guide

TABLE 15.1 Linen Par and Weight Determination Sheet Count

No. Rooms	No. Type	Total Beds/Room	Total Beds	Total Sheets	Wt/Unit Item (Pounds)	Total Weight (Pounds)
10	King Single	1	10	20	2.20	44.0
70	Queen Double	2	140	280	1.45	406.0
20	Queen Single	1	20	40	1.45	58.0
Total						
100	All types		170	340	508.0	

Pillowcases

Type Bed	No. Pillowcases per Bed	Total No. per Bed Type
King	3	3 × 10 = 30
Queen	2	2 × 160 = 320
Total no. pillowcases		350
350 cases at 0.25 pound/pillowcase = 87.5 pounds		

Terry Linens

Item	Quantity	Weight/Item (Pounds)	Total Weight
BT	350	0.714	249.9
HT	350	0.231	80.85
WC	350	0.053	18.55
BM	100	0.437	43.70
Totals	1150		393.00
One Par Total Weight			

Sheets	508.00 pounds
Pillowcases	87.5
Terry linen	393.0
Total	988.5
Approximately	1000.00 pounds

Assume one bath towel (BT), one hand towel (HT), one washcloth (WC), one pillow case per pillow, and one bath mat (BM) per room.

for determining equipment requirements. (See also Figure 15.24.)

Washer/extractor selection should be the best balance of machine capability and labor requirements; the best balance is the least machinery that allows for the smallest labor force (one person working an eight-hour shift is optimum). After setting a constraint that requires the production of **1 par linen** (the total amount of linen required to cover every bed and supply every bathroom once) in one shift, we now select a mix of washing machine capacity that is most practical.

One 500-pound washer, washing two loads, which can be completed in about one hour washing time, can handle the 1000-pound requirement, but then the washer would be idle for seven hours. The opposite extreme, one 50-pound washer working slightly less than a half-hour cycle, can produce the same amount of linen in 10 hours of operation. Neither of these is the best choice. Two 50-pound washers can produce the 1000-pound requirement in about 5 hours, and two 50-pound-capacity machines cost considerably less than one 500-pound machine and require less energy and mechanical support.

FIGURE 15.24 A bank of four 50-pound washers plumbed for automatic chemical and water intake. *(Photo taken with permission.)*

There is another consideration, which is that all linens will not be washed using the same **wash formula**. Linens must be separated by linen types and degree of soiling. *Wash formula* refers to the combination of washing time, rinsing time, temperature control, and automatic addition of chemical detergents, bleaches, and softeners.

Linens must also be weighed for proper washing. By analyzing the weights of each type of linen noted in Table 15.1, we can find the most practical loading combination for a 50-pound washer. Table 15.2 shows that two 50-pound washers, working one cycle of approximately 30 minutes, can complete all wash operations in about $5\frac{1}{2}$ hours.

DRYERS

As we mentioned earlier, in a no-iron laundry, the number of dryers relates to the number of washers in the ratio of 2 to 1. At 100 percent occupancy, the production

of up to 1,000 pounds of washed linen (22 loads of wash) can be accommodated by three 100-pound dryers in a $6\frac{1}{2}$-hour period (Figure 15.25).

LESS THAN 100 PERCENT OCCUPANCY

We have been assuming 100 percent occupancy in determining our washing and drying equipment requirements. As we know, hotel operations are not always full. How, then, do we determine the hours of laundry production as related to hotel occupancy?

Figure 15.26 equates the washing capability of the two 50-pound washers to 100 percent occupancy of the 100-room hotel example on a linear basis, thereby indicating the number of hours a laundry must operate for any given occupancy. At optimum efficiency and with no breakdowns, we see that two 50-pound washers on a 30-minute cycle can generate the linen required for 100 percent occupancy (1,000 pounds of wash) in slightly more than $5\frac{1}{2}$ hours; 70 percent

TABLE 15.2 Load Schedules for One 50-Pound Washer

Item*	Quantity	Total Weight (Pounds)	Items/Load	Total Loads
Sheets (King)	20	44	20	1
Sheets (Queen)	320	464	32	10
PC	350	88	175	2
BT	350	250	70	5
HT	350	81	175	2
WC	350	19	350	1
BM	100	44	100	1

PC, pillowcase; BT, bath towel; HT, hand towel; WC, washcloth; BM, bath mat.

FIGURE 15.25 Four 100-pound dryers make a compatible arrangement with four 50-pound washers. *(Photo taken with permission.)*

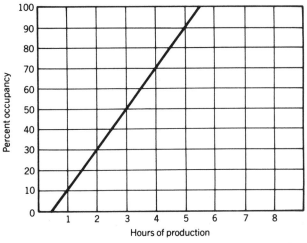

FIGURE 15.26 Washer productivity versus occupancy graph developed for a 100-room example property.

occupancy would require 4 hours of operation; lesser occupancies would require less time. Loading time and requirements due to different wash formulas for sheets and terry linen were also considered when the graph was developed.

ADDITIONAL EQUIPMENT

Having specified two washer/extractors and three dryers as basic machinery required for our 100-room example property, what other equipment may be considered essential? Mary Chew[4] recommends the following ancillary equipment:

- *1 soak sink:* Double basin, plastic formed, for soaking stained linens in special wash formulas for spot and stain removal (Figure 15.27).

- *1 folding table* (4 by 6 feet)*:* Centrally located between dryers and storage shelving; it is used primarily for folding terry linens.
- *5 laundry hampers:* Either vinyl-coated canvas or plastic-molded hamper. Two hampers are used for soiled separated linen. One is to receive washed-wet linen, and two are for washed-dry linen. These hampers should not be used outside the laundry.

In addition to Chew's recommendations, the following equipment is also recommended:

- *6 convertible/mobile linen storage carts:* Three convertible/mobile storage carts should be in the laundry to receive clean linen throughout the day. These three carts are moved to satellite linen rooms for the next day's operation. As linen is moved from the mobile carts to the maids' carts, the shelving is repositioned so as to create soiled linen hampers for the next day's housekeeping.

Three mobile linen carts should be in the satellite linen rooms to accommodate soiled linen during the day. At day's end they are ready to be moved to the laundry for washing the following day. After soiled linen has been removed and sorted, shelving on the convertible mobile carts is repositioned to accept clean linen. The cycle will then be repeated. (I.E.H.A. can provide the names of several manufacturers of this type of convertible mobile cart.) Figures 15.28 and 15.29 are examples of a convertible/mobile cart with shelves in the positions for clean and soiled linen, respectively.

Mobile shelving does not preclude the need for some permanent shelving, but it does remove the requirement for most and it does allow for transporting linen. The total need for mobile linen carts is determined by the number of satellite linen

FIGURE 15.27 Soak sink and chemical mixing center. Note detergent lines leading to washing machines. Other chemicals are arranged for proper dispensing. *(Photo taken with permission.)*

FIGURE 15.28 Convertible mobile cart with shelving positioned to receive fresh linen. *(Photo courtesy of Inter Metro Industries Corp.)*

FIGURE 15.29 Convertible cart with shelving positioned to receive soiled linen. *(Photo courtesy of Inter Metro Industries Corp.)*

rooms; two are needed for each linen storage area, one of which would be positioned in the laundry each day.

- *1 Extra Hand sheet/spread folders:* There are several ways to fold sheets. The one used is normally determined by the size of the laundry workload. When workloads are low, capital expenditures for sheet folders would usually not be warranted

or recommended, since two attendants working together can fold about 90 to 100 sheets per hour. For example, a small laundry load (50 percent average occupancy) in our 100-room example hotel yields a workload of about 150 sheets and requires two people to fold sheets for about $1\frac{1}{2}$ hours

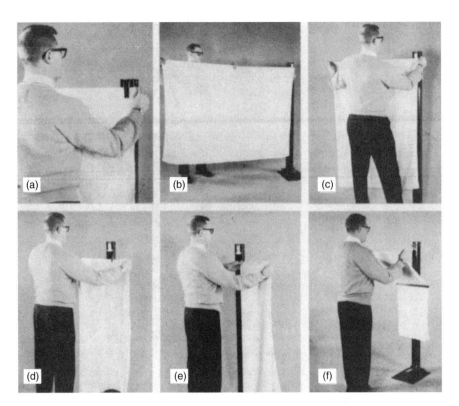

FIGURE 15.30 An Extra Hand sheet folder in operation. *(Photo courtesy of S & S Products.)*

If the workload permanently increases, it then becomes appropriate to consider purchasing an **Extra Hand** folder. The Extra Hand gives one employee about the same production capability as two employees folding sheets by hand. Figure 15.30 illustrates an Extra Hand device in use; one employee is performing six basic steps and folding approximately 120 sheets an hour.[5] The same procedure can be followed for spreads, blankets, bed pads, shower curtains, and so on.

Laundry Equipment for Larger Hotels

The previously discussed equipment for our hypothetical 100-room hotel is probably sufficient, but what could be added to the mix in larger properties of several hundred rooms and multiple restaurant outlets? Obviously, the washers and dryers would have to increase in size and number, but what else is available to reduce our dependence on labor?

Chicago Dryer Company, for example, produces a number of labor-saving devices for laundries. The Pik-Quik is an automatic **flatwork** (e.g., sheets, table linens, pillowcases) separating system (Figure 15.31). Carts of wet linen can be placed in the machine, which

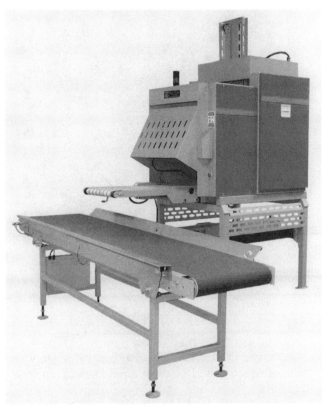

FIGURE 15.31 The Pik-Quik can be teamed with the Linen Stream™, a conveyor system that advances linen to operators who are loading a spreader/feeder like the King Edge. *(Photo courtesy of Chicago Dryer Company.)*

will automatically untangle and separate the sheets so that they can be easily introduced into spreader/feeders. There is even an optional feature that will break apart those large linen **cakes** coming from a **tunnel washer**.

The King Edge is the world's only cornerless, ergonomically enhanced spreader/feeder (Figure 15.32). This device takes laundered wet sheets, spreads them, and feeds them into an ironer. An operator takes a sheet separated by the Pik-Quik and feeds it into the King Edge. With most spreader/feeders, you have to find a corner of the sheet before you can feed it into the unit, but not the King Edge. Finding a corner takes valuable time, decreasing the amount of linen an operator can handle in an hour.

Next, the sheets fed into the spreader/feeder are automatically transferred into a flatwork ironer, such as the Century Deep Chest All Roll Drive (Figure 15.33), which automatically dries and removes the wrinkles from the linen. Because the same control system is used in all aspects of Chicago Dryer's finishing systems, operators

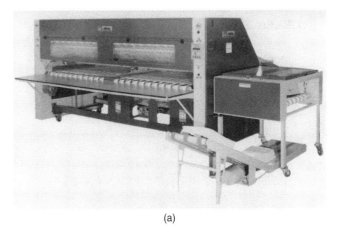

(a)

(b)

FIGURE 15.34 The Skyline 2000 comes in a wide variety of models and options to handle every application from institutional settings to hotels. *(Photo courtesy of Chicago Dryer Company.)*

need to learn only one system to control the entire finishing area.

The final stage is the automatic folding of the flatwork by the Skyline 2000 (Figure 15.34). All four units (separator, spreader/feeder, flatwork ironer, and automatic folder) linked together make up a labor-saving flatwork finishing system.

The final example of a labor-saving device in this section is the Air Chicago Triple Sort. This stand-alone unit (Figure 15.35) automatically folds bath and bed linen (e.g., towels, blankets, patient gowns, and underpads). Specific folding ability will depend on the model employed.

FIGURE 15.32 The King Edge accommodates not only sheets, but also other flatwork items such as pillowcases, napkins, and tablecloths on the bypass conveyor. *(Photo courtesy of Chicago Dryer Company.)*

FIGURE 15.33 The Century Deep Chest All Roll Drive Flatwork Ironer is microprocessor controlled. *(Photo courtesy of Chicago Dryer Company.)*

General Nonequipment Factors and Requirements

✂

LINEN SUPPLY

As mentioned in Chapter 7, about $3\frac{1}{2}$ par of linen is required for efficient housekeeping operations: One par

GREEN TIP

Turn all your laundry green

There are a number of opportunities to reduce the environmental impacts of an on-site laundry operation:

- Avoid detergents containing nonylphenol ethoxylates, which are suspected of being endocrine disrupters as they enter the environment when washed down the drain.
- Consider using hydrogen peroxide or trying ozone or ionization to replace chlorine bleach.
- Make sure that equipment is operating efficiently, including washers that efficiently spin dry clothes, dryers, vents, and automated dispensing equipment.

Thanks to Stephen Ashkin and *Cleaning and Maintenance Management* magazine for these tips.

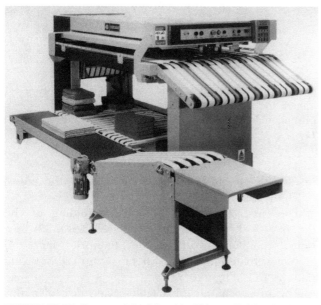

FIGURE 15.35 One model of the Air Chicago Folder Series, the Triple Sort, allows an operator to randomly feed as many as three different towel sizes. *(Photo courtesy of Chicago Dryer Company.)*

of linen is found on the beds and in bathrooms of all guestrooms; 1 par is clean and is either on maids' carts or on shelves for tomorrow's cleaning operations (Figure 15.36); and 1 par is soiled, awaiting the next day's laundry operations. The remaining half par is related to new linen in storage. (If linens are owned and have to be sent off the property to a commercial laundry each day, add 1 additional par to total requirements because of the time required to transport linen back and forth to the commercial laundry.)

A MINI CASE STUDY

Pitfalls in Linen Reuse Programs

"We aren't running an economy motel here," Tony Belcher, hotel manager at the Sea Coast Pines Resort & Convention Center, states in a strident tone to Molly Galloway, the executive housekeeper. The scene is the weekly executive committee meeting and Molly has asked for some time to argue the point that the hotel should think seriously about implementing a linen reuse program.

In essence, Galloway wants to start a program that would give guests the option of reusing their towels and bed linens for up to three days during their stay, or guests could opt to have their linens changed out each day of their stay if they so desire. Galloway wants to put "Project Planet" door hangers, table tents, and cards in each room explaining the program and urging guests to join in the program.

"I think guests will appreciate the opportunity to do something good for the planet by saving water, energy, and detergent," says Galloway. "It really is 'win-win' for everyone. The hotel benefits by saving money, the guests feel as though they have done something good for the environment, the guestroom attendants will save time and energy in what is a very stressful schedule, and of course, the environment benefits as well."

Belcher responds, "That may be okay for the Holiday Inns out there, but we are an upper-class property. Currently, we have four stars and four diamonds and we are all working very hard to make that five. Considering the money our guests are paying for their rooms, they have a right to expect to have their sheets and towels changed every day," says Belcher.

Holly Cane, marketing director at the property speaks up, "Am I hearing opinions or facts here? Who has the data to support their claims?" Belcher and Galloway look at each other and say nothing.

Cheryl Case, the GM, finally speaks up. "Frankly, I am not convinced by either side. But one thing I know, I am not going to do anything to make the guests in this hotel think we are taking advantage of them and lowering our service standards. It is going to take more than these arguments we have heard today to convince me to start a linen reuse program. If you want to

pursue this, Molly, you are going to have to provide me with some hard data. I am not going to
risk our reputation on what a few other hotels of
questionable standards may have done." Case
ends the discussion by stating that Galloway can
come back for "round 2" at next week's meeting.

QUESTIONS

Assume you are Galloway or Belcher and back
up your opinions with some facts. Be ready
to present your findings when your instructor
indicates you are going to revisit this topic. Have
the class vote on the appropriate strategy.

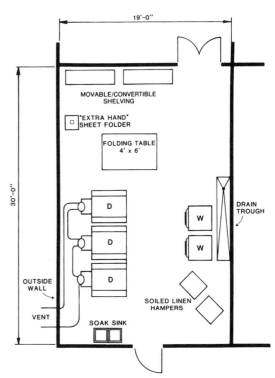

FIGURE 15.37 Small laundry floor plan layout suitable for supporting rooms operations of a 60- to 100-room hotel.

FIGURE 15.36 Fresh linen supply awaiting pickup for future use. *(Photo taken with permission.)*

FLOOR PLAN LAYOUT AND SIZE

About 4 square feet of space for each guestroom is required for the laundry facility itself, and an additional 4 square feet per guestroom is needed for linen handling and storage throughout the property. Figure 15.37 shows a typical **floor plan layout** for a small laundry with only two washers. Figure 15.38 shows the actual layout of a four-washer/dryer laundry.

Soiled linens are first moved to a sorting and wash area. After washing and drying, linen is moved to the folding area. Both folded sheets and folded terry linen are then moved to convertible/mobile storage carts for passage out of the laundry.

A third washer could be added to accommodate expansion. Dryers should be installed as shown and are part of the original equipment. (Note the venting capability.)

If a hot-water system is not sufficient to accommodate two washers, a fast-generating hot water heater will be necessary. Gas hot water heaters must be properly vented when installed.

Two soak sinks provide capability for soaking stained and spotted linen rather than using valuable washing time.

A $4' \times 6'$ folding table, positioned as indicated, is recommended.

STAFFING CONSIDERATIONS

Staffing for the 100-room hotel example laundry in this chapter (no food and beverage linen or uniforms considered) is: 1) one wash person, and 2) one laundry attendant.

The wash person handles the loading and unloading of washers and the loading of dryers. The laundry attendant unloads the dryers, folds sheets, and stacks terry linen and pillowcases in flat stacks of appropriate numbers (Figure 15.39). Folding rates for the Extra Hand sheet folder are approximately $1\frac{1}{2}$ sheets per minute. A full par of sheets (242) can therefore be folded in two hours by the laundry attendant.

The laundry attendant spends the rest of the shift stacking terry linen and pillowcases in counted stacks to

FIGURE 15.38 Laundry layout indicating how linen flows from washer to dryer to folding tables. Laundry hampers are rolled under folding table with cleaned and dried linen to be folded. *(Photo taken with permission.)*

FIGURE 15.39 Laundry attendant folds terry linen and places it in stacks of appropriate size. *(Photo taken with permission.)*

be passed to the satellite linen rooms at the end of the day via the mobile linen carts.

For the model hotel (353 rooms), laundry staffing is approximately seven people (one wash person supervisor, one utility helper, and five laundry attendants). Since this is the same number of people as in a housekeeping team (see Chapter 2), the laundry crew, with proper cross-training and working a five-day week, can be relieved on the sixth and seventh days by the swing teams.

LAUNDRY FLOORS

Even with proper drainage, washer spills and overflows will occur. It is therefore essential that the laundry floor be waterproofed (sealed).

Soiled sorted linen and even clean linen may be found trailing on the floor occasionally, and as a result, the laundry floor must be damp-mopped daily. Linen on the floor is of no consequence, provided the floor has been sealed and is kept clean.

MECHANICAL ENGINEERING REQUIREMENTS

When small-facility equipment has been installed with no attention to engineering considerations such as electrical wiring, water supply and drainage, plumbing, and ventilation, it can create a shutdown. The greatest of these unrecognized problems is inadequate water disposal drainage caused by extraction cycles of several washing machines draining simultaneously. For example, can a 44-inch floor drain accommodate the drainage from three washers, each with a 3-inch discharge line? According to most specifications, the answer is no. A drain trough or holding basin that can hold 100 gallons of water can allow for the overload of effluent water under pressure and will allow time for the drain water to pass into the 44-inch floor drain over a period of several minutes. (Refer to Figure 15.37 and note the specified drain trough associated with the two washers. There is also a provision for drainage of a third washer.)

VENTILATION REQUIREMENTS

Another requirement concerns the necessity to exhaust moisture-laden air from the three dryers out of the laundry room. Small properties usually have laundries with low ceilings, which compound the problem of dryer effluent exhaust. Most 100-pound dryers each exhaust about 800 cubic feet per minute (cfm) of air. Operating three dryers together results in 2400 cfm of this moist hot air.

Laundry rooms also require adequate space through regular doors to intake or supply an equal amount of fresh dry air. Without ample intake through regular doors or a separate forced dry air supply, dryers will not operate at specified efficiencies. Some modern dryers now provide for heat recovery equipment, which will reduce laundry energy requirements if provision is made for this type of accessory in advance.

PROVISION FOR LINT REMOVAL

It is absolutely essential that the laundry room and adjacent areas be kept clean and free of lint. Lint is a major fire hazard in laundry operations and must be dealt with accordingly. Not only must lint be removed from dryer air ventilation, but it must be dusted away from overhead pipes and hard-to-reach areas. A regular campaign must be maintained to keep lint accumulation to a minimum.

CONCLUSION

The determination of whether to have an on-premises laundry is based on cost considerations. If it is appropriate, the need for accurate planning arises. Decisions must be made concerning the proper size of equipment, facility layout, ancillary equipment, staffing considerations, work-flow patterns, and floor treatment. A critical factor in preliminary planning is a necessary concern for mechanical, electrical, plumbing, and airflow engineering to ensure proper equipment operation after construction and installation.

Frequently, once the decision is made to have an on-premises laundry, facility architects unfamiliar with hotel operational design and the need to trim capital costs ignore the necessity of seeking and obtaining professional laundry facility advice. Shortcuts in this area create problems that haunt the operator during startup operations and for some time thereafter until they are identified and corrected. The decision to have an on-premises laundry facility should therefore include the decision to contact a nationally recognized laundry consulting firm. Small operators should not become unduly concerned about the costs of such consulting services. The payback in future years of trouble-free operations far outweighs the initial cost of proper planning and foresight.

KEY TERMS AND CONCEPTS

On-premises laundries
No-iron linens
Laundry consultants
Systemeering
Linen poundage requirements
Washing capacity

Drying capacity
Handling capacity
Ironers
1 par linen
Wash formula
Extra Hand

Flatwork
Cakes
Tunnel washer
Floor plan layout

DISCUSSION AND REVIEW QUESTIONS

1. List advantages of having an on-premises laundry.
2. Discuss the characteristics of no-iron linens. Indicate why no-iron linens have made on-premises laundries more practical today than they were in the past.
3. When on-premises laundries are being considered, why are the services of a qualified laundry consultant so important? List several of the factors that are often overlooked when inexperienced people are involved in planning small laundry operations.
4. When developing the requirements for an on-premises laundry, what are the nonequipment factors that should be considered? What are the mechanical equipment factors that must be considered?

NOTES

1. Jack E. Scott, "Why You Should Install Your Own Laundry," *Lodging*, November 1976, pp. 38–39.
2. Paul Schweid, "A Laundry in Your Plans: Don't Underestimate Its Importance," *Cornell Quarterly*, vol. 17, November 1976, pp. 40–46.
3. "Baring Laundry-Valet Profile," Baring Industries, 655 NW 122 Street, Miami, FL 33268; undated brochure.
4. Mary Chew, "Those Indispensable Laundry Accessories," *Executive Housekeeper*, March 1977, p. 46.
5. "The Extra Hand," S & S Products, 8377 Neiman Road, Lenexa, KS, 66214; undated brochure.

The Full Circle of Management

After studying the chapter, students should be able to:

1. Describe what is meant by the full circle of management.
2. Describe and give examples of what it means to be a problem solver in housekeeping.
3. Define the terms leader and manager and be able to differentiate between the two.
4. Describe the executive housekeeper's role in the development of subordinates.
5. Describe why it is important to continue to personally develop as a manager and give examples of what can be done to ensure that professional development takes place.

Thus far, we have discussed the theoretical aspects of scientific management and how they are applied to the tasks of the executive housekeeper; that is, opening a hotel and operating a housekeeping department. We have seen that the executive housekeeper has to be systematic in the development of procedures, whereby most housekeeping tasks are delegated to department personnel and controls are inaugurated so that the technique of **empowerment** can be used. In addition, we discussed the special topics of safety and security and on-premises laundries.

Once these procedures and tasks are mastered, what is left for the manager to do? Nothing—provided all systems work perfectly; no problems arise; employees do not need any caring, human understanding, attention, guidance, or inspiration; morale is not an issue; and no progress is expected. Of course, such situations never exist, and thus we see that it is the manager who deals with these issues and brings the art and science of management full circle.

The integration of the art and science of management is especially important for managers of hotel or hospital housekeeping departments. This is so because of the large numbers of personnel employed, requiring orientation, training, development, guidance, and supervision, and the day-to-day problems that arise as a result of the unexpected human dynamics and interactions among personnel. There is also a need for flexibility, for recognition of occasional change in operational direction, and for application of new techniques.

This chapter thus presents topics related to the special ongoing responsibilities of managers: problem solving, managerial styles, employee development, and personal professional growth.

Problem Solving

At one particular time I was assigned responsibilities as regional director of technical services for the Midwest region of Marriott Hotels, Inc. Upon reporting for duty, I was introduced to many members of top management, including other regional directors, in an office complex in which all directors were housed. The directors' offices gave the impression of heavy and complex activity. Desks were covered with work in progress; bookshelves were full of references; walls were covered with charts and graphs; and most telephones were either being used, were ringing, or had lights flashing.

All offices except one were like this—the one that had just been assigned to the new regional director of the Midwest region. In my office were a clean desk, empty drawers, clean walls, empty bookshelf, credenza, and quiet telephone. The appearance of the office gave no clue as to the work content of this new staff position. This uncertainty lasted only momentarily, however.

The phone rang—it was the executive housekeeper of the Houston Marriott indicating that there was a problem with the hotel's recently installed laundry. From that moment on, there was never any doubt about the responsibilities involved in the new assignment. The incumbent was to become a problem solver, and within one month the office of the Midwest regional director gave the same evidence of activity as did the other offices.

Problem solving can be one of the greatest challenges faced each day by the executive housekeeper. Few, if any, days will pass that someone in the organization will not utter the infamous phrase "I've got a problem." Most problems are best resolved by ensuring that the supervisor in whose area the problem lies is not allowed to shift the problem upward. Solutions must come from that person rather than from higher authority. The characteristic of human nature whereby people tend to push their problems onto anyone who will accept them, rather than solve the problems themselves, must be avoided. In addition, the tendency for overzealous managers to take on the problems of others as their own must be overcome.

Many employees are afraid to solve problems for fear of making mistakes. Mistakes are a great teaching device, provided they are used for objective counseling as opposed to unsatisfactory performance evaluations. Most mistakes made in a housekeeping department are not costly to overcome, and the development that can occur from making and learning from a mistake far outweighs the cost of managerial and supervisory training that may be required to have prevented the mistake from happening in the first place. Executive housekeepers should therefore guard carefully against solving problems in areas in which junior managers and supervisors have simply failed to act.

Not all problems can be referred to junior managers for solution without some form of guidance, however. There are those problems that must have the direct

involvement of the executive housekeeper or they will grow in complexity and intensity. A review of some of the more common problems that require the executive housekeeper's attention is therefore in order.

EMPLOYEE ABSENTEEISM

The reasons most employees do not report for work as scheduled are usually predictable and therefore preventable. When questioned about the reasons for an absence pattern, most employees indicate "a personal problem," when in fact the roots to such problems may be found in management's insensitivity to some critical issue: poor orientation, a person's lack of understanding of his or her worth to the housekeeping operation, lack of proper observation during probationary periods of training, poor supervision or difficulties with supervisory personnel, and management's insensitivity to the personal needs of employees are among the prime causes of **employee absenteeism**.

Poor Orientation

During orientation meetings, it is essential that management convey the notion that employees are hired because they are needed and that management does not hire employees with a view toward terminating them. It should be made clear that employees are hired to perform tasks that are vital to the success of the operation and that the cost of hiring and training employees is not to be taken lightly.

Such comments made during employee orientation meetings are crucial to the initiation of morale-building environments, whereby employees can begin to motivate themselves to come to work when scheduled. In so doing, employees are allowed to consider themselves *valuable* to the success or failure of the operation. In addition, it shows employees that they are working for a company that is successful. It is thus reasonable to assume that working for a successful organization requires every employee's contribution, commitment, and dedication to that success.

Lack of Appreciation of Self-Worth

Although tasks may be different, employees who understand that their contributions are just as valuable as those of executive housekeepers and general managers will more than likely sense their own worth and role in the success of the operation. They will look forward to participation each day in that success rather than find excuses to avoid coming to work.

Improper Observation during Probation

Only employees who demonstrate technical competence and attitudes that support company objectives should be allowed to complete probationary periods of employment successfully and become permanent employees. Too often employees are allowed to slide through probationary periods when it should have been obvious that certain trainees were not in tune with company objectives and goals. In the truest sense, a company's goals include the objectives of every full-time, permanent employee who has successfully demonstrated a desire to be a part of the organization. In fact, a disservice may be done to good employees who must work with others of questionable loyalty to those ideals pledged by regular employees.

Poor Supervision

Poor or inept supervision may be another common reason for employee absenteeism. The positive measures enumerated earlier are actually put into practice by supervisory personnel, and becoming a competent supervisor requires training in personnel relationships, leadership, responsible action, and human dynamics.

How often is outstanding performance in a housekeeping department rewarded with promotion to supervisor? How seldom, however, is the new supervisor adequately trained for these new and different types of responsibilities? Sustained superior performance by a guestroom attendant (GRA) or section housekeeping aide should be rewarded with public recognition and incentive pay, not by promotion to positions in which potential in dealing with personnel problems has not been demonstrated or development has yet to take place.

This is not to say that some employees are unpromotable; it only means that promotion should be based on demonstrated professional development, rather than a reward for outstanding performance of technical skills already learned. Newly promoted supervisors should themselves be placed in supervisory training classes in which they will be exposed to new skills. Role playing should be used to familiarize the new supervisor with personnel relationship situations *before* they happen, rather than requiring the new supervisor to stumble and fall—*after* an encounter.

Chances are that 95 percent of all problems encountered by a supervisor have been encountered before; mistakes have been made and solutions have been found. Failure to take advantage of the learning available from the resolution of past mistakes of others is equivalent to reinventing the wheel. Confidence will be gained when the new supervisor is exposed to situation dynamics that have been experienced by others to the extent that the remaining 5 percent of problems yet to be faced will be tolerated well and will form the basis for new problem-solving opportunities. Temperament, attitudes about people in general, and a willingness to apply an old yet valuable management technique—the Golden Rule—should also be a part of supervisory training.

Management Insensitivity

Management must remain sensitive to the personal needs of employees. Such a premise does not require that managers become involved with the personal problems of employees, only that they recognize that different things matter more or less to different people. To understand this is to recognize that employees work for different reasons. Some employees work to support themselves, whereas others work to augment family incomes. Working mothers see their priorities differently from women who have no children. Some employees see their employment secondary to the demands placed on them by school, whereas others work to conquer boredom.

Each of these reasons for working results in a motivation from a different source, each of which should be discovered during preemployment interviews. The executive housekeeper who visits the floors with employees regularly stays in tune with individual employee concerns, is better informed as to what counts in the lives of employees, and may therefore be forewarned of impending problems. For example, it would be expected that a working mother whose child becomes ill would readjust her priorities accordingly, and as a result may need to be absent. Of major concern would not be that the working mother failed to show up for work, but whether she notified the department in sufficient time to allow for her temporary replacement.

It has been well documented that managers who demonstrate genuine respect, feeling, and caring for employees create maximum employee loyalty and productivity. Feelings must be genuine, however, inasmuch as patronization can be quickly sensed and can have the reverse effect.

William T. Scherer takes such caring a step further and cites ''love'' of employees as necessary to convey caring. Scherer states:

> Some . . . will argue that ''love'' is too strong a word to use when describing the attitude managers should have for their people. Some will even laugh at the idea. If you happen to be such a person stop and think for a moment. The late Vince Lombardi of the Green Bay Packers was a great football coach and leader of men. Many might think that ''love'' is too delicate a term to describe the feelings between a coach and his players. But listen to the men who played and won for Vince Lombardi. They aren't ashamed to say that they loved him and gave their all for him, because, to a man, they knew he loved each of them.[1]

Scherer continues by reminding us that love is usually a reciprocal emotion. When love and caring are in evidence between the manager and employees, team spirit flowers, and loyalty, compassion, and understanding are returned to the manager in the form of increased openness and successful performance.

Management's sensitivity to the needs of employees culminates with an accurate understanding of what motivates employees to take a desired action. Motivation comes from within. Motivation is a complex reaction between an individual and his or her environment.

The executive housekeepers or supervisors who feel that they can motivate their employees are allowing the shift of responsibility for motivation from the worker to the supervisor, which in itself is a poor technique. Although the supervisor may assist in motivational development by creating an atmosphere wherein the employees can motivate themselves, techniques that imply an ''I am going to motivate you'' mentality are highly suspect.

Solutions lie in those activities over which the supervisor does have control: open communication, caring, sensitivity to personal needs, and ensuring that employees understand their personal worth to the overall operation all help to create a self-motivating atmosphere.

Employee absenteeism as indicated is both predictable and preventable, provided the executive housekeeper looks in the right places. Poor orientation, lack of understanding of worth, little or no observation of attitudes during periods of probationary employment, inept supervision, and insensitive management can be found at the roots of most absenteeism. GRAs who leave work each day with quiet hearts because they know their contributions were necessary and valuable to an overall worthwhile and successful operation look forward to the next workday with great expectation, not for a way to avoid coming to work.

EMPLOYEE TURNOVER

Another problem with which executive housekeepers must become involved is **employee turnover**. The problem is an extension of employee absenteeism in that when failure to come to work becomes excessive, the cost of having to hire and train a new employee is incurred.

Employee turnover in housekeeping departments may range from 2 to 15 percent per month, which at a minimum represents one-fourth of the staff each year. Although it is true that 90 percent of all turnover occurs in less than 10 percent of the housekeeping jobs, an analysis of causes *is* important. To hire and induct an employee into the department on Monday only to have him or her fail to report for work on Tuesday is an indication that hiring practices should be highly suspect. All too often, the press of business tends to force the manager to skip important matters, such as a thorough and professional look at past work history, when reviewing an applicant's background in hopes that everything will work out. Obviously, care and attention should go into selecting employees.

After a person is hired, there are several things that executive housekeepers and managers in general can do to ensure the success and long-term commitment of the employee. First, staff members who will train others should be carefully considered. More than one potentially good employee has been discouraged by the techniques of the person assigned to do the training, causing an early and unnecessary departure. Second, job enrichment is a technique whereby the employee may see the job as important and necessary to proper functioning of the organization. Third, participative management, whereby employees are involved in discussions as to why some employees choose to leave the company, often reveals motives not readily shared or even understood by people working at the management level. Employees themselves may be able to point out matters of importance in reducing turnover.

Fourth, being looked down upon by outsiders because of the nature of the work being performed is a major cause of employee dissatisfaction, which can lead to employee turnover. This unrest usually stems from new and unenlightened junior management who openly profess distaste for the housekeeping function and would therefore not perform such duties. Junior managers' training programs that include orientation in the housekeeping department result in a much keener awareness of the value of those performing such functions.[2] For example, the close personal relationships that can develop between an expert GRA and a young sales trainee who is being taught how to service a guestroom can prove invaluable in developing mutual respect for each function. Executive housekeepers should therefore push for junior management development programs that cycle the young manager through the housekeeping department.

The underlying causes of absenteeism are at work in causing high turnover rates and should therefore be considered when looking for solutions. The executive housekeeper should first assess the level of turnover and then set goals for reduction of turnover rate. When properly addressed, most turnover rates can be reduced by one-half over the period of a year.

EMPLOYEE PROBLEMS

Employee problems involving difficulties in working with supervisors or with each other necessitate constant attention. It is not necessary that employees like each other, provided they respect each other at work.

Employees should be counseled at the onset that personal problems involving the family are best left at home and should not be aired in public at work. This is not to diminish the manager's concern for each employee; it is only to reinforce the fact that those people who expose their personal family problems at work create gossip that usually returns to haunt them.

Counseling is best used as a preventive measure rather than waiting until problems arise. Employees should be counseled to keep their professional and personal lives separate. Management should remain aloof and objective about personal relationships that emanate from working relationships, and personal relationships should not be allowed to interfere with the working environment.

POOR APPEARANCE AND HYGIENE

An **employee's appearance** and manner of dress will never be better than when applying for employment. It is surprising how many employees, once hired, assume that having their hair in curlers or under a bandana, or working in a soiled uniform is normal and perfectly acceptable. This problem must be addressed during orientation, so that every employee understands that appearance goes hand in hand with the overall quality and look of the property.

Housekeeping work differs from secretarial work in that much physical energy is expended during the workday. Employees must therefore be counseled that regardless of the type of work to be done in a hotel, they must keep themselves as neat as possible; otherwise they will look out of place with their surroundings. A sturdy, comfortable uniform that allows freedom of movement should be provided. In addition, a prescribed sweater or foul-weather jacket should be specified, rather than having employees wear odd colors over their uniforms.

To gain acceptance of such concepts of dress requires that employees themselves become involved in the selection of uniforms. Colors might be specified by hotel decor, but type and quality should be left up to employees since appearance has an important effect on morale and personal pride. A panel of employees could be used to review uniform catalogs and make recommendations as to what uniform it feels would be enjoyed by the most workers.

The care and overall treatment of uniforms should be monitored, and those not familiar with proper laundering techniques should be taught how to care for their uniforms. Some hotels require that uniforms be serviced and issued on a daily basis. Such service is costly, however, and it rules out the possibility of allowing the employee to become involved in the uniform maintenance and selection process.

Employee hygiene is another matter that must not be ignored. When employees consistently have a problem with personal hygiene, the manager should first consider that the employee may have never been counseled in how to prevent body odors when doing heavy physical work. The axiom that "only your best friends will tell you" is more true than we might expect—provided counsel is discreet and professional. The cost of holding professional classes in how to dress for success, how to wear your hair, and how to apply makeup is far outweighed by the benefit in overall appearance of each employee and in morale. Regardless of how personal a matter might be, problems in appearance and hygiene should not be ignored and must be dealt with in a personal and professional way.

EMPLOYEE CLAIMS OF UNFAIRNESS

One of the greatest causes of **employee claims regarding unfairness** is associated with a desire for information—asking questions and not receiving answers, not knowing what is happening, and going away with a feeling that "no one cares about me or what I think." Employees who ask questions deserve answers. If the answer is not currently known, then a genuine attempt must be made to obtain the answer; the employee should be informed in a reasonable period of time. Questions asked of management that go unanswered will be answered by someone else—and most often incorrectly.

Every question asked is a management opportunity to demonstrate concern for employees. Also remember that employees who feel they cannot receive answers as individuals usually seek someone to represent them, which can result in opening the door to unionism. Employees who ask questions and receive answers may not like the answers, but they are much more likely to accept them when explanations are forthcoming.

POOR PERFORMANCE

Employees who satisfactorily complete probationary periods of employment will have demonstrated their capability to perform all tasks required for the job satisfactorily. **Poor performance** after probationary periods thus indicates some reason that had been nonexistent previously.

There are many factors relating to employee behavior that end in unsatisfactory performance that have little to do with the employee's ability to do a job properly. Problems at home, poor relationships with supervisors, changes in priorities, illness, and poor morale can cause deterioration in performance.

The executive housekeeper's challenge in each case is to find the underlying cause of stress leading to substandard performance and deal with the causes before the situation becomes irreversible. The leveling technique discussed in Chapter 11 is most effective in working with employees whose performances have become substandard, especially when managers send "I" messages. "I" messages (rather than "you" messages) imply the manager's concern for how operations may be suffering as a result of poor performance as opposed to implying that the employee is a bad person. "I am troubled because your performance is not what it used to be" as opposed to "You are not performing up to standards" hits the core of the problem without implying that the employee has a serious personality defect. Actually, the employee whose performance starts to diminish may not even be aware of such deterioration because no one *until now* has given him or her an objective evaluation of what was becoming obvious over a several-week period.

THE PROBLEM-SOLVING TEMPERAMENT

Housekeeping managers need to develop a **temperament for problem solving**. Seeing a problem as an occurrence to be dreaded, as opposed to an opportunity requiring a solution, can seriously hinder the manager's development for greater responsibilities. Such feelings need to be addressed before negative attitudes begin to bring about the head-in-sand phenomenon.

I recall a junior manager who possessed excellent problem-solving abilities and was selected for promotion to executive housekeeper, resulting in a transfer to a smaller property. The young manager at first refused the promotion, which amazed many people since it appeared that he was on the fast track to rapid growth within the company. When questioned, the junior manager indicated a major concern for being assigned to a smaller property: "I would miss the hassle" was his reply, referring to the fact that the day-to-day problem-solving challenges presented by the larger property provided the major source of enjoyment in his current position. He feared that losing that challenge could prove boring. It was pointed out that promotion has seldom been the cause of a lessening of problem-solving opportunities, only a change in the type of problems that may be encountered. The young manager was encouraged to reconsider his decision, which he did, and today he is one of the company's general managers. Solving problems must be a challenge that the manager welcomes.

CHANGE AGENTS
Bob Merkt, Founder of MEGA

Bob Merkt is the owner of MEGA—the Merkt Educational Groups and Associates. He has been in the cleaning industry for 20 years and in training for more than 12 years.

In addition, he is an invited speaker at many industry events and a columnist for *Installation Cleaning Specialist* (ICS) and *Commercial Floor Care* (CFC) magazines. He is an author and regular contributor to many other industry publications including *Cleanfax* and *Cleaning and Maintenance Management* magazines.

Merkt is an Institute of Inspection, Cleaning, Restoration Certification (IICRC)–approved instructor. In addition, he is an IICRC Master Cleaner and vice chair of the IICRC Floor Care Technician (FCT) Committee.

He is a Cleaning Management Institute (CMI)–certified instructor and a member of the CMI's "All Star Speaking Team."

Merkt is also past president of the Association of Wisconsin Cleaning Contractors (AWCC) and presently sits on the board of directors of International Custodial Advisory Network (ICAN). ICAN is a nonprofit educational corporation composed of building service consultants and facility service professionals who perform a substantive educational function. ICAN's mission is to promote, strengthen, and enhance respect for the cleaning and building services industry, foster education, provide expert information, develop meaningful standards, and raise the professionalism and perceived value of its members' services and the cleaning industry.

ICAN's goals are to:

- Create a **Custodial Code of Ethics** and Pledge of Excellence to help raise the standard (qualifications and professional expectations) for workers.
- Create a **Custodial Literacy Program/ICAN Spanish site**.
- Create a **Custodial Educational Forum** that endorses and teaches standardized cleaning procedures to improve the skill level and professionalism of cleaning workers. This forum is planned as a cooperative effort with existing industry groups and associations.
- Form a **Consultants Educational Forum** that coaches and encourages consultants to improve their professional skills.
- Establish a **speakers' bureau** for member consultants.
- Create a **"Consumer Reports"**–type testing program for the commercial cleaning industry.

According to Merkt, the greatest achievement in his professional life has been the honor to serve others in the cleaning industry by being able to inform, educate, and train others in hopes of making their jobs easier and more profitable; particularly in the area of "Cleaning for Health" and educating others as to the real benefit of cleaning, that is, impacting public health through quantitative case studies and related information.

Managerial Styles

CHANGING PHILOSOPHIES

Managerial styles run the gamut from highly authoritarian to total abdication. Western philosophy about how to manage has for years concerned itself with the axiom that managers tell workers what to do, and workers do what they are told. Such philosophy has been behind the development of the entrepreneurial spirit in America, which has glorified the self-made person for being in the forefront of American industrial progress. Such people succeeded through directive leadership, and in many cases became board chairmen and chief operating officers of many successful companies—50 years ago.

It is no wonder that to succeed in such companies junior managers had to model their own management styles after these leaders; failing to do so would surely bring about mediocrity in personal development and prevent success beyond the midrange point of management.

There have been those entrepreneurs, however, who have dared to question their own employees on how their organizations might be improved and then had the courage to accept the fact that they themselves might be a part of the problem of creeping mediocrity. Let us consider four different attitudes toward power as illustrated in material gathered from managers at different companies by management experts Robert Tanenbaum and Warren Schmidt.[3]

1. I believe in getting things done. I can't waste time calling meetings. Someone has to call the shots around here, and I think it should be me.
2. I'm being paid to lead. If I let a lot of the other people make the decisions I should be making, then I'm not worth my salt.
3. Once I have decided on a course of action, I do my best to sell my ideas to my employees.

4. It is foolish to make decisions oneself on matters that affect [other] people. I always talk things over with my subordinates, but I make it clear to them that I'm the one who has the final say.

The first two statements are symbolic of military-type leadership, which may produce an instant response but may not necessarily produce the best decision. Emergencies involving life-and-death situations may require highly directive leadership, but the majority of decisions made by managers do not involve life and death and do not require the indispensability of the manager.

The second two statements are more symbolic of the manager who has chosen to share power with those who will be affected by decisions that must be made, and as a result are more likely to encourage participation by subordinates who in turn will commit themselves to the decisions.

The democratic principles advocated in the latter two positions are today identified by terms such as "participative management," "industrial democracy," and "quality circles." The sharing of power does not mean the abdication of responsibility; it means a recognition that greater employee commitment is attained by involving those who have a stake in the outcome of decisions.

THE EXECUTIVE HOUSEKEEPER AND PARTICIPATIVE MANAGEMENT

The surest way for the executive housekeeper to establish a style of patronizing benevolence is to assume that housekeeping employees, lacking in experience and education, are short on common sense or could never care about the overall success or failure of the housekeeping operation. Unfortunately, such executive housekeepers remain in evidence today. Employees are sometimes treated like children; they are stroked affectionately when their performance is above average and scolded when the quality of their work is less than desired. Assumptions are made that employees do not have the concern or inclination to get involved.

The actuality is that when employees, regardless of their level of education, are involved in decision-making discussions, they become highly contributive to successful decisions of major consequence. They are then not only committed to the outcome of these decisions, but they are involved in the success or failure of such decisions and are thereby motivated to continue their participation and personal growth.

For example, consider a case in which guestroom cleaning was being considerably slowed when beater-bar belts would break on vacuum cleaners. Engineering priorities could cause several days to pass before a broken belt would be replaced and the machine returned to the appropriate GRA. It was a GRA who pointed out that time could be saved if users could change belts rather than involving engineering in such a small mechanical task. No one changed her belt for her at home, and she never used a screwdriver, just a dime. As a result of the GRA's participation in the resolution of this common work-slowing problem, all GRAs were thereafter provided with a spare belt with a dime taped to it and were given the technical training required to make the belt change. Those employees who had complained about the breaking belt and about how long it took to receive the vacuum back in a repaired condition became involved in a contest to see who could change a belt in the shortest time. The winner received simple but public recognition, which further encouraged participation in implementing the change in this work practice.

Successful executive housekeepers who allow participation in decision making affirm that delegation does not leave people with the feeling of being stripped of power. Actually, power is held only if we can empower others. Nothing in participative decision making can remove the responsibility created for the executive housekeeper; decisions are just made with greater input.

THE EXECUTIVE HOUSEKEEPER: MANAGER OR LEADER?

For the executive housekeeper to become a manager requires only the decree from higher authority that such is the case. Such a decree empowers the manager to carry out the sequential and continuous functions of management within the department: analyzing problems, making decisions, and communicating direction regarding plans, organization, staffing, and control of housekeeping operations.

Decrees of management appointment, however, do not certify the **manager as a leader**. Such certification lies in the purview of those being led. It is difficult to assess our own leadership abilities, since proof of such attributes may remain smoldering in the feelings and attitudes of those being led. However, the following questions can be used for candid self-evaluation as to what kind of leader you might be. For each one, determine which option is better:

1. To drive employees or to coach them?
2. To take credit or give credit?
3. To be concerned with things or with people?
4. To tell employees to be at work on time or to be at work ahead of time personally?
5. To think "I" or to think "we"?
6. To inspire fear or enthusiasm?
7. To see today or look at tomorrow?

8. To know how the job is done or to show employees how to do the job?
9. To depend on authority or goodwill?
10. To work hard to produce or work hard to help employees produce?
11. To let employees know where you (the leader) stand or where they stand?
12. To never have enough time or to make time for things that matter?
13. To say "go" or "let's go"?
14. To fix blame for breakdowns or show how to fix a breakdown?
15. To use employees or to develop them?
16. To command or to ask?

Should you dare to ask *your employees* for an objective evaluation of your leadership attributes? Courageous managers do.

Development of Others

It is unfortunate that some managers erect barriers to the **development of subordinates**. In most cases, fear of being outperformed by subordinates is the cause of such behavior. Successful managers welcome the development of others as supervisors who can ultimately serve as the managers' replacement, thus allowing for their own advancement. Consider a warning given to a group of young managers: "Opportunities may come and go, but until you have trained a replacement for your current position, I consider you indispensable to your current assignment, therefore unpromotable." A comment in the group was then overheard: "I'm going to become the most dispensable person I know."

DEVELOPING EXECUTIVE HOUSEKEEPERS

The challenge of opening a housekeeping department does much for developing the executive housekeeper, as well as other employees with potential. Department openings require long hours and few days off since, at first, the abilities of subordinates are limited. Thus, the executive housekeeper's primary concern is to identify those people who welcome responsibility and then to develop them to the greatest possible extent.

Many GRAs and section housekeeping aides will do an outstanding job in their current positions, but will resist additional responsibility. Some excellent performers in current assignments balk at accountability for greater challenge. Others may welcome the recognition that promotion can bring but a week later will begin to show signs that they did not know how different a new set of responsibilities can be; the skills needed to deal with subordinates are different from those needed to make beds. As a result, performance may decline, and signs of greater deterioration may become evident.

Being promoted to supervisor in housekeeping is as close to being on the first rung of the supervisory growth ladder as you can find, and this first step is the largest step that will ever be encountered. The key, therefore, is to identify the employee who demonstrates a desire for greater responsibility. Jasper Dorsey comments on two important factors:[4] the willingness to take risks and the ability to discover a person's capabilities.

Risk taking implies that no manager can develop others without being willing to allow people to make mistakes and learn from them. Effective risk taking allows for the opportunity to fail. Unfortunately, some employees may fail completely, but failing at a task does not mean that a person is a failure. It is what happens after failing at the task that counts.

Dorsey indicates that a person's potential is "discovered by placing him or her in a position requiring a 100 percent effort. Once the person feels comfortable at that level of achievement, add to the load. Growth comes to those who welcome responsibility." Dorsey recalls these methods as "placing someone in water up to his neck and, when he becomes comfortable there, placing him in water over his head. After he becomes a good swimmer, start making waves."

TRAINING AND EVALUATING SUPERVISORS AND MANAGERS

The development of management and supervisory personnel requires planning and systematic, periodic evaluation. Some companies use a system of self-development for fast-track employees. The Marriott Corporation, for example, uses a system known as the **Individual Development (ID) Program**, whereby employees identified for advancement become responsible for their own development at a pace suitable to individual learning. The Marriott system involves the assignment of predetermined tasks (possibly as many as 100) to be performed. Many of these tasks involve hands-on work regularly performed by personnel who might later be supervised. (The trainers in the task are usually the regular performers of the function to be learned.) Some tasks involve administrative work and the study of systems and procedures, and some involve the trainee moving into other departments in which knowledge outside of the primary department may be imperative for proper understanding of the primary training area (for example, how front-desk operations relate to housekeeping).

After tasks are performed, self-critique in training performance is required through analysis of certain key points and questions regarding the tasks. In each

task area, the trainee has an advisor who coaches and counsels him or her. Periodically, the trainee meets with a counselor (usually a senior manager in the hotel) to review training performance and phase progress and to map out future training functions and goals.

Several other major hotel organizations recruit management trainees directly from university campuses and place them in formalized development programs that guide the trainees through all departments of the hotel. Some companies hire trainees into specific departments. In chain operations, successful development normally heralds transfer to another property, because a supervisor elevated from the ranks of a group of employees may have difficulty forming a supervisory relationship with that same group. In most cases transfer makes it easier to end old working relationships and begin new ones.

Often, the executive housekeeper will become involved with formal training programs created by other entities (corporate training offices) within the company. When this happens, the executive housekeeper must contribute time and effort to the development of trainees and guard against using them for personal advantage. Because one of the primary responsibilities of the manager is to develop other employees, no housekeeper should ever be too busy to devote adequate time to this important responsibility.

In small operations in which such development programs are not in evidence, the executive housekeeper would do well to establish such a program in his or her own department, regardless of what might be done in other parts of the organization. The executive housekeeper being considered for promotion has done well if, when asked for the name of a person qualified to replace himself or herself, the executive housekeeper can provide a *list* of such people.

Personal Development

Training an individual to perform the technical functions of a housekeeping department can take weeks of hard work. The **personal development of managers**, however, never ends, and progress is recognized only with the assumption of greater management responsibility. It is for this reason that executive housekeepers should take advantage of every opportunity to improve their technical knowledge of the profession and their management skills.

The executive housekeeper should keep up with new techniques, systems, and procedures being used in the housekeeping profession. Periodicals such as *Executive Housekeeping Today, Lodging, Hospitality Management*, and *Lodging Hospitality* are only some of the

TABLE 16.1 Selected Web Sites of Cleaning Industry Associations

ASHES	*http://www.ashes.org/*
BSCAI	*http://www.bscai.org/*
CIRI	*http://www.ciri-research.org/*
IEHA	*http://www.ieha.org/*
ISSA	*http://www.issa.com/*

publications that offer information regarding technical aspects of housekeeping operations. There is also a wealth of information available regarding the subject of management in general. Many hotels subscribe to management publications such as the *Journal of the American Management Association*. Sharing these publications increases tenfold the amount of information available to each manager. In addition, there are associations that cater to the needs of the professional housekeeper (Table 16.1). Membership in the International Executive Housekeepers Association (IEHA; Figure 16.1), the American Society for Healthcare Environmental Services (ASHES), and the Building Services Contractors Association Internationl (BACAI) can be beneficial not only in personal development through certification programs but also in the sharing of information about products, systems, procedures, personnel availability, and general knowledge about labor markets and personnel recruitment.

Advertisements pertaining to management seminars and forthcoming conventions in the housekeeping and management disciplines should be researched, and the conventions attended when appropriate. Most hotel companies are interested in assisting the development of their managers who show interest in developing themselves and will gladly pay for the managers' attendance at such functions.

THE PERSONAL PLAN

It is not sufficient that the executive housekeeper leave personal development to chance. A written **personal plan** should be prepared by every manager, critiqued by the manager's supervisor, and progressed over a specified period of time.

An example of such a plan, whereby the manager indicates in detail what is intended to be accomplished over a given time period, is presented in Appendix G. Appendix G relates specifically to an executive housekeeper and deals with technical expertise and accomplishments for the areas of administration, managerial skills, and personal development. It offers specific goals to be attained in a given time frame. The personal plan cites how the manager intends to carry out primary responsibilities and serves as an instrument for monitoring personal development. Thoroughly review this document and use it as a model for writing your own personal plan.

Housekeeping Managers of the Future

The recession of 1982 provides some interesting observations regarding on-campus recruitment. Whereas in the past most students received several job offers, in 1982 only a few students were lucky enough to receive even one offer.

Students who were interested in management training positions were told to consider what needs recruiters might have in the housekeeping field. To their surprise, three students were offered and did accept positions as housekeeping manager trainees with major hotel organizations. Not only were these students surprised to find such openings available, but some recruiters were surprised to find students with goals in top management who were willing to enter through the housekeeping door.

Communications from these students verify three important conditions: (1) Housekeeping was a viable career entry-level opportunity that allowed progression to higher management within a hotel organization; (2) the opportunity to supervise large numbers of people and, as a result, to develop supervisory skills was much greater than had been expected or was greater than noted in other departments; and (3) opportunities for men and women were equal.

The idea that the position of executive housekeeper is a dead-end situation is a condition of the past or of the mind. Most certainly, there are executive housekeepers who see their role as one that they favor to keep as a goal, since satisfaction in the position is reward in itself. For the executive housekeeper who wishes to advance, however, the opportunity is there more than ever because they can demonstrate management skills and ability, as well as technical housekeeping skills.

The position of executive housekeeper can be agonizing or inspiring, fraught with pitfalls or opportunities, tiring or refreshing, guarded or benevolent, interesting or boring, meaningful or pointless. Whatever it is to be will depend on the input of the person who is to aspire to, hold, and possibly progress from the executive housekeeping position. To those who wish to be the best possible executive housekeeper, I hope that this text inspires you to improve systems and techniques, that it indicates the excitement that awaits the manager who chooses to progress and become a better manager, and that it presents housekeeping as an avenue to career development to top management.

I.E.H.A. Fact Sheet

FACTS ABOUT I.E.H.A.

What is I.E.H.A.?

The International Executive Housekeepers Association, Inc. is a professional association for persons employed in facility housekeeping at the management level or suppliers to the industry. I.E.H.A. provides services for its members to achieve personal growth as well as a high level of professionalism. Members of I.E.H.A. are committed to a cleaner, safer, healthier environment. As an organization, these goals are promoted through education, leadership and research.

* N.E.H.A. founded by Margaret Barnes in New York City, 1930. (17 hotel members)

* Congresses became biennial in 1940.

* Delegates (members) voted to accept male members in 1954.

* First Newsletter, 1955.

* Education Program established, 1956.

* First Honorary Membership awarded to Mildred Chase, 1962.

* Beginning of Executive Housekeeper Magazine, 1964.

* Association Offices established with paid executive secretary, 1965, Gallipolis, Ohio.

* 320 hour education program established, 1974.

* Magazine becomes Executive Housekeeping Today, 1980.

* 330 hour education program established, 1985.

* Association Offices moved to Westerville, Ohio in 1985.

* Continuing Education Units required to maintain education status (R.E.H., C.E.H.), 1988.

* Self Study Program established in 1989.

* Frontline Program established in 1999.

* Total Membership in 2002 - 4,000.
  15 Districts
  101 Chapters

* Membership segmented by facility type:
  32.0% Healthcare
  15.0% Nursing Homes/Retirement Ctr
  13.0% Hospitality
  14.0% Education
  9.0% Suppliers/Manufacturers/Distributors
  6.0% Contract Cleaners
  11.0% Misc - (Airports,
  Housing Authorities,
  Government Buildings,
  Print Shops, etc.)

* Name changed from (N.E.H.A) National Executive Housekeepers Association to (I.E.H.A.) International Executive Housekeepers Association July 23, 1996.

* Patron and Affiliate Club members became regular members July 23, 1996.

* "Congress" changed to "Convention" July 23, 1996.

* I.E.H.A. Educational Conference and convention (in conjunction with ISSA/INTERCLEAN™ –Clean USA '03) October 14-17, 2003

* Next I.E.H.A. Association Convention: November 16-19, 2004 — New Orleans, LA.

* Current I.E.H.A. President, Paulette Collins, C.E..H., Director of Environmental Services, Tropical Builders, Mililani, HI.

I.E.H.A.'S MISSION STATEMENT: The International Executive Housekeepers Association, Inc., is a professional organization committed to a cleaner, safer, healthier environment. The mission of I.E.H.A. is to provide a professional organization for Executive Housekeepers, Directors of Environmental Services, managers within the housekeeping or custodial activities, and suppliers of custodial goods and services. Through this organization, individuals can attain education, share research, and achieve recognition for success while interacting with colleagues within the career environment.

For additional information on I.E.H.A., please contact the Association Office:

I.E.H.A., Inc.
1001 Eastwind Drive, Suite 301
Westerville, Ohio 43081-3361
1-800-200-6342 or (614) 895-7166
Fax: (614) 895-1248
Webpage: http://**www.ieha.org**
E-mail address: **excel@ieha.org**

FIGURE 16.1 Join the International Executive Housekeepers Association (IEHA) now and start working on the Certified Executive Housekeeper (CEH) designation or the Registered Executive Housekeeper (REH) designation. When you have one of those sets of initials behind your name, it will be one of the proudest days of your life. *(Courtesy of the International Executive Housekeepers Association.)*

EXECUTIVE PROFILE

Executive Profile   *A Woman of Great Beginnings . . .*

by Lisa M. Marinik and Destry Holmes, *Executive Housekeeping Today*

This article is a compilation of two articles about Kay Weirick that appeared in the October 1996 and October 2000 issues of *Executive Housekeeping Today*, the official publication of the International Executive Housekeepers Association, Inc.

Author's note: We began these profiles with a young man who is just starting his career in the housekeeping profession, and we end with a valued friend and contributor to this book who has had a long and rewarding career in housekeeping. Although Kay Weirick has seen fit to retire from business, she continues to be one of the most active and valued contributors to the Las Vegas Chapter of IEHA. She continues to serve as a role model to her colleagues here in Las Vegas, and it is hoped that her career and her indomitable spirit will also serve to inspire all who are about to read her story.

During the '50's Kay Weirick's missionary work with the Medical Mission Sisters took her to Dhaka, Bangladesh, for 10 years. It is there that she helped to establish the housekeeping department at the Holy Family Hospital. While serving the convent she soon realized that she enjoyed using her talents to promote the cleanliness and order of a public facility. Having realized her ability to provide quality service as an executive housekeeper she also recognized the need to affiliate herself with an organization that would foster her professional growth and networks.

Upon leaving the missionary field to pursue new interests, she decided to join the International Executive Housekeepers Association (IEHA) in 1970. From the start of her membership, she was determined to become certified and volunteer her services to the organization. It was not long before her ability to lead and organize programs found her serving as a chapter officer and a district leader.

In addition to earning her C.E.H (Certified Executive Housekeeper) status in '77, and her Registered Executive Housekeeper status in '90, Kay built an impressive résumé. She owned three businesses and set up housekeeping departments in several new hotels, including the Fairmont Hotel in Dallas, TX; the Four Seasons Hotel in Irving, TX; and the Kapinski Hotel in Dallas, TX. She also participated in opening the Four Seasons Hotel in Houston, TX; the Fairmont Hotel in Philadelphia, PA; the Paris Hotel in Las Vegas, NV; and she was with Bally's of Las Vegas from February 1988 to September 2000. It is fair to say Weirick is a woman of great beginnings.

Even upon her retirement, she found herself assisting Bally's with a huge remodeling project! During the last few years, Kay has been keeping herself very busy with her family, travel and her community activities. She continues to serve I.E.H.A. and is intent on helping the next generation of her chapter's leaders.

Kay has always believed that housekeeping was similar in the healthcare or hospitality fields because the common denominator is delivering quality service and a smile to the patients or guests who are ultimately served.

She also believed in empowering employees, she is an avid fan of Stephen Covey and his book, *First Things First*. "All employees need an *internal* motivator to do a good job. As managers, we need to provide the tools, resources, and ongoing encouragement to help them maximize their potential." Weirick stressed the importance of attending seminars and researching the latest in housekeeping products and equipment. Staying current with the latest trends in federal and state regulations was also a hallmark of Weirick's management style.

Ultimately, it comes down to people. Whether she was mentoring an employee or meeting with a fellow I.E.H.A. member during a convention, Weirick would tell anyone that the opportunity to work with others is what made her career and affiliation with I.E.H.A. great.

DISCUSSION QUESTIONS

1. Kay Weirick clearly believes that the key to success is to stay current in the profession. Before her retirement, she attended seminars, researched the latest trends in federal and state regulations, and was extremely active in the International Executive Housekeepers Association. Others executive housekeepers today complain that they simply have no time for these activities because of increased demands in the workplace.

Some complain that their companies do not support their membership in professional associations, so why should they join? Declining membership in many of these professional associations has been the result in the past decade. What argument could you make for the need to stay current in one's profession? Include any examples you might think of where the executive housekeeper has been confronted with new and difficult challenges during the past decade.

2. Weirick believes that employees must be self-motivated and it is management's job to provide them with the tools, resources, and encouragement to help them maximize their potential. Do you think Weirick's right? Is it true that management can only provide a climate for motivation and really cannot motivate employees?

[Covey, Stephen R., Merrill, A. Roger, Merrill Rebecca R., *First Things First: To Live, to Love, to Learn, to Leave a Legacy*. New York: Simon and Schuster, 1994.]

CONCLUSION

A large part of the executive housekeeper's responsibilities involve the creation of tasks that may be performed by other members of the housekeeping department. This text has strongly emphasized the delegation of such tasks to people within the department whenever possible. What is then left for the executive housekeeper's personal accomplishment revolves around those continuous functions of management enumerated in Chapter 1: analyzing problems, making decisions, and communicating. A major emphasis for personal involvement must therefore rest within the area of problem solving.

Problem solving does not mean taking on subordinates' responsibilities, but is the guidance of thought so as to help them arrive at solutions to problems for which they are responsible. In addition, there are specific problem areas that are the direct responsibility of the executive housekeeper and therefore give meaning to the term *full circle of management*.

Employee absenteeism, poor employee orientation, lack of employee appreciation of self-worth, inadequate employee observation during probationary periods, poor supervision, and the insensitivity of management to employee needs are the causes of most problems that regularly face the executive housekeeper. These problems must be dealt with professionally when they occur and must not be allowed to grow through neglect.

Problem solving requires the development of a unique temperament that recognizes problems as opportunities for solutions rather than as bothersome chores. It is this fact that should cause the astute manager to investigate his or her own management style and leadership qualities. The executive housekeeper may be designated as a manager by higher management, but it will be those who work for the executive housekeeper who will determine whether or not such a person is a good leader.

The full circle of management does not end with the manager's ability to solve problems; it continues into the realm of developing others for higher responsibilities and for self-development. The development of potential in others ensures the executive housekeeper's availability when higher positions of responsibility become available. An aggressive program of self-development not only signals the desire for advancement but also helps qualify the manager for greater responsibility.

Executive housekeepers of the future will be seeing their positions not only from a more professional standpoint but also as meaningful entry-level positions into the field of hospitality and hospital operations that lead to top administrative positions.

KEY TERMS AND CONCEPTS

Empowerment
Problem solving

Employee absenteeism
Employee turnover

Employee problems
Employee's appearance

Employee hygiene
Employee claims of unfairness
Poor performance
Temperament for problem
   solving

Managerial styles
Manager as a leader
Development of subordinates
Individual Development
   (ID) Program

Personal development of managers
Personal plan

DISCUSSION AND REVIEW QUESTIONS

1. The full circle of management requires that the executive housekeeper be a problem solver. How can this be done without assuming the responsibilities of subordinates to solve their own problems?

2. The success or failure of a manager as an effective problem solver may rest with the manager's style. Identify several management styles and assess their worth in dealing with various types of problems and different types of people.

3. Explain the difference between a manager and a leader.

4. Assume that as executive housekeeper you observe one of your junior managers about to make a mistake. Recognizing that most people learn greatly from their mistakes, under what conditions, if any, would you step in and prevent the subordinate from making the mistake? If the mistake were to cost money, how would you justify the mistake to your own manager after you allowed it to be made?

5. Recognizing that personal plans are written as guides to achievement, why should they be negotiated with your supervisor? As your performance year unfolds and you see that you will not be achieving your specific objectives as set forth in your personal plan, what would your actions be?

6. Some managers aspire to the position of executive housekeeper as an end; others see the position as a stepping stone to higher administrative responsibility. Which condition is more likely to cause a leadership style that is conducive to subordinate growth? Why?

NOTES

1. William T. Scherer, "Is Caring about People a Lot of Hogwash?" *Chemical Engineering*, February 14, 1977, pp. 93–94.

2. Robert J. Martin, "Recognition of Employee Worth vs. Turnover," *Executive Housekeeping Today*, March 1983, pp. 18–20.

3. John Simmons and William Mares, "Return of the Pied Piper," *Savvy*, October 1982, pp. 40–44. Adapted from *Working Together* by John Simmons and William J. Mares (New York: Alfred A. Knopf, 1983).

4. Jasper Dorsey, "Are You a Good Manager?" *Saturday Evening Post*, January–February 1981, pp. 46–47.

Job Descriptions

This appendix contains several examples of job descriptions. They may be written for unskilled, semiskilled, and skilled employees. They may also be written for supervisors, managers, and executives. The techniques of presentation may vary considerably. Simply stated, however, they are designed to set forth a group of tasks combined into one job, indicate a person's responsibility to do the tasks, provide the necessary authority to that person to do the work, and indicate to whom the worker filling the job will be accountable to for the proper performance of the work.

Position Descriptions for the Housekeeping Department

The following is typical of position descriptions for a housekeeping department.

Executive Housekeeper

Basic Function

Assumes complete direction, operational control, and supervision of the housekeeping and laundry departments and pool areas.

Scope

Operates the departments under his or her control in the most efficient manner possible through effective application and enforcement of company policies, the use of methods described in standard operating procedures, and the use of sound management principles. The incumbent is primarily responsible for the cleanliness of guestrooms and public areas assigned to the housekeeping department. Accomplishes assigned tasks through proper training, motivation, and supervision of all personnel assigned to the housekeeping and laundry departments.

Specific Responsibilities

1. Coordinates with the personnel department regarding prescreening of employees, indicating staffing needs and qualifications desired of personnel necessary to staff the housekeeping and laundry departments. Coordinates with resident manager on hiring of immediate subordinates.
2. Develops plans, actions, and standard operating procedures for the operation and administration of assigned departments. Establishes and maintains housekeeping and laundry scheduling procedures, taking into consideration percent occupancy, time and use of facilities, and related public specialty areas and events.
3. Organizes, the housekeeping department using the **housekeeping team concept**, with each housekeeper cleaning room sections.

---

4. Develops an inspection program for all public areas and guestrooms to ensure that proper maintenance and standards are achieved and sustained.

5. Coordinates the operation of the housekeeping and laundry departments in the hotel to guarantee minimum disruption in the overall operation of the hotel.

6. With assistance from the resident manager, develops budgets for housekeeping, laundry, and recreation departments to ensure that each operates within established costs while providing maximum service.

7. Establishes a training program within assigned departments that will enable positions of increased responsibility to be filled from within the department.

8. Is constantly alert for newer methods, techniques, equipment, and materials that will improve the overall operation of the departments and will provide a more efficient operation at reduced costs.

9. Stimulates within all employees a friendly and cheerful attitude, giving proper emphasis to courtesy in contacts with guests and other employees.

10. Administers time card control over all assigned hourly employees.

11. Maintains strict inventory and purchase control over all controllable items.

12. Develops job descriptions for all members of assigned staff.

13. Serves as expediter on special projects assigned by the resident manager or the general manager.

14. Communicates freely and effectively with assigned personnel, continuously passing on to assistants and subordinates any information necessary to make them feel included in the overall operation of the hotel. Reiterates, if necessary, the objectives toward which hotel employees are striving.

15. Conducts employee performance appraisals on time, showing objectivity and sincerity. Employees should be personally counseled toward improvement.

16. Coordinates with the resident manager concerning the termination of any employee.

17. Maintains control of linen rooms, storerooms, new linen, and cleaning supplies, ensuring adequate security and supply.

18. Is responsible for the proper scheduling of the department, keeping in mind the forecast of daily occupancy.

19. Develops a personal plan to carry out responsibilities.

Relationships to Responsibility

1. Reports directly to the resident manager.

2. Has access to the general manager.

3. Coordinates functions of housekeeping, laundry, and recreation departments with all other departments.

4. Supervises and coordinates the activities of assigned assistants.

Work Emphasis

Time allocation for performance of position responsibilities:
   50 percent administrative
   30 percent operations, inspections, and training
   20 percent coordination and follow-up

JOB DESCRIPTIONS FOR A HOTEL HOURLY WORKER

Here is an example of a job description for a hotel housekeeping department hourly worker.

Once an organization has been designed, it becomes necessary to set forth exactly what is expected of each member of the organization. Job descriptions ensure that every operation that needs to be performed is covered by assignment and that the operations are not assigned to more than one specific classification of individual.

Job descriptions will normally specify the **job title**, **working hours**, and position or job title of the incumbent's **immediate supervisor**, whether such supervisors are hourly supervisors or members of management. **Responsibilities** and specific **duties** are then spelled out in detail. Whether or not the incumbent is to wear a uniform and punch a time clock, and the pay scale standard for a particular job may also be shown.

Job descriptions are excellent tools for training, and a copy can be given to an incumbent as training begins. They are also excellent documents to use for periodic reviews at departmental meetings. They should not necessarily be used to evaluate performance, as they are by nature rather inflexible and are inclined to foster the concept of limiting development. Performance appraisals, discussed in Chapter 11, should be based on *meeting established* **standards**.

Job Descriptions for a Hotel Housekeeping Department

Several job descriptions for a hotel housekeeping department follow.

Senior Housekeeper (Supervisor)

Title

Senior Housekeeper

Immediate Supervisor

Housekeeping manager

Hours

8:00 A.M.–4:30 P.M.
   Weekdays and Saturdays
9:00 A.M.–5:30 P.M.
   Sundays and holidays

Responsibilities

To follow the instructions of the executive housekeeper and/or housekeeping manager in order to maintain company standards of cleanliness throughout the rooms section of the hotel. To supervise the GRAs and section housekeeping aides assigned to the housekeeping team. To relay information concerning the status of rooms to and from the housekeeping office.

Duties

1. Report to housekeeping at 8:00 A.M. in uniform and clock in.
2. Secure keys and worksheet for assigned area.
3. Note all **ready rooms** and **checkouts** on the worksheet.
4. Proceed to assigned area and check all ready rooms to make sure they are up to standard for early morning check-ins. Should a **tidy** be necessary, tidy the room. If a room needs extensive cleaning, it should be reported to the housekeeping manager and noted on the discrepancy report.
5. Report all checkouts and other information such as **early makeups** and **ASAP** (as soon as possible) **rooms** to GRAs.
6. Make a round of entire assigned area, checking for items in need of immediate attention such as burned-out lights, spots on hall carpets or walls, trash in stairwells, and spills in ice machine areas.
7. Check all GRAs' supplies and equipment to be sure they are in working condition. (All section housekeeping supervisors should know the prescribed use of all authorized cleaning equipment and chemicals.)
8. Spot-check (inspect) rooms completed by the GRA in the section. Make sure that standards have been properly met in rooms being cleaned and that a room is ready to be sold for occupancy to a guest before releasing the room to the housekeeping office.
9. Keep a record of all rooms **deep-cleaned** in each section so that rooms are periodically deep-cleaned on a rotating basis.
10. Report any damage to guestrooms, corridors, or equipment seen or reported by a GRA. Such information should be reported to the housekeeping manager or executive housekeeper.
11. Report to the engineering department, using a **Maintenance Work Request Form**, any defect or equipment failure that cannot be corrected by the housekeeping department.
12. Throughout the day, periodically telephone the housekeeping office to advise it of all **ready** rooms and to receive **checkout** rooms.
13. Inspect linen rooms and storerooms in assigned areas for cleanliness and for adequate supplies used by the GRAs. Be sure linen rooms are secured and locked when not in use.
14. At 3:00 P.M. the **evening room checks** will be collected from the GRAs. Room checks on any open section (pickups) will be taken by the section supervisor. The room check reports will be delivered to the housekeeping office promptly in order to make up the housekeeping report for the front desk. Any room not serviced that day, refused service, or requesting late service by the night staff will be reported to the night supervisor.
15. Report persistent complaints or remarks by the employees about working conditions, wages, or any other matter to the housekeeping manager.
16. Periodically report to the housekeeping manager on the quality of the performance of each person she or he (the senior housekeeper) supervises, offering remarks about which employees are performing above average, average, or below average.
17. Complete any special assignments as directed by the executive housekeeper promptly.
18. At 4:30 P.M. turn in the keys and clock out.

Section Housekeeper Guestroom Attendant (GRA)

Title

Section Housekeeper (or GRA)

Immediate Supervisor

Senior housekeeper (supervisor) of assigned section

Hours

8:00 A.M.–4:30 P.M.
    Weekdays
    9:00 A.M.–5:30 P.M.
    Sundays and holidays

Responsibilities

1. Report to the housekeeping department at 8:00 A.M. in uniform and clock in.
2. Pick up keys and **GRA's Daily Report** for cleaning assignment. Note any special instructions.
3. Remove assigned cart from satellite linen room and begin cleaning assignment. Special guest requests, checkouts, and early makeups should be cleaned first.

Entering a Guestroom

4. *Procedure for entering a guestroom.* If there is no "Do Not Disturb" sign, and if the **hard lock** is not on, knock softly with your knuckles and softly announce "Housekeeper." Wait a few moments and enter the room. Leave the door wide open. Pull cart across the doorway, with the clean linen facing the room.
5. Open the drapes for maximum light and turn out unnecessary lights.
6. Look at the condition of the room. If linens, wastebaskets, TV, and so on are missing, or furniture is damaged or broken, report it to the main linen room and senior housekeeper immediately.
7. In occupied rooms, pick up newspapers and periodicals, fold them neatly, and place them on the desk. *Never* throw away newspapers unless they are in the wastebasket.

Bedroom

8. Strip the bed linen, shaking it carefully off the bed. Pillowcases are favorite hiding places for valuables. All lost articles should be turned in to the main linen room to be labeled, logged, and locked up. Notify senior housekeeper if foam pillows, bed boards, and so on are found in the room.
9. Mattresses and box springs should be straight on top of each other and against the headboard. Bed pad should be clean and in place. Check between mattress and box spring for magazines and other articles.
10. Make the beds using the **once-around method**. Do not use torn or dirty linen. Replace soiled or burned blankets and spreads. The bed is the focal point of the room. It should not have wrinkles or lumps. Pillows should be smooth. Blanket and top sheet should be six inches from top of bed.
11. Roll-away beds are to be made up with clean linen. If the room is a checkout, make up roll-away bed and close it. A section housekeeping aide will take it from the guestroom to the proper satellite linen room for storage.
12. Dust bed area. Wipe vinyl headboard, and dust all pictures, baseboards, corners, and ledges where cobwebs gather. Dust the nightstand and telephone book. Clean the ashtray; replace memo pad, matches, and any literature as instructed. Place your own name card on nightstand.
13. Clean the telephone and plastic phone card with a clean cloth and the **one-stroke solution**.
14. Dust chairs and table near window. Remember the legs, backs, and under the cushions. Dust floor lamp, placing lampshade seam to the wall.
15. Dust the TV—screen, stand, back, and underneath the set. No liquid should be sprayed on the screen as it may damage the inside of the set.
16. Dust the desk area, including lamp, chair, and all furniture surfaces. Remove desk chair and clean sides of furniture. Dust lampshade, and be sure seam is to the wall. Clean tray and ashtray. Arrange pitcher, glasses, and matches properly. Literature on desktop and in drawer should be arranged correctly and replaced as needed.
17. In checkout rooms, drawers should be inspected for cleanliness and lost items. In occupied rooms, *do not* go into drawers.
18. Dust the coat rack. In checkout rooms, remove wire and wooden hangers not belonging to the company. Replace missing hangers. There should be eight in each room. Place two laundry bags with slips on coat rack shelf. The company logo should face the front. Dust overhead light.

19. Check that all light bulbs are working.
20. Vacuum carpet as necessary. Push the vacuum slowly and steadily over the whole area. Watch for pins, bits of string, coins, and the like, and pick them up by hand because they can damage the vacuum cleaner. Occasionally the carpet edges will need to be swept with a broom or wiped with a damp cloth.
21. Adjust the drapes and sheer panels as instructed. Be sure all hooks are in place, pulleys are working, and wands are attached. Report anything not working to senior housekeeper, who will make out a Maintenance Work Request form.
22. Adjust heater and air conditioner controls as instructed.

Bathroom

23. Turn on heat lamp and vanity lamp for maximum light. Wipe off light switch plate and soiled area on wall around switch. Report needed light bulbs to senior housekeeper.
24. Flush toilet. When water level has returned to normal, place one-stroke solution from stock solution bottle in the toilet bowl. Let it work while cleaning the rest of the bathroom.
25. Use the one-stroke solution to clean the mirror.
26. Dust the vanity light. Check that the bulbs work.
27. Wipe bathroom door and door knob.
28. Clean and polish chrome plumbing fixture under the sink.
29. Pull sink stopper and clean it thoroughly. Use the **three-stroke solution** to scrub the sink. Dry it and polish the chrome faucet. Replace the stopper.
30. Empty and wipe out the wastebasket. Be careful of glass and razor blades. Check supplies. Replace toilet paper if roll is less than half full or if it is dirty. Paper should roll outside from the top. Facial tissue may need to be replaced. Fold ends of both toilet paper and facial tissue into a "V." Each bathroom should have one ashtray with matches and two bars of soap. Place clean towels in their proper places.
31. Wash and dry the vanity top using the three-stroke solution.
32. Using the three-stroke solution, scrub tub walls, soap dish, and tub. Clean tub stopper. Wipe tub dry. Polish chrome fixtures, including shower head. Place bath mat so the name of the hotel can be read.
33. Spray three-stroke solution on shower curtains and wipe both sides dry. Position curtain neatly against the wall near the toilet.
34. Clean toilet lid, seat, and base with three-stroke solution. Clean inside of bowl using the solution that is already in it. Toilet should be dried thoroughly and a sanitary strip put in place across the seat.
35. Sweep hair from bathroom floor. Mop the floor starting at the far corner. Mop behind the toilet and the door.
36. Check the bathroom before turning out the lights.
37. Wipe off bedroom door and door frame.
38. Hook the chain lock and turn out the light.
39. Check the guestroom and close the door.

3:00 P.M. Check

40. At 3:00 P.M., the housekeeper begins her P.M. check on the GRA's daily report, which is designated "P.M." Every room on the report must be entered and the status checked. The status will be **C/O** (the room needs cleaning or tidying), **OCC** (occupied), or **R** (ready to rent). The P.M. reports are collected and used by the night housekeeping supervisor or the P.M. housekeeper to complete the Daily Housekeeping Report for the front desk. On weekends and holidays, the P.M. check is made at 4:00 P.M.
41. At 4:00 P.M. weekdays, or 5:00 P.M. Sundays and holidays, the housekeeper should take the cart to the floor linen room to clean and stock the cart for the next day's work. Sufficient time has been allotted so that a good job can be done, thus making any time spent the following morning stocking the cart unnecessary.
42. Notify section supervisor if there is anything wrong with a housekeeper's cart or vacuum.
43. At 4:25 P.M. weekdays, 5:25 P.M. Sundays and holidays, return to the main linen room, turn in keys, and clock out.
44. On occasion, a GRA may be required to function as a laundry attendant. When this happens, the job description for laundry attendant will apply.

Section Housekeeping Aide

Title

Section Housekeeping Aide

Immediate Supervisor

Senior housekeeper (supervisor) of assigned section

Hours

8:00 A.M.–4:30 P.M.
   Weekdays
   9:00 A.M.–5:30 P.M.
   Sundays and holidays—less 30 minutes for lunch

Responsibilities

To work as a member of a team in conjunction with the senior housekeeper and GRAs, maintaining a high standard of cleanliness in the guest sleeping room area of the hotel and in the public areas of that section of the hotel assigned to the team.

Duties

1. Report to the housekeeping department in uniform at the time the shift begins and clock in.
2. Receive keys necessary to perform functions for that day.
3. Check with the senior housekeeper for any special instructions.
4. Proceed to assigned area, satellite linen rooms, and determine if any supplies are needed in the room for that day (general-purpose soap, clean glasses, etc.).
5. Tour and inspect the entire area assigned, looking for items requiring immediate attention.
6. Proceed with usual cleaning program in rooms department public areas.
   a. Elevators—daily
   b. Corridors—twice weekly
   c. Ice and vending areas—twice weekly
   d. Stairwells—once weekly
   e. Any specific task assigned by the senior housekeeper
7. At least four times a day (more often if necessary), remove all trash from GRAs' linen carts. Remove trash to dumpster area and discard.
8. At least three times a day (more often if necessary), remove all soiled linen from team GRAs' linen carts. Deliver and deposit into laundry.
9. At approximately 3:00 P.M. each day, restock satellite linen rooms with bed linens needed by GRAs to load carts for the next day's work. (This linen should be picked up in the laundry and moved to the satellite linen rooms.)
10. There will be at least two rooms in each section of the hotel that will be **general cleaned** each day. Your supervisor will tell you which rooms are to be general cleaned. The section housekeeping aide helps the deep cleaner or person assigned the responsibility for general cleaning move and replace any furniture necessary during cleaning.
11. As a member of your team, recognize and assist any team GRA when it is obvious that a particular room presents an unusual problem in trash removal. Assist as necessary.
12. Take care of equipment; ensure that all mops are clean, vacuum cleaners are properly cleaned out, and all equipment is properly put away and locked up at the end of each day. It is especially important to ensure that there is no trash stored in any satellite linen room overnight. *This is an extreme fire hazard.*
13. When requested or required by housekeeping, take items such as roll-away beds and cribs that have been requested by the guest to the guest-room.
14. Return all special-use items such as roll-aways and cribs to the satellite linen rooms after they have been properly made up by the GRAs.
15. Make special setups in guestrooms (e.g., tables and chairs) when requested.
16. Remove same and return to storage upon completion of use.
17. Perform other functions assigned by your senior housekeeper.

Hotel Employee Handbook

Every organization that employs service personnel should have an employee orientation manual or *handbook* so that common questions asked by employees may be answered as soon as possible. The various rules, regulations, and procedures that are specified should apply to all members of a hotel staff.

This appendix presents a generic **employee handbook** typical of those used in many hotels. On the last page of the handbook, the employee is provided with the name of his or her supervisor and/or manager, the name of the job, the starting rate of pay, when he or she is to receive a first check, and working hours. The employee signs a receipt for this information, which is kept in the personnel file of the new employee.

The reader is cautioned not to adopt this handbook in whole, or in part, without consulting current federal and state labor laws. It is also recommended that all company policies regarding the treatment of employees be reviewed by a practicing labor attorney before being implemented.

Welcome Aboard!

Congratulations, and welcome to one of the fastest-growing companies and the most exciting of all industries—the hospitality industry.

We appreciate your desire to join us, and we wish you every success with your new career—a career loaded with opportunity to say to your fellow man or woman, "Welcome! May I be of service? I'm glad you're here and I am concerned about you while you are our guest." If you have that feeling toward people in general, then you will have it toward our guests, and you will soon learn that what you are about to do in your new job can bring happiness and self-satisfaction—regardless of whether your job has you performing directly in front of the public or in support of those who do.

The hospitality industry probably has a greater variety of jobs than any other industry you can think of, but I can assure you that no one job is any more important than another. What you will be doing is just as important as what I do every day. (We just do different things, that's all!) And that applies to every job and every person equally. Few, if any, of us started anywhere except "at the bottom"—so you will find your supervisors and managers understanding of your need to be properly trained, and ready to help you if and when you need their help. We were all beginners ourselves at one time; we know you will have many questions about your job, company policies, the do's and don'ts, promotional opportunities, and your own opportunities to grow. Don't be afraid to ask questions, because to you the answers to those questions will be important. And don't be afraid of making a mistake. It is from our mistakes that we learn our best lessons.

A well-informed employee who knows what is expected of him or her and who knows the rules and recognizes his or her contribution to the overall effort is usually an employee who is content with his or her job and looks forward to coming to work every day.

It is our hope that this booklet will help you learn more about us, helping you to keep informed and to know what you can expect from us.

AGAIN, WELCOME ABOARD!
General Manager

Employment Policies

It is our policy to implement affirmatively equal opportunity for all qualified employees and applicants for employment without regard to race, creed, color, sex, national origin, or religion.

The hiring objective of the company is to obtain individuals qualified and/or trainable for any position by virtue of job-related standards of education, training, experience, and personal qualifications, who can carry on our work competently, who have capacity for growth, and who will become a living part of our organization. We will use every reasonable means available to select the best employee for the position to be filled.

New Employees

Every newly hired employee must complete a set of employment papers in the Human Resources Department prior to beginning work. Your address, telephone number, and information about family status must be on record. Any changes in this information must be reported immediately, as it is very important for us to have it in the event of an emergency and in connection with Social Security and withholding taxes.

Please notify the Human Resources Department in the event of any change in the following:

- Address or telephone number
- Marriage, divorce, or legal separation
- Birth or death in immediate family
- Legal change of name

Your personnel records are maintained in a secured place and locked when not in use. Only certain authorized personnel have access to these records. They are confidential and as such will not be used outside the company for any purpose, including Christmas card mailing lists or city directories or for any other purposes.

After completing your employment papers, a copy of our Employee's Handbook will be given to you. This handbook is for your benefit, to inform you of what is expected of you and to help you perform satisfactorily on the job. It is to your advantage to read it carefully and keep it as a reference.

Employment Status

The following list of employment statuses, with definitions, represents the four categories of employees in our company.

1. *Full-Time Employee:* An employee who may be expected to be and is normally scheduled to work a minimum of thirty (30) hours per week. Such persons will be classified as full-time. An employee classified as full-time may on occasion be scheduled to work less than thirty (30) hours a week. This does not change the employee's status from full-time unless the average hours worked per week, over a six- (6-) week period of time, fall below 30 hours. If this occurs for a period of six weeks, the employee's status may be changed from full-time to part-time.

2. *Part-Time Employee:* An employee who is expected to be and is regularly scheduled to work twenty-nine (29) hours a week or less. Such an employee would be classified as part-time. Part-time employees may on occasion be scheduled more than twenty-nine (29) hours. If scheduling of more than twenty-nine (29) hours a week occurs more than three weeks in a row, employees will be given the opportunity to have their status changed to full-time.

3. *Temporary Employee:* An employee who is hired to work for a specified period of time. In the case of a temporary employee, the termination of employment may be predetermined at the time of employment. The number of hours worked per week is insignificant to the definition of temporary employee.

4. *Pool Employee:* An employee who is on call on an as-needed basis. The number of hours worked is irrelevant to the definition of pool employee.

Probationary Period

Every new employee and current employee transferred or promoted into a new position will be placed on a ninety- (90-) day probationary period. During this time, both the employee and the company will pass through a "breaking-in period." You will want to know how the company operates and what our methods are, and we will want to know if you can report to work regularly, follow instructions, and get along with guests, managers, and fellow employees. Therefore, your performance and suitability for the job will be carefully evaluated during these first 90 days.

Guarantee of Fair Treatment

As an employee of this company, you as an individual have the right to appeal any decision or voice any complaint you may have concerning your treatment or working conditions to your immediate supervisor. Should you fail to receive what you consider to be a fair response, you have the right to appeal through channels to the president of the company.

Bulletin Boards

We have mounted several bulletin boards throughout the hotel. These boards are intended to keep you informed on important announcements concerning company policy, procedures, organization, and changes. By making it a habit to regularly check these boards, you will be kept well informed and up to date.

Employee Referrals

If you desire to recommend a qualified friend or relative for employment, we will be glad to interview that person.

We will consider any of your relatives for employment; however, they will not be employed in the same department where you work because of conflict-of-interest situations such as transportation, scheduling, etc.

Job Security

One of our objectives is to provide job security and steady work to our employees insofar as careful planning and sound management can afford. You have the assurance that we will do everything possible to provide continued employment for you as long as you perform your job satisfactorily and follow our policies and rules.

Job Abolishment

From time to time as we grow, changes will occur. New jobs may be created, and some jobs may be abolished. Any employee who is filling a job that is to be abolished will be given two weeks' notice of job termination or two weeks' pay in lieu thereof. In addition, every attempt will be made to relocate the employee in a new job, provided the employee is qualified.

Wage and Payroll Information

Pay Rates

It is company policy to pay the highest wages possible consistent with good business practices and in comparison with companies in the same business.

Pay rates for each position are determined by degree of difficulty and responsibility. Pay rates are reviewed annually to ensure our competitiveness within the industry and local area.

Pay Scales

Employees will be shown the pay scale for the job they are performing. The pay scale will show the *start rate*, *job rate* (3-month rate), *one-year rate*, *raise increment*, and *maximum rate*.

Time Clocks and Time Cards

Every employee is provided with a weekly time card. You are required to punch in when you report to work and punch out when you leave. Since time cards are the basis for computing your pay, it is your responsibility to make sure that the time reported on your cards is accurate. You must punch your own time card and only your card. You are paid for your *scheduled time*, so make sure you obtain your supervisor's signature on your time card when you begin work early or work late.

Work Schedules

Your work schedule will be prepared and posted in advance of each workweek. Since our hotel is a seven-day operation, we cannot always account for last-minute changes or unforeseeable circumstances. Therefore, a regular shift or regular day off cannot always be granted, as last-minute changes in schedules will sometimes occur.

Paydays

Your paycheck will be issued every other Friday and distributed after 3:00 P.M. twenty-six (26) times a year. Our legal workweek begins each Saturday and ends the following Friday. In order to process time cards, complete payrolls, and issue checks, the pay period closes seven days prior to your Friday payday.

Employees are not permitted to borrow on their earnings in advance of payday. Certain emergency situations may be exceptions with prior approval of the General Manager.

Payroll Deductions

Certain deductions that we are required by law to deduct will be made from your pay. The major portion of deductions is generally for taxes such as federal income tax, state income tax, and Social Security taxes. If you are a tipped employee and receive tips amounting to more than $20.00 per month, you must report the amount you receive to the HR Department each week. A tip report has been stamped on the back of your time card for your convenience. Your check cannot be issued until you have completed this information so that the appropriate tax deductions can be made.

Other deductions are allowed if you request; however, we reserve the right of deciding what other deductions will be allowed. All deductions made on your pay will be itemized on your paycheck stub.

At the end of the year you will be furnished a statement of your earnings and the amount of taxes withheld so that you can furnish this information to the government when you file your own tax report.

Employee Conduct

Every well-run company must have rules and regulations governing the conduct of its employees in order to achieve the company's objectives. You should read this section carefully so that you have an understanding of the rules by which you and every other employee must abide.

The following is a list of important work rules. Your supervisor may have certain departmental rules to add to these.

Attendance	Prompt attendance on the job is an important part of your performance record. Failure to be on the job not only disturbs the smooth operations of your department, but also affects the jobs of your co-workers.
Alcohol and Drugs	Employees will not report to work under the influence of alcohol or drugs.
Absence	Absence without good and sufficient cause cannot be tolerated. When you are sick and unable to work, notify your supervisor immediately.

If illness is given as a cause of absence, we have the right to require a written statement from your doctor. When you return to work after serious illness, injury, surgical operation, maternity leave, or other physical condition(s), you must submit a doctor's release to work prior to your return in order to safeguard your health.

An employee who is absent for three consecutive workdays without notifying his or her supervisor will be considered to have voluntarily resigned and will be automatically terminated.

Breaks — Employees are entitled to a 15-minute break for every four hours worked.

Deadly weapons — Employees cannot carry a firearm or any other deadly weapon on company premises or in company vehicles at any time for any reason.

Following instructions — All employees are expected to follow the instructions of their supervisors. Refusal or failure to do so is considered insubordination. You are also expected to perform your work or job assignments in a satisfactorily and effective manner.

Fraternization — Employees will not fraternize with any hotel guest on or off duty. In simple terms, you should not use your job as an opportunity to build personal relationships with guests.

Hotel facilities — The lounge and pool areas and guest areas are for the guests of our hotel only. Employees will not be allowed to use these facilities, but may obtain special permission to eat in the dining room for a special occasion with prior approval of the General Manager.

Leaving work during working hours — Employees are not allowed to leave the company premises during working hours.

If an emergency situation necessitates your leaving, obtain the permission of your supervisor prior to your leaving. Meal periods are not considered working hours.

Lost-and-found — All articles found should be turned in to your supervisor for your own protection. When articles are properly identified, they will be returned to their owners.

Name tags — All employees will be issued a name tag, which is to be worn during each working shift.

Meals — All employees are entitled to one meal period (one-half hour) for each shift of work, with a minimum of a four-hour shift. All employees working a shift of nine or more hours are entitled to two meal periods. Employees' meal periods will be taken in the employees' cafeteria.

Nonsolicitation rule — For your protection and to avoid disruption of work, outside solicitors will not be permitted to solicit employees on the company's premises. The solicitation of employees by other employees will not be permitted during working hours. The distribution or circulation of leaflets, pamphlets, literature, or other materials among employees during working time or in working areas of the company is not permitted.

Off-duty employees — Upon completion of the work shift, employees are to clock out, depart the property, and not return in an off-duty

	status without prior approval from their supervisor.
Packages	We reserve the right to check all packages being taken off the property, personal or otherwise. No company property will be removed from the hotel without written authorization of your supervisor.
Parking	All employees are to park in the northern gravel lot adjacent to the hotel.
Personal behavior	Employees are expected to (1) get along with managers, supervisors, and fellow employees and guests; (2) not discuss personal or unauthorized company matters in public areas where a guest could overhear these conversations and either be offended or made to feel ill at ease; and (3) not engage in actions on or off the property that could bring discredit to the company or its employees.
Restrooms	Employees are to use the restroom facilities upstairs next to our employee cafeteria.
Standards of appearance	Every employee is expected to maintain a high standard of personal cleanliness and appearance.
Standards of cleanliness	We provide comfortable and clean working conditions in an effort to provide safe areas and promote productivity. We take pride in the general neat appearance of our facilities and equipment. In order to maintain good housekeeping, you must keep your work area neat, clean, and free of articles not being used. This includes keeping equipment in the proper place, disposing of waste in proper containers, and storing materials and equipment and supplies in an orderly manner and in their designated place.
Smoking	Uniformed employees will not smoke in public areas. No employee will be allowed to smoke in the kitchen because of health regulations.
Telephone usage	Employees will be called to the telephone only in emergency situations. Employees are to use the pay telephone located in the housekeeping department when they need to make an outgoing call.
Uniforms	Uniforms will be furnished by the company where required and must be worn for each scheduled shift.
Working areas	Employees are expected to refrain from being in areas in which their job does not require them to be.

Discipline

In order to deliver a consistently fair application of company rules and equitable treatment to all employees, a system of violation notices, called *written warnings*, will be administered to offer constructive criticism and provide an opportunity for you to improve or correct a problem, or to help you perform your job better.

A written warning will be issued for any violation of a company rule or regulation or for substandard work. Should you receive a written warning, it will be issued in writing and signed by you and your manager. Your signature on the warning indicates only that you have been informed of the violation or problem and that you understand what your supervisor is telling you in the warning. It does not necessarily mean that you agree with what is being said.

During an employee's probationary period, an employee may be terminated for any justifiable reason including a reduction in force or unsatisfactory progress in his or her position.

After the probationary period, an employee may be discharged if he or she has been given three (3) written warnings for the same or different offenses in the last twelve (12) months (except for those reasons listed under "Termination for Just Cause").

Terminations

Our employment procedures are aimed at hiring people who will become reliable and satisfied employees. Nevertheless, employees may resign or be dismissed for various reasons. Some of these terminations will be within our control; others will be beyond it.

Voluntary Terminations

Any employee who decides to terminate his or her employment is expected to give a proper notice of at least one week and preferably two weeks. Supervisory personnel should give a notice of one month or more.

When an employee resigns, continuous service is ended. If, at some point in the future, a previous employee is hired, he or she starts as a new employee. Employees who terminate without proper notice will not be considered for reemployment.

Company Terminations

If it becomes necessary to dismiss an employee (barring reduction in force), this will be a result of the employee's own actions. An employee who has completed his or her probationary period shall not be discharged without first having been given three (3) written warnings. This protects an employee from losing his or her job unfairly and provides him or her an opportunity to improve performance or correct the problem.

Termination for Just Cause

In addition, an employee may be terminated immediately for certain specific offenses. The following violations may justify discharge without warning or advance notice:

- Willful damage to company property or misappropriation thereof
- Theft of company, employee, or guest property or unauthorized removal of any of these, including lost-and-found items
- Consuming alcohol or drugs on employer premises during working hours, or possession of alcohol or drugs during working hours without authorization
- Willful falsification of company records (i.e., employment applications, payroll, financial, etc.)
- Conduct that could endanger the safety of the employee, co-workers, or a guest
- Incarceration in jail following conviction of a misdemeanor or felony by a court of competent jurisdiction
- Refusing to obey an order of a supervisor and/or insubordinate conduct toward a guest, supervisor, or manager
- Immoral or indecent conduct, soliciting persons for immoral reasons, or the aiding and/or abetting of the same
- Being absent for three consecutive scheduled workdays without notification to the supervisor
- Unauthorized entry into a guestroom
- Unauthorized removal of guest property from the guestroom or the hotel

Health and Safety

We are interested in your safety and well-being. We can all do much to prevent accidents and injuries by working safely and carefully on our jobs. Always remain alert and report any working condition that you feel may cause an accident or injury.

Any accident occurring at work, no matter how small it may seem, must be reported to your supervisor. If necessary, an injured employee will be sent to an available doctor.

Employee Benefits

Paid Holidays

There are six (6) paid holidays annually: New Year's Day, Memorial Day, Independence Day, Labor Day, Thanksgiving Day, and Christmas Day.

After thirty (30) days of employment, all full-time employees will receive eight (8) hours of holiday pay at their regular hourly rate for each holiday. Temporary and pool-status employees will not be eligible for holiday pay.

Because the hotel never closes, you may be asked to work any of these six holidays. If you do work on any one of these holidays, you will receive pay for the hours you work plus your eight hours holiday pay.

If you are scheduled to work the day before the holiday, the holiday, or the day after the holiday, then you must work your schedule in order to receive your holiday pay.

Paid Vacations

After the completion of one year of service, full-time employees will have earned the right to take a paid vacation: one full week of vacation time with pay, assuming an average of forty (40) hours per week were worked. After two (2) years of service, you will receive two full weeks of vacation each year. Thereafter, you will receive two full weeks of vacation each year. The amount of vacation pay to be received is determined by the average number of hours worked per week for that year.

Vacations cannot be saved up—you must take your vacation time each year. Every employee should take advantage of vacation time for rest and relaxation. Cash payment rather than time off will not be authorized.

If you are a part-time employee and your employment status is changed to full-time, then you will have earned one full week of vacation time with pay after one year of full-time service.

Meal Provision

Meals are provided for your convenience in the employees' cafeteria. Employees may have one meal after four (4) hours of work, and a second meal if working more than nine (9) hours.

Leave of Absence

After you have completed six months of employment, you may, in the event of illness, maternity, or military duty, be granted a leave of absence without pay, at the discretion of the company.

With the exception of military and maternity leaves, an employee may take a minimum of thirty (30) days and a maximum of ninety (90) days for leave of absence.

Vacations and holidays will not accrue or be paid during a leave of absence. Length of service will be retained at the time of the leave but will not accrue during the leave. The company cannot hold your job open for the duration of the leave. However, upon return from leave the employee will be given the first open position of like classification and pay for which he or she is qualified, if the original job is not open.

Military Service Leave

It is a policy of the company to re-employ personnel after any required military service. Personnel entering military service will be placed on military leave of absence. Upon honorable discharge and being physically able, and within ninety (90) days of date of discharge, the employee will be reinstated in the same position and at the same rate of pay, if vacancies permit; otherwise, the employee will be given the option to accept another job for which there is a vacancy or to be placed on a preferred waiting list for the next vacancy.

Military Training Leave

If you are serving an obligated period of duty with the National Guard or a reserve unit, you will be granted military leave for not more than two (2) weeks for the purpose of attending summer camp and or training. When you are absent from work because of required National Guard or reserve training, you will be paid the difference between your military pay and your company pay for not more than two weeks in any one calendar year. If a paid company holiday falls during the training time, you will receive an extra day's pay.

Maternity Leave

The hotel will grant leave of absence without pay to any expecting employee. Pregnant employees may, however, work as long as they like, with the written approval of a doctor.

Funeral Leave

In the event of a death in your immediate family, three (3) days off with pay is permitted. Immediate family includes husband, wife, children, father, mother, brother, or sister.

Unemployment Compensation

Under the State Unemployment Act, you are insured against unemployment. The company pays the entire cost of this insurance.

If you become unemployed through no fault of your own, you are eligible for unemployment compensation for a limited period under provisions and law of the State. This law is administered by the State Unemployment Compensation Commission. You must apply for this compensation from the Commission.

Workmen's Compensation

Under state laws in the United States, you are covered by Workmen's Compensation for injuries sustained in the course of your work. Be sure to report any such injury promptly to your department head. The cost of this insurance is paid entirely by the company.

For Your Information

Your employment status _____ Full-time _____ Part-time

_____ Pool _____ Temporary

Your position title _____

Your supervisor's name _____

Your manager's name _____

Your executive's name _____

Your starting date _____

Your starting pay rate _____

Your first payday _____

I acknowledge receipt of and will read the Hotel Employee Handbook, which outlines my benefits and obligations as an employee of the company.

Date_____ Signed _____

All employment papers completed on _____

Company orientation lecture completed on _____, at which time employee was briefed on rules, regulations, benefits, policies, and procedures.

Date_____ Signed _____

Director of Human Resources

Bally's Casino Resort Housekeeping Department Rules and Regulations

The Bally's Casino Resort is a luxury casino and resort hotel located in Las Vegas, Nevada. The resort has 2832 rooms and employs approximately 560 unionized housekeeping employees when operating at 100 percent occupancy. This document provides explicit details on the housekeeping department's regulations.*

What follows is a set of **departmental instructions**. In most service organizations, a proper orientation for a new employee will include a complete acquisition program by the human resources department, property tour, and presentation of a company handbook. Many organizations go further by presenting a set of hotel housekeeping **departmental guidelines**.

Appreciation is extended to the Bally's Casino Resort Hotel of Las Vegas, Nevada, for allowing the presentation of its Housekeeping Department Handbook.

* Reprinted with permission of Bally's Casino Resort, Las Vegas, Nevada.

WELCOME TO BALLY'S LAS VEGAS

You have been selected to work for Bally's Las Vegas in the Housekeeping Department. We're very pleased to have you join our team.

Prior to working in your assigned area, you will go through a ten-day Orientation Program. During this time you will be placed in the care of our Training Specialist / Supervisor and receive instructions on what we expect.

You will be taken on a tour of the Hotel and will be shown the Front Desk, Casino areas, Shopping Mall, the Employee Cafeteria, and etc. You will be advised of Hotel policies and procedures, days off, break periods and lunch schedules.

I have an open-door policy and am here to help you in any way possible. We want you to feel comfortable working with us. Our Guests should see in you a friendly, competent, caring Employee. Good work and a positive attitude will please them and that is our goal.

Again, welcome.

Sincerely,

Kay Weirick

Kay Weirick, R.E.H.
Director of Housekeeping Services
Extension 4776

KW\ris

Revised 04\23\97
a:\jobdescriptions\training

3645 LAS VEGAS BLVD. SOUTH
LAS VEGAS, NEVADA 89109-4307
(702) 739-4111

GRA TRAINING GUIDELINES AND PROCEDURES

I. *INTRODUCTION:* You will have a short meeting with the Director of Housekeeping Services or one of the Assistants.

II. *NEW EMPLOYEE PROCEDURES:*

1. DAILY

Day Shift—8:00 A.M. to 4:00 P.M.—Monday through Saturday.
Sunday and some holidays—8:30 A.M. to 4:30 P.M. or 9:00 A.M. to 5:00 P.M.

2. As you enter and leave the building, you must stop at the Time Office. You will be clocked in and out for the hours you have worked that day.

3. After changing into your uniform, you must sign the Department Payroll sheets in the Housekeeping Office before going to your assigned floor.

4. EACH MORNING—All employees must check the bulletin board outside the Scheduling Office for their assigned floors and any notations by their names. (This is for messages or special instructions.)

5. You must be on your assigned floor no later than 8:00 A.M. The <u>Red Line</u> is drawn at 8:00 A.M., and anyone signing in under the red line is considered late. (Guestroom Attendants may go on the floors to fold linen no earlier than 7:30 A.M. Please inform the Status Department what floor you will be on. You should not leave the floor until five (5) minutes before the end of your assigned work shift.

III. POLICY

A. DESIGNATE FELLOW WORKERS

You will be advised as to who the Supervisors are and what their duties and functions are: Inspectors, House Persons, Status Clerks, Payroll, Scheduling, etc.

B. ATTITUDE / APPEARANCE / ATTENDANCE

1. It is extremely important to make sure the Guest is comfortable and that the room is kept in a "0 Defect" condition.

2. RESPECT—Workers must show respect for everyone they work for and can expect to have the same in return. Treat others as you would wish to be treated.

3. DUTIES—All new Employees must read the Safety Booklet and practice all Safety Rules.

4. PERSONAL APPEARANCE—Being neat and clean is very important. You must take personal pride in your appearance. No socks, hats, headbands, or scarves, no tennis shoes or footies. Deodorant is a must. Fingernails should be no longer than $\frac{1}{4}$. No bright colors. Shoes should be black, white, or grey. If a sweater is needed, you may wear one. The color should be black, white, or grey. No personal clothing should be worn under the uniform.

5. ABSENTEEISM—Calling in sick, tardiness, and going home early without permission are considered "absenteeism." This can lead to warnings and termination. Be sure when you are unable to come to work that you call in at least four (4) hours prior to your scheduled shift. When you have made an appointment on a scheduled workday and need to be off, come in late, or leave early (you must sign an early out form), please be sure to make these arrangements with the Scheduling Office at least 48 hours in advance.

6. LOCKERS—You will be given your own locker and key. Lockers are not to be shared with anyone. If you lose your key, report the loss immediately.

C. PROCEDURES

1. SAFETY—Safety precautions must be taken at all times in order to avoid injury and loss of work.

A. If <u>SMOKE</u> or <u>FIRE</u> is detected, call **4911!**

B. It will be explained what to do and how to evacuate the Hotel in case of fire...REPORT TO THE LOCKER ROOM.

C. You will be shown how to bend in order to make beds.

D. You will be shown how to get down and back up off the floor, without hurting your back.

E. You will be shown how to change towels and clean tubs without reaching beyond normal extension.

F. BLOODBORNE PATHOGEN—If you enter a Guest Room that has blood or body liquids on the bed or in other areas, do not clean it. Please call your Inspector, who will then call the proper persons to handle this situation. Be very careful not to use your hands to remove trash. Always take the whole plastic sack and empty it. Watch out for syringe needles and other sharp objects. Each cart should have a "RED BAG"; these are to put any items in that may have body liquids, blood, or feces on them. Always wear gloves for protection.

G. THE AMERICANS WITH DISABILITIES ACT—Some of our Guests may be physically impaired and may need certain machines to help them while they stay here. At check out time, please inform the Inspectress of these items. Your Inspectress will then advise the Housekeeping Department.

H. Please report all maintenance problems to your Inspector, such as lights out, shower head broken, toilet runs, any broken furniture, any burn spots or tears. This is to be done on a daily basis. All lights should be burning at all times; in the hallway and in guestrooms.

I. Do not move heavy furniture. Ask the House Persons to help you. You may move chairs and small items. Use the wand on your vacuum to get behind heavy furniture.

J. You will be shown how to unplug the vacuum cord. It must not be pulled or yanked out of the wall socket. The cord must always be untwisted.
    <u>NO VACUUMING WET CARPET, OR TILE FLOORS.</u>

K. Check bathroom floor for water before entering the bathroom.

L. Rubber gloves are to be used at all times for your protection. Sizes are S, M, and L.

M. Rubber mats are to be used in the tub to clean shower walls. No leaning from outside the tub to clean shower walls.

N. No smoking in the hallways, guestrooms, or linen lockers. You may smoke in the service elevator corridors or in Shop Talk. You may not smoke anywhere on nonsmoking floors.

2. *KEY CONTROL:*

A. Do not give your key card to anyone!

B. Do not open a guestroom door for anyone, whether it is a guest or an employee. Advise a guest to go to the front desk for assistance to get another key.

C. If a guest wishes to enter his or her room while it is being cleaned, he or she must insert his or her key card in the door before entering. If the door lock shows green, the guest may enter.

D. If a key card is lost, a warning or termination will be issued. Lost keys must be reported immediately.

E. Each Inspectress, Guestroom Attendant, and House Person has his or her own key and/or key card for which that person is responsible.

F. Return all Guestroom keys from checkout rooms to the Inspector as soon as possible. Keep them safe while they are with you.

3. *MAID CART*—Each item on the Maid Cart will be identified, and an explanation will be given as to where it goes in the Guestroom. Each cart should have a RED BAG for hazardous waste. All carts must be clean, safe, and serviceable. Do not overload your cart.

4. *SHEETS/LINEN*—We have king sheets only for king and queen beds. You must change sheets and pillowcases daily. Blankets and bed pads must be changed if they have spots and are dirty. Do not burn strings off bundles. This practice can result in termination. Feather pillows are to be used in all suites. Qualifil pillows are used in all regular rooms. Guests may request different pillows. Remember to change them out at checkout.

5. *ROOM REQUIREMENTS*—The daily work requirement is at least 15 rooms for an 8-hour shift; approximately 25 minutes per occupied room and 25 to 32 minutes for checkouts. Suites will receive added time. The timer in the bathroom is used to help pace work. You may be asked to work overtime. Your cooperation is appreciated.

6. *TELEPHONES IN GUESTROOMS*—Upon entering a guestroom, the first thing that must be done is to dial the room status.

A.M. **or** P.M. **Room Check:**

VACANT CLEAN	811 plus your code
VACANT DIRTY	812 plus your code

When you **ENTER A ROOM** to clean:

ENTER	814 plus your code

When you have completed a room, **UPDATE THE ROOM STATUS:**

C/O CLEAN (VACANT)	811 plus your code
M/UP CLEAN (OCCUPIED)	815 plus your code

ALWAYS PUT YOUR CODE IN WHEN YOU ENTER THE ROOM and UPDATE THE ROOM STATUS BEFORE YOU LEAVE.

If a guest is using the telephone when you finish, go to the Linen Locker, call Housekeeping extension-4766, and tell the number of the room you cleaned. A personal identification number will be assigned to you in the Housekeeping Office. You will use this code at all times no matter what floor you are working on. Everyone must have a telephone code. If you do not have one, go to Housekeeping and ask for your code.

7. *TIPS*—Money left in checkouts is to be considered a tip (and only reasonable amounts.) In a makeup, if a dollar is left on the pillow, this may be considered a tip. All other monies must be turned into Lost and Found at checkout. Never take money in plastic containers. Turn it in.

8. *ROOM CHECK*—You must take room check each morning at 8:00 A.M. and each afternoon at 3:00 P.M. to see if the guestrooms are occupied or vacant. This gives the Front Desk an accurate count of the rooms that are occupied and lets your Inspectors know how many rooms are occupied on the floor, and helps guestroom attendants determine which rooms are available to be cleaned. Clean reoccupied rooms with "Red Priority" cards on the door, then C/Os and makeups. If a guest has requested the room to be cleaned at a certain time, please make note of the time on your report. If you cannot get into a room at least once during the day, call the guest on the phone. If no answer, inform your Inspector. We must be sure the guest is safe and that the room is not damaged.

9. *TV'S AND TELEPHONES*—TVs are not to be on while you are working. Telephones may not be used in the rooms, except to code in and out. Telephones for employees' use are located in the cafeteria. Radios are permitted to be played quietly. Never answer the telephone in the guestroom.

10. *BREAKING GUEST ITEMS*—If you break a guest item, immediately notify your Inspector, giving him or her a description, such as perfume name, brand, and size (ounces) so the item may be replaced.

11. *AIR FRESHENERS*—Always use air fresheners before leaving the room.

12. *CHANGE BEDSPREADS*—Change spreads, pads, and blankets as needed. Check pillows to make sure they are clean. Tell the Inspector if carpets or drapes need attention.

13. *INSPECTORS PER FLOOR*—there is one inspector assigned to two floors in the North Tower. In the South Tower there is one Inspector per five floors.

14. *REFRIGERATOR CLEANING—"A" ROOMS:* Defrost and clean the refrigerators. Clean bar sink. After cleaning, turn refrigerator back on.

15. Checkouts and makeups are to be cleaned the same way.

16. Only the guestroom attendant who is assigned to clean the guestroom should be in that particular guestroom. Special permission may be given by your Inspector for more than one guestroom attendant to be in the room.

17. *Makeups*—In the shower, take shampoo and soap out of a tub to clean properly. Change sheets every day and leave used soaps only in the makeup rooms. Replace all amenities daily and vacuum all rooms daily.

18. *NO FOOD OR DRINK*—No food or drink is to be taken out of the cafeteria, or to the floors without permission.

19. There are various lunch periods, depending on your assigned floor each day. You must go to lunch when assigned unless you receive permission for another time from your Supervisor.

20. *ROOM SERVICE*—Water on trays and tables must be emptied, and all trays and tables must be removed and placed in the hallway at the time of checkout.

21. *LOST AND FOUND*—Articles found in C/O rooms must be turned in to your Inspector immediately, and proper paperwork must be filled out. Airline tickets must be turned in at once. Liquor must not be placed outside in the hallway. Room Service must be called to remove bars. Other liquor is turned in to Lost and Found.

22. *REMEMBER*—Do not throw anything away, papers, tickets, etc., from a makeup or a checkout room.

23. Do not leave notes for the guests. Do not ask for tips.

24. Do not flush soap down the toilet.

25. Give your Inspector the room numbers of rooms with bed boards.

26. Nonsmoking floors are 9, 10, 11, 12, 14, 15 (20 and 21 only on the East Wing) in the North Tower. In the South Tower they are 6 through 10 (56–60) and 17 through 20 (67–70.)

27. Do not throw cigarette butts in the trash can. Dispose of them by flushing them down the toilet. If a toilet is not available, use water to make sure a cigarette is out.

28. You have one 10-minute break before lunch and one 10-minute break after lunch. You have a 40-minute lunch break, giving you a total of 1 hour.

29. If a guest should act strange or make you feel uncomfortable, make an excuse and contact your Inspector. He or she will help you, or will call Security.

30. *RUSH ROOMS, VIP ROOMS PRIORITY CARD (RED) ROOMS*—All rooms must be done as soon as possible. The Red Cards should be returned to the Inspectress after you clean the room.

31. Be friendly and polite to the guests.

32. At the end of the day, after 3:45 P.M. return your cart to the Locker Room. Be sure all Lost and Found items have been turned into the Inspector with the proper paperwork completed. Clean your cart of dirty glasses, trash, food, etc.

33. Go to your assigned floor to return your key to the Inspector and sign out. Do not come down until 3:55 P.M.

34. Sign out in the Housekeeping Office and go to the Locker Room to change your clothes.

35. You may not EXIT with any item from the guestrooms or other areas unless you have a note signed by the guest and a pass from the Housekeeping Office signed by the Supervisor.

36. *LANGUAGE*—It is important to be able to speak English with Guests and fellow employees. En-glish should be spoken during working hours. However, if you have difficulty with English, there are other employees or supervisors who can help you understand. Please ask for help. We also have classes for English as a second language, that you can attend at no cost to you.

37. Payday is every other Friday. Pick up your paycheck at the Time Office. You may pick up your check beginning at 12:00 midnight on Thursday. You may also want to inquire about Direct Deposit of your paycheck.

38. We hope this has been a productive learning experience. If there are any questions, please ask us. An informed employee, one who can answer the questions that guests will ask, is a great asset to us.

Thank you, and I hope you enjoy your work with us.

Ozone in the Laundry

The following article appeared in the April 2003 issue of *Executive Housekeeping Today.* Jack Reiff shows us how to incorporate new technologies into our operation that will conserve our resources, save us money, and help us to avoid polluting. I wish to thank Beth Risinger, CEO/Executive Director, and Andi Vance, EHT Editor/Ad Sales at the International Executive Housekeepers Association (IEHA) for allowing me to reprint this and other articles from *Executive Housekeeping Today* in this book.

Ozone Puts the Washroom on a Diet

By Jack Reiff

"Dilution is the solution to pollution," was a common saying in textile rental and other industries depending on water for processing. The statement may be true, but it is a costly solution considering the price and/or scarcity of water and the expense of sewage disposal in many areas.

Dilution does, however, play an important role in washroom chemistry that is often ignored in wash formula discussions. But a common test process, chemical titration, explains the dilution process and provides an opportunity to understand how a new ingredient—ozone—can put the entire wash process on a diet.

It Wouldn't Be Washing without Dilution

The chemical industry has developed a number of products and laundering techniques to remove soils from all types of fabrics that are safe and effective in cleansing the fabric without causing excessive fabric degradation. Current methods of chemical soil removal in the wash formula are emulsification, saponification, lubrication, flocculation, neutralization, oxidation and color alteration.

The general theory of washroom soil removal promoted by the chemical industry includes four processes—time, temperature, mechanical action and chemical action. The theory states that changing one process affects all the other processes. This is true. And taking the theory at face value should mean that increasing chemistry allows for the reduction of time, temperature and mechanical action.

This, however, isn't true because the theory ignores the process of dilution, which is necessary to rinse away soil that has been dislodged by the chemicals and to remove chemicals from the wash liquor to prepare it for the next chemical phase of the wash formula.

In a wash formula, chemicals (alkali and detergent) are added based on soil level and washwheel capacity. The resulting alkali activity establishes the parameters to bring the alkalinity of the wash liquor to specific levels for different activities: Removing soil, bleaching or removing stains, neutralizing, or adding fabric treatments.

The pH of the wash liquor, which is based on the amount of alkali added, is measured by titration. This analytical process uses amounts of acid of a known strength to neutralize and measure alkalinity of an unknown quantity. For example, if alkali added to the wash for medium soil creates a titration of 18 drops of normal acid in the wash process, the titration sequence might be as shown in Exhibit 1 (below):

Exhibit 1

Operation	Water Level	Titration
Break/Wash	Low	18 drops of normal acid
Carryover suds	Low	12 drops
Flush	High	6 drops
Flush	High	3 drops
Bleach	Low	2 drops (if water is clear)
Rinse	High	1 drop
Rinse	High	5 drops of 1/10 normal acid
Antichlor rinse	High	3 drops of 1/10 normal acid
Sour/treat	Low	pH 5.5

As the exhibit indicates, water levels (dilution) affect the titration arithmetically because of the water and chemicals retained by the fabric. High-water operations reduce the titration by about one-half from the previous step; low-level operations reduce titrations by about one-third.

If, according to the theory, more chemistry is used to remove and suspend increasingly heavier soils, then time, temperature and mechanical action should be reduced. However, the situation is just the opposite—the more chemicals used, the more water operations that are needed to reduce chemical and soil levels. And more operations require more mechanical action, which leads to more electrical use, longer operating hours and more wear and tear on equipment and textiles. This negatively affects the bottom line.

An equally unacceptable solution is to rely on chemistry to neutralize the alkalinity of the wash formula. This produces neutral salts that stay in the fabric, creating wash formula problems and user discomfort.

But by including dilution in the traditional washroom technology pie, operators can develop formulas that achieve the most efficient use of time, temperature, mechanical action and chemical action.

Employing high-level rinses allows for the greatest dilution of dissolved materials, which means more soil can be separated from the load and drained away. High-level rinses also create a higher ratio of water removed by draining water retained in the textiles, allowing for a higher percentage of materials, including alkali, to be removed at each rinse step. By progressive dilution, high-level rinses eliminate all but a very small amount of dissolved and suspended materials from the load (see *What You Should Know About Laundering and Textiles*, by Eugene Smith, Ph.D., and Pauline Mack, Ph.D.; pp. 77–99).

How Ozone Can Improve the Process

Ozone, a new ingredient in washroom technology, also can help improve washroom efficiency. A quick and effective oxidizer, ozone is part of the chemistry added to the break/wash cycle to remove the soil that is held by the alkali and detergents. In effect, ozone cleans up the water by cleaning the detergent chemicals so that they can be reintroduced into the washwheel and continue to remove soil from the fabric.

Ozone accomplishes this by:

- replenishing oxygen in the wash water
- decomposing fats, oil and grease
- preventing redeposition of soil
- softening the wash water
- purifying the wash water
- working like an oxygen bleach
- requiring lower wash temperatures
- removing soil attached to the wash chemicals
- and deodorizing the wash liquor and vapor.

Ozone is added to all of the operations of a wash formula to continually clean the wash liquor, putting dilution on a diet.

Ozone chemistry is simple: The three oxygen atoms that bind together by an electrical input to form O_3 are unstable and have an affinity for almost any atoms other than a pair of oxygen atoms. In the washwheel, the third oxygen atom jumps ship and joins with a carbon atom to form carbon dioxide (CO_2) or with other nonorganic atoms to form oxides. This process makes wash water cleaner by reducing soil levels and making chemicals become more effective. Cleaner water allows for formulas that use:

- less chemicals
- fewer water operations
- shorter wash time
- lower water temperatures
- and peroxide instead of chlorine for bleaching.

(This enhanced oxygen technology has a synergy with peroxide; ozone and oxygen bleaches provide superior results with less color degradation than chlorine bleach.)

An added benefit is that ozone improves the quality of the wastewater going to the sewer, both because it helps reduce the concentration of wash chemicals and because it acts as a pretreatment for the wastewater.

Ozone technology still is in development but has proven to be an effective additive to the wash process. Used correctly, it can be one tool in the ROI (return on investment) arsenal for the laundry industry.

Jack Reiff is president of Wet Tech, a laundry and wastewater treatment consulting firm in Webster, Massachusetts.

APPENDIX E

What If. . .?

"What If. . .?" is a booklet available to hotels to place in each guestroom. It is an excellent means of educating guests about what to do in case of fire.

This material is reprinted with permission of the copyright owner, the James H. Barry Co. of San Francisco, California. It may not be reprinted without written permission.

What If...?

Your Hotel Name
City

What if...
you're in a fire?

Probably it won't happen. You are in a building which was constructed to meet modern fire codes and which offers reasonable protection against such an occurrence. Your chances of being involved in a fire here may be thousands to one.

But your chances are even better if you understand, in advance, what to do in case of fire. Countless people are needlessly harmed by fires because they did *not* understand what to do.

This little booklet will tell you what to do, and it takes only three minutes to read. Increase your chances: please read it.

Andrew C. Casper
Chairman of Board of Visitors,
National Fire Academy,
U.S. Fire Administration

What if... you've just arrived?

Learn Where The Exits Are . . . before you first enter your room, look to the right and left of the door and locate at least *two* exits.

Walk To Each Exit . . . to help you remember their locations, walk to each exit from your room.

Count Doors On The Way . . . Choose a wall and, as you walk to each exit, count the doors along that wall between the exit and your room. This helps you remember the distance and location of exits—and may also help in case you have to find an exit when it's dark or smoky.

Find Alarms & Extinguishers . . . locate and walk to the Fire Alarm and Fire Extinguisher on your floor.

Find The "Off-switch" On Your Air Conditioner . . . in your own room, learn how to turn off your air conditioning system. This way, in case of fire, you can prevent smoke from being sucked into your room.

What if...
you find
a fire?

Pull The Nearest Fire Alarm . . . if you find a
fire in your room or somewhere else, sound the alarm.

Close Doors Against The Fire . . . if possible, close the
doors around the fire area, to keep the fire from
spreading.

Phone Management For Help . . . immediately telephone the front desk or building management to report the fire. If you cannot reach them, don't hesitate
to call the local fire department—its number is on the
inside front page of all phonebooks.

Fight Only Tiny Fires . . . use a fire extinguisher—*if* it
is a small fire.

Flee Larger Fires . . . if possible, exit from the building
if the fire is not small.

Always Take Your Room Key . . . before trying to
exit, be sure to take your room key. A tip—if possible,
loop the key to your wrist with a rubber band.

Stay Calm . . . don't hurry, keep relaxed, and *think*.
Your danger is almost always less than you imagine it
to be.

What if...
you hear an alarm
from your room?

Take Your Room Key ... if you're in your room, find your key. Again, if possible, loop it around your wrist with a rubber band.

Test Doors For Heat Before You Open Them ... with your hand test the door to the hallway to see if it is hot or cool.

Inch the Door Open if It's Cool ... if the door to the hall is cool, open it carefully, looking out for smoke. Slam it shut fast if there is thick smoke outside, and stay in your room.

Exit If There's No Smoke Outside ... if the hallway contains little or no smoke, head for the nearest exit.

Hug Walls While Exiting ... while moving to the nearest exit, keep close to the walls. If it's dark or smoky, count the number of doors to the exit, and feel along the walls as you go.

Exit With Caution ... test the exit door for heat before opening it—and, again, watch out for thick smoke in the stairwell. If the stairwell is safe, exit down to the street.

Avoid Elevators ... in case of fire, never use elevators for emergency exits.

Stay Calm ... don't hurry, keep relaxed, and *think*. Your danger is almost always less than you imagine it to be.

What if...
your exit's
blocked?

Go Back To Your Room . . . should the stairwell start filling with thick smoke, and your exit turns out to be unsafe, if possible return to your room—it's the safest place for you.

Or Otherwise Go To The Roof . . . if you can't return to your room from the stairwell, go up to the roof. There you can wait out the fire or be in position for a possible helicopter rescue.

Stay Calm . . . don't hurry, keep relaxed, and *think*. Your danger is almost always less than you imagine it to be.

What if...
you can't leave
your room?

Stay There ... if you can't exit, your room is the safest place to be.

Shut Off The Air Conditioner ... to prevent smoke from being sucked into your room, flip the "off-switch" on your air conditioning system.

Stuff Wet Cloth Under The Door ... wet towels, sheets or blankets can keep smoke from entering through the crack under your door

Stuff Air Vents With Wet Cloth ... this will also keep out smoke.

Remove All Drapes From The Windows ... in case fire should enter a window, no fabric will be nearby.

Fill Your Bathtub ... keep plenty of water in the tub, and have wastebaskets or icebuckets nearby for carrying water. This way, you can quickly re-moisten the wet cloths that are keeping smoke out.

Phone Your Location ... telephone the front desk or building management and tell them your location. If you can't reach them, don't hesitate to call the local fire department—its number is on the inside front page of all phonebooks.

Stay Calm ... don't hurry, keep relaxed, and *think*. Your danger is almost always less than you imagine it to be.

What if...
nothing ever
happens to you?

As Chief Andrew C. Casper said at the beginning, probably nothing will.

If you never have a bad experience with fire, there could be several reasons why. Maybe it's because this building is unusually well-constructed to guard against the outbreak of fire. Or maybe you and all its other occupants have been careful not to smoke in bed or to empty ashtrays into wastebaskets.

Or maybe it's because you've understood this booklet. We sincerely hope you have.

Thomas T. Nyhan

Thomas T. Nyhan
Public Fire Educator
Bureau of Fire Prevention
San Francisco Fire Department

Excerpts from InterContinental Hotels Group Loss Prevention Manual

InterContinental Hotels Group, as part of its concern for safety and loss prevention, provides excellent training and training outlines for its corporate property managers in order that a proper professional emphasis may be applied in areas of safety and security. These training aids are also made available to franchise holders who may either use them outright or use them as guides to write their own policies and guidelines. This appendix has three parts.

Part One contains recommendations on security issues pertinent to the **cleaning of guestrooms**.

Part Two is an excerpt on proper **key control and procedures**.

Part Three presents segments on the role of a hotel's **emergency response team** and the **emergency management plan**. The plan is used in company hotels and is made available to franchise holders as a guideline for the safety and security management of the owner's property. Note the degree of detail and formalization in these procedures. Space does not permit reprinting the entire emergency action plan.

Appreciation is extended to Wendell Couch, Vice President of Risk Management at InterContinental Hotels Group, for his unwavering support of this and prior editions of this book. Everything in this appendix is copyrighted (1978, revised 2002) and may not be reproduced without prior permission from InterContinental Hotels Group.

Part One: Cleaning of Guestrooms

To help ensure the safety of employees and guest property, room attendants and engineers should work in rooms with the doors closed unless the guest is present. A sign indicating "Guestroom being serviced" should be posted on the door. If the guest returns when the employee is in the room, the employee should ask the guest for his or her key and dip it in the lock. If the key works in the lock, the employee should allow access and offer to return later. If the guest does not have a key or the key does not work, the guest should be referred to the front desk. At no time should the employee be in the room with the guest with the door closed.

When housekeeping is being performed, the cart should be placed so it blocks the doorway. Guestrooms should never be left unsecured. The practice of opening multiple guestrooms simultaneously for cleaning should be avoided. Employees should be instructed not to smoke, make phone calls, utilize the bathroom facilities, or watch TV while in a guestroom.

In performing their assigned duties, the employees should note whether or not any hotel property has been removed or damaged. This applies whether the room is occupied or vacant. If property has been removed or damaged, the employee should call his or her supervisor or security immediately. A lock interrogation should be preformed and the guest should be billed for any missing or damaged property. If desired, hotel management may choose to block the room.

Guest Keys

If an employee discovers a key in a guestroom door, he or she should make contact with the guest and return the key. If the guest is not present, the key should be returned to the front desk.

Open Doors

If a guestroom door is found ajar, the employee should approach the room, announce his or her presence and make contact with the guest. If the guest is present, the employee should inquire if he or she can be of assistance. If the room is vacant, the door should be closed and the incident reported to either security or the manager on duty (MOD).

Room Service Trays

If room service trays are present in the corridors, hotel employees should pick them up and remove them to a service area or contact room service for pickup. Room service trays should not be left in the hallway as this might provide indication that a guest is present in the room or may create a trip hazard.

Security Check

Before leaving the guestroom, employees should check to see that all locks and/or security devices on windows and connecting and sliding glass doors or windows are in the locked position.

Do Not Disturb Signs

Each room should be serviced and inspected each day. A daily room-status report should be implemented and completed by the housekeeping department after the normal, posted guestroom checkout time. The report should indicate each guestroom, whether it is occupied and whether it was serviced. After the posted checkout time, housekeeping should review the report and the rooms that were not serviced should be called. If there is no answer to the call, the room should be entered and serviced.

Taking into account long shifts, unusual working hours and airline crews, the question often arises regarding what action should be taken when a guest asks not to be disturbed. A guest may give notice at the front desk, via telephone or with a simple sign on the door. No matter how the guest indicates a desire for privacy, to help ensure his or her safety and to protect hotel property, several important procedures must be followed. Failure to follow these procedures could have serious consequences, including delayed medical treatment for a guest, discovery of a deceased guest and legal actions taken against the hotel.

To ensure the safety of guests, rooms must either be checked once each day or contact made with the guest. In the morning, rooms for which the guest has requested privacy should be bypassed. If at the end of the shift, a privacy sign is still posted on the door, contact must be made. The room attendant or the housekeeping supervisor should call the room and ask if the guest requires anything. If the guest inquires about the call after having asked for privacy he or she should be told: "To help ensure your safety it is hotel policy to make contact with our guests on a daily basis." If there is no answer, the housekeeping supervisor should proceed to the room and again attempt contact. If there is no answer at the door, it should be opened in the presence of a witness. Often this is the result of a guest oversight or early checkout. If the door is deadbolted or the secondary latch is engaged, attempts at contact should be made through the door.

If there is no response, the MOD, security, and the chief engineer should be contacted. The room should be checked to determine if it has a connecting or exterior door which could have been used to exit the room. If none exist, or they are locked, the emergency key should be used to unlock the door. If necessary, the night chain or latch should be disabled or cut. If the room is discovered vacant, a note should be made in departmental logs and the MOD report.

If a non-responsive guest is discovered, attempts to awaken the guest should be made. If there is no response, Emergency Services (EMTs, Police, etc.) should be immediately contacted and CPR/First Aid procedures implemented by qualified personnel. Care should be taken so employees do not expose themselves to bodily fluids. If the guest is discovered deceased, the room should be immediately vacated and sealed and the local authorities contacted.

In the event that contact is made with the guest and the guest does not want his or her room serviced, consideration should be given to the use of a "Guest Refusal of Service" card. If there is concern about possible theft or damage, the hotel has the right to enter and inspect the room each day. In the event there is evidence of contraband or other crimes, the police should be contacted.

Non-Responsive Guests

From time to time a room attendant may open a room and discover the guest sleeping in the room. In the event that contact is not made with the guest, a note should be made to recheck the room later. If contact has not been made by checkout time (for due outs) or by the end of the business day, the door should be opened. If the guest is present in the room and does not respond, Security or the MOD should be contacted. Two employees should enter the room to make contact with the guest. The guestroom door should remain open. If the guest is non-responsive, Emergency Services (EMTs, Police, etc.) should be immediately contacted and CPR/First Aid procedures implemented by qualified personnel.

Housekeeping and Maintenance Carts

If, for any reason, an employee must leave the floor, his or her cart should be moved to a linen room or service area for safekeeping. Carts should not be left in guest areas or stairwells.

Housekeeping carts should be provided with a secure lock box in which the room attendant should place all room keys found in vacant rooms or public areas.

A member of management should inspect employee carts on a random basis to ensure the cart is properly maintained and to check for inappropriate or lost and found items.

Part Two: Key Control and Procedures

Key Control and Procedures

It is essential for each facility to establish sound key control procedures. These procedures should include regular inventories, secure storage, and re-keying of locks.

Electronic Locks

Hotels utilize electronic locking systems for the hotel guestroom door locks. These locks are distinguished from conventional key-accessed door locks by the presence of a credit card-sized slot or an opening designed for a computer or isolinear chip. Keys for these locks are reusable, reprogrammed at check-in and are used to gain access to guestrooms. Major benefits of these systems include:

- Ability to interrogate locks
- Ease of re-keying locks
- Conduct audit trails
- Improved security
- Automatic expiration of cardkeys

When an appropriately programmed key is inserted into the lock, the interior mechanism reads the computer code. When a valid key is removed, the lock is unlatched allowing the lever to turn and the door to be opened.

As with hard key controls, electronic locking systems in hotels allow for many levels of controlled entry. These include:

- **Guest**—access to assigned guestroom(s). The card code is changed for each registering guest.
- **Suite**—access to the main entrance door to the suite plus one of the sleeping areas; a second key allows access to the main suite entrance door plus another sleeping area of the suite.
- **Section/Floor Master**—access to a predetermined number of guestrooms in a section or floor.
- **Supervisor**—access to several designated sections or floors.
- **Grand Master**—access to all doors in the hotel.
- **Emergency ("E" key)**—Grand Master which overrides the deadbolt of a guestroom lock.

In addition to these controls, electronic locking systems offer additional features as follows:

- **Blocking**—prevents access to the guestroom by the last issued guest card. It is cleared by the next guest level key card issued for that room.

- **One-Time**—opens a specific lock only one time and then is canceled.
- **Display**—allows a member of hotel management to lock a door to a specific room preventing entry to that room by use of any hotel key except the current guest key and the "E" key. Reuse of the display key will clear this lock back into the system (can be used for vendors with wares displayed in their room).
- **Back Up**—prepared guest key cards for issuance when there is a power failure and the computer cannot function. Allows access to designated guestrooms that have a battery powered electronic door lock.
- **Programmer**—programs locks, sets date and time.
- **Interrogator**—a piece of equipment which downloads the details of recent lock openings. In some systems, a single piece of equipment functions as both the programmer and the interrogator.

Key Security

Duplicates of keys should not be made. If an additional key is required, uniquely coded keys for that lock or section should be made. Lock interrogations will reveal the exact key that was used. This will help ensure accountability.

To maintain accountability, each key should be uniquely coded and identified. Keys should be secured in a locked cabinet, signed out and signed in on a daily basis. In addition, keys may be programmed to work during designated shifts and will not work during any other time. Keys should not be removed from the property. If an employee takes a key home, he or she should be required to return the key to the property immediately.

Blank key cards for guestrooms are to be stored in a secure manner, in a locked cabinet under the control of the Guest Service Manager with restricted access as designated by the General Manager. Backup keys and blank key cards for all other levels should be stored in the General Manager's safe. The issuance of each department level card and all error/voids should be automatically recorded through the use of a printer. The record of levels and number of keys made, and by whom, should be reviewed to ensure key controls are maintained.

Security of the key cards is critical. If a master level key is lost, stolen or compromised, immediate action should be taken. The security code for that level should be changed and new keys for the affected sections should be made. The old keys will continue to function in the affected locks until the new key is inserted.

Employees should be trained that their key is for their use only. They are not permitted to admit other employees or guests to a guestroom. An employee who is authorized to be in the guestroom should have his or her own key. Guests should be informed "To help ensure guest safety, I am not authorized to open doors for guests" and referred to the front desk to obtain access.

In addition to security of the keys, key security also encompasses the ability to make keys. The electronic key system will allow anyone with knowledge of a password to make a key. With the correct password, master level keys can also be made. Therefore, each hotel should consider the following policies when allowing access to key making equipment.

- **Passwords**—Each person who is authorized to make keys should have his or her own, unique password consisting of at least 4 characters. When an electronic lock is interrogated, it will tell what key opened the lock, when the lock was opened, and who made the key that opened the lock. Therefore passwords should never be shared.

- **Timed Log Off**—Some key making systems allow the automatic log off time to, be changed. Each hotel should ensure that the automatic log off time of its key system is set for less than one minute. Therefore, one minute of inactivity will cause the system to automatically log off and subsequently require the use of a password for further keys to be made. This will help prevent someone from making a key and walking away, allowing additional keys to be made without the employee's knowledge.

- **Key Making Access**—Each person who is authorized to make keys should be granted an access level that is appropriate for his or her job description. Front desk employees should only be granted guestroom key making ability. If the person whose job description entails the making of master keys also checks in guests, then he or she should have two separate access levels (one with and one without master level access) with separate passwords. This will help prevent someone from making a guestroom key, leaving and having another person come up and make a master key before the system has logged off.

In addition to limiting the access to the key making equipment, the hotel should also keep the local time current for all guestroom locks and the central key making computer. This will help reconcile lock interrogations and give an accurate reading of when keys were made and when guests or employees entered a room. This should take a priority whenever a time change occurs (such as the beginning or end of daylight savings time).

Also, each hotel should change the master codes for all of the master keys a minimum of once a year. This helps ensure guest and employee safety by restricting the length of time master key codes are active. This task may be accomplished at the same time as a time change.

Guest Keys—If a guest requests a replacement room key, care must be taken to ensure that the individual is registered to the room. The guest should be required to produce positive identification in the form of photo ID or verification of registration information and comparing signatures on the registration card. If the guest cannot produce positive identification, additional keys should not be issued. Additionally, the hotel may choose to escort the guest to the room and allow admittance only after photo identification has been produced.

Victims of domestic abuse and other crimes often seek refuge in hotels. To help ensure guest safety, guest-room keys can only be provided to registered guests. Unregistered guests and family members should not be granted access to guestrooms. At check-in, if a guest requests more than one room key, the guest should be asked if he or she would like any additional parties registered to the room.

In the event that an unregistered guest requests access to a guestroom, he or she should be directed to a house telephone to make contact with the guest. If the guest is not in the room, the unregistered guest should be informed "To help ensure guest safety, we do not provide keys or guest information to unregistered individuals."

The hotel should offer to leave a message for the guest and may offer hotel amenities at the hotel's discretion.

The guestroom number should not appear on the room key.

Emergency Keys—The emergency key, or "E" key, should be used for emergency situations only, and should not be used in the normal course of business. The hotel should maintain two "E" keys. Additional keys should be maintained where required by the local governing authority. One "E" key should be placed in a sealed envelope with the manager's signature and date written across the seal. This envelope should be secured in the General Manager's safe or the MOD's safety deposit box. A second "E" key should be secured in a break-glass box convenient to the front desk for use in emergencies. The key box should not be visible from the lobby side of the front desk. Usage of either key should be recorded in an "E" key log.

Key Lanyards and Attachments—To help prevent the loss or theft of keys, they should be attached to employees by a thin lanyard, wrist bracelet or similar means of attachment. A small hole should be punched near the non-sensitive end of the key cards and a metal grommet or ring inserted in the hole to prevent tearing.

Department Key Control (Metal)

Various departments maintain metal keys which access their individual back of the house areas. To help protect hotel assets, key control procedures similar to electronic locks must be implemented.

Each department will have keys specific to its area. These keys should be individual and uniquely identifiable. To prevent potential removal of keys, tamper resistant rings should be used. These keys should be inventoried on a regular basis. The key rings should be signed in and signed out each day. While not in use, the key rings should be stored in a locked key cabinet within a secured office. Two separate keys should be required to gain access to the key cabinet.

Depending upon the size and complexity of the hotel, management may choose to have keys controlled at a departmental level or on a hotel-wide level by security. Regardless of which method is chosen, all keys must be accounted for daily.

Liquor Storage Keys—Due to the cost of inventory and the potential for misuse, access to the liquor storage room should be tightly controlled. There should be a limit of two keys, when possible. One key should be secured by the General Manager or his or her designee. The second key should be controlled by the Food and Beverage Director. If an electronic lock is used, keys may be programmed to work on the first and second shifts only.

Metal Key Audits—The Security Director or a member of hotel management should "spot check" storage of department keys on a random basis to ensure all keys have been returned and properly stored.

Duplication of Metal Keys—Any request for the duplication of keys should be submitted in writing to the General Manager who should thoroughly review the request before granting approval. Approval should be in writing. If the key was broken, the broken parts should be given to the General Manager for comparison with the master. If the key was lost, the circumstances under which it was lost (how, where, and when) should be discussed to determine the need for re-keying the locks. If there is any doubt as to whether the key could be recovered or used to access the hotel, the affected locks should be re-keyed.

Part Three: Emergency Response Team and the Emergency Management Plan

Emergency Response Team

The primary responsibility for protection of persons and property from injury and loss during an emergency belongs to the General Manager. Often he or she can best meet this responsibility through the establishment of an Emergency Response Team (ERT). The ERT can then be charged with identifying, planning for and responding to emergencies. The ERT should:

- Evaluate Risks and Exposures to the hotel
- Aid in fire prevention
- Train staff in emergency procedures
- Require periodic safety and security inspections of the hotel
- Ensure the maintenance and availability Life Safety equipment
- Help ensure the authorities are notified in a timely fashion
- Provide preliminary first aid and fire fighting efforts
- Provide for the safe evacuation of guests and employees
- Provide for the safe relocation and transportation of guests
- Secure hotel assets
- Evaluate and report losses
- Restore operations in a timely manner

Emergency Organization Staffing

The number of employees assigned to the ERT on a full-time or part-time basis will depend on local conditions, including the availability and response time of the emergency agencies. In smaller hotels, the ERT may consist of the General Manager and the Chief Engineer or the engineer on duty.

The ERT will not be successful unless it receives management support, adequate training and equipment.

Additionally, on each shift there should be employees trained in first aid and the use of fire equipment as well as instructed on what to do in case of an emergency.

In some hotels, these employees may be considered part of the ERT, but in general, the employees selected for the ERT should be selected with the idea of forming teams within departments that may respond to an emergency at anytime, anywhere in the hotel. It is desirable to have one team made up of persons from engineering. The Chief Engineer or his assistant should be a member of the ERT.

Every person who is a member is expected to perform physical duties, i.e., fight a fire, lifting, climbing, etc. All members should be available for duty at all times, or in accordance with a prearranged schedule.

Hotels operate 24 hours a day and the selection of ERT personnel should take into account the availability of employees during periods of reduced staffing. It is important to select persons from all shifts in order to provide adequate coverage at all hours, and that periodic checks are conducted to be sure that the rotation of personnel or changes in assignments have not depleted the ERT on any one shift.

Selecting an Emergency Organization Director

The General Manager should designate the ERT Director. The Director should be given full support from management. Responsibilities of the Director should be clearly defined and understood by the hotel staff.

ERT Director should meet the following criteria

- Technical competency in the fields of fire protection, hotel life safety and security systems, fire fighting and emergency planning
- Proficiency as a trainer
- Ability to direct the activities of others

Duties of the Emergency Response Team Director

- Organize the ERT, maintain a full roster of personnel, and provide plans of action to meet emergency situations in the hotel.
- Determine the number of persons to be placed on the various teams of the ERT on all shifts.
- Conduct regularly scheduled meetings with the ERT in order to provide special information and discuss problems with regard to the hotel's loss prevention program.
- Attend the hotel's Safety and Security Committee meetings.
- Arrange for actual fire, bomb threat and evacuation drills at least two (2) times per year designed to train the ERT members under varying conditions.
- Periodically inspect all of the hotel's life safety and security systems to assure proper maintenance and supervise the testing of these systems.
- Make monthly inspections of the entire hotel with the General Manager in conjunction with the security program. Copies of the inspection report should be filed with the Secretary of the Safety and Security Committee.
- Provide cooperation to local authorities.

Emergency Response Team Directors/Supervisors

Assistant ERT Directors

Assistant ERT Directors should be appointed by the General Manager to assist the ERT Director and to act as director during the Director's absence. The Assistant Directors should have similar qualifications and duties as the Director. The Director and the Assistant Directors should try not to be absent from the property at the same time.

Team Captains

The Director should appoint Captains of various teams within the ERT who will supervise the individuals in their teams. These individuals should be capable of taking charge during an emergency.

Phase One

In Phase One the ERT should be prepared to aid the victims, relocate guests and notify senior management and Risk Management of the emergency.

Providing Aid

- Notify emergency response agencies, such as the police, the fire department, and medical services of conditions at your hotel.
- Locate any injured persons and provide first aid within your ability to do so. Victims should not be moved unless their lives are in danger or there is a possibility of additional injury.
- Cooperate with emergency personnel as they arrive in providing any assistance they may need. Be prepared to respond to requests made by medical personnel, as they may need your assistance if there are large numbers of victims. Employees who have been trained in CPR and first aid should be available to assist. Basic first aid materials, towels and blankets should be provided to the emergency personnel for use in helping victims.

Relocating Guests

- Upon the advice of professional emergency personnel, evacuate the hotel and relocate guests to an area away from the endangered zone. Hotel staff should assist guests in moving to this pre-designated relocation center. At that time the ERT should be prepared to implement the transportation and housing plans established for such purposes. If it is necessary to move guests away from the hotel, make arrangements for guests to make calls to relatives. The hotel may wish to arrange for the hotel to pay for these calls.
- Assign management personnel to monitor the relocation of guests away from the hotel, including the relocation of injured guests. Use the materials in the emergency response kit (guest identification tags and roster) to keep track of each relocation. These records should be turned over to the General Manager.
- Assign key staff employees to assist guests and employees at the relocation center.
- Account for all guests and employees who were present at the hotel at the time the emergency occurred. Pertinent records for employees should be obtained from the hotel's personnel director. Guest records should be obtained from front desk personnel.
- To secure guests' belongings and protect company assets, security may have to be increased around the endangered zone. Contract security may be used if necessary. Initiate and coordinate procedures to secure guests' personal effects. If guests have been removed from the hotel, the guestroom doors should be "double locked." Security should conduct frequent patrols of the hotel.

It may be necessary to remove belongings from guestrooms. Inventory guest belongings (use two employees) and store belongings in a secure location. The General Manager or his or her designee should maintain the key to this location.

Phase Two

In this phase the ERT should establish an operations center, arrange for communications, establish emergency security, shut down utilities/inspect for structural integrity, and make arrangements for communicating with the media.

Hotel Operations Center

If for safety reasons the hotel cannot be occupied, a hotel operations center should be established close to the emergency area as soon as possible following the evacuation of the hotel. This will allow the ERT to continue managing and controlling the emergency while ensuring the continuation of the hotel's business. If necessary, the center should be staffed and open 24 hours a day. The Manager on Duty should remain in the operations center to coordinate hotel operations and communicate with local authorities and senior management.

Communications

- Contact the Telephone Company and arrange for installation of multiple telephones.

- Obtain several "two-way radios" for management's use.
- Staff the communications center with sufficient hotel personnel or temporary employees who are knowledgeable enough to answer guests' and employees' questions.
- If necessary, lease or purchase cellular phones. (Remember that in an emergency telephones at the hotel may not be in service. It may be possible that pay phones will be working while internal hotel phones will be out of service. Also, there is a possibility that phone calls may be placed out of the area but calls may not be able to be made into the affected area.)
- Continue to communicate the status of the hotel emergency to senior management.
- Establish necessary staffing requirements and communicate work schedules to hotel employees.

Emergency Security

In cooperation with local authorities, immediate steps should be undertaken to survey the property and provide security for guests, employees and company assets.

- Increase or recall all staff security personnel. Establish a schedule by which security is provided 24 hours a day. Establish patrol patterns that will provide coordinated security of the hotel's perimeter and buildings.
- Hire an outside private security contractor to provide additional services as required.
- If necessary, erect barriers around the affected area to control access to it.
- If the hotel has been evacuated, begin coordinated security of the hotel's perimeter, buildings, and any outside material. If the building structure is damaged or will be out of service for an extended period, it may be necessary to erect fencing around the hotel.
- Establish a badge identification system for all persons who may require access to the property. This system would allow security to identify employees and outside individuals who have a need to be in and around the emergency area. Hotel employees should wear their nametags as identification.
- Establish a policy as to who has the authority to enter the affected area and furnish this information to security. Only those individuals should be allowed to enter the affected area.

Records should be maintained by security of the name, date and time of the entry and exit of all individuals.

Utilities/Structural Integrity

In the event of structural damage these additional items should be considered:

- Have the hotels engineering staff shut down the hotel's utilities and HVAC system.
- Contact the electric company, gas company, and water department. Ask for inspections by their employees to confirm the integrity of the hotel's systems.
- Contact an electrical contractor to install temporary lighting and emergency generators, if necessary.
- Conduct a visual inspection of the building structure for any damage. Later, it may be necessary for a structural engineer to conduct an in-depth inspection.

Communications with the Media

Refer to Communications with the Media Section of this Loss Prevention Manual for instructions on communicating with the media, or contact the SIX CONTINENTS HOTELS Communications Department.

Establish a location away from the emergency area where media representatives can assemble.

Establish a rigid timetable for dispensing information or holding news conferences.

Phase Three

In this phase the ERT will arrange for an investigation of the emergency incident, conduct management reviews of the actions being taken, and conduct a review of your emergency plan to accommodate unforeseen losses.

Emergency Investigation

Prepare a report on the emergency that includes the following information:

- What happened?
- Where did it happen?
- When did it happen?
- How many people were reported injured, deceased or missing?
- What is the physical condition of the property?

Witnesses to the emergency should be interviewed and their information included in the report. The report should be sent to the hotel's senior management as soon as possible.

Once senior management has received the report, the ERT should determine what their response to the emergency is and coordinate with them to ensure that the proper resources are mobilized to help manage the emergency.

Also, note that major hotel emergencies will usually involve agencies from all branches of government (local, state, federal). Space should be made available to accommodate agencies involved with the emergency.

Once the property has been released by the local authorities, the ERT should prepare to take over its security by:

- Closing the facility or isolating damaged areas.
- Fencing in the entire property or damaged areas.

Plan for both short-term and long-term investigations of the emergency. Each investigating entity involved with losses to the hotel will need space in which to work as well as the following arrangements:

- Meeting rooms
- Food service
- Restrooms
- Secretarial and support staff (numbers will depend on the magnitude of the incident)
- Communications (telephone and two-way radio)
- Separate accounting systems for both the emergency and insurance purposes
- Computers to manage data and provide wordprocessing
- Blueprints and plans of the hotel's physical plant
- Employee assistance (such as where they can be located and when they will be needed to work)
- Fax access to supplement telephone communication

Management Review

During the first 72 hours following the occurrence of the emergency, schedule meetings with the ERT at least three times a day to ensure that all assigned duties are being carried out. After the first 72 hours, continue to meet at least daily or as often as circumstances require.

Add or restructure job duties or functions as required by the current situation. Continue meetings and critiques as long as emergency conditions exist.

Plan Review

Unexpected issues that will require your attention will emerge as additional losses to the hotel are discovered after the initial crisis. The ERT should reevaluate the emergency plan to accommodate for these issues.

Emergency Management Plan

Natural emergencies, although infrequent, do happen and the ERT should be prepared for them. Depending upon its location, a hotel may have to cope with earthquakes, floods, tidal waves, hurricanes/typhoons, tornadoes, windstorms, power failures or severe snowstorms. In some instances, natural disasters present unique problems whereby the hotel might be used as shelter or hospital for nearby residents. These situations may have a traumatic effect on the victims, their families

and the hotel. Emergency planning can greatly reduce the impact of these situations and can assist in the efforts to reestablish operations following a loss.

The hotel's ERT should develop Emergency Management Plans (EMP) for those perils likely to impact the hotel. These plans are a critical part of any hotel's operating procedures. The ERT should prepare hotel staff to implement emergency plans with little notice.

The goals of an emergency plan are as follows:

- To help ensure the safety and well being of persons which may be affected by a fire, natural disaster or other catastrophe.
- To provide timely notification to the appropriate authorities
- To provide a tool for training employees in actions that should be taken in the event of an emergency.
- To ensure the flow of accurate information to the hotel's guests, its employees, the public and any others directly affected by the incident.
- To promptly assist others in the evaluation of the cause(s) of any losses and in an assessment of the magnitude of damage.

Contingency Planning

Preparation and training are critical components of any emergency plan. An effective emergency plan will provide for the following:

Training: Employee training and drills should be conducted semi-annually and on all shifts to ensure that in the event of an emergency, employees are aware of their duties and responsibilities. The ERT should critique the employees' actions on these drills to evaluate and correct the hotel's emergency plan.

Emergency Resources: To help ensure hotel operations are restored in a timely fashion, a list of vendors, contractors and other resources should be maintained. The list should contain names, 24 hour contact numbers, and a description of the services offered. A minimum of two vendors should be listed for each resource. Each vendor or contractor should be contacted on a regular basis to confirm that they will respond to your request and are capable of providing the services or equipment required.

Relations with Local Authorities: The ERT should establish a working relationship with local authorities who will be responding to emergencies at the hotel. The ERT should know the names of individuals within the public agencies who can help coordinate the safety efforts undertaken by the hotel. In the event of a major emergency, local and state authorities might take control of the hotel property for a period following the emergency. Efforts in preparation for an emergency will help ensure cooperation with these authorities before, during and after an emergency.

Emergency Checklists: Each department manager should have a checklist of actions that he or she should perform in the event of an emergency. Where appropriate, drawings of the hotel identifying utility controls, assembly points, and any other important information should be maintained. Department managers should be trained through a practice drill to become familiar with their respective responsibilities during and following an emergency. Department managers should delegate specific responsibilities on the checklists to their employees and train them in those responsibilities.

Emergency Response Kit: An emergency response kit should be kept at the front desk that contains supplies that will enable the hotel's management to keep track of the relocation of employees and guests after an emergency. The kit should contain the following:

- Hotel drawings
- Emergency checklists
- Emergency plans
- Contact numbers
- Guest identification tags
- Guest identification roster
- Several pens
- Legal note pads
- File folders
- Paper clips

The guest identification tags are used to identify the guests or their property if they have been relocated or are being relocated to a medical facility. They should have space to record the guest's name and room number, and the name of the medical facility to which the guest was transferred. The tag should be a two-part form. One part of the form should be provided to the guest or placed on his or her property. The second part should be kept at the hotel by the General Manager to account for and identify the current location of the guests.

The guest identification roster should also be used to keep track of the location of all guests who had been staying at the hotel at the time of the emergency. It should record the guest's name, the room number to which the guest is registered, the name of the location to which the guest was transferred, and whether it was a medical facility or alternate housing.

First Aid Training and Supplies: Selected personnel on each shift should be trained in first aid and CPR procedures. This training should be kept current. A basic first aid kit should be maintained with a complete inventory of supplies.

Mutual Assistance Agreement: The ERT should develop a Mutual Assistance Agreement with several local hotels or businesses to provide for the transportation and relocation of guests in the event it is required. This agreement should be developed in advance and in writing when possible. The plan should be reciprocal for all parties.

Emergency Plan Review: Emergency plans should be reviewed by the ERT a minimum of twice each year at the time of training or drills. A post drill review should be conducted to determine if any changes to the plan are necessary. All contact information should be verified to ensure it is current.

Reporting Instructions

After an emergency occurs, the General Manager should inform the senior management and Risk Management department, company, owners, and insurance carriers of the incident by telephone, providing as much information as possible. Immediately thereafter the following reporting procedure is to be observed:

List nature and extent of all injuries, sustained or reported by guests or employees.

Assess the damage to the facility and the impact on business operations.

NOTE: Repair work, other than that necessary to protect the building and its contents, should not be started until approved by the Risk Management department.

APPENDIX G

The Personal Plan

The **Personal Plan** is a document prepared by an individual manager, indicating how he or she intends to fulfill assigned management responsibilities over a given period of time. The Personal Plan is designed by the manager after consultation with an immediate supervisor. It may then be used as a guide to performance appraisal at the end of a given time period. Of even greater significance is the use of the plan as a guide to professional development.

This appendix presents the Personal Plan I developed while employed as executive housekeeper for the Los Angeles Airport/Marriott Hotel during the opening year of the facility. The plan indicates areas in which development should occur during the upcoming year of operation.

Note the last paragraph, in which specific goals were established as *results expected*. At the end of the year, the manager and supervisor use the plan to evaluate performance against these results expected; that is, what had been specified as intended action. Once the year is complete, a new plan should be developed for the next performance period.

*The Executive Housekeeper's Personal Plan for*_____
(name)

I. Technical Skills

  A. Job and technical knowledge

    In order to perform the technical requirements of my position, I plan to do the following:

    1. Continue to review all media at my disposal for products, equipment, and techniques. Test and implement new ideas and equipment found worthy of consideration that might improve operational methods and standards and/or decrease costs.

    2. Periodically review job descriptions, personal staffing organization, and standard operating procedures (SOPs) to increase effectiveness of assigned employees.

    3. Improve effective communications with all members of my staff.

    4. Stimulate and effect career progression of qualified personnel. Set the right kind of example for all subordinates. Cross-train to increase potential for this property; increase cooperation and respect of employees for each other and develop skill depth within the department.

II. Administration

  A. I will consider my area of responsibility properly administered when:

    1. Organization charts and job descriptions are prepared and published for all positions within my area of control.

    2. Equitable work distribution and production have been balanced to provide high morale and effective operation.

    3. Correspondence, records, reports, and training objectives have been timely and efficiently accomplished.

    4. Adequate controls affect increased productivity and decreased operational expenses to the degree that high priority standards will achieve the proper balance against profits for the rooms department.

    5. Communications are free and open.

    6. Proper creation of responsibilities and delegation of authority will create effective utilization of personnel.

    7. Production standards exceed required standards.

III. Managerial

  A. My areas of responsibility will be well managed when:

    1. Administrative goals have been attained.

    2. Wages and controllable expenses are maintained at or less than authorized percent of sales.

    3. GRA hours per rooms rented is in control.

    4. Turnover rate and employee opinion reflect high morale and efficient operation.

    5. Promotions of qualified career progression employees have been made, and success in development of personnel and depth of the staff is accomplished.

    6. Standards are attained or exceeded in producing guest satisfaction with minimum guest complaints.

    7. Objectives of my Personal Plan have been attained.

IV. Personal Development

  A. I will be advancing myself in my present position when I:

    1. Have full knowledge of all operational aspects within the areas I control. To improve this knowledge, I intend to

      a. Learn other technical skills that relate to my present position.

      b. Obtain knowledge from technically competent personnel who have experience with items of equipment being used.

      c. Increase knowledge through formal educational opportunities.

      d. Grasp every opportunity that my spare time will allow to learn other departmental responsibilities.

      e. Seek out responsibility and critiques and learn by doing.

    2. Cross-train in front desk operations to develop my knowledge in areas directly affected by actions in my department.

    3. Obtain a general grounding in other areas (food and beverage) not directly related to my present operation.

4. Take advantage of every opportunity offered to enroll in training courses available through the company or educational facilities for the advancement of my managerial skills. Continue working toward certification as American Hotel & Lodging Association (AHLA) hotel administrator.

5. Reach my primary goal (promotion) by (date).

V. Expected Results

  A. I expect to accomplish the following results by the dates indicated:

1. Attain a smooth and coordinated hotel opening for all back-of-the-house operations by (completion of opening).

2. Solidify operating targets by (date).

3. Institute systems for scheduling, stock control, cost control, inventories, continued formal training of new personnel, linen control, and budget control by (date).

4. Stabilize labor turnover at 8 percent or less by (date).

This plan approved and implemented: (date)   .
Expected performance appraisal date: (date)   .
Submitted by_____.
Accepted by_____.

APPENDIX H

Microfiber Technology

The following series of articles appeared in the February 2003 issue of *Executive Housekeeping Today*. David Carmichael introduces us to a synthetic fiber, microfiber, that will change how we clean. A companion piece shows us how to maintain this wonderful new product. A third article by Robert Kravitz introduces us to microfiber and flat mops and gives us a look at a remarkable study conducted at the University of California Davis Medical Center. I wish to, once again, thank Beth Risinger, CEO/Executive Director, and Andi Vance, EHT Editor/Ad Sales, at the International Executive Housekeepers Association (IEHA) for allowing me to reprint these articles from *Executive Housekeeping Today*.

Microfiber Cleaning. . . If Not Now, WHEN?

By David Carmichael

You've read about it. You have seen products displayed at trade shows and on Internet sites. So what is it? Does it work? Is it practical? Will it work in a commercial application?

Only a century ago, rayon, the first manufactured fiber, was developed. Prior to that, the use of fiber was limited to those fibers available in the natural world. However, cotton and linen wrinkled from wear and washings; silk required delicate handling; wool shrank and was irritating to the touch. Since rayon and other synthetics, manufactured fibers are now found in modern apparel, home furnishings, medicine, aeronautics, and yes, cleaning products.

Microfiber, introduced in 1986, is a revolutionary synthetic that can be processed, woven and finished in a variety of different ways to achieve a specific result. As a synthetic, it provides mankind with control over its supply and can be manufactured to extremely fine tolerances, many times thinner than other synthetics and hundreds of times thinner than a human hair.

Rated in denier, the unit for measuring fineness of a fabric, a strand of cotton has a rating of 200. A human hair has a denier of 20 and a strand of silk has a denier of 8.

Microfiber has a denier of 0.01 to 0.02. Hundreds of times finer than a human hair, yet strong and tough, split microfiber attracts dust, grime, microorganisms and residues like a magnet.

Microfiber, by itself, would wear and shed its fiber with use. But when it is expertly combined with nylon, a synthetic thermoplastic material, the result is a cloth that exhibits the advantages of both synthetics—cleaning and absorbency of microfiber and the strength and lint-free nature of nylon.

Microfibers are tiny fibers that have been slit into millions of finer fibers that are no thicker than 1/100th of a human hair. The special slitting process produces an ultra-fine fiber with wedge shape filaments and a core of nylon. The wedge shape, the nylon core and the smaller-sized fiber are the key to their effectiveness.

When these tiny fibers are woven together into a cloth through a unique weaving method, the result is a powerful cleaning tool.

Each cloth consists of tens of thousands of tiny storage compartments that lift the dirt up, trap the waste and leave a clean, streak-free surface.

The nylon core within the microfiber form tiny cutting edges that break up surface dirt and easily absorb and remove oils and other grimy substances. The only solvent needed is water!

The conjoining of the two synthetics in just the right combination is crucial. Too much nylon will result in a cloth that will scratch fine or delicate surfaces. Too little nylon and the cloth will not last or clean rough surfaces without rapid deterioration. It is only the perfect combination of polyester and nylon, extruded and woven into microfiber cloth, that makes the cloth effective and durable.

Quality manufactured microfiber offers a unique surface structure that contains millions of micro-hooks that grab, lift and hold dust, dirt and grime. These micro-hooks can clean into the pores of surfaces and when used dry, create a positive charge within the fibers that literally "vacuum" dust and dirt from the surface and into the cloth—all without chemicals. High-grade microfiber cloth can hold as much as seven or eight times its weight in dust, dirt and moisture.

Not All Microfiber Is Created Equal

From fine fashion to biotechnology, the demand for microfiber is growing exponentially. Factories in Korea, China and other countries are flooding the American market with poor quality, low-grade "microfiber" products. So buyer beware! There are significant differences between cheap, poor quality cloths and high-grade, durable cloths. High-quality extruded microfiber is expensive to produce; with machining costs that can exceed several million dollars. Low-grade microfiber can be produced for under $100,000.

Blending ratios are an important factor in microfiber cloth quality and cleaning ability. While a blend of 80% polyester and 20% polyamide (nylon by-product) is typical, a 70/30 blend that contains more polyamide fibers can be more expensive and will clean more aggressively. Research conducted by the University Hospital, Lund, Sweden, indicated that microfiber cleaning resulted in dust, microorganism and bacterial reductions from a low of 96.9% to a high of 99.4%.

The density of the fibers per square inch can affect pricing and cleaning ability. A cloth with 50,000 fibers per square inch can cost much less than one with 220,000 fibers per square inch. Greater density translates into greater cleaning power and durability.

Finally, the quality of construction and the finish of the cloth affect cleaning ability. Cloths can be woven, hooked, knitted, and feathered, each good for specific cleaning functions. Ultra-suede, a high-fashion material is a finely polished microfiber blend that works well on fine optical glass.

Executive Housekeeping Today asked Chris Schran, president of Reliable Maintenance Services of Fountain Valley, CA, to explain microfiber cleaning and the experience RMS and their nearly 300 janitors have had using microfiber cleaning for the last two years.

"We are a 54-year old, family-owned company," said Schran, "and as any building service contractor can tell you, labor and supplies are the two costliest drains on revenues. We are constantly looking for innovative ways to increase our cleaners' productivity and decrease our consumption of chemicals and other consumables. Simply stated, transitioning to microfiber cleaning has saved our company. We have decreased our chemical consumption by over 70%, increased our worker productivity by 31% and have decreased consumable expenses by over 40%—all the while raising our customer satisfaction approval rating to nearly 99%. It has allowed us to compete nationally, and, perhaps most importantly, to differentiate ourselves from all competitors by making us a low-chemical, low moisture cleaning company.

"We experimented with several microfiber products during the test phase and found that cloths and floor tools designed to perform specific cleaning functions work best for us. One cloth is for aggressive heavy-duty cleaning; another is designed specifically for wet environments, and the third is engineered for dusting and delicate cleaning.

"Each cloth is color-coded, and that helps the cleaners easily recognize each cloth for its specific cleaning function. We added the microfiber tools to our team cleaning training and the results have been astounding. After about two weeks of using the cloths, our cleaners asked us why we hadn't given them these tools before now.

"Microfiber floor tools and mops have had the greatest impact on our productivity. We clean several million square feet of commercial and retail space daily and eliminating the wet mops, buckets, wringers and trips to the janitor closet to change dirty water has saved us over an hour per shift per cleaner.

"We have some of the most stringent environmental regulations here in California, and converting to microfiber cleaning has brought us some welcome attention. Several floor manufacturers are using the microfiber mop as their suggested maintenance tools because of the low-moisture nature of the cleaning process. Medical facilities are converting over to microfiber cleaning because of the lower incidence of cross-contamination. The EPA estimates that the typical janitorial worker uses over 240 pounds of chemicals during the course of a year. By cutting that amount 70%, we're not only saving money, we're safeguarding our workers, clients and their guests and tenants. I call that a win-win situation for everyone."

David Carmichael is a Director for REDCO, Inc. He can be reached at (714) 418-2960.

Caring for Microfiber Cloths and Mop Heads

The many benefits of microfiber cloths and mop heads are finally reaching more and more end users. Microfiber, constructed from polyester and polyamide nylon fibers, is approximately l/16th the size of a human hair. There are approximately 90,000 microfibers in one square inch of a microfiber towel. It is the resulting density of the material that allows microfiber cleaning cloths and mop heads to lift and trap grime, making them more thorough cleaning agents than traditional cleaning cloths and mops.

However, less is known about the proper care and cleaning of microfiber products. For them to work their very best, microfiber cloths and mops do need to be cleaned on a regular basis. Usually, all that is needed after one or more uses is a thorough soaking in a disinfectant, rinsing, and then wringing out until all visible signs of soil are gone. They do not need to be machine washed after every use.

Eventually (and definitely after heavy use) microfiber cloths and mop heads will require a more thorough scrubbing and should be machine-washed using household laundry detergent and hot water. "Washing in warm water is necessary because it causes the fibers to swell, releasing the dirt and soil trapped within," says Aileen Cleary, assistant global marketing manager for Unger Enterprises, a supplier of microfiber products.

Cleary suggests washing microfiber products with nothing else in the load. She explains that other fabrics can "shed" lint during the wash. The lint can become embedded in the microfiber, reducing its usefulness.

Using Bleach and Fabric Softener

Though microfiber is a very hearty material and can withstand from 500 to as many as 1000 washings, certain cleaning products are harmful to microfiber, affecting its longevity and usefulness. Bleach should not be used.

Many studies report that fabric softener should never be used to clean microfiber. According to these studies, the microfiber will treat the fabric softener as if it were soil. It will attempt to store the tiny particles of the softener in its fibers. When this happens, the microfiber becomes stiff and hard and cannot be used effectively.

Drying Microfiber

Microfiber can be dried in a commercial dryer using a low heat setting or simply hang microfiber cloths and mop heads out, allowing them to air dry. "Never expose microfiber to extreme heat," says Cleary, "Treat them as you would any other polyester fabric."

Microfiber offers another benefit of which many end users are unaware. They are positively charged. That means they attract dust, which has a negative charge. "This is another reason to keep microfiber products clean," adds Cleary. "There are so many pluses to microfiber, just a little cleaning care is well worth the effort."

Unger Enterprises, Inc., an international company with offices in the United States, Germany, the United Kingdom, and Brazil, has been manufacturing economically designed cleaning tools for more than 35 years. Unger takes pride in developing innovative and unique products and cleaning systems that allow professionals to achieve consistent quality results while saving time and energy.

Alternative Floor Maintenance Systems

By Robert Kravitz

The University of California Davis Medical Center (UCDMC) decided to reevaluate its floor mopping procedures. It was looking for a floor maintenance system that reduced chemical costs, trimmed cleaning times, and minimized custodial staff injuries and workers' compensation claims.

The hospital also was seeking a more environmentally friendly way to maintain floors. Many floor-cleaning products used in hospitals contain chemicals. Some chemicals can be harmful to human health as well as to the environment, and UCDMC wanted to reduce the amount of chemicals necessary for cleaning.

Additionally, UCDMC was seeking ways to make floor maintenance tasks less burdensome on the custodial staff. For instance, they wanted to reduce the number of times the cleaning solution and rinse water had to be changed. Traditionally, to reduce the risk of cross-contamination for patients and staff, the cleaning solution and rinse water had to be changed every two or three rooms. Because each solution-filled bucket could weigh as much as 40 pounds, establishing a floor cleaning system requiring fewer cleaning solution changes would be less strenuous for the cleaner and provide direct cost savings for the hospital.

Going Flat

Just a few years ago, the hospital would have found few alternatives to the conventional mopping methods that have been used for decades. However, they discovered that some medical facilities had recently begun using microfiber flat mops with considerable success.

Microfibers are nylon fibers that are approximately 1/16th the size of a human hair. The resulting density of a mop made with microfiber allows it to absorb up to six times its weight in liquid, making it considerably more absorbent than a traditional mop. In addition, the microfiber mop heads are lighter, making them easier to maneuver than conventional mops.

Because microfibers are so small, they can easily penetrate grout areas and uneven surfaces in floors. This allows the cleaning professional to remove soil and grime deep within the pores of the floor.

UCDMC was so impressed with the potential of microfiber technology that they decided to test the product for one year. They also instituted a floor mopping system to help achieve their goals of reducing costs, injuries, and cleaning times and finding more environmentally safe ways to maintain the hospital's floors.

This system included the use of two buckets or dual buckets—buckets with two separate compartments—one for cleaning solution and one for rinse water. With this system, the cleaning solution was not contaminated by dirty rinse water, preventing cross-contamination, reducing chemical costs, and making the process less taxing on the custodian.

Floor mopping procedures using flat mops usually included "cutting" the floor by mopping all edge areas first. The custodian then mopped using a "figure 8" or "S" movement, which allowed the flat mop to partially overlap areas just cleaned, assuring the floor was thoroughly mopped. The system assured a consistency in cleaning, allowing for easier benchmarking and cleaning standards.

Resistance and Reasons for Change

Though the hospital believed there were compelling reasons to consider microfiber flat mops and to introduce a new floor mopping system, convincing the custodial staff, hospital personnel, and even hospital patients of the merits of microfiber was not an easy task. The hospital's cleaners were averse to change and initially found using the flat mop and the new floor mopping system awkward. Doctors and nurses were unconvinced that microfiber could be as effective as claimed. Even patients expressed their concerns when they first saw custodians using the flat mop.

Though change is rarely easy, the hospital patiently worked with custodians, communicating the benefits they believed would be derived by using the new microfiber mops and floor mopping system. Eventually, two primary selling points materialized that eased the way for the transition:

1. The microfiber mops weighed five pounds less than the conventional mops.
2. The microfiber mop head could be easily changed after every room was mopped, if necessary.

This second reason benefited custodians because it reduced the time and effort required to wring a mop and, with the floor mopping system in place, there would be less need to change the cleaning solution. According to hospital studies, the solutions needed to be changed an average of seven times a day per cleaner before implementing the new restroom cleaning system.

Still, there were concerns about the effectiveness of the microfiber mops. To allay these concerns, UCDMC staff ran tests using conventional mops in specific areas and then recleaning the same area with a microfiber mop. In each case, the microfiber mop captured more dust and dirt. To further bolster their support of the microfiber mops, they performed the same test in reverse order, mopping first with the microfiber mop and then with the conventional mop proved ineffective.

Program Results

Benefits

UCDMC began tests with the microfiber flat mop in 1999. Within one year, the hospital had completely replaced loop mops with microfiber and had implemented the dual bucket floor mopping system.

There were initial costs to put the program into action. Microfiber mops can cost three times more than conventional mops, plus the new dual buckets had to be purchased. However, most manufacturers guarantee that conventional mops will withstand 55 washings; microfiber mops are guaranteed to last after 500 washings. This gave the microfiber mop a comparatively low lifetime cost.

Additionally, the purchase of additional buckets or dual buckets resulted in considerable cost savings when the floor mopping system was implemented. Floor cleaning chemicals purchased by the hospital were reduced by 46 percent, from 513 gallons in 1999 to 283 gallons in 2000. With the use of the microfiber flat mop, the dual bucket, and the floor mopping system, UCDMC saved 638 hours per year for each worker, or approximately $7,665 in wages multiplied by the number of workers.

UCDMC cut its water use by a whopping 95 percent because of the floor mopping system. Another benefit was cost savings from reduced workers' compensation claims. Because the microfiber flat mops were five pounds lighter and there was less need to change the cleaning solution, custodians suffered fewer job-related injuries. In fact, floor mopping was reclassified as "light duty" by the hospital with the switch to flat mops.

Limitations

UCDMC decided not to use microfiber mops in areas "contaminated with an extraordinary amount of blood or other body fluid" such as emergency and operating rooms, though no reason was cited. Additionally, they did not use the mops in greasy areas such as high-traffic kitchens where the hospital decided to continue using mechanical floor cleaning machines.

The microfiber mop heads could not be washed in the hospital's industrial washers and dryers because the high heat setting damaged the material. However, washing the mop heads in conventional washers with lowered heat settings and using standard laundry detergent easily solved this problem.

Cost Savings Using A Microfiber Flat-Mop System vs. A Conventional Mop

		Microfiber Mop	Conventional Loop Map
Mop Cost			
	Initial Cost:	$17.40 each	$5.00 each
	Washing Lifetime:	500 to 1000*	55 to 200*
	Rooms Cleaned:	1	22
	Total Mop Costs	$1.75 to $3.48	$0.11 to $0.41
		Per 100 rooms	Per 100 rooms
Labor Costs			
	Rooms Cleaned/Day	22 in 8-hour shift	20 in 8-hour shift
	Hourly Rate Paid	$12 per hour	$12 per hour
	Total Labor Costs	$436	$480
		Per 100 rooms	Per 100 rooms
Chemical Use			
	Quantity	1 gallon/day	21 gallons/day
	Cost of Chemicals	$0.22/gallon	$0.22/gallon
	Rooms Cleaned/Day	22	20
	Total Chemical Costs	$1.00	$23.10
		Per 100 rooms	Per 100 rooms
Water Use			
	Quantity	1 gallon	21 gallons
	Rooms Cleaned	22	20
	Total Water Usage	5 gallons	105 gallons
		Per 100 rooms	Per 100 rooms
Electricity Usage in Wash Mops			
	Cost	$0.30 per mop	$1.00 per mop
	Cleaning Frequency	Once per room	Once per day
	Total Electric Costs	$30	$5
		Per 100 rooms	Per 100 rooms
Total of all Costs		$468 to $470	$508
		Per 100 rooms	Per 100 rooms

Total Savings for One Custodian Per Day: $38 to $40 per day
Total Savings for One Custodian Per Year: $13,870 to $14,600 per year*

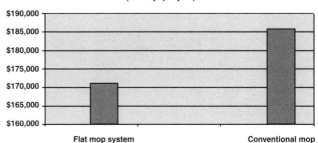

Annual Cost to Mop 100 Rooms
(365 days per year)

Source: Environmental Protection Agency: University of California Davis Medical Center.

Summary

The limitations that resulted from using microfiber mop heads were minor when compared to the benefits derived. Overall, the hospital found that microfiber flat mops were:

- Light and ergonomic
- More absorbent
- Dense and durable
- More effective for cleaning floor surfaces
- Cost-effective

They found that the floor mopping system was less work-intensive than conventional mopping, virtually eliminated cross-contamination, and drastically reduced chemical and water use while cleaning more effectively.

They also found that microfiber manufacturers underestimated the longevity of the mop heads. Use at UCDMC proved that the mop heads could withstand up to 1,000 washings, double the manufacturer's guarantees—all the more reason to change from conventional mops to microfiber flat mops and the new floor mopping system.

Robert Kravitz is a 30-year veteran of the janitorial industry. He has authored four books on the industry, lectures on JanSan and Internet issues, writes for several publications, and is a JanSan marketing and public relations consultant. He may be reached at rkravitz@rcnchicago.com.

APPENDIX I

ProTeam Articles

The articles included in this appendix are all variations on a theme: How can we become more effective and efficient at the task of cleaning? We start with David J. Frank, who reintroduces us to the father of scientific management, Frederic Taylor, and explains that Taylor's ideas are still relevant today. Then we hear from Jim Harris Sr., who declares that now is the time for the cleaning business to join the computer revolution; Jennifer C. Jones gives a detailed look at the latest activities at the Carpet and Rug Institute (CRI) and makes a very effective case for purchasing only those vacuums that have achieved CRI certification. Chris Murray presents a very compelling case to consider worker ergonomics when purchasing equipment if you want to keep your people happy and increase productivity. ProTeam, president Larry Shideler contributes two articles: one on vacuum filtration and another on the "Science of Suction" (in vacuums). John Walker explores the subject of team cleaning, which has boosted productivity in a number of operations. Finally, Robert Woellner dispels some old myths regarding vacuum cleaners and presents the results of a recent controlled study of vacuums and soil removal.

All of these articles are appearing through the generosity of Larry Shideler, president of ProTeam Inc. A sincere note of thanks to all those at ProTeam who assisted with this project.

Classic Management Science Drives New Clean Gains

By ProTeam

(This article is presented through the generosity of ProTeam Inc., a Boise, Idaho, manufacturer of backpack vacuum systems and sponsor of Team Cleaning Seminars.)

The quest for discovering how work can be best performed is nothing new. As the Industrial Revolution spawned large factories and assembly lines, prominent engineers and others began to analyze human behavior at work, in the interest of improving efficiency.

By the late 1800s, people like Frederic Taylor were analyzing tasks and human elements as if they were parts of a complex machine that could be fine-tuned for top performance. These early seeds of Scientific Management set the stage for continuing research aimed at increasing productivity. One remaining comical image of this era is that of the uptight industrial engineer—stopwatch, pen and clipboard in hand—huddling over workers and meticulously recording their every movement, to be incorporated into time and motion studies.

Yet, in truth, the core concepts of early scientific management were on the right track. Early proponents laid the groundwork for analytical approaches to workloading. Today, organizing work flows, information flows, and how people interact to fulfill job specifications are all proper domains of effective professional management. In particular, the model of breaking work into smaller pieces to be defined and performed by a team of "specialists" is not only current and useful, but also state-of-the-art in the science of cleaning. We inherited the principles of scientific management and have shaped them to meet human needs as well as production needs.

Cleaning by the Numbers

Modern managers in the contract cleaning industry have accomplished a revolution of their own by switching from traditional zone cleaning to more scientifically based specialized or team cleaning. Typical results show that zone cleaning is considerably less efficient than specialized cleaning methods. Specialists cover much greater floor space in the same period of time—and with higher overall quality of cleaning.

One of the main reasons for this high performance is that specialists know exactly what is expected of them since jobs and tasks are carefully delineated and training is systematized. Work patterns of workers are precisely routed for optimum efficiency. Guesswork and overlap are practically eliminated. The team of specialists operates like a well-oiled machine—in a sense, like the ideal model envisioned in early scientific management concepts. Also, breaking of tasks into definable, discrete units facilitates measurement, analysis, and improvements using computer software.

Multiply the Gains with Software

Just as specialized cleaning streamlines the flow of work, new computer software streamlines other technical aspects. As labor time standards for methods of cleaning become standardized, this information can be input into software for comparisons. Growing data is available on labor times for both zone cleaning and team or specialist cleaning methods (one source: ISSA—International Sanitary Supply Association 1-800-225-4772). Cost and labor analysis software is invaluable since it allows apples-to-apples comparisons between different methods of cleaning, and quantifies labor costs for different scenarios.

For example, one hospital determined that vacuuming specialists averaged 6000 to 10000 sq. ft. per hour using backpack vacuums and team cleaning, compared to 2500–3000 sq. ft. per hour using older zone methods and floor-based equipment. Workers performing light duty tasks (emptying waste containers and dusting) averaged 4000–6000 sq. ft. per hour using a team specialist approach versus 2500–3000 sq. ft. per hour with older techniques.

This kind of data can be recorded in interactive software and be used to extrapolate costs, generate bids, and demonstrate the cost-effectiveness of selected methods to customers.

Another computer advantage: Using software to project costs allows "experimentation" without capital expenditure. According to a Houston, TX–based distributor of janitorial supplies: "We use a computer program to compare the customer's existing program with the team cleaning approach we recommend. Initially, we take a survey of the building, and input the facility parameters—square footage, number of hours per shift, labor hourly rate, employees per shift, etc. Then we input the numbers required for team cleaning, show the reduction in labor and equipment, and generate a computer print out."

The results, he points out, can be dramatic. For example, in a 250,000 square foot office building, with an hourly rate of $5.40, if you increase the vacuum production *alone* from 6000 square feet an hour to 10000 square feet, the annual saving is $21,600 (based on a 20-day month). As he states, "When you show a customer that, you can be sure you have his attention."

High-Tech Bidding for Business

New third-party computer programs are invaluable to contractors for separating accurate estimates and producing convincing graphic presentations for the bidding process.

Some new software packages supply formatted templates, so the contractor simply plugs in numbers and basic information such as amount and types of floor to be cleaned, by what method, using what level of worker, and with what frequency. The contractor also fills in vacation time, projected sick pay, and other and equipment cost factors at increasing levels of detail, as needed to bid on a particular job. The program not only performs all calculations and itemizes results, produces easy-to-read charts and graphs—with suggestions on how to use in bid presentations.

Best of all, template-based software can be revised at a touch of the keyboard—literally. The user can vary the input to display "what-if" scenarios that satisfy a different set of assumptions. This permits instant rebidding when the customer suddenly changes the specs or when the contractor wants to show the prospect exactly how much can be saved (in time and in dollars) by cleaning the glass areas three times a week instead of five, or by using a backpack vacuum with a 14-inch floor tool rather than an 18-inch dust mop for cleaning vinyl flooring.

Similarly, templates and calculations can be rolled over for new jobs to produce estimates using variations of the prior calculations. In other words, the contractor is building his or her own database from every estimate to enable ever more precise estimates covering an ever wider choice of bid specifications, all available at a keystroke. We now have at our disposal hassle-free high-tech computer tools that help contractors organize work, manage information, streamline bidding, and refine the human/equipment/production/place equations to suit the needs and budgets of customers.

Seeing Is Believing and Controlling

New software packages often include a module for work scheduling. This fill-in-the-blanks onscreen approach enables managers to schedule work crews and routes, to generate printed work tickets for workers, and to monitor the status of job assignments. Of course, this work scheduling module connects directly to others for comprehensive billing, payroll and other key business functions. With the calendar screen in some programs, contractors can view scheduled tasks for an entire month—allowing effective planning and providing a means to show customers the comprehensive scope of the cleaning plan.

Modern scientific management means using computer capability to manage major projects, determine work schedules, track progress and costs, produce payroll and billing—all while improving accuracy and saving time. Managers can keep on top of the work, overseeing the business for maximum efficiency and productivity.

Besides the gains made possible by computer software applications, the new scientific approach as reflected in specialized cleaning adds hard-core gains on the floor, in daily actions.

Divide and Conquer the Work

The concept of creating a team of cleaning specialists gains power by harnessing individual focus and dedication. For example, cleaning tasks are organized into categories, typically four areas with a specialist for each: light duty, vacuuming, rest rooms, and utility. Each cleaning specialist is trained in the preferred procedures, products, and the proper equipment to be used to get the desired results. This automatically builds in consistency of method, uniformity and compatibility of cleaning products, and recommended work time frames based on known benchmarks.

Workers who specialize simply do *more* work faster. Workers learn the best and fastest ways to clean; they use the most efficient equipment. Efficiencies are gained individually and compounded by repeating the module of cleaning specialists throughout a given facility.

Modern software packages can help contractors demonstrate the savings inherent in using specialists for cleaning, and document their ability to tackle additional tasks within the same working budget due to the efficiencies gained using scientific management principles.

Conclusion

Scientific management has truly come of age in the cleaning industry as the principles of breaking work into bite-size pieces meets the computer's ability to process byte-size databases into usable decision-making information. It's transforming how cleaning is done and, in most instances, lowering its overall cost significantly. Make no mistake about the dimensions of the revolution: Contractors who remain aloof or resistive to the implications and applications of modern scientific management will dissolve in the heat of competition.

David J. Frank, the author of this article, has more then 12 years' experience in the sanitary supply industry. He is an active member of the International Sanitary Supply Association and the Building Service Contractors Association International. He is currently a marketing research consultant with ProTeam, Inc., a Boise, Idaho, manufacturer of backpack vacuum systems and sponsor of Team Cleaning Seminars. He can be reached at 303-770-6731.

Custodial Management in the Information Age

With the advent of bar codes, handheld readers, and appropriate software, modern technology has finally reached the custodial department. Why computerize? Read on.

By Jim Harris Sr., CBSE

(This article is presented through the generosity of ProTeam Inc., a Boise, Idaho, manufacturer of backpack vacuum systems and sponsor of Team Cleaning Seminars.)

Delivering high-quality services, increasing productivity, and managing resources cost-efficiently are issues faced by all businesses. The challenge to custodial service providers is keeping up with job activity and inventory data retrieval, analysis, and application. As with many challenges today, the solution can be found in technology. Electronic data collection and tracking systems using bar code technology make the gathering and sound use of information easier.

Bar coding was introduced in the 1970s, and today it is an important part of many business operations. The bars, which vary in width and spacing, represent the binary digits 0 and 1. A string of digits functions as a unit and assigns a unique identification code to an item.

Though still in its infancy in the custodial management process, a bar coding system can offer a level of data integrity previously unobtainable with manual systems. Many feel this will become the new industrystandard technology for data management.

Bar code labels are placed in areas to be monitored such as offices, classrooms, patient rooms, hotel rooms, elevators, or even storerooms; or on objects to be monitored, from backpack vacuums to vehicles. Scanning the label with a handheld bar code reader activates the system. Readers are programmed and can be reprogrammed to prompt for answers to many specific questions each time a bar code is scanned.

For example, to start a room inspection, a manager swipes a bar code sticker attached to a door jamb. The bar code reader asks if trash was emptied, dusting completed, vacuuming done, furniture rearranged, etc. Yes or no answers are entered. By also assigning numeric values to cleanliness, bar code readers enable measuring levels of clean, in effect not only asking, "Was the work done?" but "How well was it done?" A detailed inspection may take less than a minute and results for that room remain in the unit for processing.

Workers who carry bar code readers can scan a separate bar code to inform the system of their progress at a specific time during the shift, increasing accountability and scheduling precision. In a team cleaning scenario, the vacuuming specialist can also act as inspector for the light duty specialist preceding him/her.

The information collected on the portable readers is easily transferred to and from a personal computer through a simple modem connection to a telephone line, or via mobile phone.

Once data is uploaded, proprietary software can delineate results by supervisor, employee, building, floor, or other variables, providing meaningful analysis and reports of worker performance, building cleanliness, or other important benchmarks.

It can also help catch small problems before they become big. For example, if the data indicates a worker is moving too slowly in some areas and running out of time before completing his entire work circuit, managers can pinpoint where the slowdown occurs, how the worker compares to others doing the same or similar jobs, and provide additional training as and where needed.

Ultimately, the process can provide a full audit trail of essential information including the time and date of input, providing a high level of detailed reporting for analysis. Integrated software prints information as pie charts, bar graphs, spreadsheets or customized formats.

Bar Code System Advantages for Custodial Performance Management

- Measuring, tracking and improving quality of custodial services;
- Creating accountability;
- Measuring, reassessing and maximizing staff productivity; and
- Improving staff performance through better management of their skills and time.

Bar coding systems customized to your situation and goals can be effective tools to address specific, localized needs. They can also be integrated into organization-wide information systems to relay data throughout by e-mail or intranet. Uses include facilities management, construction, plant operations, grounds, and security.

High-speed bar code processing units come with versatile software programs. Here are some examples:

Computer-aided cleaning management. An overall program that keeps track of an entire operation, including personnel, assets and resources is the computer-aided cleaning management system. State-of-the-art offerings, such as Innovise Software's recently updated Comtrac 3, have internet and intranet capabilities and provide a comprehensive range of performance reports to help identify consistent area of weakness and strength. Capabilities include fast mobile phone messaging and data transfer.

The system enables the use of bar codes to speed the collection and processing of service quality and performance data, and helps ensure scheduling accuracy by recording the time, whereabouts and actions of employees and system users. It also tracks nonconformance and management response, measures productivity, processes work orders and maintains employee-training records.

Use of the information enables development of employee skills, human resource profiles, training and pictorial work schedules specific to each employee's need and routine.

Computer-aided asset tracking. Asset tracking systems help manage fixed and moveable assets, using hand-held readers and bar-code data to identify and track movement, service schedules and maintenance costs. For example, the system checks the location of the asset against the listed location to produce a variation report showing which assets have been misplaced, lost, or found. It enables you to monitor maintenance costs by asset, asset group, employee, category, and/or location. It also maintains an asset register, automatically logging preassigned asset values. Frequency, nature, and cost of repairs can be tracked for each asset, allowing for better maintenance or purchasing decisions in the future.

Programs are capable of handling multiple categories, allowing the management of many different asset types, and possess an asset search function. Equipped with the right data, you have the ability to maximize maintenance and reduce replacement frequencies and costs. With the latest systems, such as AssetTRAC, you also can create new maintenance routines and automatically compile planned preventive maintenance schedules.

Computer-aided stock management. Stock management bar coding and software programs can produce a wide variety of standard reports and analyze expenditure, revenue flow, allocation and use.

With portable bar code readers, you can perform stock audits, enter stock requisitions and factor in OSHA criteria in preparation for external audits of hazardous chemicals handling. Advances, such as the StockWATCH system, maintain inventory levels and flow for multiple stock rooms or warehouses, automatically reordering inventory when it falls below user-defined minimums. It also batches and processes purchase orders and special delivery notes.

Other advantages include the ability to process both consumable and rechargeable requisitions. A function for just-in-time ordering minimizes stockpiling.

Delivering High Quality Services

Bar coding is easy, quick, efficient and affordable. The cost savings can be significant using industry-leading software programs and technology, and when combined with proven systems of facility management, operations and cleaning. The result is a more predictable flow of information that gives managers greater control over precious resources.

Jim Harris Sr. is CEO of Concepts IV, a cleaning management and consulting group specializing in Team Cleaning training and computer-aided custodial management systems. For more information, contact him at 518-1456-7100 or e-mail: Jim@teamcleaning.com.

Raising the Bar for Vacuum Effectiveness

By Jennifer C. Jones

(This article is presented through the generosity of ProTeam Inc., a Boise, Idaho, manufacturer of backpack vacuum systems and sponsor of Team Cleaning Seminars.)

When the telephone rings at the Carpet and Rug Institute, it's often a consumer with a question. One of the most frequently asked is, "Which vacuum is best?" In the past, the answer depended upon whom you asked.

"Consumers want to take care of their carpets," says Michael Hilton, CRI's Technical Services Associate. "Vacuum marketing can be confusing. Consumers are confused about HEPA filtration, twelve amps vs. ten. Some vacuum manufacturers are making ridiculous claims about how they filtered when they didn't remove any dirt. If you don't remove anything, there's nothing to filter!"

According to Hilton, CRI members wondered about vacuum IAQ efficiencies. Schools were a special area of concern. Were children and cleaning workers being exposed to unacceptable levels of airborne particulate stirred up by vacuum cleaners?

In addition, many carpet manufacturers were branching out into carpet maintenance as well. Some of these members wondered which vacuum products to recommend to their customers or to purchase themselves.

CRI decided perhaps it was time to go looking for some more definitive answers. The Institute began work on a voluntary testing program that would allow vacuum manufacturers to test their products in three categories: soil removal, particulate emissions, and wear testing.

Carpet manufacturers welcomed the idea with open arms. "We were looking at it primarily from the fiber standpoint," says DuPont's Alan Luedtke, Product Steward for DuPont's nylon flooring systems. "Within the last ten years we've made a pretty dramatic push about how our products are used by our customers. Historically, there's never been much you could hang your hat on other than (vacuum) manufacturer claims," he says.

Dr. Howard Elder is Director of Research and Environmental Affairs for J and J Industries. "We want to provide carpet products that are environmentally friendly, including adhesives and pads. One part that's been missing is the cleaning system," he says. "We are marketing an entire system to the consumer, and that includes cleaning. As manufacturers, we want to have the entire package available to the consumer."

According to Elder, J and J's primary interest was not necessarily how much soil a certain vacuum brand would remove. "What we really want to do is understand something about how vacuum cleaners allow particles to escape into the air and be breathed," he says.

Both men felt a vacuum test conducted by the CRI, instead of individual manufacturers, would benefit carpet manufacturers. "It's not as fragmented to the consumer," says Howard Elder.

While the carpet side of manufacturing was generally supportive of the testing idea, vacuum manufacturers were much less enthusiastic. A majority of those first approached by CRI refused to participate. But a small core of vacuum makers saw the testing as a golden opportunity to promote and improve their products.

Castex was one of those companies. Mark Wierda, Key Account Sales Manager, explains why. "We see that vacuuming is the first line of defense in a good cleaning system. Most people, whether it's schools, hospitals or businesses, don't do a very good job vacuuming. Either they don't have the proper equipment or the proper program."

Michael Grubb, U.S. Sales Manager for Lindsay Manufacturing, says his company is fighting for better consumer education. "It's important that we don't just use a bunch of hype," he says. "If you're going to use hype, you better be able to back it up with good results."

ProTeam, a backpack vacuum manufacturer, was happy the industry was finally taking a hard look at IAQ. "In ProTeam's case, filtration has always been one of the biggest keys with us," says Richard Coombs, the company's Engineering Manager. We concentrate so much on filter efficiency."

Other vacuum manufacturers are also participating in the study. CRI officials wanted a good mix of vacuum models—everything from central vacuuming systems to backpacks and uprights. The Institute included models that could be purchased at local discount stores as well as commercial grade systems. Now CRI was ready to start establishing a benchmark for the testing. Mark Wierda sums it up: "Draw the line where ever you want, and we'll meet those standards."

It took vacuum and carpet manufacturers, as well as CRI officials, months to develop what they felt was an effective testing protocol. Michael Hilton recalls, "We didn't want to set something so easy everybody passed, or so tough the consumer would only have one or two options." CRI was also sensitive to the potential damage to manufacturers whose products failed the test. For that reason, each product was assigned an ID number, not a name, during the testing. In addition, the Institute decided not to release the test results. Using their ID numbers, manufacturers can get the results for their products only, not their competitors'.

Consumers who call with questions are told only that a machine passed. If a certain model fails the test, the consumer is told there is no information available on that vacuum. Machines are not rated in comparison to one another—only in comparison to the test benchmark. Vacuums receive a Pass/Fail rating. In order to pass, the machine must meet acceptable levels in all three test areas: soil removal, emissions, and wear.

The testing would be conducted at an independent laboratory—Dalton, Georgia's Professional Testing Labs—and monitored by three peer reviewers. The reviewers, Dr. Michael Barry, former Deputy Director of the EPA; Dr. Barry Ryan, Emory University, and Cornell's Dr. Alan Hedge were selected. CRI chose the men for their reputation in environmental research and testing.

The peer reviewers were responsible for examining the protocol and evaluating it from an unbiased perspective. CRI asked this team to provide input and direction, based on their technical skills. The peer review group observed the testing, analyzed the results, and recommended where the pass/fail levels should be established.

The testing protocol itself was designed to be as accurate as possible. The Institute used 400 square inch samples of both cut and looped pile carpets. For the soil removal test, the carpet sample was first weighed and then attached to the side of a cylinder. The special cylinder spread a mixture of soil somewhat like a salt and pepper shaker, dispensing $\frac{1}{10}$ of a gram of soil per square inch of carpet. CRI chose 540 Wedron sand for this test—a mix similar to that used in earlier ASTM testing, only without the addition of talc. "It's a very heavy sand and difficult to remove," says Hilton.

Next the sample is placed on a table with the vacuum locked into position on top. The table moves the carpet sample back and forth at a rate of 1.8 feet per second. The vacuum makes just four passes. The carpet test sample is removed and weighed once again to determine the amount of soil that has been captured. Contents of the vacuum bag are also measured.

Emissions testing was conducted in a state-of-the-art environmental chamber with no outside air flow. The carpet sample is once again positioned on a moving table. The vacuum is stationary. Researchers used 5 grams of ISO fine road dust as the soil base. Each vacuum was operated for ten minutes. A special sampling device measured particulate emissions at approximately five feet above the floor—a cleaning worker's breathing zone. The emphasis in this test was not the average emissions release. Instead, the test marked how much particulate was put in the air as soon as the vacuuming started. "It's going to spike when you first start the vacuum," Michael says. "It's going to jump as high as it's ever going to get, then it's going to drop off. We're concerned about the high point, not the average."

For wear testing, the CRI relied on a black and white photographic scale. Each vacuum made 200 passes across the carpet sample, moving at 1.8 feet per second. Then researchers compared the carpet sample to a photograph of the benchmark sample. They compared color and texture changes to determine a pass or fail rating.

Those who helped develop the testing protocol say this test is substantially different from earlier vacuum research. "We used some existing protocols and got as much as a 65% variation in results," says CRI's Michael Hilton. "The speed at which you pull the vacuum cleaner could produce about a 400% variation. That's why we locked the vacuum in place and put a tachometer on the table that moved back and forth."

Alan Luedtke says simple changes made a big difference in the credibility of the test. "What this test brings is better reproducibility. It will allow you to look at the relative performance."

Lindsay's Michael Grubb says the CRI program represents a new generation of testing. "Cleanability results were determined years ago by ASTM. The problem is, the carpet used at that time is almost gone. Issues like emissions and wearability have never been addressed."

ProTeam believes this test comes closer to real world conditions than other vacuum research. "The more I worked with the protocol the more I agreed with it," says Richard Coombs. "ASTM says you make ten passes. Who does that in the real world? CRI went a little bit beyond. They cut it back to four."

The result of all this testing is the award of CRI's Green Label. Vacuums that pass the test are allowed to display the special label certifying that they meet certain performance standards. "If you're on the approved list, that's the ultimate, the best you can get," says Grubb. "You can see how effective a marketing tool that could be."

With results only just beginning to be analyzed, there have been plenty of surprises. Less than half of the vacuums tested passed all three categories. Nevertheless, vacuum manufacturers remain undaunted. "We have the ability here to set a standard for vacuum cleaners which has never been done before," says Mark Wierda, "Manufacturers can look at the vacuum and determine what it would take to meet the criteria, decide whether it was worth it to modify the vacuum or start a whole new product."

"We have to find where our weak spots are," says ProTeam's Coombs. In spite of the fact the backpack had superior filtration results, the company rented the test lab for two additional days, at their own expense, to conduct even more testing. "We have to know which tool works best on which type of carpet," says Coombs, "That allows us to help our customers."

Michael Grubb says, "I believe no matter how it comes out, even if we should fail one of the tests, all that does is encourage us to improve our equipment."

That's exactly what CRI hoped would happen. "We're not out to get anybody," says Michael Hilton. "If a manufacturer submits and fails, they'll be able to go back and reengineer and retool."

DuPont's Luedtke says it's possible the Green Label program may change carpet manufacturers' cleaning recommendations. Right now the company is taking a "wait and see" position.

Test participants predict the consumer will be the big winner. "I would hope the consumers, once they find out about the Green Label program, would be a little stingy and only use products that meet the guidelines," notes Hilton.

"If you buy a vacuum with this certification on it, you're going to be assured the machine will remove the dirt, not put a lot of emission in the air, and not harm your carpet over a long period of time," says Mark Wierda.

That, says Alan Luedtke, will result in happy consumers and better-looking, longer-lasting carpet products.

Ergonomics and Backpack Vacs

By Chris Murray

(This article is presented through the generosity of ProTeam Inc., a Boise, Idaho, manufacturer of backpack vacuum systems and sponsor of Team Cleaning Seminars.)

Ergonomics involves making workers *comfortable and safe* while they work, by designing equipment and processes that integrate with the body to allow low-stress activity for extended periods. However, the definition of ergonomics is much broader. According to OSHA's (Occupational Safety & Health Administration) "Advance Notice of Proposed Rulemaking for Ergonomic Safety and Health Management," 57FR34192, August 3, 1992: "Ergonomics seeks to fit the job to the person rather than the person to the job. The aim of the discipline is to prevent the development of occupational disorders and to reduce the potential for fatigue, error, or unsafe acts through the evaluation and design of facilities, environments, jobs, tasks, tools, equipment, processes, and training methods to match the capabilities of specific workers."

For this discussion, we'll focus on equipment, process, and training aspects related to backpack vacuum cleaners that facilitate good ergonomics and high productivity levels.

New Equipment Design: Building for Bodies and Productivity

Ergonomically sound design in backpack vacuums is vital because of the close physical relationship between a backpack and its user. While using backpacks is not new—think of footsoldiers, mountaineers, and mothers of toddlers—technology has made it easier. The mobility of backpack vacuums has increased productivity (the ISSA, International Sanitary Supply Association, estimates backpack vacuuming with a 14-inch tool allows cleaning 10,169 sq. ft. of floor surface per hour).

Engineers have reduced weight and improved harness design to make the vac more comfortable to wear. Some early backpack vacs had bulky steel bodies, clumsy harnesses, and weighed 20–30 pounds. Cylindrical design, modern materials, and efficient motors have pared the weight of many backpack vacs to under 10 pounds. Aluminum floor wands are lightweight and easily handled. Padded and contoured shoulder straps and waist belts distribute weight evenly around the hips. Adjustable backplates and harnesses allow custom-fitting the tool to the worker.

The Design Process: Harnessing Comfort

As opposed to carrying an object with hand and arm, carrying objects on your back helps maintain balance and distribute weight equally to the body. Current backpack harness design, however, has less to do with the back, and more to do with the hips. Weight is transferred to the hips using a padded belt connected to the lower part of the backpack and secured around the user's waist. Shoulder straps, far from being a way to "hang" the pack on yourself, simply keep the pack from twisting or rotating.

Field studies show that shoulder straps should be curved in a natural position that does not interfere with the motions associated with vacuuming. In the field, conventional straps were reshaped from the straight position they were manufactured in to a curved position. After hours of use, operator motion while wearing the product formed the strap into a new shape. By analyzing this shape, engineers fashioned a form-fitted part, improving comfort.

Improving the Work Process: Team Methods

A 1993 NIOSH (National Institute for Occupational Safety and Health) report on backpack vacuums used at the Travelers' Insurance complex in Hartford, Conn., concluded, in part, that workers should be properly trained to use the equipment. The report also stressed that backpack fit, use, and worker complaints should be monitored and corrected, and workers be allowed some flexibility in choice of equipment.

Team cleaning seminars—focused on creating backpack vacuuming specialists as part of an integrated cleaning "team"—teach operators how to avoid unnecessary bending (a basic tenet of good lifting) and optimize labor. By training workers as specialists, operators become skilled, accustomed to the equipment, and most productive. Rotation of workers prevents burn out, and cross-trains the group. Of course, permanent specialists can be selected based on their aptitude or preference for tasks. You may wish to select backpack vacuuming specialists from among those who "take to" the process and enjoy using the equipment.

Ergonomic Training: Fit and Technique

It's crucial that any specialized tool be used properly, especially one attached to your body. Backpack vacuums must be worn and used properly for maximum comfort. The padded waist belt should fasten snugly around the hips, allowing shoulder straps to fit comfortably but loosely. The primary weight of the unit should rest on the hips, not the shoulders, since shoulder straps serve mainly to balance the pack and prevent load shifting. The backplate—a ventilated panel that rests against the operator's back and supports the vacuum unit—if adjustable, should be positioned according to the height of the operator. Backplate adjustment raises or lowers the vacuum relative to the operator to facilitate a range of torso sizes for convenient movement and use.

The upper body should stay upright with little twisting during backpack vacuuming.

For maximum productivity without fatigue, a side-to-side fanning technique with a lightweight aluminum vacuuming wand (a motion similar to mopping) allows rapid vacuuming without back bending or other biomechanical stress. Workers who can mop a floor without undue fatigue or discomfort are able to use a backpack vacuum using a similar motion for long periods.

When vacuuming underneath large desks or other furnishings, vacuumers should bend their knees rather than their backs. By bending at the knees, and using the vacuuming wand to get into hard to reach areas, no undue demands are placed on the back.

An often-neglected technique that makes vacuuming both easier and more effective is keeping the vac bag emptied. Emptying the bag frequently lightens the unit, keeps filter pores clean to trap maximum dust, and maintains airflow for good suction and motor cooling.

Knowing these simple techniques isn't enough, however. Vacuumers need time to adapt to new equipment and develop the right habits. Workers require hands on training and a practice session or two to get the feel of the backpack, and learn to use the tool without improper bending, twisting, or lifting. Observe workers, monitor complaints if any, and coach them in correct technique by studying your best vacuumers. Teach them to emulate methods that work.

Physical Fitness

Sometimes equipment, process, or technique is not at fault when workers experience discomfort or fatigue on the job. A lack of physical fitness is often the problem. Blaming cleaning tools or tasks for fatigue and discomfort in poorly conditioned workers is like blaming the road for the breakdown of a poorly maintained automobile.

Many corporations in industrialized nations, including those in the U.S. and Japan, encourage workers to exercise regularly since fit workers are more productive, injury and stress-resistant. Could cleaning and maintenance personnel benefit from company sponsored exercise programs? Could this reduce the number of "ergonomic complaints"? The answer is yes.

Exercises that strengthen the arms and legs, abdominal muscles, and lower back, are especially helpful for workers who perform tasks involving physical exertion, such as scrubbing or mopping floors, operating backpack vacuums, and emptying or carrying solution-laden mop buckets. Cardiovascular training via aerobic workouts increases endurance and mental alertness, traits vital to good cleaning.

Plainly, ergonomics is a broad discipline involving both the health of the worker and the design of equipment and processes the worker encounters. Optimizing conditions in a multifaceted approach dealing with the full reality, makes sense. Employees equipped with the right ergonomically designed equipment, processes, technique and physical training will not only feel better, they'll clean better. Like a customized exercise program, the results are worth the effort.

Chris Murray is an engineer working with ProTeam, Inc., Boise, Idaho, a backpack vacuum manufacturer and sponsor of Team Cleaning Seminars. For more information, call 208-378-0716.

What Your Customers Need to Know about Vacuum Filtration

By Larry Shideler

(This article is presented through the generosity of ProTeam Inc., a Boise, Idaho, manufacturer of backpack vacuum systems and sponsor of Team Cleaning Seminars.)

The use of *efficient vacuum cleaners and filters* can significantly improve indoor air quality (IAQ), according to an Environmental Protection Agency (EPA) study. The one-year study, conducted at the Frank Porter Graham Child Development Center in Chapel Hill, North Carolina, found that efficient vacuum cleaners, along with an organized cleaning program, can greatly reduce the level of dust, bacteria, and fungi found in carpet and ambient air.

The study is important, EPA Research Analyst Jeff Bishop said, "because it provides authentic baseline information on how specifically to improve indoor air quality with relatively simple maintenance."

Interestingly, the study found that surface and carpet levels of dust and bacteria correlate with airborne levels, showing that dust distributes itself evenly within a facility, and that the proverbial "white glove test" has validity in determining not only cleaning quality but overall IAQ levels. Important among methods of reducing whole building dust levels was the use of high-efficiency vacuum bags or filters.

Filter Factors

Few cleaning processes are as important to IAQ as vacuuming, and few internal steps are as important to the process as vacuum filtration. Without proper filters to catch dust, fine particulate is blown through the filter media and into the ambient environment. A vital factor to assess in choosing a vacuum filter is both the size of dust particles—measured in microns—and the quantity of dust particles removed from the vacuum's airflow.

Microns Matter

A micron is one millionth of a meter, 1/70th the thickness of a human hair. Single dust particles smaller than 10 microns are so tiny they are virtually invisible.

When the main interest was in removing *visible* dirt, traditional cloth or paper bags filtering down to 10 microns were widely used. Vacuums that could effectively remove particles smaller than that were considered specialty items—valued only for stringent applications like computer data centers.

Now buildings are "tighter"—with less air exchange to dilute airborne dust—and people are reacting to the respirable particles (mostly ranging between 1 and 10

microns) they are breathing in many energy efficient facilities. Statistics indicate 50 million Americans, one of every five people, suffer from allergen-related diseases. Many allergic reactions are caused by airborne carpet and upholstery fibers, pet dander, molds, spores, dust, dirt, bacteria, and the feces and body parts of dustmites, dispersed by inefficient vacuuming.

While many filters remove dust down to one micron, the critical question is, how much one micron dust is captured? Less desirable filter arrangements may capture only 30% of one micron particles, while better filter configurations allow removing 99% or more of those particles. That brings us to the issue of filter *efficiency*.

Efficiency

"Filter efficiency"—expressed as a percentage—denotes how much dust of a particular size a filter captures. For example, a filter that is 95% efficient at one micron, catches 95% of all particles that size.

By contrast, an advertised "1 micron filter" (capable of removing particles as small as 1 micron) may be retaining only 30 percent of all 1 micron particles, while the remaining 70 percent pass through the filter and escape. That filter would have a 30 percent efficiency rating at one micron. Conversely, if the filter arrangement removed 99 percent of all 1 micron particles, it would have an efficiency rating of 99 percent. Typically, old-style cloth bags have an efficiency rating of only about 30 percent at one micron.

Airflow Issues

Airflow and air volume create suction, traits relating closely to effective filtration, since dust must be adequately pulled into the filter's mesh without being pulled *through* the media by too much pressure. An integral part of the vacuum's operating system, filters are only effective when they are carefully proportioned to the airflow and volume created by the vacuum motor's fan. The filter *media* is also critical since material that catches fine dust must "breathe"—letting air pass through—to create sustained suction and cleaning ability. As you can imagine, developing materials that trap the finest dust while sustaining airflow is the goal of vacuuming engineers. Fortunately, there are several successful filter options that meet this need, depending on the intended application.

The Right Filters

In the past, when the main concern was the removal and capture of large noticeable debris and dust, old-style cloth or paper bags were considered adequate. However, with the current emphasis on IAQ and building wellness, a higher degree of filtration, usually in the form of layered micro filter media [this media is now used by a number of manufacturers of vacuum cleaners]—highefficiency filters of several layers—is necessary to effectively remove and retain contaminants smaller than 10 microns.

Micro filters greatly increase vacuum efficiency. One study showed that a standard paper filter bag removed only 39.9 percent of debris 10 microns in size, while a micro filter bag removed over 99% of these particles. Likewise, a standard paper filter bag removed only 16.3% of 1 micron particles, whereas micro filters in two to four-stage configurations removed 95–96% of one micron debris. For this reason, micro filters are now increasingly used in commercial vacuuming applications.

Even greater filtration can be achieved with high filtration disc media.

Tests show this filter medium captures 99.79% of .3-micron particles (near HEPA efficiency) at a fraction of the cost of HEPA filters. The medium also removes 99.98% of 2-micron and 99.96% of 1-micron particles.

More sensitive vacuuming applications require high-efficiency particulate air (HEPA) or ultra-low-penetration air (ULPA) filters. More costly than standard or micro filter bags or high filtration discs, both HEPA and ULPA filters are designed to remove more than 99 percent of superfine particles. HEPA filters remove 99.97 percent of particles .3-micron and larger in size. ULPA filters are even more efficient, removing 99.999 percent of .12-micron and larger particles. Both—typically installed as secondary filters "behind" primary filters that catch larger "gross" dust—rely on numerous brain-like folds or corrugations of filter media creating tremendous surface area in a relatively small package to trap fine contaminants without substantially restricting airflow. Watch out for ads for HEPA filtration, however, since many manufacturers' claims are nothing more than marketing hype. True HEPA filtration requires balancing sufficient filter media with vacuum airflow.

Ensuring Sustained Suction

Old-style cloth and paper vacuum bags catch pollens, plant spores, and visible dust. Yet, particles quickly clog the pores of these filters, restricting airflow and significantly reducing suction. As a result, vacuuming is less effective. More debris is left in the carpet or on the floor or—agitated by a beater brush—it is broken up and dispersed into the surrounding environment.

The use of micro filter technology has alleviated this problem to a large extent. Note the chart showing suction loss using a standard paper filter bag versus a bag composed of micro filter material when vacuuming 20–120 grams of fine road dust.

Suction Loss
Standard Dust Bag vs. Micro Liner

Grams of Road Dust	Standard	Micro-Linear
20	20.1%	2.1%
40	33.3%	5.3%
60	38.4%	6.1%
80	43.6%	9.2%
100	49.2%	12.2%
120	55.6%	15.8%

Despite the advances in vacuuming technology and filtration, one element of vacuuming is potentially more critical to maintaining good filtration than any other.

The Critical Vacuuming Part (People)

Having selected an appropriate filter combination for your application, the key to maintaining adequate suction and filtration is filter *maintenance*. Today's filters—as opposed to the old style disposable single-layer paper bags—can be cleaned and reused several times, and vacuum technicians should be encouraged to do this on a regular basis, perhaps as often as every 30 minutes to two hours of vacuum time, depending on the soil conditions. Regular cleaning maintains suction and prolongs the life of the filter and the vacuum cleaner, resulting in more effective vacuuming and ensuring a healthier, more comfortable environment. Regular inspection of filters also allows detecting punctures that allow fine dust to pass through and contaminate the room. Clearly, beyond equipment, ensuring effective vacuuming and filtration means training and educating the *people* using the tools.

Larry Shideler is CEO/President of ProTeam, Inc., Boise, Idaho, a manufacturer of high-efficiency filtration backpack, hip-style, cannister, and upright vacuums and more.

The Science of Suction

By Larry Shideler

(This article is presented through the generosity of ProTeam Inc., a Boise, Idaho, manufacturer of backpack vacuum systems and sponsor of Team Cleaning Seminars.)

Vacuum cleaner suction is negative airflow that removes dirt from carpeting, fabric, and other surfaces. This is achieved using an internal fan rotating at high speed to create a partial vacuum, causing air at the tool head to rush to "fill" the vacuum—sweeping away debris in its path as it does so.

Removable soil must have sufficient air resistance to be caught in the airflow, making suction effective. Difficulties with removing certain kinds of soil stem largely from either its low relative air resistance (fine powders, soot, chalk dust), adherence to the surface (mud, lint), and/or low negative airflow or suction at the tool head.

Suction Variables

Suction is a product of several variables. Ideally, the internal fan is powered and proportioned to create "vacuum" for moving or suctioning a desired volume of air (measured as CFM—cubic feet per minute) in relation to the size of the tool head, the diameter and length of the airflow conduit (hose and internal air channel), and the type, size, and configuration of filter media.

Of course, proper air volume and suction would be simpler to achieve and maintain if filtering the air and retaining the dirt weren't necessary. Without filter media (cloth and/or paper bags, HEPA, ULPA, and secondary types) to screen and hold particulate of various sizes, air passing through a vacuum cleaner would meet little resistances—suction would remain constant. The room environment would also be dirtier than ever, since dust removed from one end of the vac would simply be blown out the exhaust end.

Until recently, this occurred too frequently. Vacuum cleaner manufacturers sold equipment based largely on suction power and ease-of-pickup. Filters were "airy" and inefficient, trapping bigger particles (10 microns plus), while hefty motors and fans pumped fine particulate out the back of the unit. Exhausted particles increased the need for dusting and cleaning, prematurely clogged HVAC filters, and created allergic reactions in building occupants. Plainly, not all suction is *effective* suction.

Effective Suction—A System Approach

Effective suction is a product of an intelligent system—one that permits constant airflow with practical filtration to trap particles of soil, large or small. Hence, trying to assess the *performance* of vacuum cleaners by individually comparing CFM numbers, amp ratings, filter type or size, etc., is at best a "part smart" approach. It's how all the components work together that makes the vacuum work, not any one separately. The key component in a vacuuming system is the relationship between airflow and filtration—and the two are somewhat at odds.

Suction and Filtrations: Tips for Success

Excellent suction and excellent filtration sometimes form an uneasy alliance. High-efficiency filters that trap more fine particles often tend to clog more rapidly, choking airflow and suction, and lowering cleaning ability. Good filters, unless *cleaned* or replaced regularly, reduce vacuum performance.

Filter efficiency, filter access, and filter maintenance are important issues related to suction. Since indoor air quality affects both health and housekeeping concerns consider a four-stage system that filters at least 95–99% of dust down to one micron—most airborne dust falls into the one to ten micron range. Secondly, look for a vacuum that permits easy filter maintenance (if filters are difficult to change, operators will tend to allow them to clog reducing suction). Third, train operators to clean vacuum filters regularly (after every few hours of vacuuming or as needed to maintain optimum airflow and suction).

Conclusion

Effective suction is a product of the right vacuuming *system*, rather than any single element. So don't be drawn into a discussion about whose vacuum has the most suction. It's like evaluating a car based on which engine is bigger, and forgetting all about the suspension, the transmission, the tires, the brakes, the drivetrain, and of course, the driver!

A quality vacuum with a qualified operator is like a high-performance car with a skilled driver. A fine car, driven well, will reach its destination quickly and safely. Vacuuming programs arrive, when operators understand that effective suction is achieved through a combination of the right machine and the right maintenance to maximize performance.

Larry Shideler is President of ProTeam, Inc., Boise, Idaho, a manufacturer of four-stage filtration backpack vacuum cleaners.

Exceeding Customer Expectations and Building Profit Margins with Team Cleaning

By John Walker, ManageMen

(This article is presented through the generosity of ProTeam Inc., a Boise, Idaho, manufacturer of backpack vacuum systems and sponsor of Team Cleaning Seminars.)

Distributors can exceed expectations for value-added service combined with savings by empowering customer staff with team cleaning. Implementing team cleaning means training and deploying task specialists to clean a facility by using "assembly line" methods, sequencing workers and tasks for maximum productivity and quality.

A team, however, doesn't become a precision machine through random effort; well-defined roles for each member are essential, and those jobs must be integrated and balanced to achieve objectives.

"Team cleaning represents an absolute commitment to serve your customer," according to Jeff Rosenstein of Diversified Supply, Humble, TX, "We go in and redesign their operations plan and the way they clean."

Your function as a value-added distributor can be to assist customers in setting up teams, and recommending equipment that facilitates a team approach. Equipment manufacturers, who promote team cleaning, can also provide considerable help.

Team cleaning initially involves assessing tasks needed to produce a clean building, then distributing the workload among specialists or team members. "Instead of having one person responsible for numerous tasks, we have individuals responsible for certain tasks. It makes workers far more efficient and productive," Rosenstein says.

Specialists perform tasks better and with greater speed, and combining their respective complementary skills in the proper sequence produces time and quality benefits. When each staff member performs his/her specialty throughout a facility without interruption, momentum and straight-line efficiency are maintained.

Workloading with team cleaning typically involves four basic specialists comprising a team, who work from point-A-to-point-B covering maximum ground: 1) a light-duty specialist to empty trash, dust horizontal and vertical surfaces, clean telephones, etc., 2) a vacuum specialist equipped with a backpack unit for multiple surface cleaning who follows 30 minutes behind the first team member, spot-checks the work of the previous worker, turns out lights and secures the area, 3) a restroom specialist who also cleans hallway water fountains and other designated areas, and 4) a utility specialist who cleans and buffs floors, details entrance glass, etc.

Tools which enable multitasking—that is, performing several related functions simultaneously—optimize the team cleaning method. Modern backpack vacuum systems actually fostered the idea for and especially lend themselves to team cleaning applications. With an excellent power-to-weight ratio, suction-only backpacks, permit carpet, hard floor, stairwell and detail cleaning in one pass, with greater soil removal than conventional systems. Sealed four-stage filtration captures more dust than other systems, and reduces IAQ problems.

Lightweight backpacks increase efficiency by enabling one trained individual—the vacuum specialist—to clean up to 10,000 square feet per hour, simplifying team duties by consolidating work.

Here are examples of simple, effective products that can help your customers integrate team cleaning with four basic specialists.

- *Light-Duty Specialist—Dedicated to dusting, spot-cleaning, and emptying trash*

Suggestions: A mobile waste collection system such as a resin-molded polyethylene refuse barrel equipped with wheels and fitted with a wrap-around apron or caddy with pockets for holding spot-cleaning spray solution, dusting cloths, and poly liners of various sizes.

Application: Light-duty specialist rolls the waste collector and tools directly to the location where needed, dusts, spot-cleans, empties trash and replaces liners in fluid motions, then rolls/moves to next location.

- *Vacuum Specialist—Dedicated to vacuuming carpeting, hard floors, upholstery, other surfaces*

Suggestions: Lightweight backpack vacuuming system with four-stage filtration, ergonomic design and harness for distributing weight across hips, and strap-mounted attachments.

Application: Vacuum specialist works systematically throughout the facility, using a side-to-side six-foot fanning technique with a lightweight vacuuming wand to clean carpeted and hard floor areas with minimal fatigue. Multi-tasking—performing several tasks in one trip with the same equipment—streamlines vacuuming throughout the building. With simple tool changes, this worker can clean upholstery, carpet edges, corners, stairwells, A/C vents, etc., according to the building's cleaning specifications. Sealed four-stage filters in one-piece backpacks capture more dust than unsealed systems, enhancing indoor air quality and reducing dusting.

- *Restroom Specialist—Dedicated to cleaning and sanitizing restroom fixtures and floors, and drinking fountains*

Suggestions: A restroom cart holding plastic mop bucket with fill-line markings, mop, other tools, restroom supplies, color-coded portion control packets for point-of-use mixing, color-coded spray bottles for glass cleaner, and disinfectant, etc.

Application: Restroom specialist uses pre-measured pouches of concentrate to make additional glass cleaner, disinfectant, and mopping solution on location as needed without having to make trips to the supply closet. Color-coding of all products eliminates mistakes. Premeasured packets create ideal dilutions and facilitate point-of-use mixing, encourage prescribed mop water changes, and enable better quality monitoring and inventory control (workers return empty packets to supervisors at shift completion).

- *Utility Specialist—Dedicated to cleaning entrance glass, lobbies, other flooring, etc.*

Suggestions: Since the utility specialist is a "clean up hitter"—focusing on miscellaneous tasks according to the building's specifications—equipment is contingent on duties. For entrance glass spot-cleaning, a plastic spray bottle containing glass cleaner, lint-free cloths, a holster or apron to hold sprayer and extra trigger/head, pre-measured glass cleaner concentrate packets for point-of-use mixing, etc. For floor cleaning, mop bucket and mop, with prescribed number of concentrate packets carried in holster or apron to facilitate solution changes without wasted trips. The utility specialist often uses a backpack vacuum for cleaning entrance areas and lobbies, a cart to carry supplies and pick up bagged refuse, depending on the scope and nature of duties.

Application: Performs various tasks throughout a facility, including glass cleaning, floor care, peripheral vacuuming, etc., and picks up trash bagged by the light-duty specialist at scheduled times for each floor, depositing it in an outside dumpster.

Equipment and Staff Comparisons between Zone and Team Cleaning

Example: Eight-story office building, 12,000 square feet per floor, 96,000 total sq. ft.

ZONE CLEANING: Staff of eight (one for each floor)
Required Equipment: Eight vacuums, eight trash barrels, eight restroom carts (adjusted according to building specs)

TEAM CLEANING: Staff of six specialists (two vacuumers, two light-duty task persons, one restroom person, and one utility person)
Required Equipment: Three vacuums, two trash barrels, one restroom cart, and two utility carts (adjusted according to building specs)

Important: In team cleaning programs, fewer tools are required and workers are typically assigned their own tools, which creates ownership and better care and maintenance of equipment, leading to leaner supply budgets.

With team cleaning, efficiency is also produced through a double-check system and supervision. Forgetting to empty trash, etc., is a problem eliminated by built-in cross-checks in team cleaning. For example, since the vacuum specialist follows the light-duty specialist, this person checks the trash, and empties it if missed by the first specialist.

With zone cleaning—since each floor is cleaned by a different person—a supervisor must look at *each* floor to determine work quality, but with team cleaning, the supervisor can spot-check two floors and two restrooms at random, and assess overall quality.

In team cleaning, since the workload and equipment are streamlined, individuals have a thorough knowledge of their functions and responsibilities. As the cleaning industry becomes more complex, it's important to clearly define each employee's duties. This can be achieved simply with team cleaning.

"Team cleaning has cemented our relationship with our customers," says Rosenstein. "They know that we are constantly on the lookout for ways to enhance their productivity. You're always stretching that goal a little further, expanding the envelope. We try to set everybody up, so that liability is minimized, and compliance with new laws is met. We try to set everything up so that cleaning is as safe and simple as possible. This reduces their exposure. It's a complete integrated approach."

Improvements in Vacuum Cleaner Soil Removal Effectiveness Mean New Ways to Save on Facility Budgets

By Robert A. Woellner

(This article is presented through the generosity of ProTeam Inc., a Boise, Idaho, manufacturer of backpack vacuum systems and sponsor of Team Cleaning Seminars.)

As the quality of carpets has increased over the past decade, the quality of carpet vacuum cleaners has also improved dramatically. Although proactive representatives from the two industries have worked together, it is not uncommon for misconceptions to remain. Many representatives of each industry have not adequately kept up-to-date with the developments of the other industry, and in many cases are using the biases of decade old information.

One of the most significant misinformed theories is that upright vacuum cleaners using "beater-bars" are more effective than suction vacuum cleaners at removing soil from carpets. With this misconception, many manufacturers incorrectly recommend that their carpets be maintained with upright vacuum cleaners. Several warranties still mandate the use of upright vacuum cleaners. Numerous studies over the last five years have concluded that not only do many modern commercial and industrial backpack vacuum cleaners favorably compare to upright vacuum cleaners, but commercial backpack units are now often more effective at removing dirt from carpets.

Soil removal effectiveness is the measure of how effectively a known concentration of soil is removed from a carpet and captured in a vacuum cleaner's filter bag. An increase in the effectiveness of soil removal from a carpet not only prolongs the life of the carpet, but allows carpets to be cleaned faster. This increase in efficiency can provide a significant economic benefit to commercial buildings.

This article summarizes the results of studies conducted by an independent testing laboratory (Quality Environmental Services & Technologies, Inc., "QUEST") comparing the soil removal effectiveness of several brands of commercial/industrial vacuum cleaners. This article is not intended to provide all the supporting data, since it is provided elsewhere and is available from the author.

In the designing of testing procedures, the following test methods were reviewed and sections included as appropriate: Standard Laboratory Test Method for Evaluation of Carpet Embedded Dirt Removal Effectiveness of Household Vacuum Cleaners (ASTM Method F 608-89); Standard Test Method for Measuring Air Performance Characteristics of Vacuum Cleaners (ASTM Method F 558-88); Specification for Air Performance Measurement Plenum Chamber for Vacuum Cleaners (ASTM Method F 431-87); Specification for Test Carpets and Pads for Vacuum Cleaner Testing (ASTM Method F 655-89); and ServiceMaster Vacuum Cleaner Testing Protocol.

The purpose of the testing was to utilize reproducible testing protocols to compare the soil removal effectiveness of commercial/industrial vacuum cleaners. An attempt was made to approximate real life conditions in a controlled environment. Since no ASTM methods specifically address the soil removal effectiveness of industrial type vacuum cleaners (most test methods focus upon residential units), the following testing procedure was designed and utilized:

Soil Removal Effectiveness

Soil removal effectiveness was tested by evenly distributing 100 grams of test soil (80% silica sand and 20% talcum powder) onto a $6' \times 6'$ commercial grade test carpet, working the test soil into the carpet with a carpet rake, vacuuming the test carpet for 60 seconds, and removing and weighing the preweighed filter bag. The percent of test soil picked up and retained in the filter bag was calculated and is presented below by vacuum cleaner type.

Vacuum Cleaner Type	Soil Removal Effectiveness	Range of Results
Backpack Vacuum	95.7%	95.3–96.1%
Two-Motor Upright	94.0%	92.9–94.9%
Backpack Vacuum	93.7%	92.1–95.3%
Backpack Vacuum	93.3%	91.3–95.3%
Two-Motor Upright	92.2%	87.9–94.2%

Conclusions

Of the units tested, a backpack-style vacuum was consistently the top performer with regards to both soil removal effectiveness and filtration efficiency. The high soil removal effectiveness of the commercial backpack vacuum cleaners appears to be the result of a combination of high airflow at the point of carpet contact which is concentrated over a smaller area than with a typical upright vacuum cleaner and successful trapping of the soil in the filter bag.

This data, along with the findings of other recent studies, should encourage the carpet manufacturing industry to retest and rethink their old notions that an upright vacuum cleaner with a beater-bar helps maintain the life of a carpet. Upright vacuum cleaners are no longer the only option for optimal carpet maintenance.

Additionally, those interested in indoor air quality and the cost savings of improved efficiency cleaning should find comfort in the fact that backpack vacuum cleaners can provide improvements in both soil removal effectiveness and airborne particulate emissions.

Robert A. Woellner is Senior Scientist, Quality Environmental Services & Technologies, Inc., 3084 South Linley Court, Denver, CO 80236.

APPENDIX J

National Trade Publications Articles

These "green" housekeeping articles offer some commonsense approaches to how we conduct our business. All of them stress that protecting the environment, indoors or out, is not just good for Mother Nature—it is also good for the pocketbook.

We start with an article by Paul Amos, an interview with Stephen Ashkin, whom you met earlier in the text. Ashkin takes an unbiased look at the country's growing mold problem. In the next article, he offers some quick, but very important tips to improve your indoor air quality (IAQ).

Next we hear from the esteemed Michael Berry on the causes of poor IAQ in an interview by Michael McCagg, Managing Editor of *Cleaning and Maintenance Distribution Online*. McCagg then explores the subject of water softening and addresses the subject of odor control in a second article.

Roger McFadden contributes an excellent piece on chemicals and the restroom. The hazard value chart he presents should be used by every executive housekeeper and purchasing agent in the hospitality and health-care industries.

Finally, we hear from a very distinguished reader of *Cleaning and Maintenance Management Online*, Arthur B. Weissman, President and CEO of Green Seal, who acquaints us with the mission and goals of this most worthy organization.

All of these articles have been provided by Humphrey Tyler, Founder of National Trade Publications, Inc. National Trade Publications is the parent company CM B2B Trade Group, which publishes *Cleaning and Maintenance Management* magazine, *Cleaning and Maintenance Management Online*, *Cleaning and Maintenance Distribution* magazine, and *Cleanfax* magazine. As noted in Chapter 10, page 208, Mr. Tyler has generously offered the readers of this text a free subscription to *Cleaning and Maintenance Management*. Thanks to him and to the rest of his fine staff.

Exclusive Interview: Stephen Ashkin

By Paul Amos, Executive Editor

This article first appeared in *Cleaning and Maintenance Management Online 2003* and is presented here though the generosity of CM B2B Trade Group, a subsidiary of National Trade Publications, Inc.

One of the nation's premier experts on IAQ (indoor air quality) and indoor health issues shares his thoughts on the "mold hysteria."

CM i-Focus: At the CM Seminars and Conferences (*www.cmexpo.com*) at the ISSA show you presented a seminar focusing on a "non-hysterical look at mold." Would you characterize the current nationwide view of mold contamination as "hysteria"?

Stephen Ashkin: The definition of "hysteria" from the Random House Dictionary is: An uncontrollable outburst of emotion or fear. Many of the recent new reports that use headlines such as "Attack of the Killer Mold" that appeared in the *Washington Post* certainly contribute . . . to a "hysterical" view of the problem since they are based on emotion and fear, rather than sound science.

From the cleaning industry's perspective, I think we have to be very concerned about this. While mold may, in fact, be a real problem, it is just one of many issues we need to address along with managing bacteria, pesticides, slip/fall issues, ergonomics, environmental impacts, etc.

Our society—including the public at-large and regulators—needs to come to the realization that mold is the result of poor maintenance and cleaning, and is not the cause of the problem. Thus, if our industry finds resources are being pulled away from general cleaning and poured into mold remediation and prevention, this focus on mold may result in unexpected, but very serious consequences that may be more serious from a health perspective than solving the mold problem.

CM: Is mold a legitimate health threat to building occupants? How does mold impact IAQ? What evidence is there to suggest mold harms humans?

Ashkin: There seems to be a great deal of evidence that high levels of molds, its spores and the toxins they produce do indeed affect people's health. While I am not a doctor, my research indicates there is little scientific/medical evidence to suggest that molds, including the so called killer molds, cause death except in the cases where people have existing health conditions.

However, the health effects often resemble the flu and can trigger asthma attacks, which can be deadly, are very serious and affect building occupant health and performance. Thus, I think we have to be careful of the extremes. While I don't want us to go to the one extreme that says "mold kills," nor do I want to suggest that it is not a real problem to both health and the building itself.

Mold is serious, as are many problems the cleaning industry deals with on a daily basis. Perhaps the best thing that may come of this "mold hysteria" is to again remind us the fundamental mission of the cleaning industry is to protect health without harming the environment—rather than just cleaning as cheaply as possible to maintain appearances and minimize occupant complaints.

CM: How important do you consider certification to the mold remediation industry? What advice would you give to a person interested in becoming a professional mold remediator?

Ashkin: Because of the seriousness of the problem and the increased liability and legal issues relative to mold and mold remediation, I think if a contractor is looking to do mold remediation that . . . this issue must be taken very, very seriously.

No business should get involved in an area, especially one wrought with these types of problems, without the appropriate training and expertise. Thus, I think certification is important for any company looking to perform mold remediation. The caveat is to make sure the certification program is well recognized and provides the type of training and credentials necessary should your company get swept into a lawsuit.

CM: If a facility manager discovers significant mold contamination within a building, what steps should he/she take to deal with the problem? Should he/she seek professional guidance?

Ashkin: If the mold contamination is "significant" then by all means it is best to bring in the experts. While many building managers are quite capable of handling the problem themselves, because of the liability and other potential problems, I think it is just good business to get a qualified third-party in to do the work.

The challenge here is to recognize what is meant by "significant mold contamination" as opposed to the work people can do themselves (for example, we don't need a third-party contractor to remove a single ceiling tile) and how to identify a "qualified third-party."

CM: Mold has existed on earth for millions of years. Why has it suddenly become such a big issue? Why didn't we hear about toxic mold 50 years ago?

Ashkin: There seem to be a number of contributing factors to the increase in mold-related problems. Some of them include:

- The reduction in the amount of cleaning that has taken place in an effort to reduce cleaning costs, which allows normally occurring molds to amplify to levels where they can affect people's health.
- Changes in building designs and construction methods and materials which result in buildings with less ability to handle moisture. As a result, when moisture intrudes in the building—mold happens.
- The reduction in the amount of fresh air to reduce the cost to heat and cool our buildings is suggested as a contributor to the overall building-related problems.
- There seems to be an overall increase in the sensitivities that children and other sensitive people are experiencing. For example, the incidents of asthma have increased by 80 percent since the 1980s. Thus, whatever is contributing to these types of sensitivities is being associated with molds.
- Finally, while I think most organizations do an outstanding job, I believe at times the media, law firms, testing labs, advocacy groups, and certain companies that sell services that are benefitted by an increased concern over mold are "fueling the fire" and intentionally contributing to the heightened awareness of the problem.

CM: What's the future of this issue? Should we expect government regulation of mold remediation? Will insurance companies be able to cap mold coverage limits?

Ashkin: The government frequently acts when the public is enraged. Thus, we may very well see some type of government action taking place. A bill was introduced last year in Congress—U.S. Toxic Mold Protection Act and commonly called the "Melina Bill"—which stalled but is likely to be reintroduced. Texas, New York and other states are also looking at some type of legislation.

But the issue with mold is extremely complicated and it is going to be very, very difficult to establish standards, laws and requirements. As for insurance companies, we are already seeing restrictions, caps and other efforts on their part. But more important than government regulations, I think building owners are very, very concerned about the issue.

This creates a true opportunity for companies who can really help building owners manage the indoor environment, which includes managing the moisture and cleaning the surfaces to control mold and other potentially harmful agents (such as bacteria, viruses, pests, vermin, etc.) resulting in a clean, healthy, safe and productive indoor environment.

Monitor Your Products to Improve IAQ

Improving indoor air quality requires more than combating mold and improving ventilation systems.

By Stephen Ashkin

Even common products can contribute to poor indoor air quality.

Chemical products can evaporate indoors, leaving their toxic contaminants for us to breathe, and create health problems for the young and old alike, as well as those with chronic respiratory problems.

Cleaning products are not immune from being lumped into this category.

While cleaning is an important means of eliminating the stuff that makes us sick, and generally we need to do more of it, cleaning products themselves can add contaminants to the indoors.

Proactive Reading

That's why it's vital to read those product labels and Material Safety Data Sheets (MSDS) before you buy cleaning products and avoid those that caution us about "respiratory irritation" and/or have a high VOC content.

Some additional product considerations:

- **Use trigger sprayers as opposed to aerosols.** Aerosols containers are terrific for some applications like wasp sprays, but the propellants are unnecessary pollutants indoors for cleaning products.

- **Use water-based as opposed to solvent-based products,** such as in furniture polish and dusting products.

- **Use hydrogen peroxide-based products approved by EPA to kill mold,** rather than chlorine-containing products for mold and mildew removal. Chlorine is a known respiratory irritant, burns eyes and skin, damages fabrics and when mixed with other commonly used household products can create deadly fumes.

- **Use mechanical means rather then chemicals for cleaning** when possible. For example, use microfiber wiping cloths as opposed to chemical-based dust control products. Of course, improving IAQ is a much broader issue.

Stephen Ashkin is a principal of the Ashkin Group, Bloomington, Indiana, and is a consultant in green cleaning and IAQ matters. He is also a former vice president of chemical maker Rochester Midland Corporation. He can be reached at (812) 332-7950.

From the October 2002 edition of *Cleaning and Maintenance Management* magazine.

Berry: Chemical Mismanagement Causes Poor IAQ

by Michael McCagg, Managing Editor

This article first appeared on January 15, 2003, in *CM i-Focus on IAQ* and is presented here through the generosity of CM B2B Trade Group, a subsidiary of National Trade Publications, Inc.

LATHAM, NY—In the CM B2B Trade Group's new CM i-Focus on IAQ, Dr. Michael Berry addresses some of the issues linking cleaning chemical usage to indoor air quality (IAQ) problems. The following are excerpts from the interview. For the full interview and additional information on IAQ issues, visit the *CM i-Focus on IAQ*.

Michael McCagg: What is the link between poor indoor air quality (IAQ) and the chemicals used by cleaning personnel in the building?

Dr. Michael Berry: It's not the answer you think. The link is mismanagement, ignorance and misrepresentation of the cleaning product. Cleaning chemicals are technologies and if they have been properly formulated and properly used, they do not contribute to poor IAQ, they enhance indoor air quality. Really what you are dealing with (in instances of poor IAQ), is ignorance and a mismanagement issue and some violation of the business standards and product formulation.

MM: If ranked by importance against other factors (such as mold) in terms of impacting IAQ, where does cleaning chemical usage rank?

MB: If it's a properly formulated chemical, it's a minimal risk. What's on the top of your list are biopollutants. They are probably the biggest problems today and have been historically. Biopollutants such as bacteria, Legionella, Pontiac fever, TB or anthrax are tops on the list. Then you have very well established allergens, such as dust mites, cockroaches, and cats. Then you have your other allergens, mold. They are the risk factors that you really have to consider first.

MM: What types of cleaning products or their ingredients are the worst offenders when it comes to damaging IAQ?

MB: Today, as opposed to 20 years ago, most of the carcinogens have been taken out of cleaning products. Your issue with cleaning chemicals today is more how well do they do their job? Chemicals don't clean, they are a machine. The biggest problem is how well they carry out that supporting function in terms of maximum extraction and minimum residue. If they are leaving behind large amounts of residue, that can become a problem. Well-formulated products that have been tested don't pose a problem.

MM: What is the most important thing cleaning professionals can do to improve IAQ in the buildings they clean?

MB: To understand what cleaning is, which is basically the extraction and removal of unwanted substance from an environment to maximize the removal of unwanted substances which, when concentrated, can cause problems and to minimize residue—things left behind including water, chemicals or other particles. Maximum extraction, minimum residue, that's what must be accomplished.

MM: How can a cleaning professional convince his/her boss or a building owner that IAQ is a real threat and that additional funds for quality cleaning and green cleaning products are needed to improve IAQ?

MB: If the boss doesn't understand it by now, I would fire the boss and get a new job, but the value of cleaning is found in many different factors. Cleaning:

Is an insurance policy—it reduces the likelihood of crisis down stream
It preserves the value of real estate and valuable property
It creates a good image
It promotes productivity
It allows the use of space over and over again
It guards against disease and adverse effects
It allows people to live indoors in a comfortable, secure and productive way

It's the best investment you can make for the management of an indoor environment and that's the message that needs to be made clear by the industry as a whole.

MM: How do carpets impact IAQ? Do carpets or hard floors promote a healthier indoor environment? Why is there still so much confusion surrounding this issue?

MB: Clean carpets pose no problems at all. In fact, a carpet has one attribute in that it traps and holds dust. Dirt poses a problem whether it's in carpeting or on a hard surface. The confusion is caused because there is not a good block of research to educate the public with. There is a lot of opinion using little data, but very little sound research to point to.

Michael Berry, Ph.D., is an author and well-known advocate of IAQ issues. He served as deputy director of the National Center for Environmental Assessment at Research Triangle Park. Today, he's a research professor at the University of North Carolina, where he's doing work in the Environmental Studies program.
—M.M.

Water Softening Is a Green Cleaning Strategy: Reduce Chemical Usage and IAQ Concerns through Water Treatment

By Michael McCagg, Managing Editor

(This article is presented through the generosity of CM B2B Trade Group, a division of National Trade Group, Inc.)

From the February 2003 edition of *Cleaning and Maintenance Management* magazine.

Want to reduce cleaning chemical usage by 50 percent and address building occupant concerns over chemical usage and its impact on indoor air quality (IAQ)? Encourage building owners or facility administrators to buy a water filtration system.

Though not commonly thought of as an area of concern for cleaning professionals, water filtration can be a valuable tool to cleaners battling budget woes, IAQ concerns and building occupants' demands to adopt green cleaning practices.

Cut the Chems!

"You can save at least 50 percent of any type of cleaning product used to remove dirt, greases, anything," said Joe Harrison, Technical Director, Water Quality Association. That's because impurities in the water—calcium, iron, lead, etc.—engage the cleaning agents in the chemical. In turn that reduces the effectiveness of the agents, requiring more of the chemical to be used, said Harrison.

One cleaning educator advises cleaning professionals in buildings where hard water is a problem to increase chemical concentration by one level in dilution control systems.

Roger McFadden, a chemist and vice president of Coastwide Laboratories, Wilsonville, OR, said, "Unless controlled, hard water can diminish the effectiveness of a variety of cleaning products."

More Green Chemicals

Water filtration systems allow the use of more environmentally friendly and safe for humans cleaning chemicals, said green cleaning advocate Steve Ashkin, The Ashkin Group, Bloomington, IN.

The Soap and Detergent Association (SDA) said hard and impure water in buildings:

- Leads to the creation of "soap scum" and films on surfaces
- Creates spots on glass and windows
- Causes calcium and other buildup on metals and restroom fixtures
- Aids in the development of rust
- Leaves dull, discolored appearances on porcelain and chrome

To combat these problems, cleaning professionals often turn to more aggressive chemicals, such as acids, for cleaning. In some instances, said James Stewart, supervisor, Janitorial Services, BMG Entertainment, Indianapolis, that practice creates even more problems for cleaning professionals as the mineral deposits in the toilets and urinals capture the acids and create running water stains.

At the same time, those more aggressive chemicals are typically dangerous for cleaning professionals to use and can pose health problems for building occupants. Ashkin said that installation of a water filtration system, though, allows for the usage of more environmentally friendly, benign and safer chemicals.

IAQ Rewards

Because the byproduct of water filtration systems is reduced chemical usage and usage of safer, environmentally friendly chemicals to clean, water filtration systems can be considered a method to reduce indoor air quality (IAQ) issues. "People tend to overlook it, but it's a really good strategy," said Harrison.

With concerns over cleaning chemical usage and its impact on indoor air quality (IAQ) reaching all-time high levels, cleaning professionals can tap into this as a new marketing method, said Ashkin. Ashkin noted that the US Green Building Council considers water filtration in the certification of a building as "green."

Cleaning Rewards

Cleaning professionals can realize other rewards beyond the budgetary savings from less chemical usage and healthier environment created by water filtration systems. Areas where filtered water is key to increased productivity for cleaning include:

- Windows
- Stone surfaces
- Laundry operations
- Cooling systems and boilers

The bottom line, said Harrison, is "water is the main thing in making water work better in washing and cleaning."

Controlling Odors at the Source

Hydrogen peroxide–based cleaning solutions can eliminate the need for deodorizers

by Michael McCagg, Managing Editor

From the April 2002 edition of *Cleaning and Maintenance Management* **magazine.**

While a debate has long raged in the industry over the use of deodorizers—do they serve to cover up improper cleaning or as an added tool to proper cleaning—one thing is certain: If a foul odor is left in a room after it has been cleaned, the cleaner will be blamed for not doing his or her job thoroughly.

An emerging way to tackle odor and other concerns without adding the expense of a deodorizer is use of hydrogen peroxide–based cleaners. The all-purposed cleaning systems are gaining in popularity among in-house and contract cleaners surveyed by *Cleaning & Maintenance Management* because of their ability to clean almost any surface and control odors.

"Hydrogen peroxide is a natural odor neutralizer—it has extra oxygen that always wants to link up with foul odors," said Roger McFadden, a jan-san industry consultant and vice president of Coastwide Laboratories Inc., Wilsonville, OR.

Restrooms

For veterans of the maintenance industry, the true testing ground for a product's effectiveness is the elementary school boys' restroom. "The boys' restroom is a real problem area," agrees Elk Grove's Linda Lopez. "It's difficult to get rid of the odor created by urine."

When Lopez was piloting the hydrogen peroxide product in select schools, she was particularly interested in its performance in the boys' restroom. "We sprayed the product on the floor, walls, partitions, and urinals and waited for a few minutes to let the product work. We wiped it down, sprayed again and walked away.

"We did this for just three to five days, and the odor was completely eliminated. It wasn't just masked. It was gone. No other product or system we've ever used has delivered these results," she said.

Patrick Stewart, president/CEO of EnvirOx products, Georgetown, IL, said hydrogen peroxide systems work in restrooms because of the oxidization process:

- The hydrogen peroxide penetrates urine—the largest source of unpleasant odors in restrooms.

- It then has a chemical reaction to the bacteria in the urine, preventing their multiplication.

Carpeting

An area where deodorizers are often utilized, carpeting can also be seen as a major test for the deodorizing ability of hydrogen peroxide solutions. McFadden said the hydrogen peroxide solutions work well on carpeting in that they eliminate the odor in one application, as long as dwell time is adhered to.

"It is great on carpets and it is used by my cleaners to address carpet spots in a nightly and timely manner," said Carol Bush, an area manager for Central Property Services, Pittsburgh.

Money Savings

Besides the obvious savings of not having to purchase a separate deodorizing system, hydrogen peroxide-based cleaning systems offer money savings:

- Reduced labor from having to apply/maintain a deodorizing system
- Reduced chemical purchases—most hydrogen peroxide systems are multi-purpose systems. Bush said that she uses the systems for everything but stripping and finishing.

Environmentally Speaking

Hydrogen peroxide-based cleaning solutions are also considered environmentally preferable and can help facilities or cleaning companies meet "green" cleaning standards federal, state and other facilities are adopting.

Alien P. Rathey, Rathey Communications, West Jefferson, North Carolina, contributed to this article.

Chemical Safety in the Restroom

Eliminating hazardous chemicals and locating safer alternatives for restroom care

by Roger McFadden

This article first appeared in the May 2002 edition of *Cleaning & Maintenance Management* magazine and is presented here through the generosity of CM B2B Trade Group, a subsidiary of National Trade Publications, Inc.

Proper restroom cleaning maintains a high level of appearance, eliminates unpleasant odors, elevates the image of custodial staff and improves the overall health and safety of the facility. Proper restroom care requires:

- Establishing cleaning standards
- Developing guidelines
- Communicating expectations
- Effective training
- Selecting the right chemical cleaning products
- Including all stakeholders

The latter is extremely important to the appearance of the facility and the health of cleaning workers.

Cleaning product selection should be based upon more than a pleasant fragrance, an attractive color or cheap price. The cost of overlooking the safety and environmental impact of a chemical cleaning product can be enormous. Using hazardous acids, caustics or volatile solvents can result in on-the-job chemical injuries, contaminated indoor air and damaged restroom fixtures.

Select Safe and Effective Products

An organized and well-planned restroom care program will select and use cleaning products that:

- Are effective
- Are safe for workers
- Protect surfaces being cleaned

A trend is emerging to eliminate acids, replace glycol ethers and find sustainable earth alternatives, ("green" alternatives) to traditional restroom cleaning products. But most cleaning products are formulated using a mixture of chemical ingredients. This makes their environmental, health and safety (EHS) assessment complicated.

For example, if isopropyl alcohol were being considered for use in a cleaning operation, EHS professionals would review a variety of scientific and medical databases about isopropyl alcohol and make an informed choice about its safety. However, if isopropyl alcohol were formulated with five other chemical ingredients into a glass cleaner, the potential adverse health effects of the cleaning cocktail would need to be considered.

Since the US Department of Labor's Occupational Safety and Health Administration (OSHA) does not require full disclosure or exact percentages of all ingredients on Material Safety Data Sheets (MSDS), this can be a problem for EHS professionals.

Double Trouble

The relationship between the chemistry of one chemical and another is important. Recently, I visited a custodial closet near an area where office workers complained about unpleasant odors causing headaches and respiratory discomfort. I opened the door and immediately recognized a chemical odor that was related to ammonia and chlorine being mixed. An investigation of the closet revealed leaking containers of an aqua ammonia detergent dripping into a bucket filled with a sodium hypochlorite (chlorine bleach) mildew remover. A review of the two chemicals' MSDS indicated they should be kept away from each other. This accident could have had serious consequences on workers there.

Avoid High Levels of Corrosive Acids and Alkalis

Hydrochloric acid (HCl) and phosphoric acid are effective ingredients sometimes used to formulate tub, tile, toilet and shower room cleaners. These acids are aggressive and are capable of damaging, among other surface areas:

- Toilets and urinals
- Sinks
- Metal
- Mirrors
- Floor tiles
- Grouting

Acid toilet bowl cleaners typically have an acid content between nine and 25 percent, which may be effective in removing tough deposits from toilets and urinals, but can etch the toilet bowl and urinal surfaces. That makes them more receptive to minerals deposits and soils.

Avoid Hydrofluoric Acid and HF Salts

Hydrofluoric acid (HF) and its salts are sometimes used to formulate specialty mineral stain removers. These chemicals are effective in removing the toughest of mineral stains, but can severely damage:

- Porcelain
- Porcelain enamel
- Glass
- Glazed ceramic tiles

Care should be taken to control the contact time of products formulated with these ingredients. Proper cleaning and care of these surfaces can prevent the need to use these HF based products. Additionally, some mild abrasive solutions that contain cerium oxide . . . can be used to remove these deposits without the risk to workers and surfaces.

Use Quaternary Disinfectant Cleaners

Using chlorine bleach to clean restrooms is not a good idea. In fact, it is a bad idea. Quaternary disinfectant cleaners are currently the best choice for cleaning and disinfecting the restroom environment. Many of these products are effective against a broad spectrum of disease causing microorganisms including:

- Streptococcus
- Staphylococcus
- Pseudomonas aeruginosa
- HIV-1
- HBV
- Herpes Simplex 1 and 2
- A variety of strains of Influenza viruses

Read the product label and literature to confirm what organisms your disinfectant cleaner will kill. Many institutions do not use household chlorine bleach because it:

- Lacks detergency
- Adversely reacts with other chemicals to create toxic byproducts and gases
- Attacks hard surfaces
- Discolors fibers and colored surfaces
- Damages floor finishes
- Rapidly loses its strength
- Is expensive to use

Treat Toilets Like Teeth

There would be significantly less root canals and expensive dental care needed if patients would properly brush and floss. The same is true in caring for toilets and urinals. When toilets and urinals are properly cleaned and brushed daily, they are less likely to need expensive and hazardous remedies, such as acid cleaners. It takes unsightly rings and deposits long periods of time to form under normal water and plumbing conditions. These conditions can be prevented with milder cleaning products and proper daily cleaning.

Locate Safer Alternatives

Research is being done and databases are being developed to assist in comparing the relative hazards of ingredients used in cleaning products. One database that is particularly interesting is the Indiana Relative Chemical Hazard Score (IRCHS). This is a scoring method developed by Purdue University that evaluates an ingredient and assigns a chemical hazard value based upon the average of the Environmental Hazard Value and the Worker Exposure Hazard Value. The lower the score, the more favorable the evaluation. This allows individuals to compare the relative hazard value of ingredients in various cleaning products.

Better Efficiency

A basic rule should be, use the least amount of cleaning products necessary to meet your specific needs. The least number of cleaning products are needed when a restroom is properly cleaned and maintained.

Planning Reduces Risks

Hazardous chemical cleaning products have found their way into many restroom care programs because the other elements of the cleaning process have failed. For example, when toilets are not properly cleaned because of poor planning or ineffective training the result is mineral buildups and stains. A well-planned restroom care program will prevent the stains and eliminate the need for hazardous chemicals.

The basic rule should be to select chemical cleaning products that are effective and yet safe for workers, building occupants and environmental surfaces.

Roger McFadden is an industry educator, consultant, and chemist and is vice president of Coastwide Laboratories, Wilsonville, Oregon. What follows is the aforementioned Hazard Value Chart based on the Indiana Relative Chemical Hazard Score in McFadden's Article.

Hazard Value Chart*

Total hazard values for ingredients sometimes used to formulate cleaning and maintenance products, according to the Indiana Relative Chemical Hazard Score (IRCHS) established by Perdue University

CAS Number	Ingredient	Total Hazard Value
151-56-4	Aziridine	60.7
7664-39-3	Hydrofluoric acid	50.0
71-43-2	Benzene	48.0
50-00-0	Formaldehyde	43.1
127-18-4	Perchloroethylene	37.5
7647-01-0	Hydrochloric acid	36.7
7782-50-5	Chlorine	31.6
64-19-7	Acetic acid	29.8
7664-93-9	Sulfuric acid	29.3
108-88-3	Toluene	29.1
75-09-2	Methylene chloride	27.2
1332-21-4	Asbestos (friable)	25.6
84-74-2	Dibutyl phthalate	24.8
67-56-1	Methanol	24.7
7664-41-7	Ammonia	21.8
111-76-2	2-butoxyethanol (Butyl cellosolve)	20.5
1310-58-3	Potassium hydroxide	19.2
141-43-5	Monoethanolamine	17.2
7664-38-2	Phosphoric acid	17.2
7681-52-9	Sodium hypochlorite	16.8
64742-88-7	Stoddard solvent	16.6
6834-92-0	Sodium metasilicate	16.2
107-21-1	Ethylene glycol	16.0
67-64-1	Acetone	15.9
1341-49-7	Ammonium bifluoride	15.0
67-63-0	Isopropyl alcohol	14.2
57-55-6	Propylene glycol	14.2
4590-94-8	Dipropylene glycol methyl ether	13.4
1310-73-2	Sodium hydroxide	13.3
64-17-5	Ethyl alcohol (ethanol)	13.2
57018-52-7	Propylene glycol butyl ether	10.3
79-14-1	Glycolic acid	9.9
111-90-0	Carbitol cellosolve	9.2
68424-85-1	Quaternary ammonium chloride	8.2
5989-27-5	d-Limonene	7.8
7320-34-5	Tetrapotassium pyrophosphate	5.2
77-92-9	Citric acid	3.4
1066-33-7	Ammonium bicarbonate	2.1
7722-84-1	Hydrogen peroxide (7%)	1.9
113976-90-2	Alkyl polyglycoside surfactant	0.2
7732-18-5	Water	0.0

*The lower the score, the more favorable the evaluation.

Reader's Letter: Green Seal Has "Green" History

This letter is in response to *CM e-News Daily/CMM Online's* ongoing coverage of the Unified Green Cleaning Alliance.

Dear Editor:

Green Seal is a 13-year-old nonprofit environmental labeling organization, and Green Seal's standards are the only environmental standards for products and services that meet EPA's criteria for third party certifiers.

Green Seal operates under ISO 14020 and 14024, and is the US member of the Global Ecolabeling Network, the coordinating body of the world's 27 leading ecolabeling programs including Germany's Blue Angel and Scandinavia's Nordic Swan.

Any manufacturer anywhere in the world may apply for Green Seal certification. The Green Seal is a registered certification mark with the US Patent & Trademark Office that may appear only on certified products.

Green Seal's Environmental Standard for Industrial and Institutional Cleaners (GS-37) was developed over the course of a year, in accordance with internationally recognized procedures for setting environmental standards.

The standard was created through an open and transparent process, involved a balanced stakeholder committee, was made available for public comment, and represents a national-level consensus for identifying environmentally responsible Industrial & Institutional (I&I) cleaners in today's marketplace.

As a point of reference, the stakeholder committee for the I&I cleaners standard included representatives from:

- Seventh Generation
- 3M
- Spartan Chemical
- Clean Environment Co.
- Church & Dwight
- US Postal Service
- Aberdeen Proving Ground
- International Executive Housekeepers Association
- American Federation of State, County and Municipal Employees
- GSA
- City of Santa Monica, CA
- MN Office of Environmental Assistance
- MA Executive Office of Environmental Affairs
- US EPA
- UMass Toxics Use Reduction Institute (TURI)
- INFORM
- Global Toxics Campaign, WWF
- Washington Toxics Coalition
- Environmental Health Coalition

The current references to and uses of GS-37 include:

General Federal Guidance

1) EPA put out a statement in late 2001 supporting 5 environmental standards, three of which are Green Seal's (Industrial Cleaners, Commercial Adhesives, and Degreasers) and two are from ASTM (Standard Guide for Stewardship for the Cleaning of Commercial and Institutional Buildings and Standard Practice for Data Collection for Sustainability of Building Products). The statement read, in part, ". . . the five standards listed below are based on scientific methodology that is accurate and reproducible and provide guidance to Federal purchasers which reflect life cycle considerations and address purchasers' needs under the National Technology Transfer and Advancement Act (P.L. 104-113), and OMB Circular A-l19.

"The following five environmental standards address environmental impacts in a manner consistent with EPA's guidance on environmentally preferable purchasing (FR Vol. 64, No. 161, pp. 45810-45858, 8/20/99). They address life cycle considerations and were developed through a voluntary consensus process....EPA recommends that Federal purchasers consider these standards when making purchasing decisions . . ."

This added further weight to considering Green Seal's standards as "national" environmental standards.

Individual Federal Agencies

2) The Department of the Interior is adopting Green Seal Standard No. GS-37 for janitorial chemicals used at its offices and parks. DOI recommends following Green Seal standards, which are the best known and most widely accepted guidelines available.

"Green cleaning is still a relatively new concept, and managers who follow Green Seal standards, will be on the cutting edge of green cleaning . . ." (from a 2-day training course for Federal employees called "Greening the Janitorial Business").

3) EPA's EPP goals for 2005 and 2010 include "greening" all significant EPA janitorial and maintenance services contracts by 2010. One objective is that "All janitorial services contracts should meet ASTM Cleaning Stewardship for Community Buildings Standard and specify use of products which meet the Green Seal Cleaning Products Standard."

4) Aberdeen Proving Ground (US Army) funded GS-37 for use in identifying environmentally responsible institutional cleaners.

State and Local Governments

5) The Center for a New American Dream Cleaning Products Work Group includes Massachusetts; Minnesota; Missouri; Washington; King County, Washington; Phoenix, Arizona; Santa Monica, California; Seattle, Washington; and the Pacific Northwest National Laboratory.

They have all agreed to use the requirements of GS-37 as the requirements for cleaners in their next contracting cycle. The Massachusetts Request for Response for Environmentally Preferable Cleaning Products was recently issued and contains the Work Group contract language. Minnesota, Missouri, and Santa Monica are scheduled to issue their RFP shortly.

6) Pennsylvania is using Green Seal standards in state contracts currently and will be updating their cleaners contract to reference GS-37.

Green Building Efforts

7) The Center for Health, Environment and Justice report "Creating Safe Learning Zones: The ABC's of Healthy Schools" encourages schools to use products that meet GS-37, and the Healthy Schools Network is very close to adopting GS-37.

8) The US Green Building Council's LEED Rating System for Existing Buildings (LEED-EB) gives a credit in the Green Housekeeping Section for using Green Seal Standard GS-37 approved cleaning products.

9) INFORM's just-released report "Cleaning for Health: Products and Practices for a Safer Indoor Environment" recommends using GS-37 for specifying cleaning products.

All of the groups mentioned require that products meet or exceed the performance and environmental criteria contained in GS-37.

Previously, many of these groups had different requirements and ideas about what constituted "green," but they are now using a common set of criteria.

This not only makes it easier for purchasers (who can now spend time developing contract language for other categories where a life-cycle environmental standard does not currently exist), but also provides manufacturers with a single set of criteria instead of varying bidding requirements from numerous local, state, and federal agencies with "green" procurement programs.

With regard to Green Seal's certification fees, for the cost of an ad in something like CM/*Cleaning & Maintenance Management*, a company can get Green Seal certification.

Incidentally, Green Seal's evaluation fees have remained the same for the past six years.

As a non-profit environmental organization, our goal is to make the marketplace more sustainable while covering our expenses.

They are also flat fees, so there is no licensing fee or percentage-of-sales arrangement. Whether you sell one or one million products with the Green Seal, our fee is the same and we have no direct ties to that product's success or failure in the marketplace.

Green Seal also does not accept general support funding from manufacturers—most of our funding comes from foundation and government grants.

The goal of aggregating the demand for environmentally responsible cleaners in one set of criteria has been getting closer all the time, and we are definitely seeing a response from manufacturers to this combined demand for products that meet GS-37.

Green Seal recently certified four institutional cleaners from Rochester Midland Corp., two from Hillyard Industries, and now has several other companies in the evaluation pipeline, so competitive bidding is assured.

Arthur B. Weissman, Ph.D.
President and CEO
Green Seal

Glossary

Italicized words identify words or phrases in each definition that are defined elsewhere in this glossary.

absenteeism Employee absence from work. A high rate of absenteeism is considered to be a reliable indicator of low employee morale.

acid rain Rain or fog that contains sulfur dioxide and nitrous oxides that are damaging to plants, lakes, streams, and even buildings. Most of it is the result of burning fossil fuels (e.g., coal and oil) in electricity generation facilities.

acrylics A group of clear, tough plastic resins produced from acrylic acids.

actual expenditures Actual spending for labor and supplies to support the generation of revenue, as opposed to budgeted (planned) costs or forecast (expected) costs.

administration A *management task*. Attending to the details of executive affairs.

administrative theory First introduced by Henri Fayol, it was an attempt to apply scientific principles to a business organization. A subcomponent of the *classical school*.

aerobic Indicates a bacterium that must be exposed to, and requires, air (oxygen) to survive and grow.

all-purpose cleaner A multipurpose agent designed for several different cleaning tasks, depending on the *dilution ratio* applied.

amenity Anything that makes a guest's stay easier and more pleasant. Often pertains to items that are viewed as luxurious. An amenity is not normally categorized as a guest essential.

amortize To periodically and gradually decrease a cost or expenditure to zero over a stated period of time; for example, the preopening cost of a hotel or hospital.

A.M. room check A visual look at guestrooms that are supposed to be ready to receive guests for the purpose of verifying status. Check is made at about 8:00 A.M. Those rooms not in a ready status are called A.M. *discrepancies* and must be investigated. Some hotels conduct A.M. room checks on every room to determine each room's status. Sometimes the housekeeping department schedules workers according to the results of the A.M. room check.

anaerobic Indicates a bacterium that can live without exposure to air (oxygen).

analyze problems Gather facts, ascertain causes, and develop alternative solutions.

annual linen reorder plan System of ordering linen that provides long lead times for various items of linens; allows a hotel or hospital to deal directly with a *linen mill*; allows for the mill to weave linen at a time most beneficial to the mill.

antichlor A substance used to remove excess chlorine from fabric after bleaching.

antineoplastic agents Chemotherapy drugs used to treat cancers. They are either man-made or made from plants.

antisepsis A process by which chemicals are used on the skin for bacteriostatic and germicidal purposes.

area responsibility plan A document that geographically defines physical areas of a facility and assigns responsibility for cleaning among the various departments of a hotel or hospital organization; usually developed from the *division of work document*.

asepsis To be free from germs and infection.

asepsis (medical) A method used to prevent the spread of a communicable disease. Hand washing and isolation are examples.

asepsis (surgical) A method using sterile equipment, supplies, and procedures when entering the "sterile" interior of the body.

assets Items of value. Notations on a company balance sheet in the *books of account*, which represents the book value of assets. See also *capital assets*; *current assets*; *fixed assets*.

atom The smallest combination of nucleus (core or protons and neutrons) and surrounding electrons that is associated with a given "named element."

autoclave An ovenlike machine, using steam under pressure, in which supplies are subjected to intense heat for a specific period of time. Also called a sterilizer.

autocratic change A dictatorially mandated change. Change that is ordered by one person or group and that person or group has absolute power.

bacillus A bacterium that is rod-shaped.

bacteria Used to refer to *microorganisms* in general; also, the same as germs and/or microbes.

bacterial Soils or compounds containing active (live) *bacteria.*

bacteriostat An agent that arrests the growth of bacteria.

badge system Method of identifying employees by their identification badges. A badge usually indicates where an employee works and identification number and may contain the employee's photograph.

balance sheet a statement of financial position at a point in time; includes assets, liabilities, and owners' equity.

bed and bath linens Items such as sheets, pillowcases, hand towels, bath towels, washcloths, and cloth bath mats.

bedding All bed linens, such as sheets and pillowcases, and all blankets, shams, dust ruffles, pillows, quilts, comforters, coverlets, mattress pads, and bedspreads.

behavioral school An approach to management that seeks to apply knowledge gained from the disciplines of human psychology and sociology to the management of employees. Proponents assert that organizational productivity can be enhanced by meeting the psychological needs of the employee.

bio-recovery service A contract cleaning company that specializes in cleaning up human remains and bodily fluids.

bomb threats Malicious announcements of forthcoming explosions or bombings.

books of account Collection of all accounting ledgers, journals, and files associated with the financial accounting system established for the particular housekeeping operation.

"Botulism" Found in feces, sewers, milk improperly sterilized, or sealed foods. Also found in untreated wounds (gaseous gangrene).

budgeting Act of creating a management system used for the allocation of resources over a given period of time.

buffing The act of polishing the surface of a floor with a low-speed (175–350 rpm) floor machine.

burnishing The act of polishing the surface of a floor with a high-speed (350+rpm) floor machine to achieve an extremely high-gloss (wet-look) surface.

cakes A tunnel washer does not have a centrifuge to spin linen dry, so the linen is pressed to extract excess water. The result is a round cakelike object.

capital assets Long-term tangible or intangible assets such as land and buildings. See also *current assets; fixed assets.*

capital expenditure budget Financial statement of estimated capital expenditures over a given period of time.

capitalize Convert an expenditure into a capital item or charge the cost of an item to a capital expenditure account. See also *expense to; capital expenditure budget; fixed assets.*

carcinogen A substance that causes cancer.

card entry system Technically superior system for gaining regular entry into a hotel guestroom. Most systems use plastic devices (cards) with changeable electronic signatures that activate door locks, eliminating the need for a metal key.

carnauba wax A high-quality wax obtained from the leaves of the carnauba plant.

case goods Furniture in a guestroom that is made of wood and used for storage, such as an armoire or desk.

cationic Describes an ion that is positively charged.

central processing unit (CPU) This processing chip is the brains of the computer. The CPU is where most calculations take place.

chambermaid See *section housekeeper.*

checkout (C/O) Designation assigned to a guestroom in which the guest has permanently left the hotel and the room is waiting to be serviced, or in the process of being readied for the arrival of a new guest. Synonymous with on-change.

chemical agent A chemical added to a solution in the correct dosage that will kill bacteria, or at least stop their growth.

chief steward Supervisor of a department that specializes in cleaning and maintaining kitchens.

chlorofluorocarbons Man-made chemicals used chiefly in refrigeration, but now banned because they contribute to global warming by destroying the ozone layer.

civil disturbance In hotels or hospitals, a disturbance caused by one or more people refusing to obey the requests, commands, or demands of those in authority.

classical school The first great theoretical school of management. Characterized by a systematic approach to the management of the assets and the employees in a corporation. Henri Fayol and Frederick W. Taylor are considered by many to be the founders of this management school.

classification of accounts Arrangement of various types of revenues, expenses, and costs into meaningful groupings for accounting purposes.

cleaning and guest supply inventory A major segment of operational inventory under the direct control and responsibility of the *executive housekeeper.*

cleaning and maintenance circuits (rounds) Planned sequences for attending to the cleaning of various *public areas.*

Clostridium perfringens (clos-TRID-ee-um per-FRIN-gins) No gram stain. An anaerobic spore.

coach-pupil method A one-on-one training system of assigning one trainee to one instructor.

coccus A bacterium that is round-shaped.

communicate To pass or receive knowledge, instructions, or data and to ensure understanding.

communication symbols A series of written symbols used to communicate the status of guestrooms; for example, R, C/O, OCC, DND, RFV, OOO, MR, and T.

competitive shopping Looking critically at the alternative sources and suppliers of items and services purchased to support a hotel or hospital operation.

computer An electronic system of *hardware* components used to store and process data electronically.

conceptual thinking A *management task*. Formulating notions for the resolution of problems.

conference method A training technique whereby students participate in a workshop arrangement for problem solving. An excellent technique for supervisory training.

consolidated room sales summary Document prepared by the sales and marketing department of a hotel indicating rooms expected to be sold during the upcoming fiscal year. Used by other departments to budget salaries, wages, and *controllable costs* in support of expected room sales; a part of the overall budget package.

consumer (market segment) A market segment of hotel guests who are not usually on an expense account; for example, vacationers with or without young children. See also *group market; corporate transient hotel*.

contingency approach Management theory that holds that the appropriate management style is contingent upon the makeup and attitude of the subordinate. Closely related to the *situational leadership* model.

continuous functions of management Related actions (*analyze problems, making decisions, communicate*) that managers do continuously.

control (or incontrol) Revenues and expenses that are within the budget.

control information Data collected and used to maintain control of an operation.

controllable costs Classification of supply and expense accounts under the control of a department manager. See also *wage costs; employee costs*.

controller (also comptroller) Manager in charge of all accounting functions of a hotel or hospital. Duties include overall budget preparation, costing, and internal audit procedures and measuring performance against previously approved plans, procedures, and standards; interpreting and reporting financial data to other members of hotel management; participating in making policy decisions and executive action.

controlling Performing certain activities that ensure progress toward desired objectives according to plan See also management sequential functions.

control profit (loss) What remains after subtracting *controllable costs, wage costs*, and *employee costs* from revenue within a given department. Usually under control of a department manager.

coordinating (efforts of employees) Relating the efforts of employees in the most effective combinations. An activity of *directing*.

corporate transient hotel A hotel that is usually used by businesspeople on expense accounts. May have a transient group market in addition to some *consumer* guests.

count sheet Form used to record results when taking inventory.

coverlet A bedspread that covers just the top of a dust ruffle. It does not reach to the floor.

creating a position (job) description Identifying and defining the scope, relationships, responsibilities, duties, and authority of people in an organization. An activity of *organizing*.

critique Statement of performance analysis, usually reserved for elements or areas on a performance statement that are not in *control*. The statement should contain comments as to intended action and how *control* of the elements will be regained. A *standard operating procedure* performed by department managers of well-controlled companies.

cross-contamination Spreading germs from one location to another. This can happen when mops or cleaning cloths pick up bacteria in one location, and the housekeeper then uses the same equipment to clean another area, thereby transporting the pathogenic organisms to a new surface.

current assets *Assets* of a short-term nature such as cash, accounts receivable, and *inventory*. See also *fixed assets*.

cut loop The yarns in a carpet arranged into areas of high-cut tufts and lower-loop tufts to form a sculptured pattern of various heights.

daily routine Series of administrative and work-related events that occur between 6:30 A.M. and midnight and form the routine for a housekeeping department in the *guestroom portion* and *public areas* of a hotel. See also *housekeeping day*.

daily work assignment sheet Form that indicates special work tasks required for a given day and assigned to a specific worker.

damp mopping The use of a damp (not wet) mop for spot cleaning of spills and overall cleaning of light dirt from floors. This technique is not intended to remove heavily embedded dirt or old floor finish.

deep clean Periodic act of cleaning a guestroom in depth. Involves moving heavy furniture, high dusting, turning mattresses, vacuuming draperies and curtains, and other cleaning functions not normally performed in the day-to-day servicing of a guestroom. Synonymous with general clean.

deferring maintenance Postponing maintenance and custodial activities to create a short-term cost savings. However, the strategy ultimately results in higher overall costs.

deficiency of knowledge (DK) A reason given for nonperformance of a task. Workers could not perform the task even if their lives depended on it. Usually caused by no training or lack of understanding of what has been taught.

deficiency of task execution (DE) The failure of workers to perform a task properly after training.

defoamer Chemical added to a fabric cleaner that reduces the amount of suds produced by the detergent in the cleaner. Defoamers are often used in water-extraction carpet cleaning chemicals so that the pickup tanks are not inundated with suds.

delegating Creating responsibilities for or assigning tasks to subordinates, passing to them the required authority to act, then exacting accountability for results. An activity of *directing*.

delineating relationships Defining liaison lines within formal organizations that will facilitate relationships. An activity of *organizing*.

demonstration method Training technique in which you show someone how to do something.

denier A unit of weight of silk, nylon, or rayon that is an indicator of fineness. One denier is equal to $\frac{5}{100}$ of a gram in a 450-meter length of thread. The smaller the number, the smaller the circumference of the thread. (Fifteen-denier nylon lingerie is more transparent than 25-denier nylon lingerie.)

departmental meetings A technique of communicating with all members of a department at the same time. Housekeeping departmental meetings should be scheduled at least once each month and when unique situations warrant them. Meetings should be interesting, informative, and always under the control of management. Employees should always be allowed time to ask questions, which should receive timely replies.

department staffing guide Document that specifies positions within the organization and the number of people required to fill these positions. Used as a hiring guide.

depreciate Systematically reduce the book value of a *fixed asset* over its estimated useful life.

detergent A chemical that acts like a soap and is used for cleaning numerous surfaces. Detergents can be used effectively in hard water where ordinary soap will not produce suds and will leave a residue.

developing employees Improving the attitudes, knowledge, and skills of employees with a view toward assigning greater responsibilities or effecting promotions. An activity of *staffing*.

developing policies Making decisions that will govern when, where, and how procedures will be implemented; usually of long-standing nature. An activity of *planning*.

developing strategies Deciding how and when to achieve certain goals. An activity of *planning*.

development of subordinates Responsibility of management to ensure the professional growth of those placed under the manager.

dilution control Controlling the mixing of certain *all-purpose cleaners* with water in prescribed amounts that will enable the performance of various types of cleaning operations. See also *dilution ratio*.

dilution ratio Comparison of the amount of water that is, or must be, added to a specific cleaning agent that is recommended for a specific cleaning task. For example, a 20:1 dilution ratio means 20 parts water to 1 part cleaning agent to perform a specific task. See also *dilution control; all-purpose cleaner.*

***Diplococcus pneumonia* (dip-lo-COCK-us new-MOAN-ee-a)** Gram positive. Lobar (lung) pneumonia. Also walking pneumonia. Treatable with antibiotics.

directing Performing certain activities that bring about purposeful action toward desired objectives. See also *management sequential functions.*

discrepancy A situation occurring when the reported status of a guestroom by the front desk is different from the status actually observed by the housekeeping department during A.M. or P.M. *room checks*. For example, front desk believes a room to be *occupied* and housekeeping reports the room as a *ready* room or a *checkout* room. Discrepancies must be resolved by the front desk, or the room must be *rechecked* by housekeeping.

disinfectants A substance or means used to destroy *pathogenic microorganisms.*

disinfection A condition existing when infectious material or infection(s) are removed.

disinfection (concurrent) Process used while disease is still in progress.

disinfection (terminal) Process used when disease is ended.

dissatisfiers Items peripheral to a job, such as pay, working conditions, company policies, and quality of supervision, that if not properly attended to will demotivate employees. The positive effects on motivation caused by properly attending to dissatifiers are usually short-lived. See also *satisfiers.*

division of work document A report prepared by the *executive housekeeper* as a result of inspection and investigation of a new facility before opening. The report indicates areas that will require cleaning and contains recommendations as to who should be responsible for cleaning each area. Forms the basis for development and promulgation of the *area responsibility plan.*

documented Recorded event, happening, or inspection result.

do not disturb (DND) A verbal or written notation by a guest that he or she is not to be bothered. Refers to the guest, not the guestroom. Guest usually makes the request by hanging a small sign, which says, "Do not disturb," on the hall side of a guestroom door.

double double (DD) Guestroom having two double beds.

double occupancy Guestroom occupied by two guests. See also *single occupancy; multiple occupancy*.

double rooming Front desk accidentally rooms two separate guests or guest parties in the same room; usually occurs as a result of an unresolved *discrepancy*.

drying capacity Optimum weight of linen that should be placed in an automatic commercial dryer; for example, 50-pound, 100-pound, 200-pound, 300-pound dryers. Used in *sizing laundries*. See also *washing capacity; handling capacity*.

duvet Also known as *coverlet*. Covers the bed down to the dust ruffle. Some duvets have a pocket in which a comforter can be inserted to keep it clean.

dwell time Period of time a disinfectant has to remain on a surface to be effective.

18-room workload Size of the room-cleaning workload assigned daily to *section housekeepers* in the model hotel in this text. A typical workload that would be assigned to well-equipped section housekeepers in a *corporate transient* hotel.

electronic data processing (EDP) Processing of data by *computer* when *input* and *output hardware* are connected *on-line* to a computer's *central processing unit* (CPU).

electrowriter Electromechanical device used for transmitting facsimile handwritten messages, usually between housekeeping, front desk, and engineering.

elements of management See *management elements*.

emergencies Unpredictable combination of circumstances or resulting states that call for immediate enlightened action; can often be anticipated but seldom foreseen.

employee absenteeism See *absenteeism*.

employee appearance Aspect of employee behavior or training having to do with personal and uniformed appearance. A concern of management and supervision.

employee claims of unfairness Statements by workers that indicate less than harmonious relations with management; related to the manner in which employees are being treated. A major cause of worker attempts and desire to unionize.

employee contamination Corruption of relatively inexperienced or impressionable employees through the observance of the dishonest acts of others.

employee costs Costs occurring as a result of having employees; exclusive of per-hour *wage costs;* include costs of health and welfare, sick leave, meals, and other benefits. See also *controllable costs; wage costs*.

employee handbook Collection of facts, rules, regulations, and guidelines about a hotel, a hospital, or a specific department; usually given to an employee at the time of hiring to assist in employee orientation.

employee hygiene Personal cleanliness habits of employees that may be of concern to other employees or guests.

employee problems Problems that cause employees to have difficulties on the job; employees who cause interruptions or inefficiencies in work.

employee profile Concise biographical sketch of an employee, indicating certain traits, characteristics, and personality.

employee requisition Document initiated by a department and forwarded to the personnel office requesting that hiring procedures be started to fill a vacancy or a newly created position.

employee theft prevention Positive program or plan that anticipates the possibility of employees stealing.

employee turnover See *turnover*.

employment checklist Document used during the acquisition phase of hiring new employees; used to guarantee that no steps are omitted or overlooked in the hiring process.

employment history Written record of prior employment status; usually a part of an employment application indicating chronologically where the applicant has worked in the past, inclusive dates of employment, name of employee's supervisor, and reason for leaving the employment.

entomological Relating to insects, especially those that can cause or carry diseases.

environmental services A hospital's housekeeping department.

epoxy A synthetic, seamless flooring material. Very long lasting and extremely durable.

***Escherichia coli* (ee-shear-EEK-ee-ah COAL-i)** Gram-negative. Can grow in soap. Never use bar soap in a public washroom. Bacteria can be contracted from the droppings of animals.

establishing organizational structure Developing the formal organization plan for the accomplishment of tasks within a company. An activity of *organizing*.

establishing position qualifications Defining qualifications and preparing specifications for people who will fill positions in an organization. An activity of *organizing*.

establishing procedures Deciding and specifying how a task is to be done. An activity of *planning*.

executive committee Usually the highest level of operations management for a hotel property. Includes, but is not necessarily limited to, the general manager, resident manager, director of food and beverage, controller, and director of sales and marketing. Ex officio members may include the director of personnel, chief engineer, and security director. The top policymaking body of the property.

executive housekeeper Person in charge of management and administration of a housekeeping department or operation within a hotel. Synonymous titles include director of services, director of internal services, and director of environmental services (in hospitals).

exit interviews Management's attempt to gain information regarding working conditions and reasons for voluntary separations from former employees of the organization.

expense to To write off as an expense or expenditure or to charge to an expense account as cost of doing business on an *operating statement* over a given period of time. See also *capitalize*.

face weight The number of ounces of yarn per square yard in a carpet.

filling The threads of yarn that run the width of the fabric (also known as the *weft*).

financial statement Summary of accounts, showing a balance as of the beginning of business on a given date, the credits and the debits made, and the balance remaining at the end of the accounting period. See also *operating statement; balance sheet*.

finish Final coat(s) of either wax or a synthetic product that is intended to protect a floor from abrasion, provide a seamless and smooth top layer for the floor, and when polished, will provide a glossy and reflective surface.

finished sheet A sheet size that includes the top and bottom hems.

fire Chemical decomposition of a fuel element through combustion or burning. For fire to occur and sustain itself, there must be four elements—fuel, oxygen, heat, and a chemical reaction.

fire by-products The side effects or results of fire. They include heat, smoke, toxic gas, and fumes.

first-line supervisor One who supervises one or more *first-line workers*.

first-line worker A trained worker who performs hands-on work at the lowest level of the organization; works for a *first-line supervisor*.

fixed assets Tangible assets of a long-term nature such as land, buildings, machinery, and equipment. See also *assets; capital assets; current assets*.

fixed positions Positions that are fixed in terms of work and man-hour requirements; positions not subject to being reduced in hours because of fluctuations in occupancy.

flash point The temperature at which the vapor from a flammable substance will ignite momentarily in the air, in the presence of a small flame.

flatwork A laundry term that is used for sheets, pillowcases, and table linens.

floor plan layout Engineering or architectural drawing of the layout of machinery, furniture, fixtures, and equipment.

forecasting Establishing where present courses of action will lead. An activity of *planning*.

forecasting man-hour requirements A short-run statement of need for the utilization of man-hours to accomplish a specific task.

foundation The primary coat(s) of sealer applied to a floor. A foundation's intended purpose is to prevent spilled liquids that may cause staining and other damage from penetrating into the floor.

14-point theft prevention program Fourteen guidelines for managerial and supervisory action that may reduce employee theft and dishonesty.

fresh look Inspection conducted by people not regularly associated with an area; allows for observing and reporting deficiencies not noticed by someone regularly in contact with the area.

front office manager Person in charge of front office operations in a hotel. One of several principal assistants to a *resident manager*, who is on the same level as the *executive housekeeper*. Person in charge of the front desk, bell services, transportation, and other related activities in a hotel.

full-time employment Incumbent has attained full-time status, usually after successfully completing training and a probationary period of employment. In union-free environments, implies that the employee is committing to work and the company is committing to schedule the employee 30 or more regular hours of work each week.

function room sheet Form on which special instructions are given for setting up, arranging, or rearranging a guestroom for a special function. See also *parlor; hospitality suite*.

functions Management duties and activities. Can be divided into sequential and continuous functions.

fungus Simple plant lacking chlorophyll. Bread mold is an example.

furniture, fixtures, and equipment (FFE) Classification of *fixed assets* of a hotel or hospital that have specified depreciable lives, usually ranging from three to seven years.

general clean See *deep clean*.

global warming An alarming planetary trend precipitated by the release of chlorofluorocarbons into the atmosphere and the burning of fossil fuels.

GRA Guestroom attendant See *section housekeeper*.

gray goods Unfinished fabric directly from the loom.

gram positive/negative Refers to the color staining of test samples of certain bacteria. Gram "positive" is a "blue" test result when certain bacteria are treated with testing reagents. Gram "negative" is a "red" test indication.

greenhouse gases Primarily carbon dioxide and methane, but also nitrous oxides, hydrofluorocarbons (HFCs), perfluorocarbons (PFCs), and sulfur hexafluoride (SF_6[sbs]). These gases absorb heat in the atmosphere. This phenomenon leads to global warming.

ground warp Yarn threads that run lengthwise in a towel. They are used as the backing for the *pile warp* threads. The ground warp is usually a poly-cotton blend.

group market Market segment of hotel business, usually defined by the sale of 10 or more room nights in one group.

guest essentials *Guest supplies* that are essential in guestrooms but that the guest would not normally be expected to use up or remove upon departure. Examples include water glasses, ice buckets, and clothes hangers. See also *guest expendables; guest loan items.*

guest expendables *Guest supplies* that guests would normally be expected to use up or take away upon departure. Examples include stationery, toilet issue, and soap. See also *guest essentials; guest loan items.*

guest loan items *Guest supplies* not normally found in a guestroom but available upon request. Examples include hair dryers, razors, ironing boards, and irons. Guests sign a receipt and specify a time that the item may be picked up by the housekeeping department. See also *guest expendables; guest essentials.*

guest receipt log book Log book in which guests sign for the use of *guest loan items.*

guest request Any special request not normally included in the regular servicing of a guestroom, such as for extra towels, hair dryer, razor, roll-away bed, or baby crib.

guestroom Numbered room in a hotel provided specifically for occupancy by one or more regular or transient guests; is most often rented but can be complimented to special guests; is located in a major subsection of a hotel known as the *guestroom portion of the hotel.*

guestroom attendant (GRA) See *section housekeeper.*

guestroom portion of the hotel Specific area of a hotel in which guestrooms are located; also includes guest corridors, elevators, stairwells, vending areas, and some service areas. Not included are *public areas,* restaurants, lounge areas, recreation areas, or major service areas.

guestroom types A differentiation among the varieties of *guestroom* based on types of sleeping accommodations or equipment; usually identified by specific symbols as follows: T, room with one twin bed; TT, room with two twin beds; D, room with one double bed; DD, room with two double beds; ST, studio, room with a day bed or convertible sofa; Q, room with one queen bed; K, room with one king bed; P, parlor sitting room usually having hidden sleep equipment, may be set for a small meeting or hospitality function; S, suite, two or more rooms that connect internally and are sold as one unit; CON, rooms that are adjacent and connect internally; BS, bilevel suite, a suite on two levels having an internal stairway between levels; ES, executive suite, a high-quality suite, usually having two

or more rooms but only one with access to the hotel corridor.

guest supplies Supplies specifically needed because guests are staying in a hotel. See also *guest expendables; guest essentials; guest loan items.*

handling capacity Measure of the design of a laundry facility that relates to the amount and ease of handling of linen within the facility. See also *washing capacity; drying capacity.*

hardware (computer) Physical components of a computer system; includes *input* and *output* devices, *processor,* printing devices, and video monitors (CRTs).

HazComm Hazardous Communication Standard for chemicals and toxic wastes established by the Occupational Safety and Health Administration.

holes in the ozone layer This phenomenon is caused by the release of chlorofluorocarbons (CFCs). Since the banning of the production of this chemical, the situation has started to stabilize.

homogeneous Uniform throughout. Everything is made up of the same elements.

hospitality suite *Guestroom* that has been temporarily set up to accommodate a small party; may require the movement of some furniture; more appropriately set in a *suite* or *parlor.*

house breakout plan Document specifying the division of the *guestroom portion of a hotel* into meaningful work units for cleaning and servicing. The plan is usually a line drawing of the floor plans of the rooms section, appropriately divided into *room sections* and *house divisions* to delineate supervisory responsibilities.

house division Group of four to six *room sections* with associated and/or specified corridors, elevators, stairwells, and service and storage areas; may be assigned a color or letter designation and be placed under the control of a *senior housekeeper* (supervisor).

housekeeper's report A report made daily to the front desk by the housekeeping department and signed by a manager, indicating the correct status of all guestrooms in a hotel as visually noted at about 3:00 P.M. each day. Compilation of results obtained from P.M. *room checks* conducted of the entire *guestroom portion of the hotel.* Specifies which rooms are *ready* for occupancy, *occupied* by a guest or contain luggage, and/or *on-change* (being serviced for newly arriving guests).

housekeeping central Synonymous with *main linen room.* Central physical point of administrative and operational activity for a housekeeping department. Usually contains or is adjacent to the offices of the *executive housekeeper* and principal assistants. Under the supervisory control of the *linen room supervisor* and/or *night housekeeping supervisor.* Central point of control for all communications emanating from and received by the housekeeping department. A point of issue for selected and special items of supply. See also *satellite linen room.*

housekeeping day That period of a 24-hour day when the housekeeping department is open and operating; usually from about 6:30 A.M. until midnight.

housekeeping manager Manager who is the principal assistant to the *executive housekeeper;* person who is directly responsible for *guestroom* cleaning. May also be the person in charge of the housekeeping department in a small property.

housekeeping standing rotational scheduling form Form used to create and display a system of standing rotational scheduling, specifying regular days off for *housekeeping teams* and other individuals within the department. See *standing rotational scheduling system.*

housekeeping team (regular or swing) Group of housekeeping employees consisting of one *senior housekeeper* (supervisor), several *section housekeepers or GRAs,* and a *section housekeeping aide,* who work together as a regular team or designated swing team within an assigned *house division.* The team is usually identified by a color or number similar to that of the house division where it is assigned to work.

hypochlorite A salt or ester of hypochlorous acid. Hypochlorous acid is an unstable, weak acid that is used as a bleach and disinfectant.

idophors A variety of disinfectants.

individual development (ID) program Development program for managers being groomed for greater responsibilities and/or promotion by the Marriott Hotel Corporation.

indoor air quality (IAQ) Good indoor air quality is present when 80 percent of the occupants are satisfied and there are no harmful pollutants present as determined by cognizant authorities—according to the American Society of Heating, Refrigeration and Air Conditioning Engineers (ASHRAE). There is a growing concern about the pollution found in the air inside buildings. Air inside is generally considered to be much worse on average than the outside air.

input (computer) Data entered into a computer for processing.

inspection day One particular day of the workweek when regular inspections of *guestrooms* and other sections of the hotel are performed. See also *zone inspection program.*

inspection program Regular inspection of specified areas of a hotel or hospital. Usually formalized and specified through a *standard operating procedure.* See also *property inspection program; zone inspection program.*

inspector Person who does nothing but inspect *guestrooms* in a hotel or hospital to ensure that *standards of cleanliness* are being maintained.

integrated waste management A strategy that incorporates many different methods to solve the problem of solid waste. Solutions include source reduction, reuse, recycling, waste transformation, and landfilling.

intermediate host A transmitter of disease that is not affected by it. Also known as an "immune carrier." An example is the *Anopheles* mosquito; it can bite a person infected with malaria, then bite another victim, thus transmitting the disease.

inventory Quantity on hand of an item of value; recorded in the *books of account* as *current assets.*

inventory (verb) To count and record the quantity of items of value.

inventory control Management function of classifying, ordering, receiving, storing, issuing, and accounting for items of value.

inventory record book Record of amounts of specific items on hand; also contains pricing information and valuation of total *inventory.*

ironers Commercial pieces of machinery used for ironing linens in a commercial or *on-premises laundry.*

JCAHO Joint Commission of Accreditation of Health Care Organizations.

job descriptions Documents describing the work to be done in each of several unique jobs within a department. Specify working hours, special qualifications of the worker, if any, responsibilities and duties of incumbents to the positions to which they refer. Usually prepared for workers who do hands-on work and first-line supervising. See also *position descriptions.*

jute A strong, smooth fiber that comes from plants in Asia; used to make rope, canvas, and carpet backing.

key control program Plan or control for the prevention of loss of keys used by employees in the daily performance of their work functions.

key pouch Leather container for storing keys. Pouch usually contains an identifying mark or number to facilitate easy reference to a specific area of the facility and ease in subcustody reference and key control inventory.

labor costs See *wage costs.*

laundry consultant Expert in the development of laundry facilities and operations.

laundry supervisor Working supervisory position in a hotel or hospital *on-premises laundry;* reports to a laundry manager.

leadership *Management task* of influencing people to accomplish desired goals.

leadership style The observed behavior of the leader in an organization. Commonly observed styles have been categorized and given labels by management theorists. Examples include MacGregor's *"Theory X"* manager who has a high concern for production but little concern for the welfare of subordinates in the organization, and the *"Theory Y"* manager who has both a high concern for production and a high concern for people in the organization.

leave of absence (LOA) Authorized period of time away from work without pay; granted by management to an employee, during which time seniority is protected.

leveling technique Enlightened style of conducting a *performance appraisal* when poor, questionable, or unsatisfactory performance is the subject of the appraisal.

level loop A type of carpet in which the pile loops are of uniform height.

linen broker Person who deals in linens; may represent several *linen mills;* has knowledge and access to sources of immediate linen supplies.

linen count sheet Form used to record the results of counting items of linen. See also *count sheet*.

linen in use Specific amount of linen in circulation or being used by a housekeeping department to service *guestrooms* at the time a linen *inventory* is taken. See also *linen, new, on hand; linen on hand*.

linen mills Places where linens are woven. Linen mills usually sell to hotels and hospitals through *linen brokers*, but large or well-managed hotel organizations deal directly with mills.

linen, new, on hand Specific amount of new and unused linen that is stored in cases on the property and is available when needed; as a part of total *linen on hand*.

linen on hand Total amount of linen as reflected by *inventory* of all linen. Includes new linen on hand and linen in use.

linen poundage requirements Specified amount of linen by weight, generated from linen demands of a specific hotel or hospital based on the size of the facility (number and type of beds). Used to determine *washing capacity* and *drying capacity* and in *sizing laundries*.

linen room supervisor Working supervisor in charge of *main linen room* activities; assistant to the *executive housekeeper*. Person is in charge of the central or main linen room, linen room operations, and communications with the housekeeping department, the front desk, engineering, and the guests.

linens Traditionally, the cloth made from flax fiber; the term is now used to indicate sheets, pillowcases, washcloths, cloth bath mats, towels, tablecloths, and napkins.

linen valuation Monetary value of the linen *inventory*, including both *new* and *in-use linens*. Calculation is determined by multiplying specific linen counts of each item of linen by the last known purchase price of the item. A value of the asset linen inventories as a part of total *inventory*.

line organization The organizational structure parallels the duties and activities involved in the production of a good or service. Follows the principle of *span of control* and unity of command (every employee answers to just one supervisor).

lobby housekeeper See *public area (PA) housekeeper*.

lobby housekeeping aide See *public area (PA) housekeeper*.

lock cylinder That portion of a door-locking mechanism that contains the keyway; houses the pins that match the indentation of a particular key being used to open a door. Cylinders are removable and thus interchangeable.

loss-prevention program A plan or procedure whereby action may be taken to eliminate or minimize the loss of life or property.

MacGregor, Douglas Educator, author, management psychologist; noted for the development of the *Theory X* and *Theory Y* models for managers.

maid See *section housekeeper*.

main linen room See *housekeeping central*.

maintenance checklist Document used as a guide in the performance of a *maintenance inspection*.

maintenance inspection Inspection conducted for the sole purpose of uncovering repair needs, as opposed to cleaning needs; also conducted to ensure that preventive maintenance is being regularly performed on machinery and equipment.

maintenance work request form A three-part document used for recording the need for repairs; is transmitted to the engineering department. Form allows for the control and progressing of work and the recording of man-hours and materials involved in the repairs performed.

make ready (MR) The act of servicing a *guestroom* for occupancy. Making a room ready prepares the room for a change of status from *checkout (C/O)* or *tidy (T)* to a *ready (R)* room.

making decisions Arriving at conclusions and judgments.

management continuous functions *Analyzing problems, making decisions*, and *communicating*.

management elements Those things that a manager has to work with: ideas, material resources, money, and people.

management science The modern-day derivation of *scientific management*. Management science attempts to apply mathematical models to aid in making management decisions.

management sequential functions Group of related actions (*planning, organizing, staffing, directing,* and *controlling*) that a manager may be seen to do in a given sequence. This sequence is most appropriate when managing a project.

management tasks Continuous objectives imposed on a person who manages, such as *conceptual thinking, administration,* and *leadership*.

management triangle Relationship of three aspects of managerial activity: concern for the accomplishment of work, concern for the people who perform the work, and application of scientific techniques to the field of management.

manager (as a leader) Person assigned to manage or supervise a group of employees; must have *leadership* skills.

managerial grid Graphical presentation of five classical styles of behavior exhibited by managers when thinking through decisions in a group setting.

managerial style See *leadership style.*

managing change Stimulating creativity and innovation among subordinates that will foster cooperation when changes in policies and procedures are necessary. An activity of *directing.*

managing differences Encouraging independent thought among workers, and resolving conflict; commonly thought of as *problem solving.* An activity of *directing.*

man-hour justification Statement explaining the need for and how man-hours will be used in support of revenue-generating operations.

material Broad classification of items, including furniture, fixtures, equipment, and supplies used in or under the control of a housekeeping or other department within a hotel, hospital, or health-care institution.

material safety data sheets (MSDSs) Informational sheets available from manufacturers of chemicals that describe the toxic effects of these chemicals and the proper procedures to use when handling them. The *HazComm* Standard demands that these sheets be made available to all employees who may exposed to a potentially hazardous chemical.

measuring results Ascertaining whether there have been, and the extent of, deviations from goals and standards. An activity of *controlling.*

mercerizing A fabric-finishing process that treats cotton with sodium hydroxide (a caustic soda) to strengthen the cotton and enable dyes to better penetrate the fabric. Patented by John Mercer (1791–1866), an English fabric printer.

metal cross-linked polymer finishes Floor finishes that contain heavy metals, such as zinc. These finishes have fallen into disfavor because of their potential harm to the environment.

microbiology A natural science that began with the discovery of the microscope. It had been suggested since the thirteenth century that "invisible" organisms were responsible for decay and disease. In the latter quarter of the nineteenth century, the term "microbe" was coined to describe these organisms, all of which were thought to be related. Bacteriology, protozoology, and virology are three subdisciplines.

micron A unit of measure—10^{-6}[ss] meter, or 1/25,000 of 1 inch. (Bacteria are usually in the range of 1 to 300 microns.)

microorganisms Bacteria, rickettsiae, small fungi (such as yeasts and molds), algae, and protozoans, as well as problematical forms of life such as viruses.

mineral A solid homogeneous crystalline chemical element or compound that results from the inorganic processes of nature having a specific chemical composition.

miscellaneous charge Nonstandard charge (as opposed to a charge for room rent, food, or beverage) of a hotel guest for services rendered or product purchased.

molecule A compound created by the combination of a certain group of *atoms.*

morning activities Group of activities occurring from about 6:30 A.M. until about 1:00 P.M. during the *housekeeping day.* They include *opening the house,* commencing the assigned work, conducting an A.M. *room check,* receiving information about *checkout* rooms, making up *guestrooms,* and providing *ready* rooms to the front desk throughout the day for reassignment to new guests.

motivating employees Creating an atmosphere whereby employees are persuaded or inspired to take a desired action. An activity of *directing.*

multiple occupancy Guestroom is occupied by more than two guests. See also *single occupancy; double occupancy.*

Mycobacterium diphtheria **(my-co-back-TEER-ee-um dif-THEE-ree-ah)** Gram positive. Transmitted in milk. Not too prevalent due to vaccination now available against disease.

Mycobacterium tuberculosis **(my-co-back-TEER-ee-um too-BER-cue-LOW-sis)** Gram negative, acid-fast (cannot be killed with acid).

napery Tablecloths, napkins, and doilies.

natural disaster Event capable of causing loss of life, great material damage, destruction, and distress. May be caused by fire, flood, earthquake, hurricane, or tornado.

needles Refers to hypodermic needles.

new linen on hand See *linen, new, on hand.*

night clerk's report to housekeeping Report prepared at the front desk by the night clerk for the housekeeping department at the end of the night's activity; indicates *guestrooms* that will require service during the upcoming workday.

night housekeeping supervisor Supervisor in charge of evening housekeeping operations; an assistant to the *executive housekeeper.*

night supervisor's report of evening activities Report maintained by the night supervisor in charge of the second work shift, indicating the volume and type of activity performed by the evening shift. Includes a record of *checkouts* and *tidies* made ready, *rechecks* made and the results thereof, and a summary of special requests made by guests.

no-iron linens Specific type of linens manufactured with a certain percentage of polyester fiber. Also identified as blend linens; for example, 50-50 blend has 50 percent cotton content and 50 percent polyester fiber. If properly handled in laundering, it will appear wrinkle-free.

nonionic detergent A detergent that does not ionize in solution.

nonresilient flooring Flooring materials that do not "give" to any degree underfoot. Examples include concrete, ceramic tile, epoxy, marble, terrazzo, and all other stone floors.

nosocomial infection An infection that results from a stay in a hospital and the exposure to germs present in that hospital.

occupancy forecast Short-range estimate of guestroom occupancy expected over a given period of time, such as a day, a week, or other accounting period of usually not more than 90 days.

occupancy type Manner in which a registered guest or group of guests will occupy a room; *single occupancy* is one person only to a room; *double occupancy* is two people to a room, *multiple occupancy* is more than two people to a room.

occupied (OCC) The status of a *guestroom* indicating that a guest or guests are in residence; the presence of luggage in the room indicating the probable presence of a registered guest.

odor-pair neutralization Molecules of gas from chemical stimulate receptor cells deep inside the nose that cancel out unpleasant odors being caused by other gas molecules.

once-around method Method of cleaning a *guestroom* whereby unnecessary steps and transportation of supplies and equipment are eliminated or minimized.

on-change See *checkout*.

one par of linen Quantity of linen required to meet certain requirements; usually the total amount required to cover beds and to handle bath needs in all *guestrooms*.

one-stroke solution *Dilution ratio* of an *all-purpose cleaner* that provides a proper cleaning agent for certain operations in approximately one wipe; for example, 4:1 dilution ratio of a specific cleaning agent is used to sanitize a toilet in one wiping stroke. See also *three-stroke solution*.

on-line Computer equipment (*input* and *output* devices and the *central processing unit*) that is electronically connected and ready to operate at all times on demand of an operator; as opposed to off-line equipment, which requires the mechanical or time-scheduled entry of data into the system.

on-premises laundry Also called the in-house laundry. A laundry that is built, owned, or operated by the user of the linens processed; usually on the same premises where linens will be used, but facility may be detached.

on-scene commander Member of local fire or police protection organization or other technically competent municipal official having authority over local law or police services who takes charge at scenes of *emergencies*.

on-the-job training (OJT) Training technique whereby one or more trainees are shown what to do on the job. Employees practice the skill and are observed by the instructor, who then critiques the work. When only one trainee receives instruction at a time, the technique is referred to as the *coach-pupil method* of training.

opening the house A daily operational planning procedure whereby rooms requiring service are assigned to *section housekeepers* specifically scheduled to work that day. Procedure becomes more or less complicated depending on occupancy levels and number of *guestrooms* that must be reassigned as *pickup rooms*. This is the first of several *morning activities* performed each day and should be completed before workers arrive for work.

open section A specific *room section* created for the regular assignment to a *section housekeeper* for cleaning, but, due to lack of occupancy, has no *section housekeeper* assigned. Occupied rooms in the open section must be reassigned as *pickup rooms* to a *section housekeeper* on that day.

operating budget A financial statement of a plan giving an estimate of operating revenues, expenses, and profit (or loss) expected for a given period of time. See also *budgeting; capital expenditure budget*.

operating cost Expenses associated with generating revenues. See *operating statement; operating budget*.

operating statement Periodic financial report indicating actual performance (results) as compared with budgeted performance; reports revenues, expenses, and profit (or loss) over a given period of time; may also report utilization of other *assets* such as labor, man-hours, and material.

operational budget cycle Chronological expression of time involving budget preparation, activation, and operation. Budget cycles usually start three to six months before the beginning of the fiscal year. They include expectations of annual sales revenues and planned utilization of salaries, wages, and controllable supplies. Time is then allowed for review and critique of the new budget. Finally, budget approval precedes the beginning of the new budget year. As the year proceeds, plans are made to start the next budget cycle.

operational budget for the housekeeping department Housekeeping segment of the total operational budget of a hotel or hospital. In hotels, that portion of the operating budget dealing with guestroom revenue, housekeeping department salaries and wages, employee costs, and *controllable costs* related to the servicing of *guestrooms* and *public areas* of a hotel.

organic A substance or a product of substances of plant or animal origin. Chemically, organic compounds contain carbon "r" strings of molecules attached to one or more hydrogen molecules.

organizing Performing certain activities that arrange and relate people and work for effective accomplishment of objectives; See also management sequential functions.

orienting new employees Familiarizing new employees with their situation and surroundings. An activity of *staffing*.

osmological Relating to soils of organic or inorganic matter that emit unpleasant odors.

out of order (room) (OOO) Designation assigned to a guestroom that for some mechanical or repair reason cannot be occupied by a guest. Authority for such designation usually rests with the chief engineer.

output (computer) Data generated by a computer as a result of *input* data being fed into a central processing unit, which in turn responds to the direction of a computer program.

outsourcing Contracting with outside firms to provide services that may have originally been performed by in-house employees.

padding A layer of material placed under carpet to increase resiliency. It can be made from a number of natural and synthetic materials.

panic emotion Uncontrolled psychological departure from responsible action or behavior when experiencing fear or sudden widespread fright as a result of not knowing what to do in an emergency situation.

par A standard, specific, or normal level of stock.

parlor (P) Sitting room usually having hidden sleep equipment; may be set up for a small meeting or *hospitality suite*.

participative management Act of involving workers in discussions regarding decisions that ultimately affect the workers.

part-time employee In the hotel industry, one who regularly commits to and is scheduled to work by the company 29 hours or less per week. See also *steady extra; regular employee; temporary employee; pool employee*.

passive-aggressive behavior An obstructionist resistance to following authoritative instructions in personal or occupational situations. It can be manifested as procrastination, stubbornness, sullenness, and resentment.

pathogenic Disease-causing, disease-producing.

pathogenic microorganisms Disease-causing bacteria and viruses.

pay increases Stepped increments of pay normally awarded to an employee for satisfactory performance during specified time periods, for outstanding performance, or in recognition of cost-of-living increases.

pay scale A published table of compensation offered for jobs performed; usually indicates increments of pay based on seniority and minimum and maximum

compensation to be offered for each job. Usually developed by personnel departments as a result of wage surveys of the surrounding area, degree of difficulty of jobs surveyed, availability of labor markets, and company policies.

percale A cotton cloth that is closely woven so as to give a smooth finish.

performance analysis Breaking apart a job into its various elements of work to evaluate how the elements affect each other.

performance appraisal Formal act of notifying employees about the observed quality of their performance. May be oral but is usually written and becomes an official part of the employee's record.

performance standards Conditions that will exist when key duties are done well. An activity of *controlling*.

period Segment of time in which performance will be demonstrated and measured against a plan or budget.

period linen inventory count record Log or similar record of all items of linen counted as reported on *linen count sheets* during *period*. See also *inventory; inventory control; inventory record book*.

period statements *Financial statements* book of an operational nature covering a set period of time; indicating revenue, expenses, and *control profit (or loss)*; usually show comparisons to budget for the same period; require critique of out-of-control elements. See also *operating statement*.

personal development of managers Responsibility of managers to develop subordinates or junior managers for future assignments.

personal plan Document prepared by a manager indicating how he or she intends to carry out assigned responsibilities and meet commitments or stated objectives.

Personnel Action Form (PAF) Standardized document used for recording details about an employee such as name, address, job classification, rate of pay, and record of past performance with the company for company reference; may be computerized.

petroleum naphtha solvents Fabric cleaners and spot removers made from distilled petroleum or coal tar products.

phenolic compounds Any one of a series of aromatic hydroxyl derivatives of benzene, of which carbolic acid is the first member.

photochemical reaction A reaction of certain pollutants in the atmosphere that produces ozone, which is a lung irritant and a component of *smog*.

physical agents Nonchemical agents that will affect the growth of bacteria or will destroy it. Examples of nonchemical agents are sunlight, temperature, heat, moisture, and pressure.

physical linen inventory Actual count or supply of various items of *linen on hand*.

pickup room Occupied room in an *open section* that must be assigned to a *section housekeeper* in a nearby section for servicing.

pile The threads of yarn found on the surface of a rug. The nap. Pile density and weight are indications of quality.

pile warp Yarn threads that run lengthwise in a towel that make the terry loops on both sides of the towel. These are normally 100 percent cotton fibers.

planning Performing certain activities that predetermine a course of action; See also management sequential functions.

plies Strands of yarn that comprise a thread.

P.M. report A document used for noting the status of guestrooms in a *room section* in the late afternoon, usually about 3:00 P.M. Report forms are developed daily for every section in the hotel to indicate whether rooms are *occupied (OCC), ready (R),* or *checkouts (C/O)*. P.M. reports form the basis of the *housekeeper's report*.

P.M. room check Visual inspection of every guestroom in a hotel to determine observed status of rooms. Results of the room check are recorded on the P.M. report.

polygraph examination Inconclusive examination of a person that may give indications as to the honesty or dishonesty of that person. Federal law forbids its use for preemployment testing in all but a few occupations and has effectively limited its use to but a handful of other applications.

polypropylene A lightweight resin. It is used for making carpet backing, molded plastics, and insulation.

polyurethane A strong plastic resin that resists fire, acids, and decay. It is used in a number of applications, including insulation, a substitute for foam rubber, and a substitute for varnish.

pool employee or employment Classification of employee or employment whereby the worker is called in to work when needed. No regular schedule of work is expected or promised.

poor performance Appraisal indicating that quality of performance is less than satisfactory but not unsatisfactory.

portion control Specifying and providing to workers specific quantities of chemicals, cleaning solutions, or other measurable agents used in housekeeping operations. Some cleaning agents are prepackaged in measured proportions and may be issued to *section housekeepers* for cleaning tasks.

position descriptions Similar to *job descriptions* but written for management positions. Documents that set forth the manager's basic function, scope of activities, specific responsibilities, and reporting relationships; also indicates where the manager should apply his or her time. See also *job descriptions*.

preopening budget Plan for the use of certain fixed and variable cost items before opening a hotel or hospital. See also *preopening cost or expense*.

preopening cost or expense Those costs or expenses normally associated with opening a hotel or hospital (before revenue generation commences). Such costs are usually *amortized* over a several-year period after operation has begun. May include the cost of certain *fixed assets* as well as preoperating costs.

primary backing The surface into which carpet fibers are stitched in a tufted carpet. The backing is normally made from polypropylene.

probationary period of employment Usually the first three or four months of employment when training is being conducted and suitability for full-time employment is being established. A period of employment before the inauguration of all employment rights and benefits.

problem solving Act of seeking solutions to professional and personal problems. The end result of *analyzing problems*.

problem-solving temperament The personal and psychological emotion and attitude displayed by a manager when involved in *problem solving*.

processor (computer) Also known a *central processing unit (CPU)*.

productivity The ability to produce. Management theory is concerned with increasing productivity.

pro forma An imaginary balance sheet or system of accounts containing figures for illustrative purposes; usually provides retroactive indications of how an operation will run.

program (computer) The electronic intelligence stored in a computer that controls the processing of data. See also *software program*.

programming Scheduling of a group of tasks in a desired order. An activity of *planning*. Also, the act of developing a *software program* for a computer.

progressing work Act of keeping track of work completed by a *section housekeeper* during the *housekeeping day*.

project Element of work to be performed that is not routine or part of a *daily routine*.

property inspection program Formalized program for the inspection of an entire hotel or hospital property. See also *inspection program; zone inspection program*.

***Pseudomonas aeruginosa* (sue-doe-MOAN-us air-o-gin-O-sa)** Gram negative. Very resistant to disinfectants. A major problem in public restrooms. Disease is more prevalent in women. Bacteria will grow in standing water.

public area housekeeper One who works in *public areas* as opposed to the *guestroom portion* of the hotel.

public areas Physical areas of a hotel where the general public may congregate or walk; includes lobby area, public sitting area, public restrooms, and public thoroughfare. Does not include *guestrooms* or the *guestroom portion* of the facility.

public areas department A department in a large hotel responsible for the cleaning of all *public areas* (e.g., pools, lobbies, convention centers, casinos, restaurants).

purchasing Management function of researching and ordering items of value used in the production of revenue. Some companies have *purchasing agents* who do all purchasing; others require department managers to perform purchasing functions for their departments, allowing for better departmental accountability for expenditures.

purchasing agent Person who performs the purchasing function for all departments within an organization. See also *purchasing.*

purify the room rack Correcting the front desk room rack to reflect the correct status of all guestrooms; usually done about 4:30 P.M. each day by reference to the *housekeeper's report.*

quality circle Group of people consisting of managers, supervisors, and workers, all having an equal responsibility for quality of work or production output.

quaternary ammonium compounds Any derivative of ammonium in which the four hydrogen atoms have been replaced by organic radicals. Quaternary ammonium compounds are used as disinfectants and in various medicines.

ready or ready to rent (R) Status of a guestroom indicating that the room is vacant and has been serviced for occupancy. See also *checkout; occupied.*

reagents A group of testing solutions used to identify certain bacteria and their properties. Such tests can help determine what chemicals should be used to kill certain bacteria.

reasonable security for guestrooms A level of quality in the attributes or physical items in a guestroom that provide the guest with a reasonable measure of protection from uninvited guests.

rechecks *Guestroom* or rooms that have been identified by the front desk as *discrepancies* and that cannot be readily resolved at the front desk; requires that the housekeeping department take a second visual look at the guestroom to ascertain the correct status of the room.

recycling Breaking a product down to its essential elements and making a new product.

red tag system Control system using a red tag (form) to administer the legal removal of property from a hotel or hospital facility. The form indicates what material is being removed and who the rightful property owner is; it is signed by a manager. A receipt (second copy) of the form is collected by a door security person as the item is removed and is returned to the authorizing manager for control.

regular employee One who has attained *full-time employment* status; usually attained after successfully completing a probationary period of employment.

relief team See *swing team.*

repair and physical maintenance Correction of a physical defect in a facility; occurs under the direction of the head of the repair and maintenance department (chief engineer).

reporting systems Determining critical data that will be needed, by whom, and how often in order to follow the conduct of an operation. An activity of *controlling.*

resident manager Person in charge of hotel operations exclusive of food and beverage operations; principal assistant to a hotel manager. An executive committee member. Usually the immediate supervisor for a *front office manager* and the *executive housekeeper.*

resilient floors Floors that "give" underfoot. When dented, a resilient floor will eventually rebound wholly or partially to its original form. Resilient flooring materials include asphalt tile, carpet, linoleum, rubber, vinyl tile, and wood.

resort hotel A hotel with fine amenities and luxury flair located near or organized about social settings, geographical points of interest, or centers of activity. May be frequented by business travelers but is primarily a vacation destination.

reuse Using a product more than once before recycling or landfilling.

rewarding employees Praising or disciplining employees as necessary to show acceptance or rejection of performance. A part of *performance appraisal;* an activity of *controlling.*

room check Visual check of a guestroom by an employee to determine the status of the room. Room is either *ready (R), occupied (OCC),* or *checkout (C/O).*

room found vacant (RFV) Status of a guestroom as observed by housekeeping that was thought to have been occupied according to the front desk. This is not an unusual occurrence when guests who have made prior arrangements for payment of bills depart without notifying the front desk. Also, guests who pay in advance may depart without notifying the front desk. This creates a *discrepancy* that must be resolved by rechecking the room.

room inspections Periodic inspections of *guestrooms* to ensure that *standards of cleanliness* and servicing are being maintained.

room revenue Gross monies generated from the sale of guestrooms in a hotel.

room section Group of 13 to 20 guestrooms reasonably contiguous to each other that may normally be cleaned and serviced by one person in one eight-hour shift. The room section is normally assigned a number and assigned to a *section housekeeper.*

sales per man-hour Performance ratio of two statistics maintained by the hotel industry that can act as a measure of operational performance; reflects the amount of revenue received for the sale of guestrooms for every man-hour used in support of the hotel occupancy that generated the revenue; can be budgeted or forecast in preparation of a comparison to actual performance. See also *target statistics.*

Salmonella choleraesuis (**sal-moe-NELL-a coll-er-ah-SUE-iss**) Gram negative. A form of food poisoning that the body can usually tolerate and throw off. The bacteria are used to test germicides.

Sanforizing A patented process that preshrinks cotton, linen, or rayon fabric; invented by Sanford L. Cluett (1874–1968).

sanitizer A sanitizing substance or product. To sanitize is to prevent the spread of disease.

satellite linen room One of several service areas located in the guestroom area of the hotel used as central workstation for a *housekeeping team;* a storage area for bed and bath linens and other supplies used regularly by *section housekeepers* and aides in the performance of their work tasks. See also *housekeeping central.*

satisfiers Experiences intrinsic in a job or work that create positive attitudes and act to enhance motivation. See also *dissatisfiers.*

scenario An outline of possible events or happenings.

scientific management Systematic way of thinking about management based on obtaining information from which to derive facts, form conclusions, make recommendations, and take action.

sealer A product intended to fill in the holes in the porous surface of a floor. It protects the floor from spilled liquids.

secondary backing A second backing on a carpet that provides additional strength, usually made from polypropylene or jute.

second request Second *maintenance work request form* submitted to the maintenance department for work called for on a prior request and not yet completed.

seconds Linens and clothing that have imperfections. Most imperfections are not noticeable and have no effect on the product's use.

section housekeeper Person regularly assigned to clean guestrooms in a hotel. Synonymous with maid, chambermaid, room attendant. See also *GRA* and *guestroom attendant.*

section housekeeper's daily work report Form designed for a specific (numbered) *room section* that is used by a *section housekeeper* during the day. A copy of this form will be used to make a *p.m. room check* and will become a P.M. *report.*

section housekeeping aide Worker who is a member of and assists workers in a housekeeping team. Must be capable of lifting heavy objects and operating heavy machinery in the servicing and cleaning of major areas in the *guestroom portion of a hotel*; is not directly involved in regular and routine guestroom cleaning.

security Quality or condition of being free from danger, fear, anxiety, uncertainty, doubt, or care.

selecting employees Recruiting and acquiring qualified people for each position in an organization. An activity of *staffing.*

selvage The side edge of a towel. There is no *pile warp* present in the selvage. It is finished off to prevent unraveling.

senior housekeeper Hourly supervisor who is in charge of a *house division* and division personnel; supervises several *section housekeepers* and a *section housekeeping aide;* performs supervisory functions and ensures that division workers perform to standards; inspects guestrooms cleaning when necessary.

senior housekeeper's daily work report form A document indicating every room within a *house division* broken down into sections. Allows the senior housekeeper to progress work of *section housekeepers* throughout the day within the assigned division.

senior housekeeping aide Working supervisor assistant to the *executive housekeeper;* is in charge of all public area cleaning, project work, storeroom inventories, and training section and utility housekeeping aides.

sequential functions of management See *management sequential functions.*

setting objectives Determining desired end results. An activity of *planning.*

shams Decorative pillow covers used on a bed. Shams are often made from the same material as the bedspread.

sharps A small plastic case outfitted for a flow-through cleansing agent that is used to clean and sanitize needles, scalpels, and other sharp instruments.

shellac A *varnish* made from alcohol and refined lac, a sticky substance made from the deposits of insects.

simulation training A training technique whereby a guestroom is set aside for training purposes and various situations are presented to the trainee for resolution.

single occupancy Guestroom is occupied by only one guest. See also *double occupancy; multiple occupancy.*

situational leadership Management theory that asserts that the leadership style of the manager must vary according to the situation, that being the skill level and attitude of the subordinate.

sizing laundries Determination of proper *washing, drying,* and *handling capacities* for the *on-premises laundry.*

skip To leave a hotel without paying a bill.

smog A witch's brew of airborne pollutants including ozone, particulates, hydrocarbons, nitrous oxides, and sulfur dioxides, primarily caused by the burning of fossil fuels. The name combines ''smoke'' and ''fog.''

snoop Someone hired to work undercover for the purpose of gathering evidence against people guilty of dishonest acts.

software items Fixtures found in a hotel or hospital room that are normally considered a part of depreciable *fixed assets*, such as mattresses, curtains, draperies, pillows, and other items of soft nature; does not include bed and bath linens.

software program The program by which a computer processes data; as opposed to computer *hardware*, the physical components of a computer system.

source reduction The best strategy, when appropriate, to reduce a solid waste stream. It consists of not creating waste to begin with.

sour A substance used to lower the pH level of the laundry wash water to enhance the bleaching process.

spalling The chipping or breaking up of a stone floor surface.

span of control The number of subordinates who can be adequately supervised by a superior. Factors that influence this number include the complexity of the task, the skill level of the subordinates, distance, and time.

spirochetes Corkscrew-shaped microorganisms.

spores Microorganisms that are in a restive, protective shell.

spot check Selective inspection of guestrooms and other sections of a hotel to ensure that *standards of cleanliness* and maintenance are being maintained.

spray buffing The application of a finish solution while polishing a floor's surface to retouch worn spots and to restore a glossy look to the floor's surface.

staffing Performing certain activities that result in selecting competent people for positions in an organization; See also management sequential functions.

standard operating procedures (SOPs) A formal document of a standing nature that specifies a certain method of operating or a specific procedure for the accomplishment of a task.

standards of cleanliness Statement of the conditions that will exist when work has been performed satisfactorily. Used sometimes as a basis for constructing inspection forms. See also *standards setting*.

standards setting Prescribing the conditions that will exist when work has been done satisfactorily.

standing rotational scheduling system A continuous system of scheduling workers or teams of workers for regular days off in each week of a seven-week period. Regular days off in each *workweek* rotate forward (or back) as each week passes through the seven-week cycle. See also *tight schedule*.

Staphylococcus aureus **(staff-ill-i-COCK-us OAR-ee-us)** A grapelike-cluster organism that can cause boils, skin infections, purulent discharge, and/or peritonitis.

steady extra Classification of employee or employment for people who work in a steady but part-time manner; used mostly in union operations. See also *part-time employee*.

sterilization A process whereby all bacteria are killed by heat.

stock-out A depleted item that is normally found in inventory.

Streptococcus pyogenes **(strep-tow-COCK-us pie-O-jeans)** Chainlike round organism that causes the strep throat infection. Gram positive. Bacteria found in public places; wound and throat infections. Also associated with scarlet fever and rheumatic fever.

stewards' department Food and beverage department in a hotel operation that cleans and maintains kitchens, among other tasks.

stripper A product designed to remove old floor finish and sealer. The product often has an ammoniated base.

styrene butadiene rubber A synthetic rubber made from petroleum and used as a floor surface material.

subroutine A routine series of events or activities performed periodically in a housekeeping department, different from the *daily routine* but of equal importance. Involves controlling operations, purchasing, personnel administration, communications and training, and long-range planning.

suite (S) Two or more guestrooms that are sold as a unit and that connect internally. See also *guestroom types*.

swing team Housekeeping team that works in relief of one or more regular *housekeeping teams* that have been assigned a regular day off. Swing teams work in place of regular *house division* teams according to predetermined scheduling on a *standing rotational scheduling system*.

syringe Refers to a hypodermic syringe.

systemeering A term coined by Baring Industries (laundry consultants) relating to the service provided by their consultants when studying and establishing laundry equipment requirements for a user (customer). Service includes recommendations for equipment purchases, bid service, and mechanical rough-in drawings for utility service.

table of personnel requirements Management tool that shows the number of rooms that will require service and the number guestroom attendants needed for each percentage of occupancy.

taking corrective action Adjusting plans and counseling as necessary to attain standards. May require replanning and a repeat of the *sequential functions of management*. An activity of *controlling*.

target statistics Numerical items of data that become goals for the measurement of performance.

Taylor, Frederick W. Noted industrialist, author, and consultant recognized as the father of *scientific management*.

team scheduling System of scheduling whereby a group of employees organized into a permanent team is scheduled to perform work as a unit. See also *team staffing*.

team staffing System of staffing whereby employees are hired and combined into identifiable teams for the purpose of performing units of work that have been combined into logical relationships. See also *team scheduling; housekeeping team.*

team system of organization System of formal organization whereby several similar organizational groups may be identified and recognized as performing identical types of work tasks. See also *team scheduling; team staffing; housekeeping team.*

temporary employee Classification of employee or employment for which the period of employment will be only temporary. Employment termination date is usually established at the time of employment.

tensile strength An indicator of fabric quality. The degree of tensile strength is determined by the amount of weight it takes to tear a $1'' \times 3''$ piece of fabric.

terminal cleaning The action of cleaning a patient room or surgical suite upon completion of its use.

terrazzo A composition flooring material made from chips of marble, granite, travertine, or other materials, and portland cement.

Theory X A way of thinking about employees that implies that there is no intrinsic satisfaction found in work; that human beings avoid it as much as possible; that positive (authoritative) direction is needed to achieve organization goals; and that workers possess little ambition or originality. A Theory X manager is recognized by the manner in which he or she communicates.

Theory Y Managerial thinking that implies that work is natural and to be enjoyed by the worker; that the committed worker will exercise self-discipline and direction; that avoidance of responsibility, lack of ambition, and emphasis on security are general consequences of experience—not inherent human characteristics.

Theory Z Japanese management model that asserts that productivity can be enhanced in an organization by involving all employees in the planning and decision-making process. Term coined by Thomas Ouchi in his management text, *Theory Z.* See *participative management.*

thermoplastic Certain resins that have the potential of becoming soft when heated.

thread count The total number of threads in a one-inch-square piece of cloth. It is one of a number of quality indicators.

three-stroke solution Refers to the dilution (with water) ratio of an *all-purpose cleaner* that provides a proper agent for certain cleaning operations in approximately three wipes; for example, 40:1 dilution of a specific cleaning agent is used to clean mirrors and windows in three wiping strokes. See also *one-stroke solution.*

ticking A strong cloth used to cover mattresses and pillows.

tidy (tidies) (T) The act of tidying or identifying rooms that require tidying in order to *make ready* to rent. Tidies require only light service and usually do not require the full making of a bed or heavy service. Tidies are also rooms that have already been serviced once before a guest departs but then require light service to make them ready for reoccupancy.

tight schedule System of scheduling whereby a *standing rotational scheduling system* may be or is modified on a daily basis to accommodate a specific guestroom occupancy.

time card control The act of *controlling* use of time cards by employees so as to conform to company policy and government regulations.

time in the hole An expression of calendar days between the time a worker completes a workweek and the time that paychecks or pay will become available; ranges between 3 and 14 days; depending on payroll processing and delivery procedures.

time sheets, weekly or periodic Documents on which times from employee time cards are recorded; forms the basis for calculation of earned or benefit pay. A basis for payroll. May contain other forms of pay besides time actually worked.

torn sheet size Torn sheet size is the length and width of a sheet before the top and bottom hems are added. Top and bottom hems will subtract approximately five inches from the length of the sheet.

total linen on hand See *linen on hand.*

training employees Making employees proficient in the performance of a task through instruction and practice. An activity of *staffing.*

Tricophyton interdigitale **(tri-CO-fi-ton inter-digit-ALL-ee)** No gram stain. A fungus (athlete's foot), which can be used to evaluate a germicidal.

truck mount A portable carpet extraction system that is installed in a panel truck. It consists of a solution tank, a recovery tank, a heater, and pumps. Hoses are attached from the unit to the operator's wand.

tung oil A poisonous oil from the seeds of the tung tree. It is often used in finishing wood surfaces.

tunnel washer A high-capacity laundry washer found in commercial laundries.

turnover The number of employee separations in an organization over a period, expressed as a percentage. Calculated by taking the total number of separations that occur in a year and dividing by the average number of total positions in the organization (the total number of positions in the organization at the beginning of the year plus the total number of positions at the end of the year divided by 2). This ratio is expressed as a percentage. High turnover is costly to an organization.

turnover rate See *turnover.*

uniforms Distinctive clothes worn by employees so that they can be recognized by the general public as being part of a business.

varnish A liquid that gives a shiny, hard, transparent surface to wood or metal; made from resins that have been dissolved in oil, turpentine, or alcohol.

virus A part of the protist kingdom; includes influenza (a flu virus), herpes simplex, vaccine (cowpox), adeno virus type 2, and AIDS. Gram positive (blue stain). Major cause of infections (boils, carbuncles, ear infections) and food poisonings. Size is 0.8 to 1 micron. It is resistant to antibiotics. Best cure is heat.

volatile organic compounds (VOCs) Hydrocarbons. Unstable elements that easily turn into gases. Found in a host of products such as paint strippers, cleaners, and solvents. They constitute a major source of indoor air pollution.

wage costs Classification of labor based on the calculation of hours worked times a given or assigned wage rate, depending on the classification of the employee. See also *controllable costs*; *employee costs*.

wage department Classification system for the identification of various types of man-hours used by departments in hotels and hospitals. Classifications usually refer to the types of work that are to be performed.

warp Lengthwise threads of yarn in a fabric.

wash formula Quantitative determinants of how long a specific type or piece of linen is to be washed, rinsed, and extracted; includes temperatures of wash and rinse solutions and quantities of detergents, bleaches, and softeners to be used during the various wash cycles.

washing capacity Optimum weight of linen that should be placed in an automatic commercial washing machine; for example, 50-pound, 100-pound, 200-pound washer; used in *sizing laundries*. See also *drying capacity; handling capacity*.

waste transformation The alteration of materials in a solid waste stream. The intent is to reduce their mass. Compactors, pulpers, and shredders are used in the transformation. Can also be meant to alter the waste into another form, such as in a waste-to-energy plant.

weekly maintenance Identified housekeeping service or repair-type maintenance that is to be performed each week on schedule.

weekly wage analysis Breakdown of expended wages by departments, showing comparisons to budgeted and forecast wages; identifies out-of-control areas and indicates corrective measures to regain control of costs if necessary.

weekly wage forecast Document prepared weekly by housekeeping management indicating how many man-hours will be required or expended, and in what *wage departments* (classifications), to support a specified forecast of guestroom occupancy.

weft The threads of yarn that run the width of a fabric.

"what-if" publication Interesting presentation of emergency situations a person might encounter in a hotel or hospital. Presentation is in the form of questions asking "what if" and enlightened alternative responses.

work calendar Seven-week period of time divided into workweeks; indicating regular workdays and regular days off in each week as presented in the *standing rotational scheduling system*.

work-centered theory of management Classical theory of management that focuses on a concern for production.

workshop training Training technique used primarily for supervisors. Involves the presentation of managerial problems and allows the participants to work out one or more solutions, which are then critiqued.

workweek Seven consecutive days with an identifiable beginning and ending used to identify and separate one week from another in a continuous daily operation. Workweeks may begin on any day of the week and end six days later. The identification of workweeks is imperative in continuous daily operations for scheduling and accounting purposes.

zero-based budgeting A concept of budgeting that requires the planner to start the entire budgeting process from scratch each year. No prior assumptions regarding past years are made. Although extremely accurate in its approach, it is time-consuming and difficult to attempt in an extremely complex and/or large organization.

zone Segmented part of a facility subject to zone inspection. See *zone inspection program*.

zone inspection program A form of *property inspection program* whereby various sections of a hotel are divided into zones and assigned to several zone inspectors; usually conducted once each week.

Index